Memoire.

may 1717

a S.A.R. Mgr le Duc d'Orleans Regent du Royaume .... venüe

Monseigneur

L'Honneur j me fais V.A.R de m'ouvrir .... convenir
les Estats g.x de ce Royaume dans les embar .... m'a donné je
m'ordonner d'y bien penser f d'en dire mon avis, m'engage f repondre dignent. à la ...
d'importance de la matiere d'écrire plus ... j de parler ... un moyen contre les def-
ereux de la promptitude du discours ... de la confusion de la conversation.

Avant j d'entrer en matiere V.A.R se souviendra s'il luy plaist par deux faits
... luy avoir échapés j de tous ceux qui ont eu l'honneur de l'approcher dans ...
aucun n'a plus d'estime ny j ainsy parler plus de gens naturel f les Estats g.x d' ...
L'un est j travaillant sous les yeux defeu Mgr le Dauphin aux projets d'un f ...
parties, le principal des miens estoit des Estats g.x de gens ans ede les simplifier de
... pussent assembler sans cette confusion qui les a si souvent rendus inutiles. j' ...
... d'un corps le Surintendant des finances f les dons les impôts leur repartition la
depense, j'il fut compte de tout devant eux, j'entre chaq tenüe il en subsidsoit ...
d'un personnage de chacun des 3 ordres f faire dans l'intervale les choses journalie ...
autres pressées jusqu'à de certaines bornes par une administration d'un ils seroient ...
Estats prochains, j'ils eussent durant cet exercice un rang ede privileges qui d'une m ...
... mon respect f la Nation representée, ... ce qui seroit mis a part f les depense ...
d'un ... une espece de liste civile, f... gere, par un Tresorier qui n'en compteroit ...
Chambre des Comptes.

L'autre est celuy d'assembler les Estats g ... après la mort du feu Roy, dont V ...
... souvenir combien j'ay pris la liberté de l'en presser, f elle l'avoir resolu, f si elle ...
d'avis ça été instant. entre le mien.

Il n'est pas question icy de s'arrester sur ces deux faits j il suffit de representer en deu
memoire. Ce p ne pouvoit estre d'usage j sous un Roy majeur selon le cœur de Dieu
... de ses peuples le restaurateur de l'ordre ... un moderateur incorruptible par un dis
... de la justice ede ses interets veritable. L'explication de ce projet ne j'apprendr...
... , n'exacerbir de mon sujet ... inutilem ... ma douleur amere de la
... Prince ede l'inutilité de ce projet j j'avois ... edigeré avec plus de joye ... f
l'honneur ede l'avantage solide de la france. L'autre a esté si fort agité avec V.A.R
... mort du Roy ede cette époq est si recente j elle ne peut j ... ... au fuy ... f ...
ce qui fait maintenant naistre la pensée d'une tenüe d'Estats g est, parce j V.A.R.
... de m'en dire, subsidiairem l'estat d'engagem ede difficulté ou se trouve ...
... , ... effectivem le terme d'embarras ou se trouvent les finances. c'puisq ...
... j il s'agir reellem icy ... d'eux j il faut traiter le plus solidem f il ne ...

HISTORICAL MEMOIRS
OF THE
DUC DE SAINT-SIMON

THE REGENT, PHILIPPE D'ORLÉANS.
ENGRAVING AFTER JEAN BAPTISTE SANCERRE

HISTORICAL MEMOIRS

OF THE

DUC DE SAINT-SIMON

A SHORTENED VERSION

VOLUME III: 1715–1723

EDITED AND TRANSLATED BY
LUCY NORTON

HAMISH HAMILTON
LONDON

First published in Great Britain, 1972
by Hamish Hamilton Ltd
90 Great Russell Street London WC1

Copyright © 1972 by Lucy Norton

SBN 241 01673 8

Printed in Great Britain by
Western Printing Services Ltd, Bristol

SYNOPSIS OF CONTENTS

PART FOUR

INFLUENCE, OFFICE AND RETIREMENT

Chapter 1

1715

M. le Duc d'Orléans surprised by the King's death – The funeral pomp reduced to bare simplicity – The Session of the Parlement – The Dukes are first allowed to protest, then put off with promises – The King's Will is presented – Lord Stair attends in a box – M. le Duc d'Orléans in violent dispute with M. du Maine – Annulment of the codicil – Madame warns the Regent never to employ the Abbé Dubois – The Regent visits Mme de Maintenon – An amnesty for prisoners – Horrors of the prisons unveiled – Formation of the Council of Regency – The one-time Bishop of Troyes is nominated – Two anecdotes – Mme la Duchesse de Berry takes up residence at the Luxembourg – Marriage of Sandricourt – Dismissal of Pontchartrain – Character of Lord Stair – The Pretender escapes assassination – The Regent wishes to move the King to Paris – Balls at the Opéra – Death of Mme de Louvois – Caylus pardoned for duelling – Revaluation of the coinage – The King comes to Paris

Chapter 2

1716

M. du Maine pays me a casual visit – I visit him and Mme la Duchesse du Maine – The Abbé Dubois made a counsellor of State – Death of the Duchesse de Lesdiguières – Death and character of Coulanges – Marriage of M. de Castries's only son – Character of Mme de Castries – Mme la Duchesse de Berry assumes honours above her rank – She falls to Rions's charms – Public and private life of M. le Duc d'Orléans – His obstinate debauchery – The cabal who for their personal advantage attach the Regent permanently to England – He never aspired to the throne – I propose a permanent and indissoluble union with Spain – A treaty between France and Spain signed at Madrid – Alberoni keeps the King and Queen of Spain under lock and key – The Pretender fails in Scotland – Stair's lying report – Characters of Stair and Bentivoglio – La Force is sent to win me for the constitution – Conduct of the Duc de Noailles towards me, and mine towards him – Mme la Duchesse de Berry closes the Luxembourg gardens – Return of the Italian players – Law pronounced Las; his bank, and my advice regarding it – The Regent desires me to see Law – The poet Arouet is exiled – The King pays a call on Chancellor de Pontchartrain – The duchy of Valentinois accorded a peerage – Character of the Duc de Brancas – M. le Duc de Chartres contracts smallpox – I return from La Ferté to be with his parents – Death of the Maréchal de Montrevel – King George offers to return Gibraltar – Louville, sent as envoy to Madrid, is driven out by Alberoni – A treaty between France and England, engineered by Dubois, is signed at The Hague – Peter the Great invited to visit France

Chapter 3
1717

Chapter 4
1718

Chapter 8
1722

Chapter 9
1723

ILLUSTRATIONS

ACKNOWLEDGMENTS

As in the other volumes, my most grateful thanks to Mr. Christopher Sinclair-Stevenson, Miss Betty Askwith, Miss Irene Clephane and Mrs. Joy Law, for their unfailing support and encouragement.

THE ROYAL FAMILY
After the Death of Louis XIV, on 1 September 1715

LOUIS XV
aged 5
His father, mother, brothers, grandfather and great-grandfather having all of them died in the four preceding years

His Great-Great-Aunt by marriage
Elizabeth Charlotte of the Palatinate, Duchesse d'Orléans (Madame), Mother of the Regent
aged 63

His legitimised Great-aunts and Uncles
Daughter of Louis XIV by Mme de la Vallière:
Marie Anne, Dowager Princesse de Conti
aged 49
Children of Louis XIV and Mme de Montespan:
Louis, Duc du Maine
aged 45
Louis, Comte de Toulouse
aged 37
Louise Françoise, Madame la Duchesse
aged 42
Françoise Marie, Duchesse d'Orléans
aged 38

His Uncles
Philip V of Spain (m. (2nd) Elisabeth Farnese, 1714)
aged 32   aged 23
Charles, Duc de Berry (m. Marie Louise d'Orléans, 1710)
aged 30   aged 20

His First Cousin
Louis of Spain, Prince of the Asturias (m. Louise Elisabeth d'Orléans, 1722)
aged 8   aged 6

His First Cousins Twice Removed
Philippe II, Duc d'Orléans, Regent of France
aged 41
Elisabeth Charlotte d'Orléans, Duchesse de Lorraine (the Regent's sister)
aged 37

PRINCES OF THE BLOOD

Condé
Louis Henri, Duc de Bourbon-Condé (Monsieur le Duc)
aged 24

Charles, Comte de Charolais
aged 15
Louis, Comte de Clermont
aged 8
Six sisters who do not appear in this volume

Conti

Louis Armand, Prince de Conti
aged 20
Two sisters who do not appear in this volume

Genealogical Table showing the Relationship of the Regent to the Royal House of England

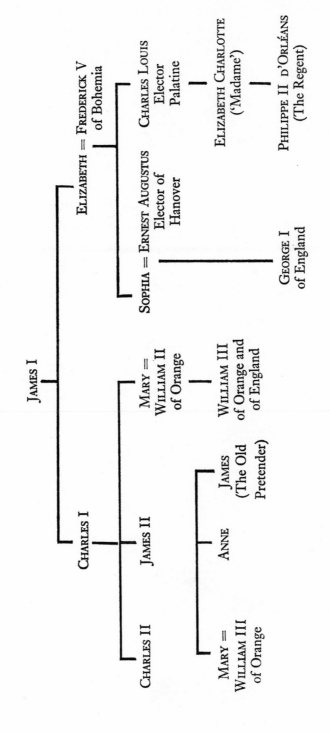

HISTORICAL MEMOIRS
OF THE
DUC DE SAINT-SIMON

INFLUENCE, OFFICE
AND RETIREMENT

CHAPTER I

1715

M. le Duc d'Orléans surprised by the King's death – The funeral pomp reduced to bare simplicity – The Session of the Parlement – The Dukes are first allowed to protest, then put off with promises – The King's Will is presented – Lord Stair attends in a box – M. le Duc d'Orléans in a violent dispute with M. du Maine – Annulment of the codicil – Madame warns the Regent never to employ the Abbé Dubois –The Regent visits Mme de Maintenon – An amnesty for prisoners – Horrors of the prisons unveiled – Formation of the Council of Regency – The one-time Bishop of Troyes is nominated – Two anecdotes – Mme la Duchesse de Berry takes up residence at the Luxembourg – Marriage of Sandricourt – Dismissal of Pontchartrain – Character of Lord Stair – The Pretender escapes assassination – The Regent wishes to move the King to Paris – Balls at the Opéra – Death of Mme de Louvois – Caylus pardoned for duelling – Revaluation of the coinage – The King comes to Paris

THE DEATH OF THE KING took the idle mind of M. le Duc d'Orléans as much by surprise as though it had been totally unexpected. He was just as I had left him,[1] having made no kind of progress in any of the decisions necessary for the affairs of State or the new appointments. As a result, and just as I had predicted, he found himself inundated with orders to give and matters to resolve, each one more trifling than the last, and all so pressing that he had no time for really important business. Two days before the King died, Mme Sforza[2] had sent one morning, asking me to call on her. She was exceedingly anxious, and Mme la Duchesse d'Orléans still more so, to know of M. le Duc d'Orléans's decisions and selections. Neither could believe that he had remained totally inactive. I assured Mme Sforza that she would learn that sad truth only too soon, and indeed, four days later both she and Mme la Duchesse d'Orléans had received ample proof of it.

I was told of the King's death when I awoke, and I went at once to make my bow to the new monarch. The first wave of courtiers had already passed and I was almost alone. I went thence to M. le Duc d'Orléans whom I found besieged, his entire apartment so crammed with people that you

[1] In other words, quite undecided. But Louis XIV had died on 1 September, and already on the 29th the Duc d'Orléans had made arrangements regarding the future with the Parlement and the officers of the household troops. It seems that Saint-Simon had not, as he suggests, or perhaps believed, been told quite everything.

[2] Louis Le Adélaïde de Damas-Thiange, a very particular friend of the Duchesse d'Orléans.

could not have dropped a pin between them. I drew him aside into his study to make one last, but useless, effort to persuade him to convoke the States-General,[1] also to remind him of his assurance to me, and to a dozen other peers, that he would approve of our remaining covered when called upon to vote,[2] and would support us in our other moves against the vile encroachments of the Parlement, to all of which he had already given his consent. I reminded him at the same time of my proposals regarding unnecessary pomp at the King's funeral, and that he had agreed to all of them. My intention was to save expense and tedious delays; to avoid the disputes inevitable in a very long ceremony, and to proceed, although the King had issued no such orders, on the lines of the funeral of Louis XIII, who had forbidden all but the simplest ceremonial. M. le Duc d'Orléans gladly consented, and no one else cared sufficiently for the dead monarch to challenge a wholesale retrenchment which he had not himself ordered.

Directly after this, I went to the Duc de La Trémoïlle's apartment, where we had arranged to meet after the King's death, and where most of the dukes then at Versailles were already assembled. Monsieur de Rheims,[3] as the senior of those ten or twelve who together had tackled M. le Duc d'Orléans on the matter of the bonnets[4], reported that the prince had promised us his entire support, and I afterwards told them of the renewed assurances he had just given me. Our unity and our determination were reaffirmed, also our total rupture with the premier président[5] in view of his outrageous conduct. After this we separated.

I went to M. le Duc d'Orléans shortly afterwards, when everyone was at dinner and he was not surrounded by callers. It was then he confessed to having made no lists and no appointments, in fact to having decided nothing whatsoever. This was not the time for scolding or reproaches. I simply shrugged my shoulders, begged him at least to beware of supplicants and ministers, and made certain once again of the total exclusion of Pontchartrain and Desmaretz from the new councils. I then spoke of the King's will and codicil,[6] asking him how he proposed to deal with them

---

[1] The États-Généraux had not been summoned since 1614, but had never been abolished, and were still part of the French Constitution. They were an assembly of the Clergy, Nobility and Commoners. Saint-Simon, who saw nothing but disaster in a continuance of Louis XIV's absolute rule assisted by professional bureaucrats, believed that they might provide a basis for a constitutional monarchy on the lines of England. The French parlements were judicial courts not legislative assemblies.

[2] An allusion to the Bonnet Affair, and to the peers' privilege of voting with their caps on their heads in the Parlement, whereas the premier président had to remove his cap when addressing them. (See II, pp. 271n, 317, 371 et seqq.)

[3] François de Mailly (1658–1721), who had been Archbishop of Rheims since 1710.

[4] Président de Novion (1618–1693) had taken to removing his bonnet when addressing princes of the blood and presidents during a session of the Parlement, and putting it on again before addressing the peers—a deliberate insult.

[5] The dukes had not been on speaking terms with Premier Président de Mesmes since the Bonnet Affair.

[6] See II, pp. 350 et seqq.; p. 490.

when we went next day to the Parlement, where both documents would be read out loud. Tête-à-tête in his study, he was the firmest man imaginable; elsewhere the very weakest. He promised me marvels; I again stressed the vital importance of the outcome, and all that it might mean for him personally. I was with him nearly two hours. I then went for a moment to Mme la Duchesse d'Orléans, who was in bed with the curtains drawn, surrounded by silent women,[1] and returned to my apartment to dine with friends who awaited me there, intending to go afterwards to Paris. It grew late, for we had a lengthy conversation after dinner; but, just as I was about to leave, M. le Duc d'Orléans sent for me and for some of the other dukes who were with me. We went to him immediately. He was in his *entresol* with the Duc de Sully, Monsieur de Metz,[2] and several more dukes whom he had likewise summoned, for he had sent messages to all those still at the château. By that time it was eight o'clock in the evening.

M. le Duc d'Orléans proceeded to address us in most flowery language, urging us to start nothing fresh on the following day (although he had previously given his consent), saying that we might distract attention from great affairs of State, such as the Regency and the administration, and bring down indignation upon ourselves for delaying public issues for our own private benefit. Many of those present were astounded at this sudden change from what he had said only that morning. D'Antin, Monsieur de Metz, and a few others reminded him of the awkward situation in which this sudden reversal placed us;[3] for M. de Sully, Charost, myself, and several others (especially Monsieur de Rheims, to whom he had promised his support) had told everyone, and had repeated his assurances only that morning to the large assembly in M. de La Trémoïlle's apartment. We asked him what advantage he hoped to gain by this sudden change, and begged him to believe that the greatest nobles in the land, who were so monstrously ill used, thought that they had deserved better of him.

M. le Duc d'Orléans appeared much embarrassed, but did not budge. We looked at one another, and said all together that, considering what had passed, he was asking the impossible. This seemed to distress him deeply. He repeated several times over that the bonnet was an intolerable infringement of our rights, and the other matters of which we complained no less so, but that we ought to choose a better moment and not disturb an important session with our personal grievances. 'But, Sir,' said I, 'when these great matters are settled you will not care about our rights, and if we do not seize this opportunity you will put us off time and again, and we shall have sacrificed our interests to no purpose.' M. le Duc d'Orléans promised marvels, giving us his solemn word to adjudicate in our favour in all disputes over encroachments by the Parlement—bonnets, advocates on

---

[1] She was probably weeping for her father, the King.
[2] Henri Charles du Cambout, Duc de Coislin (1664–1732), Bishop of Metz from 1697.
[3] Saint-Simon is still referring to the Bonnet Affair.

the bench, etc.—as soon as the public business had been dealt with. I entreated him to remember this formal promise, and not to undertake more than he intended to do, if only to avoid the complaints and demands which we should certainly not spare him if we found him inclined to break his word. He reaffirmed his promise in most explicit terms, but asked us once again not to introduce innovations at the coming session. The dukes were angry but feeble; they murmured, but dared not protest aloud. They fully understood the disadvantage of letting slip such an occasion, but so accustomed were they to obey that none dared to obstruct the prince who represented that dead monarch whose shadow still had power to paralyse them. The murmurs continued for some considerable time.

By then I had begun to despair of arriving at any settlement whatsoever, and I therefore spoke again. I told M. le Duc d'Orléans that it would be wellnigh impossible to warn all the dukes who had been present at the meeting in M. de La Trémoïlle's apartment, not to mention all those to whom they might have spoken before leaving for Paris. I said further that I saw no way of convincing them of his having promised to rule in our favour in the matter of the bonnet and other encroachments of which we complained, unless he consented to let one of us make a speech before the opening of the session, explaining our demands, but adding that in accordance with his wishes we had agreed not to press our claims until after the country's business had been dispatched. I said that our speaker would then call on him to declare the truth of what had been stated, and at the same time to repeat his promises in open session. M. le Duc d'Orléans breathed again, and made no more difficulties. He proposed me as our speaker, and gave us the strongest possible assurances of swift judgment in our favour as soon as the Regency was established on a secure and permanent footing.

Everything being thus settled and agreed, albeit to our extreme annoyance, we had to decide how best in the short time remaining before the session, to warn the absent dukes of the sudden change. In the end, we resolved that each one of us should send word to those who lived nearest, asking them to meet us wearing parliamentary dress[1] at five o'clock next morning, on a matter of the greatest possible urgency, in the house of the Archbishop of Rheims. It was ten in the evening before we reached Paris, but we all, as had been arranged, immediately sent to inform our neighbours.

Between five and six o'clock next morning most of the dukes had arrived at the Archbishop's house, at the end of the Pont Royal, behind the Hôtel de Mailly. Monsieur de Rheims informed them of what had taken place on the previous evening. There was a good deal of grumbling, but since no

---

[1] A short mantle over a tunic of the same colour, a sword, and a bonnet with white plumes, was the parliamentary dress of peers. Counsellors wore scarlet robes and high-court presidents cloaks lined with ermine. All the judiciary had the square caps or bonnets, about which there was such a rumpus.

action could be taken everyone was obliged to submit. I made one last unavailing effort to shift the responsibility of the formal protest on to someone else. They argued that nothing could be done without M. le Duc d'Orléans's permission; that he had always insisted on my being the speaker, and that there was neither the time nor any good reason to ask him to choose someone else. They ended by exhorting me to be of good courage and not too accommodating towards M. le Duc d'Orléans, since he was so careless of our interests.

That last remark made me think it desirable to bring them to a better frame of mind, and I spoke of the awkward situation in which M. le Duc d'Orléans found himself between the Parlement, as guardian of the King's will and codicil, and the bastards whose power and influence these documents were directed to increase—as no one for a moment doubted. I pointed out how essential it was for M. le Duc d'Orléans, the State, and ourselves to prevent the bastards from benefiting by the King's clear intentions, and insisted that M. le Duc d'Orléans's promise, given and repeated, was sufficient proof of his good will and sincerity. I further added that we could not reasonably blame him for being loath to set the Parlement in league with the bastards at this crucial moment when the Regent's powers were being decided, nor for refusing to let a private quarrel delay the settlement of graver and more pressing issues in which he had everything to lose.

My short oration had the desired effect. It was by then nearly seven, and we therefore went all together straight to the Parlement, with our coaches and escorts following behind. Less than a quarter of an hour after our arrival the bastards entered. M. du Maine seemed about to burst with joy. That is a dreadful expression, but I can find no other to describe his countenance. A veneer of rapturous satisfaction covered an air of bold self-confidence which was plainly visible at times, despite his seemingly polite struggle to restrain himself. He advanced, bowing to left and right, directing a piercing glance at every face, and saluting the bench with a look of jubilation which was clearly reflected in the manner of Mesmes the premier président.[1] Towards the peers, the gravity, nay the reverence, the slowness, the depth of his bow to all three sides was truly eloquent. His head remained bent long after his body had straightened—so heavy is the weight of wickedness, even when victory is within its grasp. I never took my eyes from him, and I observed that from all three sides the bows returned to him were noticeably stiff and perfunctory.

Scarcely were we reseated before Monsieur le Duc arrived, and shortly after him M. le Duc d'Orléans. I let the bustle of their entry subside a little, and then, perceiving that the premier président had uncovered and was about to speak, I raised my hand, removed my bonnet and, immediately

[1] Jean Antoine III de Mesmes (1661–1723), Premier Président of the Parlement 1712, member of the French Academy. He was the friend and supporter of the Duc du Maine.

replacing it, said[1] that I had been charged by the peers to announce to the assembly that only in consideration of the urgent and vital nature of the issues now to be discussed would they tolerate a moment longer the infamous abuse of the bonnet, and the many other encroachments of which they had to complain. In so doing they showed their very proper respect for the supreme importance of affairs of State. None the less, I continued, I now protested in the strongest possible way, in the name of all the peers, and with the approval of M. le Duc d'Orléans, who only the day before had given us, at Versailles, his absolute promise to rule on these same abuses as soon as the affairs of the nation had been dealt with. The profound silence in which I was heard bore witness to the amazement of the entire assembly. M. le Duc d'Orléans removed his bonnet, bowed rather low, seemed somewhat embarrassed, and immediately replaced it. I looked at M. du Maine, who appeared relieved at having been let off so lightly, although, according to my neighbours, he had been vexed enough when I began.

A very short pause followed, after which I saw the premier président turn and say something in a whisper to M. le Duc d'Orléans. He then loudly called on a deputation from the Parlement to fetch the King's will and the codicil, which had been kept together. The silence continued during these long and short periods of waiting; people looked at one another; but no one stirred. We were all in the lower seats and the doors should have been closed; but the great chamber was overflowing with gentlemen of quality and other people of all kinds and conditions, including the numerous retinues of those taking part in the proceedings. M. le Duc d'Orléans had been easily gulled into enlisting the help of England in case of need, and for that purpose had seated Lord Stair[2] in one of the upper lanterns.[3] That had been the work of the Duc de Noailles, Canillac,[4] and the Abbé Dubois.

Other help was also at hand, for the regiment of Guards had silently lined the approaches, and all the officers and some hand-picked troops were dispersed throughout the interior of the Palais. The Duc de Guiche[5]

---

[1] In fact it was the Archbishop of Rheims who read out a protest on behalf of the peers; Saint-Simon's only contribution was to ask the Duc d'Orléans to confirm his promise.

[2] John Dalrymple, 2nd Earl of Stair (1673–1747), the English ambassador.

[3] *Les Lanternes*: these were like the boxes at a theatre, overlooking the great chamber of the Parlement.

[4] Philippe de Montboissier Beaufort, Marquis de Canillac (1669–1725). A great friend of the Duc d'Orléans with a strong influence during the Regency. Saint-Simon says, 'Well-made, chestnut hair, rather a pleasing expression, a man of parts, eloquent, frank, and noble-looking. He spoke pithily, with a caustic wit that made his words memorable. Wonderful at telling a story, and better than anyone at describing some absurdity with a perfectly inscrutable countenance. He was also vicious and, as will be seen, completely corrupt.' Other writers of the period do not confirm this character.

[5] Colonel of the regiment of the French Guards.

was in the lower lantern by the fireplace; he had come to terms with M. le Duc d'Orléans, and was well rewarded for this service, of which he wisely made a great display. During the King's lifetime he had always professed attachment to the bastards, who had counted on his support. As you will observe, they were quickly disillusioned. In the event, these precautions served no one except the Duc de Guiche. The session itself was far from peaceful, but nothing disturbed the outer calm.

The deputation was not long absent. The will and the codicil were placed in the hands of the premier président, who presented them to M. le Duc d'Orléans without relinquishing his hold of them. They were then passed from hand to hand along the row of magistrates as far as Dreux,[1] one of the counsellors, who read them loud and clear, so that all might hear them, from his place among the high seats behind the premier président, close to the lantern of the robing-room. You may imagine how attentively he was listened to, and how all eyes and ears were turned in his direction. M. du Maine appeared anxious, despite his triumph; for him it was the beginning of a mighty struggle. M. le Duc d'Orléans displayed merely polite attention.

I shall not pause to describe those two documents which were solely concerned with the rank and power of the bastards, Mme de Maintenon's situation at Saint-Cyr, the ordering of the young King's education and the Council of Regency, all to the detriment of M. le Duc d'Orléans, and intended to deliver him stripped of all authority into the hands of an all-powerful Duc du Maine.

I observed an air of melancholy, almost of indignation, descend on every face as the reading proceeded, and I watched this turn to silent anger at the provisions of the codicil, which was read by the Abbé Menguy,[2] another counsellor of the great chamber, but also a cleric, standing where Dreux had stood so as to be clearly audible. The Duc du Maine sensed this silent indignation, and turned pale. His eyes continually scanned the faces of the assembly, and mine, as I listened, were riveted upon him, except when, now and then, I also watched the countenance of the Duc d'Orléans.

When the reading was over that prince began to speak, casting his eye round the whole assembly, removing and replacing his bonnet, and saying first a few words in praise and sorrow for the late King. Then, raising his voice, he declared that he entirely approved of all that related to the education of the present monarch and the nominations suggested for that work, also to the arrangements for the maintenance of the excellent and worthy establishment of Saint-Cyr. Regarding the provisions in the will and codicil that concerned the government of the kingdom, he would prefer

---

[1] Thomas II Dreux (1640–1731); he was the doyen of the Parlement, ninety-one, and a friend of Chamillart.

[2] The Abbé Guillaume Menguy later played an important part as appellant against the Bull *Unigenitus*.

to take each document separately, for he found them hard to reconcile with the assurances publicly given him by the King in his last days, namely that nothing in the testament would displease him; after which the King had delegated all public business to him, and had directed the ministers to come to him for their orders. It must therefore appear that King Louis did not fully understand what he had been persuaded to do (here M. le Duc d'Orléans stared hard at the Duc du Maine), since the Regent's Council was now shown to have been appointed in the testament, and the Regent's powers so much curtailed as to be virtually non-existent. So great an insult to his birth and devotion to the King, to his love and loyalty for the State, could not honourably be endured, and he felt sufficiently confident of the esteem of all those present to believe that they would now declare his Regency to be what it should be by right, namely absolute, independent, and with full authority to appoint the members of his council, whose right to a voice in the affairs of State he would never contest. His short address appeared to make a deep impression.

The Duc du Maine at this point tried to speak; but, as he raised his bonnet, M. le Duc d'Orléans put his head round in front of Monsieur le Duc and said curtly: 'Monsieur, you shall speak in your turn.' From that moment things began to go as M. le Duc d'Orléans desired. Authority over the Council of Regency, and power to appoint its members, were freely acknowledged to belong to him as Regent of the kingdom; its decisions were to be subjected to a majority vote, with the Regent's vote to count as two when the other votes were evenly cast. Thus all favours and punishments remained the sole prerogative of M. le Duc d'Orléans. When that was settled, there was such an outburst of applause that M. du Maine dared not say a word. He reserved all his strength for the codicil,[1] which, had it been declared valid, would have rendered null and void all that M. le Duc d'Orléans had so far gained.

After a moment's pause M. le Duc d'Orléans continued, expressing his great astonishment that the testament alone had not seemed sufficient for those who had inspired its terms, although these would have made them rulers of the kingdom. Perhaps the terms had seemed so outrageous even to those persons that in order to protect themselves they felt it necessary to control the King himself, the Regent, the Court, and Paris. He added that while the testament attacked his honour to a degree which the assembly appeared to feel as deeply as he did himself, the codicil wounded him even more seriously, for it left neither his life nor his liberty secure, and placed the King in the custody of men who did not scruple to torment a dying monarch in order to extort privileges which he never intended to grant them. M. le Duc d'Orléans declared finally that no regency could function under such limitations, and that he did not doubt but that the assembly

---

[1] The codicil in fact contained nothing relating to the Duc du Maine (see II, p. 490 and footnote). Saint-Simon's account of the Regent's speech does not tally with other reports.

would annul a codicil that was indefensible since by its provisions France would be thrown into great and certain disaster. While the prince was speaking a deep and mournful silence dumbly signified the assent of the assembly.

The Duc du Maine, turning every colour of the rainbow, tried once more to speak, and this time was allowed to do so. He declared that, since the King's education and consequently the safety of his person had been entrusted to him, it was only natural for him to have authority over the civil and military establishments. How otherwise could he discharge his task? He then boasted of his well-known love and devotion for the late King, who had placed in him his entire confidence.

M. le Duc d'Orléans interrupted him at this point, taking exception to that last remark, and M. du Maine thereupon endeavoured to soften it by praising the Maréchal de Villeroy, who was associated with him in the same task and shown the same trust, but in a subordinate capacity. M. le Duc d'Orléans retorted that it would be extraordinary if the chief and most complete confidence were not placed in the Regent himself, and stranger still if he were not permitted to be with the King except under the guard and authority of those who had made themselves absolute masters within and without the King's palace, and masters of Paris also, by commanding the Guards regiment.

The dispute grew angrier, with the speakers interrupting each other in half-finished sentences until, fearing an unseemly brawl, I signed to M. le Duc d'Orléans to adjourn, and to finish the argument in the fourth Chambre des Enquêtes, which was empty, and which had a door leading into the great chamber. What induced me to intervene was that I could hear M. du Maine murmuring something about sharing the responsibility, and could see that M. le Duc d'Orléans was no longer making such a good impression, now that he was on the defensive. As it happened, however, that prince was not only extremely near-sighted, but was so much absorbed in attacking, and parrying thrusts that he did not notice me. A few moments later, I therefore rose and spoke. 'Monsieur,' I said, 'if you would care to step into the adjoining room with M. du Maine you might speak more freely,' and leaning forward I gestured to him with my hand and eyes until at last he did perceive me. He nodded, and as I sat down I saw him step past Monsieur le Duc and leave the chamber with M. du Maine, as I had indicated. I could not see who followed them, for the entire assembly rose as they went out, and then sat in perfect silence without again moving. After a time the Comte de Toulouse also entered the adjoining room, followed by Monsieur le Duc, and shortly afterwards by the Duc de La Force.

The last named soon returned to the great chamber and to his place. Passing along the line of dukes, he stopped to put his head between the Duc de Sully and myself (so as not to let the Duc de La Rochefoucauld overhear), and whispered, 'For God's sake go to them. Everything is going as badly as possible, and M. le Duc d'Orléans is weakening. Go and stop them and bring him back. Tell him to adjourn for dinner, and let us use the interval to send the King's household to the Palais Royal, and to canvas the doubtful peers and the ringleaders of the magistrates.'

This advice seemed good to me, and I accordingly went into the next room, where I found a number of onlookers standing at a respectful distance from the fireplace, where M. le Duc d'Orléans and M. du Maine were disputing in low voices, but looking very angry. I watched them for a few moments and then stepped forward as though I wished to speak. 'Well, what is it?' said M. le Duc d'Orléans impatiently. 'Just a word, Sir, for your private ear.' But he continued to argue with M. du Maine, leaving me as it were eavesdropping on them. I persisted, however, until at last he turned to hear me. 'No, no,' I said, 'not here, Sir,' and taking him by the hand, I drew him after me to the other side of the chimney-piece. At that, the Comte de Toulouse, who was standing close by, took a long step backwards, and the Duc du Maine stepped back also.

I then whispered into M. le Duc d'Orléans's ear that it was useless to expect anything from M. du Maine; no arguments would ever persuade him to abandon the codicil; it was therefore unseemly, dangerous, and, what was more, perfectly futile to prolong the dispute. 'You are right,' said M. le Duc d'Orléans, 'I will end it now.' 'Do so at once,' I said, 'and do not allow them to divert you.' He left me then, and went to say a couple of words to M. du Maine, to the effect that it was late and that it was time to adjourn for dinner.

I stayed where I was, and thus saw M. du Maine make his bow and leave, and Monsieur le Duc step forward to speak to M. le Duc d'Orléans. Then, since it was necessary for them to pass the place where I stood in order to re-enter the great chamber, they both approached me. That was when I first learned of Monsieur le Duc's having asked to be appointed to the Council of Regency, and to be made head of it, if the will were declared invalid, to all of which M. le Duc d'Orléans had agreed. I think he had already promised Monsieur le Duc to give him that post, but had not dared to tell me so. Be that as it may, he briefly gave me that piece of information, adding that he intended to announce it to the Parlement before the session ended. I assumed an air of approval and congratulation, and we returned at once to the great chamber.

When the bustle of their entrance had subsided, M. le Duc d'Orléans announced an adjournment for dinner, adding that he thought it fitting for Monsieur le Duc to join the Council of Regency as its head; and that, since the assembly had done him the honour due to his birth and rank, he would later acquaint them with his views on the forms he considered most suitable for the administration. He hoped, he said, to profit by the wisdom and experience of the company there assembled, and thus he then and there returned to them their ancient right of remonstrance.[1] These words were greeted with loud and general applause, and the session rose.

I had been bidden to dinner with Cardinal de Noailles on that day, but I thought it best to spend the short time of the recess with M. le Duc d'Orléans, especially since the Duc de La Force continued to urge me not to leave him. I therefore approached him as he left, saying, 'Time is precious; I will follow you to the Palais Royal.' I then returned to my seat so as to leave with the other peers, and I sent a gentleman to Cardinal de Noailles with my excuses. Having done that, I stepped into my coach and drove at once to the Palais Royal, where an immense crowd was waiting to hear the news; but I merely said that all was proceeding according to the proper forms, and that the business was not yet concluded.

I found M. le Duc d'Orléans closeted with Canillac, who had been waiting for him. We immediately made plans, and he sent for Daguesseau, the procureur général (afterwards Chancellor), and for Joly de Fleury, the chief avocat général. It was nearly two o'clock. They served dinner at a small table laid for four, at which Canillac, Conflans (M. le Duc d'Orléans's first gentleman), and I sat down to eat with the prince—and let me say in passing that I never ate with him again, save once, at Mme la Duchesse d'Orléans's house at Bagnolet.[2]

The Maréchal de Villeroy had meanwhile remained at Versailles, where he was kept posted with the latest news. Three couriers, coming one after another, filled him with such joy and hope that he and his former mistress Mme de Ventadour[3] never doubted but that the codicil would be accepted and the will proved. They could scarcely contain their raptures, and soon spread the news that there had been a complete victory for M. du Maine. Paris was similarly deceived by messengers from the Duc du Maine himself; but his triumph was short-lived.

We returned to the Parlement shortly after four o'clock. I drove there alone in my coach a little ahead of M. le Duc d'Orléans, and I found everyone already seated. People looked at me curiously, or so I imagined. I do not know if they guessed whence I came, but I took good care not to let my face betray me. I merely said to the Duc de La Force as I passed him that his advice had been good, and that I had told M. le Duc d'Orléans from whom it had come. The prince then arrived. After the bustle inevitable with a large following had subsided, he began to speak, saying that he would take up the affair from the point at which it had been left that morning, for he must confess that he had been unable to reach any

[1] A royal edict needed to be registered by the Parlement to become law. From the beginning of the sixteenth century the Parlement had been in the habit of commenting, or remonstrating, on the edicts sent to it for registration. Louis XIV had, however, abolished that right, or rather had reduced it to making comments signifying approval.

[2] A village to the east of Paris, within the twentieth-century District of Paris. The Duchesse d'Orléans had a country house there.

[3] Louis XV's governess, who had saved him from the doctors in 1712. See II, pp. 235 f.

agreement with M. du Maine. He would therefore remind the assembly of the monstrous clauses contained in that codicil wrenched from the dying monarch, for they were even more abominable than those in the will which had already been set aside. Having annulled the will, the assembly could not rightly allow M. du Maine to control the young King, the Court, Paris, and consequently the entire kingdom, and to have power of life and death over the Regent, whom he could arrest at any time once he was made master of the civil and military households. The assembly would surely realize the disasters likely to follow from such a revolutionary situation, and he relied on the members' prudence and justice, as well as upon their love of France, to make them speak out without fear or favour.

M. du Maine, at that point, showed himself as despicable in the field as he had been formidable in the tents. He looked like a condemned man. He who was always so ruddy now appeared deathly pale, as he murmured something vastly humble and respectful, in striking contrast to his bold utterances earlier in the day. The vote was then taken without allowing him an opportunity to speak, and was given unanimously for the total annulment of the codicil. The voting was preceded, as in the case of the will, by a sudden upsurge of indignation. The King's advocates had been due to speak before the vote was taken, for they were both present and M. de Mesmes also, but they did not ask to be heard. Daguesseau and Joly de Fleury were therefore the only ones to address the assembly. The former was very brief, the latter vastly rhetorical, but since their words may be found in the libraries, I shall only say that both were entirely on M. le Duc d'Orléans's side. M. du Maine, perceiving that they were plucking him bare, made one last desperate effort, declaring with more vigour than he had yet shown, but still with moderation, that since the power given him by the codicil was to be removed, he would ask to be relieved also of the guardianship of the King's person, retaining only the supervision of his education. To which M. le Duc d'Orléans replied, 'Most certainly, Monsieur, that will amply suffice.' Thereupon Mesmes the premier président, appearing as crushed as M. du Maine himself, counted the votes.

While this was proceeding, and for the remainder of the session, the Duc du Maine sat with eyes cast down, looking more dead than alive, and quite motionless. His sons and his brother appeared completely indifferent and did nothing. As soon as judgment had been delivered there was loud and prolonged cheering from the great crowd of onlookers that had filled the building when the news was made public.

When the noise had quite abated, the Regent made a short but dignified address thanking the assembly, after which he announced that the time had come to explain the measures which he thought necessary for good government, adding that he was all the more confident of them since they expressed the wishes of Mgr le Duc de Bourgogne (he named him thus), which had come to light among the papers found after his death. He praised His Highness in glowing terms for his enlightened views, and then announced that in addition to the supreme Regency Council controlling all the nation's affairs, he proposed to set up other special councils, for foreign affairs, war, the navy, the finances, the Church, and the Interior, and to appoint magistrates of the Parlement to assist the members with their learned advice in matters pertaining to the police, the law, and the liberties of the Gallican Church. The magistrates and the crowds applauded this announcement. The premier président then brought the session to a close with a very cold compliment to M. le Duc d'Orléans, who rose and left the chamber with all the company assembled. It would be impossible to exaggerate the impression made in that assembly by the mention of the Dauphin's name, nor to describe how dear the memory of that truly venerated prince was held.

The Regent went straight to Versailles, for it was by then very late, and he wished to see and, as it were, report to the King before they put him to bed. He then received the congratulations of those one-time love-birds[1] and immediately after visited Madame, who left her apartments to embrace him and appeared vastly pleased. When the first compliments and questions were over, she said that she had one request to make of her son, for the good of France and his own reputation. She then asked him to give her his solemn promise never, no matter for how short a time, or in what capacity, to employ the Abbé Dubois who, she said, was the greatest rascal unhanged (as to which she had ample proof), and who if ever he got the chance, would certainly betray the Regent and the kingdom to serve his own selfish interests. She said much more concerning him, and pressed her son so hard that she extracted his firm promise never to employ Dubois.

I arrived at Versailles an hour after the Regent and went to Mme la Duchesse de Berry, who was in raptures, M. le Duc d'Orléans having just left her. I next called on Mme la Duchesse d'Orléans, who also appeared well pleased; but, on the plea that I needed rest, which was true enough, I avoided giving her long descriptions. It was thus only on the following day that I learned of the promise freely given to exclude for ever the Abbé Dubois. You will discover all too soon that M. le Duc d'Orléans's promises were mere words, just sounds that rent the air.

On Wednesday, 4 September, the late King's entrails were taken without ceremony to Notre-Dame by two royal almoners, in one of the State coaches, and without other escort. On Thursday, 5 September, the Parlement and the other high courts of justice presented formal addresses to the new King. On that same day there were announcements of important changes in the *Maison du Roi* and the department of buildings, and the royal hunts were reduced to the size they had been under Louis XIII.

[1] The Duc de Villeroy and Mme de Ventadour.

On Friday, 6 September, Cardinal de Rohan took the heart to the Church of the Jesuits,[1] with little ceremony and a very small escort. It was very noticeable at the service that less than half a dozen courtiers were in waiting. It is not for me, who in imitation of my father never in all my life missed attendance at Saint-Denis on the anniversary of Louis XIII's death, and who had already attended two-and-thirty times without seeing another soul there, to draw attention to such swift forgetfulness.

It was on that very day that the Regent did what would have been an action of sublime merit, had the thought of God prompted him. Since religion did not enter into it, however, it was a most shameful deed, for he should have considered his high position, and not so quickly and so publicly have shown that his persecutors would go unpunished. At eight o'clock that same morning he went to see Mme de Maintenon at Saint-Cyr. He spent more than an hour with that bitter enemy who had once demanded his head, and quite recently had wished to place him, bound hand and foot, in the power of the Duc du Maine by the most monstrous terms of the late King's will and its codicil. On that visit, the Regent assured her that her allowance from the King of four thousand francs would be continued, and would be brought to her in the first days of every month by the Duc de Noailles, who was apparently responsible for persuading M. le Duc d'Orléans to make her both the visit and the present. The prince told Mme de Maintenon that if she wished for more she had only to say so, and promised her to protect Saint-Cyr, whose young ladies he inspected before departing. You should know that besides the estate of Maintenon and the other properties belonging to that infamous and malign old witch, the convent of Saint-Cyr, endowed with an income of more than four hundred thousand livres and possessing great sums in reserve, was obliged by its settlement to receive her in her retirement, and to obey her implicitly as its sole and absolute head, to feed and house her and all her friends, also her servants, both indoor and outdoor, with her coaches, carriages and horses, keeping her table and that of her household according to her desires and wholly at the expense of the convent, all of which was carried out most punctiliously until the day of her death. Thus she certainly did not need such a munificent gift as the continuance of a pension amounting to forty-eight thousand livres. It would have been more than generous had M. le Duc d'Orléans deigned to forget that she still lived, and allowed her to rest undisturbed at Saint-Cyr.

Madame also visited her that morning at eleven o'clock; but Madame, as you will remember, had owed everything to her at the time of Monsieur's death,[2] and had good cause to show her that mark of gratitude. The Regent was very careful not to mention his visit to me, either before or afterwards, and I thought it not worth while to reproach him or make him feel

1 The Grands-Jésuites, in the Rue Saint-Antoine.
2 See I, pp. 160–161.

ashamed. It was much talked of in Society, and not with approval. The Spanish scandal[1] was not yet forgotten, and the will and codicil were still the main subjects of conversation.

The King's continued residence at Versailles greatly inconvenienced the Regent, who liked to live in Paris where all his pleasures were within reach. The court physicians, however, who were all comfortably lodged in the château, had strongly opposed the King's removal to Vincennes, on the pretext of a slight cold in his head. On the following day, M. le Duc d'Orléans sent for all the Paris doctors who had been called in during the illness of the late King. They, having nothing to gain by the King's remaining at Versailles, ridiculed the fears of the court doctors, with the result that it was decided to take the King to Vincennes on the following day, Monday, 9 September. All was ready to receive him.[2] He left Versailles at two o'clock in the afternoon, seated at the back of the coach between the Regent and the Duchesse de Ventadour, with the Duc du Maine and the Maréchal de Villeroy in front, and the Comte de Toulouse by one door, because he preferred that to the front seat. They crossed the walls of Paris, but did not enter the town, and arrived at Vincennes at exactly five o'clock. There were great crowds and many coaches lining the road to see the King pass.

Next day the Regent spent the entire morning working with each secretary of State in turn. He had ordered them to bring lists of all the *lettres de cachet* issued from their offices, and the reasons for them, which latterly had often been very slight. The greater number of the banishments were on account of Jansenism and opposition to the Bull *Unigenitus*, but there were many others of which only the late King had known the cause; others again had been issued by earlier ministers, and among these several had long been ignored or forgotten. The Regent freed all exiles and prisoners, save only those whom he knew to have been guilty of grave offences or of treachery to the State, and thus he was greatly blessed for an act of justice and humanity. Many very strange stories then came to light, and others that were vastly terrible, so that people became deeply concerned for the miseries of the prisoners and the persecutions during the past reign and by previous ministers. Among the prisoners in the Bastille was a man who had been arrested thirty-five years earlier, on the very day of his arrival from Italy, where he had lived. No one ever discovered the reason for his arrest, and he was never interrogated. It was all thought to have been a mistake. When they told him of his release, he sadly asked what he was supposed to do, for he had not a penny, knew no one in Paris, or, indeed, in the whole of France. His Italian relatives were all apparently

---

[1] See index, II, under Spanish scandal.

[2] Louis XIV before he died had ordered the little Dauphin to be taken to Vincennes to escape the 'foul airs', and had had the fortress specially furnished and arranged so that the Court could live there.

dead, and so many years had passed without news of him that all his possessions had been given away. He did not know what to do with himself, and asked to spend the remainder of his life at the Bastille with board and lodging provided for him free of cost. That favour was willingly granted, with all the liberty that he chose to take. The state of those who were taken from the dungeons, where the rancour of the ministers, the Jesuits, and the officers of the constitution[1] had thrown them, was so dreadful that all the horrors which they recounted seem perfectly credible. On the day that they were set free, the Regent held a council with the ministers of the late King, and invited the Duc du Maine and the Comte de Toulouse to attend.

Mme de La Vieuville[2] died that same day, at a not very advanced age, of a breast cancer which she heroically but foolishly kept hidden until two days before her death, thus depriving herself of all medical aid. One solitary maid knew of her illness and nursed her. I have already mentioned both her and her husband at the time when she was a lady-in-waiting of Mme la Duchesse de Berry. That princess stayed at Saint-Cloud with her little court while the Luxembourg palace was made ready for her. M. and Mme la Duchesse du Maine were given a splendid apartment on the ground floor of the Tuileries.

A few days later, the Regent's irresponsibility combined with the pressing needs of the finances to give Crozat[3] the office of treasurer of the Order, in return for a loan to the King of a million in silver bars, with a promise of another two million later. There was a general outcry at this appointment. Crozat was from Languedoc, and of very humble origin; people even said that he had begun life as a lackey. He became a bookkeeper, then a cashier in a bank and, having enriched himself there, began to move in wider spheres; but he never dabbled in ordinary finance. His great triumph was in banking and shipping, and he became the richest man in Paris. He was, indeed, enormously rich, and conceited in proportion, especially after marrying his daughter to the Comte d'Evreux,[4] even although that grand alliance gave him cause for regret all the rest of his life. It was discovered at the same time that sixteen hundred thousand francs was owing to our ambassadors and agents in foreign parts, the great majority of whom had literally not the wherewithal to pay the postage on their letters.

Soon after we had taken up residence in Paris, that is to say directly after

---

[1] The constitution refers always to the Bull *Unigenitus*.

[2] Marie Louise de La Chausée d'Eu d'Arrest. She had married the Marquis de La Vieuville in 1685. She was 'beautiful, poor, meek, and virtuous. Her particular bent was a continual desire to please everyone by boundless flattery, and a talent for ingratiating herself with anyone whom she thought capable of advancing her interests; but that was all.' See I, pp. 357 ff.

[3] Antoine Crozat (1655–1738), Marquis de Châtel, known as 'the millionaire'.

[4] In 1707, Marie Anne Crozat was married at the age of twelve to Henri Louis de La Tour d'Auvergne, Comte d'Evreux.

the King had gone to Vincennes, M. le Duc d'Orléans and I began to speak of the various councils—not without reproaches from me that so much work still remained to do. He was in some doubt regarding the post of president of the finance council, although before the King's death he had promised the post to the Duc de Noailles,[1] at my suggestion. By then I knew where I stood with that gentleman, but I thought it right to consider the interests of the State above my own, and to hold to my original plan. I still believed Noailles capable of working independently, especially since he had been trained in all branches of finance by Desmaretz for the past two years. His private fortune and establishments gave assurance of his incorruptibility; his very ambition would lead him to give of his best in a vitally important post, where I wished to place a nobleman, and for which I could see no better candidate. I thus confirmed M. le Duc d'Orléans in his resolve to appoint him.

Once the membership of the councils was finally decided, we were obliged to tackle the Council of Regency, a much more difficult problem. It had to contain few enough members to give it eminence and, because of their rank, several of M. le Duc d'Orléans's enemies had to be included—for example the Duc du Maine, the Comte de Toulouse, the Maréchal de Villeroy, the Maréchal d'Harcourt (because he had refused the presidency of the council for the Interior), and Chancellor Voysin, since M. le Duc d'Orléans had committed the appalling blunder of allowing him to keep the seals. Toulouse and Harcourt were not certain enemies; but were highly suspect, the former because of what he was and because of his brother (although their characters were very different); Harcourt because of his old friendship with Mme de Maintenon and the Princesse des Ursins. All the others were proven enemies. They had therefore to be counterweighed by men loyal to M. le Duc d'Orléans, and important enough to be treated with respect on the Council, where all the nation's affairs, both at home and abroad, would be brought from the other councils and decided by a majority vote. A further consideration was that Monsieur le Duc had as yet no authority, and when that came to him with age and experience, he might well fall a prey to intrigues and personal ambition and turn against M. le Duc d'Orléans. That prince's weakness was such that he had now consented to the Maréchal de Bezons's[2] leaving the war council, where he had been placed, and had allowed him to go over the heads of others on to the Regency Council itself.

Bezons was a commoner, a coarse and brutal fellow who had run away from the parental home when his father wished to make a priest of him. He enlisted as an ordinary soldier in a body of troops going secretly to Portugal, and fought there in the ranks. His father's inquiries soon established his identity; he was promoted, and served with keenness and industry. The Latin which he learned before joining was all the education he ever

[1] See II, p. 451. [2] See index.

received, but he none the less became a good general, especially skilful at manœuvring a wing of cavalry. His rudeness, however, and his evil temper often prevented him from seeing other men's points of view. All in all, he was a man with much personal courage, not unfamiliar with the idea of honour, but always at a loss, very diffident, a trimmer, with a great desire to arrive and make a fortune. He was also vastly mean and vastly boring, not entirely devoid of commonsense, with a small talent for intrigues of short duration, and possessed of a fairly sound judgment. He had a leonine head of huge dimensions and blubber-lips, the whole surrounded by an immense wig, which would have made him a good model for Rembrandt, and looked all of a piece with his great body. He passed among fools for being a man of sense. This man was not the kind to oppose any member of a Council of Regency, and M. le Duc d'Orléans was ashamed to tell me of his appointment. I, who never lost sight of my chief purpose, was furious to find that he gave me so little support.

Another man whom the Regent placed on the Council caused him so much embarrassment that only by stages did he reveal his identity. This was Torcy, to the surprise of the entire country. All his days at the Court he had been more violently opposed to M. le Duc d'Orléans than anyone save Mme de Maintenon and M. du Maine. The prince had often had good reason to be vexed with him, and until after the King's death neither he nor Mme la Duchesse d'Orléans had ever made the slightest attempt to secure his good will. I myself had the barest acquaintance with the Torcys for, truth to tell, since only the best and most select company went to their house, my pride was hurt at their never inviting me. Torcy came of a ministerial family; thus as it was my purpose to abolish secretaries of State and their powers, he, who had inherited from his father and father-in-law,[1] was not the kind of man to suit me. I had often urged M. le Duc d'Orléans to dismiss him, and although the prince had not agreed as heartily as I could have wished, I still had hopes until he allowed me to perceive that I must not be too sanguine. I then redoubled my efforts; but at last he confessed with a good deal of confusion that he considered Torcy necessary because, having been minister of foreign affairs for so many years, he knew all the secrets. That indeed was what saved him. M. le Duc d'Orléans showered him with favours, rewards, and powers in order to win him over. He received six hundred and fifty thousand livres for his post of secretary of State, plus a further hundred and fifty thousand, all paid in cash when he handed in his resignation.[2] His minister's pension of twenty thousand livres was allowed him, and another pension of sixty thousand, on resigning the office of postmaster, although he retained control of that department, together with the authority and the secrets.

[1] His father was Charles François Colbert, Marquis de Croissy; his father-in-law, Simon Arnauld, Marquis de Pomponne.

[2] Torcy resigned all his offices in order to join the Regency Council.

Impossible to describe the general amazement at such treatment of Torcy, who was supposed with sufficient reason to be totally free from any association with M. le Duc d'Orléans, if not actually opposed to him. You shall soon see how wrong I was concerning Torcy, and how a close friendship gradually developed between us, which endures even at the present time, March 1746.

M. le Duc d'Orléans had always been minded to place a bishop on the Council of Regency. I thought he might well have dispensed with one. In that sentiment I was in agreement with the late King and, I believe, with all prudent men, especially in the heat of the affair of the constitution. The interests of the late Archbishop of Cambrai,[1] on account of the great influence which the Duc de Beauvilliers had over me, had hitherto prevented my entering into a struggle. I was thus reduced to choosing the least harmful of the prelates, and I mentioned to M. le Duc d'Orléans the name of the one-time Bishop of Troyes.[2] Earlier in these memoirs[3] I have described how he amazed many people by his noble and courageous retirement.

Monsieur de Troyes was the son of secretary of State Chavigny,[4] and the grandson of Bouthillier, financial secretary.[5] He gained promotion at an early age, became one of the King's almoners, and soon afterwards was made Bishop of Troyes. He was something of a scholar, and knew more about the temporal affairs of the clergy than any other member of that body. Thus he was appointed to nearly all of the Church assemblies, and spoke brilliantly at every one. He was, moreover, a man of parts, able to quiz the ladies, perfectly taking the tone of the highest Society, and spending his life among the best and most distinguished people of the Court and Paris. He was much sought after, especially in gambling for high stakes, and by all the ladies. He was their favourite. They used to call him 'the Trojan', 'the dashing bishop', or 'that brute of a Trojan' when he won their money. From time to time he went to be bored at Troyes, where for decency's sake, or because he could do no other, he faithfully performed his functions. But he never stayed long, and once returned to the gay world, he found it impossible to tear himself away.

That was his life. Yet every now and then thoughts of relgiion came to spoil first his pleasures, then his diversions. He tried to live more austerely, but at last experience taught him that he would never succeed unless he burned his bridges and made a return to the world impossible. He never appeared gayer nor more entertaining than at a dinner at the Hôtel de

[1] Fénelon.
[2] François Bouthillier (1642–1731), Abbé de Chavigny, Bishop of Rennes 1676–1677, then of Troyes 1678–1697.
[3] The following description has been taken from the earlier part of the memoirs. It does not occur earlier in this version.
[4] Denis Bouthillier (died 1622), counsellor of State 1617.
[5] Claude Bouthillier de Chavigny (1581–1652).

Lorges, among a great company of the best Society; after which he spent the night at Versailles, having arranged his plans a few days earlier with Père de La Chaise. Next morning, after prayers,[1] he begged the King for a short audience, and was heard in the study, before mass. There he contrived his confession with some ingenuity:[2] he told the King of his need for retirement and penitence, and of his fears that he would never summon sufficient strength while the world still claimed him. He then handed his resignation to the King, saying that His Majesty would overwhelm him with kindness if he deigned to bestow the bishopric on M. de Troyes's nephew the Abbé de Chavigny, who was of suitable age, and still more suitable because of his ability, learning, and good character. He continued by saying that in the beginning he would help his nephew in the administration of a diocese with which he was perfectly familiar; that he would share with him his own house, at Troyes, and live there in retirement for the remainder of his life. The benefice was of little value, the King liked M. de Troyes despite his frivolity, he at once granted his request.[3] When he left the King's study, M. de Troyes went straight to Paris, visited no one, and left for Troyes on the following day. There he exactly fulfilled the plans which he had made, refusing to see anyone except his nephew and the clergy of the diocese, writing no letters nor communicating with anyone; but living entirely for prayer and penitence, and in complete solitude.

All of this happened very soon after my marriage. At my then age,[4] I barely knew Monsieur de Troyes by sight, and had no acquaintance with him; but from all that I learned of him he appeared to me perfectly adapted to join the Council of Regency, for I saw in him a prelate thoroughly familiar with the temporal affairs of the clergy, well versed in questions regarding Rome, and, best of all, a Frenchman. What is more, he had spent his life before retirement in the highest Society, and had been the friend of most of the eminent personages of his day, and of their wives also. So wide a knowledge of the world was a great point in his favour. He was also a bishop without a diocese, and nothing could be further from his thoughts than re-emergence, since for the past seventeen or eighteen years he had been living in strict retirement. Such a man appeared to me likely to be of great influence in restraining M. le Duc d'Orléans in his debauches. The prince approved the nomination, and the bishop was duly appointed. There was general gratification. He was summoned, arrived, and accepted without demur. The world that invariably expects too much would have preferred to see some hesitation, or even a first refusal. The start was

[1] The prie-Dieu: the King's private morning prayers, accompanied by some ceremonial.
[2] It was dangerous to retire from the King's service. He called it desertion, and never forgave it. Louis XIV regarded the Church, like the army, as his own personal service because he was king by divine right. See I, p. 184.
[3] (Denis) François de Chavigny succeeded his uncle in 1697.
[4] Saint-Simon was twenty when he married Marie Gabrielle de Lorges in 1695.

admirable; he was seen only at important functions; I congratulated myself on my excellent choice. These marvels were, however, of short duration, for I was as much mistaken regarding the Bishop of Troyes as I had been over Torcy, but in a different way. That must suffice for now.

The Council of Regency thus comprised M. le Duc d'Orléans, Monsieur le Duc, the Duc du Maine, the Comte de Toulouse, Voysin the Chancellor, myself (since the fact must be recorded), the Maréchaux de Villeroy, d'Harcourt, and de Bezons, the one-time Bishop of Troyes, and Torcy, all with votes; La Vrillière, keeper of the register, and Pontchartrain, neither of whom had the right to vote. Those who came from the other councils to report were: the Archbishop of Bordeaux, the Maréchaux de Villars, d'Estrées, and d'Huxelles, the Duc de Noailles, and the Duc d'Antin. You will see from the above on which and on how many members the Regent could rely as friends, count as enemies, or regard as neutral. In the event, however, the Council was nearly always unanimous and the Regent in perfect control. Desmaretz was the only one of the late King's ministers to be dismissed at that time, with a very brief note to that effect from M. le Duc d'Orléans. The other six councils were registered in the Parlement; that is to say their existence was recorded, but not the names of their members. No mention was made of the Regency Council because it was the Council of the King and the government of France.

Mme Desmaretz, who was wont to interfere in many matters under cover of her husband's office, fell with him. La Fontaine, her confidential agent, who made a fortune in her service, investing and managing the huge sums which she extracted from the State, was also ruined. She swore he had robbed her and became perfectly distraught. In that condition, smallpox attacked her, and when she recovered she had gone mad; thus, although she survived for several years, no one ever saw her again.[1] It so happened that Mmes Voysin and Desmaretz, the two competitors for the favours of Mme de Maintenon, both died, the one from despair at having been supplanted by her rival,[2] the other from despair at losing her position and her sources of supply.

None of the councillors took an oath, on the precedent that ministers of State were not sworn; and no member of the Regency Council received letters patent, or any written word from the King or the Regent. Since they could not appear at the council table without a royal summons, the members of the Regency Council were summoned on the first occasion by the usher of the King's study, after which M. le Duc d'Orléans told them of the time of the next meeting, and no further notice was given because that would have entailed too much running about. As soon as the Regent

[1] She survived ten years, dying in 1725.
[2] Mme Voysin died in 1714. According to Saint-Simon, Mme de Maintenon engineered her husband's appointment for her sake. She then preferred Mme Desmaretz, which Mme Voysin resented, and, coming from the *extrême bourgeoisie*, did not hide her pique. She was thereupon disgraced and died of misery.

appeared the meeting began. If anyone was late, which seldom happened, he came to the table from behind; the Regent asked him to be seated, and with a word of apology he sat down at his usual place, which on such occasions was left empty.

In former times, members of the councils had always been seated, and only the maître des requêtes coming to report had stood; but even before the new councils met there was unexpected trouble in the finance council, since claims for precedence, however absurd, gain strength if not immediately suppressed. To mention one example: the late King had merely ridiculed the counsellors of State when, at the signing of the treaty of Baden, they had first claimed the right to sign before noblemen. He did not, however, actually forbid them. Following that tradition, which the King himself said was no precedent but merely an absurdity, the counsellors of State on the finance council (none attended the other councils) now claimed and were granted precedence over the Marquis d'Effiat, who was indeed of their cloth, but whose grandfather had died a Knight of the Order, an ambassador, a surintendant des finances, and a Marshal of France. There was much astonishment on the first occasion when a maître des requêtes came to report to the Regency Council, for he declared his right to report sitting, and said that all who were neither dukes nor officers of the crown must stand to hear him. This was a direct consequence of the Regent's having weakly allowed the councillors' claim to precede Effiat. Everyone protested, tempers ran high; but nothing could be done, since the Regent had not been firm enough to issue a command. We were thus reduced to making the presidents of the various councils report to us in person, and none of them was capable of the task, except d'Antin, who was excellent. Let me relate two anecdotes that will show how greatly this practice hindered us in our work.

The Maréchal de Villars, head of the war council, wrote a hand that was completely illegible. He came to the Regency Council with a ruling that consisted of forty or fifty paragraphs relating to warehouses, stages, movements of troops through the kingdom, and all the relevant details. He read the document aloud item by item; and we voted on each point as he read, making several changes which he noted in the margin. When all was finished, M. le Duc d'Orléans asked the Maréchal to re-read the entire document, together with his notes, so that we might be sure he had neglected nothing and that no more changes were required. The Maréchal, sitting next to me, took up his papers and read the first paragraph again, but when he came to the note, he studied it closely, turned the sheet this way and that to catch the light, and finally asked me if I could manage to decipher it. I laughed, asking him how he expected me to proceed when he could not read his own writing, not even when it was fresh in his mind. Everyone mocked him, but he was not in the least disconcerted. He proposed sending for his secretary who, so he said, was in the ante-room and well used to his handwriting; but the Regent would not allow that. We all looked at one another in fits of mirth, quite unable to provide a solution. At last the Regent declared that we must begin all over again; and he desired me to take the pen and write down the notes as we voted for the second time on the various issues. All of this doubled the time spent on this one matter. It is true that an absurd waste of time was the only loss incurred; but the disadvantages were often far greater when, because of the bad reporting of long and complicated affairs, we were prevented from understanding them fully, and sometimes gave the wrong decisions.

The other anecdote is even more revealing. The Maréchal d'Estrées reported to the Regency Council on all the business of the council for the navy. La Vrillière used to liken him to an upset bottle of ink that flows sometimes in a trickle, sometimes ceases altogether, and then suddenly pours forth in great thick blots. One day, as he started to report on a most complicated affair concerning the capture of a vessel, the Comte de Toulouse, who was very knowledgeable on the business of that department,[1] and by nature accurate, brief, and remarkably sensible, turned to me saying that I should never understand the matter from the Maréchal d'Estrées's report; that it was of some importance, and that he would whisper the gist of it into my ear as the Maréchal proceeded. I heard M. le Comte de Toulouse clearly enough to learn his views, but not well enough to express my own opinion, especially since he was still whispering when my turn came to vote. I therefore explained to the Regent what had happened, adding that M. le Comte de Toulouse was so lucid that I felt obliged to side with him; whereupon the Regent laughed, saying that no one had ever before voted for such a reason. I laughed also, and said that if he would not take my vote in that form, he might perhaps have the goodness to count M. le Comte de Toulouse's vote as two, and so the matter was settled. Next day, I seized the opportunity to remind M. le Duc d'Orléans of the harm done to the nation by the obstinacy of the maîtres des requêtes, and of his weakness in not issuing commands to them. I had no success at all with him.

The Duchesse de Berry took up residence at the Luxembourg palace with her little court. Attempts were made to find us comfortable lodgings there; but although Mme de Saint-Simon could contrive no decent excuse for leaving, she did seize on this opportunity to live as far away as possible, and we thus continued to reside at our Paris house.[2] Mme la Duchesse de Berry still insisted on my wife's having a room at the Luxembourg, but it remained unfurnished, and she never entered it. She attended on Mme la Duchesse de Berry in the mornings; but only when

---

[1] The Comte de Toulouse was president of the council for the navy; the Maréchal (Admiral) d'Estrées was vice-president.

[2] The Saint-Simons' house was then in the Rue des Saints-Pères; they did not move to the Rue Saint-Dominique until 1719.

there were audiences or other official receptions, and she visited her nearly every evening at the time she had company for card-playing, when ladies were permitted to appear in ordinary dress and frequently stayed afterwards for supper. Mme de Saint-Simon scarcely ever supped with her, for we almost invariably had guests to dine and sup at home, as had always been our custom. On very rare occasions, my wife accompanied her when she went for drives or paid calls, unless she were visiting the King, and sometimes she went with her to the play. Mme de Saint-Simon had good reason to be firm regarding her freedom, but was always treated with great civility and consideration. As for myself, I continued as usual, calling on Mme la Duchesse de Berry once or twice during the year, staying for a moment only, but always being very well received. You already know the reason for such conduct from me.[1]

You may recollect from something I said earlier that I had taken as much trouble for the Marquis de Sandricourt as if he had been my own son.[2] We are of the same house, although the two branches of our family separated more than three hundred years ago. I have always greatly cared for my name; and have done everything possible to advance my kinsmen in my own generation. The results have not been happy. Sandricourt's parents, persons of great intelligence, but avaricious, obscure, living in complete retirement, had no other children. They possessed fine estates in Picardy, but were perpetually at my father's house, and after his death scarcely quitted mine. I procured a company of cavalry for their son when he was still very young, and the first use that I ever made of Chamillart's friendship was to get for Sandricourt the offer of the Berry regiment of cavalry, which Yolet, a very good officer, was resigning after failing to be promoted brigadier-general. Sandricourt's father was alarmed by the price; I undertook to pay it, and I asked Yolet to clinch the bargain at his first offer, saying that I would pay the difference. The father, however, guessed what had happened, and out of hurt pride concluded nearer to Yolet's price. The difference was still paid by me, but they have since repaid me. When the regiment went to Spain, I recommended Sandricourt to Mme des Ursins on whose good offices I could rely. M. le Duc d'Orléans was in command, and on that account Sandricourt was treated with marked distinction. He served with valour, and three years later Chamillart caused him to be promoted brigadier-general over the heads of many others. When he returned to Paris in the winter after M. le Duc de Berry's marriage, I took him everywhere, and obtained for him the entrée at that prince's court on the pretext that he commanded M. le Duc de Berry's own regiment. I had really begun to think that I might do something with him.

[1] There had been a terrible scene in 1711, after Saint-Simon had warned her father about scandalous rumours of incest. Orléans had repeated his words and the Duchesse de Berry had attacked poor Mme de Saint-Simon.

[2] Louis François de Rouvroy, Marquis de Sandricourt (d. 1751). The earlier reference to him in the memoirs is in 1705 (not included in this version).

His parents had for a long time been desirous of a marriage for him. I had always discouraged them, on the grounds that he was too young and too low in the service. By advancing in years and fortune he would be likely to find a far better match, and one capable of promoting his interests. More especially, I adjured them to remember their excellent situation, in being free from debt and with an income of nearly fifty thousand livres from good estates and lands extending from Paris to Abbeville. They should, I said, be under no obligation to make a misalliance, which had always appeared to me very far from their son's wishes. They were, however, so bent on a marriage that they refused to listen to reason. Mme de Saint-Simon and I therefore sought to content them in a fitting manner, and we believed that in Mlle de Richebourg we had found a prize.[1] Her father, the Marquis de Richebourg, was the grandson of a brother of that Prince d'Espinay whose son I have several times mentioned. That son had died several years before, and the Princesse d'Espinay,[2] his widow, was the sister of Mlle de Lillebonne who has appeared even more often in these memoirs.

The Marquis de Richebourg with whom we are now concerned served, like his father and his grandfather before him, in Spain, and continued in the service of Philip V. He was a Grandee of Spain, a Knight of the Golden Fleece, Colonel of the Walloon Regiment, Viceroy of Catalonia, and resided in Barcelona; what is more, he was wealthy and a widower, with only two daughters, the elder of whom, being excessively pious, had given up all idea of matrimony. Both daughters lived on their father's Flanders estates in the most suitable manner, and with very high reputations for virtue. Their father was quite set against a second marriage for himself, which was no doubt somewhat eccentric; but on that account, all his Flemish property, and all the very considerable wealth which he had amassed in Spain, would go to his daughters on his death and, even more precious, they would also inherit his grandeeship.[3]

For many years past, this Marquis de Richebourg had placed his entire confidence in the above-mentioned Princesse d'Espinay. She had authority to administer his estates in Flanders and to govern his daughters, and they continually exchanged long and affectionate letters. No one of rank had as yet contemplated this great alliance, so little known, so far distant, so uncertain because of the father's age and situation, and the possibility of

---

[1] Marie Lydie Albertine de Melun (1692–1746). Her father was Guillaume de Melun-Espinay, Marquis de Richebourg, who died in 1735.

[2] See index. Considering Saint-Simon's loathing for the Lorraine family as expressed in the early part of the memoirs, it seems strange, to say the least, that he was so anxious to have one of them in his own family. He himself had nearly married Mme d'Armagnac, a Lorraine princess, in 1695 (see I, p. 60), and one wonders whether, in that event, his loves and hatreds would have been different.

[3] When Mlle de Richebourg inherited the grandeeship, her husband would acquire the rank from her.

his suddenly deciding to remarry. We discussed the prospects with Sandricourt and his parents, who seemed to regard the match as the greatest one available and far better than they had ever dared to hope. And so indeed it was. Mme de Saint-Simon spoke to Mme d'Espinay who gladly gave her approval. She confirmed the unlikelihood of the Marquis de Richebourg's contracting a second marriage, spoke freely of his implicit confidence in her, and promised to write to him immediately. Scarcely had her letter gone than the Sandricourts came to inform us that they had no hope of our succeeding; that they urgently wished to marry off their son, and that nothing would suit them better than a connection with the law, so as to protect them against land-taxes and possible lawsuits. Their son, looking very woebegone, visited me also and begged me not to abandon him to the whims of his father and mother. He spoke to the same purpose both to my mother and to Mme de Saint-Simon, and we all thought him sincere. You may guess what we said to his parents, more especially since the Princesse d'Espinay's letter had already been posted. They appeared very much abashed but were not a whit less stubborn. They did not, however, give any definite refusal, and we hoped that before they had found anyone to suit them, and if the young man remained firm, the Marquis de Richebourg might reply and the match be made.

Our hopes did not long endure. Two days later, the young man, looking vastly embarrassed, informed us that his marriage to a Mlle de Gourgue[1] had been arranged. I violently expostulated, asking if he had given his consent. He said he dared not go against his parents, who wanted the law at any price. I took him to my mother and to Mme de Saint-Simon, both of whom used every conceivable argument in vain. In the end, I said that if they were so mad for the law as to prefer it to the immensely wealthy daughter of the House of Melun, who without doubt would make her husband a Grandee of Spain, and were too impetuous to wait for the Marquis de Richebourg's reply, after making us beg Mme d'Espinay to write to him, they might at least choose a decent family capable of assisting them. The father[2] of this girl, I said, was a maître des requêtes so thoroughly discredited that Chancellor Pontchartrain had actually received a formal deputation from the magistrates asking for his dismissal; since when he had never dared to appear before the council. I added that his father's reputation was little better; that his uncle, the Bishop of Bazas, was the mock and scorn of all Gascony; that if, in short, they were determined on the law they should at least allow us time to give some courteous explanation to Mme d'Espinay, and that if they cared to have Mlle Le Peletier,[3] I could easily arrange that match through Coëtanfao, who was

[1] Louise Marie Gabrielle de Gourgue (1699–1754). She was interested in chemistry and died of asphyxiation in her laboratory at Saint-Germain.
[2] Jean François de Gourgue, Marquis d'Aulnay-les-Bondy (1670–1734).
[3] Louise Françoise Le Peletier. She married the Marquis de Salignac, great-nephew of Fénelon.

their close friend and mine also. She was the daughter of a premier président, and the sister of a président-à-mortier, the granddaughter of a minister of State and contrôlleur général, the great-niece of Le Peletier de Souzy and niece of his son des Forts,[1] both of them counsellors of State, in office at that time, and with the highest reputations. The Le Peletiers, at any rate, were a famous family of that kind and condition, and in positions where they might be useful.

My mother and Mme de Saint-Simon echoed my arguments; but we spoke to deaf ears, and, what was worse, to a lover, although we did not know that at the time. All this happened during the morning. After dinner, Mme de Sandricourt came to me bursting with rage. I suffered her tirades as one suffers fools. She then went upstairs to my mother, who was less forbearing, and who told her flatly things about her future daughter-in-law which she was loath to believe (although they were known to all her father's servants and to many other people besides), finally prophesying all that has since happened. Mme de Sandricourt left us more furious than ever. Her husband never came at all. Five or six days later the wedding took place.

The cream of the story is that the gallant bridegroom went round to all the lawyers of his acquaintance, saying that I had such a horror of their kind that I had broken with his family rather than allow the connection. At that time the affair of the bonnet was at its height; you may therefore well imagine the effect of his remarks. After such black ingratitude, treachery, and revolting slanders, we refused to let the Sandricourts be mentioned in our presence, and never since have we so much as clapped eyes on them. The parents lived long enough to see and feel the truth of my mother's prophecies, and both died in sorrow. Their more amiable son was for a short time in love, then went in mortal fear of his wife who cared nothing for prudence or restraint; at last he followed the fashion by becoming her docile and obedient servant. Children were not lacking to them, but money often was, although they spent little, and lived in total obscurity in their own part of Paris. Sandricourt continued in the service and rose to be a lieutenant-general during the Bohemian war;[2] but his lack of parts, his shabby marriage, and the resulting obscurity caused him to be overlooked and to go unrewarded. Mlle Le Peletier, whom I had proposed to him, has since married the Marquis de Salignac, for a long time ambassador to Holland and now lieutenant-general, Governor of Quesnoy, counsellor of State, and a member of the Order.

On Friday, 25 October, the state funeral of Louis XIV took place at Saint-Denis. Everything about it was so disordered, so unlike what was done at the funerals of Louis XIII, Henri IV, and all their predecessors,

---

[1] Michel Le Peletier de Souzy (1640–1725) was Mlle Le Peletier's uncle; Michel Robert Le Peletier des Forts was her first cousin.

[2] The War of the Austrian Succession, 1740–1748.

that I shall spare you a description, since it would lead only to a long digression.

At this same time, M. le Duc d'Orléans lost Homberg, one of the greatest chemists in Europe, and the most honest man imaginable, as well as the most simply and steadfastly devout. It was with Homberg that the prince gained the disastrous knowledge of science that kept him so long and innocently employed, but was used against him so wickedly. Following the treacherous advice of Effiat, M. le Duc d'Orléans had wanted, after the deaths of Monsieur le Dauphin and Madame la Dauphine,[1] to send this same Homberg to the Bastille; but he later made him his chief physician. M. le Duc d'Orléans chose to succeed him Chirac, reputedly the best doctor in the world, who had accompanied him to Italy and Spain. Chirac was indeed conversant with every branch of medicine, and possessed all possible brilliance and learning. I enter into so much detail because after M. le Duc d'Orléans's death this same Chirac became the King's first physician.

Pontchartrain,[2] safe in the shelter of his father's reputation and protected by Effiat and Bezons, continued undismayed to clutch at the remnants of office. He was at that time completely without responsibilities; yet he still survived, tirelessly swallowing insults and rebuffs, living on the hope of one day recovering functions that were still nominally his. He never missed a meeting of the Regency Council although he had no voice in it, although no one regarded or spoke to him, and although his only self-imposed duty was to trim the candles, which had become a habit with him, and a source of unconcealed amusement to all the company present. Everyone marvelled at his being willing to present so mean and contemptible an appearance, and at his insensibility in thus surviving his official self in that profoundly mean capacity, so very far removed from the pride of his past splendours and authority. All the members wished him gone, and seized every opportunity to dismiss him after their own fashion by showing him their supreme contempt, as though to compensate for the respect and servility with which he had been treated earlier. M. le Duc d'Orléans, like everyone else, marvelled at his endurance, but seemed to have no idea of dismissing him. The Comte de Toulouse and I frequently mocked him in whispers, especially when the navy was in question, and the Comte de Toulouse or the Maréchal d'Estrées directed cutting jibes straight at him. They even sought such opportunities, and the Comte de Toulouse and I, in full assembly, would lament together over the Regent's

---

[1] See II, pp. 241 et seqq. When the Duc d'Orléans realized that he was seriously suspected of having poisoned the Dauphin and the Dauphine, he took the bad advice of the Marquis d'Effiat and went to Louis XIV asking that both Homberg and himself be arrested and sent to the Bastille, pending an inquiry. When the King refused, Orléans asked for Homberg alone to be arrested; but that too King Louis refused to hear of.

[2] For descriptions of Pontchartrain, secretary of the Navy under Louis XIV, his ill treatment of the Comte de Toulouse, and Saint-Simon's reasons for loathing him, see index, I and II.

THE DUC DU MAINE.
BY FRANÇOIS DE TROY

LOUIS HENRI DE
BOURBON-CONDÉ, MONSIEUR
LE DUC. BY PIERRE GOBERT

LOUIS XV'S ACCESSION TO THE THRONE. ENGRAVING

A MEETING OF THE REGENCY COUNCIL. EARLY EIGHTEENTH-
CENTURY FRENCH SCHOOL

Photo : Artaud Frères

THE RUINS OF SAINT-SIMON'S CHÂTEAU AT
LA FERTÉ VIDAME

THE PALACE AND GARDENS OF THE TUILERIES.
BY FRANÇOIS RAGUENET

Photo : Bulloz

CARDINAL DUBOIS.
STATUE ON HIS TOMB IN SAINT-ROCH, PARIS
BY GUILLAUME COUSTOU

mistaken kindness in allowing a useless outsider to hear our deliberations, a man malicious enough to disclose our secrets, and in every way meriting dismissal. In the end such tolerance of Pontchartrain's presence became quite unendurable, and I resolved to make a great effort to be rid of him. On Sunday, 3 November, I went to M. le Duc d'Orléans, at Vincennes, before the Regency Council, which met in the morning, and asked him if he were not weary of seeing Pontchartrain, unable to speak, listening to everything, with no one addressing him, merely snuffing our candles when it grew dark. Would he not, I asked, make an end to this ludicrous situation? And I pointed out that by refusing to take action he sickened and defiled us with the presence of this poisonous insect, whose expulsion every one of us most heartily desired. I said further that it was disgraceful to leave him undisturbed after the many well-justified and repeated censures which for the past two months he had been unable to confute. I ended by stressing the indignation felt against that ex-pasha, the general surprise that he should still be tolerated, and the universal applause with which his dismissal would be greeted. The Regent agreed with what I said, but objected on account of the father,[1] saying that he could not bring himself to give the Chancellor so much pain. I replied that if he so wished, I could show him a way to dismiss the son and at the same time earn the father's undying gratitude. The Regent, looking vastly astonished, asked how that could be. I proposed that he should order Pontchartrain immediately to hand in his resignation as secretary of State, and then forthwith bestow that office on Maurepas,[2] his eldest son who, being only fifteen years old, could not fulfil even the rudimentary duties remaining. La Vrillière[3] might well undertake them for the time being—they would not occupy more than half an hour a week, and the Chancellor could be made to feel the exceptional favour of an appointment that was not merely a reversion, and the solicitude shown by placing his grandson until he came of age in the hands of a kinsman who, being himself a secretary of State, would not feel tempted to snatch the post for his own benefit.

The Regent opened his eyes and ears very wide at this suggestion and thoroughly approved of it. I said that nothing prevented his taking action on the following day, and again he agreed; but he desired me to compose

---

[1] Louis II Phélypeaux, Comte de Pontchartrain (1643-1727), Chancellor of France 1699-1714.

[2] Jean Frédéric Phélypeaux, Comte de Maurepas (1701-1781). He married La Vrillière's daughter, Marie Jeanne Phélypeaux de La Vrillière.

[3] Louis II Phélypeaux, Marquis de La Vrillière (1672-1725), a secretary of State like his father and grandfather before him, in 1700 had been made Commandeur-Secrétaire des Ordres. 'He was little taller than a dwarf, tubby, perched on high heels, somewhat absurd-looking. He was, however, intelligent, if too impulsive. He understood his work, which consisted only in being the secretary of the Conseil des Dépêches. He had no department of his own. He was also honest, loyal, obliging, eager to please and make friends.' His grandfather and Saint-Simon's father had been good friends; Saint-Simon was therefore prepared to be lenient towards him.

a letter for him to send to Pontchartrain's father, and to show it him that same day at the Palais Royal. I took great care not to appear reluctant, for I was eager to be finished with the matter and to have it kept absolutely secret.[1] Moreover, the Chancellor was in Paris, which made me fear lest someone get wind of my plan in time to frustrate me; for I well remembered how once before Pontchartrain had escaped me at the eleventh hour. When the Council rose we all went to dine in Paris. I composed M. le Duc d'Orléans's letter to the Chancellor. It was honest, affectionate, full of respect and consideration; but ended by stating very firmly that since he could not be other than gratified by the concern shown for himself and his family, and since the matter was now settled, His Royal Highness desired his son before noon on the following morning to be at the Chancellor's lodging at the Institution,[2] to hand his resignation to the Abbé de Thésut[3] who would bring it forthwith to the Palais Royal. La Vrillière would be waiting there to receive it, and would see that everything was in order and the office conferred on young Maurepas, whom he would take to thank the King that same afternoon. Lastly, being anxious to avoid the fatigue of useless appeals, the Regent forbade Pontchartrain to attempt to see him, write to him, or ask any other person, no matter whom, to speak on his behalf until the entire matter was closed.

I took the draft of M. le Duc d'Orléans's letter, complete in every detail, to the Palais Royal. His Royal Highness changed nothing. I dictated it; he wrote it with his own hand; signed it, sealed it, addressed it, and gave it back to me to be delivered. He then immediately summoned La Vrillière and the Abbé de Thésut and gave them their orders secretly. Thus no more remained than to act.

Next morning at half-past eight, I sent M. le Duc d'Orléans's letter in a sealed envelope, which I myself addressed to Chancellor de Pontchartrain, with a message to say that I would call on him within the hour. I had no wish to be the bearer of bad news, and I thus purposely allowed an interval of half an hour to elapse before starting. At the Porte Saint-Michel, I met La Vrillière, returning from his mission. We both stopped. He stepped into my coach, and I asked him why he came back. He described the Chancellor's surprise and distress, said he had admitted that Pontchartrain well merited dismissal, and that the favour shown to his grandson was immense; but he was a father witnessing his son's shame, and he had exclaimed that it was my doing, because I had sworn to ruin him. Yet he had spoken without rancour. La Vrillière said these lamentations had made

---

[1] Saint-Simon does not appear at his best in this vengeful affair, especially considering how great and old a friend the Chancellor was; but he shows a good deal of moral courage in going to face him with the hurtful news. Moreover he had once before rescued Pontchartrain for the Chancellor's sake when he was on the very brink of dismissal. See II, pp. 166–169.

[2] Chancellor Pontchartrain's apartment at the Oratory.

[3] The Abbé Louis de Thésut (1663-1729) who had been the Duc d'Orléans's private secretary since 1708.

him so unhappy that he had decided to return. 'You made a great mistake,' said I, 'Turn round now, and go back with me. He is certainly wretched on account of his son; but very soon he will be gratified by the regard shown for himself, and because the office remains in his family, which it would not otherwise have done.' Thus conversing we reached the Chancellor's lodging, and found him alone, pacing up and down his study. 'This is your doing!' he exclaimed; 'I recognize your handiwork. You expel my son, and save my son's son for love of me and of his mother. Did you not always say you would ruin him?' 'Monsieur,' said I, 'I swore to that long before the King's death. I have not deceived you; I have simply kept my word; but I have done better, for your family is saved, and your grandson has been given office in such a way that he cannot be robbed of it. That should greatly comfort you; and what an honour, what a mark of distinction for yourself!' 'Indeed, I feel that,' he replied, 'and I realize that I owe it to your affection'; whereat he flung his arms round my neck. 'But I am also a father, and although I know my son, it cuts me to the quick to see him disgraced.' At that point he was moved to tears; but before long thoughts of his grandson had intervened.

When he was slightly calmer, I pointed out that this would be the making of his family, for Pontchartrain could not long have retained his office, and, once dismissed, no one would have considered replacing him with a boy of fifteen whose father was ruined. The Chancellor admitted this, embraced me again with great affection, and we three began to talk somewhat disjointedly in an attempt to kill time. Every now and then he returned to his son and the matter in hand, saying to me, 'You wrote that letter; I recognized your style from all those precautions. You wanted to prevent my interceding with M. le Duc d'Orléans, that is why you made it impossible for me to approach him; and you also wished to keep my son muzzled until the order was carried out. Oh! I recognize you in all this, and also in the kind attentions to myself, with which the letter is packed.' 'Well, Monsieur,' said I, 'admitting all that to be true, was I so very wrong? You stopped me once before by appealing to M. le Duc d'Orléans; I did not want you to deflect me a second time. Believe me, you will get over your grief as a father; and as a grandfather and the head of the family you will be glad and live to thank me.' 'Yes, indeed I shall!' he exclaimed impatiently, 'I do so already; it overwhelms me to think that I owe my grandson's appointment and the welfare of my family entirely to you.' He then once more embraced me, adding that he would tell his grandson of his obligation to me and bid him never forget his debt of gratitude. He did in fact do so, and in such a way that I ever afterwards observed affection and confidence in M. de Maurepas's manner towards myself.

At that moment the Abbé de Thésut arrived, and almost immediately the Chancellor glanced at the clock, remarking, 'I have sent for my son, and he will soon be here; he will know that this crushing blow comes from your hand; spare him the pain of finding you here at this bitter time.' He embraced me once more, saying, 'You are a terrible man; yet I must again declare that I love you, for indeed I cannot help it.' I thereupon departed, leaving him with La Vrillière and the Abbé de Thésut, who were both to witness the signing of the resignation. On my way out I passed Pontchartrain, in a great hurry to go to his father and looking extremely alarmed. La Vrillière told me later that he had taken it very badly and was not at all comforted by his son's good fortune. He none the less dared not make a scene in the presence of his father and M. le Duc d'Orléans's confidential secretary, who took the document and delivered it to that prince between eleven o'clock and half-past the hour.

Paris, and later the provinces, were overjoyed by the news. Everyone said that it should have happened long ago; and many declared that he had been let off lightly. There was general astonishment that his son should have inherited his office. At the Council of the Regency we mutually congratulated one another. The Maréchal d'Estrées was particularly pleased, and so was the Comte de Toulouse, to whom I had told all. From that moment Pontchartrain lived in complete obscurity in the back regions of his house, and became increasingly isolated. He lives there yet in solitude[1] and absolute retirement, still harbouring feelings of jealousy and resentment towards his son who treats him with proper courtesy— no more. That ex-pasha, once so rude and arrogant, now fills his empty hours in counting his money and other such trivial distractions, and seldom allows himself to be seen elsewhere. He has never acted in a more becoming manner. Let us now turn to foreign affairs.

After the death of Queen Anne and the dismissal of all those who had formed her council and enjoyed her trust, Louis XIV had reverted to his earlier view of England. King George had reinstated her previous advisers; the Whigs were once again in power, and the Tories out of favour. Such a fundamental change, not only in the government but throughout the whole of that contentious country, was bound to create malcontents of all kinds, more especially so because the new ministers and favourites were bent on revenge against those who in the last months of Queen Anne's reign had ruined them and seized their offices. They wished for nothing less than to arrest and condemn all the men who had done most to secure peace, and to whom France thus owed a debt of gratitude. As for the Scotch, they still bitterly resented their country's having become a mere province of England. The Duke of Ormonde[2] lay hidden in Paris, biding his time until the Earl of Mar[3] felt safe to act in Scotland where there was the beginning of

---

[1] Jérôme de Pontchartrain died 8 February 1747. Saint-Simon wrote this in the previous year.
[2] James Butler, 2nd Duke of Ormonde (1665–1745). See index.
[3] John Erskine, Earl of Mar (1675–1732). He had begun as a Whig, but changed sides so often that he came to be known as 'Bobbing John'.

a rebellion, and the Pretender[1] (to use the accepted term), secure in the knowledge of King Louis's help and protection, waited at Bar[2] for a suitable moment to cross the sea.

The death of Louis XIV upset all these plans. In the sorry condition in which France was left, the interests of a small minority did not seem to warrant the risk of a war with England without the certainty of what could not be known in advance, I mean of a sudden and complete revolution of the kind that had placed King William[3] on the throne of his uncle and father-in-law. Such a revolution would have bound together England and France, leaving the Elector of Hanover their only enemy, supported by those who, from outside the British Isles, cared to risk taking up arms in his cause. The late King, as you already know, had left Philip V secure upon the throne of Spain; there was a perfect union between the two crowns, and both countries were at peace with all Europe —a settlement brought about by the treaties of Utrecht and Baden. M. le Duc d'Orléans when he became Regent was absolutely determined to preserve this essential unity.

There was another reason why M. le Duc d'Orléans was reluctant to follow the King in giving help to the Pretender. The Earl of Stair[4] had come to Paris as George I's ambassador more than a year before the King's death, but had not so far presented his credentials. He was a plain gentleman of Scotland, tall, well built, thin, still of middle age, carrying his head high and proudly. Quick to act, fearless, bold by nature and by principle, Stair was a man of parts, shrewd, devious, but above all alert, informed, secret, master of his face, speaking many languages when he might do so becomingly, pretending to enjoy the social world, good eating and debauchery, in which he never exceeded. He was eager to make acquaintances and form such attachments as might be used in the service of his master and to promote his own interests. His affiliation was to the Whigs, especially to those whom King George had returned to office, and to the family and friends of the Duke of Marlborough, to whom he was devotedly attached, for he owed everything to him, had served under his command, and had received promotion, a regiment, and the Scottish Order,[5] all at the duke's request. Stair was poor but a great spender, keen and ambitious

---

[1] The Old Pretender, James Francis Edward (1688–1766), only son of James II of England. His mother was James II's second wife, Mary of Modena. He was called James III by English Jacobites, James VIII by the Scots.

[2] In Lorraine.

[3] William III of Orange, William III of England (1650–1702). He was appointed joint sovereign with his wife Mary II, elder daughter of James II by Anne Hyde, in 1689, after the abdication of James II (VII). His mother was Mary, eldest daughter of Charles I. He was thus nephew and son-in-law of James II; he was also a first cousin once removed of Louis XIV.

[4] Lord Stair had fought at Ramillies and greatly distinguished himself at Oudenarde and Malplaquet. Winston Churchill, in *Marlborough: His Life and Times*, says that he was 'one of the most capable ambassadors Britain ever sent to Paris'.

[5] The Order of the Thistle, founded 1687.

to excess; his chief desire was to run his embassy in such a way that with the help of his powerful supporters he might make a large fortune in England, where the great offices of State were held by patrons who found him all the more valuable because his hatred of France was equal to their own.

You already know that the King had taken a dislike to him[1] at first sight, and had continued to be displeased by his conduct. Torcy hated him so much that he would neither see nor have dealings with him. Stair had therefore witnessed the King's last illness only from afar. He conjectured that there was nothing to gain from M. du Maine, for if that bastard prevailed he would certainly be guided by the principles and sentiments of Louis XIV. Stair therefore decided that the man to cultivate was M. le Duc d'Orléans, and he proceeded to ingratiate himself by offering his master's help in case of trouble, winning the Regent thus early for King George by promising support at a time of danger, and fostering a firm attachment by stressing their common interests. To speak frankly, so he said (Stair never minced his words), two usurpers who were close neighbours needed to hold together since both were in the same boat—King George versus the Pretender, and M. le Duc d'Orléans (faintly justified by the Renunciations)[2] against the King of Spain, should the sickly infant who had succeeded Louis XIV fail to reach maturity.

Acting on these principles, Stair early sought for men likely to serve his purpose, and he considered none too base for that employment. One such was the kind of creature who scarcely merits any other description. This fellow, a little man, risen from the gutter and in countenance even lower, had insinuated himself, by dint of some knowledge of Greek and Latin and a small acquaintance with literature, into certain houses where he was allowed entry. Then, by debauchery of all varieties and the expression of sentiments now unhappily in fashion, he had contrived to meet some noble ladies and to move in some sort of good Society. He pretended to gallantry, composed verses, was something of a philosopher, but also a thoroughgoing voluptuary, extremely coarse in his behaviour, although very fastidious and choosy in his speech. Professing to admire the English scholars, he became a dinner-guest of Lady Sandwich,[3] who found life far pleasanter in Paris than ever she had done in London, and it was at her house that he formed an association with the Abbé Dubois. Through that prelate he graduated to an acquaintance with Mme d'Argenton and M. le Duc d'Orléans. Thus, in course of time he made a niche for himself at the Palais Royal and at Saint-Cloud, where he would often retire to play the hermit, being very careful not to miss M. le Duc d'Orléans on the rare occasions when that prince

---

[1] See II, p. 409.

[2] See II, editorial note, pp. 259–260; p. 288.

[3] Elizabeth Wilmot (1665–1757), daughter of the Earl of Rochester, and wife of Edward Montagu, 3rd Earl of Sandwich (1670–1729).

walked there in the park. Artful, discreet, capable of bold action when he saw fit, the creature had moreover a smooth tongue, and little by little grew to be Dubois's right-hand man. His name was Rémond,[1] and before very long he was knocking at every door.

Stair gathered Rémond up, and Rémond courted Stair, first with his smooth tongue, then with his company, until, in the end, Stair had surrendered to him completely, at which Dubois was altogether enchanted. At that particular moment he had alienated M. le Duc d'Orléans by his meddling, and was vainly searching for a means by which to retrieve himself. It now appeared to him that an alliance with Stair and thereafter with England would produce the desired result and bring him great rewards. To that end he gave instructions to Rémond, who found little difficulty in bringing together two men whose interests were so similar. Dubois was already in league with both Canillac and the Duc de Noailles. He persuaded them that England provided the only security for M. le Duc d'Orléans against those who questioned his authority (by right of birth) over the young King, and Rémond made many journeys to England in order to cultivate a friendship with Stanhope,[2] whom he had already met, first in Paris, then in Spain, when Stanhope was commanding the English troops there, and Dubois was on the staff of M. le Duc d'Orléans. Dubois's particular hope was that by inclining the Regent to favour England, he might become first an intermediary, then the negotiator of a treaty of alliance, from which great advantage to himself would accrue. He was, alas!, not mistaken.

All this was happening in Paris during the last year of the King's life, towards the end of which M. le Duc d'Orléans was shown the kind of support which he might expect from King George. After that came proposals, followed by definite offers from Stair, until the point was reached when the Regent saw that nobleman in the back offices of the Palais Royal. He told me of this quite casually; but since he well knew that my sentiments regarding England coincided with those of the late King, he spoke too late, as though merely to keep me informed. The deed was done; it was of no use to object; but I did entreat him not to be precipitate, and to remember that Stair thought only of himself and his party. That was the cause of Stair's presence in the lantern gallery at the Parlement, at the beginning of the Regency. He wished to appear unbidden in support of M. le Duc d'Orléans; so as to show an understanding with England, and hold the Parlement and the Duc du Maine in awe.

At the beginning of October, after the King's death, Stair had a long audience of the Regent concerning the alarms of King George, who claimed that the Earl of Peterborough[3] had discovered a plot to burn his

---

[1] Nicolas François Rémond, the son of a partisan, and well known at the court of the Duchesse du Maine at Sceaux. He filled many posts at the Parlement, in a judicial capacity.

[2] James Stanhope, 1st Earl Stanhope (1673–1721). See index.

[3] Charles Mordaunt, Earl of Peterborough (1658–1735).

palace, rob the Bank of England, seize the Tower of London, and proclaim the Pretender as James III. Letters had been intercepted from Mr. Harvey[1] to the Pretender and the Duke of Ormonde, and Harvey had attempted suicide, but his wounds had not been mortal. A vast number of malcontents loudly complaining in London and the provinces seemed to King George to give substance to the rumours of a conspiracy.[2] He asked the Dutch for the body of troops which they had covenanted to give him, and proposed sending them to the Duke of Argyll,[3] to use against the Earl of Mar who, with a large following, had gained many victories and was acting in Scotland with caution and good sense. The States General supplied the king with three thousand Swiss and the promise of a further three thousand in accordance with the treaty.

Spain, since the death of Louis XIV, had been noticeably less well disposed towards the Pretender. The intention was to gratify King George by every outward show of friendship without, in the present state of uncertainty, quite breaking with the unhappy Stuart prince. England was being equally cautious in her dealings with Spain. The Abbé Alberoni, employing the methods of the Princesse des Ursins, had already begun to rule that kingdom. Like her, he used his influence with an ambitious queen to incite her to possess the king, body and soul; keeping him to herself and for herself day and night, without a moment's respite; preventing even his personal staff from approaching him alone; accustoming him always to work with ministers in her presence, and so dominating and controlling him that nothing could reach or be sent by him without her full knowledge and consent. This system the queen adopted to the very letter, and Alberoni thus skilfully managed to keep the royal couple apart from the Court and under his sole guidance, and prevented everyone else from having access to them, as you shall see in due course.

Meanwhile, in England, the troubles were increasing, and the Earl of Mar had several successes. Stair fixed his entire mind on dissuading France from giving aid to the Pretender, and on preventing his passage through that kingdom in order to cross the sea. Efficient spies kept him well informed, and as soon as he learned that the Pretender was preparing to leave Bar, he hurried to M. le Duc d'Orléans demanding his arrest. Stair had already proposed a treaty to guarantee the succession in France and England, and had been given authority to sign it; but the Regent wished first to include a defensive alliance between Holland and England, thinking

---

[1] Edward Harvey, a member of Parliament.

[2] From this point until towards the middle of 1718 Saint-Simon made great use of the notes and papers from which Torcy compiled his memoirs. They seem to have given him a wider view of foreign affairs and to a certain extent changed his style. He said that 'the clarity, fluency, and nobility of Torcy's style, by its polished charm marked a contrast with my own', and that he 'felt obliged to copy every word'. In fact he did not always strictly adhere to that obligation.

[3] John, 2nd Duke of Argyll (1678–1743). Pope said that he was 'destined to shake alike the senate and the field'. He had played a principal part in bringing about the Act of Union, 1707.

this necessary to provide a firm basis for the guarantees. Buys,[1] the Dutch ambassador, was willing, but Stair, eager for a settlement, fought shy of the alliance lest it delay matters. He feared moreover that the Regent was waiting to see what would happen in England, and he went so far as to tell His Royal Highness that if he cared so little for England's troubles, England might well come to feel the same regarding his own. They were on those terms when news came of the Pretender's departure. Stair went forthwith to M. le Duc d'Orléans complaining bitterly and clamouring for an arrest. At that time, the Regent was very skilfully engaged in running with the hare and hunting with the hounds. He had already promised to close his eyes to the Pretender's journey and even to help him on his way, provided secrecy was maintained; but he now wished to appear ready to grant Stair's request. He accordingly dispatched a certain Contades,[2] a major of the Guards and a most intelligent and trusty agent, and his brother,[3] a lieutenant of the same regiment, with two hand-picked sergeants, to Château-Thierry, through which city, according to Stair, the Pretender was bound to pass. Contades left Paris on the night of 9 November, firmly determined and instructed not to find the man whom he appeared to be seeking. Stair, who only half-trusted him, took measures on his own account and, as you shall see, was very nearly successful. This is what occurred.

The Pretender left Bar in disguise with an escort of only three or four persons, and reached Chaillot, where M. de Lauzun owned a small, very ancient house which he never visited, though he kept it for sentimental reasons. The Pretender went to this house at Chaillot, spent the night there, and saw his mother who paid long and frequent visits to the convent of the Filles de Sainte-Marie in that neighbourhood. Thence he continued his journey to the Brittany coast, by the Alençon road, in one of Torcy's post-chaises.[4] When Stair received the news of the Pretender's departure, he resolved by any means to seize the person of this sole survivor of the House of Stuart. He posted spies on several roads, and particularly on that from Paris to Alençon, for which he made Colonel Douglas,[5] an Irish officer, dismissed that service and now in the pay of France, personally responsible. This Douglas, screened by his name and his wits, his tact and cleverness in intrigue, had, since the beginning of the Regency, managed to insinuate himself into many of the great houses of Paris, and was on terms of intimacy and esteem with the Regent himself. He used often to come to my house. He was excellent company, had married while on the Metz

[1] William Buys (1662–1749), the Dutch ambassador to Paris from 1713 to 1715.
[2] Georges Gaspard de Contades (1666–1735). He had served as a major-general in Villars's army in 1713, and became Governor of Guise in 1727.
[3] Charles Pierre Erasme, Chevalier de Contades (1683–1765).
[4] Torcy was also master of the posts, and could therefore supply post-chaises secretly.
[5] The Earl of Douglas. He took service with the French army in 1707. In 1708, he married Mlle d'Orthe. In 1715 he was bribed by the English to assassinate the Pretender; later that year he was imprisoned for debt and was not released until 1731.

frontier, was excessively poor, polite, much in the social world, with a reputation for distinguished service that gave no grounds for thinking him capable of murder.

Douglas hired a post-chaise, and accompanied by two mounted men (all three of them heavily armed) slowly patrolled his section of the Alençon road. Nonancourt is a small hamlet on that same road, nineteen leagues from Paris, between Dreux, three leagues farther on, and Verneuil-au-Perche, four leagues back on the Paris side. At Nonancourt he halted, ate a meal at the posting-house, asked anxious questions regarding a post-chaise which he carefully described, saying how it would be escorted, expressing fear lest he might have missed it, despite all that was said to the contrary. After exhaustive inquiries, he posted a third horseman who had arrived in the interval, with orders to warn him when the said chaise appeared, adding threats, and promises of rewards for the post-boys if they did not fail him by negligence. The postmaster's name was l'Hospital.[1] He was away, but his wife was in charge, a very decent woman full of spirit, courage, and good sense. Nonancourt is a mere five leagues from La Ferté; and when we took a short cut, it was always our practice to warn them at the inn, so that they might send a relay to meet us on the by-road. I was thus well acquainted with the postmistress, who played a greater part than her husband in this affair; and she later more than once told me what happened.

She did her best to discover the reason for so much anxiety. All that she could learn was that the travellers were English and in a tremendous hurry; that something vastly important was afoot, and that some crime was being plotted. She guessed immediately that it concerned the Pretender, made up her mind to save him, worked out a plan, and put it successfully into execution. She first made it her business to please her visitors, refusing them nothing, agreeing to all they wished, promising solemnly to alert them in time. So amiable was she that Douglas departed, telling no one but the third man (the one who had joined them) where he was going; but he did not go far because he wished also to be warned. He took with him one of the two grooms; the other remained with the third man to wait and watch. This extra man was a great embarrassment to the postmistress; but she was not daunted. She invited him to take a glass, seeing that Douglas had already left the table when he arrived. She served him attentively with her best wine, and kept him as long at table as she could manage, fulfilling his every wish even before he could express it. In the meantime she posted one of her own head-grooms on sentry duty, with orders to appear silently if he saw a chaise in the distance. Her plan was to lock up the third man and the servant, and then to intercept the chaise and provide it with a relay of fresh horses on a back road. But no chaise appeared, and the Englishman grew weary of sitting so long over his wine. She then

---

[1] Pierre de l'Hospital, whose wife was Suzanne Delacour.

managed to induce him to get some sleep, trusting in herself, her servants, and the groom left behind by Douglas to give him ample warning.

The Englishman ordered this groom on no account to stir from the outside door, and to call him as soon as the chaise appeared. The post-mistress made him warm and comfortable in the back part of the house and, still looking perfectly carefree, went to one of her neighbours in a side street, to tell her the whole story and all that she suspected. This neighbour promised to take into her house and keep hidden the man whom they awaited, and the postmistress forthwith went to find a priest, their mutual friend and cousin, from whom she borrowed an abbé's cassock with a wig to match. That done Mme l'Hospital returned to find the English servant at the door. She engaged him in conversation, condoled with him on his tedious vigil, murmured that the inner door was only a step farther back, promised that she would keep his watch as though his own eyes were on the road, and gave him wine, leaving him in the care of a trusty postilion who never moved until he had seen the Englishman lying dead-drunk beneath the table. During the interval, that sagacious woman listened outside the room where the Englishman slept; softly turned the key in the lock, and then returned to watch by the front door. Half an hour later her sentinel reappeared, saying that the long-awaited chaise was arriving with its three outriders, having been persuaded, without explanation, to slow down to a walking pace. It was indeed King James, and Mme l'Hospital spoke to him, telling him that he was expected and in mortal danger, but would be safe if he trusted and followed her. This he did, and so entered her neighbour's house, where they told him what had happened and concealed him and his three companions to the best of their ability.

Mme l'Hospital, returning home, sent for the local magistrate, who on hearing her suspicions arrested the drunken English groom and the sleep-ing Englishman, and dispatched one of her postilions to Torcy. The magistrate, meanwhile, had drawn up his report and sent it to the Court. Impossible to describe the rage of that Englishman when he found himself arrested and incapable of doing what he had come to do, or his fury with the drunken groom. As for Mme l'Hospital, he would gladly have strangled her, and she went for some long time in dread of his vengeance. The Englishman absolutely refused to say what business had brought him or where Douglas might be found; naming him only so as to impress by his title. He declared that the English ambassador (who had not yet claimed that office) had sent him, and loudly proclaimed that that minister would not allow him to be so insulted. He was gently reminded that there was no proof of his coming from the ambassador, and that all the evidence pointed to a highly dangerous plot against civil liberties and the freedom of the highway; that no wrong or injury had been done him, but that he must wait under arrest for further orders; and thereupon they most politely conducted him to the gaol, along with the drunken English groom.

No one ever learned what had happened to Douglas, save that he was seen at various places on that road, crying out desperately that someone had escaped—whom he would not say. Growing anxious at hearing nothing, he had apparently sent, or was coming himself, for news, but the commotion of such a scandal in a tiny village like Nonancourt reached him where he was resting, and that was what had set him chasing up and down the road, in a vain attempt to catch up with his prey. King James remained in hiding at Nonancourt, where he became so captivated by the kind attentions of the noble postmistress who had saved his life, that he revealed his name to her and gave her a letter for the queen his mother. He stayed for three days, until the excitement had somewhat abated and no hope remained for his pursuers; he then continued his journey disguised as an abbé, in a hired post-chaise which Mme l'Hospital summoned as though for her own use. He was followed, but luckily not recognized; thus he reached Brittany safely and at once embarked for Scotland. Douglas, exhausted by his fruitless journeyings, returned to Paris to find that Stair was making a tremendous rumpus over the Nonancourt incident, declaring that it was a deliberate attack on civil rights, and a most impudent proceeding into the bargain. The wretched Douglas, who could not be ignorant of what people said of him, had to bear the humiliation of appearing everywhere as usual, even at the play, and of presenting himself also before M. le Duc d'Orléans.

That prince chose to ignore, so far as was possible, a cruel and dastardly plot, which he could not but regard as a personal insult. He said nothing publicly, but in private he told Stair to shut his mouth, and then returned to him his English murderers. Douglas himself sank considerably in the Regent's esteem, and many important people closed their doors to him. He tried in vain to break down mine; and made so bold as to complain to me; but that did him no good. Soon afterwards he disappeared from Paris. His wife and children remained, living on charity. Long after his death overseas, the Abbé de Saint-Simon,[1] happening to go from Noyon to Metz, found his widow living there in very miserable circumstances.

The Queen of England summoned Mme l'Hospital to Saint-Germain, thanked her and made much of her, as well she might, and presented her with her portrait; that was all. Be that as it may, the Regent, and very much later King James, also wrote to her and sent their portraits. To conclude: she remained postmistress of Nonancourt, exactly as before, for another twenty-four or twenty-five years, until she died; and her son and daughter-in-law now occupy that post. She was a very truthful woman, much esteemed in the neighbourhood, and nothing that she said of this incident was ever contradicted by anyone. I would not hazard a guess how much she was left out of pocket; for she was not paid a brass farthing. She did not complain of this; but when anyone questioned her she related the

---

[1] Claude de Rouvroy (1695–1760), Abbé de Saint-Simon, became the Count-Bishop of Noyon and a peer of France in 1731. In 1733 he was made Bishop of Metz.

affair exactly as it occurred, simply and honestly. Such is the niggardliness of dethroned sovereigns, and their total indifference to the terrible risks taken on their behalf, and to the services rendered them. Many decent people avoided Stair after that, and his insolent airs put many others against him. He went beyond all bounds in attempting to explain the affair, for he dared neither admit the truth, nor disclaim it altogether, nor yet express any regret other than for his failure.

On Tuesday morning, 12 November, below the terrace of the Tuileries, Ferrand, a captain of the King's regiment,[1] and Girardin de Vauvré, a captain of the Guards,[2] fought a duel in a private quarrel. One of them belonged to the Parliamentary Ferrands, the other was a son of that Vauvré who had a seat on the navy council because he had long been intendant of Toulon. Two such men, by their bad conduct and low rank, would have seemed cut out for the severest penalties as an example against duelling, and so the Regent appeared to think. But very soon his good-nature overcame his better judgment. Both were dismissed, but by that the service lost nothing. This bad example had the effect of reviving duelling, which had almost died out. Strange to say, M. le Duc d'Orléans did not seem to object. Yet when M. de Richelieu and the Prince of Bavaria[3] quarrelled a few days later, and prepared to fight in the Bois de Boulogne, on a day when Monsieur le Duc had arranged a great hunt for the ladies, the Regent sent for them, gave them a good dressing-down, took their promises, and declared that if they broke their word to him, he would not fail them, which was the end of that quarrel.

The Chevalier de Bouillon,[4] who since the death of the Comte d'Auvergne's son had begun to call himself the Prince d'Auvergne, asked the Regent to allow public balls at the Opéra three times a week, with payment on entry, masked or unmasked, the boxes making a convenient refuge for those who wished to watch without joining the dance. It was thought that public balls, supervised as the Opéra always is during performances, would be safe from scandal, and might discourage people from attending shady little dance-halls scattered over Paris, where scandals so often originate. The Opéra balls were duly inaugurated, with huge crowds and all the desired effect. The proposer was at once given a pension of six thousand livres, and a wonderful new machine was invented that swiftly and easily covered the orchestra pit, bringing the stage and the auditorium to the same level, and perfectly flat. What was most unfortunate was that M. le Duc d'Orléans had only to walk a step to go there after his suppers, and very frequently showed himself in a most unseemly

---

[1] Guillaume Ferrand, b. 1683. He fled to Lorraine after this duel, and subsequently became chamberlain to the King of Prussia.

[2] Alexandre Louis Girardin de Vauvré (1685–1745). He was forgiven later and was made a brigadier-general in 1719.

[3] Emmanuel Francis Joseph, natural son of the Elector of Bavaria by the Countess of Arco.

[4] Frédéric Jules de La Tour d'Auvergne (1672–1733).

condition. The Duc de Noailles, ever anxious to pay his court, appeared at the first one of all, so drunk that there was no filthiness he did not commit. M. le Duc d'Orléans found himself greatly inconvenienced by Vincennes, and therefore wished to have the King in Paris. I did my best to have him returned to Versailles, where he would have been with the Court, and far from those who never sleep out of Paris unless they go to the country. Anyone going to Versailles on business could see everyone he needed in the space of an hour; whereas in Paris, one might go ten times to the same house and cover any number of different districts. The men in charge of the affairs of State would not there be a prey to the distractions and waste of time inseparable from life in Paris, and, what I also considered highly advantageous, there would be no danger of such adventures as those which befell Louis XIV in his boyhood, when he was forced to leave the town secretly one Twelfth Night.[1] I was anxious moreover to keep M. le Duc d'Orléans as much as possible from the bad company with whom he supped every evening, and from the state in which he allowed himself to appear at the Opéra balls, as well as prevent the waste of time caused by his attending every performance. Unhappily, this was precisely why the Regent wished to remain, and there was no way of extracting him against his will. He went so far as to call a grand consultation of all the doctors in order to have the King brought back to Paris, but they all agreed it would be unwise to move him until the first frosts had cleansed the air and destroyed the smallpox that was still raging.

His Royal Highness had no cause to congratulate himself for having disbelieved my words regarding Père Tellier and Père Doucin.[2] Their arrogant and threatening behaviour now obliged him to banish them; but once again his good nature prevailed, and he allowed Père Tellier to retire to Amiens, where the bishop,[3] as fanatical as he but a veritable dunce, was quite under his thumb. You shall see that it became necessary to drive Père Tellier from that refuge also, for he did far worse there than in Paris. Meantime, the Jesuits comported themselves with such impertinence at Metz and Verdun that Monsieur de Metz was compelled to lay them under an interdict; and the Bishop of Verdun,[4] to the horror of his cousin Charost (more fanatically bigoted, if possible, than the rest), quickly followed suit.

Mme de Louvois died at this time.[5] Her death was a great loss to her family and friends, as well as to the poor, and provided a notable example of what wisdom and dignity may achieve when guided over a long period

---

[1] In 1649, when Paris was besieged by Condé's troops during the rebellion of the nobles, the Queen and her sons, Louis XIV and Monsieur, fled from the Palais Royal to Saint-Germain. Louis never forgot or forgave this insult; it was one of the reasons he would never live in Paris. He was eleven years old at the time. See also II, p. 372n.

[2] Le Père Louis Doucin (1652–1726), a Jesuit.

[3] Pierre Sabatier (1654–1733).

[4] Hippolyte de Béthune (1647–1720), Bishop of Verdun from 1680.

[5] Mme de Louvois was ninety-nine years old when she died. Her maiden name was Anne de Souvré, and she was the mother of the Duchesses de Rochefoucauld and de Villeroy.

by honour and plain commonsense. She was a great heiress of a family whose distinction did not go back beyond the Maréchal de Souvré,[1] her grandfather's father. But that Maréchal was illustrious indeed, and his children also, and it was they who placed the name of Souvré on a pinnacle which deeper probing could scarcely have enhanced. She had the most stately bearing imaginable, the tallest and most graceful of figures. A brunette and handsome, she made up for lack of wit by possessing most excellent good sense, which had not been evident during her marriage, although Louvois invariably treated her with the consideration he accorded to all his personal belongings.

Instead of sinking after that minister's death, Mme de Louvois contrived to gain for herself a position of real personal esteem, first in her family, among whom she reigned supreme, and then at the Court and in Paris, where she lived retired, the mistress of a great house, never overstepping the bounds imposed by her rank and her widowhood. There she entertained her family and friends, filling her life with good works performed without fuss or advertisement. The sums she gave in alms were truly astronomical, and she dispensed them royally and with method. Once or twice every year she spent a night at the Court, accompanied by her entire family. Her arrival was news. She attended the King's supper, and invariably received a warm welcome, which was imitated by the whole Court. She paid scarcely any other visits, not even to Paris; but spent each summer at her great house near Choisy, with very excellent company, her guests being always respectable, select, and suitable to her age. In a word, her life was so noble, so proper, so dignified and worthy, without a single lapse, that her death came as a tragedy for the poor, a grief to her family, and a cause of sincere regret to the general public. With her death ended the House of Souvré.

Another consultation of the doctors was held on the question of the King's return to Paris. They insisted on waiting a few weeks longer, which made M. le Duc d'Orléans decide to have only two sessions of the Regency Council each week at Vincennes, and to hold the other meetings at Paris, in the King's apartment at the Tuileries. This came as a great relief to all the members, because the constant journeyings to Vincennes and back in the depths of winter were most uncomfortable and a great waste of time.

M. le Duc d'Orléans's leniency regarding duels, which I have already mentioned, caused him to allow Caylus[1] to return and purge his quarrel

---

[1] Gilles, Maréchal de Souvré (1542–1626). He was made a Marshal of France in 1615, and was the governor of Louis XIII. Mme de Louvois's great-grandfather was Jacques II de Souvré (1600–1670), Marquis de Courtenvaux, Grand-Prieur de France, and religious ambassador to France, Holland, and Lorraine.

[1] Claude Abraham de Tubières Grimoard de Pestels de Lévis, Chevalier de Caylus. His duel, in 1697, was a shameful affair because the Comte d'Auvergne's son ran away at the very start, waving his sword, through the streets of Paris. The quarrel was over some harlots in a tavern. His father disinherited him, and he ended his days in the Order of the Knights of Malta.

with the eldest son of the Comte d'Auvergne, who died long ago. He came for that purpose from Spain, where he had lived and served, always with distinction, during the intervening years, having risen to be a lieutenant-general. Three or four days' imprisonment in the Conciergerie put an end to that affair, and three or four more were all he required to visit such friends as remained to him, after which he returned to Spain, where King Philip had given him command of Estremadura, in succession to the Marquis of Bay. He has since made a great fortune. I shall have occasion to speak of him again. He was the brother of the Bishop of Auxerre,[1] and brother-in-law of Mme de Caylus, Mme de Maintenon's favourite cousin, who has already appeared more than once in these memoirs.

At one session of the Regency Council, when it was meeting at the Tuileries on foreign affairs, we were astonished to hear the Duc de Noailles ask to have an urgent matter included in the agenda. He spoke for a moment to M. le Duc d'Orléans in a corner of the room, and then proposed a depreciation of the coinage. There was general astonishment. The Regent spoke after him, deploring the need for revaluation, but as though he had already decided on it. The voting was somewhat uncertain, since the members were torn between their feeling of repugnance and fear of giving offence. When it came to my turn, I exposed all the disadvantages of juggling with the coinage, giving examples from history and our own times, and stressing how illusory it would be to seek immediate relief if it were to entail such long-drawn-out and disastrous consequences in foreign exchange and markets, and in every kind of commerce. I concluded by urging that the coinage should be left as it then was, since there was no possibility of bringing it nearer to its real value by a devaluation. I was applauded, but cut short. The measure caused a good deal of grumbling, especially among the people.

M. le Duc d'Orléans, like his father before him, attended all the Christmas services at Saint-Eustache and the Oratory. Fewer prayers by the almanac, and less dissipation at night, would have produced a more settled and respectable way of living. It is not yet the moment to speak of that, or of his daily life.

At last, on Monday, 30 December, the King left Vincennes after his dinner and drove to Paris. The arrangements in his coach were as improper as they had been on the outward journey. He sat at the back, between M. le Duc d'Orléans and the Duchesse de Ventadour; the Maréchal de Villeroy was in front, between M. du Maine and Prince Charles,[2] a master of the horse; the Maréchal d'Harcourt, captain of the guard, sat by the

---

[1] Daniel Charles Gabriel de Tubières Grimoard de Pestels de Lévis de Caylus (1669–1754), made Bishop of Auxerre in 1704. Saint-Simon said at that time that by his promotion God displayed 'how insignificant are the instruments by which He deigns to support His truth and His Church'. Saint-Simon continues, 'The libraries are full of him; there will be occasion to speak of him in due course.'

[2] The so-called Prince Charles was Charles de Lorraine-Armagnac (1684–1753).

door on the King's side—on the right, that is. Monsieur le Premier[1] nipped quickly into the opposite side before the Lord Chamberlain, the Duc d'Albret, whom M. le Duc d'Orléans had nominated. In conclusion, let me add that neither M. du Maine nor the Maréchal de Villeroy had any right to be in the coach while the King was still under the care of women. Their places should rightly have been occupied by the Duc de Tresmes, first gentleman of the bedchamber on duty, and the Duc d'Albret. Preparations for the tutors had already begun at Vincennes, and they had been given lodgings there. At the Tuileries, the Maréchal de Villeroy was granted a very fine apartment, and later took over the Queen's rooms, which were next to those of the King; and M. du Maine had the Dauphin's splendid apartment on the floor below. Monsieur de Fréjus[2] had his lodging on the top floor; the assistant governors, etc., were also supplied with rooms. The King was harangued on his arrival by the citizens of Paris; great crowds lined the way as far as his apartments. Thus ended the year 1715.

[1] Monsieur le Premier was the court name for the master of the horse: in this case, Jean Louis, Marquis de Beringhem (1651-1723). He was a member of the council for the interior, and director-general of the Ponts et Chaussées.

[2] André Hercule de Fleury (1653-1743), Bishop of Fréjus 1698-1715. He had just given up his bishopric of Fréjus, and was about to go to the Abbey of Tournus, when, in 1715, he became tutor to Louis XV. In 1726 he was made a cardinal, and the same year was appointed minister of State, and first minister to the King.

CHAPTER II

1716

M. du Maine pays me a casual visit – I visit him and Mme la Duchesse du Maine – The Abbé Dubois made a counsellor of State – Death of the Duchesse de Lesdiguières – Death and character of Coulanges – Marriage of M. de Castries's only son – Character of Mme de Castries – Mme la Duchesse de Berry assumes honours above her rank –She falls to Rions's charms –Public and private life of M. le Duc d'Orléans – His obstinate debauchery – The cabal who for their personal advantage attach the Regent permanently to England – He never aspired to the throne – I propose a permanent and indissoluble union with Spain – A treaty between France and Spain signed at Madrid – Alberoni keeps the King and Queen of Spain under lock and key – The Pretender fails in Scotland – Stair's lying report – Characters of Stair and Bentivoglio – La Force is sent to win me for the constitution – Conduct of the Duc de Noailles towards me, and mine towards him – Mme la Duchesse de Berry closes the Luxembourg gardens – Return of the Italian players – Law pronounced Las; his bank, and my advice regarding it – The Regent desires me to see Law – The poet Arouet is exiled – The King pays a call on Chancellor de Pontchartrain – The duchy of Valentinois accorded a peerage – Character of the Duc de Brancas – M. le Duc de Chartres contracts smallpox – I return from La Ferté to be with his parents – Death of the Maréchal de Montrevel – King George offers to return Gibraltar – Louville, sent as envoy to Madrid, is driven out by Alberoni – A treaty between France and England, engineered by Dubois, is signed at The Hague – Peter the Great invited to visit France

BEFORE EMBARKING on the events of this present year, 1716, I must for a moment return to the past, in order that you may be prepared for what follows. M. du Maine and I were still on the same footing as after that dreadful visit[1] when we were forced to trip him with the self-same rope which he had prepared for our discomfiture in the matter of the bonnets. We saw one another regularly at the Council of Regency, where he continually strove to gain some return for those marks of recognition which he showered upon me, though he dared not speak to me. He invariably found me cold and unbending, responding to his many deep and respectful bows in a most perfunctory manner. The King was dead; Mme de Maintenon no longer need be feared; in their time I had not considered

[1] See II, pp. 371 et seqq.

his feelings, and I had shown him no greater courtesy after that secret quarrel. He knew that I should take even less care to restrain myself now. He saw me on intimate terms with the Regent, and so well esteemed that I had become a figure of no small importance; his cowardice was roused; he longed to appease me, but did not know how to begin.

That being our situation, I was vastly surprised when one morning, towards the end of a visit to Vincennes, I found him in my room. He concealed his embarrassment beneath a friendly smile, and with great politeness began to converse as though nothing were amiss, and without any reference to the past. He was a master of small talk, and thus addressed me in the manner best calculated to please, but he said nothing of any interest. Since we were in my room, I was obliged to repay him in the same coin, and I managed it reasonably well, with sufficient courtesy to avoid actual rudeness, and little enough in the way of compliments to prevent advances. We were alone more than half an hour; and this was before the meeting of the Council and at an hour not usually given to visits. That he should choose this time appeared to me most pointed; I was thus much relieved when he left me after what had amounted to no more than a social call. I told the Regent what had happened before we entered the Council, and we laughed to think of the terrors of this gentleman who had once thought the prince of little account, and myself, with better reason, of no account at all. M. le Duc d'Orléans none the less urged me to return the call and, since M. du Maine had made the first move, to be somewhat less distant and curt with him when we met in public. Although such counsel was reasonable enough, it pained me to have to abide by it after all that had passed. I was no hypocrite; it seemed the grossest mendacity to behave towards the Duc du Maine as though he were an ordinary person. I made the effort for the sake of propriety, yet with indifferent success, or so I believe, and I took good care to remain out of range of his conversation; but I was greatly embarrassed by his loathsome bows and scrapes, and vastly annoyed by his attempts to fawn on me.

At this time, the Arsenal was being pulled down to provide him with a fine new residence; the other house which he was building by the river, at the end of the Rue de Bourbon,[1] was hardly begun, and he was lodging meanwhile in the Rue Saint-Avoye,[2] at the house of the premier président, that gentleman being at his official residence in the Palais de Justice. It was therefore in the Rue Saint-Avoye that I visited him a few days after the King's return to Paris; and I chose to go late in the morning so as to provide myself with an excuse for not seeing Mme la Duchesse du Maine. It was of no avail. I was received with joy, even with gratitude, and when I made to leave after a very short time, he said that Mme la Duchesse du

---

[1] Later the Rue de Lille.
[2] In the old quarter of Paris, now the 3rd and 4th *arrondissements* where there are still many ancient houses.

Maine would never forgive him if he let me depart without seeing her. Despite all my protests he then conducted me to her room and seated me in an armchair by the bed-head, while he sat down on the other side. She gave me an equally enthusiastic welcome, for, like her husband, the Duchesse du Maine was adept, when she so pleased, at all the social arts and graces. I had hoped to escape with such civilities; but not so. From flattery they turned to something more serious which greatly surprised but in no way embarrassed me. There were seven or eight members of their household present. Mme du Maine, on the pretext of their temporary place of residence, broached the subject of the premier président; for it was she who led the conversation, with M. du Maine merely making comments. I replied that her well-known partiality for that magistrate reduced me to silence; but she continued to press me until we both had had enough. She did nothing but laugh, and M. du Maine, who excelled in repartee, would not let the matter rest. When I tried to take my leave, they declared that they enjoyed my visit too much to let me go so soon. It was indeed a rare occasion for them. Since M. du Maine's visit I had not seen him once; before the affair of the bonnets I visited him very seldom, and never, at any time, had I called on Mme la Duchesse du Maine, who rarely came to the Court.

At that point, as though eager to proceed, Mme la Duchesse du Maine broached the subject of their differences with M. le Duc; for differences there were, although they had not yet become apparent. I would not speak of that, but she plied me with innumerable questions, urged on by the Duc du Maine, and I found myself being cross-examined before the attentive ears of the little group surrounding us. I managed to extricate myself at last by saying that they must both have long known my opinions on that matter, since I had expressed them more than once. I hoped by this to stop them; but Mme du Maine still persisted and, with the laughing excuse that her husband did not tell her all, begged me to speak frankly. This made me furious. I said that if she insisted on my repeating yet again something which I felt sure M. du Maine had already told her, I would do so, but only on condition that she would remember that I spoke at her express orders. I thereupon stated that I was very glad of their having been made princes of the blood in the line of the succession; we dukes had no objections on that score. So long as they retained their rank, we should say nothing. Let them, however, take good care to guard that rank; for should they fall from that high estate we would tolerate no intermediate place for them, but would do all in our power to prevent their inserting themselves between us and the princes. Then, both speaking the exact opposite of their thoughts, they agreed that I was right, and that they had no complaints, since we accepted their present position. 'But,' said the duchess, 'will you truly not set the princes of the blood against me?' 'Madame,' said I, 'that is a matter for the princes, and none of our business. They neither need our advice nor have they asked it.' I was thus kept dancing on the tightrope of that most delicate question. They were pleased because they wished so to be, I was still more so because I had managed not to budge a single inch. The pretty speeches (on their part) continued, and I left them after a full hour that had seemed to me at least twice as long.

I have never since visited Mme du Maine at her house, and only very rarely M. du Maine, at the Tuileries. At the meetings of the Council, and whenever I encountered him in Mme la Duchesse d'Orléans's drawing-room, he lavished attentions on me, and I was as pleasant to him as possible, which, to tell the truth, was not saying much, for I held aloof, never attacking him, almost never coming near him and, as far as I decently could, preventing him from approaching me. It was quite otherwise with the Comte de Toulouse, for he, as I have already mentioned, was a very upright and honourable man. He had done nothing to support his brother's titanic efforts to reach the heights; still less was he concerned in the affair of the bonnets. His manner of giving his opinion; choosing good for its own sake, and justice for the sake of justice, had quite won me over. I saw him nearly every day in the company of Mme la Duchesse d'Orléans, and had become friendly, although never intimate, with him. At the Council, my place was next his, and there also we talked very freely, and were sometimes alone together both before and afterwards.

The other affair that requires me to retrace my steps was that of the post of Church-counsellor of State, left vacant by the death of La Hoguette, Archbishop of Sens.[1] As you have seen earlier in these Memoirs, the Abbé Dubois[2] had always toadied me, and since the death of the King had fawned upon me still more. At the time of that historic event he had fallen out of favour with his master, and Madame, as I have recounted, had succeeded in ousting him completely. Being thus abandoned he turned to me, and until the moment when he was made a secretary of State, and for several years previously, I had been apt, even in midwinter, to find his coach standing in the road outside my house, awaiting my return; for he would not enter before me, and refused to drive into the courtyard. It is a fact that I had thought him hardly used after so much intimacy, and I had said so to M. le Duc d'Orléans, urging him to be kinder to Dubois, but at

---

[1] Hardouin Fortin de La Hoguette (1632–1715). He was eighty-two, 'grave, pious, devoted to his duties and his diocese', and Saint-Simon's old friend. Saint-Simon greatly admired him for refusing the Order so as to save the King from breaking the rule that limited membership to the nobility.

[2] The title abbé is muddling. Some abbés, e.g. the Abbé de La Trappe, were abbots and ruled monasteries. But most of the abbés mentioned in the memoirs were nothing of the sort. The title was used by all who wore clergyman's bands because they had studied theology. At this period, except for the very rich, everyone had to go to a theological college for higher education, which is why abbés were so abundant in seventeenth- and eighteenth-century France. Few were ordained, and thus their conduct was not expected to be holier than that of laymen. Indeed as they were usually unmarried, it tended to be a good deal worse.

all costs to keep him away from State affairs. I had succeeded on the first point; would to God that I had been believed as to the last! At the time in question, Dubois had a longing to become a counsellor of State, and came to me begging for my support with the Regent. At that I could not contain myself. I said I wished him all the good in the world, but for that particular post I must urge him to consider the circumstances. Could he face the scorn of the other counsellors? Would not his attachment to M. le Duc d'Orléans bring down on him the hatred of the entire council and the rival claimants? What would the world say of him? What affronts and unkindnesses would he be likely to receive? He seemed astounded; but we soon separated because he could find no answers.

Four days later he returned in raptures, and at once exclaimed, 'I have come to tell you that I am a State counsellor.' 'My dear Abbé,' said I, 'I am delighted; all the more so because I had no hand in your appointment. This satisfies us both. Take care for the future; but since the deed is done, rejoice and never fear.' I then embraced him, and he left me well pleased. I said nothing to the Regent, nor did he speak of it to me. Once a thing was over and done with, it was my practice to be silent, however much I may have disapproved. The Regent for his part never mentioned it when he felt he had blundered. Where favours and rewards were concerned, I wished to harm no one, and thus never attempted to parry them,[1] reserving all my strength for affairs of State, and preventing such measures as I disapproved of. The consequences for the Abbé Dubois were as I had foretold. Everyone, from the Chancellor down to the most junior maître des requêtes, conceived himself to be personally affronted, and displayed hurt feelings. Neither they nor the other claimants curbed their complaints or their language. Dubois, who thought only of himself, cared neither for the scandal nor for his master's honour.

The Duchesse de Lesdiguières[2] died at Paris, at her magnificent house. She was not old, but had long been a widow, and had lost her only son, who had been M. de Duras's son-in-law.[3] She was also prodigiously wealthy. From every point of view, she was a mean old harridan who, despite all her advantages, would scarcely see a soul, let alone provide any refreshment for the few persons whom she did consent to entertain. She never appeared at Court, and was seldom seen outside her own home.[4] Her front door stayed wide open before a locked grill, through which one

---

[1] '*Je n'allais point à la parade.*' Saint-Simon uses this fencing term, an unusual one for him; but there had recently been several duels, and he was cross with the Regent for not suppressing them more vigorously. The subject of duelling may have been much in his mind at the time.

[2] Paule Marguerite Françoise de Gondi (1655–1716), a niece of Cardinal de Retz. She was a little over sixty when she died and had been widowed in 1681.

[3] Jean François Paul de Bonne de Créquy, the last Duc de Lesdiguières, who had died in 1703.

[4] The Hôtel de Lesdiguières was in the Rue de la Cerisaie, near the Arsenal.

saw a veritable fairy palace, such as we read of in tales. It appeared totally deserted, furnished with articles of the utmost beauty, comparing in splendour and strangeness with the magnificent liveries of her servants, the yellow covers on her coaches, and her two huge blackamoors in gorgeous uniforms. She left vast sums to her staff and to charity; nothing to her daughter-in law,[1] although she was poor and had always cared for her devotedly. All the rest went to the Maréchal de Villeroy and his children, who inherited incomes of more than three hundred thousand livres, apart from that wonderful house and a great quantity of exquisitely beautiful furniture. The Maréchal de Villeroy's mother had been a sister of the Duc de Lesdiguières, the father-in-law of this old horror, and her mother and the mother of Mme de Villeroy were sisters.[2] The Lesdiguières and Gondi families thus both became extinct, and the Villeroys inherited from both sides. Had anyone predicted such riches to the various dukes, marshals, and cardinals of Gondi and Retz, not to mention the Connétable de Lesdiguières, all of whom knew the Villeroys and the stock from which they sprang, they would have turned in their graves.[3]

Coulanges[4] also quitted the world at this time. He was a very short man, stout, and with a jovial countenance, one of those happy-go-lucky people who are always friendly and cheerful, continually uttering delightful nonsense, and for ever inventing new and original jests. Everything save learning and self-discipline came easily to him, all the rest was inborn. Thus he matured very early. He soon rid himself of his post of maître des requêtes, abandoning all the advantages that close kinship with M. de Louville might have brought him simply in order to live an idle life in the best company in Paris, and at the Court, where he had the sense to make only rare appearances among his intimates. Pleasantness, a gay and original wit, good breeding, good manners, and the ability to know his place and refuse to be spoiled; a light touch, singing his little songs at every opportunity, but never malicious, completely charming at table, without the least trace of drunkenness or debauchery, the life and soul of every party, enjoying travel, particularly sound in business matters, with the kindness of one who is incapable of doing harm, but cares only for his pleasures, he was, throughout his life, sought after by the best people, and won a reputation far higher than his futility merited. So he lived, admirably sound in mind and body, until the age of eighty-two, and died a speedy

---

[1] Bernardine de Duras, who had married the Duc de Lesdiguières in 1696.

[2] The Duchesse de Lesdiguières's mother was Catherine de Gondi, Duchesse de Retz, who was a sister of Marguerite Françoise de Gondi, Duchesse de Brissac, the Maréchale de Villeroy's mother.

[3] The dead lady does not seem to warrant so much abuse. Saint-Simon might not have called her an 'old harridan' (*vieille fée*) had not so much money accrued to the Maréchal de Villeroy whom he hated for having been a member of the Meudon cabal. See index, I, under cabal.

[4] Philippe Emmanuel, Marquis de Coulanges (1633–1716). He was the cousin and lifelong friend of Mme de Sévigné who called him '*le tout petit Coulanges*'. He was generally known as '*Le Chansonnier*'.

death. His wife[1] was equipped with better understanding and more sense, and like him had many friends in good Society and at the Court, although she never set foot there. They lived in perfect harmony, broken by occasional tiffs that gave zest to their existence and brought intense pleasure to their friends. They had no children. She survived him by many years. Although once remarkably pretty, she was always virtuous and highly respected.

Parabère died also at this time.[2] Considering the kind of figure he cut in this world, he would have done better to have quitted it sooner. He was the son-in-law of Mme de La Vieuville, Mme la Duchesse de Berry's lady-in-waiting. I shall have reason to speak later of Mme de Parabère, his wife.

The beginning of this year also produced several marriages, including that of young Castries[3] to the daughter of Nollent, a counsellor at the Parlement. This alliance produced the most absurd rumpus, to understand which you must know that the young man's grandfather was Governor of Montpellier, and made a Knight of the Order, in 1661.[4] His grandmother was a sister of Cardinal de Bonzy, the Queen's chief almoner. That prelate, after the death of his sister's husband, secured the governorship of Montpellier for her son; after which M. du Maine married him to one of M. de Vivonne's daughters.[5] That connection eventually gained for young Castries's parents the posts of groom-in-waiting and lady-in-waiting to Mme la Duchesse d'Orléans, who became extremely fond of both of them. Mme de Castries, the mother, was totally lacking in shape and size; but was all heart, all charm, all wit, completely original, with that inimitable flavour of the Mortemarts, and exceedingly well-read and scholarly into the bargain, though she never let that appear.[6] She was a mere scrap of a woman, flat as a pancake, well enough proportioned, but so extremely tiny that you might have passed her through a ring of medium size; no bosom, no bottom, no chin, monstrously plain, always appearing anxious and perplexed, yet a face that sparkled with intelligence and gave even more than it promised. She knew everything—history, philosophy, mathematics, the dead languages—yet she never seemed to know more than how to speak French correctly, which she did with eloquence, grace, and wit, even in the most everyday matters, and with that unique turn of

[1] Marie Angélique de Gué de Bagnols, Dame de Coulanges, also a friend of Mme de Sévigné. She died, aged eighty-one, in 1728.

[2] César Alexandre de Baudéan, Comte de Parabère (1671–1716). His wife Marie Madeleine de La Vieuville became the Regent's mistress.

[3] The Comte de Castries, Jean François Joseph de La Croix (born 1693). He married Marguerite du Monceau de Nollent. They both died within this year, 1716.

[4] Gaspard René de La Croix, Marquis de Coulanges (1611–1674). His wife, the Comte de Castries's grandmother, was Elisabeth de Bonzy (1626–1708). Her brother Cardinal de Bonzy had died in 1703.

[5] The Comte's parents were Joseph François de La Croix, Marquis de Castries (1663–1728), and Marie Elisabeth de Rochechouart, daughter of the Duc de Mortemart, later the Maréchal-duc de Vivonne (1636–1688). She had married M. de Castries in 1693 and died, aged fifty-five, in 1718.   [6] The portrait that follows has been transferred from the year 1696.

phrase which only the Mortemarts possess. Agreeable, diverting, grave, or gay, she could be all things to all men, fascinating when she wished to please, genuinely droll, brilliantly and apparently quite unconsciously funny, delivering her sallies in a manner that made them unforgettable. She was also imperious; liable to be shocked by a thousand trifles, protesting in a plaintive tone that brought the house down. She could be cruelly snubbing when she so desired; but was a very good friend, cultured, kind, always ready to oblige, not a coquette, but sensitive, delighting in other people when she felt drawn to them. She had a charming talent for story-telling; when she cared to invent some impromptu romance people were amazed by her inspiration, variety, and humour. For all her pride,[1] she thought herself well married because she loved her husband. She boasted of everything concerning him, and was quite as vain about him as about herself. He returned the compliment, treating her with every possible care and consideration.

M. de Castries did in fact greatly distinguish himself during the war, and would have gone far, had not asthma and indifferent health compelled him to leave the service. Despite his unimportant post and a mind not far removed from the commonplace, his good nature and merit earned him a vast number of eminent friends, and personal esteem such as is rarely acquired. They had this only son, exceedingly handsome, a young man of much promise, whom they loved to the point of idolatry. They were poor; they wished him to marry money. They found perfect beauty, adorned by every grace, with, so they say (for she came and vanished like a flower), a heart and mind even more admirable than her body. The match once made, Mme la Duchesse d'Orléans had to be told, but only from politeness and because the parents were in her service. They did not need to seek permission. Now that princess was like Minerva, in that she acknowledged no relation except Jupiter. Thus however fond, however intimate she might become with the Castries, however great the trust she reposed in them, she appeared completely unaware of any shadow of a relationship, and they, on their side, would have committed an unpardonable crime had they so much as hinted at its existence. At the first mention of this marriage, she seemed suddenly to perceive that Mme de Castries might conceivably be her cousin, and immediately she started to rant and rave over the disgrace of an alliance with the Nollents. It was not as though she had any better match in view, still less any intention of providing the wherewithal for the Castries to claim one. This particular marriage was what she would not countenance, seeming to regard it as a personal insult, and making such a rumpus that it had to be postponed. The engagement was none the less continued, for both parties desired it; and in the end, the Duc du Maine and the Comte de Toulouse managed to have the ban lifted and the

[1] In being a Mortemart. She was a niece of Mme de Montespan, and was thus a first cousin of the Duchesse D'Orléans, a legitimized daughter of that lady by Louis XIV.

marriage took place. From that moment onwards Mme la Duchesse d'Orléans treated them all with such contempt that the young bride scarcely dared to show herself, and even M. and Mme de Castries began to find the situation intolerable. The poor young couple did not long survive; but it was only after their deaths, separated by no more than four days,[1] that Mme la Duchesse d'Orléans consented to make it up with M. and Mme de Castries, who had nearly died of grief and could never afterwards be comforted.

D'Antin married his second son[2] to the only daughter of Verthamon,[3] premier président of the grand council, a millionaire, and, had that been possible, even stingier than he was rich. In her father's house the bride had gone barefoot, living in an attic without so much as a fire to warm her. Thus her greenness (though she was not stupid), and her amazement at the luxury and splendour of d'Antin's abode gave us much entertainment over a long period. Her husband took the title of Marquis de Bellegarde.

The King left the Tuileries for the first time to visit Madame, and M. and Mme la Duchesse d'Orléans, at the Palais Royal. A few days later he called on Mme la Duchesse de Berry, at the Luxembourg. Because of rival claims and uncertainty, the folding seat in his coach had been removed, leaving only the two back-seats, with the result that the King was squashed between the Duchesse de Ventadour and the Duc du Maine. The Duc du Maine's two sons rode in front with Mme de Villefort, the under-governess. None of them had any right to a seat, except the Duchesse de Ventadour. I have already explained that there are only two rules for places in the King's coach—rank and necessity. But now there was disorder in everything, and it grew worse as time went on.

Mme la Duchesse de Berry took advantage of the confusion to claim a queen's honours, despite Mme de Saint-Simon's protests and her warning that disgrace would follow. She came into Paris with kettle-drums beating all along the Quai des Tuileries, where the King was in residence. The Maréchal de Villeroy complained next day to the Regent, who promised him that when the King was in Paris no drums but his should be heard; and Mme la Duchesse de Berry never afterwards had them. When she attended at the playhouse, she had the floor of her box raised, with four guards posted on the stage, and others in the auditorium; the whole theatre was far more brilliantly illuminated than usual, and the actors addressed their speeches to her. This created as great a scandal in Paris as did, a few years later,[4] her raised seat in her box at the Opéra. She dared not continue in this way at the playhouse, but rather than admit defeat, took a

[1] Saint-Simon forgot. Castries died nearly two months after his wife. Saint-Simon refers to them again.
[2] Gaspard François Balthazar de Pardaillon, Marquis de Bellegarde (1689–1719).
[3] Michel François, Duc de Verthamon (1654–1738). His daughter, Elisabeth Eugénie, died in the same year as her husband.   [4] This happened in 1718.

small private box at the Opéra, where she could hardly be seen and might pretend to be incognito. She never saw plays elsewhere, but since they were sometimes performed at the Opéra for Madame's benefit, the little box served her for both entertainments.

One day, when she arrived, her guards stopped M. le Prince de Conti's coach when it drew up in front of hers, and set about the coachman while the prince was still inside. The truth is that people were everywhere struggling for precedence. The princes of the blood dared not positively deny their duty to make way for a Daughter of France (there being no Sons of France at that time); but they avoided encounters and, in the event, refused to pull up for her. It was, however, one thing to stop M. le Prince de Conti's coach by force, and quite another to set on his coachman while the prince was inside. He too sought redress from M. le Duc d'Orléans, who ordered Mme la Duchesse de Berry to receive him. He visited her, but their public conversation was far from cordial, and to say truth, for all her wit she came very badly out of it. She reproached him for not having spoken to her in the first place, tried to blame his coachman and excuse her own guard. Then, seeing that M. le Duc d'Orléans must be obeyed, she told M. le Prince de Conti that if he were determined to put her servant in gaol, to gaol he should go; but only, she hoped, for a very short time. It was all most despicable. In the end he did go to gaol, but was released immediately at M. le Prince de Conti's request, the excuse being that, having had him arrested, there remained nothing to complain or argue about.

After several love-passages, Mme la Duchesse de Berry became violently enamoured of Rions,[1] a younger member of the Aydie family, a youth with neither charm nor good looks, and a nephew of Mme de Biron. He was short, and stout, and pale, with so many pimples that he resembled one vast boil. He did, however, possess excellent teeth; but he never dreamed of arousing a passion that soon became positively mad, and proved lasting, despite other more fleeting fancies on the side. Rions was almost penniless, with numerous brothers and sisters no better off than he. M. de Pons and his wife, who was one of Mme la Duchesse de Berry's ladies, were related to him and from the same province; it was they who had sent for this lad, when he was still a lieutenant of dragoons, in order to see whether something might not be made of him; but no sooner did he appear than the princess became infatuated, and there he was, master of the Luxembourg. M. de Lauzun, his great-uncle,[2] gave a sly chuckle. He was secretly enchanted, for he could imagine that the old days at the Luxembourg were back, and Mademoiselle alive once more.[3] He issued certain instructions.

---

[1] Armand Auguste, Comte de Rions (1692–1741). In 1717 he was made master of the horse to the Duchesse de Berry, became Governor of Cognac, then of Meudon, and later married that princess morganatically.　　　　[2] Rions's grandmother was Lauzun's sister.
[3] He is referring to Lauzun's famous affair with La Grande Mademoiselle, Anne Marie

Rions was a gentleman, polite, respectful, a very decent fellow. He soon became conscious of possessing charms that appealed only to the princess's depraved taste. He used his influence to hurt no one; everyone commended his good manners; but he treated Mme la Duchesse de Berry as Lauzun had treated La Grande Mademoiselle. He was soon wearing the finest lace, the richest stuffs; his pockets were filled with money, snuff-boxes, and jewels. He played fast and loose, amused himself by making his lady jealous, showed still more jealousy himself. Gradually she feared to do anything without his permission, even the most ordinary everyday actions. Sometimes, when she was about to leave for the Opéra, he would make her stay at home; at other times he would force her to go against her will. He made her be kind to ladies whom she disliked, and maltreat those whom she cared for, on the grounds that he was jealous. She had no freedom, not even to choose her clothes. He delighted in making her take down her hair, or change her gown when she was ready to go out, and he did this so often and so publicly that she fell into the habit of asking each evening for his orders for the following day. Then, next morning, he would change all, and the princess would weep time and time again. At last she took to sending messages to him by trusted servants, for he lodged by the gates of the Luxembourg, and she sent several times while she was dressing to know what ribbons she should wear, what gown, and what style for her hair; and nearly always he forced her to act against her wishes.

When, occasionally, she chose some small thing for herself he would rate her as though she were a servant, and then her tears flowed for several days on end. That princess, who was once so imperious, who had loved to treat people with the utmost rudeness, stooped to taking her meals with persons of no breeding—she, with whom no one, save only the princes of the blood, had the right to eat. A Jesuit named Père Riglet, whom she had known as a child, was admitted to her private suppers, and he was not ashamed, nor was she embarrassed. Mme de Mouchy[1] was her confidant in these most shocking matters; she and Rions between them invited the company and fixed the dates. The Mouchy woman frequently acted as a go-between in their quarrels, and treated the lover far the better, which the princess dared not object to, for fear of losing them both at one stroke. All these brawls took place in public. Everyone at the Luxembourg dealt through M. de Rions, who took immense care to offend no one, treating all and sundry with a respect which he denied, even in public, to his princess alone. In company he gave her such short answers that bystanders lowered

Louise d'Orléans, Duchesse de Montpensier (1627–1693), daughter of Gaston d'Orléans, brother of Louis XIII. She was one of the leaders of the *Fronde* (the nobles' revolt).

[1] In 1712, 'the Duchesse de Berry had a common little favourite, who was well made, pretty, and clever, and had been brought up with her. She was the daughter of Mme la Duchesse de Berry's head waiting-maid. She found a husband for her in Mouchy, a man of quality, advanced in age and high up in the service.' The Saint-Simons gave the reception for the Marquis and Marquise de Mouchy, who were married in the chapel at Versailles. Saint-Simon says, 'as you will see in due course, the Mouchy woman was a little vixen'.

their eyes, and her own were filled with tears. Yet her eager, submissive manner towards him did not at all change on that account.

Something most shocking was that while living this life she had rooms at the Carmelite convent in the Faubourg Saint-Germain, where she sometimes went in the afternoon, and always spent the night there during the Church festivals, often staying for several days on end. She took with her only two ladies, very occasionally a third, and very few servants indeed. She and the ladies ate such food as the convent could provide, attended all the daytime services, in the choir or the tribune, and sometimes the night offices as well, she remaining long afterwards at her prayers, and very strictly keeping the fasts on days of obligation. Two Carmelite nuns of high intelligence and with a knowledge of the world were instructed to welcome her and spend much time with her. One was beautiful, the other had been so; both were young, especially the more beautiful of the two, and both were excellently religious. They performed this duty very much against their will. When they came to know her better, they spoke freely, saying that had they known no more of her than what they could see, they might have venerated her as a saint, but having heard from other lips of her wicked life, they failed to comprehend why she came to the convent.[1] Mme la Duchesse de Berry laughed at them and was not at all displeased.[2] They sometimes took her to task, calling people and things by their names, and exhorting her to change her mode of life. Cleverly and tactfully, they encouraged or corrected her, and never quitted her without some plain speaking. Later, they told such of her ladies as were capable of understanding their difficulties that Mme la Duchesse de Berry left them completely baffled because she continued to come to the Carmelites, yet still lived the same evil life at the Luxembourg.

The princess made her father pay dearly for the cruelty and insolence of her lover; yet, in his weakness, he remained as attentive and compliant as ever, and, shame to say, appeared both submissive and afraid. It grieved him deeply to witness Rions's tyranny and the public scandal of his daughter's depravity; but he dared not interfere, and when on rare occasions, after a particularly shameful scene, he plucked up the courage to protest, he was abused like a pickpocket, forced to endure her sulks for days on end, and snubbed in every attempt to make his peace. Yet not a day passed without their meeting, more often than not at the Luxembourg.

It happened about this time that M. le Duc d'Orléans, who was extremely short-sighted, with one eye far worse than the other, struck the good eye with his racquet while playing tennis, a game which he greatly enjoyed at that period. The blow was such a hard one that he was in danger

---

[1] One of them, Mme Pulchérie, is reported to have said to her, 'When I hear you speak I think you are a saint; but I do not think so any longer when people speak to me of you.'

[2] The Duchesse de Berry was only twenty-one in 1716. One imagines that she was mad. Poor girl, she had recently lost her husband and her babies; this story makes one feel how unhappy she must have been. Cf. II, p. 333 and footnote.

of losing the eye altogether, and although that was averted, he did not greatly benefit because for the rest of his life he saw almost nothing with it. Thus the bad eye, which he had used less, became the better of the two, although the sight from it did not at all improve.

It is now the moment to say something of the public and private life of the Regent, his conduct, pleasures, and daily routine. The mornings were devoted to affairs of State, and the various departments had their special days and hours. He worked alone before he was dressed, and received company at his *lever*, which was kept short, but always preceded and followed by audiences that wasted a great deal of time. After that, the men who bore direct responsibility visited him one after another until two o'clock in the afternoon. These included the heads of the different councils, first La Vrillière;[1] then Le Blanc,[2] whom he used as a spy; the officials with whom he worked on the business of the constitution and the Parlement; often Torcy for letters and the posts; others as the need arose; occasionally the Maréchal de Villeroy, in order to let off steam. Once a week the Regent saw the foreign ambassadors; sometimes he attended the councils or, especially on Sundays and feast-days, went to mass in the chapel. At the beginning he rose early; but gradually he grew more dilatory, then uncertain, or positively late, according to the time when he had gone to bed. At two or two-thirty in the afternoon all might come to see him drink chocolate, and he conversed with the assembled company. This lasted as long as he chose, but usually not more than half an hour. Thereafter he gave audiences to ladies and gentlemen, visited Mme la Duchesse d'Orléans, worked with someone, or attended the Regency Council. He sometimes visited the King during the morning, but if not then, in the evening, either before or after the meeting of the Council. He saluted him, talked with him, and, on leaving, bowed with such profound respect that it was a pleasure to watch, even for the King himself, and taught the world how it should behave.

After the Regency Council, or about five o'clock if there were no meeting, he was done with work. Now was his time for the Opéra or the Luxembourg, if he did not go there before his chocolate. Sometimes he visited Mme la Duchesse d'Orléans and occasionally supped with her. At other times he went out by the back offices, or had people admitted that way. If it were fine he used to go to Saint-Cloud or some other country place, and supped either there or at the Luxembourg, or else returned home. When Madame was in Paris, he called on her for a moment before mass, and always saw her when he went to Saint-Cloud, lavishing attentions on her and showing deep respect. At home he ate his suppers in shocking bad company, with his mistresses or girls from the Opéra, often with Mme la

---

[1] See note 3, p. 33 above.
[2] Louis Claude Le Blanc (1669–1728). A maître des requêtes and Intendant of Dunkirk. He was also a secretary of State, and minister for war 1719–1723.

Duchesse de Berry[1] and some dozen young men, not always the same, whom he invariably spoke of as his *roués*.[2] These included Broglio,[3] elder brother of the Broglio who died a duke and Marshal of France;[4] Nocé;[5] four or five of his officers, but not the best; the Duc de Brancas;[6] Biron;[7] Canillac; a few wild young men; some fashionable ladies of relatively easy virtue, and various persons of no importance who shone by their wit or their depravity. The food was delicious, prepared in special kitchens on the same floor. All the utensils were of silver and the guests often joined the cooks to make experiments.

At these suppers everyone was discussed, ministers and friends alike, with a licence that knew no bounds. The past and present love-affairs of the Court and Paris were examined without regard for the victims' feelings; old scandals were retold, ancient jests, and absurdities revived, nothing and nobody was sacred. M. le Duc d'Orléans played an active part in all this, but it must honestly be said that he seldom took much account of the talk. The wine flowed, the company became heated; they talked filth and out-rivalled one another in blasphemy; and when they had made sufficient noise and were all dead drunk, they were put to bed, and on the following day began all over again. As soon as supper-time arrived, the outer doors were bolted and barred so that, no matter what occurred, the Regent could not be disturbed. I do not mean for private or family matters only, but in case of danger to the State, or to his own life; and his incarceration lasted all night and well into the following morning.

The Regent thus wasted an infinity of time with his family, his diversions, and his debauchery. He wasted still more in audiences too easily obtained, too long, far too widespread; and became inundated with details similar to those which we had so often discussed and deplored during the late King's lifetime. I reminded him of this sometimes and he remembered; but it made no difference, for he could not stand firm. Small matters that might have been settled in half an hour were long drawn out either because he could not decide, or from his unhappy desire to set people against each other, following that fatal maxim, *divide et impera*, which he sometimes confessed was his favourite. All this derived from his suspicious

---

[1] Madame was deeply distressed by the rumours about her son and the Duchesse de Berry, but did not, of course, believe a word of them (there was never any proof). She hated to hear that notices were stuck on the Palais Royal: 'Here be Lotteries and most subtle poisonings.' 'By lotteries,' she wrote, 'they imply that my son lives with his daughter after the manner of Lot.'

[2] His boon companions were born to be broken on the wheel: see II, p. 438.

[3] Charles Guillaume, Marquis de Broglio. He was Voysin's son-in-law.

[4] François Marie, Duc et Maréchal de Broglio (1671–1745). In 1725 he became the French ambassador in London.

[5] Charles de Nocé, Seigneur de Fontenay (1664–1739). He became Master of the Regent's wardrobe, 1717, and his first gentleman, 1719.

[6] Louis III, Duc de Villars-Brancas (1663–1739).

[7] Charles Armand de Gontaut, Marquis, later Duc, de Biron (1663–1756), Maréchal de France 1734. He became a member of the war council in 1715, and joined the Regency Council in 1721.

nature, and a general distrust of everything and everybody, that led to trifles' developing into hydras, and landed him in appalling difficulties. His friendliness and approachability were extremely pleasing and made him much liked; but people abused his complaisance, sometimes showing a want of respect all the more unseemly because, in trying to rebuke them, he was often the most embarrassed. Among the chief sinners were Stair, the officers of the constitution, the Maréchal de Villeroy, the leaders of the Parlement, and the great majority of the magistrates. I brought to his notice many such personal matters, whenever I found the opportunity; now and again I advanced a step, and I avoided all unpleasantness; but nearly always he wriggled free. He knew that I spoke the truth, but his weakness ruled him.

What was most extraordinary was that neither his mistresses, nor Mme la Duchesse de Berry, nor his *roués*, not even when he was quite drunk, ever extracted anything at all from him concerning the government or the business of the State. He lived openly with Mme de Parabère, and with many other women too. He revelled in their jealousies and complaints, but continued on equally good terms with all of them. Thus the scandal of his public harem, and the lewdness and impiety of his nightly suppers soon became generally known throughout the whole of France.

At the beginning of Lent, I foresaw that when Easter came there would inevitably be either a public scandal or the most dreadful sacrilege, and that the Regent's already evil reputation would be further harmed. I therefore decided to remonstrate, notwithstanding that for a long time past I had ceased to do so, having lost all hope of altering his way of life. I now depicted the perplexity[1] in which he would find himself at Easter, saying how damnable it would be in the sight of God, how supremely shocking to a world that was quite prepared to sin, but not ready to let others do the same, especially not its betters. Thus, although it went against my will and custom, I could not abstain from showing him the danger. I then spread myself on the world's reactions, for to speak of religion would, alas!, have had no effect. He heard me out most patiently and anxiously asked what I proposed. I said I could offer only a palliative that would not entirely prevent a scandal, but might at least reduce it, and prevent the worst from being said. My idea was not wholly disagreeable; merely that he should spend the last five days of Holy Week, and Easter Sunday and Monday, at his house at Villers-Cotterets, and return on the Tuesday. He should take neither women nor his *roués*, but six or seven decent people of good standing, who would be able to converse with him, play cards, go for walks, generally amuse themselves, but keep the fasts— although, at Villers-Cotterets, the food on fast days was as good as at a feast elsewhere. Bawdiness at meals should be avoided and his stay at table

[1] Whoever might be perplexed, it was unlikely to be the Duc d'Orléans who appears to have been quite happy in that respect.

not too much prolonged. He should go to church on Good Friday, and to High Mass on Easter day. I asked no more, and I guaranteed that he would thus escape censure.

The doings of princes of such high rank, I continued, were known to all, and everyone would learn that he had not taken the Sacraments; but there was a vast difference between refusing them scornfully, head held high, in the centre of Paris, and an escape into the country, with a look of shame and embarrassment. To remain would arouse horror, even among libertines; to go would make respectable folk feel sorry for him, and still all tongues. I even offered to accompany him if he so wished, and to sacrifice the holiday at my home, which I took every year at that season. The State, I said, would not suffer, since no business was done on those days; Villers-Cotterets was not far and the country very beautiful; he had not been there for several years, and it would be in every way desirable to visit his estate. M. le Duc d'Orléans received the proposal with joy; was effusive in his thanks for my offer to go with him, seeming even relieved, for he had had no idea of what I had in mind. He raised no objection; thought it even pleasant. We discussed his companions; it was not hard to choose, and the thing was settled. We agreed that he should issue no orders until the week before. We spoke again later, and he appeared quite convinced that the excursion would be wise, and that he would certainly go.

Sad to relate, his good intentions rarely took effect because they seldom suited the rakes surrounding him, whose vital interests required his constant presence, and constant entertainment—if no worse. When I spoke to him a few days before Palm Sunday, I found him stiff, embarrassed, unable to answer me. I knew at once what had happened, and I redoubled my efforts, impressing upon him the horror with which people would regard him if, in the centre of Paris, he failed in his Easter duties, and how such vile conduct would alienate all decent men. It was of no avail. I was net with silence, dejection, and arguments so futile that I shall not repeat them. In fact, he had changed his mind as soon as he saw the disgust on the faces of his mistresses and *roués*. Do not be surprised at my so often using that word; M. le Duc d'Orléans never spoke of them otherwise, nor did Mme la Duchesse de Berry, nor even Mme la Duchesse d'Orléans. Those rascals were afraid to let him enjoy the company of respectable men lest he should cease to wish for theirs alone. His mistresses were equally alarmed, and the whole group had raised such a rumpus at the first mention of the excursion, that there was no further talk of it.

When I took my leave of him before going to my home, I entreated him to be careful at least during the four holiest days, and above all not to commit sacrilege.[1] I then immediately left for La Ferté, hoping at least to

---

[1] Before receiving absolution he would have had to promise to send away his mistresses. It was sacrilege to take Communion intending to keep them.

have fended off the worst. I learned with sadness, however, that after spending the last days of Holy Week in a more than shady fashion, if less publicly, he had attended most of the church services after the manner of Monsieur, who had nearly always been in Paris at that season. On Easter Sunday he had gone to High Mass at his parish church of Saint-Eustache and, with much ceremony, had taken the Sacrament. That, alas!, was the last communion ever taken by this unhappy prince and, in this world, the result was as I had foreseen. Let us now leave this distressing subject and turn to events abroad.

Let me first mention that on 20 January of this year, at Madrid, the Queen of Spain gave birth to a son, her first child. He was named Charles, or Don Carlos, and has since become King of Naples and Sicily.[1]

Partly from necessity, partly to give you a better understanding of things, I have, at various times, described the persons of all conditions who have taken part in the events recorded. You must now recall the following, who will henceforth play leading roles, and in particular the characters of the Duc de Noailles (II, 203–204), Canillac (III, 10, note 4), the Abbé Dubois (II, 434–435), de Nocé (see below), d'Effiat (II, 412–414), Stair (II, 408–409), even of Rémond (III, 39), and lastly of the Maréchal d'Huxelles (II, 347f).

[*The page numbers here given refer to this edition. Saint-Simon quotes from his own manuscript. The only portrait not already included is that of Nocé; this is what Saint-Simon says of him : 'Nocé was a tall man with a once magnificent figure that had served somewhat to enhance his reputation. He had wit, a certain degree of culture, and charm also when he wished to please. M. le Duc d'Orléans had known him a long time (he was the son of Fontenay, the prince's tutor), and greatly appreciated his dislike of all restraint, his epicurean philosophy, his brusque manner, that when it did not become brutal (as it too often did) could seem pleasant enough, masquerading as candour and independence. All in all, Nocé was not a bad fellow, but eccentric. He absolutely refused to suffer fools, was abominably idle, disinclined to accept any restraint, denying himself nothing. Climates, seasons, delicious viands only to be found in certain districts and temperatures, circles that pleased him, a mistress, bracing air, drew him in one direction or another, and held him for years or even longer).[2] He was civil, ready to keep his place, caring for nothing but money— and even there he was not too greedy—to enable him to indulge freely in his many caprices of many different kinds, none of which he was ever able to resist. All this was exceedingly pleasant to M. le Duc d'Orléans. Nocé was one of the people whom he saw whenever he went to Paris. I had no acquaintance or dealings with him, since at that time, I never saw M. le Duc d'Orléans in town, and people like Nocé never came to Versailles. During the Regency I had scarcely more to do with him. His sphere was the Regent's supper-parties and his other diversions; mine was the affairs of State. I never shared in the Regent's pleasures.'*]

[1] This eldest child of Elisabeth Farnese, Philip V's second wife, became King Charles III of Spain in 1759 on the death of his half-brother Ferdinand VI, second son of Marie Louise Gabrielle of Savoy, Philip V's first wife.

[2] One of Saint-Simon's more attractive characters. He was always going after the honey-pots.

You already know the beginning of the Scottish adventure; how the Pretender made a secret journey to embark from Brittany, and how he escaped from Stair's assassins thanks to the skill and courage of the post-mistress of Nonancourt. The enterprise had originated with the late King and King Philip of Spain, who had offered to defray the expenses. The death of Louis XIV was one of the greatest misfortunes that James III could have suffered; but at the time of his journey that monarch's memory was too green for French policy to have changed. He was allowed to go, although there was no intention of assisting him unless a sudden revolution in Great Britain should force the government's hand. The news of the attempted assassination prevented embarkation in Brittany, but Bolingbroke,[1] who controlled the Pretender's private affairs and was his secretary of State, had chartered a ship in Normandy also. In the event, King James went not to Normandy, but to Dunkirk, where the vessel was sent secretly.

If you will recall Stair's behaviour at the end of 1715, you will know that the English ambassador lost no time in forming attachments in Paris that were likely to serve him in the future; and he did not neglect the lesser men, for they led him to the greater. As for Rémond, that fop, libertine, sham scholar, and general dogsbody, he had struck up an acquaintance with the Abbé Dubois who used anyone at hand, and had formed a kind of friendship with Canillac. He wooed both men with praise and flattery; won the abbé with intrigues, and Canillac by sharing his interest in the obscurer forms of debauchery. Overjoyed at their conquest, he boasted to them of Stair's genius, while to Stair himself he bragged of his influence with M. le Duc d'Orléans. To all three he spoke as though he were commissioned to approach them, and he succeeded so well that he brought them together, at first only socially, but soon to discussing affairs of State. Canillac, as you may have gathered, had singularly little sense for all that he was so clever. Brilliance in conversation, a startling ability to unmask affectations or absurdities took the place of sound judgment with him, and a continual flow of words dammed up his reasoning powers and left him most often in the wrong. Stair, well coached by Rémond, lavished upon him all the attentions best calculated to please, and this method succeeded, for Canillac could not resist a great ambassador who admired and deferred to him. He, in turn, admired Stair's intellect and capability, and Stair's quarrel with the entire government of the late King was a most powerful attraction, for Canillac had hated the men then in favour and office, and almost hated the King himself for having appointed them. Before long, he was agreeing with Stair on every issue; at which point, his attachment to

[1] Henry St. John, Viscount Bolingbroke (1678–1751). Created Viscount Bolingbroke in 1712, he negotiated the Peace of Utrecht 1713. He was a great schemer, and during Queen Anne's reign had plotted a Jacobite restoration, but her sudden death in 1714 upset his plans. Threatened with impeachment, he fled to France.

the Duc de Noailles made him eager to include him also. Thus a circle was soon formed and the talk was all of politics.

With the Abbé Dubois the connection was quickly made; he was as anxious for Stair's friendship as Stair was for his. Stanhope[1] at that time was a secretary of State and confidential adviser to George I. He had lived in Paris, and had met Dubois in the drawing-room of Lady Sandwich,[2] who for many years had been living in France and was on amorous terms with that abbé. After Stanhope's return to England, he and Dubois often exchanged greetings through her; and when M. le Duc d'Orléans was in Spain, it so happened that Stanhope had been commander of the English forces. Even in that relationship they had had all the friendly dealings possible, despite their situation as enemies. Now that Stanhope was in office, Dubois placed all his hopes on their old attachment, and it was purely for that reason that he wished to bring M. le Duc d'Orléans over to King George. He was as yet in no position to be consulted on State affairs; Stair, so he hoped, would contrive some pretext to remind the Regent of his old friendship with Stanhope, and thus involve him in their discussions. Nothing, indeed, better suited all the parties concerned than the attachments effected by Dubois and Rémond with Stair and Canillac, and by Canillac with the Duc de Noailles.

As for Noailles who was always attracted by novelties and, like M. le Duc d'Orléans, thoroughly enjoyed circuitous methods, he had one, maybe two, personal reasons for advocating a change of policy. First, he was finding the finances a thankless task, with all the worry of trying vainly to make ends meet. He now saw an opportunity for great economies by refusing further assistance to the Pretender, thus ruining an attempt that, if successful, would require support and large grants of money for several years to come. The other reason, or so I believe, concerned myself.[3] M. de Noailles had known me too long to be unaware of my pro-Jacobite sentiments; for I was perfectly convinced that it was in France's best interests to keep England too busy at home to think of foreign conquest or interference with our commerce and that of Spain. What is more, we had no common bond with the English king who, because of his estates and other interests in Hanover, was more German than English;[4] who feared

---

[1] Earl Stanhope was George I's favourite minister.

[2] See note 3, p. 38 above.

[3] Saint-Simon's life was at a crisis. The time for planning and theorizing was past; he was now part of the administration and needed to work with other people. He may have begun to realize that he had not those capabilities. He was also for the first time since his boyhood without advisers who protected him against himself, his malice, his impulsiveness. Beauvilliers and Chevreuse were dead, Chamillart and the Chancellor were in retirement, even the King whom he feared and respected had gone. There was no one to lean on except his wife. No wonder if he felt lost and began to imagine persecution. There is evidence to show that Noailles was not an enemy plotting his downfall. Saint-Simon was clearly digging his own grave in politics, having nothing to offer but the lessons of past history.

[4] George I and the Regent's mother were first cousins. Saint-Simon is inclined to forget their close family relationship.

and was influenced by the Emperor and, so far as he was able, remained in permanent alliance with him. Noailles may indeed have learned of Stair's vain attempts to win me through M. de Lauzun, who loved foreigners and, despite all that he owed to the court of Saint-Germain, had a particular relish for Englishmen of all kinds. Lauzun saw a good deal of Stair, dined at his house, and invited him in return; but he entirely failed to get any response from me to the advances he made on that gentleman's behalf, or to his pressing invitations to dine with them à trois.

Thinking as I did on the subject of England, I could not accept the friendship of the English ambassador, quite apart from the fact that his conduct and his insolence repelled me, more especially since the affair at Nonancourt. Noailles none the less had good reason to believe that with the help of Canillac and Dubois the Regent might be brought over to King George, and in so doing he hoped to make me appear hostile. His Royal Highness's confidence in me might then be shaken, and he would hide from me his alliance with England. However that may have been, Noailles began dealings with Stair simultaneously with Canillac and Dubois, and between them they persuaded M. le Duc d'Orléans to take this great step, suggesting motives of personal interest that were in themselves infamous. The argument they offered was as follows: George I was a usurper of the throne of Great Britain; if anything should happen to our King, M. le Duc d'Orléans would likewise usurp the French crown. Their interests were thus identical; they had every reason to cultivate each other's friendship, even to the point of guaranteeing each other's thrones, and of doing nothing likely to disturb that security. The plotters emphasized that the Regent had everything to gain, whereas the English king would gain very little. He had only a Pretender to reckon with, a prince without lands, money, or support; M. le Duc d'Orléans, on the other hand, might find himself facing a King of Spain, powerful and secure, whose kingdom bordered on France itself by land and sea.

M. le Duc d'Orléans swallowed this poison, presented with great skill by men on whose capabilities and devotion he was entitled to rely, but who thereby demonstrated that their brilliance was a fraud, their capability non-existent, their devotion a pretence, and that they were guided only by personal advantage. The prince had too much intelligence not to see the trap; the miracle was that he allowed himself to be attracted by the tortuousness of the manœuvre; for he had not the least wish to reign. I can well imagine that if ever these memoirs are published, people will laugh at that statement, and that my entire narrative may therefore be discredited. They will think me a fool if I aspire to convince my readers, and a madman if I myself was deceived. Yet such is the plain unvarnished truth, and to it I sacrifice whatever others may think of me. Incredible though it may seem, it is none the less true, and I owe it to that truth which reigns supreme in these memoirs to say that M. le Duc d'Orléans never desired the crown;

that he most sincerely wished the King to live and, moreover, as will be seen from what follows, that he wished him to reign unassisted. He never willingly contemplated the possibility of the King's death, nor the events following on such a tragedy; for a tragedy he would have considered it, and for himself also, had it ever come to pass. All he did was to reflect on the ideas put before him. He was quite incapable of originating such thoughts or of acting as though the event were possible.[1] I do not say that had it occurred he would have surrendered the right given him by the Renunciations,[2] and guaranteed by the whole of Europe; but I must emphatically state that for him possession of the crown would have been the least attraction, and that honour, courage, and his own integrity would have meant all. This is the truth which my very complete knowledge of him, my conscience, and my honour oblige me to set down.[3]

Let us quickly finish with the subject of this private agreement that throws light on much of what follows. The plotters were not entirely successful in their designs against me, assuming that I am right in my suspicions of the Duc de Noailles. The Regent did not long try to hide from me his new affection for England. I approved of it to a certain point, for the sake of the peace which our exhaustion and the King's minority made so infinitely desirable, also in order to counteract King George's highly dangerous bias towards the Emperor; but I could go no further. I had more than once said in private to the Regent, and again at the Council of Regency, that it was of the first importance for France to have a close and permanent union with Spain, whose ruler was of the same house, attached by bonds of a very close blood relationship to our own monarch, and without rival claims or conflicting interests to make him look elsewhere. The real enemies of France, I maintained, were the Austrians and the English; the entire course of our history clearly displayed their hatred and suspicion of a country that alone had the power to frustrate their ambitions.

The Regent heard me with great attention, and could find no answer. He agreed both with my assertions and my arguments. He promised me that he firmly intended to remain closely attached to Spain, but said that while that country continued to be ruled by an ambitious queen and a most dangerous minister,[4] he must guard against their knowing too much of our affairs. In agreeing, he reminded me that, since the Peace of Ryswick[5] especially, it had been the policy of the Viennese court to be strongly allied with the maritime powers Holland and England, for the

[1] Yet so many little children died young from contagious diseases and the ignorance of the doctors, so many had recently died in the royal family itself, that it seems scarcely likely that the Regent had not thought Louis XV's death a strong possibility.   [2] See note 2, p. 38 above.

[3] The European powers were highly suspicious of the Regent, believing that he had in mind the crime of which Saint-Simon says he was incapable. One feels that Saint-Simon was right, and that the Regent's kindness to the little King is a further proof that he was no Macbeth.

[4] Alberoni.

[5] The Peace of Ryswick, 1697, by which Louis XIV was forced to recognize the heretic William, Prince of Orange, as William III of England (see index, I).

purpose of ruining our commerce. I approved of these sound precautions, provided that they were precautions only, and that he saw the need to follow the policy which I had described. He said that such was indeed his intention, and the conversation ended by his telling me once more how secret and how careful he must be in helping the Pretender to land in Scotland, and in disguising any support given him by France, unless, of course, he should have a swift and unexpected victory.

The treaty that had been under negotiation for the past year between the King of England and the King of Spain was signed at Madrid and, judging by the extreme satisfaction with which it was received in London, appeared to herald the closest possible alliance between the two countries. Monteleoni,[1] the Spanish ambassador in London, counted on its increasing his reputation and influence in the King of Spain's service, not only at that time, but also in the future, should that event occur in France for which their Catholic Majesties and some of their ministers kept ever on the watch. Stanhope had many conversations with him on that subject, urging Spain to take a firmer line with France, in view of the Regent's supposed aid to the Pretender, at the same time ignoring, or pretending not to know, that Spain was also doing much to support him.

Meanwhile, in Spain itself, Alberoni had induced the queen to keep her husband completely secluded, just as the Princesse des Ursins had done in her time. It was the one sure way to govern that prince; for by temperament and conscience he felt bound to cleave only to his wife, who like her predecessor led him wherever she pleased, having discovered that the safest course was to prevent his hearing anything from other lips than hers, or Alberoni's, which amounted to the same thing. All the officers of his guard, all the entrées and members of his household were kept away from him. At his palace the king saw only the same two or three gentlemen of his chamber, and them only at their hours of duty—one or two at his *lever*, fewer, even, at his *coucher*, and four or five valets, including two who were French. The three gentlemen of the chamber were as follows: the Marquis of Santa-Cruz,[2] the queen's major-domo and very much in her confidence, a man of parts, with a sound understanding of affairs, and a particular hatred of France; the Duke of Arco,[3] the master of the horse, a keen huntsman and governor of the royal residences. Arco was greatly liked both by the king and the queen; but he never toadied Alberoni, who would gladly have removed him had that been possible. His gentle, tolerant, rather mediocre intellect was, however, no great danger, for he kept his place and was very careful not to interfere. The third gentleman was Valouse[4] who had been page and personal equerry to Philip

---

[1] Isidore Cassado de Azevedo, Marquis of Monteleoni.
[2] Alvarez Antonio da Bazan Benavidès y Velasco, Marquis of Santa-Cruz (died 1737).
[3] Alphonzo Manrique de Lara, Duke of Arco (1672–1737).
[4] Hyacinthe Boutin, Marquis de Valouse (1671–1736).

as Duc d'Anjou in France, and was promoted to first equerry on following him to Spain. Valouse was honest enough, but very limited, frightened to death of everyone, and always on the side of those with power. He loved the king; was the friend of all men; particularly attached to the Duke of Arco, and quite incapable of any kind of interference.

I shall return in greater detail to King Philip's isolation in the midst of his courtiers when the time comes to describe my mission to Spain; to recount it here would take too long. Suffice it to say that the king allowed himself to be immured in a very real sense, living under the eye of the queen every hour of the day and night. By that means she became at one and the same time his gaoler and his fellow-prisoner; for since she was always with the king no one could approach her without also approaching him. Alberoni thus kept them both in captivity, and kept the key of their prison in his pocket. And this was the same Alberoni who, beginning as the humble envoy of the Duke of Parma to Madrid, had now become the chief and all-powerful minister of Spain itself. This tremendous ascent and the dangers of his situation tempted him to raise his eyes to the cardinalate in order to be safe; and he confidently expected to gain the King of Spain's nomination. There was, however, a temporary obstruction. He longed to act, but could do so only with the queen's support, and, at the beginning, that royal lady found it hard to adjust her mind to the idea of an upstart foreigner's climbing over the heads of many Spaniards with far better claims. Thus for the moment Alberoni remained greatly discomfited.

King James, in the meantime, was in hiding near Paris,[1] his enterprise having failed. Despairing of any help coming from the Regent, he had turned to Spain for support, and had, with the utmost difficulty, secured a secret interview with Cellamare,[2] at a corner of the Bois de Boulogne. There he had described his unhappy situation in moving and pathetic terms, stressing his predicament at finding neither a place nor the wherewithal to live. He threw all the blame for his failure on Bolingbroke, whom he had dismissed from his post of secretary of state, and bitterly complained of the Duke of Berwick for refusing to join him in Scotland. Meanwhile, he said, he could not continue as the Duc de Lorraine's guest; but retirement to Rome would destroy his cause in England. His hopes were all for some place of refuge in Spain; but wherever he went he would need monetary support, not only for himself, but for those who had lost all in his service. He ended by begging the King of Spain to send him a hundred écus. Cellamare extricated himself as best he could, but made no promises; he well knew what the result would be. King George had formally required the European powers to refuse all help or refuge to the Pretender and his

---

[1] The Old Pretender had landed at Peterhead, in Scotland, during December 1715; but the Earl of Mar mismanaged the rebellion, and James was forced to take flight from Montrose six weeks later. By the terms of the Treaty of Utrecht, he could no longer remain in France. He spent the rest of his empty life in Rome, where he died in 1766.

[2] See II, pp. 403, 420.

followers. Stair had recently presented that demand to the Regent in a strongly worded letter, and the English ambassador to the King of Spain had been charged with a similar message.

At that particular time, the English court was ultra-sensitive regarding the Pretender. They realized the discontent among the English people and their horror of the past bloodshed, which had forced the government to keep as many as thirty-five thousand men under arms in the three kingdoms, and forty ships of war. In this dangerous situation they tried with might and main to gain the friendship of Spain. Flattery and confidences were lavished on the Spanish envoys, even to the extent of hinting at distrust of the Emperor's Italian ambitions. There was even the offer of an alliance to prevent his influence from spreading, coupled with a suggestion that England had refused to sign a treaty with Austria only because it included a guarantee of Tuscany that might have prejudiced Spanish interests. The final lure to the King of Spain was a suggestion of assistance should events in France give him an opportunity to claim his royal rights. Nothing, indeed, was better calculated to please the Spaniards than the hope of such an alliance.

At this point Stair committed an act of the utmost wickedness; for he sent a report to his master King George to the effect that France was arming with all speed to restore the Pretender, adding false details of ports, vessels, and troops. This lie raised the alarm in England, causing a fall in the public funds, and the king thereupon decided to ask Parliament for the subsidies necessary to prepare for an inevitable war with France. Monteleoni, who saw the urgent need to prevent a rupture, spoke so firmly to Stanhope that all preparations were stopped, there being no foundation for that wicked lie save in the malice of its perpetrator. Stanhope then proposed a firm alliance between England and Spain to preserve the neutrality of Italy, with a guarantee of the King of Sicily's[1] enjoyment of the territories he had acquired by the Treaty of Utrecht. Stanhope realized that the whole of Great Britain was in a ferment against the government, and saw the need to calm the people's fears lest France and Spain should join together to assist the Pretender. He therefore reasserted his hopes that France would join the above-mentioned alliance, and guaranteed the Protestant succession to the English throne, in conformity with the act of Parliament. Thus Stair's villainy had an effect quite contrary to his intentions, and marked the beginning of that alliance between France and England on which the Abbé Dubois had pinned his hopes. It was also the first step in the the rise of that vulgar nobody, who managed to extract from it most disgraceful benefits for the State, and very great advancement for himself.

---

[1] Victor Amadeus II (1666–1732): see index, II. He married Anne Marie d'Orléans, a daughter of Monsieur and Henrietta of England, and was the father of the Duchesse de Bourgogne, who became Dauphine in 1711, and of Philip V's first wife, Marie Louise Gabrielle of Savoy.

Although Stair took extraordinary pains to hide his treachery from the French court, he did not escape being regarded as a meddler who presumed on his official standing, and for that reason was much disliked, more especially since he appeared to be abominably arrogant. At the Palais Royal, however, he was safe enough, for his three supporters would have thought it harmed their interests to seem to change their view of him. Dubois desired of all things to succeed with England; he saw no other road to success. Noailles had long ago realized that sooner or later the abbé would be restored to favour. He therefore made it a principle to defend him when necessary, never to contradict him, and to help him in every possible way, for the sake of repayment later. Canillac, incapable of so much duplicity but totally lacking in judgment, remained as credulous as ever, completely deceived by Stair's apparent admiration. As for the Regent, he may well have seen through Stair and his friends, but he had not the will-power to refute that vile comparison of the two usurpers, which they continually harped on, sometimes together, sometimes separately, steadily denying everything that did not suit their views concerning England. I often tackled him on that subject. Had I not known his weakness, I might have thought to change his mind; but they were three to one, and their efforts easily nullified whatever I might say to enlighten or convince him; for M. le Duc d'Orléans, though he hated making up his mind, could sometimes be caught on the rebound. He made amends to me by mocking them. Dubois, however, was used to that; Noailles shrugged it off, but Canillac's pride was sometimes wounded. The Regent would let him sulk for a time, then laughed at him, and afterwards made much of him. Canillac's pompous manner made people listen to him and consider his hurt feelings.

As for Stair and Bentivoglio,[1] they were hot-heads to whom nothing was sacred, so long as it could advance their interests. Their only wish was to ruin France, and if one was more corrupt, more wicked, more treacherous than the other, that one was Bentivoglio. Both were notorious impostors, both were in disgrace at their own courts, where they had lost all credit. Had a firm demand been sent for their recall, they must both have left France. But Stair was protected by his three declared advocates, and Bentivoglio had supporters just as powerful. Effiat, though an unbeliever, was his creature and deceived his master, while that prince, in his weakness, deferred to the Maréchal de Villeroy, and the Cardinals de Rohan and Bissy, who were Bentivoglio's eager and self-seeking protectors. Thus the Regent kept by him, under the disguise of papal nuncio and British ambassador, two most notorious and explosive firebrands, the worst enemies of France and his own person. You shall hear more in due course of that most infamous

[1] Cornelius Bentivoglio (1668–1732), papal nuncio in France, 1711, made a cardinal 1719. He originated in Ferrara; and was nuncio in Paris in 1713, in pursuance of the constitution (the Bull *Unigenitus*).

nuncio, how he thought nothing of publicly keeping an opera-singer, and of having two daughters by her, who were known to be such, and went by the nicknames of 'La Constitution' and 'La Légende'.[1] Had I filled these memoirs with all the details concerning the constitution and the nunciature of Bentivoglio, it would not be too much to say that your hair would stand upright on your head as you read of the true conduct and daily life of that legate.

Soon after the King's death this faction had tried to win me over, or at least to avoid having me as an enemy. They knew my feelings regarding the constitution, for I had never sought to conceal them, and before long Cardinal de Bissy had tackled me, and later both Prince and Cardinal de Rohan visited me. I answered that I was no bishop to pass judgment, nor even a learned divine, and thus I extricated myself. That, however, did not completely satisfy them, and they loosed the Duc de La Force upon me for one last effort. It was not as though I had ever raised my standard in the affair; I had kept firmly in my place as a member of the Council of Regency, and in my private talks with M. le Duc d'Orléans; but even during the King's lifetime they had known my sentiments, and they distrusted my attachment to Cardinal de Noailles.

La Force accordingly came to do battle with me. He knew his subject and spoke well enough; but since politics was his only religion and he would have needed faith to shift me, it is not surprising that he failed. When all his arguments were exhausted, he urged the Regent's need to deal gently with Rome, the Jesuits, and the majority of the bishops, who all eagerly desired the constitution. But politics and personal advantage can never replace truth and religion, and his appeals had as little effect on me as his doctrine. At a loss where next to turn, he produced his final effort which, as I later discovered, he and his masters were convinced would prevail with me. I was, he said, the sworn enemy of the Duc de Noailles, never sparing him, quite unmoved by all his attempts to placate me; I showed every sign of being proud of my attitude, quarrelling with him continually at the meetings of the Council, and wherever else I encountered him; yet, although I never concealed my desire to ruin him, I neglected the one sure means of so doing, by persisting in being the friend and supporter of Cardinal de Noailles.

I begged La Force to explain this 'one sure means' of destroying the Duc de Noailles, vowing that I should be enchanted to know it. 'Destroy the uncle,' said he, 'and to do that you have only to join us. Without the uncle, the nephew cannot last long, and vengeance will be yours.' Horror brought the blood rushing to my cheeks. 'Monsieur!' I exclaimed, 'Is that how you treat matters of religion? Let me say once and for all, and you may tell this to your friends, that were I quite certain of the total and permanent ruin of the Duc de Noailles by removing one hair from his uncle's head, he would be safe from me. No, Sirrah!' I repeated in a burst

[1] La Légende Dorée, the 'Golden Legend' of the lives of the Saints.

of indignation, 'though I shall neglect no honourable means of crushing the Duc de Noailles, he may live and rule two thousand years before I strike at him across the body of Cardinal de Noailles.' M. de La Force appeared greatly upset, and since that time he has never tried to win me over. I never spoke of all this to the Cardinal, nor to anyone who might have repeated it to him.

It is true that in my conduct towards the Duc de Noailles I may have gone too far in stamping upon the involuntary movements of remorse in a man who had greatly offended me. We met only at those sessions when our troubles with the Parlement were discussed;[1] but Noailles's treachery, and the folly or jealousy of certain others, soon brought such discussions to an end, and even before they were discontinued my remarks, aimed publicly straight at him, had driven him from them, for he could never find any answer. At the last meeting which he attended, he told the Duc de Charost, who was sitting next him, that if I continued to press him so hard he would be obliged to seek satisfaction sword in hand. Satisfaction he never got, nor did he demand it, and his sword remained peacefully in its sheath.[2] Whenever we met he bowed with deep respect, and I merely glanced at him, passing on without even the most perfunctory salute. In one place or another this scene was repeated without any variation, and although people became accustomed to it, it always created a drama. If I approached him, he at once drew back; but I took not the slightest notice, and we never exchanged a word except in public at the Council, on affairs of State: I, speaking curtly and to the point, he, infinitely polite, I might almost say with an air of deference, flattery, and all the tact that he could muster.

He came to the Regency Council one day, on the pretext of some urgent matter concerned with the finances. The meeting had already begun. He sent his name to the Regent, who bade them admit him. I rose because the entire Council rose; he sat down below, but next me, and began to explain his difficulty, which did not seem to amount to much. As he finished I whispered into the ear of the Comte de Toulouse, who sat next me on the other side, that the Duc de Noailles was making this an excuse to stay for the whole meeting. 'I think I agree with you,' he answered smiling. 'Well!' said I, 'we shall see, just leave it to me.' When the question of finance had been settled, the Duc de Noailles still remained, and after a moment's pause, M. le Duc d'Orléans turned to the Maréchal d'Huxelles and said, 'Now, Sir, let us proceed.' Monsieur de Troyes usually acted for the Maréchal by reading the dispatches because he had a good voice and intonation, and read aloud extremely well. He began; but at the second word I interrupted, saying, 'Wait, Monsieur, do you not see that M. de

---

[1] These troubles included the affair of the bonnet, ducal precedence in general, and the usurpations' of the magistrates.

[2] Fascinating to imagine the duel! Would the tiny duke really have fought? What would the Regent have done?

Noailles is still present?' and I turned round to gaze fixedly at that nobleman. I then moved my folding armchair[1] a little way so as to give him
room to rise, and after a moment's silence, observing that Monsieur de
Troyes and the Regent made no objection, he hastily turned his back on me
and left the room without a bow to anyone. I looked at M. le Comte de
Toulouse, and he laughed; M. le Duc d'Orléans was not frowning, and the
entire assembly looked at me either laughing or smiling. After that the
main subject of gossip was that he had tried to join the Council and that I
had dismissed him. The Comte de Toulouse, M. du Maine, Monsieur le
Duc, the Maréchal de Villeroy and several others congratulated me as we
left the meeting. They all said I had done well; but I blamed them for not
taking action themselves. I later spoke to the Regent, and even he did not
have the courage to reproach me. I reproached him, however, for his weakness, asking whether to be a member of the Council one needed only to
enter on some pretext, and then have the impudence to remain. Noailles was
neither liked nor respected; people laughed at him for being disagreeable
and hard to approach. He was aware of that because he liked to know
everything; but what almost reduced him to despair was that such scenes
were often repeated. I have given you one example of many; the subject is
not worth expanding.

It appeared that Mme la Duchesse de Berry, living as I have earlier
described, wished to spend the summer nights in the gardens of the
Luxembourg. She had every gate boarded up, with the sole exception of
the grille at the foot of the stairway in the middle of the palace. The
gardens had hitherto been a public park where all the Faubourg Saint-
Germain had been used to take the air, and thus very many people were
deprived of a pleasure. Monsieur le Duc, by contrast, opened the gardens
of the Hôtel de Condé to the public; but there was a loud outcry, and
many very insolent remarks were made about this exclusion. Mme la
Duchesse de Berry also felt the inconvenience of wearing mourning for so
long, whereat the drapers seized the opportunity to make her ask M. le
Duc d'Orléans to shorten the periods, which with his usual amiability he
did. The result has been that because the ramifications of kinship are so
widespread and uncertain, people wear mourning for those who are not
their relations, and do not wear it for their immediate families. It has all
become vastly improper. But since evil invariably outlasts good, this cur-
tailment of mourning periods is the only law of the Regency that still holds
today. It first took effect at the death of the Queen-mother of Sweden.[2]

[1] His *siège ployant*, the ministerial folding armchair, called a *perroquet*, was much more
elaborate than the usual camp-stools provided for the courtiers. There was also a very inferior
ployant, called a *respect*, on which noblemen allowed such inferior persons as doctors, architects,
and curés to sit when they called on business.
[2] Hedwig Eleanora of Holstein-Glucksburg (1636–1715). She was the daughter of Frederick
I, Duke of Holstein, and of Maria Elizabeth of Saxony. She married, in 1654, Charles X (Charles
Gustavus) King of Sweden.

Mme la Duchesse de Berry, for all her pride, was the first Daughter of France to admit the ladies of princesses of the blood into her box, and to let them sit behind their mistresses. This certainly applied only to her small box, at the Opéra; but the step taken on that most insecure foundation has been allowed ever since.

The Regent sent for a troop of Italian players on the recommendation of Rouillé, a counsellor of State closely concerned with the finances.[1] You will remember that the late King banished them for publicly mocking Mme de Maintenon, in a sketch entitled *The False Prude*.[2] The players now returned under Rouillé's protection and subject to his censorship; and so as to keep them independent of the first gentlemen of the chamber they were known as M. le Duc d'Orléans's players, and not the King's. The Regent and all the fashionable world went to their first performance, in one of the smaller rooms of the Opéra. They played there until their old theatre, at the Hôtel de Bourgogne (where they had acted until the King banished them), was put to rights. The novelty and high patronage made them at first the fashion, but gradually decent folk were disgusted by their bawdiness, and they ceased to be popular. None the less, they still continue, and perform as before at the Hôtel de Bourgogne.

A Scotsman of birth unknown to me, a great gambler and a great schemer who had made fortunes in the various countries where he had lived, had come to France at the end of the late King's reign. His name was Law,[3] but as people learned to know him better they called him Las, and the name Law ceased to be used.[4] He was spoken of to M. le Duc d'Orléans as a man deeply versed in matters of banking and commerce, the fluctuations of currencies, and finance in general, which made the prince most anxious to see him. He interviewed Law on several occasions, and was so much impressed with him that he mentioned him to Desmaretz as a man to be consulted. I recall that the prince spoke of him to me at about that same time. Desmaretz had several long talks with Law, but I never

[1] Hilaire Rouillé du Coudray (1651–1729). The son of an intendant, he began life as a principal clerk, under M. de Pomponne (see index, I) in the ministry of foreign affairs, became director of finances, 1701, a counsellor of State and member of the finance council, 1716–1718.

[2] See I, p. 92.

[3] John Law (1671–1729), the son of an Edinburgh goldsmith and banker, and owner of the estate of Lauriston. He fled from London in 1694, after a duel. In Amsterdam he studied credit operations at the bank; then, in 1700, he returned to Scotland eager to establish a paper currency. He failed and returned to the Continent, where he made and lost vast sums in gambling. He settled in Paris in 1716, and with his brother William set up a successful private bank. In 1718, the Regent adopted his plan of a national bank. In 1719, Law originated a joint-stock company which came to be called the Mississippi Scheme, for the colonization and exploitation by the French of the Mississippi valley. This scheme turned into the French equivalent of the English South Sea Bubble. In 1720 Law was made Controller General of Finances; when later that year the 'Mississippi Bubble' burst, he was forced to fly from France (see text, below, p. 298).

[4] Since w is pronounced as v in French, Law must first have been called 'Lav' to rhyme with love, then 'Las' to rhyme with the French '*pas*'. In view of what happened later it was perhaps a good thing that they so soon stopped referring to him as 'Love'.

learned what transpired, only that Desmaretz also was impressed by him, and developed a respect for his mind. For some time after that, M. le Duc d'Orléans rarely saw him, but when the first rush of business after the King's death had somewhat subsided, Law presented himself again; was seen by M. le Duc d'Orléans, and proposed various measures for the finances. In the end, the Regent was so much delighted by Law's plan for a national bank that he decided to adopt it, and discussed it privately with the heads of the finance department, who were all bitterly opposed to it. He spoke to me also, but since I was little interested in such matters, and consequently did not properly understand them, I merely listened. Indeed, at that time,[1] the prospect had seemed very remote. M. le Duc d'Orléans, however, had made up his mind to act. He summoned a meeting of the departments of finance and commerce, and made Law explain his idea to them. He was listened to for as long as he wished to speak. Some, seeing that the Regent was so eager, voted in favour, but the majority opposed. Law was, however, not at all discouraged; he explained once again, and this time very few went against him.

Thus the national bank was decided on; but it had to be passed by the Regency Council. M. le Duc d'Orléans took the trouble to speak to each member separately, letting it be known that he wished there to be no opposition. He spoke a long time to me, and I was thus obliged to give an opinion. I had never concealed my dislike and ignorance of all that concerned the finances; none the less, what he said appeared sound policy, in so much as without new taxes, extra expenses, dishonesty, or distress to anyone, the currency might be doubled by means of notes issued by the said bank, and easily negotiable. I did, however, perceive two drawbacks: first, the problem of administering the bank with wisdom and foresight, so as to prevent more notes from being printed than could be cashed on demand; secondly, that what might be excellent for a republic, or for a monarchy like that of England where the finances belong to the people, might be disastrous in an absolute monarchy, like France, where the needs of a war unwisely begun and ill-sustained, the greed of a first minister, a favourite, or a mistress, the display and extravagance of a king, might soon exhaust the bank's resources and ruin the note-holders, that is to say, the entire population.

M. le Duc d'Orléans did not dissent, but at the same time he stoutly maintained that a monarch's personal interests would so much depend on never drawing, nor allowing any minister, mistress, or favourite to draw on the bank, that this great obstacle might be discounted. We argued the point for some time without either of us yielding; and thus, when he proposed the measure at the Council, I gave my opinion much as I have given it here, but more firmly and at greater length, ending by stating that the founding of a national bank would be fatal in an absolute monarchy,

[1] 24 October 1715.

whereas in a free country it might be a wise and profitable undertaking. Few members dared to side with me, and so the motion was carried. M. le Duc d'Orléans reproached me later for speaking out; but he was not angry. I said I owed it to my honour and my conscience to speak according to my lights. The measure was forthwith registered at the Parlement—the members of the Council being sometimes willing to bow gracefully to the Regent's wishes, in order to stand firm against him at other times.

To tell all at once, the Regent shortly afterwards desired me to see Law, asking me as a favour to allow him to explain his idea. I said that he would be using an unknown language, because I knew nothing of his subject; and that it would be a great waste of our time. I tried in this way to avoid meeting him. The Regent, however, returned to the point again and again, and at last ordered me to see him. Thus Law came to my house. Although there was much that was foreign in his bearing, language, and accent, he expressed himself excellently, with clarity and precision. He spoke long on the subject of the bank which was, in truth, a brilliant plan for any other country than France, and with a ruler less easy-going than the Regent. Law had no remedies for my two objections other than those which the Regent himself had offered, which had not satisfied me. But since the motion had been carried, all that remained was the administration, and we spoke mainly of that. I did my best to impress him with the importance of strictness, in order to prevent anyone from taking advantage of a Regent as kind, as lax, as artless as M. le Duc d'Orléans. So far as I was able, I disguised what I wished him to gather from my words, and thus I mostly stressed the need always to be in a position to cash on demand every bank-note presented for payment in every part of France; for on that would depend the prosperity or ruin of the bank.

The Regent, who continued to speak to me with enthusiasm of Law, said later that he had a favour to ask, nay, to demand of me, namely that I would allow Law to pay me regular weekly visits. I said that this would be perfectly useless in view of my ignorance; but it was of no avail, I had to give in. Law came, readily admitting that he had begged the Regent to intercede for him, because he dared not ask me himself. A vast number of compliments were exchanged; it was arranged that he should come every Tuesday morning at ten o'clock, and that I should close my door at that time to all other callers. On the following Tuesday he duly appeared, and he kept the appointment punctually, every week, until the day of his disgrace.

These conversations usually occupied an hour and a half to two hours. He invariably told me of the good impression that the bank was making in foreign countries, of its profits, plans, and administration; of the opposition he encountered from the heads of the finances and the magistrature; of his personal opinions, and above all of the bank returns, in an attempt to convince me that he was, indeed, in a position to meet all demands. I had understood well enough that when Law asked to see me regularly, it was not with any hope of turning me into a financier; but that as a clever man. which he truly was, he wished to attach to himself that one of the Regent's helpers who was most in the prince's confidence, able to converse freely and frankly with him on all occasions. He hoped gradually to gain my friendship and thus be able to consult me regarding his difficulties, and the men with whom he had dealings. More especially, he hoped to profit by my hatred of the Duc de Noailles who, while continually embracing him, was all the time bursting with spite and jealousy, doing his best to hinder and obstruct him, and who would gladly, were it possible, have strangled him, Now that the bank itself was functioning and doing well, I thought it only right to support it. I subscribed to the policy put forward by Law, and soon we were conversing with a freedom I never had cause to regret. I shall not go into all the financial details, the new plans, the subsequent trans-actions. Volumes might be filled with these matters. I shall mention only such affairs as immediately concerned the history of that time or affected me personally. At the moment of the King's death, I explained the reasons that persuaded me to omit from these memoirs the innumerable details of the finances and the constitution. They are already fully recorded by writers who concentrate on such affairs, and explain them better than I can do. Indeed, I could not include them without long and frequent digressions from that history of my own times which, from the beginning, has been my sole purpose. I might here describe the eventual fate of Law; but this I shall defer until a more appropriate time, when its interest is immediate.

Arouet,[1] the son of a notary who until his death was my father's lawyer and mine also, was exiled and sent to Tulle for writing monstrously satirical, monstrously impudent verses.[2] I should not waste my time over such trifles, had not this Arouet, now a famous poet and academician under the pseudonym Voltaire,[3] also become, after many disastrous adventures, something of a personage in the world of letters, even winning a kind of reputation among certain sorts of people.

The Maréchal de Villeroy took the the King to see the Observatoire.[4]

---

[1] The famous passage about Voltaire, which shows how little Saint-Simon respected con-temporary literature. Voltaire was, however, in good company for Racine and Boileau were treated with equal contempt. See also p. 118 below.

[2] Voltaire was generally supposed to be the writer of all scurrilous verses, and he usually denied having had anything to do with them, as he denied the authorship of this particular effort, aimed at the Regent and his daughter:

> Regnante Puero
> Veneno et incestis famoso
> Administrante
> Ignaris et instabilitus consiliis
> Instabilosi Religione
> Oerario exhausto
> Violata Fide publica, etc., etc.

[3] Reading v as u, and i as j, the name Voltaire is an anagram of Arouet l.j. (le jeune).

[4] The Observatoire de Paris was founded by Louis XIV in 1667, for the study of celestial and atmospheric phenomena.

He was a lifelong friend of Chancellor de Pontchartrain, then in retirement at the Institution;[1] that is to say, living in an adjoining house, having doors communicating with it from inside. On the way from the Tuileries to the Observatoire they had to pass Pontchartrain's front door, and he happened to be in Paris. The Maréchal remembered that once when the King's grandsons[2] were going sight-seeing to Paris, from Versailles, he had ordered the Duc de Beauvilliers to take them to see old Beringhem,[3] so as to show them a man whom the King loved, one who had earned a glorious reputation and, without in any way deserting,[4] had had the wisdom to live as befitted his years, never leaving his Paris house, where he was surrounded by his friends and family.

Villeroy, for once, was struck with the excellent thought of showing the little King a man, still hale and hearty, so well in mind and body that he might have held office many years longer, filling with distinction and without undue fatigue the posts of Chancellor and keeper of the seals; yet who had chosen to resign all in order to put a wise and pious interval between life and death, in complete retirement, concentrating entirely on his soul's salvation, without diversions of any kind. Such a visit, the Maréchal believed, would teach the King to honour virtue. He accordingly sent word from the Observatoire to Chancellor de Pontchartrain, that the King would pass his house on the return journey and intended to visit him. Nothing was simpler than to receive this extraordinary favour, which he was very far from expecting; but Pontchartrain, firmly defending his modesty and seclusion, gave orders to be alerted in time, and was in the street, at his door,[5] when the King drove up. In vain he strove to prevent him from leaving his coach; but by a mixture of tact, obstinacy, and respect, he managed so that the visit took place in the street, and lasted no more than a quarter of an hour, after which the King climbed back into his coach. Pontchartrain saw him go, and immediately retired to his humble abode, wherein complete spiritual withdrawal caused him at once to forget the enormous honour which had just been paid him, and the pious cunning with which it had been avoided. Everyone who knew the circumstances

---

[1] The Institution de l'Oratoire. For Pontchartrain's retirement there, see II, p. 339. At this time he was seeing virtually no one except his children, got up at four in the morning and went to bed at nine o'clock, attending all the services, and having not a moment's leisure. He scarcely ever went out even into his little garden, and never read anything except religious books. He never had anyone except his children to meals, and sent them away the moment the clock timing their visits had struck. One may imagine the appalling disruption caused by the idea of having to entertain the monarch.

[2] The Dukes of Bourgogne, Anjou, and Berry.

[3] Henri de Beringhem (1603-1692). His career was as follows: head-valet (c1620), Brigadier-general, counsellor of State, Marshal of the Royal Household and Postmaster General. He was for a time exiled by Richelieu. His son Jean Louis, Marquis de Beringhem (1651-1723), was Master of the Horse (Monsieur le Premier) to Louis XIV.

[4] *Sans rien quitter*: Louis XIV always called a man who left his service for any reason whatever, including age and infirmity, a deserter.

[5] In the Rue d'Enfer.

admired him and praised the Maréchal de Villeroy for his happy thought and the dignified way he had put it into execution.

Monsieur le Duc and Monsieur le Prince de Conti contracted smallpox one after the other at a very short interval; and Mme la Duchesse d'Orléans gave birth to a daughter who died Princesse de Conti,[1] leaving an only son, the Comte de La Marche.

On 1 September, the anniversary of the late King's death was kept as by tradition, but with a very scant, much curtailed ceremony. Only the heralds saluted. The mourning princes were M. le Duc d'Orléans, Monsieur le Duc, and M. le Comte de Charolais.[2] The Duc du Maine, his two sons, and the Comte de Toulouse attended, and almost no one else. The entire proceedings at Saint-Denis were over in less than two hours.

Shortly before his death, the King had given a solemn promise to Matignon's only son[3] to create a new peerage for the duchy of Valentinois, on his marriage to the eldest daughter of M. de Monaco.[4] So many additional clauses were agreed that the favour was quite unprecedented.[5] The King had not lived to see the marriage consummated; but the announcement had been made, and, in December 1715, as soon as both families were ready the letters patent were dispatched. The new duke went to Monaco for his wedding, and on his return found the princes of the blood and the bastards at loggerheads over the bastards' claim for equal precedence in the Parlement.[6] To prevent awkward situations arising, M. le Duc d'Orléans deferred the registration of Valentinois, at which formality both sections

[1] Louise Diane d'Orléans, known as Mlle de Chartres. She married Louis François, Prince de Conti (1717–1776), in 1732, and died in 1736. Her son Louis François Joseph de Bourbon (1734–1814) became Prince de Conti on his father's death.

[2] Charles, Comte de Charolais (1700–1760), was the younger brother of Monsieur le Duc (1692–1740).

[3] Jacques François Léonor Goyon de Matignon (1689–1751). His bride was Louise Hippolyte Grimaldi, Princesse de Monaco (died 1731).

[4] Antoine Grimaldi, Duc de Valentinois, Prince de Monaco (1661–1724). He was one of the 'foreign princes', so called because of the size of their estates, of whom Saint-Simon disapproved, on the ground that there was nothing royal about any of them. See I, p. 226n; II, p. 44.

[5] One of the complications was that the Valentinois dukedom and peerage was for males only; females were excluded from the succession. Thus the Prince of Monaco could not pass the peerage over to his daughter on her marriage, so that Matignon's son, simply by marrying her, would inherit. Another difficulty was that the original creation had been for the Prince of Monaco's grandfather, in 1642, when he had turned out the Spanish garrison of Monaco, exchanged it for a French one, and put himself under French protection. There was thus already one Duc de Valentinois in the Prince of Monaco himself, and a second one could not be *created*. A third problem was that the Prince might yet produce a son and heir. The first two difficulties were solved by digging for precedents and discovering them. The third was very neatly dealt with by stipulating that should M. de Monaco have a son, all the titles and dignities would revert to him, with seniority from 1642. Matignon's son would keep the title for his life, as a 'retired duke', but no son of his would have any right to the dukedom or the peerage. Saint-Simon remarks that M. de Monaco made a very good bargain and sold his daughter extremely dear; however, he did not have a son, and so all was well.

[6] They were claiming to cross the floor of the chamber and sit on the same bench as the princes of the blood.

had resolved to be present. The quarrel grew heated when the princes petitioned to deprive the bastards of the succession, and of many another of their fraudulent claims; there was thus no further need for a confrontation in the Parlement, and M. de Valentinois's affair was quietly settled.

The granting of this favour, so long deferred for reasons quite unconnected with the grace itself, gave rise to many new demands, and the Duc de Brancas,[1] always so irresponsible, and his equally futile son were among those who fell to temptation. Brancas was an idle fellow, devoid of malice or kindness, love or hatred, without system, without aims, save that of making money, provided it could be done with no great effort, and spent quickly, with the maximum of enjoyment. To those who had not to deal with or rely on him, he was agreeable, amusing, obliging, with the most witty sallies and repartee imaginable, a charming and often quite crazy fancy, denying himself nothing, conversing all the while with admirable originality and sometimes inimitable naïveté. He would speak home truths of himself so as to be able to do the same of others, but never from malice or jealousy. Outrageously and evilly debauched, he was avoided by most decent people, and although now and again, by some flash of invention, he retrieved himself in High Society, where the greater number were willing to accept him, his ignoble pastimes drove him back into obscurity, where he often remained invisible for years on end.

Although his brand of licentiousness was different from that of M. le Duc d'Orléans, the prince always enjoyed his society, and after he became Regent continued to admit him to his suppers and companionship. Yet showed him no more consideration than the others. Brancas used to say that the Regent ruled and controlled the affairs of State as though he were juggling; and once, when pressed beyond endurance by some vulgarian to sue for a favour, and when, as is usual with such vermin, the man assured him that everyone knew he could get all he wanted, Brancas retorted impatiently: 'Yes, Sirrah! true enough; since you already know, I shall not pretend to deny it. M. le Duc d'Orléans showers me with favours; he wants me to have all that I desire. The trouble is he has so little influence with the Regent—so little, so very little, it would amaze you. It is a great pity, but there's no hope of getting anything that way.' The first statement was not untrue, and he said as much to M. le Duc d'Orléans. The prince learned of the second, which was not entirely wrong, and he laughed at both most heartily. Brancas, when talking to the Regent, warned him that he was a veritable sieve; the prince, he said, should be most careful not to confide in him; he had no head for State affairs, they bored him, and he wished only to be amused. This made M. le Duc d'Orléans feel so much at ease with him that he could not have too much of his company at his private hours, and his suppers. Brancas used to say whatever came into his

[1] Louis Antoine de Brancas-Céreste, Comte, then, from 1709, Duc de Villars-Brancas (1682–1760). From 1708–1709, he had been the Duc de Bourgogne's aide-de-camp.

head regarding himself or others, and spoke his mind with what passed for wit and candour. His sayings were afterwards repeated by the other supper-guests, who then mocked whomsoever had been his butt.

Chamarande[1] lost his only remaining son; and the Comte de Beuvron[2] died also at this time, extremely young, unmarried, losing blood even through the pores of his skin, a disease relatively unknown to the doctors.[3] He had brought back from Spain his uncle Sézanne's Golden Fleece, having been given it there, and the Maréchal d'Harcourt had secured for him the lieutenancy-general of Normandy, and the governorship of the Vieux-Palais at Rouen, which had formerly been his. The Regent allowed the Maréchal d'Harcourt to redispose of these appointments, which he passed on to one of his younger sons.

Mme de Lussan,[4] whom I have already mentioned, died in extreme old age. I never heard that with the years she had become any less giddy, sly, or pertly insolent. Another cheerful soul to be taken with great suddenness into the presence of God was the Abbé Servien,[5] whom also I have described. The Duchesse d'Olonne[6] died at this time from sheer terror after shutting herself up with her husband, who little deserved this kindness considering the way he had behaved to her. She was a daughter of Barbezieux's first marriage, young, well built, amiable, virtuous, and a slave to duty. Her death was a thousand pities.

I had taken the opportunity of a fortnight's respite from the Regency Council to go and enjoy myself at La Ferté, and other country houses, when M. le Duc de Chartres[7] developed symptoms of smallpox. It vexed me to have to interrupt my short holiday; but they pressed me so hard that I returned to spend an entire day in Paris with his parents. I called at the Palais Royal on the morning after my arrival, and found M. le Duc d'Orléans in the state apartments. He appeared moved to see me. We were conversing alone together when the Duc de Noailles was announced; I was in the middle of a speech. M. le Duc d'Orléans interrupted me to say that he had given him an appointment, even stating the hour, and simultane-ously the Duc de Noailles entered and stood on the threshold. 'Oh! as to that, Sir,' said I, loud enough for Noailles to hear, 'I have travelled fifty leagues for the honour of seeing you; I return tomorrow; we were in the

---

[1] Louis d'Ornaison, Comte de Chamarande (1660–1737). His son, Ange François d'Ornaison, was only twenty-one.

[2] Louis Henri d'Harcourt, Comte de Beuvron, second son of the Maréchal d'Harcourt. He was twenty-four years old.

[3] Possibly a case of haemophilia, which was not recognized until 1854.

[4] Marie Françoise Raymond, Comtesse de Lussan. In 1707, Saint-Simon went to law with her over some property. It rankled still, after nearly ten years. See II, pp. 26, 59.

[5] The Abbé Augustin Servien: see II, pp. 266–267, 318.

[6] Anne Catherine Eléonore de Tellier de Barbezieux, Duchesse d'Olonne. She was only twenty-three when she died. Her husband the Duke was Charles Paul Sigismond de Montmorency-Luxembourg; he married again and lived on until 1785.

[7] Duc de Chartres was an Orléans title used by the Duc d'Orléans's eldest son.

middle of a conversation; all you have to do is to send M. de Noailles away; it will not hurt him to wait.' We had not risen from our armchairs. The Regent made a slightly apologetic gesture towards the Duc de Noailles, who left the room forthwith, closing the door after him.

Our conversation turned almost entirely upon foreign affairs, and upon one aspect of particular importance, the negotiations between France, England, and Holland. When we had reached that point, M. le Duc d'Orléans rose, saying, 'I am afraid they may overhear us from the next room' [the door of which was close beside his table]; 'let us go into my study.' We were at that time in the great room overlooking the Rue Saint-Honoré; he led me into the adjoining study which also overlooks that street, and closed the door after me. It was a room with which I was unfamiliar, for it formed part of the small suite he used for the supper-parties which I never attended.[1] We talked there for the better part of an hour. As we left, we passed through the ante-room where the Duc de Noailles, the Maréchal d'Huxelles, and other gentlemen were waiting, but they were at some distance from the door by which we entered. I took my leave of M. le Duc d'Orléans for the remainder of the holiday, and then went up to the Maréchal d'Huxelles, to whisper somewhat maliciously of the drift of our conversation, and he whispered back to me. I was all the while watching the Duc de Noailles, and I saw him turn every colour of the rainbow. I bowed to the company and was most civilly saluted by everyone in return; but as I passed the Duc de Noailles, I made no sign at all, though he stepped back and made me a most particularly low bow.

Soon after dinner I visited Mme la Duchesse d'Orléans, who gave me a remarkably warm welcome. M. le Duc d'Orléans had asked me to call on her, and had even hinted that she wished it. He feared lest my having sought him out might have angered her. On the contrary, she seemed far from being annoyed. She had just come from M. le Duc de Chartres's bed-room. My own two sons had had smallpox during the previous year, and the younger had been in danger for some considerable time. I had used Frère du Soleil, a Jesuit and the apothecary of the Jesuit college,[2] an extremely able man who had refused to become a doctor. I was so well satisfied with him that I had strongly advised M. and Mme la Duchesse d'Orléans to consult him for M. le Duc de Chartres, should the need ever arise, and they had done so with complete success. This Frère du Soleil was excellent for his learning and experience, also because he took great care of his patients, with a simple kindliness that won their hearts. He was moreover a man of great humility and a very godly friar.

The recovery of Monsieur le Duc and M. le Prince de Conti was responsible for a most unseemly novelty. Their families had *Te Deums*

---

[1] Saint-Simon rubs it in at every possible opportunity that he knew nothing of the Regent's goings-on. One is almost, but not quite, persuaded that he knew more than he says.

[2] Frère François du Soleil (1647–1720), apothecary at the Jesuit College of Louis le Grand.

sung in their parishes, and in other places also, something that had never before been done save in times of national rejoicing, the recovery from illness of a King or Queen of France or their extreme danger, very rarely for their children. Nothing now was sacred, however, and following the example of the princes of the blood, there was no private person that did not demand the same. It was allowed to pass; *Te Deum*s are still sung everywhere, and for every Tom, Dick, or Harry.

The Maréchal de Montrevel[1] whose name will be found in no book of history, that favourite of fools, the world of fashion, the Maréchal de Villeroy, and even to a certain extent of the late King, from whom he extracted more than a hundred thousand livres annually by way of grants, died at this time, still enjoying those favours. His only advantages were not his own making—a figure that enabled him to live most of his life on women, high birth, and a name for brilliant courage far in excess of the reality. His death swindled his creditors, for he was worth no more than the three thousand louis which he had by him, and some silver and porcelain dishes. He had been having trouble with the women who supported him, and consequently dreaded nothing so much as spilt salt. On the eve of a journey to Alsace, he had been dining with Biron (since made duke and peer, and a Marshal of France), and had happened to overturn a salt-cellar. He went pale, felt ill, said that he was dying, and had to be carried from the table and taken back to his home, where it proved impossible to restore what few senses he possessed. That same night he developed a fever, and four days later was dead, regretted only by his creditors. He had no children by either of his two wives, and had been sucked dry and made monstrously unhappy by both of them.

The negotiations between England and France went smoothly enough. Both countries, for different reasons, were eager to draw Spain into the alliance. The Regent to further this end extracted a promise from England to restore Gibraltar, which was the Spaniards' chief desire,[2] and the King of England consented, for it was something of a burden despite his friendship with Barbary, and the fact that his navy was far superior to that of Spain. He made one condition, however; namely that the arrangement be kept a profound secret until all was safely accomplished; that Alberoni should therefore be kept in ignorance, and all matters be treated directly between the Regent and the King of Spain, using a confidential agent selected by the former and given opportunities for private talk with King

[1] Nicolas Auguste de La Baume, Marquis de Montrevel (1645-1716), Maréchal de France 1703. He was Saint-Simon's pet abomination for having dared to claim the command in Saint-Simon's sacred governorship of Blaye: see II, pp. 284-286.

[2] These negotiations appear to be mentioned only by Saint-Simon. In Louville's memoirs, however, is the following entry: 'The Abbé Dubois reports that my sudden departure to Spain has caused a temporary delay in drafting the treaty, at Hanover. There are doubts regarding the Regent's sincerity, or at least of his determination in making an alliance, after the great sacrifice of Gibraltar, which King George authorized us to propose in his name.'

Philip. This agent was to be the bearer of a letter listing King George's trifling requirements, and a firm command, written and signed with his own hand, directed to the Governor of Gibraltar, bidding him surrender that fortress to the King of Spain, and retire forthwith to Tangier, taking with him his entire garrison, etc., etc. In order to facilitate the transfer, a Spanish general was to appear suddenly at Gibraltar, on the pretext of preventing raids by the garrison. He was to summon the governor, and give King George's letter into his own hands, thereafter taking possession of the fortress. The excuse was scarcely plausible; but that seemed a matter for the English king.

Louville[1] was the man chosen; he already knew Spain, and in the past had been the trusted friend of King Philip. I do not profess to be brilliant, but speaking personally, I should have doubted the King of England's good faith in making such an offer. He must have known how jealously the queen and Alberoni guarded the king's ear, and that the surest way to fail was to attempt to see him secretly, alone, and against their wishes. As for Louville himself, to my mind he was the very last man to entrust with such a mission. The more intimate he had once been with King Philip, the greater the confidence once reposed in him, the more his appearance would seem alarming to the queen and Alberoni, who would do their utmost to prevent him from approaching the king. I said as much to Louville, and he did not contradict me, saying only that he was so much astonished he had not dared refuse; and that if he succeeded, the acquisition of Gibraltar was of such importance that the arrears of his Spanish pensions would certainly be made up to him, which meant a great deal.

His selection and his departure were almost simultaneous. After a very swift journey he arrived at Madrid, and went immediately to lodge at the house of our ambassador, the Duc de Saint-Aignan, who was astounded to see him, having received no previous warning. By pure chance a courier, happening to pass Louville when he was still some distance from the city, had informed Alberoni. You may imagine that cleric's alarm, and the panic that gripped him. He knew Louville's history; the esteem and affection which the king had once felt for him, and the violence which the late queen and Mme des Ursins had been forced to use in order to remove him. So great, indeed, was his dismay that he lost all restraint.

His first impulsive act was to send an order by courier, forbidding Louville to approach any nearer to Madrid. That message was sent too late; but a quarter of an hour after Louville's arrival, a letter came from Grimaldo,[2] enclosing the King of Spain's command to leave within the

---

[1] Charles Auguste d'Allonville, Marquis de Louville (1664–1731). A very old friend of Saint-Simon; he had been Philip V's *gentilhomme de la manche* when that monarch was still a child in France, and was his most trusted friend when he first went to Spain (see I, p. 153).

[2] Joseph Guttierez, Marquis of Grimaldo (1660–1733). He was a secretary of State, and the Queen of Spain's private secretary.

hour. Louville answered that he was the bearer of letters for King Philip from King George of England and M. le Duc d'Orléans, together with a personal message for His Most Catholic Majesty, which he was bound to deliver before leaving. M. de Saint-Aignan wrote in similar terms. In response, couriers were sent forthwith to the Prince of Cellamare, the Spanish ambassador to France, bidding him require Louville's immediate recall, on the grounds that King Philip found him so intensely displeasing that he would neither see him nor allow his ministers to treat with him.

The fatigues of that long journey followed by his rude reception brought on an attack of colic, from which Louville occasionally suffered. He ordered a hot bath to be prepared, and towards the end of the morning immersed himself in it. At that precise moment Alberoni appeared, with the firm intention of forcing him to depart at once. Reports of poor Louville's condition did not at all mollify him, and despite protests he insisted on going to him in the bath. The words he then spoke were all honey and concern; but their meaning was harsh, forbidding, and peremptory. He said that he pitied Louville's discomfort; wished that he might have known it sooner and so spared him that pain; deeply regretted that he could by no means overcome the king's aversion, nor even gain a few days' respite. His orders were plain, to bid Louville depart immediately and to see that he did so. The wretched man was clearly in no state to travel, which Alberoni was obliged to concede, but he would permit no delay beyond the duration of the illness, after which Louville must instantly depart.

Louville continued to urge the letters of credence, giving him authority to deliver an important message to King Philip from the King of France (King Philip's own nephew), with secret papers of such vital consequence that His Most Catholic Majesty would all his life regret it if he did not see them. The argument persisted despite Louville's sufferings; but at last both he and Saint-Aignan realized that no audience would be granted, and that to stay longer might lead to a scandal involving both crowns. At the end of a week he returned to France. Alberoni recovered from his panic and breathed again. He could comfort himself with the thought that after such a victory no one would be able to approach King Philip without his permission, nor any State business be transacted except as he wished. That is how Gibraltar was lost to Spain. It has never been recovered. Such are the results of having a first minister.

Immediately after Louville's return, a report was sent to King George of all that had happened in Spain, and the reason for the Gibraltar negotiations having ended in nothing. Their only effect was to set Alberoni against the Regent for attempting to send the king a secret letter by the hand of a possible supplanter, and the Regent against Alberoni for intercepting the message and provoking so great a scandal. Alberoni had displayed his power, and neither of them ever forgot the incident. Their enmity brought disastrous consequences, as in due course you shall see.

Suffice it now to say that a treaty of alliance between France and England was signed at The Hague at the end of November, and for a month was kept secret. I did my utmost to prevent it, for I sincerely believed that the Regent's best policy was to assist the Pretender, thus keeping England so fully engaged with domestic affairs that it would be unable to interfere with those of the Continent. I had long and frequent talks with the Regent, but although my arguments appeared at the time to convince him, they were soon forgotten under the Abbé Dubois's growing and pernicious influence. His palm had been so well oiled by the English that he dared all. It thus came about that the treaty in every way tended to England's advantage, and not at all to that of France. Among other conditions the Regent agreed to banish the so-called Pretender from our country, thus compelling him to seek shelter abroad, and this particular clause was most rigorously fulfilled. James III and VIII, who for some time past had been living in retirement at Avignon, now crossed the Alps and established himself at Rome, never more to return to France. I could only deplore a policy so detrimental to France's true interests; but the deed was done, and I remained silent. There was indeed nothing more that I could do.

[*We now enter a part of the Memoirs in which, off and on for hundreds of pages, Saint-Simon describes with infinite care and endless detail the ebb and flow of Spanish diplomacy under the influence of Alberoni—a diplomacy that ended in a French enthusiasm for England which Saint-Simon thought misplaced, because it went against all tradition. 'Those English,' he says, 'who under the guise of pretended friendship are our oldest and most natural enemies.' 'The fatal charm of England.'*

He was convinced that the well-being of France lay in strengthening the old alliance between France and Spain, through the cousinship of their two rulers. But although the Regent may never have plotted to dethrone Philip V, as it was rumoured, his imprudence had made a breach in the alliance with incalculable effect. The two princes became increasingly unfriendly, and the Queen of Spain seems to have inherited all the Princesse des Ursins's hatred of Orléans. To make matters worse, when the Duc d'Orléans was serving in Spain, his courage and ability had greatly impressed the Spaniards, making King Philip appear even duller by comparison; some, indeed, would have been glad of a change of rulers. From all these personal antipathies there resulted a complete reversal of the customary European alliances.

The negotiations between England, the Empire, Piedmont and Sicily, France, and Spain were so complex that Saint-Simon needed not just a lengthy digression, but almost an entire volume to describe them. They seem now remote and wearisome, and this editor gladly lets most of them go, especially since the memoirist relied heavily on Torcy's reports.[1] On the other hand, those who dare to tackle them in the original may find them fascinating and rewarding, for Saint-Simon shows such a masterly grasp of all the intricacies, and is so brilliant a writer, that he gives life to this part also,

---

[1] 'Congresses without issue; campaigns without visible objectives; open tactics; secret articles; public alliances; private combinations.' Lord Morley was writing of the political scene a few years earlier; but it continued throughout the greater part of the Regency. The fact is that politics which lead to no result are very dull to read about.

*and the subsidiary characters, Cellamare, Stair, Stanhope, the King of Sicily, are as
vivid and alive as the leading figures of the Memoirs.*]

It was revealed at this time that Peter I, Czar of Muskovy,[1] had wished
to visit France in the lifetime of the late King, but had been most courte-
ously discouraged. The chief obstacle being now removed, the Czar felt
free to satisfy his curiosity, and therefore informed the Regent, through
Prince Kurakin[2] the Russian ambassador, that he proposed to leave the
Netherlands and visit our present King. The Regent would gladly have
dispensed with such an honour; but there was nothing for it except to
simulate delight, and an invitation for the following year was accordingly
dispatched. The expense would be prodigious, and the trouble scarcely less
so with a prince so powerful, so capricious, so inquisitive, and still tinged
with some remnants of barbarism.[3] The behaviour of his staff would
greatly differ from the conduct agreeable to western countries. They were
certain to be full of strange whims and outlandish customs, as prone to
take offence as their master, and very positive about their rights and dues.
To make matters worse, the Czar was at daggers drawn with King George;
their enmity went beyond all propriety, and was all the more violent
because it was rooted in personal dislike. Thus the Regent, whose accord
with the English king had been publicly proclaimed, was more than a little
apprehensive.

[1] Peter the Great (1672–1725), joint Czar with his half-brother Ivan V 1682–1696, Czar from
1696. See also below, p. 120 et seqq.

[2] Boris Ivanovich, Prince Kurakin (1671–1727), who was also ambassador to London. His
wife Aksina was the sister of Peter's first wife, Eudoxia Lopukhina (see index).

[3] Barbarous in the eighteenth century did not usually mean savage, but rather lacking in
good taste, uncultured, brutal, or merely rude and foreign.

CHAPTER III

1717

Extraordinary meeting of the Chapter of the Order – I prophesy that the constitution will be made a rule of faith – Death of the Abbé de Castries – Death of the Abbé de Saillans – Death of Chancellor Voysin – Daguesseau the new Chancellor – Character of Daguesseau – Remarkable interview with M. le Duc d'Orléans – Alliance with England is approved – Death of Callières – I prevent the destruction of Marly – Explanation of the Entrées – Marriage of Mortagne – Mme de Maintenon ill – Alarms of the Queen of Spain and Alberoni – Daily life of the King and Queen of Spain – M. le Duc d'Orléans consults me regarding the constitution – Extraordinary conversation at the Opéra – Outrageous neglect of etiquette – Judgment on the rank of the bastards – They are excluded from the succession – Monsieur de Fréjus rides in the King's coach – Voltaire is sent to the Bastille – Death of Mme Guyon – Contades and Brilhac – The Regent's diamond – Visit of the Czar – Kidnapping of the Governor and Intendant of Martinique – Death of Harlay, counsellor of State – The feast of Saint-Louis – The King is taught a bad lesson – Mme la Duchesse d'Orléans renews her claim for precedence – Alberoni made cardinal – The Duc de Noailles's jealousy of Law – Disputes in the King of Spain's household – Unrest in Brittany – Mysterious interview with Mme d'Alègre – Grave illness of the King of Spain – Alberoni's skirmish with the Marquis of Villena – Dubois and Law scheme to be rid of the Chancellor and the Duc de Noailles

THE YEAR 1717 began with a small event that had great significance. The late King had always treated the children of the King of Spain as though they were Sons of France, even though they were, in fact, no more than great-grandsons. The Renunciations of the Treaty of Utrecht had made no difference to this rule. The Allies apparently had not noticed, and the King of Spain, who had signed them, seemed unaware of any need to change. According to tradition, every Spanish infant had hitherto worn the blue ribbon from birth, after the manner of the Sons of France, and King Philip, with thoughts of a possible return never far from his mind, and encouraged by the arrival of the herald[1] bearing the ribbon, took care to say nothing.

---

[1] Alexandre Chevard (1687–1740). He had been Herald of the Order of the Saint-Esprit since 1714. The Infante, Don Carlos, later Charles III of Spain, had been born in 1716.

A meeting of the chapter is unnecessary for this first ceremony, nor is there a nomination. The prince does not become a knight until he receives the collar of the Order. Our King[1] was not yet a knight, nor was the Prince of the Asturias; but since the latter was rising ten years old, King Philip urgently requested the collar for him, and was unwilling to wait for King Louis's coronation, when both might have received it together. The Regent accordingly convened a meeting of the knights of the Order, in the chamber at the Tuileries where the Regency Council ordinarily met. The King came after his mass, and sat in his armchair at the head of the table, hatless. M. le Duc d'Orléans stood uncovered on his right, and the other knights, also uncovered, stood along the sides in no special order, with the commanders at the foot, opposite the King. The Regent then proposed sending two collars to Spain, one for the Prince of the Asturias, the other for his governor the Duke of Popoli,[2] to whom the late King had promised it. The Regent had not wished to hold a meeting without the little King, and he followed the precedent created by Louis XIV who, by standing hatless, had prevented such of his ministers as were knights from having to stand without hats before the covered and seated dukes. That is why on this occasion the King was uncovered (he sat only because of his youth). There is of course no comparison between the King and his subjects, but since the very beginning, our Kings have never sat nor worn their hats at meetings of the Chapter of the Order, without desiring all the other knights to sit and wear their hats also. This has also been the practice, and still continues, at all Chapters of the Order of the Garter, and of the Golden Fleece likewise.

Although, for reasons already given, the affair of the constitution does not come within the scope of these memoirs, certain events must be included, either because I was personally concerned in them, or because I had first-hand knowledge which, so I believe, does not appear in the official accounts. Despite the fact that the whole question was negotiated in the Regent's study with Effiat, the premier président, the King's personal advisers, various prelates, the Abbé Dubois, and the Maréchal d'Huxelles, some reference to it was made from time to time at the Regency Council. Monsieur de Troyes invariably supported both the constitution and the claims of Rome, apparently to punish himself for having until then always bitterly opposed them, and he faithfully reported every word to Bentivoglio, the nuncio. Considering how old he was, his aim was obscure.

On one of the first days of that month of January, the whole matter came before the Regency Council. As I have already said, I shall not enter

---

[1] Louis XV.

[2] Rostaing Cantelmi, Duke of Popoli (1651–1723). He was the brother of Cardinal Cantelmi, and had brought the Italian company of the bodyguard over to King Philip, in 1703. He was a member of the councils for war and finance and, in 1721, was appointed High Steward.

into details; but I observed an angry determination to command obedience
without explanations or argument, and a great increase in the numbers of
those willing to submit. My own views were exactly contrary to those of
Monsieur de Troyes; he grew heated, we began to argue; he turned so
violent that I bluntly stated that the constitution would evidently soon
reign supreme, for I could see its becoming first a dogma, and then an
article of faith. There was Monsieur de Troyes protesting at the slander,
declaring that I went beyond all bounds, and thereafter explaining at great
length that the constitution could never be either dogma, rule, or article of
faith; that such a thing was never contemplated, even at Rome, and that
Cardinal Tolomei, a lifelong Jesuit, had laughed scornfully when that note
had been sounded. When he had finished scolding me, I looked around the
assembly, and said, 'Messieurs, I hold each and every one of you witness to
what I have said regarding the future of the constitution and Monsieur de
Troyes's assurances. Permit me to remind you of what has just been said
when, as is bound to happen, the constitution becomes all those things.'
Monsieur de Troyes again declared that I was talking nonsense.

To be brief, six months later, or even less, my prophecy was amply
fulfilled. The question of dogma and rule of faith was presented. The mani-
pulators of the constitution had already mentioned them in their writings
and speeches, and in next to no time the claim had reached the point
where it now stands. As soon as that claim had been clearly stated, with
official support, I duly reminded the Council of my prophecy, and of
Monsieur de Troyes's contrary assertions. Then, turning towards him, I
exclaimed with a bitter smile, 'Next time I say something, perhaps you will
believe me. Alas!' I added, 'there will be other occasions.' No one answered,
and the Regent also was silent. I never saw a man more hurt and confused
than Monsieur de Troyes as he, blushing scarlet, bowed his head, and
remained utterly mute. These two scenes created some interest in their
time. They disclosed no secrets of the Regency Council, and I therefore
had no compunction in describing them, and other Council members did
the same. M. le Duc d'Orléans was not displeased. He had pretended to
think, or did really think, like Monsieur de Troyes, that I went too far, and
he was, or pretended to be, astounded when my prophecy was fulfilled.

At that time Cardinal de Noailles had frequent audiences of M. le Duc
d'Orléans, for the Abbé Dubois had not yet succeeded in bringing about
his downfall. Smallpox, of which Paris was full, had invaded the Archbishop's palace and forced him to leave it, since M. le Duc d'Orléans, who
saw the King nearly every day, would have no contact with the least
suspicion of foul air. The Duchesse de Richelieu's first husband had been
the Marquis de Noailles,[1] the cardinal's brother, and she had remained on
excellent terms with the entire family. She now offered a temporary home

---

[1] Jean François, Marquis de Noailles (1658–1696). His widow Marguerite Thérèse Rouillé
married the Duc de Richelieu in 1702.

to the cardinal, which he was pleased to accept, in the fine new house she was constructing at the end of the Faubourg Saint-Germain.

Being thus in residence at her house, he invited me to visit him there, in his study, in order to hear the procureur-général[1] read aloud a memo-randum, recently composed, on the subject of the constitution. That magistrate had felt unable to tackle me on his own account because of my anger over the Parlement's encroachments. It was with some difficulty that I persuaded myself to comply; but in the end I submitted, and a meeting was arranged for the following day, at three o'clock in the afternoon. When I arrived, the doors were firmly closed behind me, and thus we three were uninterrupted. The reading took two hours. The purpose of the document was to show that a bull, such as the Bull *Unigenitus*, that went contrary to the laws of our Church and the maxims and customs of our country, must be wholly unacceptable. Apart from the scholarship, and the extreme elegance of the style, so simply expressive, the memorandum was most admirable for the lines of evidence that appeared to flow naturally one out of another, forming a chain that was impossible to refute. What was more, it stayed within the limits which Rome's superiority over other Churches could justifiably demand, showing due respect to papal authority and to the Holy Father himself. The final recommendation was to return the Pope's bull, after a vain search for some means of rendering it acceptable. I was greatly heartened by this document;[2] and I allowed the procureur-général to see my pleasure and the deep impression it had made. Cardinal de Noailles was equally pleased, and we discussed it at some length before we separated. Sad to relate, religion and truth were not at the helm of this tragic affair, nor were they the guides of those at Rome who had originated it. Their cause was not the inspiration of the men who, from personal ambition, made it their business to press and support the bull, bringing it ultimately to the point it had then reached, regardless of truth, justice, the Church and State, the bodies of learned ecclesiastics and laymen, not to mention the many thousands of individual saints and scholars.

The Abbé de Castries,[3] chief almoner of the Duchesse de Berry, and on excellent terms both with her and with Mme la Duchesse d'Orléans (who, as you know, greatly relished his brother and sister-in-law), was appointed to the bishopric of Tours. I supported his claim with all my strength, and I never could imagine why he also needed the assistance of the two princesses. He was well made, with an exceedingly wise and gentle wit, and an excellent head for business. He and his brother (with whom he lived) had a very large circle of friends, and were sought after by the best Society. This

[1] Henri François Daguesseau (1668–1751), who was made procureur-général in 1700. See index, II.

[2] This memorandum still exists and confirms Saint-Simon's account of it.

[3] Armand Pierre de La Croix, Abbé de Castries (1659–1728). He was made Archbishop of Albi in 1719.

had so shocked the late King, infatuated as he was with unknown names and the sweepings of the seminaries, that until his death the Abbé de Castries had had no chance of promotion. Cardinal de Noailles, his old friend, now consecrated him and immediately afterwards he took his seat on the Conseil de Conscience, where only one of the two episcopal seats was filled at that time. The advocates of the constitution set up a loud outcry because the cardinal had officiated, and had sponsored his nomination to the council. That, however, did not prevent the rich see of Albi from going to him when, later, it fell vacant, and it thus transpired that he never went to Tours at all. Many years afterwards, he received the Order of the Saint-Esprit. He still lives, though very old, adored by his diocese where he very scrupulously resides, wholly occupied by his duties and his ministry.

At this same time I was able to arrange for the little abbey of Andecy to be given to one of Mme de Saint-Simon's sisters,[1] then a nun at Conflans, near Paris. She was a saintly woman, but not well adapted to rule a larger community. When I brought her the news she first fainted, then refused, and we had the greatest possible trouble in persuading her to accept. Very few nuns greet promotion in that spirit.

The Abbé de Saillans[2] died only a little past middle age. Had his morals been better, he would have been worthy enough. Debauchery, a pleasant wit, and honest dealing won him many powerful friends, including the Maréchal de Luxembourg, who almost forcibly snatched a few abbeys for him, including Senlis, which was a good one. I was then lodging in a house belonging to the Dominicans of the Rue Saint-Dominique, with windows that overlooked their garden, to which I had a door. The front of the house was occupied by blind Fourilles,[3] captain of the guard, who had retired with a *cordon rouge*. I saw him walking for two or three hours every day in the Dominicans' garden, led by his son, an abbé without benefice, who read to him all the while they were walking. Both were men of culture, particularly so the father. Such filial devotion moved me deeply and I quietly set myself to discover something of the young fellow, for he was not yet twenty years old. I learned nothing but good of him—that he never left his father's side and spent all day reading to him. I had no acquaintance with either of them and knew none of their friends; no member of their family had ever entered my house; I had never spoken to any of them. It suddenly occurred to me to give the Abbey of Senlis to that excellent son; and when I asked M. le Duc d'Orléans I obtained it for him instantly. When I went to tell them, never were two people more astounded than they. It was indeed a pleasure to be able to reward such

---

[1] Elisabeth Gabrielle de Durfort de Lorges (d. 1727), Prioress of Andecy [Marne].

[2] Charles Alexandre d'Estaing, Abbé de Saint-Vincent de Senlis from 1692 (d. 1717).

[3] Henri de Chaumejan, Marquis de Fourilles (d. 1720). His son Louis de Chaumejan (1690–1765) was Abbé de Fourilles, then Abbé de Saint-Vincent de Senlis.

LOUIS XV WITH THE DUCHESSE DE VENTADOUR WATCHING
THE SWISS AND FRENCH GUARDS EXERCISING IN THE
PARK AT VINCENNES. ENGRAVING

DAGUESSEAU. BY ROBERT TOURNIÈRES

JOHN LAW. BY ALEXIS SIMON BELLE

CARDINAL ALBERONI. ENGRAVING

devotion, and as time went on the wise and virtuous conduct of the new abbot and the gratitude of both of them made me still more delighted.

On the eve of Candlemas, several of us went to sup informally at Louville's house. Soon after dessert was served, they came to whisper something in the ear of Saint-Contest, counsellor of State,[1] who hurriedly left the table. He was not long gone; and when he returned, looking exceedingly worried and promising to explain later, our only thought was to finish the meal as quickly as possible. As soon as we were back around the fire, he told us what had happened. Chancellor Voysin, supping at home with his family and apparently in excellent health, had suddenly been stricken with apoplexy, and had fallen like a log upon Mme de Lamoignon, a Voysin like himself,[2] with no more than two hours of life left in him. Indeed, he did not live so long, and never regained consciousness. Of Voysin I have already said enough; no more is needed.[3] Saint-Contest's wife was a Le Maistre,[4] of the ancient and famous line of Paris magistrates; she was also aunt-in-law of the procureur-général, on whose promotion Saint-Contest now set his hopes. When he had told all, he went off to warn that magistrate; but found the entire house shut, and all its occupants asleep. He returned early next morning, and dragged Daguesseau out of bed to hear the news. That worthy, however, never believing that he would be chosen for such great employment, took no action, but quietly dressed and went with his wife to hear high mass at the parish church of Saint-André-des-Arcs.

The Duc de Noailles, who was notified that same evening or later that night, thought it a magnificent opportunity to advance one step further towards becoming first minister, which was ever his heart's desire. The procureur-général was his old friend, for his brilliant reputation had not escaped the notice of the Noailles. He could not hope for a Chancellor more eager to assist him; what is more, he felt that he could rule that mild spirit, who would at first feel insecure, groping blindly amidst cabals and intrigues, and certain to be grateful for a guide of the stature of the great Duc de Noailles. Imbued with that idea, in which he was not mistaken, M. de Noailles sought out M. le Duc d'Orléans, who had just risen from his bed, and was seated on his chaise-percée, suffering with acute indigestion, his head still confused by sleep and the previous night's supper (his usual state in the early morning, and for some hours thereafter). The Duc de Noailles dismissed the handful of valets, reported the death of the Chancellor, and without drawing breath demanded the office for Daguesseau, who was that instant sent for to come to the Palais Royal,

---

[1] Dominique Claude Barberie de Saint-Contest (1668–1730).

[2] His first cousin Marie Jeanne Voysin (1654–1727). She was the widow of François Chrétien de Lamoignon (1644–1709).

[3] See index, I and II.

[4] Marie Françoise Le Maistre (1670–1736), who had married M. de Saint-Contest in 1702.

where Noailles awaited his arrival, so as to run no risks. During the interval, Rochepot, Vaucourt and Trudaine, counsellors of State, the first being Daguesseau's son-in-law, the two others his brothers-in-law,[1] brought the seals, which the Regent placed on the table, in their box, dismissing the bearers with his thanks. The messenger sent to find Daguesseau, having failed at his home, proceeded to the parish church, and was more successful. Daguesseau came at once to the Palais Royal, where the Regent had already ordered his coach, and was putting on his coat. The Duc de Noailles was in the study beside M. le Duc d'Orléans when he, with the flattering compliments that always accompany such enormous favours, informed Daguesseau of his sudden elevation.

Very shortly afterwards they all three left the study, and the Regent, taking Daguesseau's hand, announced to the assembled court that they might see in him a new and very worthy Chancellor. After that he took him to the Tuileries, praised him to the King, and proffered the box of seals, on which the King placed his hand as M. le Duc d'Orléans made the presentation. Daguesseau received it with fitting modesty, but escaped as soon as he decently could, bearing the precious box to his home, which was teeming with friends and relations, all of them in raptures because of M. le Duc d'Orléans's message, the news having spread like wildfire on account of the festival. As for the new Chancellor, he had at first been in a state of such complete bewilderment that his mind was a blank, and it was not until he was alone in his coach with the precious box on the seat beside him that he recovered himself. After his return, when the first unavoidable wave of congratulations had spent itself, he went upstairs to tell his brother,[2] a kind of philosopher-voluptuary, a man of vast wit and learning, but as odd as it was possible to be. He was sitting in his dressing-gown, smoking his pipe before the fire. 'Brother,' said Daguesseau as he entered, 'I am come to tell you that I am the new Chancellor.' 'New Chancellor?' exclaimed his brother, 'what have you done with the old one?' 'He died suddenly in the night.' 'Really! I'm uncommonly glad to hear it; but sooner you than me.' And that was all the congratulation he received. The Duc de Noailles, on the other hand, was paid a vast number of compliments, for it was perfectly clear that he was the one who had chosen Daguesseau, and he was very glad that all should know it.

I heard the news early that same evening, and went after dinner to the Palais Royal, to find that M. le Duc d'Orléans was still with his wife. I went down by the back stairs to join them. He was sitting by her bed, for she had a touch of migraine; but he began at once to tell me what had happened. As the matter was already settled, I kept to my rule of saying

[1] Louis Le Goux de La Berchère, Comte de Rochepot; Jean Baptiste Desmaretz de Vaucourt; Charles II Trudaine.

[2] Joseph Antoine, Seigneur de Valjouan, who died aged sixty-five in 1744. There was also another brother, the Abbé Daguesseau (1671–1728).

nothing in opposition, merely stating that he could not have selected for that high office a more learned, enlightened, or more honest man, and that the appointment would be sure to please. I added only that his age might annoy some people by blocking their ambitions;[1] and that I wished Daguesseau would now forget his lifelong devotion to the Parlement, and remember only his new functions and his debt of gratitude. M. le Duc d'Orléans's own enthusiasm, or else the general chorus of congratulation, prevented him from considering my words; but he had good cause to remember them later. He rather nervously asked me how I myself stood with him; but I had made up my mind to think only of the country's welfare. I therefore replied that Daguesseau had won my liking and esteem because he had pleaded our case so well against M. de Luxembourg, in 1696;[2] I said I felt the same about him now, although a coldness had arisen because of the affair of the bonnet, and the encroachments of the Parlement. Now that he was Chancellor of France, I hoped he would be that, and that alone, and drop all his earlier prejudices. I could then live in harmony with him for the sake of our work, and would go that very day to call on him with my congratulations. This I did; M. le Duc d'Orléans appeared mightily relieved, and the new Chancellor deeply touched.

A Chancellor should cut a splendid figure. In a regency he can scarcely do otherwise. This one has for so long been a personage, since he still lives, and has been so buffeted by fortune in that high office, that I have decided to break my rule against writing of the living. He was born on 26 November 1668; was made avocat-général, 12 January 1691, when he was two-and-twenty; became procureur-général at thirty-two, and Chancellor of France on 2 February 1717, at the age of forty-eight. His father's father was head of the audit office—better to probe no deeper.

Daguesseau is stout, of medium height, with a large, plump face, very pleasant to see until the time of his disgrace; and even afterwards looking wise and humorous, in spite of one eye being considerably smaller than the other. It is noteworthy that until he became Chancellor he had never possessed the right to speak or vote in the Parlement, and that it had become a point of honour to dispute his findings, because jealousy of his swiftly growing reputation overcame respect and personal liking. Brilliance, industry, learning of all kinds, judicial gravity, piety, and good morals form the basis of his character. One might fairly say that his mind is acute and incorruptible; yet he is, at the same time, kind and gentle, easy of access in public, and in private gay and witty, but never so as to cause offence. He is also exceedingly sober, quite without arrogance or self-seeking; but temperamentally lazy, which may account for his slowness.

---

[1] Daguesseau was only forty-eight years old, and might be expected to be Chancellor for another ten or fifteen years. In the event he was dismissed a year later, but reinstated in 1720.
[2] This case against the Maréchal de Luxembourg was a continuation of the first lawsuit, and does not appear in this version of the memoirs. See I, pp. 42 et seqq.

Who would ever believe that a magistrate so amply endowed with virtues and talents could fail to make the greatest Chancellor for centuries past? Truly, he might have been the best premier président that ever was. Strange to relate, as Chancellor, he caused even such men as Alègre and Boucherat to be regretted. This is a paradox hard to understand; yet in all the thirty years that he has held office, the facts have been abundantly clear. Indeed, if facts so incredible did not require explaining I need say no more. That happy union of talents was marred by failings, at first concealed, but plain to every eye once he had reached the heights. His long schooling in the heart of the Paris Parlement had so deeply imbued him with its maxims and ambitions that he came to regard it with as much love and veneration as the English do their own Parliament which has nothing in common with ours, beyond the name. It would not be too much to say that he viewed its every edict as the faithful do the decrees of the œcumenical councils. This blind loyalty was at the root of certain grave failings that became abundantly obvious. For example, he was always on the side of the Parlement in its attempts to undermine the King's authority, which was to say his own, for as Chancellor he was the King's mouthpiece, the superior and moderator of the Parlement, with the duty to restrain it when it overstepped its functions. He had the intelligence and equity to see clearly enough when the Parlement erred; but he could never bring himself to utter a rebuke. All his talents were turned to keeping the peace, concealing, excusing, giving false interpretations, negotiating with the Regent, taking advantage of M. le Duc d'Orléans's indecision and good nature to bore and plague him with every detail. As a result, instead of a strong chief magistrate to support his authority, the Regent found in Daguesseau a mere apologist, who strengthened and encouraged the Parlement in all its claims and encroachments.

Long practice in the law courts spoiled the keenness of his mind. Their business is to gather information, examine and compare the arguments of the two opposing parties, and of others also, supposing, as often happens, more than two are concerned in a suit; to strike a balance, so to speak, and lay the facts before the judges with such accuracy and art that the views of the advocate are unknown until he reaches his conclusion. A procureur-général writes down his opinion and need not speak in public; but in his study, he too must examine, compare, and weigh evidence before reaching a conclusion. After twenty-four years' practice, this process had become engrained in Daguesseau's pernickety mind, engendering doubts which he could by no means throw off, with the result that he spent an unconscionable time on his cases. He was the first to suffer, for it truly was hard labour for him to reach a decision; but to those whose fate hung in the balance the effect was often disastrous. When hard pressed, at the Regency Council, for example, or by the need to finish at a certain time, he would ramble on, offering first one opinion, then another, and at the very last moment pronounce as though the truth had suddenly dawned on him.

His silence and indecision marvellously combined to leave his cases unsettled; and another weakness, a perfect mania for seeing difficulties, also contributed to that end. So many obstacles of every imaginable variety came to his mind that they often brought him to a complete standstill. As I once said of the Duc de Chevreuse, he could split a hair in four. No wonder they were such dear friends. Not only were they painfully precise; they looked everywhere for difficulties, with the same eagerness that other men show in avoiding them, and the least interruption drove them to a frenzy. Their dearest friends, their personal affairs, were not immune; this perverse delight in discovering obstacles poisoned everything they touched. The old Duchesse d'Estrées Vaubrun,[1] a clever woman and Daguesseau's close friend, was once asked to intervene on someone's behalf. She demurred, saying that the ground was too stony. 'But Madam,' said the client, 'Daguesseau is your friend.' 'He is indeed,' she replied, 'but you must know that he is a sheep in wolf's clothing.' It was a perfect description of him.

That is already a great deal about Daguesseau; but just one touch more. The elder Duc de Gramont,[2] a man of considerable intelligence, told me that he had found himself alone with the Chancellor, at Versailles, one morning when the King was at mass. In the course of conversation he had asked him whether, having so long an acquaintance with all the pettifoggery and unnecessary prolongation of lawsuits, he had never wished to speed them by legislation, thus curbing the dishonesty of lawyers. Daguesseau had answered that he had indeed considered the matter, and had even started to compose just such a ruling, but as he continued he had thought of the great host of attorneys, prosecutors, and ushers who would be ruined, and compassion for them had stayed his hand. He might as easily have argued that there should be neither provosts, nor archers[3] to arrest thieves and put them in the way of certain punishment; compassion being even more desirable in such cases. In short, he was maintaining that on the length and number of lawsuits depended the power and wealth of the lawyers, and that they must consequently be encouraged to increase and extend themselves *ad infinitum*. This has been a long digression, but the matter is of great interest, and I felt it might profit you to see how a man of such excellent parts, talents, and reputation as Daguesseau could, by moving outside his proper sphere, render his integrity questionable and his talents worse than useless, explode his fame, and gradually become nothing more than a straw blown by the wind.

[1] Madeleine Diane (died 1753), daughter of the Marquis de Vaubrun. She married Louis Armand, Duc d'Estrées, as his second wife.

[2] Antoine Charles, Duc de Gramont (1645–1720).

[3] The royal company of archers, who acted as constables of the watch in the royal residences, and were sometimes used to arrest people of quality and escort them to the Bastille.

The treaty between France and England (which I have already mentioned) was kept a profound secret in the hope of persuading the Dutch to participate. The news could not, however, be confined entirely to the Regent's study, and long before it was announced to the Regency Council, some of the facts were known. This secrecy was the work of the Abbé Dubois, taking his first long stride towards power. He had so feared obstruction that he had extracted M. le Duc d'Orléans's promise to tell no one, although I never doubted but that the Duc de Noailles and Canillac were excepted. Be that as it may, the silence lasted too long for the members of the Council to remain in perfect ignorance. The Maréchal de Villeroy spoke of it to me in great indignation; he was extremely angry at having been kept so long in the dark. I had no wish to share a grievance with a man so ill disposed towards M. le Duc d'Orléans; but I allowed him to see my total ignorance. Dubois and his associates distrusted me regarding England;[1] and had taken precautions to prevent the Regent from confiding in me. Nothing at all had been said, and after the signing I had not so much as opened my mouth.

Once the signatures were appended it was necessary for the Regency Council to debate and approve the terms. Not one member had learned more of them than was known to the general public, namely, that a treaty was being negotiated.[2] This was scarcely flattering to the members, and M. le Duc d'Orléans feared obstruction, perhaps even a scandal. He accordingly spent the whole morning of the day when he was to present it at the Council in interviewing one after the other all the members, explaining the terms, conciliating, apologizing for the secrecy, in short, nobbling votes by a display of graciousness.

I was summoned like the rest, and found him alone in his study, at eleven o'clock. He began as soon as I entered, saying with a propitiatory smile, 'You of all men will not wish to raise difficulties over this treaty with England.' I replied that like many others, I had known of its existence only a few days earlier; and that since he had told me nothing, he might well suppose that I knew nothing. Thus I was in no position to approve or disapprove. I added that in order to do either I should need to examine the terms at leisure; weigh the possible drawbacks; discover the full scope of the promises on either side; compare the probable outcome with the effects of other treaties; in short, study the entire matter in peace and quiet, and so reach a considered opinion. Not being able to do any such thing, since I had known of it only a few minutes before it came to the Council, I could say nothing either for or against, but must leave it to his better judgment, as he alone knew all. It appeared to me that he was much relieved by my words.

[1] The views of Cardinal Dubois and Saint-Simon were almost always at variance.
[2] Saint-Simon must surely be exaggerating; something would have emerged from the official reports.

I had more than once been obliged to stand against the Regent when he wished to coerce the Council into passing some particular measure. One day, when I had firmly opposed him, carrying my fellow members with me, I visited him at the Palais Royal. As soon as I appeared (he was quite alone), he burst out, 'What the devil possessed you to let off that squib under my feet?' 'Monsieur,' said I, 'I am extremely sorry, but your arguments made no sense.' 'Who are you talking to?' he exclaimed; 'as though I did not know it! But I dared not tell those fellows my true reasons,' and he proceeded to explain. 'Once more I apologize,' I answered, 'Had I known, I could have overlooked your fancy talk; but next time, give me warning; for fond though I am of you, once I have taken my seat on the Council, I must speak for God and the State, according to my conscience and my honour. Thus, despite all I owe you, and all the good I wish you, never doubt but that I shall speak my mind. If you need to have some suspect or difficult measure passed, without explaining it, tell me beforehand, and give me your true reasons; I can then either accept your opinion, or tell you frankly why not. If I find myself completely unable to swallow something on which your heart is set, I will absent myself from the Council on that particular day, and offer some valid excuse so that nothing is suspected.' M. le Duc d'Orléans thanked me for my candour, saying that I spoke like an honest man and a good friend, adding that he would take me at my word on the next occasion.

That same afternoon we all met in Council. The Regent opened the session with a word as to the need and advantage of the treaty, and proceeded to ask the Maréchal d'Huxelles, who was at the head of foreign affairs, to read it aloud. The greatest objection was having had to sign without the Dutch. The Maréchal proceeded to read in a low voice, with some hesitation. The Regent asked for his opinion. 'In favour,' he said between his teeth, bowing as he spoke. Everyone else did the same. When it came to me, I said that since I could not possibly form an opinion on a vitally important matter, which I was now hearing for the first time, it appeared more prudent to rely on the judgment of His Royal Highness. Then turning to face the Maréchal d'Huxelles, and looking him straight in the eye, I added, 'and on that also of Monsieur le Maréchal, who has doubtless brought all his wisdom to bear on the subject'.[1] I could not resist this malicious sally against that travesty of a Roman citizen. All the rest looked at me, and immediately lowered their eyes; some could scarcely repress a smile, and several spoke to me as we left the Council.

Callières died at this time, which was a thousand pities. I have already spoken of his honesty and skill.[2] He had been a secretary in the King's study,

[1] The Maréchal d'Huxelles had been at The Hague negotiating the treaty, and was known to have objected to signing without the Dutch. Saint-Simon thought he was being double-faced.
[2] See I, p. 279n.

and had held the pen since 1701.[1] 'Holding the pen', as it is called, means being a kind of licensed forger, and doing in the course of duty what would cost other men their lives. The work consists in imitating the King's handwriting so perfectly that no difference is observable, and then writing all manner of letters which the King himself would wish to write, were no labour involved. Such amanuenses are employed by many sovereigns and foreign princes, and by some subjects also, for example by army commanders, philanthropists, and many important persons, for their private correspondence. It was after the death of Rose[2] that Callières first took the pen. The Abbé Dubois was already aspiring to reach the heights; but he felt the need to rise step by step. He therefore made application for this post, although it ill became a counsellor of State for Church affairs. He had only to ask. His great hope was to insinuate himself into the council for foreign affairs, like certain plants that insert themselves into walls and eventually bring down the entire structure. There were difficulties, however; the Maréchal d'Huxelles was likely to be jealous and indignant, and some of the other counsellors were unlikely to welcome him. He was not yet in a position to bare his claws.

Ever since the affair of the English treaty, d'Huxelles had pleaded indisposition, being too much ashamed to leave his house, except for meetings of the Council. Dubois, seeing a chance to pay his court, persuaded the Regent to visit him, on the grounds that the old gentleman might indeed be ailing; that a visit would be greatly appreciated, and that Society would highly approve. No more was needed to activate the Regent. He called on the Maréchal d'Huxelles. Since the only motive was to caress him, a feat at which M. le Duc d'Orléans was past master, and since d'Huxelles was vain enough, and foolish enough, to be moved by the honour, he began to purr again. After that there was no difficulty in promoting the Abbé Dubois to the council of foreign affairs. He immediately paid his round of official visits, protesting earnestly that he had nothing further to desire. For once he spoke truly. All he wanted at that time was to join the council without arousing the customary ill feeling for new brooms, who had no intention of remaining with them long.

I now remember having forgotten something that merits inclusion because, in itself, the event was so noteworthy. I shall recount it here, lest once again it escape my mind. One afternoon, just before a meeting of the Regency Council, the Maréchal de Villars took me on one side, to ask me whether I had heard that Marly was to be pulled down. I said I knew nothing, and could not believe it. 'Then you would not approve?' he inquired. I said that on the contrary I should most strongly disapprove. He repeated that the destruction of Marly had been decided, and that if I wished to prevent it there was not a moment to lose. I replied that I would

---

[1] See *Saint-Simon at Versailles*, p. 104.
[2] Ibid. pp. 69–74.

speak at once to M. le Duc d'Orléans. 'Immediately,' he exclaimed, 'Do it this very moment; the orders may already have gone.' The Council was in session, but I made my way round the back of the table and whispered what I had learned into the Regent's ear, not saying who had told me. I begged him to suspend all orders until he had spoken with me, and promised to go to the Palais Royal directly after the meeting. He muttered something, as though he were cross at having been found out; but he agreed to wait for me. When the Council broke up, I had a word with the Maréchal de Villars, and then went straight to the Palais Royal.

M. le Duc d'Orléans denied nothing. I said I would not ask who had given him such bad advice. He urged the need for economy; the cost of maintenance; the immense amount of water flowing through the pipes; the building materials and other things which might with advantage be sold; the disadvantage of preserving something which the King would not visit for years to come, and the fact that many other fine houses, none of which could be pulled down, had to be maintained at vast expense. I replied that had he been the guardian of a private individual such advice might have been good; but it was the worst possible for the governor of a King of France since, even admitting the huge expense of Marly, it was no more than a cipher on a king's budget. Let him put from his mind any thought of selling the materials, for all the profit would vanish in bribes and pilfering. It was not such trifles that he should consider, but how many millions had been thrown into that old sewer to turn it into a fairy palace, unique of its kind in the whole of Europe, unrivalled for the beauty of its fountains and the glory lent it by the late King. It was, I said, the admiration of every foreigner who visited France. All Europe would greet its destruction with dismay, and a disapproval which mean excuses of petty economy would do nothing to appease. The French nation would be indignant to see that splendid artifact destroyed. It behoved us both, I declared, to be infinitely careful of all that represented the taste and most cherished dreams of Louis XIV. We should do nothing to detract from the memory of one who by so long a reign, so many brilliant years, such terrible disasters heroically borne, and the incredible good fortune of issuing so gloriously from them, had left the entire world holding him in veneration. Lastly, I argued, he must realize that every malcontent, every neutral even, would side with the late Court to cry 'Murderer!'; that the Duc du Maine, Mme de Ventadour, the Maréchal de Villeroy, etc., would make sure that the young King counted it a crime; that they would carefully nurture the grudge throughout the Regency, along with many others, and use it to harm him on the King's majority.

I could see clearly enough that such ideas had not entered M. le Duc d'Orléans's head. He admitted that I was right; promised that Marly should be spared and maintained, and thanked me for preserving him from so great an error. When I was quite sure of him, I remarked, 'You must admit that if the late King is looking down on us from another world, he will be mightily surprised to see the Duc de Noailles persuading you to destroy Marly, and I preventing you.' 'Indeed! indeed!' said he warmly, 'He would never believe it.'[1] Marly was thus preserved and maintained, and it is Cardinal Fleury, like any cheese-paring college bursar, who has despoiled it of the river that gave it its extraordinary charm. I left M. le Duc d'Orléans and hurried to bring the good news to the Maréchal de Villars. The Duc de Noailles, who would have benefited most from the saving,[2] was furious to see his prey escape him. In order to avoid total defeat, he gained permission (very secretly, for fear of a second failure[3]) to sell the furnishings, curtains, linen, etc., on the grounds that everything would be spoiled and rotten by the time the King came of age; that, by the sale great sums would immediately become available, and that the King would later be able to refurnish as he best pleased. There was not much beautiful furniture; but the various lodgings, the bedrooms of the courtiers and of the senior and junior officers, and the wardrobes and closets also, were all supplied by the King with curtains, linen, etc. The grand total was thus enormous;[4] yet because of favour and pillage, the amount realized was very small, and the replacements since have cost millions. Anyone who chose might buy at the sale. I learned of it only after it had begun; thus I could not prevent that extremely mean and wasteful event.

Mortagne,[5] Madame's groom-in-waiting, owned a kind of country house at the end of the Faubourg Saint-Antoine,[6] and spent the greater part of his time there. M. de Guéméné,[7] who abominated making matches for his family, and had by no means been converted by the example of his sisters[8] who eventually married without his assistance, had placed one of his daughters[9] in a convent nearby. Mortagne came to be acquainted with her, and, seized with compassion for her misery and total lack of comforts, had begun to give her presents. Thus, by degrees, their friendship had blossomed into an affection of such a nature that they wished to marry.[10] The Rohans made a great commotion, for although Mortagne was in every way

---

[1] Considering what he had said about Marly, in 1715, 'a haunt of snakes and vermin', 'typical of the King's bad taste in everything', Saint-Simon was showing great integrity, and a pleasant glimpse of his sense of humour.

[2] The Duc de Noailles was controller of the finances.

[3] On the contrary, everyone knew.

[4] During the bad times, 1709, the King announced that the courtiers would have to pay for everything in their apartments, and for alterations and decorations by the royal workmen. Only Marly was excepted.

[5] Antoine Gaspard de Colins, Comte de Mortagne (1663–1720). He was born in Brussels.

[6] It was in the Rue de Charonne.

[7] M. de Guéméné was Charles III de Rohan Guéméné (1655–1727) who, in 1699, became Duc de Montbazon.

[8] Charlotte Armande, who married the Comte de Jarnac, in 1688; and Elisabeth, who married the Comte de Melun, in 1690.

[9] Charlotte de Rohan-Montbazon (1680–1733).

[10] They were married in 1717. In 1729, after the Comte de Mortagne's death, she married the Comte de Canaples.

a gentleman, with a fine record in the service, his surname was only Colins, and he thus amounted to very little in the neighbourhood of Liège, whence he had sprung. Mortagne, however, took no offence. Declaring that his desire to marry the lady arose purely out of pity[1] for the misery that drove her to despair at the age of thirty-five, he said he would wait one year, after which, if no better match was found, he would marry her. The family made no effort to arrange an alliance, hoping that he would be frightened away; but he feared them not at all. The lady gave them respectful notice, and a year later the couple were publicly married, according to all the proprieties. They lived very happily together, for he was a good fellow, and his wife thought herself already in paradise. There resulted a daughter who was later married to the eldest son of Mont-boissier, appointed captain of the black musketeers in succession to his cousin Canillac.

The ill feeling between the princes of the blood and the bastards was increasing daily. The princes wanted a ruling, and constantly pestered the Regent to give one. The bastards merely played for time. The peers, deplorable though their conduct had been, were, as you know, defending themselves against the innumerable encroachments which they had been forced to swallow in the previous reign. I saw that the Regent was harassed by the princes' continual attacks, but was finding it extremely hard to resist them. That being so, we peers decided to present a petition to the King himself, and to send a copy to the Regent, the whole document couched in terms that were restrained, but none the less exceedingly strong, regarding our exact demands. The petition ended thus: 'For the above reasons, Sire, may it please Your Majesty to revoke and annul the edict of July 1714 and the proclamation of 23 May 1715; revoke and annul also the proclamation of 5 May 1694, in its entirety, and the edict of May 1711, which edicts granted to MM. the Duc du Maine and the Comte de Toulouse and their male descendants the right to represent the senior peers at the King's coronation (excluding the other peers of France), and per-mitted them to take the oath at the Parlement, at the age of twenty.' This was demanding most explicitly that they be reduced to exactly the same level as the other peers, taking seniority according to the date of their creation and their first reception by the Parlement.

When this document had been revised, examined, and approved, it was signed at a general meeting held at the house of the Duke-Bishop of Laon, in the absence of Monsieur de Rennes who, like the other absentees, signed by proxy. As soon as this was done, Messieurs de Laon and de Châlons, with six lay peers, took it to present to the King. When they arrived, the Maréchal de Villeroy introduced them, and the King graciously received the petition from the hands of Monsieur de Laon, who explained very

---

[1] He wished them to understand that he was not trying to better himself by marrying into the Rohan family.

shortly what it concerned. The King did not reply, just as he never replied to the princes of the blood or the bastards when receiving their petitions.

At the same time as these eight peers left to go to the Tuileries, the Duke-Bishop of Langres and the Dukes of La Force, Noailles and Chaulnes went to the Palais Royal, where M. le Duc d'Orléans, expecting them in his study, received them with all his customary, inscrutable graciousness. Few of the renegades dared to show themselves in their true colours on that occasion, one exception being the Duc de Rohan, who differed from them all, himself included. The Duc d'Estrées and the Duc de Mazarin[1] were the dregs of humanity, whom no one ever spoke to. Estrées never joined us; Mazarin had literally been thrown out of one of our meetings by Monsieur de Laon, and since that unexampled disgrace, had not risked an appearance. D'Antin's situation was so difficult that we could not mention the affair to him.[2] The Prince de Rohan[3] owed too much to Louis XIV's love-life, and had too much to gain from disorder, encroachments, and meddling of all kinds to be able to stand for truth and honesty. The Duc d'Aumont was so utterly discredited by his behaviour in the affair of the bonnet, and his treachery during the conference at Sceaux,[4] that none of us was speaking to him. It thus cost him little, by not signing, to add the final proof of his infamy.

Mme de Maintenon, forgotten and already as good as dead, in her grand and costly retirement at Saint-Cyr, fell seriously ill, although hardly anyone was aware of it, and those who knew felt total unconcern.

The English and the Dutch were treating the King of Spain with great consideration and, like the French, kept him informed regarding the Treaty of the Triple Alliance. King Philip guessed that there were secret clauses, inserted by the Regent, and that they formed the real importance of the treaty. He was, however, too intent (both at home and abroad) on hiding his hopes of succeeding to the throne of his ancestors not to display complete indifference. It was generally believed that his main interest was in Italy, and the recovery of some of his lost lands in that country. This view was supported by the advantage to the queen, which Alberoni had so much reason to promote, and by her eagerness to settle the dispute, at Rome, over that prelate's elevation to the cardinalate. He continually proclaimed himself frustrated by the delays which, so he said, the queen felt to be a personal slight, not so much for their effect on a loyal and devoted subject, as by her need to arm a confidential servant with the authority to deal firmly in the dangerous situation now confronting her.

[1] Paul Jules de La Porte, Duc de Mazarin (1666–1731). Until his father's death in 1713, he had been Marquis de La Meilleraye.

[2] The Duc d'Antin was on the King's staff as assistant to the Maréchal de Villeroy.

[3] Hercule Mériadec, Prince de Rohan-Soubise who, in 1714, became the Duc de Rohan-Rohan. His mother, the Princesse de Soubise, had been a mistress of Louis XIV.

[4] See p. 176.

This was a reference to the moods of black melancholy that were once again afflicting King Philip,[1] making them fear consumption and an early demise. Burlet, his first physician, was banished for expressing himself too freely on that subject.

The Queen, hated as she was by the Spanish people, had therefore good cause to dread the future, and so had the foreigners who looked to her alone for protection. For Alberoni himself the peril was extreme; although lord of all under her protection, he was the object of universal loathing and jealousy, and, having no official position, his downfall would necessarily be very great. He persuaded her that her honour was at stake, and that if the Pope, despite all his promises, should give Borromeo the purple,[2] it would be the final insult. Indeed she had written to the Pope, recommending Alberoni in terms as strong as though she were asking God for paradise. Meanwhile, knowing the Pope's proneness to take fright, Alberoni had given an order to Daubenton,[3] as coming from the king himself, bidding him inform Aldrovandi[4] that unless the queen received immediate satisfaction neither he nor Alessandro Albani[5] would be permitted to come to Madrid.

Alberoni now embarked upon a campaign of self-congratulation, ably assisted by his supporters, praising the wisdom and secrecy of his rule, the admirable order in which he had placed the nation's affairs, and the government's vigorous policy after so long a period of weakness. He had it put about that his only care was to strengthen the Spanish navy and encourage commerce. More especially, he deplored the conduct of previous ministers, who had blunted King Philip's talent for government; but he greatly praised the king's regular life, year in year out the same—a routine which Alberoni himself had established in order to keep Their Catholic Majesties in close confinement. This same routine, persisted in until it became deeply engrained, deserves to be better known. I shall describe it from Alberoni's own account.

The King and Queen of Spain who, in sickness, pregnancy, and good health, invariably shared the same bed, woke at eight o'clock, and immediately took breakfast. The king then went to dress and afterwards

---

[1] He may have inherited these moods from Monseigneur le Grand Dauphin, his father, whom Saint-Simon describes as 'drowning in gloom'.

[2] There was only one vacancy. The Pope's difficulty was to choose between Alberoni, the King of Spain's candidate, and Gilbert Borromeo (1671-1740), who was supposed to be favoured by the Emperor, and whose niece was married to the Pope's nephew Charles Albani. Borromeo was, in fact, made cardinal in this year, 1717.

[3] Père Guillaume Daubenton (1648-1721), Philip V's Jesuit confessor. He was assistant-general of the Society, a friend of Alberoni, and, according to Saint-Simon, in constant secret correspondence with the Pope.

[4] Pompeo Aldrovandi (1668-1752), a native of Bologna. He had a somewhat chequered career in Church diplomacy. In 1715, he was the Papal nuncio to Spain; in 1717, he was Archbishop of Neo-Caesarea. Alberoni had him banished; but in 1733 he became Patriarch of Jerusalem and Governor of Rome. He was made a cardinal in 1734.

[5] Alessandro Albani (1692-1779), the Pope's third nephew; made a cardinal in 1721.

returned to the queen, who had remained in bed (when we come to my embassy, I will note such very few changes as I then observed). He entered his study and held his council; if it was finished before half-past eleven, he once more returned to the queen. At that point she rose; and while she dressed, the king gave various orders. As soon as she was ready they went together to hear mass, after which they dined together. The hour after dinner they spent in private conversation, and then said their prayers, before going hunting. When they returned, the king summoned one or other of his ministers, and worked in the queen's presence, while she embroidered or wrote letters. This continued until half-past nine in the evening, when they supped together alone. At ten o'clock, Alberoni entered, and stayed with them until their bedtime, at about half-past eleven. Here let me add that the officers of the court had entirely ceased to perform their functions, for no one any longer had access to Their Most Catholic Majesties; and so it continues even today. If I ever reach the time of my embassy, I shall give further particulars.

I shall abide by my decision to speak of the constitution only on those rare occasions when I felt obliged to intervene. I knew the Regent's weakness and that, although in spite of himself he believed, he liked to make a mockery of religion. I saw that he was falling a prey to his enemies in this affair as in so many others. He was ruled by the Jesuits because he feared them; by the Maréchal de Villeroy, whom he had looked up to from early childhood, and who, although profoundly ignorant, made a point of supporting the constitution to parade his respect for the late King and Mme de Maintenon; by the Abbé Dubois, already dreaming of a cardinalate and eager to smooth his path to Rome. He was deceived by the intrigues of Cardinal de Rohan; by the rages of Cardinal de Bissy, and the chicanery of many prelates who, calmly contemplating their future hats, used the present to impress their personalities, strengthen their positions, and win favour. Lastly, M. le Duc d'Orléans was completely misled by that rotten trunk the miserable Bishop of Troyes, whose return to Society had putrefied his very bowels, leaving him without aim or reason, quite divorced from all the principles that had guided him until the moment of his joining the Council. There was no one of any kind or condition to provide a counterweight.

Cardinal de Noailles was too good, too devout, too simple-minded to use his influence. Through intrigue and menaces, the small band of clergy who thought like him had begun to dwindle away. They had no support, being without access to the Regent, and thus having no chance of stating their case. All they could do was trust in God, for they failed to understand how a matter of religious doctrine had become one of plots and double dealing —none of their training had been for that. Against them was Bentivoglio the nuncio, feeding the flames in France and, at Rome, doing his utmost to make the Pope use force. Poor, fiercely ambitious, vulgar, utterly immoral—as you already know, he had given ample proof.[1] His only religion was self-interest. Believing, as he did, that his hat and his fortune depended entirely on the bull's causing a conflagration in France, he stopped at nothing to bring one about, even to the point where the Pope had begun to find his furious homilies an infliction, and the patience of Cardinals de Rohan and de Bissy was becoming exhausted. There remained besides a few desperate men who, like the Jesuits, lived only for bloodshed, wealth, and the destruction of the Gallican Church. Step by step, from one violent deed to the next, they brought the affair to the point at which acceptance of the constitution was made an article of faith.

The Pope, against all the traditions of his greatest and most holy predecessors, grew obdurate, refusing to explain his bull, or allow any of his bishops to do so, lest his so-called infallibility be questioned—not to mention the difficulty of finding any valid excuse for the edict. He simply demanded blind obedience, and his nuncio, at the head of the Jesuits and Sulpicians, seized on that as a pretext for suppressing our liberties, and making France, like Italy, Spain, Portugal, and the Indies, a humble slave of Rome. Their first move was to obtain the bishops' consent to having the constitution proclaimed an article of faith. A few protested, as they had done when the bull was first published; but in the end, even that small minority was, by intrigue and flattery, persuaded to comply, and thus the article of faith was swallowed in the same way as the constitution itself.

In this crisis, the Sorbonne and four bishops[2] felt it was time for that desperate remedy which Mother Church has at all times freely allowed her children, to give a breathing-space in which the truth may emerge—a remedy that was used by the late King himself to save France from the clutches of Rome. I speak, of course, of an appeal to a general Church council. Bentivoglio and his henchmen cried aloud. They foresaw the ruin of their ambitions, and all hell broke loose. The Regent, so prone to be alarmed, so easily misled, allowed his pernicious advisers to take action against the Sorbonne and to banish the four bishops; but he afterwards allowed them to return to their dioceses.

It was at this point that Cardinal de Noailles let slip, as so often, his one great chance. I used often to see him, either at his house or mine. On this occasion he came to me in order to discuss the affair. I begged him to appeal, telling him that he might count on the support of the chapters and priests of Paris, the foremost prelates, the largest and most important congregations, and the various lay and religious communities. I said he must surely see the treachery lurking beneath the mask of obedience to Rome, that planned to make France the slave of Papal power. He had been patient long enough; the time had come for him to save our Gallican

---

[1] Saint-Simon is referring to his illegitimate daughters, 'La Légende' and 'La Constitution'. See p. 75 above.
[2] They were the Bishops of Boulogne, Montpellier, Senez, and Mirepoix.

liberties and calm these furious storms. I could see that I had shaken him. He confided to me that a document of appeal was drawn up and ready for dispatch; but that he would not send it yet, for fear of losing patience too soon. Nothing I said had any effect, and he offered no other reason for delay. Thus after a very long discussion, I predicted that such patience was folly; for he would appeal too late, all his supporters having by then been intimidated or enticed away.

M. le Duc d'Orléans well knew my thoughts regarding the constitution, and those of the late King also, as I have recounted earlier.[1] He thus found my company something of an embarrassment. It was not hard for him to avoid the subject, since I never faced him with it, except for an occasional request (invariably granted), to mitigate the harsh punishment of individuals that was being demanded of him. Once I had discovered how deeply he was involved, I did not try to interfere. But as always when in a dilemma, or driven beyond a certain point, he could not help returning to me with absolute frankness, even when his own feelings, or the influence of his advisers, made me appear most prejudiced.

Thus in his immediate state of distress and uncertainty, torn between the appeal and the raging furies of whom I have spoken, he stopped me one afternoon, as I was tidying my papers and preparing to leave after working alone with him, as I usually did two or three times a week. He said he was going to the Opéra, and asked me to accompany him because he had important matters to discuss with me. 'To the Opéra, Monsieur?' I cried, 'What a place to talk business! Talk to me here as long as you please. Or if you wish to go to the Opéra, what could be better? I will come to you tomorrow, or whenever else you choose.' He none the less persisted, saying that we could shut ourselves up in his little private box, where he often went alone, and that we should be even more comfortable than in his study.[2] I begged him to consider that the performance would be distracting, and the music too; that everyone would see him talking and arguing, his mind not on the singers; that they would draw conclusions from his gestures; that people coming to pay their court would wonder at finding me shut up with him alone; that the Opéra was for diversion and entertainment, to allow people to see and be seen; certainly not a proper place to discuss State affairs and provide a rival spectacle to the one on the stage. It was all in vain. He merely laughed; took his hat and cane from a sofa with one hand, and my arm with the other, and carried me off.

Before entering his box, he told them not to let anyone in, or open the door on any pretext whatsoever, and, in particular, to keep people away from the entrance. This was tantamount to saying that he wanted no

---

[1] See index, II, under *Unigenitus*, the Bull.

[2] A crowded place is good for talking secrets, and the audience would not have dared to hush them; but it does seem possible that the Regent, with experience of Saint-Simon's homilies, could not bear to start one without providing himself with the means to end it.

eavesdroppers, and quite enough to show that closeted with me, who was never one for music or the drama, he was not so much at the Opéra as in his study, engaged on affairs of State. He thus most indiscreetly provided matter for gossip, which spread through Paris like wildfire, just as I had predicted.

He sat down in what he called his accustomed place, facing the stage, and set me with my back to it, so as to face him. In that position we were plainly visible to all;[1] he to those on the stage, in the neighbouring boxes, and in a section of the stalls. My back could be seen by everyone on the stage, and my profile by the entire audience. I was a stranger at the Opéra, and people did not at first recognize me. After a while, however, some sharp eyes detected who it was, and whispered confidences revealed me to the rest. The piece had barely begun. We glanced around for a moment before sitting down, and observed that the house was crowded; after that we became so utterly absorbed that we neither saw nor heard anything until all was over.

M. le Duc d'Orléans began by explaining his difficulties regarding the appeal, which the Parlement, certain bishops, and all the lower clergy, following the example of the Sorbonne and other religious and secular bodies, were urging him to allow. I did not interrupt him; but when he had finished began to speak. Soon, however, he interrupted me, saying that the great majority, led by the Pope, most of the bishops, the Jesuits, and all the seminarians of Saint-Sulpice and Saint-Lazare, favoured the constitution. Thus the consciences of the people had been awakened by innumerable confessors, curés, and vicars. A successful appeal might provoke that great majority who desired the constitution to join with the King of Spain against him; and by force of numbers, by secret plots, and by the power of Rome, they might finally prevail. I told him how shocked I was to hear a matter of doctrine and religion treated as mere politics. Such methods, I declared, would bring down God's curse upon those who used them, and upon the entire population. I reminded him how horrified he had been at the wickedness of a similar plot, and the violence that had accompanied it, in the reign of Louis XIV, and of our feelings when we believed we should have to accompany that monarch to the Parlement—an event prevented only by the King's death. I showed him how wrong he was. . . .

[. . . *and so on, and so forth, for more than thirteen pages of the Édition de la Pléiade, rehearsing yet again the familiar arguments, and the dangers of a secession on the lines of Henry VIII and the English Reformation, or the revolt of the North European protestants; then, as always, returning to the iniquity of the Duc de Noailles and his treatment of his saintly uncle the cardinal; winding up with detailed instructions as to how the Pope should be answered. The Regent had already*

[1] In the early eighteenth century it was fashionable to watch performances from the sides of the stage. As Saint-Simon says, one went to the opera or the play as much to be seen as to see.

heard Saint-Simon's views at great length; yet he had now subjected himself to still
another long homily and apparently relished it. 'M. le Duc d'Orléans listened with
deep interest and seemed glad of my words. He was indeed deeply perturbed. He
needed the support of an honest friend.' Yet one wonders at his powers of endurance
—two and a half hours? Perhaps Saint-Simon's voice was more palatable to the
strains of Lulli or Rameau than as a regrettably squeaky solo in the silence of the
study.]

At length I ceased to speak; I had no more to say, and I wished to judge what impression my words had made. It far exceeded my expectations, but did not wholly convince me. I saw a man who felt deeply the weight of my arguments (that he did not deny), but was still in the clutches of those wicked men, and quite unable to free himself. He spoke of the present state of the affair, and of the drawbacks to either course of action; he admitted the urgency of all that I had said. I produced counter-arguments, so as to keep him talking, and enable myself to watch him intently. I beheld a man to whom the truth had been brought home; who could not answer any of the points presented to him, but was in the very throes of anguish. We were at that stage when the curtain descended, to our mutual surprise and disappointment. Amid all the bustle of the audience hurrying to go, we could not for some moments bring ourselves to end the discussion. Finally, I declared that the nuncio was not wrong when he said that the man who spoke last to the Regent was always in the right, and I warned him that he was closely watched by relays of men whom he believed to be loyal but who were, in fact, loyal only to themselves and their personal advantage. They would now watch him like vultures, and he must beware lest he become their tool, for he had no one about him equally strong in defence of the truth. Let him remember, I said, the nuncio's remark, and not allow himself to be swept away. Thereupon he left the little box, and I left with him. Outside were crowds of people, either trying to enter or wishing to see him leave. Most of them gazed earnestly into his face; and they gazed at me also. He was still so full of our talk that he appeared very grave as he passed through them. He entered his apartments with that great throng at his heels, among them Effiat and Bezons who presumably had learned of our *tête-à-tête*, and were eager to buttonhole him in the few remaining moments of his official day, before the time of his supper and his *roués*. I do not know what happened next, because I went home immediately.

Returning for a moment to the appeal. What I had said to the Regent as we left the box was only too true. He was so closely watched, set about, and tormented that they worked him up into a passion. Effiat, the premier président, and the rest finally won the day. The Regent cancelled the appeals, used his supreme authority to forbid the debate in the Parlement, and revoked summonses taken out against the Archbishop of Rheims,[1] and

[1] François de Mailly. See index.

other fanatical constitutional bishops, for monstrously cruel and vindictive actions. I had to be content with having impressed him; there was nothing more I could do. What use to argue with a prince so surrounded that his light, indeterminate nature had lost all will to resist? In the end, he became what they desired, and all that I had predicted came to pass. Had he believed me or, rather, had he been able to summon sufficient strength, the constitution with all its intrigues and disorders would have ended in nothing, and the Church of France been left in peace. Rome, moreover, would have learned by bitter experience to cease from troubling us with her plots and ambitions. I shall not recount the fate of Cardinal de Noailles's appeal, nor its results which, because of his delays, I had also foreseen. All that is part of the history of the constitution, and nothing that concerned me personally.

The King went driving on Cours La Reine. He sat squeezed in between the Duc du Maine and the Maréchal de Villeroy, on the back seat of his coach, with a most indecent disregard for etiquette. The only persons whom the late King had ever allowed in his coach were the Sons of France; never at any time princes of the blood. The last Monsieur le Prince[1] once entertained the King and the entire Court, at Chantilly. It so happened that this excursion coincided with a solemn Church festival, which the King attended at the local parish church, driving there alone in his open carriage with room for two only on the back seat, the front one having been removed to hold his shooting-dogs.[2] No one ever drove with him, save only Monseigneur[3] and Monsieur,[4] and they so rarely that it was as good as never. It was therefore regarded as the greatest honour imaginable, due to the magnificence of the party at Chantilly, and the recent marriage of Madame la Duchesse,[5] that when the King saw Monsieur le Prince at his carriage door, as he left the church, he ordered him to step in beside him. That was positively the only occasion when such a thing occurred. The Maréchal de Villeroy, as governor, certainly had the right to a place in the King's coach; but he could not claim precedence over the master of the horse, the great chamberlain or, for that matter, over the gentlemen of the bedchamber on duty for that year. But everything[6] had gone to rack and ruin, and things grew steadily worse as time went on.

On Wednesday, 30 June, the premier président, with the présidents-à-mortier and the gentlemen of the household, went to the Tuileries at eleven o'clock, in order to report to His Majesty on the affair of the princes of the

---

[1] Henri Jules de Bourbon, Prince de Condé (1643–1709).

[2] Louis XIV loved English setters. They lived in a special dog-room in his personal apartments, and he always carried biscuits for them in his pockets. His favourites were Nonne, Ponne, and Bonne.

[3] Louis, the Grand Dauphin (1661–1711), son of Louis XIV.

[4] Philippe I, Duc d'Orléans (1640–1701), Louis XIV's only brother.

[5] Louise Françoise (1673–1743), the eldest legitimized daughter of Louis XIV by Mme de Montespan, widow of Louis III de Condé, Duc de Bourbon (1668–1710), called Monsieur le Duc. The marriage was in 1685.

[6] That is to say, court etiquette.

blood and the bastards; to present the petition and protest regarding the bastards' claim to nobility, and to hear his orders. M. le Duc d'Orléans was present with the Chancellor, into whose hands the King gave the documents when he had received them from the premier président. The Chancellor then announced that the King would make his will known.

On the afternoon of the same day, an extraordinary meeting of the Regency Council was held to hear the verdict, and was continued on the following morning, 1 July. The verdict was not unanimous. Saint-Contest made an admirable speech, wholly on the side of the princes of the blood; and most of the magistrates supported him. But M. le Duc d'Orléans's great benevolence, which so many criminal deeds, so many open attacks, had been unable to destroy, his sympathy for those who importuned him on the bastards' behalf,[1] a certain feeling of alarm, and his favourite maxim, *divide et impera*, moved him to return the verdict for modification. The succession to the throne was then declared wholly unlawful, the rank of the children abolished, and that of the bastards themselves considerably reduced. This judgment, now become an edict, was thought to be altogether too mild by the Parlement, and there was some trouble over the registration, on Tuesday, 6 July. Yet despite its softer terms, M. le Duc d'Orléans used his authority to have it still further modified, with the result that the bastards lost only the right to succeed. Monsieur le Duc had forbidden the royal butlers to allow the Duc du Maine's sons to hand the King his napkin; the Duc de Mortemart, the first gentleman, had stopped the princes of the blood from waiting on them, and it was hard, in the guardrooms, to find men willing to present arms when they passed. M. le Duc d'Orléans issued orders that they were to be treated exactly as though they were princes of the blood—in fact, exactly as heretofore. That immense favour did not prevent Mme du Maine from shrieking like a lunatic, or Mme la Duchesse d'Orléans from weeping day and night; shutting herself up for two whole months; refusing to see anyone except her cronies, very few even of them, and only towards the end. M. du Maine had a talent for concealment, and good reason for displaying nothing on this occasion. He failed, however, to appear at the next meeting of the Council, and sent to say that he was indisposed. He came as usual to the one after. The Comte de Toulouse looked no different, and absented himself from nothing. Everyone except the supporters of M. du Maine was deeply disappointed, the princes of the blood most of all; but since they could extract nothing more, they were thankful for what they had managed to secure.

The dukes took no part in all these agitations and remained perfectly calm; they had nothing either to win or to lose, and thus let others do the barking and growling. As for me, I pursued my policy of silence with the

---

[1] After all, Orléans's wife was herself one of the bastards; he was fond of her; one feels he might naturally have wanted to avoid a tremendous family row.

Regent, for the reasons I have mentioned earlier,[1] and to show him my indifference to conduct which I could neither approve nor change. I simply gave him short, cold answers whenever (which was rare) he tried to talk to me of those two great questions.[2] Although both were being dealt with at that time, I have thought it best to treat them one after the other, keeping them quite separate.

It is high time that I mentioned new assaults of the most outrageous kind on the laws of etiquette. Monsieur de Fréjus[3] and the under-governors had claimed the right to ride in the King's coach, wherein no one, at any time, had been permitted to sit. They founded their claim on the tradition that the under-governors had been allowed, one at a time, to ride in the coach belonging to Monseigneur's royal sons. That was true; but neither M. de Fénelon nor M. de Beauvilliers had ever dreamed of taking such a liberty, although, as you know, both were on terms of the greatest intimacy with them. Saumery,[4] insolent, dare-all, first cousin of the Duc de Beauvilliers, took to inserting himself in the duke's absence—but under-governors are so necessary that without any claim to precedence they come before others. When the governor appears, the under-governor becomes a nobody: the need for him is gone. Yet Saumery continued to ride in the royal coach even when the Duc de Beauvilliers was present; but he sat on the very front seat and excused himself each time; and often the Duke de Beauvilliers apologized for him, explaining that he could not take the place by the door because an old wound prevented him from bending his knee. I saw this happen time and time again, when I was in the coach. He was the only one of the three under-governors to do this. He made it appear to be pure chance, and always he made his stiff knee the excuse for stepping in last but one, so that the last of all had to sit by the door. Riding in the coach included the privilege of eating with the prince; but as the sons of Monseigneur had no occasion to eat with anyone, Saumery's effrontery was made easy for him. There was no precedent for any tutor to use the King's coach, and, as you see, only the very feeblest one for an under-governor. Moreover, great though the Sons of France were, they were very far from being on a level with the King. Yet M. le Duc d'Orléans, trampling on rules of etiquette, allowed the entrée of the King's coach to the under-governors, and to Monsieur de Fréjus, a mere tutor. True, he had the honesty to say that the grace was given as a personal favour, and not at all as to a tutor or a bishop. God only knows to what dregs and gutter-scum the honour of driving and eating with the King will not now be extended.

---

[1] Because the matter was over and done with.

[2] The constitution and the bastards' rank.

[3] See note, p. 49 above. Bishops were addressed as Monsieur (written in full), followed by the name of their diocese. Not so the Archbishop of Paris, since Monsieur de Paris was the executioner.

[4] Jacques François de Johanne de La Carre, Marquis de Saumery (1652–1730). He had been made under-governor of Monseigneur's sons in 1690, and of Louis XV in 1715.

I should not think it worth while mentioning that Arouet was sent to the Bastille for writing scurrilous verses,[1] had not the world seen fit to give him some sort of a name for poetry. He was the son of my father's notary, whom I many times saw when he brought deeds to be signed. Nothing could be done with this dissolute son, whose rake's progress ended by his making a fortune under the name of Voltaire, which he took in order to conceal his true name.

The death of another, and far more illustrious personage, though of a very different kind, made less sensation than it would have caused some years earlier. This demise was of the notorious Mme Guyon. She was exiled to Anjou after all the rumpus over quietism had died down;[2] had lived there prudently, in complete obscurity, and had set no one talking. Eight or ten years later, she was allowed to reside at Blois, where she continued in the same way, and died no different from anyone else. Still deeply religious, living in absolute retirement, she very frequently took the Sacraments, and survived most of her great protectors and her more intimate friends.

Contades and Brilhac,[3] the one a major, the other a captain of the regiment of guards, had spent their lives in the same corps with the most hearty loathing for one another. Contades was by far the cleverer of the two. Brilhac had a vast number of influential friends—his brother was premier président of the parlement of Brittany; but he was not much considered. I do not know what had occurred between these two relatively ancient generals, but at four o'clock in the morning of Saturday, 12 June, Brilhac called on Contades, in the Rue Saint-Honoré, and forced him to dress and go out. They entered a little alley[4] that ran from the Rue Saint-Honoré towards the end of the Tuileries gardens, near the Orangery, and went at it hammer and tongs. Brilhac was only slightly wounded and soon recovered, but Contades was so dangerously hurt that his family had to be notified. There was a terrible shindy. A certain rope-maker and his wife, who found the alley convenient for their craft, had been up and working, and had witnessed the duel. They had talked, which had proved so troublesome that they were reprimanded.[5] Contades lay concealed at the back of the Hôtel de Noailles, which stands close by, and his many friends

---

[1] He stayed in the Bastille for a year, and was released 18 April 1718. The Regent had been very patient with him. Voltaire said 'twenty scavenging, starving black crows' (in reality two policemen) appeared in his bedroom and carried him off to gaol. This, in the parlance of the time, was his first Bastille. He was not excessively uncomfortable; prisoners could furnish their rooms and bring servants. Voltaire did a great deal of work and dined every night at the governor's table. See *Voltaire in Love*, Nancy Mitford, Hamish Hamilton, 1957. See also p. 81 above.

[2] See index, I and II.

[3] Georges Gaspard de Contades (1666–1735) who was made a lieutenant-general in 1713; and François de Brilhac, maréchal de camp 1710. He died 1731.

[4] Possibly the present Rue du Mont Thabor.

[5] The French word is *enlever*. *Enlever quelqu'un* means to reprimand but also of course to remove or abduct. The reader must make his choice.

combined together on his behalf. The Gramonts, the Noailles, the Villars, the premier président, and numbers of others made it their business to save him, and the Regent was as pleased as anyone to have him extricated. It took time, trouble, and a good deal of money; but in the end the affair came to nothing. During the interval Contades recovered. He and Brilhac then appeared once before the Parlement as a matter of form, and no more was heard of it. It was none the less decided to separate two men whose temperaments were wholly incompatible, yet who had to meet almost daily in the course of their duties. The Governorship of the island of Oléron[1] then happened to fall vacant. It was a good post, but entailed residence. That last obligation persuaded them to give it to Brilhac.

To record an extremely rare event: one of the workers in the diamond mines of the Great Mogul[2] managed to secrete a stone of enormous size in his hinder parts and, even more astonishing, to reach the sea and embark without undergoing the searches imposed on all passengers whose rank and occupation do not guarantee immunity—I mean of course purgings and *lavements*, obliging them to render up whatever they may have swallowed or otherwise concealed. It appears that he convinced everyone that he had not been to the mines, and was in no way connected with precious stones. To complete his phenomenal luck, he arrived safely in Europe with his diamond. He showed it to several reigning princes, but the price being too high for them, he took it to England, where the king greatly admired it, but could not bring himself to buy it.[4] An imitation was made in crystal, and the man, the diamond, and the imitation (an exact copy) were all sent to Law, who offered it to the Regent for the King. The price alarmed him also, and he refused it. Law, who in many fields had grand conceptions, came to me in dismay, bringing the copy with him. I agreed that it ill became a King of France to be put off by the cost of a unique and priceless jewel, and that since so many rulers longed to possess it, we ought not to let it escape us. Law was enchanted, and begged me to intercede with M. le Duc d'Orléans. The state of the finances was certainly an obstacle, and on this M. le Duc d'Orléans laid great stress. He feared to be blamed for such a vastly expensive purchase at a time when urgent necessities could hardly be supplied, and many people were in actual want.

I applauded those sentiments, but urged him not to rate the greatest king in Europe as though he were a private individual; I said that it might

---

[1] Oléron is near Rochefort, at the mouth of the Charente.

[2] The title given by Europeans to the Emperors of Delhi.

[3] This is the famous 'Regent's diamond'. The story is that it was bought by Thomas Pitt, Governor of Fort St. George (Madras) in 1701. He sent it to his son Robert, who had it cut. It remained in that state for two years. The jewel was worn in King George's crown, at his coronation, and was then offered to Louis XIV, who refused to buy it, perhaps on account of its price. M. Gonzague Truc, in his note to the Édition de la Pléiade, says that the transactions between Law and Saint-Simon are nowhere else recorded.

indeed be wicked to sink even a hundred thousand francs in a diamond for one's own adornment, at a time when one's debts remained unpaid. On the other hand, we must not lose this unique opportunity of acquiring a precious jewel that outshone every other diamond in Europe. It would, I said, be the everlasting glory of the Regency. No matter what the state of the finances, saving this amount would not much relieve them, and the spending of it would scarcely be noticed. In short, I did not leave M. le Duc d'Orléans until he had promised to buy the stone. In the meanwhile, Law had managed to convince the vendor that his price was an impossible one, and that he would lose heavily by cutting the diamond into smaller pieces. The sum was reduced to two million francs, to include the chips inevitable in cutting. In that way the bargain was clinched. The man was paid interest on his two millions until such time as the whole sum could be given him; and during the interval, two millions' worth of jewels were passed over to him as security. M. le Duc d'Orléans was most agreeably surprised by the public rejoicing at this splendid acquisition; and the stone was called 'The Regent', in his honour. It is the size of a greengage plum, almost circular, as thick as it is wide, perfectly white, free from all stains or cloudiness, indeed quite flawless, a diamond of the first water, weighing five hundred grammes. I was extremely elated at having persuaded the Regent to make this magnificent purchase.

Peter the First, Czar of Muscovy,[1] has won so much fame in his own country and throughout Europe and Asia, that I shall not attempt to describe him. This illustrious prince, comparable to the heroes of olden time, the admiration of his century, will continue to be admired for centuries to come. His journey to France was such an astonishing event that I must not omit any portion of it, or interrupt in any way the flow of the narrative. I shall therefore place it here, although rather earlier than it actually took place. You already know that this monarch had made journeys to Holland, Germany, Vienna, England, and many parts of northern Europe,[2] and you will remember that he wished to visit France also during the last years of Louis XIV's reign, but was politely discouraged. Now that the King was dead, he proposed to satisfy his curiosity, and informed the Regent to that effect, through Prince Kurakin, his ambassador. The Regent would gladly have dispensed with his society but there was nothing for it except to appear pleased.[3]

Kurakin came of a branch of the Jagellons, the ancient dynasty that reigned so long over Poland, Denmark, Norway, and Sweden. He was tall and very handsome, extremely conscious of his high birth, a man of parts,

[1] See above, p. 91.

[2] In fact Saint-Simon has not mentioned these journeys before: they took place 1697–1698 when Peter worked with his own hands in the shipbuilding yards of Holland and at Deptford, London.

[3] The French people were immensely interested by the Czar's visit, but they found the Russians' manners and habits extremely alarming, and occasionally rather funny.

capability, and learning. He spoke French moderately, and several other languages well; had travelled a great deal, served in the wars, and been given employment at many different courts. He was none the less still unmistakably Russian, and his extreme avarice greatly marred his talents. The Czar and he had married two sisters, and each of them had a son. The Czarina had been repudiated and sent to a convent, near Moscow;[1] but her disgrace had not affected Kurakin, who perfectly understood his master, and had established with him a relationship of intimacy, trust, and latterly of affection.

As soon as the Regent learned of the Czar's imminent approach by sea, he sent a large consignment from the King's stables—horses, coaches, carriages, waggons, table and room furniture, under de Liboy,[2] one of the King's gentlemen—to meet him at Dunkirk, and defray all expenses as far as Paris, ensuring that he everywhere received similar honours to the King of France himself. The visit was expected to last a hundred days. They refurnished the Queen-mother's apartments at the Louvre for his occupation, and the councils that ordinarily met there were forced to assemble at the houses of their heads. M. le Duc d'Orléans consulted me as to what great noble he should choose to attend the Czar during his visit, and I recommended the Maréchal de Tessé because he was un-employed, well bred, used to the ways of the world and to foreign royalty as a result of his wartime travelling and his diplomatic posts in Spain, Rome, and Turin. He was, I declared, a perfect gentleman and sure to do admirably. M. le Duc d'Orléans agreed, and immediately sent for Tessé to give him his orders. Tessé, bored with idleness, was dividing his time between his house in Paris and his country home at the Camaldolite monastery, near Grosbois. In both he had room enough to lodge his entire family, and at both he entertained as many guests as he could muster, thereby hoping to pass for having retired.[3] He was naturally enchanted at being chosen to attend on the Czar, accompany him everywhere, and make the presentations. It was an excellent job for him and he did it to perfection.

When the Czar neared Dunkirk, the Regent sent the Marquis de Nesles[4] to welcome him at Calais and accompany him on the way to Paris until the arrival of the Maréchal de Tessé, who was ordered to go no farther than Beaumont. It was then decided to prepare also the Hôtel de Lesdiguières

[1] The Convent of Susdahl. Peter the Great had repudiated her in 1692. Their son Alexis Petrovich (1690–1718), a studious young man, despised by Peter, fled abroad, but was persuaded to return, when he was imprisoned and knouted to death.

[2] Étienne Rossius de Liboy La Rochefoucauld, Marquis de Liboy. Borne at Liège, and naturalized French in 1701, he was a gentleman-in-ordinary to the King.

[3] Tessé, in the fearful quarrel between Orléans, Mme de Maintenon, and the Princesse des Ursins, had been on Mme des Ursins's side, and had never afterwards been on good terms with the Regent, which was why he had been given no post on any of the councils.

[4] Louis III de Mailly, Marquis de Nesles (1689–1767). He was Capitaine-lieutenant of the Scottish division of the gendarmes (the Maison du Roi).

as a lodging for the Czar and his staff, in the belief that he would prefer a private residence, surrounded by his own people, to sleeping at the Louvre. The Hôtel de Lesdiguières, a fine large house, adjacent to the Arsenal, belonged to the Maréchal de Villeroy, who lodged at the Tuileries, which was how the house came to be empty, for Villeroy was not an active man, and had found it too far from his work. It was completely and magnificently refurnished, with pieces from the King's collection.

Tessé waited an entire day at Beaumont lest the Czar should arrive early. He at length appeared on Friday, 7 May, at noon precisely. Tessé made his bow at the coach door, had the honour of dining with him afterwards, and that same afternoon escorted him to Paris. When they arrived, however, the Czar chose to enter the city in one of the Marshal's coaches, but not in his company, preferring to drive with three members of his own staff. Thus Tessé followed in a second coach. They alighted at the Louvre at nine in the evening. The Czar inspected every room of the Queen-mother's suite, but thought them too luxurious and too brightly lit. He at once stepped back into his coach and went to the Hôtel de Lesdiguières, where he decided to lodge. There also he thought the rooms much too grand; and he had his camp-bed set up in one of the closets.[1] The Maréchal de Tessé, whose duty it was to do the honours of his house and table and accompany him everywhere, also had rooms in the Hôtel de Lesdiguières. He had his work cut out in trying to stay with the Czar, and was sometimes reduced to chasing after him. Verton,[2] one of the King's stewards, had charge of the service, and of the tables for the retinue, numbering altogether forty persons, twelve or fifteen of whom were of sufficient importance either by birth or function to eat at the Czar's table. Verton had his wits about him, and figured large in certain circles. He was a great one for good eating and gambling high. He ordered the household so efficiently and showed so much tact and goodwill that the Czar became remarkably friendly with him, and so did the suite.

Everyone marvelled at the Czar's insatiable curiosity about everything that had any bearing on his views of government, commerce, education, police methods, etc. His interests embraced each detail capable of practical application, and overlooked nothing. His intelligence was most marked; in his appreciation of merit, or the reverse, he showed great perception and a most lively understanding, everywhere displaying extensive knowledge, and a logical flow of ideas. In character he was an extraordinary com-

[1] Changing out of the royal coach, leaving behind Tessé, with his glittering uniform, inspecting every room at the Louvre, refusing the state bedroom at the Hôtel de Lesdiguières and choosing to sleep in a small closet—did he fear assassination? On the other hand, royalties often seem to have disliked their bedrooms—Monseigneur used a cupboard under the stairs; Mme la Duchesse d'Orléans redecorated her privy; later, Louis XV, Napoleon, and Francis Joseph, all slept on camp-beds. One wonders whether this practice still continues.

[2] Louis François de Verton (1670–1751). He had been major-domo of the Duchesse de Bourgogne and then of Louis XV. Later he became grand master of woods and forests.

bination: he assumed majesty at its most regal, most fastidious, most unbending; yet, once his supremacy had been granted, his demeanour was infinitely gracious and full of discriminating courtesy. Everywhere and at all times he was the master, but with degrees of familiarity according to a person's rank. He had a friendly approach, which one associated with freedom, but was not exempt from a strong flavour of his country's past lack of culture. Thus his manners were rough, even violent, his wishes unpredictable, brooking no delay, or the very least opposition. His table manners were unseemly, and those of his staff still less elegant. He was determined to be free and independent in all that he wished to do or see, without the slightest regard for the comfort or convenience of others. His dislike of being recognized was such that he frequently chose to use hired coaches, sometimes even *fiacres*,[1] or the first vehicle that came to hand, no matter to whom it belonged. Mme de Matignon[2] discovered this to her cost when she went to gape at him, for he took her coach out to Boulogne[3] and other country places, and left her stranded, much disgusted at having to return home on foot. It was at such times that the Maréchal de Tessé and the suite were forced to chase after him, and more often than not failed to catch up with him.

Peter the Great was a huge man, very well proportioned, on the thin side, with a round face, a broad forehead, and very well marked eyebrows; his nose was short, without any distinguishing feature, but rather thick at the tip. His lips were thick also, his complexion reddish-brown; he had very fine black eyes, large, piercing, wide open; when he was attentive his glance was royal and gracious, at other times it appeared fierce and severe. He had a kind of nervous tic that contorted his entire face and was most alarming; it lasted only a moment, accompanied by a most ferocious stare; then it was gone. His whole appearance suggested brilliance, thoughtfulness and nobility, and was not without grace. He wore a simple linen collar, a brown and unpowdered wig, falling short of his shoulders, a jacket of plain material with gold buttons, a waistcoat, breeches, and stockings; neither gloves nor shirtcuffs. The star of his order was worn outside his coat, and the ribbon beneath.[4] His coat was usually unbuttoned all the way down; his hat was always on a table, never on his head, not even out of doors. For all the simplicity of his attire, his humble conveyances and companions, there was no mistaking the air of nobility that was his by nature.

It was incredible how much he drank and ate at his two regular meals, not counting all the beer, lemonade, and other beverages which he consumed in between. As for the suite, they drank even more: one or two

[1] Paris street-cabs were called *fiacres* because the first stand for them had been outside the Hôtel de Saint-Fiacre, in 1640.
[2] Charlotte Goyon, Comtesse de Matignon (1657–1721).
[3] To the Bois de Boulogne.
[4] The order was the Star of Saint Andrew.

bottles of beer, the same amount or even more of wine, various liqueurs to follow, and after meals a brew of punch, half a litre per head, sometimes nearly a quart. That was their usual ration at all their meals. Those at his own table drank more copiously and ate correspondingly more at eleven in the morning and at eight o'clock at night. When they stuck to that, they appeared sober enough. There was an almoner-priest, twice the size of the others, who ate at the Czar's table and hugely diverted him. Prince Kurakin went every day to the Hôtel de Lesdiguières, but lodged at his own residence. The Czar understood French, and I think could have spoken it had he so wished; but to preserve his dignity he always used an interpreter. He spoke Latin and other languages very well indeed. There was a guard of honour from the King's bodyguard posted in one of the rooms, but he rarely availed himself of it when he went abroad. Eager though he was to see everything, the Czar refused to leave the Hôtel de Lesdiguières or show any sign of life until after the King had visited him.

It was on the following Monday, 10 May, that the King called on the Czar, who received him on the steps; saw him get out of his coach, and walked on his left side to the state drawing-room, where two identical armchairs had been placed. Prince Kurakin acted as interpreter. All were astounded to see the Czar pick the little King up under his arms, and swing him up to his own level in order to embrace him. The King, young as he was,[1] was quite unafraid. It was very moving to see the Czar's gentleness with him; he appeared to grow fond of him, showing innate courtesy, mingled with royal dignity, equality of rank, and some slight superiority because of his age. All this was clearly visible. He praised the King very highly, seemed enchanted with him, and convinced everyone of his sincerity. He several times kissed him. The King said his little speech very well, and M. du Maine and the Maréchal de Villeroy, assisted by some of the entourage, helped to keep the conversation alive. This interview lasted less than a quarter of an hour. The Czar then escorted the King to the front door, in the same way as on his arrival, and saw him enter his coach.

On Tuesday, 11 May, the Czar returned the King's visit between four and five o'clock. The King welcomed him at the coach door and conducted him in similar fashion, giving him precedence everywhere. The Czar was as gentle and as fond as before, and the visit lasted no longer; but he was greatly astonished to see such crowds of courtiers. At eight o'clock that same morning he had been to see the Place Royale, the Place des Victoires, and the Place Vendôme, and next day he went to the Observatory, the Gobelins factory, and the garden of the Royal Apothecaries.[2] He was vastly interested in all that he saw, examined everything, and asked innumerable questions.

[1] Louis XV was seven on 15 February 1717.
[2] The present Jardin des Plantes, then only a botanical garden, and without the zoo. Earlier still it had been a herb garden only.

On Thursday, 13 May, he took physic;[1] but that did not stop him from going to see some highly skilled craftsmen.[2] On Friday the 14th, he went at six in the morning to the great gallery of the Louvre to inspect plans and models of the King's fortresses, which were shown him by Asfeld[3] and his engineers. The Maréchal de Villars was there also for the same reason, with some of his lieutenants-general. The Czar spent a long time examining the plans in detail. He then went to the other departments of the Louvre, and afterwards out into the Tuileries gardens, which were shut to the public. At that time they were working on the revolving bridge. He very carefully inspected that, and stayed there a long time asking questions.

After dinner he visited Madame at the Palais Royal. M. le Duc d'Orléans called for him there to go to the Opéra, and sat alone with him on the front seats of the royal box, with a most magnificent carpet spread before them. Shortly after the beginning, the Czar asked if he might have some beer. A large goblet, on a salver, was immediately produced. The Regent rose; took it, and offered it to the Czar who, without rising, but smiling and bowing politely, received it, drank, and put it back on the salver, which the Regent had continued to hold. After relinquishing it, he handed a dish with a napkin on it to the Czar who, again without rising, took it as he had taken the beer. It was really an astonishing sight. When the fourth act had begun, he departed to his supper, but desired the Regent not to leave the box. Next day, which was Saturday, he leapt into a hired coach and went to inspect a great number of curious and beautiful objects in the process of manufacture.

On Whit Sunday, 16 May, he went to the Invalides and insisted on seeing and examining everything. In the refectory he tasted the soldiers' soup, and tried their wine; drank to their health, patted them on the shoulder, and called them his comrades. He especially admired the chapel, the dispensary, and the infirmary; and appeared altogether enchanted with the way in which the hospital was governed. The Maréchal de Villars did the honours. Mme de Villars attended, but only as an onlooker; the Czar recognized her, however, and paid her many polite attentions.

On Monday, 17 May, he invited Prince Ragotzi[4] to dine with him. They went afterwards to Meudon, where some of the King's horses were in readiness to enable him to see the park and gardens at his leisure.

Tuesday, 18th: the Maréchal d'Estrées called for him at eight o'clock and took him by coach to his house at Issy, where they dined, and spent a

[1] No doubt his monthly purge.

[2] In the Faubourg Saint-André, for example, there was the looking-glass factory.

[3] Saint-Simon's friend. See index, I and II. He was a member of the council for war, specializing in fortifications.

[4] Prince Francis Leopold Ragotzi (1679–1735). He was a Hungarian whose father had been one of the candidates for the Polish throne in 1688. This prince, chief of the 'Malcontents' who attacked Vienna in 1703 (see index, I, under Hungary) had taken refuge in France, and played no further part in politics.

most interesting afternoon examining various matters concerned with the navy.

Wednesday, 19th: he busied himself with numerous craftsmen. Later in the morning, Mme la Duchesse de Berry and Mme la Duchesse d'Orléans sent their first equerries with their compliments. They expected some polite message in return, or perhaps a visit; but no answer was forthcoming, and they were obliged to lower their sights. The Czar finally sent word that he would call and thank them another day. As for the princes and princesses of the blood, he took no more account of them than of the other nobility at the Court.

Thursday, 20th: he had intended to go to Saint-Cloud, where M. le Duc d'Orléans waited to receive him; but a touch of fever, contracted on the previous evening, forced him to send his excuses.

Friday, 21st: he visited Mme la Duchesse de Berry, at the Luxembourg, and was received with the same honours as the King. Later, he walked in the gardens. Mme la Duchesse de Berry went out hunting, so as to enable him to explore her entire residence, which he did with keen interest. In the expectation that he would leave France on 16 June, he ordered barges to be in readiness to convey him down the Meuse.[1]

Saturday, 22nd: he visited, at Bercy, the house of Pajot d'Ons-en-Bray,[2] head of the post office, because it contained all manner of rare and curious objects and contrivances, some natural, others mechanical. The celebrated Carmelite, Père Sébastien,[3] attended to show him everything, and the Czar spent a very happy day, admiring many strange and marvellous things.

On Sunday, 23 May, he dined with M. le Duc d'Orléans, at Saint-Cloud, and was shown the house and gardens, which greatly pleased him. On the return he stopped to see the Château de Madrid,[4] and thence went to visit Mme la Duchesse d'Orléans at the Palais Royal. Although extremely polite, his manner to her was infinitely more condescending than it had been either to Madame or to Mme la Duchesse de Berry.[5]

Monday, 24th: he went early to the Tuileries, before the King was awake, and was shown the crown jewels in the apartments of the Maréchal de Villeroy. He said that they were finer and more numerous than he had

---

[1] Travelling by barge up or down the great rivers was a normal mode. Generals, during Louis XIV's wars, often came and went in that way at the beginning and end of campaigns. It will be remembered that Marlborough was for a moment taken prisoner when his barge was ambushed. See I, p. 205.

[2] Louis Léon Pajot, Comte d'Ons-en-Bray (1679–1754). He had been made intendant-général des postes in 1708.

[3] He was Jean Truchet (1657–1729), very famous for his mechanical inventions, especially hydraulic machines.

[4] A charming little house in the Bois de Boulogne, built and named by François I who was taken prisoner of war by the Spaniards. He was allowed home on parole after giving his word of honour to return to Madrid at stated intervals. And so he did, but to his little château, and not the Spanish capital.

[5] Because her husband was not a Son of France, or perhaps because she was born illegitimate.

supposed; but admitted that he knew little of such things. In fact he showed very little interest in objects whose beauty was confined to their value or artistry. Afterwards he desired to see the King, who was brought to him in the Maréchal de Villeroy's apartment. This was done purposely, so as to make their encounter seem informal, as it were by accident. They met in one of the offices and stayed there to converse. The King held a roll of paper in his hand, and gave it to the Czar, saying that it was a map of his dominions. This enchanted the Czar, who was as polite, friendly, and affectionate as before, and as gracious, but also very royal, speaking to the King as to an equal.

That same afternoon he went to Versailles, where the Maréchal de Tessé left him with d'Antin to do the honours. Mme la Dauphine's apartments had been prepared for him, but he slept in the corridor outside Monseigneur le Dauphin's room. I am speaking of the father of the present King. Those same rooms are now the offices of the Queen's apartments.

Tuesday, 25th: he was up very early, and had been through the gardens and in a boat on the canal by the time d'Antin arrived. He saw all over Versailles, Trianon, and the Menagerie. The suite were lodged in the château. They brought young women with them, and bedded them down in Mme de Maintenon's old rooms, quite near to where the Czar slept. Blouin, Governor of Versailles, was horribly shocked to see that temple of chastity so defiled. He and its late goddess were old now; they might not have been so particular in days gone by.[1] It did not suit the Czar or his Staff to restrain themselves in any way.

Wednesday, 26th: the Czar spent a busy day seeing Marly and the Machine,[2] and hugely enjoyed himself. He sent to inform the Maréchal de Tessé that he would return to the Hôtel de Lesdiguières next morning at eight o'clock, and wished to see the Corpus Christi procession. The Marshal was there to greet him on his arrival, and escorted him to Notre-Dame.

The expenses of the Czar's visit amounted to six hundred écus a day, even though, after the first few days, he greatly reduced the number of his guests. At one moment he had thought of sending for the Czarina,[3] for he was deeply attached to her; but on further reflection he sent to tell her to

[1] Saint-Simon was always accusing Mme de Maintenon of being nothing better than a prostitute when she was the Widow Scarron in 1660. It was all hearsay. Saint-Simon was not born until fifteen years later.

[2] The famous hydraulic machine (still existing in 1971) on the banks of the Seine, by means of which the waters of underground streams were brought to Versailles.

[3] Peter's second wife. An orphan named Martha Skavronskaya (c. 1684–1727), she was born in Livronia, brought up by a Lutheran pastor at Marienburg, and married a Swedish dragoon; when in 1702 the Russians captured Marienburg she attracted the notice of a Russian general who sold her to Prince Menshikov at whose house Peter saw her and fell in love with her, making her his mistress. She was received into the Orthodox Church in 1710 and renamed Catherine; in 1711 Peter divorced Eudoxia and married Catherine. Crowned empress consort in 1724, she succeeded Peter as Catherine I.

go either to Aix-la-Chapelle or else to Spa, whichever she preferred, and to take the waters until his arrival.

Sunday, 30 May: he went with Bellegarde[1] (d'Antin's son and reversioner) to dine at Petit-Bourg, and thence to Fontainebleau, where he slept. He did not much enjoy Fontainebleau, and positively disliked the hunt for, not being a very expert rider, he nearly tumbled off his horse. He said the exercise was altogether too violent. On his return, he insisted on eating alone with his suite, on the island in the lake of the Fountain Court, so that they might recover from their fatigue. He then drove back to Petit-Bourg in a coach, alone with three of his staff. From the state of the coach, it appeared that they had eaten and drunk a very great amount.

Tuesday, 1 June: he embarked from the terrace at Petit-Bourg, and returned to Paris by water. When they reached Choisy, he desired to stop and view the house and gardens, which obliged him to pay a short visit to Mme la Princesse de Conti who was in residence. He walked a little while in the gardens, re-embarked, and asked to be taken beneath all the bridges of Paris.

Thursday, 3 June: the eighth day after Corpus Christi. He watched the procession from the parish church of Saint-Paul, standing on the balcony of the Hôtel de Lesdiguières. Later that day he returned to Versailles, being anxious to explore it at greater leisure. He was enchanted by everything, and asked to sleep also at Trianon. He next spent three or four nights at Marly, sleeping in the pavilions nearest the château, they having been made ready for his use.

Friday, 11 June: from Versailles he went to Saint-Cyr; inspected the school, and watched the young ladies at their lessons. They received him with the same honours as though he had been the King. He desired to see Mme de Maintenon who, at the first intimation, retired to bed and drew close all her curtains, with the exception of one, which they left half-drawn. The Czar entered, flung wide first the window-curtains, then all the bed-curtains,[2] took a long, leisurely look at her, uttered not a word, nor she to him, and then went his way, without the smallest suspicion of a bow. I learned afterwards that she was at first stunned and, later, greatly mortified; but Louis XIV was no longer alive.[3]

On Sunday, 13 June, the Czar went early to d'Antin's Paris house. This was one of the days when I customarily worked with M. le Duc d'Orléans; but I was finished in half an hour. He appeared surprised and tried to keep me; but I said that I should always have the honour of waiting on him, but not of seeing the Czar, for he was about to leave France. I had not yet

[1] Gabriel François Balthazar de Pardaillon, Marquis de Bellegarde. He died in 1719, aged only thirty.

[2] Poor Mme de Maintenon; she was then eighty-two. On the other hand, she must have felt a ghost of the past. She always felt the cold. Louis had liked fresh air. His first action had always been to fling wide open all the windows, regardless of the weather or her feelings.

[3] There exists another version of this interview: according to Mme de Louvigny, one of the nuns at Saint-Cyr, the Czar was perfectly charming to her.

Photo : Archives Photographiques

THE PALAIS ROYAL FROM THE GARDEN SIDE. ENGRAVING

LOUIS XV VISITING PETER THE GREAT IN THE HÔTEL DES LESDIGUIÈRES:
A LATER RECONSTRUCTION. BY LOUISE MARIE JEANNE HERSENT

Photo : Cliché des Musées Nationaux

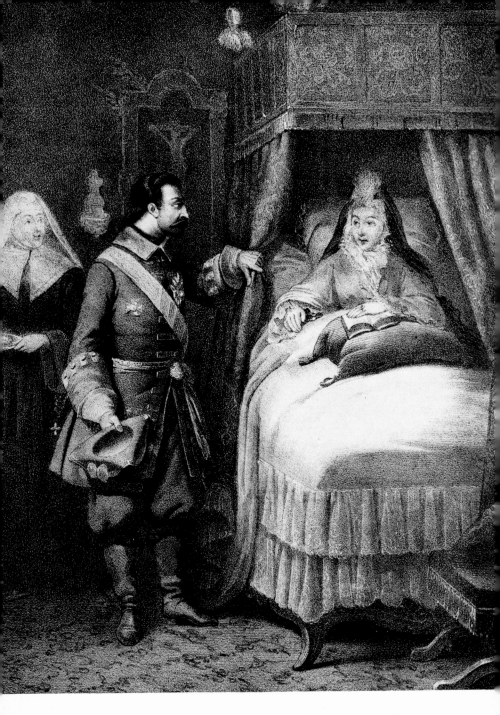

THE CZAR VISITING MME DE MAINTENON AT
SAINT-CYR. LITHOGRAPH BY LAFOSSE AFTER PINGUET

PHILIP V OF SPAIN.
BY JEAN RANC

Photo : Museo del Prado

ELIZABETH FARNESE,
PHILIP V OF SPAIN'S
SECOND WIFE.
BY JEAN RANC

Photo : Museo del Prado

LOUIS XV AND THE SPANISH INFANTA

Photo: Bazzech

clapped eyes on him, and planned to go to d'Antin's so as to have my fill of gazing at him. No one was present who had not been invited, except for some ladies accompanying Madame la Duchesse and her daughters, who like myself had come to stare. The Maréchal de Tessé, seeing me across the room, came over, all eagerness to present me; but I begged him on no account to do so, because I wished to be free to gaze at my leisure, going on before, and, whenever possible, letting him pass in front of me, so as to give me the chance of a good long look, which I should not have if he knew me. I begged him to warn d'Antin and, thus protected, I was able to satisfy my curiosity. I thought the Czar reasonably affable, but behaving as though he were everywhere the master. He then retired into one of the studies, where d'Antin showed him maps and other documents of interest. He asked many questions. That was when I noticed the tic I remarked on earlier; I asked Tessé whether it happened often, and he said several times a day, especially when he was off his guard.

They went into the garden, and d'Antin made as if to take him past the ground-floor windows, informing him that Madame la Duchesse was inside with some ladies who much wished to see him. He made no reply, but let himself be conducted, walking more slowly, with his head turned towards the drawing-room where everyone was drawn up to attention, but merely as spectators. He looked at them all individually, but made only a very slight inclination to the company in general, not letting his eye travel down the row, and passed on somewhat haughtily. I surmised from the manner in which he had greeted other ladies that he might have shown more courtesy had Madame la Duchesse not been there. It is possible that he considered her presence an intrusion.[1] Indeed, he made a pretence of not knowing her, or the names of the other ladies. I spent nearly an hour there, never letting him out of my sight; gazing at him continually. Towards the end of the time, I seemed to observe that he noticed me,[2] which made me rather more cautious, for fear lest he should ask my name. When he re-entered the house, I went on ahead into the room where refreshments had been prepared. D'Antin (so like him)[3] had managed to find a portrait closely resembling the Czarina, and had hung it over the chimney-piece, with verses in her praise, which hugely delighted and surprised the Czar. He and the suite said that the picture was very like.

The King presented him with two magnificent tapestries from the Gobelins factory; and wished also to give him a beautiful sword with a diamond hilt, but this the Czar politely refused. He on his part distributed about sixty thousand livres among the King's servants who had attended him; gave d'Antin, and the Maréchaux d'Estrées and de Tessé, each his

---

[1] Saint-Simon is hinting once again that the Czar drew the line at bastards.

[2] He could scarcely not have noticed. One feels that the tiny figure of Saint-Simon, somewhere round his knees, must have been as obvious as a crouching press photographer of today.

[3] D'Antin, the perfect courtier! The reader will remember how he felled a whole avenue of beautiful trees because the King remarked that they spoiled the view. See I, p. 339.

portrait set in diamonds, with five gold and eleven silver medals depicting the greatest actions of his life. He gave a personal present to Verton, out of friendship, and earnestly requested the Regent to send him to Russia on the King's business,[1] which the Regent promised to do.

Wednesday, 16 June: he reviewed on horseback both regiments of the guard, the horseguards, light horse, and musketeers. M. le Duc d'Orléans alone attended him. The Czar scarcely looked at the troops, a fact which they observed. Thence he went to Saint-Ouen, to a splendid banquet given by the Duc de Tresmes,[2] where he acknowledged having been so overcome by the heat and dust, and the crowds of people riding and on foot, that he had left the review sooner than he had intended. On learning that the Marquise de Béthune (who was present only to see) was the Duc de Tresmes's daughter,[3] he begged her to be seated at the table. She was the only lady amid a very great company of noblemen. Several other ladies attended merely as spectators, and he was exceedingly civil to all of them, once he had discovered who they were.

On Friday, 18 June, the Regent went early to the Hôtel de Lesdiguières to bid the Czar farewell. He remained with him some little time, Prince Kurakin making a third. After that, the Czar went to the Tuileries to visit the King. It had been arranged beforehand that there should be no ceremony. No one could have been sweeter or gentler than the Czar on all the occasions when he and the King met, and so he was on the following day, when the King visited the Hôtel de Lesdiguières to wish him a pleasant journey.

Sunday, 20 June: the Czar departed and slept at Livry, going thence straight to Spa, where the Czarina awaited him. He refused to have any escort, even on leaving Paris. He was astounded by the display of wealth, and visibly moved at parting from the King and leaving France; but he said it grieved him to think that so much luxury must before long be the ruin of our country. He was delighted with the welcome given him, the sights he had seen, and the freedom allowed him, and he expressed a strong desire to be closely allied with our King. The interests of the Abbé Dubois and of the English tragically prevented that; for which we have had, and still continue to have, good reason to be sorry.

One might go on for ever expatiating on this truly great man and emperor, with his remarkable character and wide range of extraordinary talents. They will make him a monarch worthy of profound admiration for countless years, despite the severe handicaps of his own and his country's lack of culture and civilization. Such was the reputation he gained everywhere in France, where he was considered a veritable prodigy, and remembered with enduring pleasure.

[1] In other words, as ambassador to Moscow. He was not, however, sent.
[2] The Duc de Tresmes, governor of Paris, was renowned for his banquets. See II, pp. 89, 329.
[3] She was Marie Françoise Potier de Tresmes (1697–1764).

I learned that the Czar visited M. le Duc d'Orléans, at the Palais Royal, very soon after his arrival, and that he never went again. I know that M. le Duc d'Orléans received him at the door of his coach, and saw him off in the same way; that they conversed alone in one of the studies, with Prince Kurakin acting as interpreter, and that the session was a long one, but I forget the actual day. The Czar did earnestly wish to be allied with France. Nothing would better have suited our commerce, or given us greater influence in the North, in Germany, and in the rest of Europe; for Russia was in a position to restrict British trade, and King George feared for his Hanoverian possessions. No one can deny that France would have gained much by the Czar's friendship. He had no liking for the Emperor, and hoped gradually to detach us from our servitude to England. It was England itself that made us deaf to his appeals and to his constant invitations which continued long after his return.

It was in vain that I repeatedly pressed the Regent on that point, offering reasons which he agreed were sound, and for which he had no answer. Unhappily, the influence of the Abbé Dubois prevailed. His mind was set on the cardinalate, though he had not yet dared to confess this to his master. England provided his best hope in that direction, and had already greatly assisted him, encouraged by his long acquaintance with Stanhope. The English understood his ambitions and his power, and were eager to make him their friend. Dubois's aim was to use the strong attachment existing between the King of England and the Emperor, in order to persuade the latter to nominate him to the Pope. It was that joyful prospect which kept us chained to England, in terms of such complete subjection that the Regent dared do nothing without King George's permission, which would certainly not have been forthcoming for an alliance with the Czar. We have since had much time in which to deplore the fatal charms of England, and our folly in scorning Russia. Our misfortunes have followed one upon another, and when at last our eyes were opened, they beheld our total ruin, made final by the ministry of Monsieur le Duc, and later by Cardinal de Fleury, both of them corrupted by England—the former with vast sums of money paid to his mistress;[1] the latter by downright, mad infatuation.

In Martinique, an event so extraordinary occurred that one might truthfully say it was unique. La Varenne[2] had succeeded Phélypeaux[3] as governor and captain-general of that island; Ricouart[4] was the

---

[1] After the Regent's death in 1723, Monsieur le Duc for a time took over the direction of affairs. He was entirely under the thumb of his mistress, Agnès Berthelot de Pléneuf, Marquise de Prye (1698–1727).

[2] The Marquis de La Varenne. He had been a naval captain.

[3] Raymond Balthazar Phélypeaux du Verger, who had died in Martinique in 1713. He had been ambassador to Cologne, and later to Turin.

[4] Louis Balthazar de Ricouart (d. 1759): he later changed his name to d'Héronville. The intendant was the King's representative in a province.

intendant. They lived in perfect harmony and busied themselves making immense fortunes. The inhabitants they maltreated abominably. Many complaints were sent to France, but all went unanswered. At last, driven beyond endurance by tyranny and pillage, and despairing of ever receiving justice, the islanders decided to take the law into their own hands. Nothing could have been more deliberate than the plan, more secret in direction, quieter or more devious in execution. The culprits were suddenly arrested at their houses, both at the selfsame moment; their papers were placed under seal, likewise all their belongings; nothing was stolen; no harm came to any of their servants. They were put into a vessel about to leave for France, and the anchor was immediately weighed. The captain was given letters for the Regent, full of protestations of loyalty and obedience, asking forgiveness for the action they had taken, reminding him of their unavailing complaints, pleading that they were no longer able to endure such cruel afflictions. Picture, if you can, the astonishment of those two, so lately the lords of their island, now seized and transported in the twinkling of an eye! Imagine their fury on the voyage, their shame on arrival! The islanders' conduct could not be approved, but it could scarcely be blamed, since clearly they had had great provocation, and their calm and restraint had been most admirable; moreover their behaviour while waiting for a new governor and intendant was so quiet and submissive that it merited only praise. Varenne and Ricouart dared not show themselves after their first formal appearance, and were not re-employed.[1] Their successors (who had been taught a good lesson) brought no reprimand for the inhabitants when they landed at Martinique—a tacit admission of regret for disregarding their just complaints and thus forcing them to seek their own salvation.

At this time, a man died to a round of applause for ridding society of his unwanted presence—and this although he was in no position to do good or harm to anyone, being merely a counsellor of State, without other office. I speak of Harlay,[2] only son of the former premier président, and the bane of his father's life, as his father had been the bane of his, and as each continued to be throughout their entire lives, which they spent always in the same house. You already know the father. His son was less brilliant, but his ambition, fed by most insane vanity, was beyond measure. By nature he was priggish, precise, pedagogic, malicious, and affected, always searching after epigrams, none of which was original, or else humourlessly repeating his father's witticisms. He was an extraordinary mixture of the outward gravity of the old-fashioned magistrate, and the foppishness of the modern practitioner, for he combined all the dreariness of the first with all

[1] Saint-Simon must have forgotten. In 1720 Ricouart became intendant of the navy at Dunkirk, then the King's lieutenant at Le Havre. M. de La Varenne became a commodore in 1720.

[2] Achille IV de Harlay (1669–1717), son of Achille III de Harlay (1639–1712). See index, I and II.

the absurdity of the second. His voice, his posture, his whole bearing were those of some wretched half-trained actor. A great gambler and hunter (by his own report), aping the glory of princes, he made the worst of himself (if that were possible) by using a severe expression to cover a sad, despondent heart, and a disposition that was utterly insupportable. Yet at the same time he was the most hardened libertine imaginable, and as open regarding his vices as any young student at the Academy.[1] You might fill a book, and an extremely funny one too, with tales of the domestic life of this father and son. They never conversed on any subject; but notes flew from one to the other, so bitter, so malevolent, that more often than not they appeared merely facetious. When his son entered the room, the father invariably rose to his feet, even when they were alone, solemnly removed his hat, ordered a chair for M. de Harlay, and covered and reseated himself only when the chair was in position. After that came endless compliments, and for the rest, just words. At their meals it was the same, one continual masquerade. In their heart of hearts, they loathed one another, and both had good reason to do so.

Harlay died as obscurely as he lived. He owned a large and excellently stocked library, with a great number of manuscripts on different subjects which he left to Chauvelin, later keeper of the seals,[2] who cleverly used them as a rung on the ladder to fortune. Since he cared little for religion, he left Chauvelin his religious books also;[3] the remainder of his library he left to the Jesuits. Harlay was not yet fifty when he died, and the thought of this ridiculous bequest thoroughly amused him. I may perhaps have dallied too long with this essentially unimportant person, but I could not resist portraying his quite extraordinary character.

25 August was the feast of Saint-Louis, when it is the custom for the orchestra of the Opéra to give a free concert to the public, in the Tuileries gardens. The King's presence in the palace drew larger crowds this year than usual, in the hope of seeing him appear on the terrace outside his apartments. A new feeling of loyalty was in the air, as was shown by the swarms of people assembled not only in the garden itself, but beyond, in the streets and on the Place. Not a seat was left empty, not only at the windows, but even on the roof of every house with a view of the Tuileries. The Maréchal de Villeroy, with some difficulty, induced the King to show himself from time to time, to those either in the garden, or in the streets, and whenever he appeared there were repeated cries of 'Long live the King!' The Maréchal pointed to the enormous crowds and solemnly said,

---

[1] The riding academy where young gentlemen (including Saint-Simon) learned equitation: the *Académie des Sieurs de Mesmont et Rochefort.*

[2] Germain Louis Chauvelin de Crisenoy (1685–1762). At the time of his bequest he was avocat-général of the Parlement; he became a président-à-mortier in 1718, and keeper of the seals 1727–1737.

[3] In 1755 Chauvelin gave his part of Harlay's library to the Abbey of Saint-Germain des Prés. During the Revolution, it was sent to the Bibliothèque Nationale.

'Look, Sire, at these crowds, these hosts of people. They all belong to you; you are their master.' And over and over again he repeated that lesson, until he was sure of having driven it into the King's head. It seems that he feared lest the King forget his sovereign power. The wonderful Dauphin, father of the King, was very differently taught, and profited by the lessons. He firmly believed that although kings have power to rule and command, their people do not belong to them, but they to their people, that they may give them justice, keep them under the law, and make them happy by the wisdom, equity, and moderation of their government. How often have I heard him say this from the heart, with absolute conviction, and the fixed determination to be guided throughout his life by that maxim! This he said, not to me only, in the privacy of his study as we prepared for his future reign; but several times in public, out loud, in the drawing-room at Marly, to the admiration and intense delight of all who heard him.[1]

The marriage of Chalmazel,[2] a man of quality (now the Queen's steward), to one of Harcourt's sisters,[3] revived a claim to precedence, by the wives and daughters of princes of the blood, which the late King had judged and expressly disallowed. You will remember this attempt,[4] and the King's ruling that had never previously been challenged. At the signing of Chalmazel's contract, however, Mme la Duchesse d'Orléans made her daughters sign so close after her name that no space remained above theirs for the wives of the princes of the blood when the document was presented for their signatures. Mme la Duchesse d'Orléans, as you know, had been completely shattered by the late King's decision; but secretly she had never relinquished hope. Her aim was to create a new rank of Great-grandchildren of France for her children, which would give them precedence over the children of the princes of the blood; and then, by almost imperceptible stages, to raise herself to the level of a Daughter of France. M. le Duc d'Orléans's regency appeared to her an excellent time for the first step. She was mistaken. The princes and their wives made an appalling rumpus, and came brandishing the royal decree to complain to the Regent. He apologized, and promised that such a thing should not occur again. Personally, he cared nothing for the claim. On the first occasion he had let his wife have her way because he hated to upset her when her heart was set on something. It did not distress him that the late King had refused her, and he had not given the matter another thought. In any event, the continual and pointless scenes between Mme la Duchesse de Berry and

---

[1] Saint-Simon had twice been invited to become governor of the little King. Strange that, with such strong feelings, he should have refused, especially since the revered Duc de Beauvilliers had been governor of the Duc de Bourgogne. Did he feel incapable of taking responsibility? Had court intrigues made him frightened of more criticism? Was it that he was so much an artist by temperament, so solitary a person, that he shunned the active world?

[2] Louis II de Talaru, Marquis de Chalmazel (1681–1763).

[3] Catherine Angélique d'Harcourt de Beuvron, who died in 1718. She was the daughter of the Marquis de Beuvron.

[4] See II, pp. 36 et seqq.

Mme la Duchesse d'Orléans exhausted his patience. Thus the only out-come of Mme la Duchesse d'Orléans's renewed assault was her extreme mortification, which her husband did nothing to alleviate.

In the black mood that followed, she took a violent dislike to her apartments at Montmartre,[1] from which the only view was over roofs, and to having to endure the nuns' petty agitations over keys and access; not to mention the distance of the garden, which she had reconstructed with perfect taste and at great expense. She now purchased the house at Ba-gnolet, and little by little other houses in the neighbourhood, making for herself a large and charming country estate. Madame spent most of the year at Saint-Cloud, which was her only country residence within range of M. le Duc d'Orléans. What Mme la Duchesse d'Orléans wished for was a place of her own, near enough for her to visit whenever the fancy took her.

All that winter they[2] had been pestering me to present my sons to the King and the Regent, and indeed they were of an age when that formality could no longer be deferred. None the less, I still held back because I wished first to teach them what they owed to Louis XIII, of precious and sacred memory to us,[3] and to let them pay homage first to him. I accord-ingly took them on his anniversary to Saint-Denis, which, following my father's example, I never failed to attend. When that (to us) paramount duty had been done, I presented them. I learned at the same time of two regiments for sale, both of cavalry and the property of their colonels. The Regent approved, and I therefore purchased them from the Duc de Saint-Aignan, then in Spain as our ambassador, and from Villepreux,[4] who was retiring on account of old age.

The Abbé Dubois returned to his post in England,[5] and we heard that the Earl of Peterborough[6] had been arrested, in Italy, by order of the legate to Bologna. He was a notorious adventurer, and all his life had been involved in politics, in both England and other countries, in war and peace alike. He had played a part in various schemes and expeditions, by reason of which his long and very frequent journeys abroad had cost him nothing. He had the Garter; was alternately in and out of favour with the English government, but was always a man whom they feared and treated with caution.

At this point, the Pope found it impossible any longer to stand firm against the threats of the King of Spain, or to risk the vengeance of

[1] She had rooms in the Abbey of Montmartre.

[2] Presumably his wife and mother.

[3] Because it was Louis XIII who had raised the marquisate of Saint-Simon to a dukedom and peerage, for Saint-Simon's father, in 1635.

[4] Jean de Villepreux, a Gascon, Colonel of the Royal-Piémont regiment.

[5] Dubois had been acting as ambassador extraordinary to England and Holland for the past year, negotiating the treaty of alliance.

[6] Charles Mordaunt, 3rd Earl of Peterborough (1658–1735). He had been one of the first to plot for the overthrow of James II. He commanded the Dutch and English army attacking Barcelona in 1705 (see I, p. 279). He was a friend of Pope.

Alberoni. He capitulated on 12 July, and Alberoni became a cardinal. Not every one applauded his elevation when it was announced at the Consistory. No cardinal was found willing to speak in praise of the new member. Some openly objected. Giudice[1] said that his conscience would not allow it, and Cardinal von Schrottenbach, the Emperor's envoy, absented himself. These events received various interpretations. What is certain is that Giudice had formed some kind of opposition, but that when it came to the pinch they all deserted him, a fact which Acquaviva,[2] who disliked him and wished to please Spain, would not allow to be forgotten.

The Duc de Noailles was jealous of the Regent's confidence in Law and of the success of Law's bank. He made all possible trouble for him. Law gave way, sometimes uttering a mild complaint; Noailles, however, was determined on his ruin, so that he himself might be absolute master of the finances in all their ramifications. He used every imaginable device to bring about Law's disgrace, even though his bank was at that time one of the foremost means of administering the kingdom. The Regent desired the two men to be friends. Law made advances in all good faith; the Duc de Noailles found it impossible to refuse them, and put up the best front imaginable. At that time, precisely, Mornay,[3] a lieutenant-general, and Governor and Captain of Saint-Germain in succession to Montchevreuil, his father, died very suddenly. The Duc de Noailles, never one to be caught napping, ran that instant to M. le Duc d'Orléans, begging for the appointment. It was immediately given him. My father had held it at one time; but I did not hear of Mornay's death and the Duc de Noailles's alertness until later that afternoon. You needed to be up very early to get the better of him.

A childish game of the King's brought on a serious quarrel when they spread a tent outside his windows, on the terrace of the Tuileries. The games of little kings always have to do with giving favours. He wanted medals made to present to little courtiers of his own age, who would always wear them, and thus gain the right to enter his tent without a special summons. It was to be called the Ordre du Pavillon. The Maréchal de Villeroy commissioned Le Febvre[4] to design the medals. He did so and brought them to the Maréchal, who presented them to the King. Le Febvre was the royal silversmith, and thus came under the first gentleman of the chamber. It happened to be the Duc de Mortemart's year in waiting. He had already crossed swords with the Maréchal de Villeroy. He

---

[1] Cardinal del Giudice (1647–1725). (See index, II.) He was the legate to Bologna referred to above. He deserted Philip V in 1716, when Alberoni replaced him as governor of the Prince of the Asturias. In 1719 he became chargé d'affaires for the Empire, at Rome.

[2] Cardinal Francisco Acquaviva of Aragon (1665–1725). He was the Spanish chargé d'affaires in Rome and Bishop of Cordoba. See II, pp. 361–362.

[3] Léonor, Comte de Mornay-Montchevreuil (died 1717). He had been Governor of Saint-Germain since 1706.

[4] Philippe Le Febvre, the Comptroller-general of the silver plate, and treasurer of the King's household.

now claimed that it was he, by rights, who should have ordered the medals, and presented them to the King. He was furious that everything had been done without his knowledge. Picture him mad with rage, going to M. le Duc d'Orléans with his complaint. The whole thing was a trifle, not worth a thought, and the three other first gentlemen of the chamber did nothing. Alone against the Maréchal de Villeroy, he stood no chance, for M. le Duc d'Orléans, eternally seeking a compromise, decreed that Le Febvre had cast the medals and taken them to the Maréchal not in the role of royal silver-smith, but in obedience to the King's direct command, and that therefore nothing had been done amiss. The Duc de Mortemart was outraged and expressed his feelings to the Maréchal.

A new quarrel then broke out. The Duc de Mortemart claimed the right to stand behind the King, and ejected a colonel of the bodyguard who was about to step into that place. The captains defended their superior officer, and the Duc de Mortemart suspended their right to the entrée. The three other gentlemen of the chamber supported the Duc de Mortemart. All eight then went to complain to M. le Duc d'Orléans, not once, but several times, grumbling that the throne was not in the same position as at Versailles. M. le Duc d'Orléans produced another compromise, by removing the throne itself; thus neatly removing the bone of contention. M. de Mortemart, bursting with rage, refused to wait on the King, although it was his year of service, and the gentlemen of the chamber composed a memorandum, which they presented to M. le Duc d'Orléans. So things remained, until yet another dispute between the Duc de Mortemart and the Maréchal de Villeroy blew up a month later, over some trivial question of attendance. The other gentlemen took up arms, and, after that, all ceased to attend on the King. That state of affairs lasted a week or more, after which they reappeared. The Regent was reluctant to issue a repri-mand; and the Maréchal had certainly been winged; thus for a time there were no more controversies. Yet M. de Mortemart remained exceedingly annoyed, and proposed sending in his resignation. M. le Duc d'Orléans spoke very angrily to me about him, and indeed he started some new trouble every day. I pacified the Regent as best I might with recollections of M. le Duc de Beauvilliers,[1] and so averted the storm.

There was still another dispute, this time between the first gentlemen and the royal butlers, regarding the right to announce the King's dinner; and, since the butlers came under the grand master of ceremonies, Monsieur le Duc supported them—for rights and claims are paramount everywhere. In the old days, I had always been used to see the butler speak to the first gentleman of the chamber and to see the latter enter the King's study alone to announce his meal. In the evening, when the King was with Mme de Maintenon, the butler would warn the captain of the guard,

---

[1] The Duc de Mortemart had married a daughter of the Duc de Beauvilliers and was a nephew of Mme de Montespan.

who alone entered the room where the King was sitting, and warned him that his supper was served.

The Estates of Brittany opened in such a way as to give credence to the rumours of unrest, and to the fact that something had been brewing in that province. The nobles who went ahead to meet the Maréchal de Montesquiou,[1] coming from Rennes to preside, took offence at his not removing from his post-chaise in order to ride with them on horseback, and at his being borne in a chair to the Estates from his lodgings, instead of walking with the company of nobles waiting to escort him. On those two points they were not wrong; but they made it an excuse to treat him with scant courtesy, and to dispute his every ruling, continually harping on their discontent, and on their ancient privileges at the time when they had had a duke, demanding that many of the laws be altered to suit them. Nine battalions were sent in addition to the two already stationed in Brittany, and eighteen squadrons of cavalry were given marching orders. The Maréchal de Montesquiou had been commanded to break up the assembly if he saw it prepared to disobey the King's will. He delayed a few days, but when the Estates affirmed that they would never change, he dismissed them. That was the start of all the troubles in Brittany, and it was the work of M. and Mme du Maine.

For some time past I had been engaged in secret and most mysterious commerce with a lady who, while wishing to acquaint me with the facts, and showing me enough to disclose dangerous intrigues, yet made a perfect enigma of all that could truly have enlightened me. Mme d'Alègre,[2] whose husband was long since made a Marshal of France, had sent a priest to me one morning, soliciting a very private, very secret interview; but not on any account at her house. I had the barest acquaintance with her in Society; her husband I knew not at all. The whole idea appeared to me most eccentric, and the lady herself prodigiously so. I have already mentioned her on the occasion of her daughter's marriage to Barbezieux, and the events that followed.[3] Mme d'Alègre came therefore to my house at an appointed hour. She began with interminable pretty speeches combined with fulsome praise. I replied briefly, trying to bring her to the point; but I soon discovered that nervousness was causing the extreme length of her preamble. She praised M. le Duc d'Orléans, my devotion to him, the constitution, the government. Having dealt with the ins and outs of all these subjects whilst I grew more and more impatient, she next proceeded to adopt the tone and manner of an oracle, pursing up her lips,

---

[1] Pierre de Montesquiou-d'Artagnan (1640–1725). Made a Marshal in 1709. He was a member of the Regency Council and Commandant of Brittany and Languedoc; he was a cousin of the d'Artagnan of Alexandre Dumas's *The Three Musketeers*.

[2] Jeanne Françoise de Garaud de Donneville, Marquise d'Alègre (1658–1723). Saint-Simon thought her common, her father having merely been president of the Toulouse parlement. Her husband had been a lieutenant-general commanding in Haut-Languedoc since 1707.

[3] See I, p. 116.

rolling her eyes, adjusting her coif, brushing her muff, giving me searching glances, lowering her eyes to play with her fan, uttering two short words, leaving the sense hanging in the air, finally relapsing into a brooding silence. This business was repeated at all the visits I subsequently received from her, which were fairly frequent for the next four or five months. In the end, she allowed me to understand that very dangerous plots were being hatched against M. le Duc d'Orléans and his administration—of that she had no doubt; but she would neither quote facts, nor name persons or places. She insisted on the perfect accuracy of her information; exhorted me to be on my guard, and to warn M. le Duc d'Orléans, swearing her abiding devotion to his interests, and the sense of duty that had made her come to me, because of my attachment to him and his confidence in me.

Needless to say that, since she gave me no inkling of what precautions to take, I could do nothing beyond worry. It was totally impossible to extract more from her, except that she would return in the same mysterious fashion, and would send me word when and how, concluding with compliments and assurances, urging absolute secrecy on M. le Duc d'Orléans and myself; earnestly forbidding me ever to visit her, because on the least suspicion she would be totally lost. All this verbiage filled the greater part of two hours, and the mystery deepened to the point of her requiring me to shut my study-door upon her, and not accompany her one step of the way. I had already known that plots were hatching in Brittany, although at that time the Estates had not been summoned; but Mme d'Alègre was from Toulouse, and her husband from Auvergne; I could see no Breton connection. Her singularity, her pious life in semi-retirement, her brains, for brains she had, though she was reputed to be fanciful, made me suspect that she wished to meddle. I did not therefore pay great attention to what she said and, on account of her vagueness, I thought it of no use to alarm the Regent.

After the disturbance in Brittany, she returned to tell me that she had known in advance of what would happen, and for what motives; that the Regent would be in error if he thought this was the end, or that the assembly's claims were the prime object. Then, grasping both my hands and pressing them down upon my knees, she declared with much rolling of the eyes, 'Be assured, Monsieur, that this is true; let the Regent know that it is only the beginning; you will see much more; but . . . , alas ! . . . , indeed . . . ,' and other broken phrases, like a woman who knows but will not say. Suddenly she rose and made to leave. Do what I might I could extract no more from her. But as she went through the doorway—'The time is not yet come, I shall see you again; be on the watch, and see that M. le Duc d'Orléans stays alert.' Thus speaking she shut the door and was gone. Perplexing though this latest visit was, I thought it best to report it to M. le Duc d'Orléans. Although he knew Mme d'Alègre by reputation, and could no more understand her words than I, he took them more seriously than I had expected. He desired me to continue my conversations with her; that is to say, to receive her and listen to her at any time, seeing that she forbade me her house; desired me to express his gratitude, and to do my utmost to discover more. I shall have occasion to describe several other such interviews.

At this time the King of Spain fell seriously, even dangerously ill. Alberoni had taken immense pains to keep him in the way instituted by Mme des Ursins, namely, living shut up with the queen, inaccessible not only to his court and the great nobles, but even to those who, by their functions, were responsible for his personal service. That was how she had come to rule his kingdom, manage all State affairs, and dispense all rewards, as Alberoni had witnessed at the time of M. de Vendôme, and, later, when he was the Duke of Parma's envoy. Profiting by Mme des Ursins's example for the sake of the new queen and for his own advantage, he kept Philip V still more closely segregated, in a kind of solitary confinement that continued for the remainder of his life. This is something which I shall describe in greater detail when I come to my embassy; if God gives me grace to continue so far. For the moment I shall restrict myself to the matters in hand.

No one at all was admitted to the private life of the King of Spain; I mean to his *lever*, *coucher*, and meals. The necessary service was limited to three or four French valets; two only of his gentlemen; no minister other than Alberoni; his confessor, for a quarter of an hour each morning after his *lever*; the Duke of Popoli and the other governors and assistant governors of his children, but only for a quarter of an hour while the queen's hair was being dressed; Cardinal Borgia,[1] Patriarch of the Indies, and, very occasionally, the Duke of Villena, the major-domo mayor.[2] The same persons, but not the children or their governors, sometimes appeared at his dinner and supper, but did not stay long. The chief physician, chief surgeon, and apothecary had similar entrées, but seldom used them. As for women, only the nurse,[3] after the king had risen, saw the queen in bed, and put on her stockings. That was the only time that they were alone together, and they prolonged it as much as possible while the king was dressing in the adjoining room. The queen then went to her dressing-table, where her duenna[4] and three or four palace ladies awaited her. At dinner and supper, she was served by the duenna, two palace ladies, and two señoras de honor. The waiting women carried the dishes and wine from the door and handed them to the ladies on duty. The king's taster

---

[1] He was made a cardinal only in 1719.

[2] Juan Manuel Fernandes Pacheco, Marquis of Villena and Duke of Escalona (1648–1725), a Grandee of Spain and major-domo mayor to the King since 1713. He held the highest post in the household.

[3] Elisabeth Farnese's nurse (called the *azafata* in Spain) Laura Piscatori (1667–1748). She had come with the queen from Parma.

[4] The Duchess of Cordoba, called Countess Altamira. See II, pp. 402–403.

prepared nothing for him, and was entirely superfluous. King Philip was served by the queen's ladies, unaided.

The major-domo mayor was thus excluded; likewise the king's steward, whose service is more personal than that of the other high officers. The royal household was therefore reduced to a very limited number of valets and doctors; the two gentlemen of the chamber; the queen's major-domo mayor, and a very few ladies, who waited in turn. Two or three others whose names I have mentioned, were allowed occasional entry while the queen dressed, or during dinner. The king's major-domo mayor, the Duke of Escalona (always known as the Marquis of Villena), was in every way considered one of the greatest nobles of Spain, revered and esteemed more highly than the rest, and with good reason because of his character, appointments, and military career.

The king's illness had still further reduced this very small court, until it comprised only the queen and her nurse, the two gentlemen, the doctors (four in all because the queen's physician was also included), and four or five personal valets. Alberoni ruled over them. The remainder, without exception, were banned; even Père Daubenton was obliged to be sparing in his appearances.

The king's doctors come under the major-domo mayor, and should report everything to him. He should be present at consultations, and the king should not take any remedy except in his presence, and with his knowledge and approval. Alberoni now hinted to the Marquis of Villena that His Majesty preferred to be at liberty, and that he would best pay his court by remaining at his home, or else should refrain from entering the royal bedroom, but merely stand at the door to receive health reports. That kind of language was more than Villena could tolerate. They had placed the king's bed, with the king in it, at the extreme end of the great mirror-hall, facing the door opposite. Thus, since the room is of immense width and also exceedingly long, there was a vast distance between the bed and the entrance door. Alberoni once more informed the marquis that the king found his frequent intrusions most wearisome; but when that had no effect, he resolved with the queen's connivance to bar his entry. Accordingly, when the marquis presented himself on the following afternoon, one of the valets stuck his head through the half-opened door, and with some hesitation said that entrance was forbidden. 'Impossible!' cried the marquis, 'What impertinence!' and so saying, he pushed the door back upon the man and entered. He found himself facing the queen, who was sitting on the king's bed, with the cardinal standing beside her, and the very few others allowed (and not all of them) grouped together at a great distance. Villena who, despite his dignity, was not good on his legs, hobbled slowly forward, leaning on a little cane.[1]

[1] The Marquis of Villena had been taken prisoner by the Austrians in 1707, and had spent a long time in captivity with his legs in chains.

The queen and the cardinal saw him, and looked at one another. The king was too ill to take notice; what is more, his curtains were closed, except on the side where the queen sat. As the marquis came near, the cardinal motioned impatiently to one of the valets, to make him leave, and leave quickly. Then, seeing that Villena still advanced, he went forward himself, exclaiming that the king desired to be alone and wished him to go. 'Not true!' cried Villena, 'I was watching. You did not go near the bed, nor did the king speak to you.' Alberoni insisted, but without success; then took his arm as if to turn him. Villena declared that it was intolerable to be prevented from doing one's duty. At this the cardinal, who was by far the stronger, managed to turn him completely round, and half-dragged, half-carried him towards the door, with further verbal exchanges, during which Alberoni remained moderately civil, but Villena simply let fly. At last, having had enough of the pulling and shoving, he began to fight, shouting that Alberoni was a villain who must be taught proper respect; but what with the heat and the manhandling (for he was not strong) he collapsed altogether into an armchair that most fortunately stood in his path. Furious at this upset, he lifted up his short cane and began to rain blows, thick and fast, with all his might, on the ears and shoulders of Alberoni, crying that he was a rogue, a swindler, a low fellow who deserved a good thrashing. The cardinal, who by this time was in Villena's grip, freed himself after a struggle, but the marquis continued to hurl abuse and threaten him with his cane. At length one of the valets came to Villena's rescue and helped him to rise from the chair and reach the door which, after such an encounter, was his only desire.

Meanwhile from her seat on the bed, the queen had watched the brawl from start to finish, without moving or uttering a single word.[1] I heard this from everyone when I went to Spain; but to make doubly sure, I begged the Marquis of Villena to tell me the whole story, with all the details. He was the most upright and truthful of men, moreover he had taken a great fancy to me; he therefore gladly described all that happened, exactly as I write it here. Santa Cruz and Arco,[2] the two gentlemen present, also described the affair, and privately thought it very funny. Santa Cruz had refused to order the marquis to leave, and after all was over had accompanied him to the door. What was extraordinary was that, angry though he was, and utterly confused by the rain of blows, the cardinal made no attempt to retaliate; merely endeavoured to free himself. The marquis shouted at him as he made off that, were it not for the respect due to the king on his bed of pain, he would give him a hundred kicks in the stomach and throw him out on his ears. I forgot to mention that episode. The king,

[1] This scene, and her cruel manner of dismissing Mme des Ursins (II, pp. 397-398) seem to suggest that Elisabeth Farnese was a most cold and unfeeling person.
[2] The Marquis of Santa Cruz was the queen's major-domo mayor, Villena's opposite number, The Duke of Arco was Philip V's master of the horse, and first gentleman-in-waiting.

however, had been so ill that he perceived nothing. A quarter of an hour
after the marquis reached his home, he received the order to retire to one
of his estates, thirty miles distant from Madrid; but during all the rest of
that day his house was filled with ever-increasing crowds of Madrileñe
Society as news of his encounter spread. There was indeed a most appalling
scandal. He left next day with his children.

The cardinal, nevertheless, was in such a state of fear that he remained
content with being rid of Villena by exile, and did not proceed further
against him for the blows. Six or seven months later, he sent him permission to return, although the marquis himself had made no efforts in
that direction. What was really incredible was that the brawl, the exile, and
the return, went quite unnoticed by the King of Spain, until the moment
of Alberoni's disgrace. After his return, Villena refused to see the cardinal, or hear him mentioned on any pretext whatsoever; and even though
Alberoni was absolute master in Spain, his pride was deeply hurt by such
just and well merited disdain. He was even more humiliated when the
continual efforts he made to patch up their quarrel met only with snubs
that greatly added to the already high reputation of that virtuous nobleman.[1]

The king was ill enough to write his testament, at the dictation of the
cardinal, seconded by the queen. This became known to all, and no one
doubted but that the regency and all authority would go to her, with the
cardinal as her adviser. There was general dismay, for few believed that a
stepmother's regency[2] would be accepted in the event of the king's death,
especially not that of a stepmother as much hated by the entire nation as
was Elisabeth Farnese whose only supporters were the Duke of Parma and
the truly abominated Alberoni.

Towards the end of November, however, the king completely recovered.
Sleep, appetite, vigour, stoutness, all returned to him; but his spirits had
been so shattered by the seeming imminence of death that he insisted on
having his confessor near him at all times, often retaining him until the
very moment when he stepped into bed beside the queen. Sometimes he
had him fetched in the middle of the night; but this weakness did not
extend to anything else and, to all appearances, he might never have been
ill. Let us now return to France.

An event soon to take place, since it occurred on 28 January 1718,[3] the
year we are about to enter, would seem to require some recapitulation of its

---

[1] Saint-Simon had a particular loathing for Alberoni as a low-class climber who had arrived
where only dukes should be. But it was his earlier record as the lick-spittle secretary of the
revolting Vendôme that had really damned him in the eyes of the memoirist. See index, I.

[2] Philip V's heir, Louis Philippe de Bourbon, Prince of the Asturias, then ten years old, was
the elder son of Philip's first wife, Marie Louise Gabrielle of Savoy. He married the Regent's
daughter, Louise Elisabeth d'Orléans, Mlle de Montpensier, in 1722. It was to arrange the
details of this marriage that Saint-Simon went to Spain in 1721 as ambassador extraordinary.

[3] He is referring to the disgrace of Daguesseau, the Chancellor (see below, p. 155).

causes, without too much concern for repeating what I may have said only a short time ago.

You will remember the discord between the Duc de Noailles and Law; the peace patched up between them, and the real gratitude felt by M. le Duc d'Orléans for the Duc de Noailles because of his complaisance and protestations. For a long time past, Noailles had been jealous of Law and interfering with his bank and his future plans.[1] Not only did he everywhere impede him with the full weight of his authority on the finance council, but he stirred up all possible opposition in the Parlement, and very often caused Law's most reasonable proposals to be rejected. Law, as I have explained, came to me every Tuesday morning, always full of complaints. It was not difficult for him to persuade me of the harm done to the kingdom by his continual frustration, more especially in view of my bad relations with the Duc de Noailles and frankly admitted ignorance of finance. Certain matters, however, depend more on commonsense than professional aptitude, and Law, although very Scotch in his way of speaking, had the rare gift for explaining so clearly, simply, and intelligibly that he was perfectly understandable. M. le Duc d'Orléans liked him personally, and, having a taste for devious and original methods, was the more ready to fall in with his ideas because he saw that the usual operations were failing to provide for the country's most urgent needs. The Regent's approval of Law deeply wounded the Duc de Noailles's pride; he felt it reduced his influence. He wished to have sole command of the finances. Law was independent; his independence pleased the Regent, and Noailles, whose one ambition was still to rule M. le Duc d'Orléans, as a first step towards becoming chief minister, found him an insuperable obstacle.

At this time Dubois's credit was running low with the Regent. He needed an ally. His desire also was to be first minister, and he wanted no rivals nor adversaries. The man he most feared was the Duc de Noailles, who had similar ambitions and far better hopes of realizing them. Dubois accordingly determined to be rid of him without a personal quarrel; but the fight was too unequal, and, moreover, he could find no pretext. For that reason he attached himself to Law. It was to their mutual advantage, because Law, as a foreigner, with many influential people in full cry after him, had good reason to dread M. le Duc d'Orléans's fickleness. Dubois, on his side, by appearing to favour Law, flattered the Regent's judgment, and incidentally played a low trick on the Duc de Noailles, whom he wished to ruin, without daring to say so. All of this took place behind a veil which Noailles for all his brains was unable to penetrate; nor were the Regent's suspicions aroused.

Law informed me of Dubois's growing attachment, and the use to which he was putting it, though he concealed how much it cost him to cultivate and establish it; but money was beginning to pour in from that budding enterprise, so disastrous because of its misuse, later to become

[1] See note, p. 136 above.

notorious as the Mississippi Scheme. It was indeed a fine thing for the Abbé Dubois thus to find a secret ally, needing support as much as he did himself, and possessed of the means to hamstring a rival candidate for that highest of all posts, which he was then in no condition even to approach. In these circumstances a liaison developed between him and Law that was to bear them very high, or should I say very far. I am not sure that Noailles saw through the antics and flatteries of Dubois; but what makes me believe that he suspected something was an event that touched me personally, and that, considering my relations with the Duc de Noailles (not bowing or speaking and, as you know, never ceasing to taunt him in public), took me wholly by surprise.

One Saturday afternoon, towards the end of the summer of 1717, at a finance meeting of the Regency Council, I was seated as usual between the Comte de Toulouse and the Duc de Noailles, when Noailles suddenly put his lips to my ear and asked whether I was not still deeply attached to the Abbey of La Trappe. A curt 'Yes' was all the answer he got from me. 'Are they not,' he continued, 'in a bad way financially?' 'Could not be worse,' I replied. 'Would you not be glad to see them firmly established?' 'Nothing,' I said, 'would please me more.' 'Very well!' said he. 'As it happens, I care as much for the Abbey of Septfonds,[1] which is also in difficulties. Would you like to ask La Trappe for a list of their debts and let me have it? I shall then try to find a way to mend the fortunes of both places.' Without the least expression of gratitude I declared that I would gladly do so, and would write to La Trappe accordingly. Our turn then came to vote, and no more was said. It was a Saturday evening, and a perfect time to write. I duly received the list for which I asked, and gave it a week later to the Duc de Noailles. As he took it, seated at his place at the table, he advised me to do nothing more, adding that he would inform me later. On the very next Saturday, seated in the same place, he told me that he had tackled M. le Duc d'Orléans, and that I might safely speak. I did so, and successfully, the path having been well smoothed for me. A fortnight later the money began to flow in from Law. It was a cause most dear to my heart, and one which I should have found it hard to plead with a man of M. le Duc d'Orléans's nature. Providence[2] had now intervened in this almost miraculous way. There is no time to say more at present.

During the remainder of that year, 1717, there was continual strife between Law and the department of finance. The Abbé Dubois returned from London and spent the month of January in Paris, very much to his own advantage. The Chancellor[3] was proving a failure in his high office,

---

[1] The Abbey of Septfonts was near Moulins.

[2] If it was Providence that had engineered the payment of La Trappe's debts, it certainly did 'move in a mysterious way'. One feels that Saint-Simon might have allowed Noailles some share of the credit.

[3] Daguesseau, whom Noailles had persuaded the Regent to appoint earlier in the year. See p. 98 above.

for his adulation of the Duc de Noailles dismayed all, even including M. le Duc d'Orléans. His indecision and tactlessness in dealing with State affairs caused him to be underrated; his eternal quibbling, born of long practice in the law courts, bored all his colleagues and put people quite out of patience, while the difficulties he constantly raised in order to impede Law's operations made him vastly unpopular, and left him wide open to the Abbé Dubois's attacks. At this point, Dubois spoke to the Maréchal de Villeroy, whom he was eagerly courting, and persuaded him to intervene with the Regent;[1] he also allowed me to perceive his future intentions regarding the Duc de Noailles, which were enough to secure my support. Law, too, exhorted me to act against Noailles for the public good, since, quite apart from the damage he was causing, we faced disaster under Daguesseau's mismanagement. On rare occasions the Regent consulted me also, although he was wary of me because of my hatred of Noailles—yet in all probability I was the one who did him least harm. However that may be, I learned all that was happening through Law, the Maréchal de Villeroy, and sometimes, with greater caution, from the Abbé Dubois himself. Let this suffice as a prelude to what follows; it will serve also to introduce the year 1718, which we are about to enter.

[1] See p. 77 above for Villeroy's disapproval of Noailles's efforts to sit on the Regency Council.

CHAPTER IV

1718

Edict to establish the Banking Company of the West – The Regent works with Law, the Chancellor, and the Duc de Noailles at La Roquette – Madame la Duchesse ousts the Maréchale d'Estrées from her box at the Opéra – Disorders in Brittany – The Regent is deceived – Obstruction from the Parlement – Character of Argenson – The Chancellor deprived of the seals and exiled – The Duc de Noailles resigns the finances – Argenson is given both the seals and the finances – Madame's unseemly conduct in attending the reading of the Abbé de Saint-Albin's thesis – Visit of the Duc and Duchesse de Lorraine – M. le Duc d'Orléans diverts himself at my expense – What he really thought of me – Law pleases me even better – Death of Fagon – Death of the Abbé d'Estrées – A startling conversion – Argenson's unpunctuality – Death of Mme de Vendôme – The Abbé de Saint-Pierre's book infuriates the Duc de Villeroy – A fire at Petit-Pont – Death of Mme de Castries – Death of the Queen of England – Foreign affairs – A sarcastic remark of mine repays the Convent of Denain – The Parlement's reckless protest against a financial edict – First suggestions of a Lit de Justice *– Weakness and inertia of the Regent – The Regent summons me to confer with him – Monsieur le Duc desires to remove the Duc du Maine – I object – Preparations for a* Lit de Justice *– The Cellamare conspiracy – Secret meeting of the Regency Council – Terror of M. du Maine – The bastards to be reduced to the rank of their peerages – The* Lit de Justice *– I am ordered to tell Mme la Duchesse d'Orléans at Saint-Cloud – I tell Madame also – Mme d'Alègre reappears with more good advice – I gain a post for the Chevalier de Rancé – Fête at Chantilly – Marriage of the Old Pretender – Death of the Maréchal d'Harcourt – Meudon given to the Duchesse de Berry – The Duchesse de Berry queens it at the Opéra – Alberoni's designs – Cellamare's precautions – Arrests at Poitiers – Cellamare arrested – Arrest of the Duc du Maine at Sceaux, and of Mme du Maine in Paris – They are separately imprisoned*

THE VERY FIRST DAY of this year, 1718, saw the publication of an edict to establish the Western Banking Company, with funds fixed at a hundred millions, non-distrainable save in the event of the bankruptcy or death of the partners. This was the name finally given to the Bank of Mississippi,[1]

---

[1] Law's plan was for a national bank. It was not until 1719 that he originated a joint-stock company for reclaiming and settling lands in the Mississippi valley, to be called the 'Mississippi Scheme'. The edict here mentioned was for the adoption of Law's first proposal.

although that title was still constantly used. Possession of its shares ruined or enriched very many people, including the princes and princesses of the blood, and more especially Madame la Duchesse, Monsieur le Duc, and M. le Prince de Conti, who found there more gold than in all the Peruvian mines, and, clinging to it, made the company a liability to the State by destroying commerce. The support they publicly gave it throughout their lives, despite the vast profits they took without sharing the losses, kept it afloat; and after them powerful ministers of finance have had the control of it, and also the profits, until the present day.

In the meantime, Madame la Duchesse, in the most high-handed manner, had commandeered the Maréchale d'Estrées's little box at the Opéra, notwithstanding that that lady's husband's sisters[1] had been her lifelong friends, and in daily and affectionate intercourse with her. There was a terrible rumpus, and the Estrées's friends and relations ceased to visit Madame la Duchesse. They appealed to the Regent who refused to intervene. Such a thing had never before been contemplated, much less essayed; but what no one would have hazarded in the late King's lifetime (indulgent though he was to his daughters and the princes of the blood), was practised very frequently after similar trials of Society's patience and cowardice. Madame la Duchesse let everyone howl and held fast to the spoils, and gradually those who had ceased to visit her came again. Even the Maréchal d'Estrées and his lady eventually forgave her after absenting themselves longer than most. Thus the princes' arrogance far exceeded the pride of the late King, who was always extremely careful to observe the rights of everyone, even in matters of this kind. He would never have countenanced such piracy; not even the greatest in his own family would have dared to attempt it.

The disorders in Brittany were increasing as the people came to believe that unity and firmness might gain them their independence. The local nobility wrote a letter to the Regent which was submissive and respectful enough in appearance but in reality was monstrously determined, and thousands of copies were distributed throughout Paris. Two presidents and four counsellors, deputies from the Breton parlement, arrived with a second letter, couched in similar terms, and a few days later were admitted to the Regent's presence, but forbidden to speak. The Maréchal de Montesquiou, who commanded in Brittany, experienced great difficulties with the local parlement whose members were for ever making trials of their strength. MM. de Piré, Noyant, Bonamour, and du Guesclairs were arrested by *lettres de cachet* and brought to Paris to account for their conduct. They were separately exiled to Burgundy, Champagne, and Picardy; all except Piré, who was lying ill at his home, and thus escaped both the journey to Paris and exile.

---

[1] Mlle de Tourbes (1673–1750) and the Marquise de Courtenvaux (1663–1741), the wife of that Marquis de Courtenvaux who was turned out of his lodging at Marly. See II, pp. 420–421.

As hopes rose in Brittany, so did the unrest in the Paris Parlement. That body, which invariably attempts to upset the government during regencies,[1] had, in Président de Mesmes,[2] a leader eaten up by ambition, a man as poor as he was extravagant, who despite complete ignorance of his juridical calling had plans ready made, the ability to please whomsoever he wished, and all the arts of the best Society. His sacred oath, his so-called honour, his integrity, he regarded as less than nothing. To his mind, duplicity and deceit were virtues necessary to those in high office, and in that, alas!, he was not unlike the Regent, and had charmed that prince with the very quality which should most have shaken his trust. As you already know, he was the willing slave of the Duc and Duchesse du Maine; he knew all that happened in Brittany and elsewhere,[3] and turned all his great intelligence to acting in their interests at the Parlement, taking due precautions to preserve the Regent's trust while all the while he was fleecing and betraying him. This was made all the easier because the Regent's go-between in all his dealings with the Parlement was d'Effiat[4]—d'Effiat who, for years past, had been the Duc du Maine's ally, continually plotting with him to destroy his master. Thus, for all his wit, the Regent had placed entire confidence in two rascals who night and day schemed to ruin him. Yet he never once suspected either of them, believing that the vast sums constantly extracted from him by the premier président were well spent because they served to maintain his loyalty, and that his attachment to M. du Maine was simply ordinary courtesy towards a one-time friend.

D'Effiat, a crony both of the premier président and of the Duc du Maine, encouraged the credulity of M. le Duc d'Orléans who therefore continued to pour gold into de Mesmes's pockets. Such was the blindness of a prince who pretended to believe that every man was a rogue at heart (save for a very small number whom too strict an upbringing had narrowed and repressed) and who really preferred to use known deceivers, in the assurance of having the ability to manage them and not be duped. This preamble is needed to understand what follows concerning the Regent and the Parlement, for, as you will now have learned, everything possible was being done to embarrass M. le Duc d'Orléans, and finally to overthrow him.

Dangers threatening at home, and from abroad, in Spain, followed the course set by these men's ambition and desires, while the rumours skilfully spread among the rash, the vulgar, and the stupid (always in the majority)

---

[1] It will be remembered that the Parlement was a court of law, not a law-making assembly. Until Louis XIV had removed the right, it could 'remonstrate' against new laws; but it carried on a never-ending struggle to gain the same functions of government as the English Parliament possessed. Meanwhile the members had no governmental responsibilities and, in a Regency, no King to keep them in order.

[2] Jean Antoine III de Mesmes, premier président since 1712. See index, II.

[3] This refers to the intrigues against the Regent in Spain.

[4] Antoine Coiffier-Ruzé, Marquis d'Effiat (1638–1719). See II, pp. 412–414.

helped to produce the wished-for effect. The understanding between Alberoni and M. and Mme du Maine was complete; the attachment they had formed during the lifetimes of the late King and M. de Vendôme had never lapsed. Their methods, first used against Mgr le Duc de Bourgogne, and after his death against M. le Duc d'Orléans, remained the same and were continually put into practice. You will know, from what I have said regarding foreign affairs, of Alberoni's genius, his supreme power in Spain, his hatred of M. le Duc d'Orléans, who rashly persisted in dealing with him through d'Effiat; lastly, of the King and Queen of Spain's passionate longing to rule France should aught befall our King, and how Alberoni charmed and flattered them by his encouragement and plans, fostering their hatred of the Regent, reviving old hurts and inventing new injuries, making his every move appear suspect, even those that benefited Spain.

The Maréchaux de Villeroy and de Villars, with many other great and ambitious persons, now rushed blindly in, out of a desire for power which nothing that the Regent ceaselessly did for them could satisfy or appease. The Maréchal de Villeroy, anxious to play his part, descended to the lowest depths by giving renewed life to long-forgotten slanders.[1] Thus he proceeded to keep locked up the King's linen, bread, and other essential commodities. Day and night he kept the key upon his person; making a great show of remaining behind to let people see with what care he shut such things away, provoking admiration for his wise precautions against assassins, never admitting that the King's meat and its seasonings, his drinks, and all the thousand other things that could not be kept under lock and key, might equally well be used for such a crime. Anything served him to keep alive such rumours, suspicions, and gossip as might assist towards the desired end of destroying the Regent.

I could see clearly enough the substance of the plot; that is to say, the aims of M. du Maine, the Parlement, and the Maréchal de Villeroy. I dimly apprehended the ambitions of Spain, and silently trembled at M. le Duc d'Orléans's indolence and blindness. That prince's trust in me had not lessened; but he was wary of me, knowing my opinion of the Duc de Noailles, Effiat, the premier président, and the Parlement. As I had long since understood that his suspicions would neutralize any advice I might give him, I took care to say nothing. If he questioned me, I answered vaguely, briefly, changing the subject as speedily as possible.

---

[1] This refers to the idea obsessing many people of that time, that the members of the royal family who died in 1712 had been poisoned, probably by the Duc d'Orléans. In fact their deaths were clearly caused by measles and the bleedings and purgings insisted on by the doctors—perhaps helped by dirty instruments. It is said that in England at the same period, people survived who were cut for a stone at the beginning of the month; those operated on at the end mostly died. There was much mystification: was it to do with the moon? The answer was that most surgeons sent their knives and lancets to be cleaned and sharpened on the first of the month, and they were never washed in between for fear of blunting them.

The Parlement was the chosen field for the development of these far-reaching intrigues. It had to be aroused as though for the common good; then stirred to anger at the extravagance and debauchery of the Regent. Law's system, and the fact that he was a foreigner by race and religion, proved most effective in inducing the more decent members to oppose him—vanity at the thought of becoming moderators of the government moved the others. It was essential to proceed slowly if the entire Parlement were to be enlisted in a policy of continual obstruction, aimed at exasperating and wearing down the Regent, but keeping the great majority of those involved unaware of the true purpose. Under the protection of the law and Parlement, those whose aim was to destroy both might safely act; none the less it was necessary to make accomplices of the whole body before they could be cheated with impunity. Such was the well-laid plot that gave every appearance of succeeding perfectly; but Providence, the protector of kingdoms, and of kings also when they are young and feeble, willed it otherwise.

When the time came for action, the Parlement raised a whole series of remonstrances in order to prepare the public. Some were directed against Law himself, others against the new form of government by councils which, it was said, wasted more time and money than the older method. At that point, two sessions were held on the morning and evening of 14 January, and continued throughout the following day. Remonstrances were uttered, and joined to most brazen demands, after which the provost of the merchants was summoned to report on the state of affairs at the Hôtel de Ville. The premier président and the King's men visited the Regent after each session to render an account of the day's business. There were further sessions on the two following days and on part of the next, but these took place at the premier président's house, and were for the purpose of putting the remonstrances and demands into written form. Law, although he was not mentioned by name, was fiercely attacked, and the administration also. Indeed, there was criticism of everything, as though by right, and a challenge to the Regent's authority that threatened to leave him with the merest shadow of his former power.

As soon as M. le Duc d'Orléans understood what was afoot, he spoke to me with more warmth and resentment than he usually displayed. I said nothing. We were walking up and down Coypel's gallery[1] and the great hall at the end, overlooking the Rue Saint-Honoré. He continually urged me to say something. At length I replied that, as he perfectly well knew, I had refused for a long time past to open my mouth regarding the Parlement or anything concerning it, and that whenever he had spoken of it I had changed the subject. Since he now absolutely insisted, I could say only that nothing in their conduct surprised me, for as he would recall I had

[1] This ran the whole length of the Palais Royal, on the first floor, on the side of the Rue de Richelieu. Coypel had been Louis XIV's court-painter.

predicted it, warning him long ago that his indolence would leave him Regent in name only, or force him to use highly dangerous methods to recover his rightful powers. He stopped dead in his tracks and turned towards me blushing scarlet. Then he stooped down ever so little, placed his hands on his hips, and gazing at me with real anger, said, 'Damn you! It is easy for you, who are as unchanging as God, and insanely tenacious.' I gave him a smile even colder than before: 'Monsieur,' said I, 'you do me too much honour. But if I have too much tenacity and firmness of purpose, I wish I might pass the excess over to you; then we should both be perfect, and you might acquire what you so badly need.' This felled him like an ox; he was left incapable of speech. He then returned to pacing up and down with long strides, head down, as was his custom when vexed or embarrassed, from the hall where this exchange had taken place to the farther end of the gallery. Coming back he talked of other matters, which I seized on eagerly so as to be quit of the subject.

On 26 January, the Parlement sent a deputation, at eleven in the morning, to utter their remonstrances to the King, in the presence of M. le Duc d'Orléans. The premier président read them in a loud voice. They strongly criticized the government and pressed their wholly unlawful demands. The Regent did not speak. The King replied through his Chancellor that he would issue his commands, and hoped (most feeble, unbecoming verb) they would be implicitly obeyed. That same evening, M. le Duc d'Orléans had copies distributed of the edict registered at the Parlement on 21 February 1641, in the presence of Louis XIII, reducing that body to the status of an ordinary court of justice, to try lawsuits between the King and his subjects, with no other functions and no power to meddle in any way with the administration. This prohibition and the reduction in authority was supported by similar decrees in the reigns of Francis I and Charles IX, and by other rulings of Louis XIII. They might, indeed they should, have included those of Louis XIV, more especially on the occasion when he took his seat at the Parlement wearing a grey coat, and in his hand a riding-switch, with which he constantly threatened the assembly as he uttered his commands to their faces.[1]

Meanwhile the Regent was becoming increasingly harassed, and spoke to me more freely regarding the persons and matters of which I had warned him, more than once complaining of Noailles's jealousy of Law, and of the Chancellor's weakness and eternal quibbling. Law also kept me informed of all that happened. Whatever may be said against his system, he was a most honest man, not swayed by personal ambition, but at heart true and simple. He came often to tell me his troubles, and was many times on the verge of resigning. The Regent grumbled angrily about them all, but drew nothing from me except sympathy for his difficulties, and

[1] It appears that this scene is apocryphal, although Louis XIV did reject the Parlement's right to remonstrate. See II, p. 352n.

regret that my total ignorance of finance prevented me from offering any advice.

So things continued until at last M. le Duc d'Orléans realized despairingly that the time had come when he must choose between them; but he resolved first to bring the three men together in one last effort to obtain some sort of unity, and to discover for himself the rights and wrongs of the matter. In order to have peace and leisure for an uninterrupted session, he arranged to spend an entire afternoon with them at La Roquette,[1] and be entertained there to supper by the Duc de Noailles. The date was fixed for 6 January.

La Roquette is an extension of the Faubourg Saint-Antoine, where M. de Noailles borrowed for the occasion a charming house belonging to a rich banker named du Noyer[2] who had recently been sweetened with a post as registrar at the Parlement. This Croesus, for his sins, had sacrificed his wealth in order to prop up the Birons who, to put it bluntly, sucked him so dry that in the end he died on a midden without any of them knowing or caring. But that was their way; and many others who contributed their entire substance to the Birons' support were similarly treated. Mme de Biron[3] would airily laugh about them and pass the subject off, feeling apparently that she had quite sufficiently honoured them.

De Noailles and the Chancellor arrived early at La Roquette. They all had a long, hard session; but for the two friends it proved a fatal one. After hearing them out, the Regent protested that the Duc de Noailles had deceived him from the start, that the Chancellor was obstructive, a slave to technicalities, deaf to Law's most convincing arguments, blind to his wisest plans. I have already said that this Scotsman, despite his uncouth speech, had such a clear way of explaining, such delightful simplicity, so much natural wit, that one was easily disposed to agree with him. He now claimed that the frustrations he met with at every turn were ruining all his schemes, and he succeeded so well with the Regent that the prince was won over, and induced all the ministers to let him have his way.

It was then, at last, that M. le Duc d'Orléans spoke to me with complete freedom, more especially of the finances and the seals, and to whom they had best be given if Law were not to be further obstructed. Law himself had discussed that question with me, saying that he often had dealings with d'Argenson[4] who thoroughly understood his aims. It was therefore to him

[1] La Roquette was near the present Rue de Charonne.
[2] Nicolas du Noyer was the brother-in-law of Mme du Noyer, author of the *Lettres Historiques et Galantes*. He died in 1731.
[3] Marie Antonine Bautru de Nogent (d. 1742). She was the wife of the Duc et Maréchal de Biron who at this time was a lieutenant-general and a member of the war council.
[4] Marc René de (or le) Voyer de Paulmy, Marquis d'Argenson (1652–1721). He had replaced La Reynie as lieutenant of the Paris police in 1697, and was made Chancellor of France in this year, 1718. The Voyer family came from Touraine, and could be traced back to the fourteenth century. See index, I and II.

that he hoped the finances would pass, believing that they could work together in harmony.

Argenson was a man of great intelligence and an accommodating disposition, very easy to work with, always provided that his fortunes were thereby advanced. He was better born than most men of his employment, and for many years past had directed the police and the inquisition in a supremely excellent manner. He was not afraid of the Parlement although many times attacked, and had often befriended persons of quality by concealing from the late King and Chancellor Pontchartrain the crimes of their sons and nephews, when these were merely youthful pranks, but might have meant ruin had d'Argenson not used his power to keep them hidden. He had a truly alarming countenance, resembling that of the three judges of Hades,[1] but he everywhere mitigated the harshness of the laws. He kept the innumerable populace of Paris in such good order that there was not one whose daily life he did not know, along with each one's conduct and habits. He thus showed great discernment in treating each separate case with severity or lenience, but always with a bias towards gentleness. Yet he had the ability to make even the innocent tremble before him. In riots he displayed boldness and physical courage, and thus easily mastered the rabble. His ways were not unlike those of the people who were brought before him, and I do not know that he acknowledged any other deity than the goddess of Fortune. Performing functions often distressing and always harsh in appearance, he was easily moved to kindness, and when among friends, most of whom tended to be obscure and of low birth (for he seemed to prefer such-like to people of high rank), he gave himself up to pleasure and was excellent company. He was tolerably well informed, not otherwise cultivated, but his wit sufficed for all, and his wide acquaintance with the arts of Society was most unusual in a man of his condition.

Under the late King Argenson had gone over to the Jesuits, but had managed to do the least possible harm by making a great show of religious persecution, under which he actually performed very little, and sometimes even assisted those who were attacked. Fortune being his only guide, he had nurtured with equal care the King, the ministers, the Jesuits, and the public. When M. le Duc d'Orléans was so unjustly suspected, he had been sufficiently far-sighted to earn his gratitude; and since then had courted me also, not fawning on me or paying me visits, but at every turn showing me consideration. For example, he voluntarily took charge of the affairs of the Convent of the Visitation, at Chaillot, where Mme de Saint-Simon had a sister[2] of great piety to whom we were most devotedly attached.

[1] Rhadamanthus, for Asiatics; Aeacus, for Europeans; and Minos presiding. According to Cicero, there was a fourth judge, Triptolemus.
[2] Marie Louise Gabrielle de Lorges. See I, p. 490. Saint-Simon's mother-in-law, the Maréchale de Lorges, and her family had set the convent on its feet financially.

His office made him wholly repugnant to the Parlement, who bore him great ill will; thus he and the Regent had often needed one another's support. By nature a royalist and careful of the King's purse, he was decisive, hating verbosity and needless ceremony, despising people who were neutral or hesitant. In his endeavour to be on good terms with everyone, he had, during the King's lifetime, and since also, cultivated an attachment with the bastards that was very much closer than either M. le Duc d'Orléans or myself had supposed. Because I was ignorant of their intimacy and impressed by his good qualities, especially his aversion to the Parlement, which it was so essential to subjugate, I decided to support him for the finances and the seals also, so as to increase his powers and give the Regent a firm and courageous Chancellor. I named him to Law, who highly approved, and then to the Regent, to whom I explained all my reasons. The matter remained a secret between us three, and our plans were soon laid. I then urged M. le Duc d'Orléans to act quickly, for I feared lest he change his mind, and it was decided to strike the blow on Friday, 28 January, so as to allow time for the Parlement to make their remonstrances to the King, as I have already mentioned.

On that morning, at eight o'clock precisely, La Vrillière,[1] who had been summoned to the Palais Royal late on the previous evening, went to reclaim the seals from the Chancellor, ordering him, in the name of the Regent, to retire until further notice to his country estate at Fresnes, on the road from Paris to Meaux. The Chancellor said simply that La Vrillière was a fatal name for Chancellors.[2] He then humbly asked whether he might see the Regent, and on being told no, begged permission to write a letter. La Vrillière promised to be the bearer of it; whereupon the Chancellor wrote it, read it aloud, sealed it in La Vrillière's presence, and gave it into his hand. He then wrote to warn the Duc de Noailles, and went to tell his wife, who was in labour. Next day he departed to Fresnes, having seen no one, except his immediate family and a few intimate friends. His wife joined him as soon as her health permitted.

After receiving the Chancellor's letter, the Duc de Noailles had no doubts of what his own fate would be; but he determined to soften the blow and make the best of a bad situation. He went at once to the Regent, at the Palais Royal, and had the temerity to ask why the seals were on the table; to which the Regent amiably replied that he had just taken them from the Chancellor. Noailles, looking as cheerful as was possible in the circumstances, asked who would next receive them, and once again the Regent was good enough to satisfy his curiosity. At that point Noailles declared that as the other side had evidently won, it might be best for him to resign the finances. 'Do you want anything else?' said the Regent.

[1] See note, p. 33 above.
[2] His grandfather had on two occasions—in 1650 and 1651—been sent to collect the seals from Chancellor Séguier.

'Nothing at all,' replied de Noailles. 'I mean to give you a seat on the Regency Council,' said the Regent. 'I shall hardly ever use it,' said Noailles impertinently, taking full advantage of M. le Duc d'Orléans's good nature, and lying most foully, for he attended the very next meeting, and never afterwards missed one; although for the next few days he kept his front door barred and bolted.

I sent to the Palais Royal for the news, because I always liked to hear that things were safely over and done with, and as I was sitting down to dinner with a great company of guests, one of d'Argenson's servants brought me a letter. In composing this missive, which I opened and showed to the assembled company, he had imitated the exquisite modesty of Cardinal d'Ossat,[1] who owed his advancement to the Maréchal de Villeroy.[2] On emerging from the papal audience at which he received his hat, he sent both a letter and the hat to M. de Villeroy, addressing that nobleman, although for the last time, as Monseigneur. So it was with d'Argenson, writing to tell me of his promotion. He ended his letter with expressions of gratitude and attachment, inscribing it both within and on the cover with the title, Monseigneur.[3]

It was thus that Chancellor Daguesseau fell a victim to the Duc de Noailles and became the scapegoat for all that lord's sins. Noailles used him as a shield, making him believe and do what best suited his own interests, without the least pity or compunction. That was how he repaid the friendship, gratitude and trust of a decent, honourable man who, perfectly ignorant of the finances and the Social World, blindly groped to fulfil his new duties, relying for honest guidance on the so-called friend who had raised him to his exalted office.

M. le Duc d'Orléans had a bastard by the actress Florence.[4] He had never recognized the young man who had none the less risen in the Church, and was known as the Abbé de Saint-Albin. Madame, who loathed all bastardy and all bastards, capriciously took a great fancy to this one, so much so, indeed, that when he submitted a thesis for oral examination at the Sorbonne, she made a public exhibition of herself of the most novel and scandalous description, at a place where, until then, no woman, however distinguished, had ever appeared or dreamed of appearing. Such was the wilfulness of that royal lady. The entire Court and all Society were invited to hear the thesis, and there was a vast audience. M. de Conflans, M. le Duc d'Orléans's first gentleman, did the honours; it was just as though M. le Duc de Chartres[5] had been the person concerned. Madame

---

[1] Arnaud d'Ossat (1537–1604), made cardinal in 1598. He was Bishop of Rennes 1596–1600, of Bayeux 1600, retiring 1603.

[2] Nicolas III de Neufville, Seigneur de Villeroy (1543–1617).

[3] See Saint-Simon's talk with the new Dauphin, II, p. 175.

[4] Florence Pellerin (died 1716). She was the daughter of a tavern-keeper in the Faubourg Saint-Germain. See I, pp. 356f.

[5] Legitimate son of the Duc d'Orléans.

sat on a specially built dais. The cardinals, bishops, and the other eminent spectators had benches with backs instead of armchairs.[1] M. le Duc and Mme la Duchesse d'Orléans were the only ones missing, and I also did not attend. This extraordinary performance made a great stir, but M. le Duc d'Orléans and I never mentioned it.

The Maréchal de Villeroy, who had adored everything about the character of Louis XIV, including the smallest details, took great care to foster them all in the present King, even at his tender age.[2] He thus made him dance in a ballet, a pleasure for which he was far too young, and which confirmed him in a dislike for balls, ballets, spectacles, and entertainments of all kinds.[3] Even though this particular performance was the greatest success imaginable, the King found it tiresome to learn the steps and try on his costume; still more did he dislike appearing in public.

The Duc de Lorraine et Bar,[4] although permanently attached to the Court of Vienna, was not one to lose any advantages that might flow from the good-natured Regent his brother-in-law, from that prince's devotion to the sister with whom he had been brought up, or his indulgence towards Madame who, Germanlike, cared only for her daughter's husband and his greater glory. M. de Lorraine's previous reception, when he came to pay homage for the duchy of Bar, provided the excuse for another visit to Paris, under the shabby incognito of a Comte de Blamont. He and his retinue arrived on Friday, 18 February, and were met on the far side of Bondy by Madame, with M. and Mme la Duchesse d'Orléans, M. le Duc de Chartres, and Mlle de Valois,[5] all in her coach. She made room in it for M. and Mme de Lorraine, the latter not under an incognito, because she ranked as a Granddaughter of France. She was thus the equal of Mme la Duchesse d'Orléans, who did the honours of the coach, seating her beside Madame on the back seat. Mme la Duchesse d'Orléans took the front seat with M. de Chartres and Mlle de Valois. M. le Duc d'Orléans could not squeeze in beside them, but sat by one of the doors, while M. de Lorraine sat by the other. They were set down at the Palais Royal, and were lodged in the Queen-mother's apartments, which M. de Chartres vacated for them.

Directly they arrived they were all taken to the Opéra, to Madame's state box, from which M. le Duc d'Orléans took M. de Lorraine to pay Mme la Duchesse de Berry a short visit in hers. When it was over, Mme

---

[1] To keep up Madame's royal rank; no one, except the King and Mme la Duchesse de Berry, could sit in an armchair when she was present.

[2] Louis XV was eight on 15 February 1718.

[3] He continued to dislike them until Mme de Pompadour converted him.

[4] Léopold, Duc de Lorraine (1679–1729). He had yielded his estates to Louis XIV in 1692, and was made Duc de Lorraine by the Treaty of Ryswick in 1697. His duchess was Elisabeth Charlotte d'Orléans (1676–1744), the Regent's sister. She, like the Regent, ranked as a Grandchild of France because Louis XIII had been their grandfather. (The Duchesse d'Orléans also enjoyed that rank after her marriage.)

[5] Charlotte Aglaë d'Orléans, Demoiselle de Valois (1700–1761). She was the Regent's third daughter and, in 1737, married the Duke of Modena.

la Duchesse de Lorraine received callers at her rooms where, on arrival, she had found an entire wardrobe of the most supremely elegant garments, a present from Mme la Duchesse de Berry, and much exquisite lace from Mme la Duchesse d'Orléans. She went later to that princess for a grand supper-party, with gambling for the highest stakes to follow. Before retiring she watched the Opéra ball from one of the boxes. They dined each day with Madame, and supped with Mme la Duchesse d'Orléans. The Regent seldom put in an appearance for supper and never dined with them. He drank chocolate in public, between one and two o'clock in the afternoon, which was the best time to speak to him. It was an arrangement that permanently upset the dinner hour, for once such irregularities became habitual they were never put right.

On the following day, the Regent took M. and Mme de Lorraine to the Luxembourg to call on Mme la Duchesse de Berry, a visit during which all stood.[1] On the Sunday, Madame escorted them to the Tuileries. The King was at dinner, but he rose and kissed the duchess. He then sat down again, and they all watched him eat, seated on their *tabourets*. When the King left, they went to dine at Madame's where the duke was waiting for them. On Tuesday, the duchess called on all the princesses of the blood, who had previously visited her in her apartments. After dinner they put on masks and went onto the floor at the Opéra ball. Large numbers of ladies were invited to all the suppers given by Mme la Duchesse d'Orléans. On Saturday, 26 February, they attended a most magnificent banquet at the Hôtel de Condé. Monsieur le Duc invited a host of ladies all most richly and beautifully attired, as was Mme de Lorraine herself. Numerous tables, generously supplied either for fasting or feasting, were an innovation that aroused some criticism.[2]

On Monday, 28 February, Mme la Duchesse de Berry gave the most charming and splendid entertainment that can possibly be imagined, magnificent in the very highest degree, and in perfect taste. Mme de Saint-Simon arranged the whole thing and did the honours, receiving all the compliments and congratulations that such trifles may command, for refinement, discrimination, and most admirable organization. One table, set with a hundred-and-twenty-five places, was for invited ladies, all most exquisitely dressed, not one in mourning;[3] another, similarly set, was for as many invited gentlemen.[4] The ambassadors, all invited, refused to

---

[1] Thus surmounting an awkward moment; for by the rules of etiquette, the Duchesse de Berry, as a Daughter of France, would have had an armchair, while her mother and aunt perched on *tabourets*.

[2] It was Lent. There should have been no temptation to feast.

[3] Louis XIV liked Versailles to be a happy place—therefore no mourning. The argument, Miss Mitford says, was that nearly everyone might have cause to mourn some relation or friend, but that it would be selfish to spoil other people's pleasure by displaying it.

[4] Those with special invitations had a 'sit-down supper'. People of quality might join such royal revels uninvited, and eat and drink at the various buffets, provided they were in court-dress, and that one person of every party gave his name on entering.

sit there, claiming that they had the right to eat with the princes of the blood, who sat with the Duc de Lorraine in no particular order at a table with their ladies, including Mme la Duchesse de Berry, a Daughter of France. Ambassadors might not sit with her; nor, indeed, should M. de Lorraine have done so because of his incognito; but no one made any difficulty about that. The Palais du Luxembourg was most brilliantly illuminated both without and within. The supper was preceded by a concert and followed by a masked ball. There was, however, no confusion until Mme la Duchesse de Berry and Mme de Lorraine wished there to be, for their amusement. All Paris came in masks. Mlle de Valois did not appear at the supper, and went only to the ball. I never was able to discover or guess why.

Three or four persons, neither invited nor fit to be so, boldly inserted themselves at the gentlemen's table. Saumery,[1] Mme la Duchesse de Berry's steward, showed his opinion of them with a curt command as they rose from table. None of them replied, and all very swiftly vanished, with the exception of Magny,[2] who was so insolent that Saumery seized him by the cravat to take him to Mme la Duchesse de Berry; and he would have done so had not Magny escaped into the streets, where all next day he continued to utter foolish abuse. He had purchased some very minor post as head of protocol from the Baron de Breteuil, which had been his excuse for claiming a place at the table, but his impertinence earned for him two days' Bastille. When he emerged he was dismissed from his place on the grounds that someone more prudent was needed to deal with foreign ambassadors. This so infuriated him that he joined the enemies of the government and very shortly afterwards departed to Spain, where he was welcomed and made much of, and although never more than an attorney in France, he became first a colonel, then a brigadier-general in the service of Spain. I have dwelt on his character because when I went to Spain I found him acting as the queen's major-domo. He was a man to ruin with extreme promptness all he touched. He complained that wealth had come to him too late; but in reality, his poverty was all of his own making. Ill temper made him insolent in Spain also, with the result that he was discharged with ignominy, and remained permanently in disgrace. After the Regent's death he recrossed the Pyrenees, hoping to profit by the change; but firebrands were no longer needed by those who had used them in M. le Duc d'Orléans's lifetime. Magny therefore remained unemployed, scorned, heavily in debt, to the great distress of the very decent, wealthy lady[3] whom he married when he was Intendant at Caen, and deserted after sucking her dry. Since then he has dragged on in want and obscurity, and

---

[1] Jean Baptiste de Johanne, Comte de Saumery (1678–1726). In 1720, he was made one of the King's assistant governors.

[2] Nicolas Joseph Foucault de Magny (1677–1772).

[3] Catherine Henriette de Ragaru (1683–1755). She had married Magny in 1705.

finally has returned to Spain, where the same poverty and scorn still attend him.

In the midst of this visit to Paris by M. and Mme de Lorraine, I must recount a very minor incident because it so well portrays the character of M. le Duc d'Orléans. One day when Mme la Duchesse d'Orléans was away on an excursion to Montmartre,[1] which she soon afterwards vacated, I was walking alone with M. le Duc d'Orléans in the little garden of the Palais Royal. We had been discussing State affairs for some considerable time, when suddenly he stopped and turned to face me. 'I am about,' he said, 'to tell you something that will greatly please you.' Whereupon he declared that he was tired of his present way of life; that his age and desires no longer required it, and other similar statements. He had resolved, he said, to give up his drunken evenings, and spend them decently, soberly, and more suitably, sometimes in his own apartments, often with Mme la Duchesse d'Orléans. He said this would improve his health, and give him more time for work, but he would not make the change until after the departure of M. and Mme de Lorraine, because he would die of boredom if he had to sup with Mme la Duchesse d'Orléans every single night among a pack of women. As soon as the Lorraines were gone, I might be sure that there would be no more supper-parties with *roués* and harlots (his very words), and that he would be leading a good, quiet life, more becoming to his age.

I must confess that I was astounded; also enchanted because of my deep concern for his welfare, and I demonstrated my heartfelt joy as I thanked him for telling me. I said he knew how for a long time past I had ceased to mention either his debauches or his wasted time because I realized this merely wasted my own. His behaviour, however, had made me most unhappy, as I had had no hope of his ever changing. He might therefore imagine my delight and surprise. He said again and again that his mind was made up; and I left him at that point because it was his supper-time.

The very next day, I learned from persons whom the *roués* had told, that no sooner was M. le Duc d'Orléans seated with them at supper than he burst into a loud peal of laughter, saying that he had just pitched me a tale and that I had fallen for it completely. He then recounted all our conversation to everyone's huge amusement, his own included. This was the only time he ever diverted himself at my expense (not to say his own) with a thumping lie which I was fool enough to swallow, in a moment of joyful astonishment that had quite destroyed my reasoning power. The incident did some little honour to me; it did him none at all. I did not choose to gratify him by telling him that I had discovered his joke, or reminding him of his words; and I never learned what had possessed him to speak to me in that way, simply to make a jest of it—to me, who for years past had not mentioned his way of life.

[1] Her apartments at the Abbey of Montmartre.

It is true that very occasionally he had let slip some word of complaint when he was alone with his valets—never with others, saying that I bullied him, or spoke roughly, just that, two words only, never resentfully or calling me unjust. And what he said was true, at certain times when he exasperated me by his false reasoning or his incurable weakness in some important matter concerning himself or the State; when, for instance, I had given him sound arguments for taking or avoiding some course of action, and had then seen him twist out of my grasp and do just the opposite. That he very well knew his own faults was one of the things that drove me to be so hard with him; but what vexed me most (although more often than not we were alone when it happened) and always made me lose my temper, was when he suddenly interrupted an important argument with an odiously misplaced jest. I simply could not stand it; I got so angry that I almost left the room. I used to say that if talking nonsense was what he wished, I would jest with him gladly; but to mix tomfoolery with State affairs was something I could not tolerate. Then he would laugh until his sides shook, especially since this was no rare event. For although I should have been on my guard, I never was so, and thus had the double annoyance of the thing itself, and of being caught napping. He would then return with all seriousness to the argument, at the point where he had broken off.

Princes must sometimes relax and tease those whom they deign to treat as friends. He very well knew that I was his friend, and although he sometimes concealed things from me when he thought I would oppose them, he never failed to show me all the affection, esteem, and trust of which he was capable. What is more, his friendship was proof against all the plots and attacks of intimates, such as the Abbé Dubois, Noailles, and Canillac.[1] His fits of annoyance, and they were infrequent, took the form of icy politeness, sulks, and silence, but they never lasted long. I used to inquire who had been making mischief, and what nonsense they had told him. He would then speak openly as to his friend, and feel ashamed. Indeed, on such occasions I always left him on even better terms than before.

It was quite by chance that I discovered what he really thought of me. I shall recount it here so as to be done with such trifles once and for all. One afternoon, M. le Duc d'Orléans was returning to the Palais Royal with M. le Duc de Chartres and the Sheriff of Conflans,[2] after a meeting of the Council. They were alone in his coach, just the three of them. He began to speak of me to his son as they left the courtyard of the Tuileries, and in terms of such high praise that I dare not repeat them. I forget what had occurred at the meeting, or what had started him off. Suffice it to say that he stressed his happiness in having so faithful a friend in fair weather or

<hr />

[1] See note 4, p. 10 above.

[2] Philippe Alexandre, Chevalier, later Bailli (sheriff), de Conflans (1676–1744). He became the Regent's first gentleman after his brother's death in 1723.

foul, so useful, loyal, and steadfast, so firm; a better friend, he said, did not exist, for all through his life he had been sure of my affection, and I had rendered him the best service of all by speaking the truth as I saw it, freely and frankly on all subjects, and wholly devoid of selfish motives. This eulogy ended only with their arrival at the Palais Royal and his telling his son that he wished him to know me, for the comfort and support he would find in me. What I have written are his exact words. The Sheriff of Conflans was truly amazed by such a flow; he repeated it all to me two days later, under the seal of secrecy. I must confess that I have never been able to forget it.

It is indeed true that despite all they could do; despite my own conduct even, when sometimes I was furious and indignant with him for doing wrong, he always returned to me and nearly always was the first to make an advance, apologetic, affectionate, trustful; and he was never in any kind of a dilemma but he opened his heart to me and told me everything; though he did not always abide by my advice when, later, other people misled him. Yet this did not often happen, and at such times he felt ashamed and embarrassed; then, when I had let fly at him a little, he would humbly confess that he had followed different counsel. You have seen this happen many a time already, and will do so again in what follows.

He was not a man to be satisfied with one mistress, for his nature needed the spice of variety; but I knew them no more than I knew his *roués*. He never mentioned them to me, nor I to him. Most often I was not even aware of such affairs. His *roués* and valets presented many women to him, and among the crowd he would single out one or another. Mme de Sabran,[1] however, was different because she sometimes had business at the Court. She had run from her home to marry a man with a noble name but no fortune or merit, who left her free to live as she chose. You never saw a lovelier creature, more perfect, more amiable, more moving, with a nobler or a more dignified appearance. She gave herself no airs, but was simple and natural, for all the world as though she was unaware of her beauty and her figure, for she was tall, exquisitely proportioned and, when she so pleased, of a deceptive modesty. Possessing a very pretty wit, she was most attractive, comically pathetic, wanton but without malice, and delightful company, especially at table. In short, she was everything best calculated to delight M. le Duc d'Orléans and, without prejudice to his other loves, soon became his mistress.[2] Since neither she nor her husband possessed a penny nothing came to them amiss; but they none the less failed to make a large fortune. When Montigny, M. le Duc d'Orléans's chamberlain with a salary of six thousand livres, was pro-

---

[1] Madeleine Louise Charlotte de Foix-Rabat, Comtesse de Sabran (1693–1768). She married the Comte de Sabran in 1714.

[2] Saint-Simon becomes quite lyrical. On the whole he was uninterested in the appearance of women. With few exceptions, the clichés, 'lovely as the dawn', 'pretty as a picture', serve to describe them. One feels that if he had had any wild oats he might have sown them here; but as far as one can gather he never strayed, nor wished to, from the matrimonial path.

moted to be high-steward, Mme de Sabran considered six thousand worth snatching for a husband of whom she thought so little that she constantly referred to him as 'my watchdog', and M. le Duc d'Orléans at once gave him the post. Once when she was supping with the Regent and his *roués*, she remarked very pleasantly that very evidently God had set aside a special mould at the Creation for princes and their lackeys, for they were totally different from the rest of humanity.

All the current mistresses had their turn. It was fortunate indeed that they had so little influence and no knowledge of State secrets; all they extracted was money, and not much even of that commodity. The Regent was amused by them, and set a fitting value on their company. Let us now return to the point at which the visit of M. and Mme de Lorraine and other such trifles caused me to deviate.

I was becoming more and more pleased with Law. Now that the Duc de Noailles no longer controlled the finances, it was to Law I went for the business of La Trappe and Septfonts, and he obliged me with all the pleasure in the world. The payments came in promptly; I took great care to give Septfonts its portion, and when later I secured a supplement for La Trappe from the Regent, I gave Septfonts part of that also. To tell all at once, La Trappe received altogether forty thousands écus, and Septfonts more than eighty thousand livres,[1] which saved those pious houses from certain and imminent ruin, and set them on their feet again. Although I was still on the worst possible terms with the Duc de Noailles, I felt obliged to remember that he had been the moving spirit of this excellent action, and accordingly, every time I received a payment from Law, I drew the Duc de Noailles on one side at the next meeting of the Regency Council to tell him the amount, and how I intended to divide it. He used to thank me, bowing deeply several times, but I neither spoke nor bowed in return and did not address him again until the next payment. These brief colloquies, at long intervals, vastly surprised the onlookers and provided food for speculation. On the first occasion we were thought to be reconciled. Later, no one knew what to think. I merely smiled, and let them imagine what they pleased. The Abbot of Septfonts[2] lived in Paris, and it was to him that I made the payments. He had never expected to share in the La Trappe supplement; thus when he learned from the amount I sent him that he was receiving a part of it, he was surprised and very deeply touched. These dealings led to our striking up an acquaintance which soon turned to warm friendship. He was a most amiable and saintly man.

Chancellor Pontchartrain arranged a match between his grandson Maurepas[3] and the daughter of La Vrillière, with whom the young man

---

[1] An écu was worth five livres.
[2] Joseph Hargenvilliers had been Abbot of Septfonts since 1710.
[3] Jean Frédéric Phélypeaux, Comte de Maurepas (1701–1781). He married Marie Jeanne Phélypeaux de La Vrillière (1704–1793).

lodged while learning the work of a secretary of State. He far outstripped his master, absorbing much from his grandfather, whom he greatly reverenced. He still, today, graces that office with all imaginable brilliance, and capability; what is more, he is now a minister of State. It would be small praise to say of him that he is by far the best of those who have sat on the King's Council since the death of M. le Duc d'Orléans. It was his good fortune to find a wife whose wit, good manners, and winning nature made her all that he could desire, and who, with him, made their marriage a most happy union. I cannot myself feel it was a disaster that they should have had no children.[1]

When Fagon lost his post as first physician (the only appointment that changes hands with the death of a King), he lived retired, in the Faubourg Saint-Victor, in fine apartments attached to the King's garden, where he continued to superintend the herbs, and the rare and medicinal plants. He still lived in solitude, happily occupied with the arts and sciences, especially those subjects connected with the profession that had always so deeply interested him. He has been described so often and at such length in these memoirs that no more need be said of him, except that he died in great piety, and at a considerable age for a body so deformed and dyspeptic, one which learning and absolute sobriety, with the constant aid of hard work and study, managed to drive so very far. What is surprising, considering the close attachment and entire confidence always existing between Mme de Maintenon and himself, which had caused him to be appointed first physician and held in continual favour, is that after the King's death they never met.

You will remember the Abbé d'Estrées, whose character and employments I have many times described.[2] He enjoyed robust health at a time when old age gave him ample leisure to savour his wealth as Archbishop of Cambrai. He was in residence, awaiting bulls from Rome, when he was attacked by an inflammation of the bowels, brought on by taking, totally without cause, just as a general precaution, the remedy of some quack of whom he had become enamoured. Another quack of better repute so thoroughly convinced him that his pain was of no consequence that he invited several of us to a grand and exceedingly delicious dinner; but just as he was about to sit down with us the pains gripped him again. He none the less insisted on remaining. Soon after the fruit appeared, a sudden and violent change was so noticeable in his countenance that we hastened to leave him free to think seriously of his condition. An hour later, Cardinal de Noailles, who had been notified earlier, came to calm him. Little time was allowed him in which to collect his thoughts, but he made good use of

---

[1] This indicates that Saint-Simon was revising this part of the memoirs shortly after the death of his elder son, Jacques Louis de Rouvroy, Duc de Ruffec (1698–1746).

[2] Jean, Abbé d'Estrées (1666–1718). He was chosen Archbishop of Cambrai in 1718, but died before he could be consecrated. See also index, I and II.

what remained. He completed his will, received the Last Sacraments the following day, and died the night after. I grieved for the loss of one who was my friend, and who, despite a certain foolishness and a good deal of smugness, had many excellent qualities, including sincerity, steadfastness and integrity. In him M. le Duc d'Orléans lost a most loyal servant; he consulted me first regarding the new appointment to Cambrai. I advised him to decide quickly, so as to avoid being pestered for that most important see which, because of its situation, required careful selection.[1] I then suggested Cardinal de La Trémoïlle, although I had no acquaintance with him. I told the Regent that having been in charge of the King's affairs in Rome, without a fortune of his own and with a natural propensity to spend freely, he would stand in great need of pensions and rich benefices that would cost the King money; that the emoluments of the Cambrai diocese would avoid the need for costly favours and spare the treasury; that he was not a man who need be feared at Cambrai, for he would never reside there—as indeed happened. The Regent believed me, and forthwith appointed him.

This death procured a startling and permanent conversion, by which good works and penitence daily increased in all humility, though still retaining pleasantness in such little social intercourse as was permitted, and with peace and joy abounding amid many most repugnant austerities. I speak of the Marquise de Créquy,[2] a childless widow, daughter of the Duc d'Aumont and of the sister of M. de Louvois, the late Archbishop of Rheims,[3] who gave her a fortune and was everywhere suspected of being rather more to her than an uncle. He was succeeded in both those ways by the Abbé d'Estrées. Once the most worldly of women, the vainest of her hair and appearance, the most fastidious regarding her jewels and other adornments, the most passionately devoted to gambling, she became most humble and retiring, abundantly generous to the poor, mean only towards herself, always at her prayers at home or in church, a tireless worker in the prisons and deepest dungeons, and also in the hospitals, amid the most disgusting natural functions. She steadily persisted in such good works until her death, which did not come until she had spent many years in repentance.

Argenson, in charge of the finances and the seals, was unconcerned with punctuality. The lieutenancy of police, which in his hands became a kind of general inquisition, had accustomed him to working at all hours of the day and night, for he was often wakened from sleep. He had no fixed times for his meals or audiences, which was vastly upsetting for those who had to deal with him. The treasury officials and their clerks were especially put

---

[1] Saint-Simon was remembering Fénelon's popularity and immense influence when he was in exile at the Archbishop's palace at Cambrai.

[2] Anne Charlotte Fare d'Aumont, Marquise de Créquy (1665–1724), daughter of Louis Marie Victor, Duc d'Aumont, and Marie Le Tellier de Louvois.

[3] Charles Maurice Le Tellier (1642–1710), Archbishop of Rheims. He was Louvois's younger brother.

out, for he often made nocturnal appointments with them. One, two, or three o'clock in the morning were the times he particularly favoured;[1] indeed, I have more than once seen Fagon very much distressed. Argenson adopted the habit, which he never afterwards abandoned, of dining in his coach on the way from his home (near the professed house of the Jesuits)[2] to the Tuileries for the Council, or else to work all through the afternoon at the Palais Royal. For years past he had been the intimate friend of Mme de Veyny,[3] perpetual prioress of the Madeleine de Trainel, in the Faubourg Saint-Antoine. He had a lodging on the outer side, did great things for the Convent, and slept there often when he was Lieutenant of Police. The change of office made no difference in that respect, for in all his leisure moments he hurried off there, and stayed the night whenever possible. On more than one occasion he left the seals behind, and was obliged to return to fetch them. By and large he wasted an immense amount of time, which caused much grumbling, especially over the difficulty of seeing or speaking to him. Had I realized these hindrances before his promotion, I should certainly have spoken to him; but now that he was Chancellor it was too late. He and Law administered the finances jointly; they often worked with the Regent, but rarely both at the same time; usually the two of them were alone, and their proposals and decisions were ratified without further consultation. The Duc de La Force, who in the Duc de Noailles's time had borne the empty titles of president of the finances and trade councils, no longer had a department to rule; moreover, the meeting of the Regency Council on Saturday afternoon (one of the two weekly sessions for matters of finance) ceased to be held, for lack of business.

Mme de Vendôme[4] died in Paris on 11 April of this year, without benefit of clergy or leaving a will. This was due to her own carelessness, largely caused by her love of strong drink, of which her cupboards were full. She was in her forty-first year. All that may be said of this death is that thereafter one less princess of the blood remained. She died immensely rich, for M. de Vendôme had endowed her with all his worldly goods by the marriage contract. You read at the proper time of how they entered into matrimony[5]—he from pride, she to gain her freedom, with M. du Maine supporting them for the greater glory of bastardy. In the two years of their union, you might count the days (no more) which they spent together. Since there were no children, and his brother the Grand Prieur[6] could not

---

[1] From all that one reads, his habits were somewhat similar to those of the late Sir Winston Churchill.   [2] In the Rue Saint-Antoine.

[3] Gilberte Françoise de Veyny d'Arbouze de Villemont (1666–1724). She was a daughter of the steward of the duchy of Montpensier and became prioress in 1706.

[4] Marie Anne de Bourbon-Condé who had married the Duc de Vendôme in 1710.

[5] See II, pp. 50–51.

[6] Philippe de Vendôme (1655–1727), a character even more dissolute than his brother the duke. He none the less held the position of Grand Prieur de France, the highest foreign rank in the Order of the Knights of Malta. He could not inherit because he belonged to a religious order.

inherit, all that vast estate went to Madame la Princesse[1] and her family.

A very trifling affair at this point caused an appalling commotion. I have already mentioned the Saint-Pierres,[2] one of whom was master of the horse to Mme la Duchesse d'Orléans; the other, his brother,[3] was Madame's chief almoner. That individual was endowed with wit, learning, and imagination. He had long been a member of the French Academy, and was somewhat puffed up, but for all that, a good and honest gentleman, a great writer of books, full of projects for reforms in politics and the administration, all directed to the public good. In the change of government he saw his chance to give free rein to his ideas. He accordingly produced a work entitled *La Polysynodie*, in which he clearly revealed the autocratic, often tyrannous power wielded during the last reign by secretaries of State and controllers-general of finance. He called these gentlemen viziers, and their departments vizierates, and extended that comparison with more veracity than prudence. When the book appeared, every member of the late administration vigorously protested, especially those who still saw hope of a return to power after the Regency. These one-time courtiers of the late monarch prided themselves, to the detriment of others, on a gratitude that cost them nothing.

The Maréchal de Villeroy made his views known in a burst of fury, sending the entire pack of the old Court in full cry after Saint-Pierre. No one else was at all disturbed by a book which might perhaps be thought wanting in prudence, but which lacked nothing of what was due to the memory of the late King. It dealt only with proven facts, well known to those alive at that time, and entirely incontestable. Academicians, and scholars from other places of learning, and many private individuals also, were outraged to see that gentlemen of the late Court were so crushed by oppression that they could no longer stomach truth and candour. The Maréchal de Villeroy, however, continued to make such a terrible rumpus, with angry speeches in public and private, that a vast number joined in the chorus of abuse, and M. le Duc d'Orléans, who disliked the Saint-Pierres, was not inclined to protect them. The Abbé de Saint-Pierre was accordingly expelled from the Academy, despite feeble protests from the members; but not from other learned bodies, although none that he belonged to was of any great importance. The book was suppressed, but the Academy, turning to good account the Regent's preference for doing

[1] Anne of Bavaria, Princesse de Condé, mother of the Duchesse de Vendôme, and widow of Monsieur le Prince. The Duchesse de Vendôme must have been one of the unhappiest women in the Memoirs—daughter of a tyrant and bully and then wife of the unspeakable Duc de Vendôme. Her spirit was so crushed, one feels, that she could not have enjoyed even her widowhood.

[2] Louis Hyacinthe de Castel, Comte de Saint-Pierre (1659–1748). He was a Knight of Malta, and had been attached to the Duc d'Orléans in 1695 when the latter was still Duc de Chartres. He was appointed Madame's master of the horse in 1706.

[3] Charles Iréné de Castel (1658–1743), Abbé de Saint-Pierre. He had been an academician since 1695; but this is Saint-Simon's first mention of him.

nothing, managed to ensure that there was no election. Thus the abbé's place was not filled until after his death, despite the fury of his persecutors.

On 27 April, the Petit-Pont[1] caught fire. Some careless fool, searching with a candle in the dark corners of a hay-barge, managed to set it alight. Terrified lest the flames should spread to the surrounding barges, he hurriedly pushed out into mid-stream. The current brought him up against one of the wooden pillars of the bridge; the rising flames caught one of the houses above, and a fairly big fire developed. The Duc de Tresmes,[2] Governor of Paris, the police magistrates, and many others rushed to the spot. When some of the hospital was endangered, Cardinal de Noailles spent part of the night in organizing the removal of patients from the Hôtel-Dieu to his residence, looking after their comfort like the good shepherd and father that he was. The Archbishop's palace was full of sick people; even the private apartments were invaded. At one moment it seemed as though the whole hospital would be destroyed, but thanks to prompt and efficient action, only a very small portion of it, and about thirty houses, was burned down or gutted. The Capuchins gave admirable service, and the Franciscans did well also.[3] The Duc de Guiche sent for the regiment of guards, who proved exceedingly useful, and the Duc de Chaulnes set the light horse to stand guard over the furniture and other effects. Everyone ridiculed the Maréchal de Villars because he had a cannon brought up to demolish the houses, a remedy that would have been little less disastrous than the fire itself, for they were made of wood and crowded together. The chief of the fire-brigade did not distinguish himself.[4]

Mme de Castries,[5] Mme la Duchesse d'Orléans's lady-in-waiting, was one morning discovered unconscious in her bed and, despite all remedies, did not return to her senses until eight that evening, at which time she died, leaving no children. Her health had seemed particularly robust, and Mme de Saint-Simon had spent part of the previous evening with her. What was still more surprising was that she had been all soul and spirit, with no body worth mentioning; for hers was so slender and small that a breath might have blown it over. Her death was the greatest pity imaginable. I have spoken elsewhere of her and of her husband, who was inconsolable, and no wonder. She looked like a little doll, and was thoroughly learned in every subject; but she never allowed this to be seen. She sparkled with wit, and occasionally with malice, and possessed all the graces, more especially that fascinating turn of phrase so original, so much admired, so

---

[1] It was the oldest bridge in Paris.

[2] The Duc de Tresmes seems always to have been on hand when needed in times of trouble in Paris. See I, pp. 475f; II, pp. 148f.

[3] Friars, especially the Capuchins and the Franciscans, were in those days volunteer firemen.

[4] François Dumouriez du Perier was the creator of the first Paris fire-brigade. He had formerly been Molière's footman, and secretary of the Comédie Française.

[5] Marie Elisabeth de Rochechouart-Vivonne. See II, p. 140; III, p. 56.

particularly belonging to the Mortemarts. Two days after her death, Mme d'Espinay[1] was appointed to replace her. One of Mme de Castries's footmen, hearing this news in the courtyard of the Palais Royal, cried out: 'Oh! my poor mistress; if she knew, she would turn in her grave.' Mme la Duchesse d'Orléans had insisted on having her because she was the daughter of M. d'O;[2] I have already reported on that family's link with the bastards. She tried hard to pretend that Mme d'Espinay was the Regent's choice; but he denied it and was the first to mock. The poor victim did extremely well, however, and in the end was liked by everyone.

The Queen of England[3] died at Saint-Germain on 7 May, after an illness of ten or twelve days' duration. Her life since she came to France at the end of 1688 had been one long succession of disasters, which she bore heroically, praising God, resigned, and penitent. She devoted herself to good works, with every saintly virtue concealing great natural sensibility, and an innate pride which she learned to subdue with the noblest, most majestic dignity, and very delightful modesty. Her death was as edifying as her life. Out of the six hundred thousand livres which the King allowed her annually,[4] she gave all she could spare to the impoverished English who filled Saint-Germain. It was they who took her body, next day, to the convent of the Filles de Sainte-Marie de Chaillot, where it has since remained, and where she had made many retreats. The Court took no notice of her death and paid no tribute at her obsequies. The Duc de Noailles went to Saint-Germain as governor and captain of the guard, but only to see that all was decently performed. The mourning period was no longer than three weeks.

Mme de Chalmazel died.[5] I note this because of the remarkable coincidence that as well as being a sister of the Maréchal d'Harcourt's father, she was also the sister of his wife's mother.

The Regent granted an increase of eight thousand livres on the twelve

---

[1] Marie Anne d'O (1687–1727) who married François Rodrigue, Marquis d'Espinay (1675–1745), in 1705.

[2] Saint-Simon was always exceedingly catty about the d'Os. He thought them social climbers who had sucked up first to the Montespan, and then to Mme de Maintenon. This M. d'O was Gabriel Claude, Marquis de Villiers d'O (1654–1728). He had been the governor of the Comte de Toulouse and comptroller of his household. He and his wife had been given a lodging in Toulouse's grand apartment at Versailles, with access to Louis XIV at any time through the backstairs. Of Mme d'O, Saint-Simon says that at the time when the Comte de Toulouse was reaching manhood, she much pleased him by her accommodating nature.

[3] Mary of Modena, widow of James II.

[4] Louis XIV was extraordinarily generous with money and kindness to the English court at Saint-Germain. He and James II were first cousins and, what is more, James's sister Henrietta of England had been the first wife of Monsieur, Louis XIV's only brother. They were also of the same religion. One imagines that Louis was genuinely fond of them.

[5] Catherine Angélique d'Harcourt, Dame de Chalmazel, married 1717, died in childbirth 1718. The daughter of Louis Henri d'Harcourt, Marquis de Beuvron, her elder brother was the father of the Maréchal d'Harcourt. By an earlier marriage, her father had a step-daughter who became the mother of the Maréchal d'Harcourt's wife.

thousand livres pension of the Duchess of Portsmouth.[1] She was exceedingly old, converted and penitent, in very poor circumstances, and reduced to living in the country. It was very right and proper to recognize the important and repeated services she had gladly rendered to France at the time when she was in England and the highly influential mistress of Charles II.

It is now time to speak of foreign affairs, which will necessitate our returning to the beginning of the year. You will recollect that in various parts of the memoirs I have quoted from Torcy,[2] who ruled that department, first jointly with his father and father-in-law, then alone until the King's death. Later he kept himself informed through the letters passing through the post-office, of which he was first the director, then the superintendent. He made extracts of all the important communications, and continued in that practice until the end of August 1718. It was the greatest pity that he should have ceased while he still controlled the posts, which, as you will learn, Dubois seized from him in 1721. Had he not done so, you might have known many interesting details of those last three years that now lie buried—for example, the whole story of the intrigues and disgrace of Alberoni, and of the Spanish double-marriage. Torcy lent me his extracts, from which I have drawn freely in all I have said of foreign affairs after Louis XIV's death. More often than not, I have abridged them so as to give only what was necessary; but the events of 1718 appear to me so extremely important that I have neither shortened nor extracted, but faithfully copied, without omitting a single word.

Although the clarity, flow, and nobility of Torcy's style must jump to any eye,[3] I do not wish to leave the reader in ignorance should these memoirs ever come to be read. I have such a profound contempt for plagiarists that I prefer to say at once from whom I have taken the following report, so that I may keep strictly to my rule of setting down only what has passed through my hands or beneath my eyes, or else was taken from completely authoritative sources which I name, explaining in what manner I use them.

[*This editor proposes to skip the next four hundred pages for precisely the same reasons that Saint-Simon inserted them. Torcy's style may be noble, but it is dull, and certainly seems far from clear, although that may be due to the complications of the politics he describes. It deals at immense length with the Franco-British alliance*

---

[1] Louise Renée de Penancoët de Kéroualle, Duchess of Portsmouth and Aubigny (1649-1734). Her country house was Aubigny-sur-Nère, not far from Bourges.

[2] Jean Baptiste Colbert, Marquis de Torcy (1665-1746). His father was Charles François Colbert, a younger brother of the great Colbert, and had been secretary of State for foreign affairs in 1679. Torcy's father-in-law was Simon Arnauld, Marquis de Pomponne (1618-1699), who was secretary of State for foreign affairs from 1671 to 1679, when he was dismissed. See I, p. 442.

[3] Extraordinarily modest from the writer of the greatest memoirs in the world, with a style so vivid that after nearly three hundred years they remain, in the original, alive and sparkling.

and British foreign policy in the Baltic during the early years of George I's reign. King George himself seems to have played a leading part, with an ambition, for the sake of Hanover, to annex Bremen and Verden, and involve Britain in the Northern War fought by Hanover, Prussia, Saxony, Russia, and Denmark against Sweden. In 1719, however, the influence of George I's Hanoverian advisers was checked, British naval intervention ceased, and the war itself ended with the Peace of Nystad, 30 August 1721.

In 1717, there had been a split in the Whig party in England between Stanhope and Sunderland on the one hand, and Townshend and Walpole on the other. It was Stanhope who had struggled to make the French alliance in 1716, partly in order to gratify King George's ambitions for Hanover, but also for the greater good of England in Europe.

It may seem as strange to us as it did to Saint-Simon that, with so much to draw France and Spain together, they did not hold fast. It must be remembered, however, that until Louis XV grew up and had a son, there were strong suspicions that if anything happened to him Philip V, despite his renunciations, would seize the French throne, and no one in Paris wanted him. That fear, in 1716–1718, was enough to split the two Bourbon powers, and sustain the very fragile alliance between France and England.

One great danger came from the ambitions of that most masterful woman, Elisabeth Farnese, Philip's second wife, brilliantly abetted by the inspired energy of the disgusting Alberoni. If they had gained what they wished, the Austrians would have been driven from Italy and the Regent from France, and the Stuarts would have replaced the Hanoverians on the throne of England. All three countries would then have come under the domination of a new, revitalized Spain. The Franco-British alliance thwarted these schemes, by destroying a Spanish fleet off Sicily. A storm in the Bay of Biscay dispersed another taking help to the Scottish Jacobites; while in 1718 a conspiracy to kidnap the Regent was unmasked in Paris. Alberoni was forced by the joint influence of France and England to leave the service of Spain, and was finally disgraced in 1719.]

Before continuing in all seriousness from the point at which I digressed, I must not forget a trifle that wonderfully portrays M. le Duc d'Orléans's character. It has hitherto escaped me, and will do so again if I do not seize this moment. In the last year of the late King's life, Denain Abbey sent two canonesses to Versailles to crave compensation for the damage and destruction to their convent, incurred during the battle that marked the beginning of France's recovery.[1] I saw those ladies often in the tribunes at the King's mass and knew their identity and their reason for coming. Mme de Dangeau had taken them under her protection; but the King had died before they were able to put their case. At the beginning of the Regency, they applied to the Maréchaux de Villeroy and de Villars, and to the Duc de Noailles also, because their claim came under the finance department. They tried other doors as well for more than a year without success; and according to what they later told me, had been ill-received

---

[1] At Denain, Villars in 1712 won the decisive victory over Prince Eugene which marked the end of the War of the Spanish Succession. See index, II.

and rudely dismissed. At last, dismayed by their long stay that was costing too much for persons of their condition, but being loath to leave any avenue untried, they approached me. The name of one lady was Mme de Wignacourt, the other was a Mme d'Haudion.[1] I gave them the kind of welcome one owes to people who are in distress or harassed, and the courtesies due to their rank. They were so much astonished that I perceived it; for they were not accustomed to civility from those whom they addressed. I was especially surprised to hear them mention the Duc de Noailles in that way, because although his breeding needed no prop, he plainly set great store by a rather sorry connection with the Wignacourts. He would not otherwise have hung in a most prominent position at his house a full-length portrait of one of the two Wignacourt Grand-masters of Malta, an uncle of Françoise de Wignacourt who married Antoine Boyer and had a daughter Louise Boyer[2] who became the mother of the Cardinal and the Maréchal de Noailles—the only, but most glaringly conspicuous, blot on the long line of the Noailles family.

To return to the canonesses, when I had learned their business, I reported it to M. le Duc d'Orléans, urging the merit of their claim and the injustice of keeping them waiting so long, adding that our good or bad reputation in the Low Countries might hang on the way we treated them. I said everything needful as to the pious fame of their convent, and the extreme poverty of its well-born nuns, especially that of the two deputies then in Paris. All this was well received and most attentively considered. But it none the less took me six months to settle their business for them.

The canonesses began to despair of gaining anything through me, while I gave them such assistance as they would accept by letting them become accustomed to dining fairly regularly at my house. They gradually spoke more frankly, at last confessing that they were being turned out of their lodging, and knew not what might become of them. Next day, I went very early to call on Mme la Duchesse d'Orléans, whom I had made a practice of visiting once or twice a week, generally alone, sometimes in the company of Mme Sforza or M. le Comte de Toulouse. I found her with M. le Duc d'Orléans, sitting by the door to their little private garden at the end of their apartments. I sat down with them, and we conversed for some considerable time. As I rose to go, I asked M. le Duc d'Orléans to give me two écus, speaking with a gravity that gave astonishing weight to the request. When they had done inquiring about my joke (I all the while insisting that there was none), I at last told him of the misery to which the two pious ladies had been reduced by their long stay in Paris, and the endless delays. I declared that although they would take no money from

[1] Marie Jeanne Adrienne de Wignacourt, daughter of the Baron de Pernes, and Madeleine Thérèse Julienne d'Haudion, daughter of the Seigneur de Chibrechies.
[2] Louise Boyer, Duchesse de Noailles (1631–1697). She had married in 1646. Her son the Maréchal was Anno Jules de Noailles (1650–1708). See index, I.

me, they might from him, and that they would thus have a crust to eat in
the next few days. M. and Mme la Duchesse d'Orléans laughed at me;
but I continued to describe their dreadful situation because I would not
leave without being sure of satisfaction. When I did go, I took away with
me a firmer promise than any I had hitherto extracted, and I took good
care to press it home. By the end of a month, I had received a grant for all
their convent claimed, and a generous allowance to enable the two pious
ladies to leave Paris and return in comfort to their abbey, and I saw to it
personally that they were paid. No two women were ever more relieved and
delighted; and when I told them of my sarcastic request for two écus they
laughed heartily. I earned the grateful thanks of their abbey and chapter;
and every year for the remainder of their lives the two canonesses sent a
letter of remembrance. Let us now return to graver issues.

For some time past, there had been complaints from the offices of the
farmers general[1] regarding illicit salt-makers. The usual precautions were
of little use, for these people had formed themselves into armed bands, and
disturbances continually increased. There had been an open battle in the
forest of Chantilly, with the archers[2] and the Swiss Guard[3] brought in from
neighbouring garrisons. The salt-makers were defeated, their salt confiscated, and the prisoners branched;[4] but there were also many casualties
among the archers and the Swiss. The only effect of the executions was to
increase the salt-makers' numbers, inure them to violence, and discipline
them. Because they did no harm to anyone, they were favoured and
protected by the local populations. It was even rumoured that certain
high-ranking persons were supporting and encouraging them, so as to have
armed force at their service if required. The Comte d'Eu,[5] in particular,
was said to be in league with them and to have recruited great numbers.

The Parlement, banking on the promised support of M. and Mme du
Maine, some so-called noblemen, and the Maréchaux de Villeroy, de
Tessé and d'Huxelles; on the discontent of the Duc de Noailles, and the
unrest in Brittany, resolved to gain their hearts' desire by destroying the
Regent and establishing their power on the ruins of his own. With that aim
in view they proceeded to display themselves as the protectors of the poor—
always the cry of those who for personal advantage seek to harass and
overthrow the government. Their first move was to summon Trudaine,[6]
provost of the merchants and a counsellor of State, to report to them on
the funds and accounts of the Hôtel de Ville. He, however, declared that

---

[1] The privileged association which, until the Revolution, leased the public revenues.
[2] *hoquetons*: see I, p. 97.
[3] The Swiss Guard (see index, I and II) were used in civil disturbances to prevent Frenchmen from having to fight Frenchmen.
[4] Hanged from the branches of trees.
[5] This is clearly a reference to the Duc du Maine to whose son the Comté d'Eu belonged.
[6] Charles II Trudaine (1659–1721), provost of the merchants since 1714. He was Voysin's
brother-in-law.

the payments had never come in with greater regularity, and that he had no complaints. That having failed, they seized the excuse of a new edict on the reminting of the coinage; appointed commissioners to study it and, though the Parlement was not empowered to meddle, sent deputies to the Regent, declaring that it harmed the country's interests. I have abridged, and shall continue to abridge all these manœuvres because, were I to tell all, a separate volume would be needed, and a monstrously big one at that.

The Parlement's next move was to meet on the morning and afternoon of Friday, 17 June, and to send another deputation requiring the Regent to leave the said edict in abeyance until certain changes had been made, and to return it afterwards to the Parlement for registration. Receiving no reply, they met again on the following day, sending still another message to the effect that they would not rise until they had the Regent's answer. That answer, when it came, was that His Royal Highness could not tolerate the Parlement's interference (he might have used a stronger word), and that he had given the entire force of the *Maison du Roi*, in Paris and nearby, their marching orders, because the King must be obeyed. The order to be ready had indeed been given, with another to arm the men with powder and shot.

Next day, which was Sunday, the premier président marched to the Palais Royal with all the présidents-à-mortier and many counsellors of State. He was the strong supporter of M. and Mme du Maine, and ring-leader of this revolt. On the other hand, self-interest required him to be on good terms with His Royal Highness, and to keep the members under control. His address to the Regent started therefore with most fulsome compliments and flattery to pave the way for three outrageous demands: first, that the edict be sent to the Parlement for prior examination; second, that the King should heed their remonstrances; third, that the work of recasting at the Mint should be suspended. The Regent's reply to all three points was a firm refusal, stating once more that the King must be obeyed. Nevertheless, when the Parlement met next day (Monday), they pro-nounced judgment against the edict; but the Regency Council, meeting that same afternoon, quashed the shameful motion. Thus, as it were, a state of war existed between the Regent and the Parlement, with the one authority cancelling the other's decrees, and vice versa. Orders were then issued forbidding the printing or posting up of the Parlement's judgment, and soldiers of the guards regiment were posted in the market-places to see that no one refused the new money. As a matter of fact, by the original edict, the Louis (worth thirty livres) was established at thirty-six livres, and the écu (worth a hundred sous) at six livres instead of five. What is more, a certain number of government notes had to be accepted as legal tender with the new coins, until such time as the work at the Mint was finished and all the necessary money reminted and recast. The King and the finances greatly benefited by the use of paper money; but private individuals lost because of the increased values, which much exceeded the worth of the metal, and caused a general rise in prices. Thus the Parlement had an excellent chance of parading its pretended care for the public good. You may be sure the opportunity was not lost. During the night, one of the counsellors named Ville-aux-Clercs[1] rode through the streets tearing down and defacing the Council's decree. He was immediately arrested and thrown into prison.

On Monday, 27 June, the premier president with all the other presidents and forty counsellors went to the Tuileries and, in the presence of the Regent, read aloud to the King the Parlement's high-falutin[2] remonstrance. Argenson, as keeper of the seals, announced that he would give the King's answer in a few days' time. On Saturday, 2 July, the same company returned to hear it. The Regent, the princes of the blood, and the bastards were all present. Argenson, who had so often been brutally handled by the Parlement in earlier days,[3] made his present superiority more than plain. He answered in the King's name, announcing that the original edict would stand unaltered by change of any kind, and the deputation, who had not expected so stiff a reply, retired deeply mortified.

But the Parlement was not yet defeated. They met again on 11 and 12 August, venting their anger in a decree, now famous, aimed specifically at the Regent's authority. You may imagine the commotion! By its terms, the control of the finances was to be transferred *in toto* to the Parlement. All those appointed by the Regent were henceforth to be accountable to that assembly; the powers of Law were to be restricted, and all his activities made subject to the discretion of the Parlement, which was certainly lacking in that commodity. After this opening volley, it would have been no more than a step to demanding the guardianship of the King, and the government of the kingdom, with the Regent more tightly in their grip even than the King's person, and probably in as much danger as had been Charles I of England. The members of the Paris Parlement were acting as defiantly as the English Parliament had earlier done and, although they were originally established as a mere court of Justice with the same limitations as other law courts in the realm, they thought themselves no less important than the English Parliament, which is a legislative body, representing the entire nation.

In the midst of this rumpus, Mme la Duchesse du Maine had the temerity to complain in no uncertain terms to M. le Duc d'Orléans,

[1] The Comte de Ville-aux-Clercs had been a parliamentary counsellor since 1716, and later became a maître des requêtes (a judge of appeals).

[2] The French word is *ampoulé*, literally blistered, or in nursery language, 'puffed up with windy pride'.

[3] When Argenson was lieutenant of police. Now that he was Chancellor of France he was superior to the Parlement because he was the King's mouthpiece. What is more, he had power to try individuals without the Parlement's intervention. This was in order to prevent a judgment on a private person becoming an affair of State. Saint-Simon came increasingly to distrust him, as he discovered how strong Argenson's attachment to the bastards had been.

because she had discovered that he blamed her for much of what was happening. By the events that soon afterwards erupted, you may judge the validity of a defence which her dangerous but cowardly husband dared not present on his own account. After the Regency Council's edict removing the bastards from the succession, both husband and wife had done all in their power to bring about a state of rebellion. Did she not confess as much, at Sceaux,[1] when she told the Ducs de La Force and d'Aumont that she would set the whole kingdom ablaze, rather than lose the royal prerogative? All M. le Duc d'Orléans's recent kindness had seemed to them mere weakness, signifying fear, and therefore one more reason for renewing their attacks. Many circumstances appeared to favour them: the fact that certain nobles had joined them; the disorders in Brittany; the Paris Parlement, at loggerheads with the Regent; the support which Alberoni gave them from Spain; the general feeling against the English alliance; the disapproval of the way in which the finances were administered, and the revival by the Maréchal de Villeroy of those wicked suspicions, when he so ludicrously guarded the King's food and linen. They believed they had only to wait until these different elements combined to open the way to a future equally pleasing to their vengeance and their ambitions. Their next move was to spread the deadly soporific[2] required, in Mme du Maine's judgment, to gain time for that highly desirable but perhaps not immediately forthcoming result. She left the Regent's study well pleased with her efforts; and left M. le Duc d'Orléans equally delighted because he thought he had appeased her.

The Parlement, encouraged—no doubt of that—by the support of that evil couple, pursued its headlong career. It met on the morning of 22 August, sending the King's officers to inquire of the Regent what had become of all the banknotes that had been approved by the Chamber of Justice; those assigned for the monthly lotteries; those assigned for the Mississippi or Western Bank, and those that had been taken to the Mint since the change in the currency. This message was delivered to the Regent when the assembly rose. His only reply was to turn his back and retire into his study, which left the King's officers mystified. It was immediately after this that the first rumours were heard of a possible *Lit de Justice*.

The Regent's lethargy left his friends deeply despondent and incapable of doing anything to serve him. It had brought both him and the kingdom he governed to the brink of a serious rebellion. For a long time past I had been aware of what would happen. As you will remember, I had warned him at the first signs of trouble from the Parlement and the bastards, and I had spoken again when I guessed their real intentions. I showed him the inevitable result if he refused to act, urging how easy it would be to nip

[1] See II, pp. 382–383.
[2] 'Mortifères pavots', literally 'mortiferous poppies'! Saint-Simon is coming up to the boil for the greatest moment of his life.

this revolt in the bud, how hard to stop it later, especially for a man of his easygoing nature. I found, however, that at this juncture I could not serve him. True, I was his oldest, most devoted friend, able and willing to speak more frankly than all the rest (he had strong proof of that); but he feared what he called my violence, my passionate defence of my rank and dignities, so foully encroached upon by the bastards and the Parlement. When I saw him still in doubt, I warned him a third time, adding that having done my duty as a citizen and his most humble servant I should not speak again; and I had kept my word, for in the past twelve months I had not opened my mouth, except under compulsion. On rare occasions when someone had broached the subject in my presence, I had been forced to utter, for fear of seeming sulky or offended; but I made only some dull and careless remark, designed to mean nothing and to change the subject.

At this point Dubois returned from England. The Regent's decline harmed his personal ambitions, and he therefore joined with Law, who dreaded being left unsupported, and with Argenson, whom the Parlement still hated. Law had enlisted Monsieur le Duc, who was deeply committed to 'the System',[1] and saw in the prevailing circumstances a chance to overthrow his enemy the Duc du Maine and supplant him with the King.[2] These different influences, all aimed at the same result, so powerfully affected the Regent that he suddenly became aware of the dangers and their only remedy, and allowed himself to be convinced that he had not a moment to lose. Law and Dubois shielded him from those bad advisers in whom he had put too much trust,[3] and all was quickly decided before anyone realized what was afoot.

Since I had not known these latest events, you may picture my surprise when, as I worked with the Regent one afternoon, he suddenly exploded in bitter complaint against the Parlement. He had opened the subject, and thus, after much urging, I said coldly that he had indeed just cause, and would perhaps remember my prophecy that he could rule that body with a frown, but that weakness and lenience[4] would bring him to the edge of an abyss. I concluded that if he wished to recover his authority he must act at once, or else be finally defeated. These strong words, torn from me as it were after my long silence, and pronounced slowly and icily, as though I had no interest in his movements, made him believe that I thought him

---

[1] Law's system for the French finances.

[2] Since 1715, the Duc du Maine had been superintendent of the little King's education.

[3] The Duc de Noailles, Canillac, etc.

[4] Boislisle, in his notes, quotes the following that sheds a good deal of light on one side of the Regent's character: 'It is true that if I listened to my heart I would have every man happy and no one displeased with me. But experience has taught me that most people will take advantage of that sentiment in a prince. This idea, in theory so delightful, has great disadvantages when put into practice, for in government, firmness is better than gentleness since it inspires respect and a sense of justice supported by sovereign power, in those who are not sufficiently reasonable or wise to be ruled by gentleness and equity.' Sad that the Duc d'Orléans could not live up to his excellent principles.

incapable of doing right or sustaining a course of action; also that I had no intention of advising or helping him. He was wounded, but because my words had deepened the impression (of which I was unaware) made by Dubois, Law, and Argenson, they had a marvellous effect.

Shortly before this, the Duc de La Force, a friend of Law, had joined in the struggle against the Parlement. Apart from the usual reasons he had hoped thus to ensure his full membership of the Regency Council. He came to ask for my support, explaining that the Regent had promised him a seat when the time came to oppose the Parlement, but only a temporary one, and that he required my services to change his status. On an earlier occasion I had strongly disapproved of his appointment to the finance council, and his subsequent conduct had made me very angry. Now, however, I agreed because the moment for concerted action was more than ripe. We had just learned that the Parlement had made an edict, not yet published, appointing a commission to inquire into the running of the finances; that a number of witnesses were being questioned; that Law was to be seized by bailiffs with a parliamentary warrant, and would be hanged within the precincts of the Palais de Justice after a three-hour trial.[1]

Without delay, the Duc de La Force and Fagon,[2] a counsellor of State, went to the Regent and pressed him so hard that he ordered them to bring Law to my house that same day, and there decide what best to do, which was the first intimation I received that M. le Duc d'Orléans understood the gravity of the situation and was preparing to act. During the meeting I observed that Law's courage, hitherto so firm, had been badly shaken, and that tears were running down his cheeks. At first we could not decide; armed force appeared necessary, but the Regent might not agree, and although Law had provided himself with a safe-conduct, that would not for one moment check the Parlement. Thus the way seemed blocked on every side; and Law, more dead than alive, could suggest nothing, let alone act. His safety was of paramount importance. Had they seized him, he would have been dead before negotiations opened, certainly before a detachment of the guards could have broken into the Palais de Justice, a dangerous business at any time, extremely unpleasant even when successful, truly terrible had they found Law's body at the end of a rope. I therefore advised him to go at once to the Palais Royal, there to occupy the room of his friend Nancré[3] who was abroad in Spain. That suggestion restored Law somewhat, and he went straight there from my house. He would have been as safe at the Bank, but I believed that retirement to the

[1] The Palais de Justice was the locality of a special jurisdiction whose head was the sheriff of the Palais, acting under the authority of the Parlement.

[2] Louis Fagon (1680–1744). He was the son of Guy Crescent Fagon, Louis XIV's doctor. He had been made intendant of finances in 1714, and became commissioner general of finances to the Regency Council.

[3] Louis Jacques Aimé Théodore de Dreux, Marquis de Nancré (1660–1719). He was ambassador to Spain in 1718.

Palais Royal would create more stir, and encourage the Regent to be firm, besides giving Law the chance to see and fortify him at all times.

That settled, I proposed a *Lit de Justice*,[1] which was eagerly welcomed by the other three as the sole means of enforcing the annulment of the Parlement's latest decree; but as our discussion proceeded, a new thought came into my mind, and I interrupted to say that since the Duc du Maine was secretly the moving spirit of the Parlement, and the Duc de Villeroy his faithful ally, both would oppose with all their might a *Lit de Justice* aimed at frustrating their plans. In order to prevent it, they might plead the heat (which was indeed very great), the fear of crowds, exhaustion, foul air, etc., striking a pathetic note of concern for the King's health.[2] If the Regent persisted, they might refuse to accompany him and, at their prompting, the King might take fright and refuse to go without them. Thus we should be defeated. That consideration halted the discussion; but I was fortunately able to produce a remedy, namely to hold the *Lit de Justice* at the Tuileries itself; by which arrangement there would be no need to announce it until the morning of the appointed day, no difficulties with the King, and none over the movement of troops.

At that point the meeting broke up; Law left us, and I dictated all the details of my plan to Fagon, thus securing absolute secrecy, and disposing of all further difficulties. By nine that evening everything had been settled, and I asked Fagon to take the document at once to the Abbé Dubois, whose influence over the Regent was rapidly increasing.

Next morning, Saturday, 20 August, M. le Duc d'Orléans sent a message bidding me attend him at four o'clock that same afternoon, and I went to him at the Palais Royal at that hour. A moment later La Vrillière appeared, relieving me of the company of Grancey and Broglie,[3] two of the *roués*, looking quite at home in the great hall, extremely untidy, and without their wigs. Shortly afterwards, we were ushered into the new gallery, the one painted by Coypel,[4] where Asfeld[5] was displaying maps and plans of the Pyrenees to the Regent and the Maréchal de Villeroy. M. le Duc d'Orléans greeted me with an embrace that showed his need, and soon after whispered that he had much to say to me before the meeting, but that we must wait until the Maréchal had gone. That was the first I had heard of any meeting and I had no idea whom it concerned. La Vrillière asked whether I had business with the Regent, to which I replied 'Yes', and he said that he himself had been summoned for four o'clock. 'I, too,' said I. The Maréchal de Villeroy took me aside at that point to babble as usual of the precautions he was taking for the King's safety, and the

---

[1] The King's bed used as a throne in the Parlement of Paris, for a session at which he presided, chiefly to witness the registration of his own decrees.

[2] *Lits de Justice* were usually held at the Palais de Justice.

[3] François Rouxel de Médavy, Marquis de Grancey (1666–1728), a lieutenant-general and recently appointed Governor of Dunkirk; and Charles Guillaume, Marquis de Broglie (1668–1751).   [4] See index, II.   [5] See index, II.

anonymous letters (probably concocted by himself and M. du Maine)
which he daily received—all this in very loud and spiteful tones.

At last he left with the rest of the company, and M. le Duc d'Orléans,
visibly relaxed, led me into the offices behind the great hall overlooking
the Rue de Richelieu. There he took my arm, saying that he had come to
the crisis of his Regency and needed every assistance. I said I knew that
only too well, but that, fundamentally, every decision was his. After that
short preamble we began to talk business. He declared that he was determined to strike the Parlement a crippling blow; that he entirely approved
of my suggestion for holding a *Lit de Justice* at the Tuileries, and that all
should be done as I had proposed. He added that Monsieur le Duc wished
to take the King's education from M. du Maine, a change which he welcomed because the King was fast growing up, and it was important to be
rid of an enemy so near him. He ended by announcing that he intended
to hold the *Lit de Justice* on the following Tuesday, and to replace the Duc
du Maine at the same time.

'Sir!' I exclaimed, 'I do not advise that.' 'What?' he cried, 'Why ever
not?' 'Because,' said I, 'that would be too much at once. What is your
most pressing need? Undoubtedly it is the Parlement. That is the important issue, be content with that. If you can manage to strike them a hard
blow, and thereafter keep them at bay, you will have regained all your old
authority. Then will be the time to deal with the Duc du Maine. Do not
confuse him with the Parlement; for if you disgrace them both at once you
will make them allies. By the way, what does Monsieur le Duc most want,
to have the King's education, or will it suffice him to see the Duc du
Maine disgraced?' 'He does not care which,' replied the Regent. 'Capital!'
I exclaimed, 'Try to make him see reason, and do not undertake too much
at once. Only reflect, Monsieur,' I said in conclusion, 'when I oppose the
immediate disgrace of M. du Maine, I go against my best interests, for it is
only a short step from stripping him of his office to depriving him of his
rank, and you know how I long for that. I loathe that man with utter
loathing, because out of sheer, deliberate spite he duped us over the
bonnet,[1] and purposely occasioned all the deprivations we afterwards
suffered. Yet the good of the realm and your personal well-being mean
more to me than rank and vengeance, and thus I do implore you to reflect
on what I have just said.'[2]

M. le Duc d'Orléans was probably as much impressed by my restraint as
by my arguments. He embraced me and yielded absolutely, declaring that I

[1] For the 'affair of the bonnet', see index, II.
[2] One feels that Saint-Simon thought his dreams had come true, and that at last he had
'become something'. There he was, the Regent's adviser, sitting to rule beside him, the highest
officers of the State kept kicking their heels waiting to be admitted. It was his ideal of government, the ruler of France with, at his side, a duke and peer to warn, counsel, and support. But,
as will be seen, the great artist was not as influential as he believed, or as skilled in statesmanship.
It was sad for him that he thought of his memoirs as a second best.

spoke like a true friend, and not only as a duke and peer. I took advantage of this to reproach him gently for ever doubting me, and so we decided to leave the disgrace of the Duc du Maine for another and less critical time.[1]

The arrival of the keeper of the seals had been announced much earlier. As our conversation was now ended, the Regent went into the adjoining room and, from the doorway, called to him, and to La Vrillière and Dubois, who were waiting alone at the farther end. This was the office in which M. le Duc d'Orléans preferred to work in summertime. He sat with his back to the wall of the room we had been in, at the centre of the long side of a huge writing-table, placed lengthwise before him. It was his usual seat; I sat beside him, the keeper of the seals and Dubois sat opposite, and La Vrillière at the end nearest to me. After a few preliminaries, Monsieur le Duc was unexpectedly announced. M. le Duc d'Orléans put on his wig and went into the next room to greet him. The keeper of the seals suggested our walking up and down in the gallery, and we had begun to do so when I heard the opening of the door by which His Royal Highness had left us. I quickly stepped forward and saw the Regent enter with Monsieur le Duc behind him. Knowing all, I asked M. le Duc d'Orléans with a smile what business he had with Monsieur le Duc, and why he was bringing him to hinder us at work. 'At any rate he is here,' he answered, 'and we shall see much more of him in future,' and so saying, he put his arm through Monsieur le Duc's. Then, looking them in the eye, I congratulated them warmly on their alliance, adding that this was where their true interests lay, not in the question of bastardy. 'Oh! indeed yes,' said the Regent to Monsieur le Duc, putting his arm round my shoulders, 'You may speak your mind to him, because of all men he cares the most for the legitimates and their close accord, and he cordially hates the bastards.' I laughed at that, and fervently agreed. Monsieur le Duc said something respectful to His Royal Highness, something pleasant to me, and we returned to the writing-table to continue our discussion.

When we had finished, the Regent rose and called Monsieur le Duc to go with him to the other end of the gallery, and a moment later called for me also. He said that they had been trying to arrange for a *Lit de Justice*, but that there were many difficulties, and he requested me to go at once to consult with Fontanieu.[2] As I crossed the portrait gallery,[3] I heard some-

---

[1] Saint-Simon's opposition to gaining his heart's desire as soon as possible does seem strange. Perhaps, certain of victory, he wanted to draw it out so as to enjoy his triumph as long as could be. Probably he was still unsure of the Regent, and indeed of Monsieur le Duc. The wife of one, the mother of the other, were bastards, and devoted sisters of the Duc du Maine. Family pressure might have made life intolerable for them had anything leaked out.

[2] Moïse Augustin Fontanieu (1655–1725) was superintendent of the King's furniture and would therefore be much needed in arranging the seating, etc. He had had the same post under Louis XIV, 1697–1701. His daughter was married to a nephew of Lauzun, and was thus in the social circle of the Saint-Simons and the Lauzuns.

[3] In the second court of the Palais Royal, and so named because of the portraits that decorated it, in their gilt frames, thickly covering the crimson silk walls.

one call my name; it was the Abbé Dubois. He asked me nothing, nor did I question him; but both of us were longing to know why the other was leaving. As I stepped into my coach, one of Law's footmen who was lying in wait for me begged me to go to his master, in Nancré's lodging. Law was there alone with his wife,[1] who immediately left us together. I told him that all was well and that Monsieur le Duc was now with the Regent, for he had told me that Law had united them. I added that I had an important mission to accomplish on His Royal Highness's behalf, but that one or other of us would come to tell him the rest. I could see that he was mightily relieved.

I then went straight to the Place Vendôme in search of Fontanieu. He was out, and I was terrified at the thought of having to chase after him to a lawyers' meeting at the other end of Paris, lest my liveries betray something. His porter, however, went to a neighbour's house, where he luckily still was, and brought him back to me. Meanwhile I had had the pleasure of conversing with his wife[2] on the subject of her house at Passy, which she sometimes lent Mme de Saint-Simon to break her journey to Forges,[3] for the waters; also of an estate which M. and Mme de Lauzun were thinking of buying, which last offered her a pretext for my coming to consult with Fontanieu. You may imagine my feelings, with my head buzzing with such very different matters.

Fontanieu arrived at last, and we went into another room. When the servants had left us I locked the door, explaining that I had come not on his business, but on another affair of the very highest importance, to which he needed to give his whole mind. First, however, His Royal Highness must know whether he might trust him implicitly. It was terrible to see how deep an impression even the most absurd rumours can make when they are brilliantly exploited.[4] Fontanieu's first reaction was literally to tremble the entire length of his body, and to turn whiter than his shirt. He stammered out something to the effect that he was His Royal Highness's obedient servant—so far as his duty allowed. I looked him in the face and smiled, which seemed to reassure him, for he evidently felt he owed me an apology for suspecting what might come through me. When I had fully explained, he promised everything right willingly, and faithfully kept his word in every way. After spending a full hour discussing the arrangements, I returned to the Palais Royal, pretending to have left something there, in order to deceive my servants. A red footman escorted me to the head of the stairs, but d'Ibagnet,[5] the keeper of the Palais Royal,

---

[1] Catherine Knollys. She lived with Law, but seems not to have married him. She died in 1747, and was never mentioned as a member of his family.

[2] Catherine Geneviève Dodun, Dame de Fontanieu.

[3] Forges-les-Eaux, a spa in Normandy.

[4] Still the same rumours of the Duc d'Orléans's murderous intentions. In fact he was charming to the little King, and very fond of him.

[5] Jean d'Ibagnet was concierge of the Palais Royal 1710-1722. Red was the colour of the Orléans liveries.

stopped me at the door of M. le Duc d'Orléans's apartments, asking me to write down my business. It was the sacred hour for his *roués* and his supper, and I wrote my message, feeling some indignation that he had not thought it worth while to postpone his pleasures for an affair of such importance. I was even reduced to asking d'Ibagnet to wait to give him my note until he was in a condition to read it, and to see that it was burned afterwards. Thence I went to Fagon, but he was out, and so back to my home, where I found that he had called during my absence. Soon afterwards, M. de La Force arrived to hear the latest news, and was greatly cheered by it.

Next day, Sunday, 21 August, as I was getting out of bed at half-past seven, they came to say that one of Monsieur le Duc's valets was waiting with a letter to place in my hand; that he had come still earlier, but finding me asleep had gone to hear mass at the Dominicans, next door. I was not then, nor ever had been, in communication with Monsieur le Duc, either directly or indirectly. It is true that I had had some dealings with him in the affair of the bastards; but considering that we gained no advantage thereby, I had since ignored those princes to the point of discourtesy. I now took the man to my study, and read the letter, written in Monsieur le Duc's own hand. This is what it said: 'I think, Monsieur, that it is absolutely imperative for us to consult regarding the business of which you know, and I believe the sooner the better. If possible may it be tomorrow, Sunday, preferably in the morning? Say at what hour you will come to me, or shall I come to you? Whichever you think will be least remarked, for it would be most unwise to give food for gossip. I eagerly await your answer, and beg you, in the meantime, to believe me your sincere friend, as I think you are mine. Signed: H. de Bourbon.'

I reflected a few moments, and then decided to go myself to Monsieur le Duc. After questioning his valet as to the time and length of his *lever*, I sent a verbal message (I preferred not to write) to say that I would attend him immediately afterwards. This seemed a safer course than to risk his being seen at my door, which was opposite the house of Président Portail who might well be at home on a Sunday morning. Fagon arrived at that moment. He was delighted by the news, especially by Monsieur le Duc's letter, for he thought that M. le Duc d'Orléans would feel supported and strengthened by an ally of such high rank. I then went to the Hôtel de Condé, where I found Monsieur le Duc, still not dressed, but fortunately with only his valets. He greeted me in a remarkably sensible way, for one so young[1]—civil, but not gushing. He even said that it was a novelty to see me; to which I replied that since the councils filled most of my mornings, and that at other times he was seldom in Paris, I had seized on this moment to do myself the honour of visiting him. He led me to his study and closed the door; drew up an armchair for me; another exactly similar for himself, and we sat down facing one another. After excusing himself for

---

[1] Monsieur le Duc (1692–1740) was twenty-six at this time.

treating me with such scant ceremony, and paying me a few compliments, he began on the business in hand.

[*For the next four days, Monday, Tuesday, Wednesday, Thursday (22–25 Aug.) Saint-Simon spent from two to three hours every morning arguing with Monsieur le Duc, who wished him to agree to include the disgrace of the Duc du Maine at the Lit de Justice. Saint-Simon was adamant in opposition: 'I turned neither to right nor left.' What is more, every afternoon he saw the Regent and, 'however long my conversation with Monsieur le Duc had been that morning, I repeated the whole of it to M. le Duc d'Orléans, omitting nothing, and adding my own reflections.' I have severely trimmed this portion of the memoirs which fills more than fifty pages. Saint-Simon was defeated; but having once, 'no, twenty times', made his protest, he was really delighted to have been overruled.*

The point of the Lit de Justice *was for the King in person publicly to deny the Parlement's claim to remonstrate on edicts presented to them by the government for registration, and to quash the decrees they had already issued regarding the administration of the finances. Once the words* Le Roy le veult *had been pronounced in the King's presence there was no going back.*]

Meanwhile, preparations for the *Lit de Justice* continued swiftly but secretly. In the course of a vast number of discussions it had been decided, despite all my endeavours, to strike at M. du Maine also. Monsieur le Duc, who was admitted to our councils, was heart and soul against the bastards, and he would have it so. I was therefore, in the end, obliged to yield. M. du Maine was to be stripped of the title of prince of the blood, with all the privileges belonging to it, and reduced to the level of an ordinary duke and peer, with precedence dating from his elevation. Thus, at one thrust he would sink to become the lowest in rank of all the peers. We did, however, decide that the blow should fall on him alone, and that the Comte de Toulouse, although similarly stripped of his title, should immediately receive it back again, in recognition of his services as a counsellor of State, and as a well-deserved tribute to his many excellent qualities.

No reader, if such there ever be, will fail to understand how perfectly this decision satisfied my heart's desire. No man hated M. du Maine more than I; yet I had opposed Monsieur le Duc, thinking it safer to strike one blow at a time. The Duc du Maine had powerful friends, he was even leader of a party—of a kind. Stripped of rank and office, what might his fury, chagrin, and disappointed ambition not urge him to attempt? It seemed to me conceivable that a civil war might yet be the result.

After that first interview with Monsieur le Duc, I returned to my house and then went to hear mass at the Dominicans' church, to which I had an entrance from my garden. My mind was far away; but God gave me the grace to pray to Him with my whole heart and in all sincerity, asking Him to guide me so as to act for His greater glory and the good of the State, without consideration for my personal feelings. Let me say here and now that my prayer was answered, and that in all that followed, supported by my virtuous intentions during the entire course of this affair, I did nothing with which I needed to reproach myself.

Fontanieu was awaiting me when I got home, and I had to answer his questions as though nothing else was on my mind. I arranged my bedroom as though for the *Lit de Justice*, with a coverlet over the bed, and I explained the many parts of the ceremony which he had not understood, and which it was essential to include. I had hoped he would see the Regent that same morning; but so many things had to be made clear to him that he did not receive firm orders until late that afternoon.

Early in the morning of Thursday, 25 August, the Duc de La Force arrived, bringing the decree that would reinstate the Comte de Toulouse. It was excellently worded, just as I had intended, and was sent at once to the printers, together with the one Millain[1] had already shown me, reducing the bastards to the level of their peerages. Millain himself came soon afterwards with a message from Monsieur le Duc, desiring me to go to M. le Duc d'Orléans's apartments that evening at eight o'clock, and to enter by the back door. Monsieur le Duc would use the front, and we three would then make final arrangements for next day. I agreed with the greatest alacrity and considerable relief; for I had earlier heard a rumour to the effect that the Duc du Maine and some members of the Parlement were plotting to declare the King of age, and immediately to form a council with Monsieur du Maine at the head to rule the country in his name. This appeared mad to me, since all the laws, as well as tradition and common-sense, opposed it. But the hatred of these people for the Regent; their contempt for his weakness (in which they were not wrong); their claim to be protecting the poor against the finance department; the cowardice of M. du Maine; the frantic audacity of his wife; and the alarms of the Maréchal de Villeroy all gave weight to the story. There were also reports of a conspiracy by the Prince of Cellamare, the Spanish ambassador, and Cardinal Alberoni, whom his master the Duc de Vendôme had long since enlisted in the cause of M. du Maine. I had therefore taken these rumours seriously enough to repeat them to the Regent.

[The Cellamare Conspiracy: *Although it has gone down in history under the name of the Spanish ambassador, who was to have remitted the plans and documents to Cardinal Alberoni at the Court of Madrid, the centre and organizer of the plot was the Duchesse du Maine, one of the 'Royal Dolls'. Ever since the edict that excluded the bastards from the succession, and reduced their children to the level of ordinary peers, she had fought for reinstatement. She was a princess of the blood, daughter-in-law of Louis XIV, a woman with a furious temper, and her pride was at stake. In her opinion, her husband was most deplorably indolent in the affair, and, finding no*

---

[1] Jean François Millain. He had been the King's secretary in 1695, secretary to the Chancellors Pontchartrain and Voysin, and was now Monsieur le Duc's secretary at the Regency Council.

chance of support in France, she turned to Spain. The plan was to persuade Philip V
to intervene, as the uncle of Louis XV ; to summon the Estates General, and declare
him Regent in place of the Duc d'Orléans. That accomplished, she and the Duc du
Maine would rule France as best suited their own interests. To modern minds it
appears like treason ; at that time, it was not regarded quite so seriously in France,
although the danger was real enough. Many agents, including Cardinal de Polignac,
were employed in drafting the letters to Spain, and messages in invisible ink were
written between the lines. A coach with a false bottom crammed with documents was
seized at Poitiers and, as will be seen, the entire affair was handled in an almost
unbelievably amateurish fashion.

The Abbé Dubois and Argenson seem to have been aware of the conspiracy, and it
was they who finally convinced the Regent of the need to arrest the Duchesse du
Maine. That was the true reason for holding the Lit de Justice, and for all the
secrecy in uttering the edict 'declaring null and void all titles and functions conferred
on the legitimized princes since 1714', thus stripping the bastards of their royal
prerogatives. Saint-Simon seems not to have understood the magnitude of the plot,
or the great need for haste. In his loathing of the bastards' claim to rank higher than
the peers, he seems blind to the wider issue, and to Mme du Maine's complicity. His
genius was not for politics, and it is perhaps significant that when he speaks of
foreign affairs, he shelters behind the expert opinion of Torcy.]

I went that evening to the Regent, as he had desired me. D'Ibagnet was
waiting to admit me by the secret door to the back offices; but just as I
entered, La Serre, Mme la Duchesse d'Orléans's equerry, most unfortunately encountered me on the stairs, and I could plainly see his surprise.
This meeting upset me at first; but since Mme la Duchesse d'Orléans was
at Saint-Cloud, I took comfort from the reflection that in twenty-four
hours' time all would be over. We found M. le Duc d'Orléans in bed
complaining of fever; but I must confess that I rather suspected his
courage. I therefore somewhat roughly seized his pulse. He did indeed
seem feverish, but I told him it was nothing but fatigue, and that he would
soon be able to rest. He declared that, come what might, he should still
hold the *Lit de Justice.* Monsieur le Duc then entered and went to stand by
his pillow. There were just the four of us, including Millain, who had come
in case of need. The light was a solitary candle. Monsieur le Duc and I
sat down to go through the orders already given, and those still to be
issued; but I could not help feeling considerable anxiety regarding a fever
which had appeared at such a critical juncture in a perfectly healthy man
who was seldom, if ever, indisposed.

Monsieur le Duc d'Orléans explained to us his time-table for the rest of
the night until eight the following morning, when he was due to go to the
King, wearing his robes.[1] I urged him to rest as much as possible, and on
the morrow to think only of France; to be firm, to keep his wits about him
and, above all, to control himself. With that, I wished him good night and,

---

[1] For a *Lit de Justice*, the proper dress for princes and peers was a short mantle, linen bands,
and a hat with white plumes.

stepping down to the foot of the bed, I thanked Monsieur le Duc for all the visits he had paid me, with protestations of heartfelt devotion, and two most fervent embraces.[1] I then took my leave with Millain, who had spoken with excellent good sense and great tact, retiring at ten o'clock precisely, by the same way as I had come. Monsieur le Duc left also, but by the front door. As soon as I found myself alone with Millain in one of the offices, I embraced him, too, with all the pleasure in the world. These demonstrations of friendship with Monsieur le Duc and Millain were necessarily muted for fear of being overheard, either by the Regent, when we were at the foot of his bed, or by Ibagnet, who was waiting for Millain and myself in an adjoining room, to light us to the door. We groped our way down the steps,[2] and after one last embrace—I could not resist that—we separated and went each to his home.

Towards five in the morning drums were heard in different parts of the town, and soldiers were seen marching. At six o'clock, Desgranges[3] delivered a *lettre de cachet*[4] to the Parlement. Those gentry, as they liked to call themselves, were only just beginning to assemble. They called upon the premier président and declared themselves to be in session. That took half an hour, after which they returned the answer that they would obey the King's command. At the same time, messengers on horseback went to all the peers and officers of the crown, the Knights of the Order, and the governors and lieutenant-governors of provinces, who were to accompany the King, informing them of the hour of the *Lit de Justice*. French and Swiss guards were posted under arms at various points, with mounted constables of the watch, and two companies of musketeers stood to arms at their barracks. The French and Swiss guards at the Tuileries were on duty as usual.[5]

I had had little sleep during the past week, and that night I had even less, in the expectation of such tremendous happenings. At six o'clock I rose, and soon after received my own summons to attend. On the back of the paper Desgranges had most thoughtfully recommended them not to wake me; he said later that he knew the order would not surprise me. All the others were roused, you may imagine with what astonishment. Just before seven, a messenger arrived from M. le Duc d'Orléans, informing me of a meeting of the Regency Council at eight o'clock, when robes would be worn. I chose a black mantle because that was the only short one I possessed, except for one very fine one made of cloth of gold which I preferred

---

[1] But Monsieur le Duc was not a friend. On 3 June 1723, he had Saint-Simon's name erased from the first promotions of the new reign to the Order of the Saint Esprit.

[2] In the ordinary way, Saint-Simon would have had an escort of footmen carrying torches.

[3] Michel Ancel Desgranges, the King's master of ceremonies.

[4] An order signed by the King or, in the King's minority, by the Regent.

[5] Boislisle says in his notes that the military precautions were a great deal more serious than Saint-Simon would have us believe. One cause for alarm was that the Duc du Maine was colonel-general of the Swiss Guard.

not to wear, lest it be said, however wrongly, that I wished to insult the Parlement and the Duc du Maine. I was accompanied in my coach by two gentlemen, and prepared myself to be a witness of great events. My feelings were a mixture of fear, hope, joy, concern. I dreaded the weakness of M. le Duc d'Orléans, and all that might result from it; but I firmly determined to do my best whatever might befall, to seem unknowing, and to remain perfectly calm, trusting in my presence of mind, concentration, prudence, and modesty, being very careful always to preserve a great appearance of gravity.

On leaving my home, I went to Valincourt's house,[1] the front door of which faced the back door of the Hôtel de Toulouse.[2] Valincourt, a most honourable man of the highest intelligence, mixing with the best people, and paymaster-general of the navy, had been with the Comte de Toulouse since his boyhood, and had always been implicitly trusted. I did not want the Comte de Toulouse to fear for himself, or to be persuaded to accompany his brother. I therefore asked my old friend Valincourt to come out and speak to me. He emerged half-dressed, much alarmed by the commotion in the streets, and urgently asking what was afoot. I leaned from the coach and took his head between my hands. 'Listen,' I whispered, 'Do not lose a word! Go quickly and tell M. le Comte de Toulouse to trust me and be calm. Things will be done to others that may no doubt distress him, but not a hair of his head will be harmed. I want him to have no fear. Go! Go at once!' Valincourt embraced me as closely as the circumstances permitted. 'Ah! Monsieur,' he said, 'we knew a storm was brewing. Others may have deserved it, but not M. le Comte. He will be eternally grateful.' He went that instant to tell him, and the Comte de Toulouse, who later discovered that it was I who had saved him from his brother's disgrace, did indeed always remember.

I arrived at the great courtyard of the Tuileries as eight o'clock was striking,[3] having observed nothing remarkable on the way. The coaches of the Duc de Noailles and the Maréchaux de Villars and d'Huxelles were there already; I saw only a few people as I went upstairs, but I made the servants open both doors[4] of the Council chamber for me, and the doors into the guardroom as well. The *Lit de Justice* had been set up in a large ante-room where the King usually dined; although since the great heat began he had used it as a bedroom because his own little room was oppressively hot.[5] On this important day, they had taken him to dress in his bedroom, and thence into the string of offices beyond. Coverlets had

<hr>

[1] Jean Baptiste Henri du Trousset de Valincourt (1653–1730), an old friend of Saint-Simon. A member of the French Academy, he was appointed the King's chronicler in 1699.
[2] Near the Place des Victoires. The Comte de Toulouse bought the house in 1713.
[3] Eight o'clock on the morning of 26 August 1718.
[4] For dukes and above, both sides of the double doors were opened by the waiting footmen. It was a very important sign of rank.
[5] The heat that summer had been terrific.

been placed over his bed and that of the Maréchal de Villeroy, and the council table had been set at the foot. I looked carefully to see that all was in order, and whispered my congratulations into Fontanieu's ear. Entering the first of the suite of offices, I saw a crowd of people, attracted no doubt by the news of this unexpected ceremony, and among them were some members of the Council. M. le Duc d'Orléans was with a circle at the farther end, and, as I learned later, had just left the King, with whom he had seen the Duc du Maine in his robes. That lord followed him to the door, but neither said a word. After a quick glance at that cluster of people, I entered the Council chamber, where I found a scattering of the members, looking so grave and serious that my own gravity was enhanced. Hardly anyone spoke, and no one stirred from where he sat or stood in various parts of the room. I remained apart, the better to observe them all.

A moment later M. le Duc d'Orléans entered looking cheerful and untroubled as he surveyed the assembled company. I thought this a good omen and went at once to ask how he did. He replied rather loudly that he felt pretty well; then, speaking into my ear, he added that except when they woke him for orders (which had happened fairly often), he had slept soundly, and had come determined to be firm. This greatly cheered me, for his manner was sincere, and I added a couple of words exhorting him to be strong. Monsieur le Duc then appeared and came straight up to me, asking if I felt confident of the Regent, and whether we might trust him to be steady. He seemed a trifle over-excited, quite noticeably so to those who knew him well. The Prince de Conti, gloomy, listless, envious of his brother-in-law,[1] looked pensive, but about nothing in particular. The Duc de Noailles scanned every face, his eyes blazing with anger at finding himself part of the crowd on so great a day, for he had deliberately been kept in ignorance. I had especially asked Monsieur le Duc to tell him nothing, believing their attachment to be greater than it really was. It turned out that Monsieur le Duc distrusted him, esteemed him not at all, and cared nothing for him, apart from fearing a possible recent alliance with M. du Maine.

That gentleman, wearing his robes, now entered by the King's little door. Never were bows deeper or more frequent than those he now made (though he was not normally ungenerous with them), as he went to stand alone propped on his stick[2] by the council table, on the side near the beds. There, I, standing facing him with the width of the table between us, made him the most radiant inclination of my entire life, every inch of it full of most voluptuous enjoyment. He returned it in the same manner, and continued to search the faces with staring eyes and twitching muscles, talking to himself almost continuously.

[1] The Prince de Conti had married a sister of Monsieur le Duc.
[2] The Duc du Maine was lame. He had infantile paralysis as a child and developed a club foot.

No one had inquired the reason for this supplementary meeting of the Regency Council. Everyone knew of the decision to annul the Parlement's decrees, and it seemed reasonable for the members to witness the annulment. All believed that at the forthcoming *Lit de Justice* they would hear it registered at the King's command, and that pain would be suffered by some who had thought themselves specially favoured by the Regent.

The Comte de Toulouse now arrived wearing a mantle, and saluted the assembly. He looked grave and abstracted and neither spoke nor was spoken to. M. le Duc d'Orléans, who was facing him, turned to me (though I was some distance away) as if to focus my attention on him and express his own concern. I nodded slightly, as much as to say, 'Well! It cannot be helped.' M. le Duc d'Orléans went over to him and said loud enough to be heard that he was surprised to see him so dressed, for he had not informed him of the *Lit de Justice*, knowing how much he had disliked attending the Parlement since their last edict. M. le Comte de Toulouse replied that that was true, but where the good of the State was concerned he put all personal considerations aside. M. le Duc d'Orléans turned away without answering and, pushing me still farther back, whispered very low, 'That man tears my heart. Did you hear what he said?' and he repeated the words. I added my praise, but reminded him that the Comte de Toulouse would at once be reinstated; there was thus no need for pity. He interrupted to say how much he wished he could tell him so. I said that the matter was most delicate, and that he should wait, at all events, until the last possible moment. I then turned and brought him back to the rest of the company, so as to cut short our private talk, which I feared might have been noticed. The Comte de Toulouse saw us, but stayed where he was, and so did the rest, keeping intentionally at a distance.

The Duc du Maine was with the Maréchal de Villeroy and d'Effiat, they seated and not moving from their places, he standing before them. I watched that little colloquy in a fever of excitement; but he soon left them and motioned to his brother to join him at the foot of the Maréchal de Villeroy's bed. He appeared agitated. The Comte de Toulouse consented with a gesture, but doubtfully. The Duc du Maine insisted; whereupon his brother moved from between the beds and the table, and going to the fireplace where M. le Duc d'Orléans stood talking to Monsieur le Duc, stopped a few paces away, as though wishing to speak. M. le Duc d'Orléans went to him as soon as he perceived him. They turned their faces to the wall, and remained so a goodish time; but seeing only their backs, one could discover nothing for they showed no emotion and seldom made a movement.

The Duc du Maine stayed where he was, his face livid as he furtively watched the conference he had occasioned. From time to time he turned wild eyes on the assembly with all the desperation of a condemned man. So we remained, I narrowly observing the Duc du Maine, but sometimes twisting my head to see the Regent and the Comte de Toulouse. At last they separated, and I had an opportunity to watch the two brothers at closer range, for the Comte de Toulouse passed quite near me on the opposite side of the table, on his way to join M. du Maine, still propped on his stick at the foot of the Maréchal de Villeroy's bed. M. de Toulouse looked much upset, even angry; and seeing his expression, the Duc du Maine turned as white as a sheet.

I continued on the alert, trying to read their lips, but soon I heard my name called. It was M. le Duc d'Orléans who wished to speak to me. Approaching him, I could see that he was deeply troubled. 'I have told him all,' he said, 'I could not do otherwise. He is the best fellow in the world, and it breaks my heart.' 'Why, Monsieur?' I exclaimed, 'What have you said?' 'He came to me from his brother, who guesses that something is prepared against him, and wishes to know whether I want him to go or stay. That is why I told all and, since he asked, I thought it only decent to say he had better go; did I do wrong?' 'No,' I answered, since it was useless to reproach a man who much needed encouragement. 'I am really very glad of it,' and I added, 'It is best to speak frankly, like one who knows his own mind and has nothing to fear. But now you have spoken, you must at all costs be firm.' I thought he was resolute enough, but that he ardently desired to be rid of the bastards, which, I believe, had been his real motive in all that had passed.

The Duc du Maine, as pale as death, looked about to collapse as he limped painfully to the head of the table, while his brother returned to say a brief word to the Regent before retreating down the entire length of the room. This was quickly over, and the Regent, now standing beside the King's chair, said loudly, 'Pray, gentlemen, let us take our seats.' Everyone sat down; but just as I grasped the back of my armchair, I noticed that both brothers were at the door and apparently about to leave. I leapt, so to speak, into the space between the King's chair and that of M. le Duc d'Orléans, so as to prevent the Prince de Conti from overhearing, and whispered urgently into the Regent's ear, 'Sir, they are leaving!' 'I know that,' he replied calmly. 'Yes,' I said, 'but what will they do outside?' 'Nothing at all,' he answered. 'The Comte de Toulouse asked leave to go, and promised that they would be prudent.' 'And if they are not?' I asked. 'They will be, but I have given orders to watch them.' 'But what if they do something rash, or try to leave Paris?' 'Then they will be arrested. I have given the orders.' After that I felt calmer and returned to my place; but he called me back to say that he had decided to warn the Council. When I agreed, he leaned across the table and the King's chair to speak in a whisper, first to Monsieur le Duc, then to the keeper of the seals.[1] All was then ready.

So much movement to and fro had greatly increased the apprehension

[1] Argenson.

and curiosity of the remaining members; but since all eyes had been fixed on the Regent, no one had noticed the departure of the bastards. Thus when I sat down in the chair of the Comte de Toulouse, the Duc de Guiche, who came next to me on the other side, left a chair empty between us, looking about him for their return. He bade me move down, saying that I was in the wrong chair; but I did not reply because I was observing the rest of the company. They presented a truly astonishing spectacle. At the second or third appeal, I motioned him to move up beside me. 'What about M. le Comte de Toulouse?' he hissed. 'Move up,' I said; but seeing that he stood transfixed, staring in amazement at Argenson, who had taken the Duc du Maine's seat at the other side of the table, I, still sitting, tugged at his coat, exclaiming, 'Come on and sit down!' Indeed, I pulled him so hard that he sat down with great suddenness, still uncomprehending. 'What is afoot?' he asked, when at length he was settled. 'Where are they?' 'I don't know,' I replied impatiently, 'they are not here, at any rate.' At that point, the Duc de Noailles, sitting on his other side and furious at being left in ignorance, seemed to divine that I was in the secret, for he leaned across the Duc de Guiche to say to me, 'For heaven's sake, Monsieur le Duc, tell us what is going on!' As you know, I was not on speaking terms with him, but on the contrary, apt to treat him with extreme discourtesy. I therefore turned upon him a cold, disdainful eye, and after hearing him out, merely looked away. That was all my reply. The Duc de Guiche begged me to speak, if only to say I knew something. I continued, however, to deny all knowledge, while the rest slowly took their places, looking around quite bewildered by the situation, and for a long time unable to comprehend that the meeting could begin without the bastards. No one said a word.

Before going any further, let me give you a plan of the seating at the Council meeting, and of the room itself, in order that you may better appreciate what had occurred so far, and what was to come later [see opposite].

When everyone was at last seated in his place, and every eye fixed upon him, M. le Duc d'Orléans announced that the meeting was being held as a prelude to a *Lit de Justice*, since that appeared the only way to secure registration of the Council's edict on the finances. After a short pause, he explained why at their previous sitting the Council had resolved to annul the Parlement's decree, adding that the keeper of the seals would read the act of annulment. The keeper then spoke, stating in what manner the Parlement might legally remonstrate; its powerlessness in all matters of government and finance, and the need to quash illegal remonstrances by means of a code (that was his word) that might serve in future as an inviolable guide.

The reading over, M. le Duc d'Orléans, against his usual practice, expressed his views by praising the motion. Then, assuming an air of

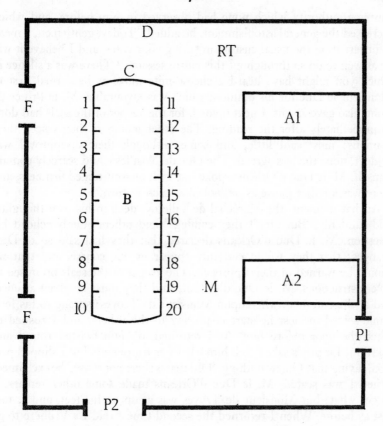

AI bed of the King
A2 bed of the Duc de Villeroy
B council table
C the King's armchair
D fireplace
F windows
 1 the Regent
 2 the Prince de Conti
 3 the Duc de Saint-Simon
 4 the Duc de Guiche
 5 the Duc de Noailles
 6 the Duc d'Antin
 7 the Maréchal d'Huxelles
 8 the Bishop of Troyes
 9 the Marquis de La Vrillière
10 the Marquis d'Effiat
11 M. le Duc

12 M. d'Argenson
13 the Duc de La Force
14 the Duc de Villeroy
15 the Duc de Villars
16 the Duc de Tallard
17 the Maréchal d'Estrées
18 the Maréchal de Bezons
19 M. Pelletier de Souzy
20 M. de Torcy
 M marks the spot where the Duc du Maine stood with the Comte de Toulouse
RT is where the Regent and the Comte de Toulouse confabulated, noses to the wall. Toulouse left by the little door, at P1. P2 marks the big doors of the usual entrance

supreme authority which none had observed in him before, and which increased the general astonishment, he added, 'Today, gentlemen, I mean to depart from the usual custom in taking your votes, and I believe it will be as well to do so throughout this entire session.'[1] There was a silence in which you might have heard a cheese-mite move as he turned first to Monsieur le Duc for his opinion, which was favourable. M. le Prince de Conti also gave assent. I next opined, for the keeper of the seals had done so immediately after the reading. The other members then voiced their opinions; most said little, and some, although their disapproval was evident, none the less agreed. The Duc de Noailles could scarcely contain himself. M. le Duc d'Orléans spoke last with unaccustomed firmness, and there was another pause as he looked at each in turn.

At that moment, the Maréchal de Villeroy, deep in his own thoughts, said suddenly, 'But aren't they coming?' and others quietly echoed his question. M. le Duc d'Orléans declared that they had said so to Desgranges; that they would certainly appear in due course, and that we should be warned of their approach. The keeper of the seals promised to give instructions. M. le Duc d'Orléans said they must be given at once, and at the entrance; whereupon Monsieur de Troyes[2] sprang to his feet. Panic seized me lest he start chattering to the ushers, and I rushed to reach the door before him. As I returned, d'Antin twisted round and asked me for pity's sake to tell him what was happening, but I slipped past him, saying that I knew nothing. 'Oh! that is sheer nonsense,' he exclaimed. When I was seated, M. le Duc d'Orléans made some other remark, I forget what; but Monsieur de Troyes was again on his feet, and I, too, just as before. When I returned the second time I told La Vrillière to go himself thereafter, because the position of my chair made my movements too conspicuous. D'Antin, his hands clasped as in prayer, was still begging for an explanation, but I remained firm, simply saying, 'You will know soon enough.' After I was seated, the Duc de Guiche continued to press me, but I was deaf to every word.

After this slight commotion, M. le Duc d'Orléans, sitting up very straight, addressed the meeting in still firmer and more authoritative tones. He said he had another, and far more important motion to propose. No one stirred; there was complete silence. He then continued that having given judgment in the suit between the princes of the blood and the 'legitimates' (he deliberately omitted the word princes) he had done no more at that time. He was, however, bound to see justice done to the peers of France, a body composed of the greatest men in the country, invested with the highest honours, most of them having served with distinction in the wars. For some time past these noble lords had had just grounds for complaint against certain persons (his very words), his own relations, who had risen

---

[1] At meetings of the councils, it was usual the custom for the member of lowest rank to vote first.
[2] For the portrait of Monsieur de Troyes, see pp. 23-25 above.

by unprecedented favours to extraordinary heights, and to rank that was
not rightfully theirs by birth. It was now time, said the Regent, to correct
such an anomaly, for which purpose an instrument had been drawn up.
The keeper of the seals would read it and afterwards it would be registered
in the King's presence, at a *Lit de Justice*.

A profound silence followed this totally unexpected statement that
served somewhat to explain the absence of the bastards. A deep gloom
settled on many faces; others, including those of the Maréchaux de Villars
and d'Estrées, flushed scarlet with anger. Tallard appeared for a moment
to be fainting, and the Maréchal de Villeroy looked completely crushed.
As for me, I had difficulty in keeping my countenance as all eyes turned
towards me; but I assumed an air of becoming sternness and modesty,
directing my gaze with the greatest care so as never to let it stray above the
horizontal. At the moment when the Regent had first begun to speak,
Monsieur le Duc shot such a triumphant look in my direction that I wellnigh lost my composure. It served to make me doubly careful not to meet
his eye. Thus, wholly self-possessed, my eyes searching every face,
sitting motionless in my seat, my pose most formal, wrapt in the keenest
and most enthralling pleasure, the most delightful fears, in joy so ardently
desired, so long awaited, I sweated in a perfect agony of restraint—an
agony so intoxicating that I have never, either before or since, experienced
anything to equal it. How far inferior are the pleasures of the senses to
those of the mind! How true it is that the pain one endures is proportionate
to the joy of its cessation!

When the Regent had finished, he asked the keeper of the seals to read
the proclamation, which he immediately did. No sweeter music ever
reached my ears; but my attention was bent on discovering the effect it had
on other listeners. Their changed expressions showed me what they felt. It
took but a few moments to persuade me, from the evident despair of the
Maréchal de Villeroy and the rage of Villars, that some moderating
influence was vitally necessary. I had the remedy in my pocket, from which
I extracted our lawsuit against the bastards, placing it on the table before
me, open at the last page, that contained our signatures printed in very
large capitals. The two marshals saw them at once and recognized them
for what they were, judging by the hopeless despair that suddenly showed
in their eyes, following the almost threatening stare of the Maréchal de
Villars. Everyone contemplated the strange document; yet no one
questioned it, for it was plain to all. I had hesitated to produce it, torn
between the fear of my part in the plot becoming known, and the risk, now
so apparent, that the marshals might raise an outcry and possibly succeed.
Nothing was more likely to restrain them than the sight of their own
signatures; but to display these after they had spoken might only have
excited their anger. I had taken the more prudent course, and had reason
to observe that I had acted for the best.

After the reading, M. le Duc d'Orléans said that it grieved him to be forced to such extreme measures, since they concerned his brothers-in-law; but the peers as well as the princes must have justice. Thereupon he turned to the keeper of the seals who spoke shortly and worthily, as nervous as a cat on hot bricks; but ending by giving his vote for registration. Monsieur le Duc was short, excited, and very civil regarding the peers. M. le Prince de Conti assented even more shortly; and M. le Duc d'Orléans then turned to me. I made a deep inclination without rising (which was against my usual practice), and proceeded as follows: that having the honour to be the senior peer on the Council on this occasion, I offered His Royal Highness my most humble thanks on behalf of the peers of France for thus giving judgment in our favour, begging him to believe in our true gratitude for an act of justice so long awaited, and now so completely satisfactory. I ended my brief oration[1] with another low bow, again without rising. The Duc de La Force copied me in this, and the rest of the Council assented one after another, although it was most evident that the majority were very far from approving.

M. le Duc d'Orléans spoke again. 'Gentlemen,' he said, 'that having been settled, justice has been done, and the rights of the noble lords are secure. I now propose an act of clemency towards the Comte de Toulouse, making an exception of him in consideration of the services he has rendered and the esteem in which you hold him. I move to restore to him, but not to his children,[2] the honours which he has hitherto enjoyed.' So saying, he bade the keeper of the seals read that part of the proclamation also, and so the motion was passed. That accomplished, M. le Duc d'Orléans let his glance travel round the table before saying that Monsieur le Duc had a request to make, which appeared to him both just and reasonable. The Duc du Maine, he continued, has been reduced in rank, the Maréchal de Villeroy will henceforth precede him everywhere, and thus cannot serve under his orders. The superintendence of His Majesty's education should be the task of a prince of the blood, and none in the Regent's opinion was more worthy than Monsieur le Duc, who now applied for it. M. le Duc d'Orléans called for votes; I spoke cordially in assent; the rest dumbly signified their agreement; the two marshals did not stir, but Villars's eyes were bright with anger.

A silence of blank dismay followed, during which the Maréchal de Villeroy, looking pale and distraught, continued to mutter under his breath. At last he managed to pull himself together, as with head bent he turned despairing eyes on the Regent, saying faintly, 'I have no arguments left. The late King's wishes have been set aside; I am deeply grieved; M.

---

[1] One particular joy for Saint-Simon was that the Duc du Maine after his reduction would rank lower than himself in the peerage.

[2] The Comte de Toulouse was unmarried at this time; he married Marie Victoire Sophie de Noailles, Marquise de Gondrin, in 1723. It was a love match. They had one son, Louis Jean Marie de Bourbon, Duc de Ponthièvre (1725–1793).

du Maine is most unfortunate.' 'Monsieur!' retorted the Regent in ringing tones, 'M. du Maine is my brother-in-law, but I prefer an open to a hidden enemy.' At those terrible words many bowed their heads. Effiat shook his vigorously. The Maréchal de Villeroy nearly fainted. Suppressed sighs were heard from one member or another on the farther side of the table. All knew that swords had been drawn; none could tell where the quarrel would end. A servant entered at that point to inform the keeper of the seals that he was wanted at the door. He returned with Desgranges to announce that the Parlement was approaching on foot, and that the head of the procession had already reached the outskirts of the palace. This news served somewhat to revive the spirits of the meeting.

The members of the Parlement came into view; and like children we crowded together to watch them from the windows. They entered two by two,[1] in their scarlet robes, by the great gate into the courtyard, and across the Salle des Ambassadeurs, where the premier président awaited them. Our two windows were packed with spectators, but I was careful to lose nothing of the events within the Council chamber, for fear of conspiracies or sudden exits. Desgranges several times came to tell me how matters were proceeding, whilst I walked up and down scanning every face with close attention. A few persons, either from necessity or because it had been forbidden, asked the Regent's permission to leave the room, to which he readily gave his consent, on condition that they said nothing and returned at once. He went so far as to order La Vrillière to caution the Maréchal d'Huxelles and a few other suspects; but he meant to watch them, which La Vrillière understood and obeyed very well. I did the same with the Maréchaux de Villars and de Tallard, and when I observed Effiat opening the little door to the King's room for the Maréchal de Villeroy, I rushed forward, ostensibly to help him, but in reality to see that he sent no message to the bastards. I even stayed with him until the Maréchal de Villeroy's return, and I closed the door firmly after him. I may truthfully say that all this exercise of mind and body, this concentrated alertness so as to be ready to intercept or warn, this continual surveying of an enormous room and a concourse of people, who had without their noticing to be controlled and manœuvred, caused me some anxiety and no little fatigue. M. le Duc d'Orléans, Monsieur le Duc, and La Vrillière did their share; but they did not much relieve my labours.

When at last the members of the Parlement were seated, the peers all present, and the présidents had been in two relays to fetch their furs from behind the screens in the adjoining room, Desgranges announced that all was ready. He had had some trouble in deciding whether or not the King should dine while he waited; but I had managed to prevent this, fearing

[1] There were a hundred and fifty-three of them, and they came to the Louvre by way of the Rue Saint-Honoré. They had hoped to win the sympathy of the rabble, but Madame said they were greeted by shouts of 'Look at the lobsters!'

lest, the *Lit de Justice* coming immediately after, he might feel unwell, which would have been very awkward. As soon as Desgranges had made his announcement, the Regent bade him warn the Parlement that it was time to send their deputation to greet the King at the farther end of the hall of the Swiss Guards; then, turning to the assembly, he said in a loud voice that he was about to admit the King.

At these words I felt a thrill of joy at the thought of the tremendous drama I was about to witness. It made me doubly careful to behave with propriety. I had told Villars[1] to walk with us, and reminded Tallard to accompany the Marshals of France and to give precedence to his seniors, because on such occasions dukes do not count unless they are also peers. I fortified myself with the strongest possible dose of calm, soberness, and modesty as I followed M. le Duc d'Orléans through the little door to the room where the King was. As we went, the Duc d'Albret[2] and others were remarkably civil to me in their eagerness to know what was preparing. I repaid their courtesies, complained of the crowd, the discomfort of my uniform, etc., and so reached the King's presence.

He was wearing neither a mantle nor bands, just his ordinary dress. M. le Duc d'Orléans talked with him a little, and then asked if he would be pleased to start; whereupon the way was cleared. One or two courtiers who were there because they had found no room in the audience-chamber, drew to one side, and I motioned to the Maréchal de Villars, who slowly led the procession to the door. The Duc de La Force followed close behind him, and then myself, making sure that I walked immediately in front of M. le Prince de Conti.[3] Monsieur le Duc walked behind him and, last of all, M. le Duc d'Orléans. Then came the gentlemen ushers[4] with their maces, then the King surrounded by the four captains of the bodyguard,[5] the Duc d'Albret as Great Chamberlain, and the Maréchal de Villeroy as Governor. Following them came the keeper of the seals, and the Maréchaux d'Estrées, d'Huxelles, de Tallard, and de Bezons, who were allowed in as part of the King's retinue. After them walked the Knights of the Order, and then such of the provincial governors and lieutenants-general as it had been possible to notify. It had been arranged for these officers to sit on the lowest bench, uncovered and voteless. In that order we processed by way of the terrace of the Tuileries to the hall of the Swiss Guards, at the entrance to which a deputation from the Parlement, headed, as is customary, by four judges and four counsellors, waited to greet the King.

As they advanced, I said to the Duc de La Force and the Maréchal de

---

[1] Because Villars was a peer as well as being a Maréchal.

[2] Emmanuel Théodore de La Tour, Duc d'Albret (1667–1730), later Duc de Bouillon on the death of his father in 1721. He was the Great Chamberlain of France, and Governor of Auvergne.

[3] Leaving no intermediate space for bastards. The highest-ranking walked nearest the King.

[4] There were sixteen altogether, with four always on duty.

[5] The Ducs de Noailles, Charost, and Villeroy, and the Marquis d'Harcourt (François, Duc d'Harcourt-Beuvron, 1690–1750, who succeeded to the dukedom later in 1718).

Villars that we had best take our seats before the King entered the Council chamber, and they accordingly processed behind me in single file, and in order of seniority. We three were the only ones with the right to enter in procession, d'Antin being absent, and the Duc de Guiche retired.[1] Tallard was not a peer, and the four captains of the bodyguard always surrounded the King at important ceremonies. But before going further, I think it would be advisable to give you a plan of the *Lit de Justice*; you will then understand at a glance the spectacle which I am about to describe [see pp. 200–1].

It would, I think, be of little use to enter into further detail. This should suffice for you to understand what follows.

As the Parlement was already in place and the King about to enter, I used the same little door by which I had gone out. There was room enough, but the officers of the guard cleared a passage for me and the Duc de La Force and the Maréchal de Villars, as they entered after me in single file. As I crossed the threshold I paused for a moment, enraptured at the sight of that noble scene and the thought of the great events about to take place. Indeed, I needed to brace myself in order to take stock of all I saw, and apply to my countenance a fresh veneer of soberness and becoming modesty. Well did I know how intently I should be scrutinized by that assembly so long accustomed to dislike me, and by the eager onlookers who waited to learn the hidden reason for the hasty summoning of an obviously momentous session. Everyone was aware that I must know the truth, if only because they had just seen me leave the Council of Regency.

I was not mistaken. The moment I appeared, all eyes were riveted on me. I walked slowly towards the clerk of the Parlement, then, turning back between the two benches, I crossed the width of the chamber, passing in front of the King's councillors who saluted me gleefully, and mounting the three steps to the high seats where the peers whom I have noted were already in their places. They all rose as I approached the steps, and I bowed to them with deep respect from the top of the third step. As I slowly moved along the row, I took La Feuillade by the shoulder (though I had no understanding with him) and whispered in his ear to listen carefully and show no surprise, for he was about to hear a proclamation concerning the Parlement, after which two more decrees would follow. At that point we should at long last reach the most joyous and unexpected moment of our lives, for the bastards were going to be reduced to the bare level of their peerages. The Comte de Toulouse would afterwards be reinstated, but only for his lifetime, and not for his children. La Feuillade was at first bewildered, then seized with such joy that he became incapable of speech. He pressed up against me, and as I moved away, murmured, 'But why the Comte de Toulouse?' 'You will see,' I answered, and passed on.

---

[1] The Duc de Guiche had given up his dukedom to his son, the Duke de Louvigny. D'Antin's absence was due to his awkward situation: he was the half-brother of the bastards.

Plan of the Lit de Justice

Seconde Antichambre du Roi où était le dais. Vuide entre le
grand Cabinet du Conseil et la grande Antichambre, où fut tenu le Lit de justice representé ici

Cheminée bouchée

L

M.M. les Evêques D et E de Laon & Noyon.   *M.rs d'Estrées, Huxelles, Tallard, Besons*

A   C   V   F   P   P   D   D   M

B   E   G   G   H   Q   K

M. le Regent   *Mesmes p. 7.be Novion.*   *Hostigue, Lamoignon, Portail, Amelot, Pelletier, Maupeou*

M *M. a Duc*   G   H   J   S

   N   Q

M. le Prince de Conti   R   M

M.M. les D. de Sully   D

S.t Simon

La Rochefoucauld

La Force

Rohan

Grammont

M *Mazarin*   T   M

Gevres

Tresme

Aumont

Villars M.al   D

Chaulnes

Rohan Rohan

Hostun

Rouanois

Valentinois   Z

Y

Secr. d'Etat.   *Secr. du P.t*

Conseillers de toutes les Chambres du P.t

M   K   *Gens du Roi:*   *Id. pour le P.t*   M

Id. pour le P.t

Spectateurs de marque.

Spectateurs de consideration.

Porte toujours ouverte, mais fermée   *Porte ordinairement fermée: mais ouverte ce jour*
ce jour là, excepté pour les seuls Pairs   *là pour la séance, et les spectateurs, et par où*
qui entrèrent et sortirent par là.   *aussi le Roi entra et sortit.*

Salle des Gardes du Corps
Les Ducs de Noailles, de Charost, et plusieurs autres entrèrent avec le Roi et vinrent
se mettre en place parmi ceux qui sont marqués ici, et qui y étaient avant l'arrivée du Roi.

Key to the Plan

a   The King on his throne.

b   The steps to the throne with carpet and cushions.

c   The Great Chamberlain reclining on the cushions, covered, and voting.

d   The high benches to left and right.

e   Low steps, covered by the end of the King's carpet, but without cushions.

f   The Provost of Paris with his staff, seated on these steps.

g   The King's ushers, kneeling and shouldering their silver maces.

h   The keeper of the seals in his backless armchair.

i   The small writing-table placed before him.

k   The steps by which one ascended to the high benches.

l   The ordinary entrance door (not used on this occasion) through which Messieurs de Troyes and de Fréjus, also M. de Torcy, viewed the scene, standing, and outside. Before them, a little to one side, but within the chamber, stood the Marquis d'Harcourt, uncovered, holding the bâton of a captain of the bodyguard and without a vote.

m   Windows with steps for the spectators; the Duchesses de Ventadour and La Ferté;[1] the King's assistant governors; the first gentlemen of his chamber, and the captain of the Regent's bodyguard were all at the window behind him.

n   The Maréchal de Villeroy seated on a stool, as the King's governor, covered and voting.

o   The Duc de Villeroy,[2] Captain of the guards on duty, seated, covered and voting.

p   Beringhen, Master of the Horse, representing the Grand-master,[3] seated, uncovered, and not voting. The two last places had been assigned because of the King's youth, and the old age of his governor.

q   The heralds in their tabards.

r   The Grand-master, or Master of Ceremonies, uncovered and not voting.

s   Entrance to the high benches on the left, for bishop-peers and officers of the crown.

t   Floor, or empty space in the centre of the assembly.

v   Passage on a level with the high benches, which led into it from either side.

y   Extra bench on a level with the high benches, in case they should be needed for lay peers.

z   Chief clerk of the Parlement; there to register the decrees after the session.

There in my high seat with no one before me, because the second bench for the peers extended no farther than the Duc de La Force, I was able to contemplate the whole assembly, and did so with all my powers of penetration. One thing alone restrained me; I dared not look too long at certain individuals lest they should grasp the meaning of my delighted gaze. Moreover, noticing that all eyes were turned in my direction, I

---

[1] They were sisters.

[2] Louis Nicolas de Neufville, Duc de Charost et de Villeroy (1663–1734), son of the Maréchal. He had become Duke in 1694.

[3] Charles de Lorraine-Armagnac, so called Prince Charles (see p. 48 above).

was still more careful to let discretion blunt their curiosity. Yet I shot one dazzling glance at the premier président and the high bench of judges, which I was admirably well placed to examine. Then I let my eye travel across the entire Parlement and perceived wonder, silence, and dismay such as I had not expected, and which appeared to me a hopeful sign. The premier président, looking insolently dejected, the others, deeply perturbed and anxious, provided me with the most enchanting spectacle.

I had little time in which to study them, for the King entered at that moment. The bustle of his arrival lasted until he and all his retinue were seated, and was in itself exceptional. All eyes were then fixed on the Regent, the keeper of the seals, and the chief officers. The bastards' departure from the Council chamber had indeed been noticed, but not by everyone. Now all remarked their absence, and the consternation of the Marshals, when they saw that their leader was missing from his seat as the King's governor, was great indeed. All this added much to the distress of the premier président. He looked in terror at M. de Sully and myself, sitting in the seats where the two brothers should have been, and immediately the entire assembly turned towards us. I saw heightened anxiety on every face. As for the Regent, he wore an expression of quiet, dignified determination that was quite new to him. The King, grave and stately, cut the most charming figure imaginable, for in all his bearing there was grace and serious attention. He did not seem at all bored, but most perfect in his public demeanour, and with no sign of shyness.

When all was quiet, the keeper of the seals uncovered, rose, and mounted the steps to kneel before the King and receive his orders. He then returned to his seat, replaced his cap, and delivered the opening speech of that great drama. The official report, drawn up and published by the Parlement, relieves me of the need to quote his words. Suffice it to say that as the force of them struck home, consternation spread over the faces of the members, few of whom dared even to whisper to their neighbours, while acute suffering, plainly caused by mortification, clouded that of the premier président whose whole countenance expressed humiliation and defeat.

When the votes had been counted and announced by the keeper of the seals, I observed a great commotion on the 'High Bench', as it is called in the jargon of the Palais de Justice. The premier président was making ready to utter the protest that has since been printed, full of most subtle and impudent spite towards the Regent, most insolent to the King's majesty. Yet the rascal trembled as he spoke. His broken voice and nervous glance, his shocked and troubled air, conflicted with his venomous words, that last libation which he could not deny himself or his colleagues. Then it was that I savoured with inexpressible joy the spectacle of those proud jurists, who once had dared to refuse us the salutation that was our due, humbly kneeling to render at our feet their homage to the throne, while we, seated and covered, remained in our high seats beside the King. Our situations, our postures, so entirely different, were the outward and visible signs of the acknowledged rights of those who are most truly *laterales Regis*, in contrast to the *vas electum* of the third estate. My eyes fixed, nay riveted, upon those arrogant persons, traversed all that 'High Bench' of kneeling or standing figures, their fur robes billowing out with each long, ever deeper genuflection, until the King, through the mouth of the keeper of the seals, gave them leave to stand once more erect. Cony aping ermine! Their heads, humbled and uncovered, were at the level of our feet.

The protest made, the keeper of the seals once again mounted the three steps before the King, and without pausing for orders came down them again. Then, looking towards the premier président, he announced in a loud voice, '*Le roi veut être obéi, et obéi sur-le-champ.*' Those tremendous words fell like a thunderbolt, annihilating presidents and councillors alike. They all bowed their heads, and it was a long time before most of them stood upright. The witnesses, with the exception of the Marshals of France, appeared little moved by their discomfiture.

Yet this was a petty triumph compared with what followed. After a short pause, the keeper of the seals once again mounted the steps to the King, and, returning to his place, stood in silence. Everyone now clearly perceived that although the business of the Parlement was done, more remained to do. Some thought it concerned the affair of the bonnets, and that a ruling would be given in our favour. Others, noticing the bastards' absence, rightly concluded that the matter affected them. No one guessed the truth; still less its full scope.

At last the keeper of the seals opened his mouth to speak, and with his first sentence proclaimed the downfall of one brother, and the reinstatement of the other. Impossible to describe the effect upon his hearers! But although I had more than enough to do in controlling my feelings, I let nothing escape me of what went on. Amazement seemed to be the prevailing sentiment. Many appeared glad, either from a sense of justice or because they hated the Duc du Maine and esteemed the Comte de Toulouse. Some were aghast. As for the premier président, he was completely out of countenance; his face, normally so haughty and self-confident, began to twitch convulsively; only extreme anger prevented his collapsing in a swoon. As the reading continued, matters became far worse for him; for every word was law, and each brought fresh discomfiture. The rest of the assembly listened intently, sitting motionless for fear of missing a single word, with all eyes turned upon the reader. Towards the middle, the premier président, grinding what few teeth remained to him, leaned his forehead upon the stick which he held between his hands, and in that singular and most revealing posture heard the rest of the reading, so deadly for him, so revivifying for us.

In the meantime, joy was nearly killing me. I was truly terrified of swooning, for my heart swelled within me, and there seemed no room for it to expand. I did violence to my feelings in order not to betray myself; yet at the same time the torture was a delight. I remembered the long days and years of servitude, those unhappy times when, dragged like a victim to the Parlement, I was forced to witness the triumphs of the bastards, as by degrees they were promoted to that pinnacle above us. I savoured once again, and with exquisite pleasure, the words I had dared to use to the Duc du Maine[1] on that vile day of the bonnet affair, under his father's tyrannous rule. Now at last, I saw my prophecy come true. I told myself that all of this had been my doing, and I was glad. I contemplated that shining hour in the presence of the King and that noble assembly. I had won; I was avenged; I wallowed in my vengeance, delighting in the gratification of my unfaltering heart's desire, and keenest hope. I was tempted to think of nothing else. Yet I did not cease to listen to those life-giving words that made my heart quiver like a fiddle-string beneath the bow, or fail to notice their effect upon other hearers.[2]

At the first words of the keeper of the seals my eyes met those of the two bishop-peers.[3] Never have I seen men more astounded, nor more unmistakably joyful. I had not been able to warn them in advance, for our seats were far apart; thus they were hard put to it to conceal their excess of emotion. My eyes took in one delicious draught of their gladness, and then I turned away for fear lest I be overcome. I dared not look at them again.

When the reading was over, the keeper of the seals called on the head clerk to bring his paper and writing-desk, so as to finish all the formalities in the King's presence, with the registration and signature of the various decrees. There were no objections, but since five or six had to be dealt with, it was a lengthy business.

I had observed the King closely when the question of his education arose; but I saw no change in his expression nor any sign of distress. This was the last act of the drama, and was only just completed when the registrations were inscribed. Then, since there were no more speeches to listen to, he began to laugh with those around him and seemed greatly amused, especially by the Duc de Louvigny[4] who was sitting some distance from the throne, wearing a velvet robe. He joked about how hot that nobleman must be feeling, and all in a most delightful way. Everyone was struck by his lack of concern regarding the Duc du Maine, which flatly contradicted those who said that his eyes were red; that he had been too frightened to say anything at the *Lit de Justice*, or after. The truth is that his eyes were

---

[1] See II, pp. 385–386.

[2] Considering that the Duc du Maine was reinstated five years later (see pp. 445–446 below), it says much for Saint-Simon's addiction to the truth, as he saw it, that he did not tone this down in his revision.

[3] The Bishops of Laon and Noyon.

[4] He figures on the plan as the Duc de Gramont, his official title.

perfectly dry; and the only time he mentioned the Duc du Maine was after dinner that same day, when he asked very carelessly where he was going, never afterwards referring either to him or to his children.

During the registrations I quietly surveyed the whole assembly; but although I kept myself under strict control, I could not resist venting some of my feelings on the premier président. I had annihilated him with long blistering looks a hundred times during the session. Glances of mockery, contempt, scorn, and triumph had shot from my eyes, piercing him to the very marrow of his bones. Sometimes he had shifted his gaze when it encountered mine, and then I had loved to insult him with a stealthy and malicious smile that completed his mortification. I basked in his anger and delighted that he should observe me. Often I mocked him, pointing him out to my two neighbours with a sly wink when I thought he was sure to notice it. In a word, I bore down upon him unmercifully to the utmost limit of my powers.[1]

When all was over, the King came down from his throne and left by the door through which he had entered. The two bishop-peers, moving in front of the empty throne, placed themselves at the head of our procession, and as they passed me, they clasped my hands and embraced me in warm congratulation. We followed after them, marching two by two in order of rank along the rows of benches, down the three steps, and out by the opposite door, which was the one through which the King had come and gone. The way was cleared for us as far as the steps. The crowds, the people of fashion, the place itself prevented conversation and expressions of delight, which deeply disappointed me. I therefore went at once to my coach, drawn up close at hand, and thus had no delay in leaving the courtyard, arriving back at my home in less than a quarter of an hour.

It was half-past two, and there, at the foot of the stairs, was Louville and my whole family waiting for me, even including my mother, whom curiosity had brought downstairs, although she had not left her room since the beginning of the previous winter.[2] We went to my bedroom on the ground floor where, whilst I changed my coat and shirt, I answered their eager questions. Suddenly Biron was announced, despite the fact that I had forbidden them to disturb me until I had rested. Biron, however, stuck his head round my study-door, and begged me to spare him a moment. I accordingly went with him into the study, only half-dressed. He told me that M. le Duc d'Orléans had been expecting me at the Palais Royal when he had returned from the Tuileries; he had said I had promised to go there at once, that he was surprised not to see me, but that it did not much matter. Now, it seemed, he desired my presence. I asked Biron if he knew why, and he replied that I was to go to Saint-Cloud to break the news to Mme la Duchesse d'Orléans. That was an unexpected horror, and so I

---

[1] This was all very disagreeable when Président de Mesmes's daughter married Saint-Simon's brother-in-law, the Duc de Lorges. See p. 295 et seqq.   [2] She was seventy-three.

said to Biron. He sympathized, but advised me to hasten with all speed to the Palais Royal, where I was impatiently awaited. He said further, though he hated to tell me so, that M. le Duc d'Orléans had declared that only I could do it, and in such a way that there could be no hope of his excusing me, or taking kindly to any objection.

I took Biron back to my bedroom, where everything had changed, and Mme de Saint-Simon was weeping, in the conviction that something terrible had occurred. I told them all, and when Biron had conversed a little longer, exhorting me again to be prompt and obedient, he went off to his dinner. Ours was ready. I waited a short time to recover from my surprise, and decided that it would be best not to vex M. le Duc d'Orléans by any further delay, but none the less to try by every means to avoid that most painful task. Then, having first swallowed some soup and an egg, I went straight to the Palais Royal.

M. le Duc d'Orléans was alone in his big study, striding up and down, waiting impatiently for my arrival. He came to me at once, asking if I had seen Biron. I replied that I had, and had come forthwith to receive his orders. He asked if Biron had told me what he wanted. I said yes, and that to show my readiness I had brought six horses, prepared for anything, although my conviction was that he had not sufficiently reflected. To this he replied that he quite understood my unwillingness to break news so distressing to Mme la Duchesse d'Orléans's way of thinking; but that he dared not write to her since he could not be sure that she would destroy the letter or prevent others from seeing it. He insisted that I had always been a peacemaker; that they both trusted me, and that for the love I bore them he begged me to undertake his mission.

I paid him all the usual compliments, but declared myself to be the last man for such a task. I was excessively conscious and proud of my rank; the bastards' position had always been anathema to me; I had ardently desired and worked for their ruin, and had many times said so to Mme la Duchesse d'Orléans,[1] and even to Mme du Maine herself. Mme la Duchesse d'Orléans would know only too well how happy this day had made me; thus it not only showed lack of respect to her, but was positively insulting to make me impart such news. 'You are mistaken,' retorted M. le Duc d'Orléans, 'and that is no argument. It is just because you have always been so frank about the bastards that you may now speak without fear. Mme la Duchesse d'Orléans is very fond of you; she will not take offence, but on the contrary thank you for your candour. She knows you want peace and harmony between us, and that no one would do this better than you, who are such a great friend of the family. I know it is difficult, but do not refuse me; one should always oblige one's friends.' I demurred, I protested; there was great argument between us; in the end I was forced to yield. I left him, declaring that he was making use of me, overruling my

[1] See II, pp. 463–464.

repugnance and my personal wishes, and exposing me to malicious gossip; he, swearing eternal affection, and infinite distress at having to ask so much from my love.

As I went out, I saw one of Mme la Duchesse d'Orléans's pages, just arrived from Saint-Cloud, and still with his boots on. I asked him to go back at the gallop, find the Duchess of Sforza and, informing her that I was bringing news from M. le Duc d'Orléans, beg her to be ready to see me privately the very moment I arrived. My idea was to see no one but her, and to give her all the papers, on the pretext of showing greater respect for Mme la Duchesse d'Orléans who, I felt sure, would not wish to see me in those circumstances. I thought M. le Duc d'Orléans would not take it ill if I acted thus. But all my poor precautions were confounded by the page, who was equally prudent. He took good care not to become involved in the bad news he had learned at the Palais Royal. All he did was to say that I was coming from M. le Duc d'Orléans, and he never so much as breathed a word to Mme Sforza, but very quickly fled.

I travelled at a slow jog-trot to give plenty of time for him to arrive first, and for the Duchess of Sforza to prepare to receive me. And all the time I was congratulating myself on my cleverness; though I could not help anticipating that I might, in the end, be forced to see Mme la Duchesse d'Orléans. It did not occur to me that Saint-Cloud might not have heard of that morning's work; but none the less, my anxiety was beyond expression and it increased with every mile.

At last my coach drew up in the great courtyard, and I saw most of the inhabitants at the windows, while others came running up from all sides. I stepped down and asked the first person to take me to Mme Sforza, for I did not know her lodging. They said she was at prayers with Mme la Duchesse d'Orléans whose apartments were separated from the chapel by the ante-room in which I was standing. I immediately made a dash for the Maréchale de Rochefort's apartment, which gave on to this same ante-room, begging them to bring Mme Sforza to me. A moment later they returned to say she could not be found anywhere, but that Mme la Duchesse d'Orléans had learned of my arrival and was waiting to see me. She sent another servant for me; then another and another. I had sent only one in pursuit of Mme Sforza, and was preparing to wait for her, when suddenly the Maréchale de Rochefort came stumping along on her stick. Mme la Duchesse d'Orléans had sent her personally to fetch me. We had a fierce argument because I still wished to wait for Mme Sforza who could no-where be found. I tried to pursue her myself in order to gain time; but the Maréchale dragged me inexorably after her, asking what news I brought. At last I replied impatiently, 'Only what you already know.' 'What do you mean? We know nothing except that there has been a *Lit de Justice*; we are dying to hear why, and what has happened.' In my intense astonish-ment, I made her promise and swear three and four times over that she spoke the truth, and that no one at Saint-Cloud had heard anything. When I told her the facts she nearly fell over backwards. I made one last effort to avoid going to Mme la Duchesse d'Orléans; but six or seven messages had come during our exchanges, and in the end I was obliged to follow the Maréchale; for she, appalled by the event, still gripped my wrist, whilst I truly pitied myself in the scene I was about to witness, indeed to occasion.

Thus numbed with terror, I entered the fountain rooms[1] of Mme la Duchesse d'Orléans, where the faces of the company reflected the fear on my own countenance. The Maréchale left me as I entered the bedroom. They told me there that Her Royal Highness was in the marble room, three steps down from where I stood. I turned, and from the farthest possible distance bowed to her in a manner very different from my usual. At first she noticed nothing, but gaily invited me to draw near, in a perfectly natural way. When, however, she saw me stop at the bottom of the steps, she cried out, 'Heavens! Monsieur. What a terrible look! What news do you bring?' Seeing that I neither moved nor spoke she became still more alarmed, firing question after question at me. At the third, I took a few slow steps towards her, saying, 'Madame, is it possible that you have not heard?' 'No, Monsieur, I know only that there has been a *Lit de Justice*, nothing more.' 'Ah! Madame,' said I, 'then I am even more wretched than I had supposed.' 'What is it, Monsieur?' she said quickly, 'What has happened?' and she rose to a sitting posture on the sofa where she had been reclining. 'Come and sit down.' I drew near, saying that I was in despair. 'But tell me,' she cried, 'it is best to hear bad news from one's friends.' That word cut me to the quick, and made me conscious of the suffering I was about to cause.

I moved still closer, and said at last that M. le Duc d'Orléans had reduced M. du Maine's rank to the bare level of his peerage, but at the same time had restored to M. le Comte de Toulouse all the titles he had hitherto enjoyed. There I paused, adding after a moment that Monsieur le Duc was given control of the King's education. Her tears began to flow abundantly. She said nothing, did not cry out, but wept bitterly. She pointed to a chair, on which I sat down, silently gazing at the ground. After a while I continued that M. le Duc d'Orléans, who had more or less compelled me to undertake this most unhappy mission, had expressly ordered me to say that he had very strong proof of M. du Maine's guilt; that out of consideration for her, he had held back; but that further delay was impossible. She said softly that her brother was indeed unfortunate, and soon after inquired whether I knew what he had done. I said that M. le Duc d'Orléans had told me nothing, and that it was a matter on which I felt I had no right to question him.

---

[1] The *Appartement des Goulottes*, at the lower end of the park of Saint-Cloud, where there were pools and reservoirs.

After a pause I said that M. le Duc d'Orléans charged me to tell her how deeply he felt for her, adding whatever in my hapless state I could invent to make that dreadful sympathy more palatable. She said she knew I should not expect gratitude from her at that moment. In the interstices[1] I spoke of my own distress at her grief, and of my reluctance at having to bring her such news, explaining how I had tried by all means to avoid it. Her only answer was by gestures, and a few kind words between sobs. I then declared that she should think now only of herself and her grief, and seek such consolation as she might. M. le Duc d'Orléans, I continued, desired her to do exactly as she pleased; to see him, or not to see him, just as she preferred; to stay at Saint-Cloud, or go to Bagnolet or Montmartre, and remain there as long she desired, in a word, to feel free; and I said I had been given firm orders to urge her to let no other considerations weigh with her. Thereupon, she asked me if I knew M. le Duc d'Orléans's intentions regarding her brothers, and whether he would mind her seeing them. I said I had no instructions on that point, and for that very reason was sure that he would approve, especially with regard to M. le Comte de Toulouse; even concerning M. du Maine, I thought there would be no objection and, if necessary, I would bear the responsibility. She then spoke of him again, declaring that he must indeed be guilty of some great offence, and that she was almost reduced to hoping so. A fresh outburst of tears followed these words. I remained a few minutes longer in my chair, in the greatest discomfort imaginable, trying to decide whether to stay or go. At length I confessed my embarrassment, saying I thought she might prefer to spend some time alone before giving me her orders, but that respect prevented my leaving her. After a moment she signed to me to summon her women. I rose and sent them to her, saying that if Her Royal Highness desired to see me again, I should be with Mme Sforza or the Maréchale de Rochefort; but as I found neither of those ladies at home, I went upstairs to visit Madame.

I could see on entering that I was impatiently expected; but I said nothing to the very few persons collected in her bedroom, while my name was announced at the door of the little boudoir in which she was writing, as she nearly always was.[2] I was admitted at once. She rose as I appeared, crying, 'Well! Monsieur; this is news indeed!' Her ladies immediately

[1] *interstices* (for *intervalles*): this is Saint-Simon's own word. In the Roman Catholic Church it means the spaces between the reception of the various degrees of divine orders.
[2] Letter-writing was Madame's hobby. She wrote in German three or four letters a day, some of them fifty pages long. In earlier days she had written chiefly to her aunt the Electress of Hanover. Now her letters were to her daughter, the Duchesse de Lorraine, and to Caroline of Anspach, the Princess of Wales. Saint-Simon liked her on the whole; she liked him because of his loyalty to her son, and he gained useful pieces of information from her. She had particularly loathed Mme de Maintenon, whom she called *die alte Zote* (the old whore), which may have coloured Saint-Simon's exaggerated language when he referred to her as *la vieille ordure* (the filthy old creature).

left her, and we were alone. I excused myself for not calling on her first, as her rank required, saying that M. le Duc d'Orléans had assured me that she would wish me first to visit Mme la Duchesse d'Orléans. She wholly approved, but it then transpired to my vast surprise that she knew only of the *Lit de Justice*, and nothing of what had taken place there. When I told her all, her countenance was suffused with joy, and she emitted a great 'At last!',[1] twice repeated, with the remark that her son should have acted long ago, but was altogether too soft-hearted. She went on to say that Mme du Maine's insane pride had egged her husband on; spoke of the princes of the blood and their lawsuit against the bastards, and told me of Mme du Maine's fury after the verdict, and of how she had brought her two sons[2] up to M. le Duc d'Orléans, swearing she would never forget that day, and would be revenged for the wrong he had done them.[3] After more talk of the hard words, the injuries, and worse, directed at M. le Duc d'Orléans by the Duc and Duchesse du Maine, Madame begged me to tell her all, moment by moment—those were her very words—of the events of that famous morning. I reminded her that she was still standing (out of courtesy to me she had refused a chair),[4] and that the recital would be a long one; but she would not be disturbed, so eager was she to listen. M. le Duc d'Orléans had ordered me to describe the meeting of the Council as well as the *Lit de Justice*, and I accordingly began at the very beginning. After a quarter of an hour, Madame did consent to take a chair, but with the greatest possible civility. I was with her nearly an hour, talking the whole time, and occasionally answering questions. She was truly enraptured over the humiliation of the Parlement and the bastards, and especially so because His Royal Highness, her son, had at last shown firmness.

The Maréchale de Rochefort then entered bearing Mme la Duchesse d'Orléans's excuses, and asking Madame's leave to remove me because Her Royal Highness desired to speak to me. Madame dismissed me at once, but begged me to return later. I went downstairs with the Maréchale to Mme la Duchesse d'Orléans's room, where I found her sitting on the sofa just as I had left her, with a writing-desk across her knees and a pen in her hand. As soon as she perceived me she said she had decided to go to Montmartre, on my assurance that Monsieur le Duc d'Orléans would not disapprove; but she was none the less writing to obtain his leave. She read

---

[1] Madame had a deep, manly voice. Many years earlier, the Elector-Palatine of Bavaria had described her as 'a noisy, rough and wayward girl'.

[2] The Prince de Dombes (1700–1755) and the Prince d'Eu (1701–1775).

[3] Saint-Simon's hatred of the Duc du Maine (in which he was not alone) led him to make out that du Maine had a far greater part in the Cellamare conspiracy than the evidence would show. His wife was at the bottom of it, and she later confessed that one of her greatest problems was to keep him in ignorance of what was going on. Du Maine was crooked in mind and body, but his greatest crime seems to have been his failure to control his uncontrollable duchess.

[4] If she had sat down, Saint-Simon would still have had to remain standing. He could not sit in the presence of royalty.

me her letter, or rather the start of it—six or seven lines in a very large hand on very tiny paper; then, looking at me affectionately, she continued, 'I cannot stop crying. I have asked you down to do me a kindness; my hand will not write; please finish this for me,'[1] and she handed me the desk with her letter on top. I took it; she dictated the rest, which I wrote down as she spoke. Her letter surprised me to the last degree; it was so concise, so full of becoming sentiments, so elegantly expressed. It could not, indeed, have been bettered by the finest writer after long and calm reflection; yet she had composed it in the most violent agitation, amid sobs and a perfect torrent of tears. All my life I have regretted not making a copy; but although I remember it perfectly, I dare not reproduce it for fear of distorting it in some way. How sad that with so much spirit, good sense, and integrity, she should have made herself useless, or worse, by a mania for bastardy that had corroded and ruined her entire character! When her letter was finished, I read it over to her. She would not seal it, but asked me to deliver it. I said that I would certainly do so, but must first go up to see whether Madame had orders for me.

As I was finishing with Madame, the Duchess of Sforza came to speak to her on behalf of Mme la Duchesse d'Orléans about her visit to Montmartre, and to ask her to keep with her Mlle de Valois.[2] The mother and daughter were on none too good terms, since the young lady had a truly royal loathing for the bastards and their rank. Madame gave most kind consent to all that Mme la Duchesse d'Orléans asked, and pitied her distress. After this interruption I continued my narrative. I was just bringing it to a close when the Maréchale de Rochefort returned to ask Madame to be so good as to go down to Mme la Duchesse d'Orléans, she being in no fit state to climb the stairs. She told us that it had now been decided to remain at Saint-Cloud, and not go to Montmartre. The Maréchale then withdrew; I ended my speech, and followed Madame; but I did not go in with her to Mme la Duchesse d'Orléans as I did not wish to put any restraint upon them. Mme Sforza, when she emerged, told me that there had been another change and that she was going to Paris;[3] whereupon I wrote to take my leave, and drove straight back to the Palais Royal, where the Regent was entertaining Mme Duchesse de Berry. He came to me in the large study, and I told him all that had happened.

On my way home, I thought it would be wise to call at the Hôtel de Condé. There I found Madame la Duchesse confined to her bed, having chosen that singularly inappropriate day to take physic. I was received in much the same way as on my visit to Saint-Cloud when Mme la Duchesse

---

[1] In Saint-Simon's minute handwriting, he might almost have written the Lord's Prayer on a postage stamp if he had so wished.

[2] The Orléans's third daughter, aged eighteen, who married the Duke of Modena.

[3] One imagines that Madame had persuaded her daughter-in-law to go back to her husband at the Palais Royal.

de Berry's marriage was announced.[1] Such is the way of the world! Monsieur le Duc took me into his private study; everyone tried to buttonhole me. The frequenters of their circle, people whom I hardly knew, saluted me admiringly. I could scarcely credit my environment. Later I had long, confidential talks with d'Antin and Torcy, and as I was leaving, Mme de Laigle[2] urged me to make friends with Madame la Duchesse. I would not hear of that, however, and answered that I had always been too close a friend to Mme la Duchesse d'Orléans to make that possible, since the sisters were not on loving terms. Notwithstanding that Madame la Duchesse had neither known nor wished to know anything concerning these dramatic events, and would greatly have preferred her brother's rank to be higher than ours, her dislike for Mme la Duchesse d'Orléans and her family increased to a totally excessive degree, and soon became publicly known.

On the day after the *Lit de Justice*, Monsieur le Duc took over the control of the King's education; and a few days later seized possession of the Duc du Maine's apartment at the Tuileries. That same afternoon, the Maréchal de Villeroy, accompanied by Monsieur de Fréjus[3] and the entire tutorial staff, went with much pomp, though inwardly raging, to the Hôtel de Condé, where their servile deference and Monsieur le Duc's lying compliments presented a most unedifying spectacle. Next day, the King drove out on Cours-la-Reine with Monsieur le Duc beside him in the place of the Duc du Maine, and thus the change was made public.

It was not long before Mme d'Alègre[4] reappeared. Wrapping up her words in the usual mysterious fashion, with sentences broken, and often unfinished, she finally allowed me to understand that her repeated and sometimes enigmatic utterances had been intended only to warn me, and through me the Regent, of the dangerous conspiracy being prepared against him. It had lately, she said, become far more serious; it was high time that it was crushed. She besought me not to allow the Regent to rest on his victories. She knew his enemies; no matter that they had been stunned by that unexpected blow, it had made them more rabid than before, and united them even more closely.[5] They might well decide to take violent action to gain their ends more quickly, counting on Spain's indignation at our treaty with the Empire and the maritime powers, and on the general discontent in France.

---

[1] See II, p. 73. Saint-Simon must have been nearly dead with exhaustion, after all the excitements of the morning, the great heat, the long drive to Saint-Cloud and back, and now this party.

[2] Marie Charlotte de Raray, Marquise de Laigle (1642–1724). She was lady-in-waiting to the dowager Madame la Duchesse and a great friend of Saint-Simon. She kept him supplied with much fascinating information.   [3] Later Cardinal Fleury.   [4] See p. 138 above.

[5] Saint-Simon says that Mme du Maine 'gave full vent to her passion, sometimes screaming with rage, sometimes stiff with suffering. She was mad enough to say that it was only those vermin the dukes who minded her husband's rank. I kept far away from both of them, leaving her to her folly, and her miserable husband a prey to remorse, weeping like a calf because of the swingeing reproaches and appalling insults that she daily hurled at him in her transports.'

I took care to repeat exactly what she had said to M. le Duc d'Orléans, and added my own conclusions. I found him, however, so thankful for having survived the crisis, so puffed up by a display of authority quite contrary to his nature, that he was completely relaxed, like a man home from hunting who lies stretched out on his bed, and refuses to consider anything but repose. He bade me thank Mme d'Alègre, at the same time declaring that after such a stroke he need fear nothing from anyone. It was in vain that I tried to shake such a dangerous conviction. I showed Mme d'Alègre herself more gratitude than I was empowered to do, and thought it no harm to go beyond my instructions in urging her most strongly, on the Regent's behalf, to keep her eyes open and report anything that she might discover or suspect. I then added the praise and flattery most likely to encourage her, and thus our interviews continued, all of them shrouded in the same deep mystery.

At this time I obtained a favour which I can never forget because it gave me quite extraordinary pleasure. You will recollect from the beginning of these memoirs that the saintly and famous Abbé de La Trappe was the man whom I admired and esteemed more than any other, loving and being loved by him with the deepest and tenderest affection. He had a brother,[1] whom I neither knew nor had ever seen, who lived far away, and was in every respect the most senior of the galley-officers,[2] having won the affection and esteem of the entire corps. He was their commodore, commander of the port of Marseilles for many years past and was, at the age of eighty-four or -five, most perfectly healthy, both in mind and body. The whim seized him to visit Paris, where, to the best of my knowledge, he had never been before, and Monsieur de Troyes,[3] whose father's first cousin he was, informed me of his arrival. I quickly went to call on him, and then invited him to dinner. He so greatly resembled Monsieur de La Trappe that I dare say in all propriety that I fell in love with him, so much so indeed, that they laughed at me for never taking my eyes from his face. The only sign of age in him lay in the wisdom of his thoughts, for he had all the air and gallantry of the world of fashion.

It came to me all of a sudden to do something for him that would give him infinite pleasure and extraordinary distinction. There had never been more than one vice-admiral of the galleys, a purchasable commission, then belonging to the Marquis de Roye;[4] but I there and then resolved to ask the Regent to appoint a second, in the person of the Chevalier de

---

[1] Henri Bouthillier, Chevalier de Rancé, who died, almost a centenarian, in 1726. For the Abbé de La Trappe, see index, I and II, under Rancé.

[2] The galley-service corresponded approximately to a merchant service. The ships were long and low, propelled by sails or oars. Until the end of the seventeenth century, there was always an *Amiral des Galères de France*.

[3] François Bouthillier, Bishop of Troyes, was the son of Léon Bouthillier de Chavigny (1617–1652), whose cousin was Denis de Rancé, father of the Abbé and the Chevalier de Rancé.

[4] Louis de La Rochefoucauld, Marquis de Roye (1671–1751).

Rancé, on condition of the post remaining vacant after his death. I first consulted Monsieur de Troyes; it would have been impolite to do otherwise. He was delighted and promised to support me, but I begged him to let it be kept a secret between us, so as to give rise to no false hopes. Affection when it is very strong lends one eloquence; I described so well the merits, capabilities, and great age of Monsieur de La Trappe's brother, with the rather feeble seconding of Monsieur de Troyes, that M. le Duc d'Orléans at once granted my request, with a salary of ten thousand livres in addition to what he was already receiving. I was really enchanted, and my joy was vastly increased by seeing that of the Chevalier, who was amazed beyond words. You may imagine the trouble I took to see that his promotion was properly registered. He spent two months in Paris, far less than I could have wished, and lived to enjoy his high rank for several years.[1]

Ségur,[2] master of M. le Duc d'Orléans's wardrobe and considerably the richer for that appointment, married the latter's unlegitimized bastard[3] by the actress Desmares. The Regent gave him a sum of money and the reversion of his father's governorship of La Foix.[4] Ségur's father, who had lost a leg in the wars, was good-looking and a fine figure of a man, even at the age of eighty;[5] he was that same musketeer who had played so delightfully upon the lute, and whom you met earlier in these memoirs, at the time of his adventure with the Abbess of La Joye, the Duc de Beauvilliers's sister.[6] But recounting these favours has led me on too far; we must now go back two whole months for more important matters. I must add, however, that Mme la Duchesse d'Orléans, after keeping herself under lock and bolt since the *Lit de Justice*, grew bored at last, re-opened her doors, and set up her card-tables. She also visited M. du Maine, who was living quite deserted at Sceaux, protesting his entire innocence, but declaring that he would see no one. They did everything possible to obtain an audience of M. le Duc d'Orléans so that he might justify himself, but all their efforts were unsuccessful.

Monsieur le Duc, to show his extreme gratification, offered to give a great fête for Mme la Duchesse de Berry, whom he invited to spend a few days at Chantilly. She stayed for ten, and brought her entire court with her, refusing to sacrifice even one vestige of her royal privilege. Yet she had good cause to be satisfied by all the honours and the pleasure she received. The lavishness, gaiety, and magnificence, the fantasies and

---

[1] Saint-Simon has forgotten: the Chevalier held the appointment for only two years, until his retirement in 1720, and not until his death in 1726.

[2] Henri François, Comte de Ségur (1689–1751). See index, I.

[3] She was Philippe Angélique, Mlle de Froissy (1700–1785); her mother was Christine Antoinette Desmares of the Comédie Française, who died in 1753.

[4] The district and town of Foix [Ariège] lie about twenty-five miles north of Andorra.

[5] In fact he was fifty-six, and died in 1737 aged seventy-six.

[6] See I, p. 162.

delightful surprises continued without cessation. Lassay, who for years past had been to the Dowager Madame la Duchesse what Rions was to Mme la Duchesse de Berry, received orders to do the honours of Chantilly for that gentleman with most particular attention. Thus he was given a special table, and there was a carriage for the pair of them, with relays. Such marks of distinction were considered delightfully absurd. The festivities were nearly marred by tragedy. Monsieur le Duc kept a fine menagerie on the farther side of the canal, equipped with a very large number of rare birds and beasts. A beautiful great tiger escaped into the gardens and prowled about among the musicians, actors and actresses. You may picture the terror and confusion; but the tiger's keeper ran forward and most skilfully returned the beast to its cage before it had caused any harm beyond spreading considerable panic.

The Chevalier de Saint-Georges[1] was at last persuaded to marry in order to have issue and thus maintain some remnant of hope for his followers in England. His unhappy state precluded his making the kind of match that was his by right of birth, and a marriage was therefore arranged with the daughter[2] of James Sobieski; her mother was a sister of the Emperor Leopold's wife.[3] This James Sobieski was the eldest son of the famous John Sobieski, King of Poland,[4] and of Marie Casimire de La Grange, Cardinal d'Arquien's daughter. He was a Knight of the Golden Fleece, Governor of Styria, and lived at Ohlau, in Silesia, where he had vast estates. He gave the bride a dowry of six hundred thousand livres, to which the Pope added nine hundred thousand, together with a pension of eighty thousand and some furniture. She was married by proxy, at Ohlau, and left there accompanied by her mother on 12 September, on her way to Rome. At Innsbruck, however, both were arrested by order of the Emperor, who was most basely eager to please King George. At the same time, he stopped Prince James's pension, banished him from his dominions, and forbade the Duke of Modena to give effect to the signed contract of his son's marriage to another of James Sobieski's daughters. This was carrying persecution too far, and in a way which the whole of Europe, including England, thought dishonourable, to say the least. Even the Pope was indignant.

Madame la Duchesse, despite her grief on Mme du Maine's account, continued to attend the Opéra in M. le Duc d'Orléans's small box. She never used the large one unless she accompanied Madame; the reason being that Madame had a carpet, and she none, which proves that until then carpets had been reserved exclusively for the use of Sons of France.

---

[1] The Old Pretender. The saying was that he lived on faith, hope, and charity—faith in his divine right, hope for his return to the throne, and the charity of the French government.

[2] (Maria) Clementina Sobieska (1702–1735).

[3] Hedwig Elisabeth Amelia of Bavaria-Neuburg, Maria Clementina's mother, was a sister of the Empress Eleanor Magdalen Theresa. Their mother was Dorothea Sophia, Duchess of Parma, wife of Charles Philip, Elector Palatine.

[4] He saved Vienna from the Turks in 1683.

Princesses of the blood had surmounted that obstacle in their tribunes at the Paris churches, but had not yet dared to put carpets in their boxes at the play. The difference is not immediately apparent, but may perhaps be that whereas in church they are alone, at the play their ladies accompany them and would sit with them on the carpet unless, of course, the princesses sat in front alone, which even now they dare not attempt. The best expedient seemed never to use their state boxes, but to hire small ones by the year, at the back of the theatre, where they could not be seen. Thus they avoided the issue of carpets or no carpets, and that is why, if you remember, the Dowager Madame la Duchesse forcibly ousted the Maréchale d'Estrées from her little private box, at the Opéra.[1]

The Maréchal d'Harcourt[2] died at last, on 19 October, aged only fifty-nine. Several apoplectic seizures had rendered him so totally incapable of speech that he could not utter a single syllable. He used to point with a stick at a large alphabet, placed before him by a secretary (always in attendance), who wrote the letters down and formed them into words, thus becoming the victim of all the Maréchal's impatience and misery. For a long time past, he had seen only his immediate family and two or three intimate friends. Such was the terrible fate of one who had seemed born for high office because of his brilliant intelligence and ability—not to mention his skill and tact in diplomacy, and the gentle charm that made him such a joy to Society. He has so often been mentioned in these memoirs that I need say no more. He died poor, for he had lived on an income of sixty thousand livres, granted him by the King, none of which passed on to his children. The Abbé de Louvois[3] followed hard upon his heels, dying of a stone. It was the greatest of pities, for he was a man of parts, learned and amiable. The Jesuits obstructed his advancement, although he was fully worthy of a bishopric and would have honoured and adorned the episcopate.

On the pretext of the King's being so extremely young and owning very many large houses, Mme la Duchesse de Berry asked for Meudon[4] and was awarded it by M. le Duc d'Orléans in exchange for Amboise, which had been given her as a country house in her marriage contract. This most extraordinary favour immediately created a scandal. She made Rions the governor; but Du Mont, who had hitherto held that post, continued to receive the same emoluments as before.

It could scarcely be expected that M. du Maine would remain inactive after the humiliations heaped upon him at the *Lit de Justice*. It soon

---

[1] See p. 148 above.

[2] Henri I, Marquis de Beuvron, Duc d'Harcourt (1654–1718): he was in fact sixty-four. See index, I and II.

[3] Camille Le Tellier, Abbé de Louvois (1675–1718), keeper of the King's library and medals, and member of the French Academy.

[4] Meudon had been the country home of Monseigneur le Grand Dauphin, the only legitimate child of Louis XIV to survive beyond the age of five. See index, I and II. It had abominable memories for Saint-Simon as the haunt of the cabal intriguing against his friends, the Ducs de Bourgogne and d'Orléans, and encouraging his enemies the bastards.

transpired that for a long time previous to that ceremony he had been involved in a most treasonable and wicked plot and, since his disgrace, had returned to it with renewed energy. Towards the end of that memorable year, 1718, it was learned that Cardinal Alberoni had been using Cella-mare,[1] the Spanish ambassador, a man of spirit and intelligence, to raise a revolt in France. The design was no less than to set the entire kingdom in revolt against the regency of M. le Duc d'Orléans and, without explaining their intentions towards his person, to put the King of Spain at the head of French affairs, with a council and ministers of his own choice, under one who in all but name would be the new Regent—none other than the Duc du Maine himself. The conspirators looked for support to the parlements of Paris and Brittany, and to the old Court that had for so many years endured the rule of the bastards and Mme de Maintenon. Latterly, they had been trying by hook or by crook to win Frenchmen to the service of Spain, offering promises, hope, and patronage. You shall see that their organization did not equal the magnitude of their plot, which was fortunately discovered before it matured. It is true that they dared not wait for that to happen. A rupture was imminent between France and Spain. The plotters were forced to seize their opportunity, and hasten the revolt by all possible means. They were discovered in the very nick of time; but the Regent and the State were horribly betrayed, and M. le Duc d'Orléans showed himself unbelievably weak.

In the last stages, it became necessary for the conspirators to speak plainly to Madrid of plans and persons. Cellamare was too prudent to entrust letters of such importance to his servants, vastly preferring that Madrid should send him an agent of a kind not likely to be suspected. Thus it came about that a young priest was chosen, who either called himself or was truly named the Abbé Portocarrero;[2] and he was given as a partner a son of Monteleone;[3] since it would appear entirely natural that these two young men, the one returning to Madrid after a short visit to France, the other coming from The Hague, should elect to travel together. Ever since the time of the famous Cardinal Portocarrero,[4] that name had been esteemed and respected in France; the other youth was son of the Spanish ambas-sador to England who had previously been ambassador to France, and possessed many influential friends in our country. Nothing would seem less likely than that an ambassador with couriers at his disposal should entrust secret papers to such persons; and you may well imagine that the

[1] Antonio Joseph del Giudice, Prince of Cellamare (1657–1733), a nephew of Cardinal del Giudice. He was ambassador to France 1715–1719.
[2] The Abbé Vincente Acuña Portocarrero (died 1723). He was the second son of the Count of Montijo, and related only by marriage to the Cardinal del Giudice.
[3] Antonio Cassado di Monteleoni. Because of the Spanish possessions in Italy, very many Spaniards had Italian names.
[4] Cardinal Luis Manuel Fernandez de Portocarrero influenced Charles II of Spain to be-queath his throne to one of Louis XIV's grandsons. See I, p. 123.

youngsters themselves were ignorant of the contents of a packet given them, almost casually, at parting.[1]

They set out early in December, armed with passports from the King, lest relations between France and Spain should deteriorate, and in company with a Spanish banker,[2] who had long lived in England, and been made bankrupt there for so large a sum that the Regent had given leave to arrest him should he be discovered in France. You will think me badly briefed in this affair; but I neither can nor will say more than I know; the rest would be pure conjecture. The Abbé Dubois was becoming more and more the master of M. le Duc d'Orléans. He had insisted on absolute secrecy, and M. le Duc d'Orléans had faithfully obeyed him. As you shall learn, even he knew only what Dubois chose to tell him.

Now whether Portocarrero's surprisingly short stay in Paris had aroused the suspicions of Dubois and his spies; whether some great man at the Spanish embassy was in Dubois's pay and sounded the alarm, or whether the action was due simply to the presence of that banker, and Dubois's wish to please the English, I cannot tell. Be that as it may, the young men and the banker were certainly arrested at Poitiers; their papers were seized and brought immediately to the Abbé Dubois by the same courier as made the arrests.

Grave issues are often decided by chance. The courier from Poitiers happened to arrive at a moment when M. le Duc d'Orléans was ready to go to the Opéra. Dubois glanced through the papers and told him the news after the performance was over. It was, however, the Regent's invariable practice to lock himself in with his *roués* at that time, and he did so then, on the pretext that Dubois had not had sufficient time to study them—thus clearly displaying his total want of interest. It was always hard to gain his attention early in the morning. When his wits were still fuddled by the fumes of the wine and his supper still not digested, he was never in any state to comprehend; and secretaries of State have told me that at such times he could be made to sign anything. Dubois chose that precise moment to report on the papers seized at Poitiers; but he was careful to allow none of them to remain in the Regent's keeping; and still more so to prevent others from handling them. M. le Duc d'Orléans's blind trust and fearful negligence on this occasion seem incomprehensible; but it is even harder to credit that he remained passive throughout the entire course of this affair, allowing Dubois to be the sole judge of all the evidence, with power to convict, absolve, or punish.

The only persons admitted to Dubois's confidence were the keeper of the seals and Le Blanc[3] because he could not do without them; but he

---

[1] Their carriage had a false bottom which is said to have been packed with papers.
[2] Joseph Hodges, Chevalier de Mira.
[3] Louis Claude Le Blanc (1669–1728). He was a counsellor of State, and minister for war 1719–1723 and 1726–1728.

told them no more than what suited his personal interests. D'Argenson was his friend and completely under his influence; Le Blanc was his slave and only boasted of friendship. Both were stunned by Dubois's conduct; but neither dared to question him, or go against his orders in the smallest particular. Their offices depended on his favour; he never let a day pass without reminding them of that. All their proceedings, interrogations, and personal reports to the Regent, everything they recommended, allowed, or condemned; all that they said or left unsaid—in brief, all their conduct, actions and words were in every detail governed by Dubois, who was their absolute master and demanded slavish obedience. People were arrested or freed by the King's orders, issued by the Regent at Dubois's sole behest. There were neither trials nor other legal proceedings, since that would have entailed others' knowing. The keeper of the seals, who had enjoyed Dubois's confidence to a greater extent, died before him, taking his secrets to the grave. Le Blanc, whom Dubois later persecuted to the brink of ruin, had known very little, infinitely less than d'Argenson. When under new skies[1] he returned to favour and office, he took care to reveal nothing of an affair in which the guilty parties had not only been released from prison, but restored to their former rank and dignities.[2]

Perhaps the Regent knew more than he let it appear; perhaps he acted as he did fearing the numbers, names, and importance of the persons involved; perhaps his natural indolence and extraordinary subservience to the Abbé Dubois kept him really in ignorance of the danger and size of the plot. However that may be, neither I nor anyone else ever extracted a word from him regarding that monstrous conspiracy which I now describe. Yet out of the prevailing darkness one fact emerges, namely that M. and Mme du Maine were at their treacherous work long before the recent *Lit de Justice*, and even before the beginning of the Regency.

On the day after the courier's return from Poitiers, the Prince of Cellamare, knowing of the arrests, but still believing that they were due to the presence of the absconding banker, called on M. Le Blanc and with a great appearance of calm asked for the return of a packet of letters which he had entrusted to the young men travelling to Spain under the protection of the King's passports. Le Blanc, well instructed by Dubois, replied that the packet had certainly been found, but would not be returned since it contained secret papers. Moreover, the ambassador must now be asked to go immediately to his residence[3] in the company of the Abbé Dubois, who that instant entered Le Blanc's office. Cellamare was then put into Le

---

[1] Saint-Simon was thinking of the time in June 1720 when Fleury gave Le Blanc back his post as minister for war, after Monsieur le Duc's resignation.

[2] On 22 February 1723 there was yet another *Lit de Justice*, to register the King's majority. Dubois, who was still in office, took an action two months later which, by restoring the Duc du Maine to his former rank, wiped out Saint-Simon's greatest victory. No wonder Dubois was anathema to him, no wonder Saint-Simon hung his portrait in the privy, facing his *chaise-percée*!

[3] The Hôtel Colbert, in the Rue Neuve-des-Petits-Champs.

Blanc's coach, and all three drove there together. Although he well knew that such language was the prelude to a search, Cellamare remained calm during the three hours of rummaging among his chests, and writing-desks, from which some papers were removed and others listed. During the whole of that time, he treated Le Blanc with the utmost civility. As for the Abbé Dubois, it was useless to flatter him since he plainly knew all, and he therefore pretended to view him with supreme contempt. When M. Le Blanc was preparing to open a small letter-case, Cellamare actually exclaimed, 'Monsieur Le Blanc! Monsieur Le Blanc! Let that alone, it is not fit for a gentleman like you! Better leave it for the Abbé Dubois' (who was there present). Then looking Dubois full in the eye, 'He's been a womanizer all his life; and there is nothing in that box but women's letters.' The Abbé Dubois had to laugh, for it was a joke which the ambassador had been storing up against him. Cellamare was already an old man,[1] and looked even older than his age. He was one who had turned his considerable wit, learning, and ability to excellent account, never yielding to debauchery, but using his great charm in Society to extract secrets, make and protect supporters of the King of Spain, and sow distrust of the Regent in France. Most of his time was spent at home, either working or reading. When everything had been sufficiently examined, the seals of the King and the ambassador were affixed to all the desks and boxes that contained documents; the Abbé Dubois and Le Blanc went to report to the Regent, and a detachment of musketeers was left on guard in the house. One of the King's gentlemen arrived with them, as is customary when ambassadors are in painful circumstances. This individual, Liboy[2] by name, had wit and sympathy, and was often chosen for such distressing tasks.

I learned of the arrests that same morning, at my home, but not of the names. One of M. le Duc d'Orléans's red footmen had come with a message while I was at table, summoning me to a meeting of the Regency Council at four o'clock. It was not the usual day, and I asked for details, at which the man had appeared surprised, saying only that the Spanish ambassador had been arrested. As soon as I had finished I left my guests and went to the Palais Royal, where M. le Duc d'Orléans explained everything, as I recount it here. I inquired about the documents. He replied that the Abbé Dubois still had them, but had had no time as yet to study them or report. He added that there was something he wished to reveal personally to the Regency Council. These and other vague statements took some time, and I immediately afterwards went to the Tuileries, for the meeting.

M. le Duc d'Orléans arrived soon after. More than any man I ever knew, he had the gift of oratory, needing no preparation, but able to say immediately exactly what he wished, neither more nor less, in clear and suitable terms, with unaffected grace, and always the greatest courtesy.

---

[1] Cellamare was sixty-one.   [1] See note 2, p. 121 above.

He now opened the meeting by describing the persons and documents seized at Poitiers, the treacherous plot discovered on the eve of being put into execution, and the fact that the Spanish ambassador was the prime mover in it. He explained what orders had been issued to inform the foreign ministers at Paris, and bade Dubois tell of all that had been done at the ambassador's house, offering to read aloud letters from Cellamare to Alberoni which had been found among other papers at Poitiers.

Dubois stammered out a short, ill-expressed account, stressing the dangerous nature of the conspiracy, so far as that was known, and reading out two letters, that showed beyond all doubt the leading part played by Cellamare, with Alberoni in every way assisting him. The Council was deeply shocked by allusions to M. le Duc d'Orléans, who was not spared either in words or accusations. The Regent then declared in most moderate language that he did not suspect either the King or the Queen of Spain of being concerned in the plot, but attributed it all to Alberoni's mad ambition, and Cellamare's desire to gratify him. He should, he said, ask Their Catholic Majesties for justice, and ended by urging the members to help in uncovering every detail of a dangerous conspiracy aimed at destroying the peace of the realm. When he had finished there was prolonged applause; but I am sure that some people felt relieved to know that he did not intend to give names, or voice suspicions until all the facts were known.

None the less, on Saturday morning, 10 December, Pompadour[1] was arrested on waking and taken to the Bastille, and so also, later in the day, was Saint-Geniès.[2] D'Aydie,[3] the widower of Rions's sister, and lodging at the Luxembourg, disappeared. A certain Abbé Brigault, a man of no importance, escaped, but was captured at Nemours and sent to the Bastille. Magny,[4] a head of protocol, also fled, and was dismissed, but he was merely a fool. Men such as these last three were unlikely to strengthen any plot. Apart from d'Aydie's rank, no one could imagine what use the plotters hoped to make of them.

On the afternoon of Tuesday, 13 December, Cellamare was put into a coach with Liboy and two officers, chosen to escort him to Blois and to remain with him there until news came of Saint-Aignan's[5] safe arrival in France. A few days later several other officers were sent to the Bastille.

---

[1] Léonard Héile, Marquis de Pompadour (1654–1732). He had been Monseigneur's friend and companion, and would therefore have hated the Duc d'Orléans. His wife had been governess to the Duchesse de Berry's children, all of whom died in infancy. See index, II.

[2] Louis César de Montault, Marquis de Saint-Geniès (b. 1664), had been Villeroy's aide-de-camp. He was born illegitimate, and had made a great to-do in trying to be legitimated. Saint-Simon says he was 'not a bad fellow, but with no head, just the sort to take part in an adventure'.

[3] Antoine, Comte d'Aydie (1686–1764). He had been a lieutenant-general in the French contingent of the Spanish army, and in 1741 became Captain-general of Old Castile.

[4] Nicolas Joseph II Foucault de Magny (1677–1772), fled to Spain and became a lieutenant-general in the Spanish army. Later, he was a gentleman-in-waiting to King Philip.

[5] Paul Hippolyte de Beauvilliers, Duc de Saint-Aignan (1684–1776), the French ambassador to Spain. News had reached Paris that the Spaniards had arrested him.

On Christmas Day, which was a Sunday, M. le Duc d'Orléans sent asking me to go to him at the Palais Royal, at four o'clock. Monsieur le Duc was there, also the Duc d'Antin, the keeper of the seals, Torcy, and the Abbé Dubois. We discussed several points regarding Cellamare and his return to Spain; the measures to be taken so as to disarm complaints from the foreign ministers (none of whom had shown the least disposition to complain); the best way to demand justice from the King of Spain who, we perfectly well knew, would never grant it. All this business was dispatched with so much calm and cheeriness by the Regent that I did not suspect there was more to follow. Our little meeting lasted quite a long time. When it was over, everyone left; but as I rose to go, M. le Duc d'Orléans called me to him. The others departed; I remained behind with M. le Duc d'Orléans and Monsieur le Duc. We sat. We were in the small study he used in wintertime, at the end of the little gallery. After a pause, he told me to look and see if everyone had gone, and whether the door at the end (the one leading to his private rooms) was shut. I went to see, and it was shut, and there was no one in the gallery. That being established, M. le Duc d'Orléans informed us that we should not be surprised to learn that M. and Mme du Maine were at the bottom of the affair of the Spanish ambassador; that he had written proof to that effect, and that their aim was exactly as I have described it. He said that the Abbé Dubois, the keeper of the seals, and Le Blanc were sworn to secrecy, and that before taking action he wished to confer privately with Monsieur le Duc and me.

I said to myself that since the other three already knew of the plot he might well have discussed it first with them, and had probably made a plan with the Abbé Dubois. I thought he wished to flatter Monsieur le Duc by appearing to seek his advice, and would tell him some small part of his intentions. As for myself, I thought he wished to argue with me in earnest, for the sake of hearing a different opinion. You will remember how accustomed he was to sharing state secrets with me, especially when he was troubled by having to make quick decisions. Monsieur le Duc went straight to the point, saying that both must immediately be arrested and sent to secure prisons, where they could cause no further alarms. I supported him, stressing the danger of not acting at once. M. le Duc d'Orléans assented, but spoke of Mme du Maine's birth and sex,[1] mainly, or so I supposed, to hear the views of her brother's son. His hesitation was, however, soon dispelled by Monsieur le Duc's expressing loathing for his aunt (which admittedly was well deserved) and her husband, and by his horror of their plot, aimed, as it was, at the overthrow of the government and the revoking of those Renunciations[2] that had saved his line from

---

[1] (Anne) Louise Bénédicte de Bourbon-Condé, Duchesse du Maine (1676–1753) was terrifying in her passions. She was the daughter of Monsieur le Prince who had a horrible temper. Louis III de Bourbon-Condé (1668–1710), known as Monsieur le Duc, was his son, and father of the Monsieur le Duc mentioned here.

[2] See note 2, p. 38 above.

subjection to that of Spain. The Regent, after that, accepted our advice without further argument.

The question of the prisons then arose. The Bastille and Vincennes were unsuitable because of their nearness to Paris; these prisoners needed to be beyond the reach of their supporters, the sympathy of the Parlement, and the manœuvres of the premier président. Several other fortresses were mentioned, for the need to have them arrested and imprisoned separately had been accepted from the beginning. When M. le Duc d'Orléans suggested Doullens[1] for the Duc du Maine I welcomed the idea, more especially because Charost[2] and his son were the governors. No gentlemen more loyal and honourable could anywhere be found, and Charost had long been my close friend. That being settled, we turned our minds to find a prison for the wife.

I maintained that this presented far greater difficulties on account of her breeding and sex, her courage and furious temper. She would do every-thing to escape, moving heaven and earth, relying on her birth and womanhood to protect her. M. du Maine, on the other hand, so dangerous in plotting, so cowardly in action, would be overcome by terror and remain quietly incarcerated, in perpetual fear of the scaffold.

After considering and rejecting a number of fortresses, M. le Duc d'Orléans turned to Monsieur le Duc with a smile, saying that he must try to accommodate him in an affair of State, which concerned him personally, as much as it did the Regent, and he then proposed the Château de Dijon. Monsieur le Duc was aghast, for although the security of Mme du Maine's prison was vital, the thought of becoming his aunt's gaoler was altogether repugnant. He none the less managed to smile, which gave M. le Duc d'Orléans an excuse to press him further. I remained silent, watching them both with close attention. Eventually Monsieur le Duc asked if I did not agree with him; whereat I smiled, too, saying that I did most heartily agree, but that M. le Duc d'Orléans's reasoning was better. All this time I had been thinking hard, and had decided that M. le Duc d'Orléans would greatly benefit by having Monsieur le Duc as a partner in this particular matter, and by sending Mme du Maine to the very centre of her nephew's governorship, where she would be his sole responsibility and far beyond the reach of outside help. I must confess to enjoying the situation, as I remembered the successive stages of the bastards' rise, from their obtain-ing rank equal to that of the princes of the blood, to their being made capable of the succession; and now to see Mme du Maine herself, who had threatened to set the kingdom aflame rather than lose those ill-gotten rights,[3] raging in prison under the governance of Monsieur le Duc, her own nephew. After some further discussion, that prince unwillingly

[1] Not far from Amiens. It was a particularly strong fortress.
[2] Armand II, Duc de Béthune-Charost (1663–1747). See index, I and II.
[3] See II, p. 383.

consented to keep his dear aunt in strict confinement at his country house; and these vital issues having been settled, we departed.

On Wednesday, 28 December, we had another long session, at which the arrest of M. and Mme du Maine was fixed for the following day. Accordingly, at about ten o'clock on the Thursday morning, guards were secretly and quietly posted all along the walls of Sceaux. La Billarderie,[1] a lieutenant of the bodyguard, then entered the house and arrested M. du Maine as he was leaving the chapel after mass, asking him most respectfully not to return to his room, but to step immediately into a stage-coach provided for that purpose. M. du Maine, having expected this event, had made sure that nothing incriminating would be found either at his house or in the houses of his people, and offered no resistance. He was alone at Sceaux. He said he had been awaiting them for some days past, and at once entered the coach. La Billarderie got in next, with a warrant-officer on the front seat, followed by Favancourt,[2] a sergeant of the first company of musketeers. M. du Maine, who did not at first perceive that individual, showed surprise and extreme alarm. He would not have minded the warrant-officer alone, but Favancourt unmanned him completely.[3] He began to question La Billarderie who was obliged to tell him that Favancourt had been appointed to escort him, and to remain with him after arrival. Favancourt chose that moment to pay his respects—to the best of his ability in those circumstances—and the Duc du Maine mumbled something polite, looking very nervous. This exchange took them to the end of the Sceaux avenue, where the detachment of the bodyguard was drawn up. M. du Maine grew visibly paler when he saw them.

There ensued, in the coach, periods of absolute silence, broken every now and then by M. du Maine assuring them that he was perfectly innocent, deeply attached to the King, and no less so to M. le Duc d'Orléans. It was, he said, tragic that His Royal Highness should give credence to his enemies—but he named no one. All this emerged amid gasps and sighs, signs of the Cross, low murmurs as of prayers, and duckings of the head whenever they passed a church or wayside shrine. He never so much as mentioned Mme du Maine, his children, or any members of his household. They ate all together in the coach (he very little); but they left him alone at his supper, taking many precautions at his *coucher*. He did not learn of his destination until next day, and then made no comment. All this, and of his conduct in prison, I learned after his

[1] Charles César Flahault, Marquis de La Billarderie (1670–1743), who was made lieutenant-general in 1734, arrested the Duc du Maine. It was his younger brother, an aide-major (assistant medical officer), who was sent to escort Mme du Maine on her road to prison.

[2] Claude Bernay, Le Sieur de Favancourt. The musketeer regiments were compose of gentlemen-troopers. Noblemen when they joined the army were expected to spend their first years in the ranks before becoming officers.

[3] The Duc du Maine realized for the first time that he was being sent to a State prison. Prisoners were always taken there by officers of the musketeers. It had so happened with Fouquet and Lauzun.

release, from Favancourt. I knew that officer well, for he had been a corporal in Cresnay's[1] platoon, in the first company of musketeers, and had taught me my drill when I served in the regiment. He had courted me ever afterwards. M. du Maine was given two valets to wait on him, and nearly always they kept him within sight.

At the precise moment of his arrest, Ancenis,[2] who had just inherited his father's post of captain of the bodyguard, went to Mme du Maine's house, in the Rue Saint-Honoré, to arrest her. A lieutenant[3] and an ensign of the footguards, and a squadron of the bodyguard arrived at the same moment to take possession of the house and guard the entrances. The Duc d'Ancenis's compliments were not well received. Mme du Maine desired to take with her some cash-boxes; Ancenis was obliged to refuse her. She demanded at least her jewels; there was an argument, very noisy on her side, very calm on his; in the end she had to give way.[4] She then flew into a passion at the insult to a person of her rank, but was careful to say nothing offensive to M. d'Ancenis, and mentioned no names. She delayed as long as possible, despite d'Ancenis's urgings, and at last he was obliged to give her his arm, declaring politely but very firmly that they must go at once. Two stage-coaches were drawn up before the entrance, each with six horses, at the very sight of which she was disgusted; but she was none the less obliged to enter. Ancenis sat beside her, and the lieutenant and the ensign in front. Two of her maids, chosen by her, and her clothes, after they had been searched, went in the second coach. They took the road by the walls so as to avoid the main streets, but none of the passers-by showed the slightest interest, greatly to her surprise and annoyance, though it drew no tears from her, only exclamations, between gasps and sighs, at the violence done to her feelings. On the road, she complained continually of the discomfort and indignity of the coach, asking time after time where they were taking her, to which they replied that she would sleep at Essonnes—no more. At her *coucher* all the necessary precautions were taken. On the following morning the Duc d'Ancenis bade her farewell, leaving the lieutenant and ensign to escort her thereafter. When she asked d'Ancenis where they were going, he merely said 'to Fontainebleau', and returned to report to the Regent.

The farther they went from Paris, the greater became Mme du Maine's

---

[1] Armand Jean Fortin de Cresnay (died 1714). See I, p. 7.

[2] Paul François de Béthune, Marquis d'Ancenis (1682-1759). He was the son of Armand II, Duc de Béthune-Charost, and became Duc de Béthune in 1724, which is probably why Saint-Simon, a few lines later on, makes the mistake of calling him a duke.

[3] Jérôme François Flahaut, Chevalier, later Comte de La Billarderie (1672-1761), the younger brother of the officer who arrested the Duc du Maine. He was not a lieutenant but an assistant medical officer. This seems to show kindness and humanity on the part of the authorities who arranged the arrest, very different from the Spaniards' treatment of poor Mme des Ursins (see II, pp. 397-400).

[4] In fact, she did manage to take some of her jewels with her, but they were confiscated at Dijon.

anxiety, and when she discovered that they were in Burgundy, and learned that their destination was Dijon, she burst into a torrent of complaints. It was far worse when she entered the château and realized that she was Monsieur le Duc's prisoner. She nearly choked with rage, inveighing furiously against her nephew and the place chosen for her detention. After these first transports, however, she controlled herself remembering that she was in no place or condition to derive benefit from such tantrums. Having managed to restrain her violent temper, she displayed supreme indifference to everything, and said nothing at all. The King's lieutenant at the château was wholly devoted to Monsieur le Duc. He kept her well guarded, and set a close watch on her and her two attendants.

Her good friend Cardinal de Polignac, who was more than that to her, or so it was always supposed, received orders that same morning to betake himself to the abbey of Anchin, accompanied by one of the King's gentlemen, who remained beside him throughout his exile in Flanders. At the same moment, Mlle de Montauban[1] who had been attached to Mme du Maine as a kind of unofficial woman of the bedchamber, and one of the head-maids,[2] a great favourite (almost on the footing of a gossip, for she passed for being something of a wit), were taken to the Bastille with one or two more of M. and Mme du Maine's servants. It had been decided to send Mlle du Maine[3] to Maubuisson Abbey, and her two brothers to Eu, with a King's gentleman in charge of them.

Le Blanc kept his promise to tell me of his return. I was waiting at home with the doors locked, not daring to see anyone, walking up and down in my study, and consulting my watch every five minutes, when they announced one of his footmen, come merely to inquire concerning my health. That enormously relieved me, though I was still ignorant of what had happened. My coach was harnessed and ready. I stepped in, and drove at once to M. le Duc d'Orléans, who also was alone, and striding up and down his gallery. It was nearly eleven o'clock. Le Blanc and Dubois had just left him. He seemed much upset by an interview he had had with Mme la Duchesse d'Orléans, and I was very thankful to be no longer in communication with her, since he might otherwise have laid the blame on me. I heartened him as best I might, and half an hour later, when M. le Comte de Toulouse was announced, I left him.

I afterwards learned that that gentleman had behaved most admirably, stating only that he regarded the King, the Regent, and France as one and

---

[1] Mlle de La Tour du Pin, Demoiselle de Montauban (1690–1750). She was the daughter of a lieutenant-colonel in the Duc du Maine's regiment.

[2] Marguerite Jeanne Cordier, called Mlle de Launay (1684–1750), who married the Baron de Staal. She was in the Bastille until 1720, and said she had never been so happy or so comfortable in all her life. Service with the Duchesse du Maine had been a dog's life.

[3] Louise Françoise de Bourbon (1707–1743); for her brothers, see index under Dombes, Prince de, and Eu, Prince d'.

the same, and vowing that he would never be found doing anything detrimental to their service either by intrigue or conspiracy, or against the peace of the realm. He said he could not help grieving at the unhappy state of M. and Mme du Maine; but must believe that His Royal Highness had strong proof of their guilt, since otherwise he would not have used extreme measures. In his opinion, Mme du Maine might, alas!, have been imprudent; but without seeing the evidence, he could not believe his brother a traitor. In the meantime, he would preserve the strictest silence, and do nothing without His Royal Highness's permission. The Regent was much gratified by such words from a man whose honesty he had never doubted. He spoke to him with great kindness and consideration, never mentioning the scandal, and they parted on excellent terms. Madame happened to be in Paris, and M. le Duc d'Orléans was thus able to break the news to her himself. As for Mme la Duchesse d'Orléans, remembering her state of mind after the *Lit de Justice*, you may easily picture how she bore this latest blow.

CHAPTER V

1719

Behaviour of the Duc and Duchesse du Maine – Conduct of the Duc de Noailles – Death of the Marquise de Charlus – Bogus manifesto of the King of Spain – The Philippiques *– Stair's audacity snubbed – Death of Puysieux – Illness of Mme la Duchesse de Berry – Her secret marriage to Rions – Death of Mme de Maintenon – Prodigies of the Mississippi Scheme – Pécoil dies the right death for a miser – Death of Mme la Duchesse de Berry – Mme de Saint-Simon's illness – We are lent Meudon – Confessions of the Duchesse du Maine – I propose a smaller Council of Regency – Conversion of Law – The Abbé Tencin and his sister – I talk with Fleury, Bishop of Fréjus – I make a suggestion for the King's education – M. le Duc d'Orléans wishes to dismiss the Maréchal de Villeroy and to give me charge of the King's education – I refuse*

THE DUC DU MAINE, as I have already mentioned, escorted by the elder La Billarderie, lieutenant of the bodyguard who had arrested him, was taken to Doullens and imprisoned there in the charge of Favancourt, my old comrade-in-arms. Once arrived, he spent his time praying, or pretending to utter long prayers, frequently prostrating himself, treating Favancourt as a little schoolboy does his master. He had with him three valets to divert him, a few books, but no writing-paper. He seldom asked for any, and always gave his letters to Favancourt to read and seal. At the least noise, the slightest unexpected movement, he grew pale and prepared for death.[1] He well knew that he merited execution and judged the prince he had such good cause to fear by his own nature, forgetting how often M. le Duc d'Orléans had proved vastly different from himself.

Mme la Duchesse du Maine, travelling in the charge of the younger La Billarderie, found him very willing to be kind. She made ill use of his gentleness; but M. le Duc d'Orléans bore that too from her with his accustomed meekness. From her airs, one might have imagined her a Daughter of France, hated without cause, and subjected to every kind of indignity. On the road, she played the lady in distress, being well practised in that rôle from having acted it for the past twenty years in theatricals at Sceaux. She used the language of melodrama, for the strongest adjectives in current speech seemed to her too mild to express her indignation. On the third day, when she learned that Dijon was her destination, there was

---

[1] For the Duc du Maine's cowardice, see I, p. 69.

an eruption. The discovery and failure of her conspiracy, the rudeness she claimed to have endured since her arrest, all the intolerable accompaniments of captivity, of which she unceasingly complained, were as nothing to her compared with imprisonment in a fortress ruled over by her nephew. She spat forth all the venom that her fury could devise; forgot she was his father's sister; damned their common ancestry, and appeared enchanted at the idea of disinterring the thirteen months' baby.[1] She feigned illness, perpetually changed coaches, insisted on stopping at Auxerre and everywhere else that they allowed her, hoping, perhaps, that Madame la Princesse[2] might still procure her a change of prison, lest she do herself an injury. That lady, meanwhile, was plaguing M. le Duc d'Orléans to such effect that three more maids were sent, and her lady, Mme de Chambonas,[3] was permitted to share her imprisonment. Later, her personal physician and three more maids were dispatched; but they all went to Dijon, any change of prison being flatly refused. Kindness was wasted on her, as M. le Duc d'Orléans must have known it would be. Yet his nature was so deplorably weak that he could not stand firm for long. Very soon, that is to say at the beginning of April, Madame la Princesse wrung from him permission to remove her, on the plea of ill health, to Chalon-sur-Saône, and shortly after that she was allowed visits.

The arrests continued and many people were sent to the Bastille or Vincennes. Dismay at the fate of M. and Mme du Maine was widespread, and faces were even longer than they had been after the *Lit de Justice*. The most visibly afflicted were the premier président and d'Effiat (who for so long had duped the Regent), the Maréchaux de Villeroy and de Villars, and Mme de Ventadour, grieving for her one-time lover;[4] but many others of lesser importance showed their discomfiture. No one, however, dared to protest. They avoided public places, but their fearful countenances betrayed them. Casting off their pride, they became polite, almost affable, eating out of our hands; and by that sudden change and their manifest uneasiness, amply revealed themselves for what they were.

I do not know where the Duc de Noailles had stood, but he presented a better front than the rest. Although plainly anxious, he was greatly assisted by his voluntary retirement, to which everyone was by then accustomed. Whether or not he had known of the conspiracy, he was certainly much put out by its detection. The loss of the finances and Law's triumph had not been redeemed in his view by all the favours showered on him by the Regent; moreover, he bitterly resented not having been

---

[1] Saint-Simon is here referring to a long-past quarrel, when Charles de Bourbon, Comte de Soissons (1566–1612), contested the legitimization of Charlotte de La Trémoïlle's son Henri II de Condé (1588–1646), on the grounds that when he was born she had been separated from her husband for thirteen months.
[2] Her mother.
[3] Marie Charlotte de Fontanges d'Auberoque, Comtesse de Chambonas (1670–1738).
[4] Meaning the Maréchal de Villeroy.

informed in advance of the *Lit de Justice* or of the arrest of M. and Mme du Maine, and I believe he would not have been displeased to see the Regent in trouble had part of the plot succeeded. On the other hand, he was, I think, too prominent, and too much despised by the parties concerned, to have been invited to share their secrets.

The fate of M. and Mme du Maine caused the dispersal of those so-called nobles whom they had so skilfully used and patronized.[1] The majority saw the light without assistance from outside, and the small band of conspirators who had acted as their leaders were terrified into quiescence. From that moment, the salt-smugglers, who had formed themselves into armed bands and often beaten the troops sent against them, gave up their arms, begging for and receiving pardons. Such promptness showed clearly enough who their employers had been, and for what purpose. I had often warned M. le Duc d'Orléans of the truth regarding them, and he now confessed that I had been right. Unfortunately I was so all too often where he was concerned.

The Marquise de Charlus, Mézières's sister, and mother of the Marquis de Levis,[2] now a duke and peer, died rich and old. She was always dressed like an old-clothes woman, and endured many snubs because people failed to recognize her, which she thought vastly ill-bred of them. By way of relief from more serious matters, I shall tell a story about her of a very different kind. She was abominably greedy and adored gambling. She would gladly sit up to all hours, madly doubling against mounting odds. They used to play *lansquenet* for extremely high stakes in the drawing-room of Mme la Princesse de Conti, Monsieur le Prince's daughter.[3] Mme de Charlus was supping there one Friday night, between two sessions, in a large company of guests. She was ill-dressed as usual, and at that time they wore head-dresses called *commodes*, which were unattached, capable of being put on and taken off as men put on and take off their wigs and nightcaps, and it was the fashion to wear them immensely high.

Mme de Charlus was sitting next Le Tellier, Archbishop of Rheims. She helped herself to a boiled egg and cracked it open; but as she leaned forward for the salt, she stuck her head all unawares into the flame of a nearby candle. The Archbishop, seeing her alight, hurled himself at her head-dress and knocked it to the ground. Mme de Charlus, furious and astounded at finding herself thus dis-wigged for no apparent reason, flung her egg into Le Tellier's face, so that it ran down all over him. He, however, did nothing but laugh, and the company was in fits over the dirty,

---

[1] The gentlemen of Brittany.

[2] Charles Eugène, Marquis de Levis (1669–1734), who became a duke and peer in 1723. He was the nobleman who had the disconcerting experience of undergoing the ceremonies of christening, first confession, and first communion, with marriage following at midnight, all in the same twenty-four hours. See I, pp. 100–101.

[3] There were two Princesses de Conti: see II, Index and p. 405, note 3.

grey old head of Mme de Charlus and the omelet she had made on the archbishop. Especially funny was her fury and abuse of him, for she imagined that he had insulted her without cause, and would not listen to explanations, and then all at once perceived that she had been peeled of hair before the whole world. The head-dress was quite burned up; Mme la Princesse de Conti sent for another; but before it was in place, everyone had time to contemplate her charms, and she to continue her angry mutterings.

Games of chance were once more forbidden, on pain of most severe punishment.

On 4 February the Parlement registered a decree suppressing four most atrocious documents, forbidding their publication, sale, or being read aloud, under threat of arrest for disturbing the peace of the realm, and for *lèse-majesté*. The first was entitled *Copy of a letter from His Most Catholic Majesty written in his own hand, which Prince Cellamare, his ambassador, has orders to present to His Most Christian Majesty*, dated 3 September 1718. The second was headed, *Copy of a circular letter from the King of Spain to all the Parlements of France*, dated 4 September 1718; the third, *Manifesto from his Most Catholic Majesty, addressed to the three Estates of France*, 6 September 1718. The fourth was entitled, *Petition presented to His Most Catholic Majesty in the name of the three Estates of France*. You did not have to be an expert to perceive that none of these documents emanated from Spain. They were not found at Poitiers in the baggage of the Abbé Portocarrero or in that of his companions, nor were they among Cellamare's papers when his house was searched. Spain, indeed, disclaimed all knowledge of them, and apart from the style, so unlike that of a great king, too much was known there of our government to allow such a misconception as that the French parlements were in the nature of legislative bodies. The papers clearly were not of the kind to have come from the King of Spain; but were very probably composed at Sceaux, judging by the spirit of them and the style employed. They caused a certain amount of disquiet, but were quickly forgotten. M. le Duc d'Orléans regarded them with contempt and was not perturbed.

This could not be said of some verses that appeared about that same time, entitled *Philippiques*, which were distributed with great speed and in enormous quantities. La Grange,[1] once a page of Mme la Princesse de Conti, the King's daughter, was the author and did not attempt to deny it. Everything true or false that Hell could spew forth was there expressed in exquisite verse, in the style of great poetry, and with all imaginable elegance. M. le Duc d'Orléans heard of them and desired to see the whole poem, which was very long, but no one would show it him. He several times mentioned it to me, and finally ordered me so peremptorily to bring

---

[1] La Grange-Chancel (1677-1758). He was indeed imprisoned, but managed to escape in 1721, and did not return from exile until 1729.

it that I had no choice but to obey. I brought it, but utterly refused to read it aloud. He therefore took it, and read it standing by the window of his little winter study, where we happened to be at that moment. As he read, he saw it for what it was, and from time to time paused to make some remark without seeming unduly distressed. Suddenly, I saw him change colour, and he turned to me with tears in his eyes, very nearly overcome.

'Oh!' he exclaimed, 'this is too much; I cannot endure this horror!' He had come to the place where the scoundrel describes M. le Duc d'Orléans as plotting to murder the King and about to put his vile plan into action. It is a passage in which the writer lets himself go in poetic fervour, with curses and invocations terrifyingly but most beautifully expressed, with horrible descriptions and touching images of the youthful innocence of the King, and the hopes that he inspired, all coupled with solemn appeals to the nation to save the dear victim from the bloody hands of his murderer.[1] At that point, when M. le Duc d'Orléans had relapsed into a most dismal silence, I tried to take the paper from him, but without success. He burst into justifiable complaints about this most vile slander, at the same time protesting his deep affection for the King. He then returned to his reading, but very soon appealed to me again. I have never seen a man more outraged, more deeply hurt, more overwhelmed by a sense of injustice; indeed I could scarcely contain my own feelings. Seeing him so, even his worst enemies, provided they were honest, could never have believed him guilty of the intended crime imputed to him. When I say that I found it extremely difficult to compose myself, and still harder to bring him to some degree of equanimity, I am saying only the truth.[2]

The scoundrel La Grange was soon afterwards arrested and sent to the Île Sainte-Marguerite; but towards the end of the Regency he was released,[3] and had the audacity to show himself publicly in Paris. Yet even while he appeared at the play and in the streets for all to see, most insolent rumours were spread that M. le Duc d'Orléans had had him killed. Indeed, the Regent and his enemies were equally active in his disservice, they in concocting lying reports of unbelievable villainy; he in displaying profitless leniency, to use no plainer word.

At about this time, Stair tried to make a State entry into the courtyard of the Tuileries. Either through ignorance that ambassadors are allowed only two horses when they enter the King's palace in Paris, or else attempting an encroachment, his coaches, each pulled by eight horses, made a bid to drive inside. There was a lively struggle, but in the end he was obliged to

---

[1] In this passage Saint-Simon's style turns dark purple with indignation. He of course exaggerates.

[2] It does seem strange that Saint-Simon should not mention the two verses in which he himself was personally accused, and which occur in the second of the two *Philippiques*. One wonders whether he knew of its existence, or whether he deliberately concealed it from the Regent.

[3] He was not released, but escaped: see note, p. 231 above.

unharness six of them and proceed with two only, according to protocol. On the following days he drove in the manner prescribed to visit the princes of the blood. M. le Prince de Conti returned the call, but not seeing Lord Stair waiting to receive him at the foot of the steps, as is the rule, he remained a few moments in his coach, and then drove straight to the Palais Royal to lodge a complaint. Stair had already asked for audiences of both Mmes les Princesses de Conti;[1] but M. le Duc d'Orléans directed them not to receive him unless he had first greeted the princes in a suitable manner. Monsieur le Duc postponed his formal visit also. Stair claimed that it was not in his protocol to wait at the foot of his front-door steps; and he managed to obtain support from the other ambassadors. After two months of argument and negotiation, Monsieur le Duc and M. le Prince de Conti paid separate calls on Lord Stair and were properly received. The audacity of this English ambassador was clearly reflected in his bearing, speech, and actions. It revolted the entire French nation.[2]

Prye and his wife[3] returned from the Turin embassy. I mention this only because of the scandal and harm caused by the wife, who became the official mistress of Monsieur le Duc, queening it over the Court and the kingdom, during the entire time that he functioned as first minister. Prye received a pension of twelve thousand livres, and a gratuity of ninety thousand.

The foundation of Belle-Isle's[4] great wealth was established by the death of Puysieux,[5] whom I mentioned earlier as having won the Order in a most extraordinary manner by his consummate tact and daring.[6] It was a mere trifle, but amusing enough at the time, and most extraordinary with a prince as grave and dignified as Louis XIV. Such little anecdotes of court-life do have a certain interest. Let me remind you of this one:

Puysieux, arriving home on leave, was most amiably received by Louis XIV. He knew the King well, and therefore boldly decided to try his luck. When King Louis expressed affection for him and praised his work, he asked if His Majesty were truly pleased or merely making polite speeches. On the assurance that every word was meant, Puysieux put on a dissatisfied expression and said that for his part he could not be equally pleased with the King. 'Puysieux, why ever not?' said King Louis. 'Why, Sire? Because

---

[1] See II, p. 405, note 3.

[2] For Saint-Simon's portrait of the Earl of Stair, see II, pp. 408–409.

[3] Louis, Marquis de Prye (1671–1751), French ambassador to Turin 1713–1719. He married Agnès Berthelot de Pléneuf (1698–1727), who was appointed a 'palace-lady' in 1725. She was also the mistress of Voltaire in the early 1720s.

[4] Charles Louis Auguste Fouquet, Comte, later Duc and Maréchal de Belle-Isle (1684–1761). He was the grandson of Nicolas Fouquet, Marquis de Belle-Isle (1615–1680): see p. 414 below.

[5] Roger Brûlart, Marquis de Puysieux (1640–1719). He was ambassador to the Swiss Confederation 1698–1708.

[6] For the full story of Puysieux's obtaining the Order of the Saint-Esprit by sheer cheek, see *Saint-Simon at Versailles*, pp. 95–96.

though I am the most honest man in your kingdom, you have not kept the promise you made me fifty years ago.' 'How so, Puysieux? How do you make that out?' 'Sire,' replied Puysieux, 'you have a long memory, you cannot have forgotten that when you played blind-man's-bluff with me at my grandmother's you placed your ribbon on my shoulder to escape being caught, and promised to give me one of my own when you became the master. It is a long while since you have been master—no doubt of that—but I am still waiting for my ribbon.' The King remembered and laughed, confessing that Puysieux was perfectly right, and he promised there and then to call a special meeting of the Order and to admit Puysieux before the end of the year. Indeed, on that very same day he appointed a date for it, announcing that it was to be a special meeting for Puysieux's benefit.

The Carthusians occasionally gave great banquets, and they did so at this time for a large number of distinguished members of the Court and councils. I was bidden, and Puysieux also, for everyone found him a most jolly, good-natured table-companion. The meal was both abundant and delicious, the company, though great, extremely merry. Puysieux was its life and soul; but for a short, stout man of nearly eighty, he did eat a most prodigious amount; so much so, indeed, that that very same night he developed an attack of feverish indigestion that carried him off in a matter of days. It was the greatest pity, for his valour, integrity, and modesty, combined with an amusing and most sensible mind, made him not only a good soldier, but a man capable of handling extremely delicate negotiations, and the best company imaginable, esteemed and sought after in the highest Society.

His father[1] ruined himself by idleness; thus very little had descended to Puysieux, who was a counsellor of State for war, and governor of Huningue.[2] His family, seeing him about to die and without an heir, promptly decided to make hay while the sun still shone. Cheverny quickly secured the ministerial post, and Belle-Isle, ever watchful for a chance of promotion, claimed the governorship. He was Le Blanc's bosom friend, and acquainted with Law and Dubois. Thus although only a brigadier-general, and not in the running for any governorship, especially not one of such great importance, his three protectors gained the Regent's consent, and the whole affair was so rapidly and secretly managed that no one dreamed of it until the appointment was announced. This incredible promotion raised a great howl from those who had been meaning to apply as soon as the place fell vacant. Those without expectations admired Bell-Isle for his cleverness; others with better claims reproached him. These included the Maréchaux de Villeroy, Villars, and Huxelles, who protested as vehemently as they dared, considering their complicity with the Duc and Duchesse du Maine. In other words, they let fly in private, and encouraged their friends to complain aloud. There was so much commotion that the Regent had second

---

[1] Puysieux's father was Louis Roger Brûlart, Marquis de Sillery.
[2] Huningue is in the *arrondissement* of Mulhouse, not far from Basle.

thoughts and was inclined to refuse his consent; but the order, by then, was signed and sealed, and he could do nothing about it without using his authority and confessing to a change of mind. Belle-Isle thus remained in tranquil possession of his governorship; but M. le Duc d'Orléans persisted in bearing him a somewhat profitless grudge.

It was only their guilty consciences that kept the three marshals so quiet amid the turmoil. More and more people were being arrested and sent to the Bastille, to be joined by others taken in the provinces—even the young Duc de Richelieu[1] was not spared. The conspirators lived in terror lest something else should leak out, or one of their more trusted accomplices be seized. It was even rumoured that the Maréchal de Villars would be the next to go. His face and conduct certainly betrayed alarm, for he durst not leave his home and asked with despicable earnestness what people were saying of him. He and his wife, despite my rudeness regarding his dukedom, and still ruder comments on his peerage,[2] had always tried their hardest to win my friendship; they now courted Mme de Saint-Simon and myself with renewed ardour. They sent one day, entreating me to visit them. When I arrived, I found the Maréchal shivering in his shoes and completely deflated. He said flatly that they were about to arrest him, and might come at any moment; that he left his house only to go to the Regency Council and the Palais Royal; that even at home he felt unsafe, having received warnings from all sides. He added that it was becoming a public scandal, ruining his health and making his life not worth living. He further declared that the Regent no longer cared for him, though he could not tell why, and at last begged me to plead on his behalf. His wife made the same request, but more calmly. I assured them, as indeed was the truth, that I had observed nothing different in M. le Duc d'Orléans, saying that I thought they wronged themselves and him too, by displaying such evident anxiety. At the same time, I did not feel entirely sure of their safety. I therefore spoke to M. le Duc d'Orléans, who seemed not at all displeased to hear of the Maréchal's alarm; but he allowed me to say what was needed to comfort them, and I immediately returned to them with his message. They both thanked me sincerely; but Villars still felt afraid. Indeed so great was his agitation that he grew visibly thinner; his blood turned putrid, and he developed such a pain that it seemed to portend a cancer. Garus's remedy[3] protected him from that; for he took a vast number of doses and carried it with him ever after. None the less, his health remained weak until the release of the Duc and Duchesse du Maine, when he immediately put on flesh and entirely recovered; thus plainly showing the cause of his indisposition.

[1] Louis François Armand, Duc de Fronzac and de Richelieu (1699–1788).

[2] Saint-Simon's main objection to the Maréchal de Villars, after his lack of breeding, was that he was cock-a-hoop about everything.

[3] Garus's remedy was a strong elixir from a recipe that may have come down from Paracelsus. It was being prescribed by Joseph Garus.

It was learned at that time, when M. le Duc d'Orléans made a public announcement, that four letters from the Duc de Richelieu to Cardinal Alberoni had been seized, three of them signed, in which M. de Richelieu pledged himself to surrender the fortress of Bayonne, which his regiment garrisoned. The cream of it was that just four days after this statement (during which the Regent said that if M. de Richelieu had four heads, there was enough evidence in his pocket to remove them all), a personal valet, several books, a backgammon board and his bass-viol were sent to that nobleman in the Bastille, at his own request. People were amused at the notion of a young colonel's imagining himself capable of inducing an entire regiment—and the Bayonne Regiment at that—to surrender its fortress. Had anyone told me that ten years later I should be made a Knight of the Order at the self-same moment as the Duc du Maine's two sons, the Duc de Richelieu, and Cellamare, I should never have believed them.

Meanwhile Mme la Duchesse de Berry was living in the manner to which she had made herself accustomed, a mixture of haughty magnificence and most servile degradation, with strict retreats (frequent but short) with the Carmelites of the Faubourg Saint-Germain, and suppers in the vilest company, where blasphemy and shameful debauches mingled with horrid fears of death and the devil. Such was her life when she fell ill. I must needs tell all for the sake of history, more especially since you will find no such scandals in these memoirs, except where they are needed to explain the general situation. Mme la Duchesse de Berry made no attempt to control herself. She was furious that people should dare to discuss what she did not try to conceal; yet it much distressed her that her conduct should be known. She was big with Rions's child, but disguised that fact as best she might. Mme de Mouchy[1] was her confidant, though in the circumstances none was needed. Rions and Mouchy were in love, living in perfect intimacy, and with every facility accorded them. Together they mocked the princess whom they were deceiving, extracting from her whatever they could obtain. In a word, they ruled her and her household with an insolence unchecked even by M. and Mme la Duchesse d'Orléans, who hated, feared, and pampered them.

Mme de Saint-Simon lived very much apart from all this.[2] She was loved and esteemed by all at the Luxembourg, including even that redoubtable couple; but she saw Mme la Duchesse de Berry only to greet her when she entered the palace. Her duty done, she returned home, shutting her eyes to all else, though she well knew what went on.

The pregnancy of Mme la Duchesse de Berry reached its appointed end, and the labour, ill prepared for by countless suppers drenched in wine and strong liquors, was at first violent, then dangerous. When the danger

[1] See p. 60 above.
[2] Mme de Saint-Simon had been most unwillingly forced to become the Duchesse de Berry's lady-in-waiting: see index, II.

became acute, Mme de Saint-Simon felt obliged to render more diligent service; but the combined efforts of M. and Mme la Duchesse d'Orléans and the entire household failed to persuade her to sleep in the room reserved for her (where she had never yet set foot); nor would she spend all day at the Luxembourg, making the excuse that she needed to rest at home. Mme la Duchesse de Berry lay confined in the last and smallest room of her suite because it possessed convenient exits, out of the public eye. No one was admitted save Mouchy and Rions, with one or two of her most trusted maids. The necessary assistants were brought in from outside. Neither M. nor Mme la Duchesse d'Orléans, nor even Madame, was allowed in without special permission; and still less welcome, for obvious reasons, were Mme de Saint-Simon, her other ladies, and the royal doctors. All were allowed access at various times, but none for very long. A violent headache, or a desire to sleep served as a pretext to deny entry or expedite departure. Since all knew the real cause of the trouble, few tried to force an entrance, but were content to speak to Mme de Mouchy through the crack of the door; and this risible contrivance, watched by all the inhabitants of the Luxembourg and the Palais Royal, not to mention the many who from politeness or curiosity came to inquire, was the main topic of conversation.

When the danger became extreme, Languet,[1] the famous curé of Saint-Sulpice, who had shown himself most assiduous, mentioned the Sacraments to M. le Duc d'Orléans. The first difficulty was to gain access; but a far greater one soon presented itself when the curé flatly refused to administer them until Rions and Mouchy had left, not only Mme la Duchesse du Berry's room, but the palace itself.[2] He spoke loudly so that all might hear, and accordingly M. le Duc d'Orléans was not merely shocked, but most horribly embarrassed. He drew the curé on one side in a fruitless attempt to describe his daughter's temperament; then, when Languet was still inflexible, he proposed referring the matter to Cardinal de Noailles, Archbishop of Paris, to which Languet agreed, stipulating only that he should be allowed to explain his reasons. There was no time to lose for Mme la Duchesse de Berry was already making her confession.[3] M. le Duc d'Orléans had perhaps imagined that the Cardinal-Archbishop of Paris might prove less strict than his priest, who was at variance with him over the constitution, a matter in which Cardinal de Noailles was in the Regent's power. If those were his hopes, he was doomed to disappointment.

The cardinal arrived. M. le Duc d'Orléans took him aside with the curé, and they conferred for more than half an hour. As the curé's refusal had

---

[1] Jean Baptist Joseph Languet de Gergy, Curé of Saint-Sulpice (1675–1750). He founded a school for noble orphans.

[2] The Last Sacraments of course always meant repentance and the permanent removal of lovers and mistresses. Compare *Mme de Pompadour*, by Nancy Mitford, p. 30 (1968 edition).

[3] The Duchesse de Berry's confessor was a Franciscan, le Père Binet.

been publicly made, M. de Noailles thought that his words should be public also, and the three of them accordingly took up a position near the bedroom door. There the cardinal-archbishop praised his priest out loud for his firmness, saying that he had acted like a true and enlightened churchman, exhorting him not to be swayed by other considerations, but to watch over Mme la Duchesse de Berry and prevent her from receiving the Sacraments by any means whatsoever, until M. de Rions and Mme de Mouchy had been expelled from the palace. You may picture the effect in that crowded room, and M. le Duc d'Orléans's discomfiture. Yet no one at all, not the staunchest advocates of the constitution, who were M. de Noailles's worst enemies; the fashionable bishops; the Society ladies, not even the unbelievers, blamed the curé or his archbishop. On the contrary, they seemed overcome with horror at the conduct of Mme la Duchesse de Berry, and deeply shocked by her arrogance.

The question now arose, which of the three, the Regent, the cardinal, or the curé (all standing by the bedroom door), should break the news to the princess herself who, having confessed, was every moment expecting the doors to open for the entrance of the Holy Sacrament. After a short discussion, hastened by the invalid's condition, the cardinal and the curé retreated a little so as to allow M. le Duc d'Orléans to open the door a crack and summon Mme de Mouchy. There, through the half-open door (he without and she within), he told her the entire matter. The Mouchy, outraged and astonished, loudly proclaimed her own merits, bitterly complained of the insults showered on her by canting hypocrites, and on Mme la Duchesse de Berry also, who would never agree to so cruel a proposal, indeed, might immediately die if it were put to her. Yet in the end she did consent to inform her mistress. A negative response was in due course returned and communicated through the chink to M. le Duc d'Orléans. Considering the messenger, what else could have been expected? The curé, being in the presence of his diocesan, merely shrugged his shoulders, but the cardinal told M. le Duc d'Orléans that it was now for him, her father, to persuade his dying daughter to do her Christian duty. You may well believe that his eloquence achieved nothing; the prince feared his daughter so much that at any time he would have made a very feeble apostle.

For more than two hours Cardinal de Noailles waited with M. le Duc d'Orléans and the curé, while the chief persons in the room gradually drew nearer. Mme de Saint-Simon remained sitting in the embrasure of a window watching from a distance, with one or two ladies of the household, and now and then was told what was happening. At last it became evident that the door would yield only to force, and the cardinal decided that it would be improper for him to remain longer. He accordingly left, after repeating his orders to the curé, and urging him to be vigilant. M. le Duc d'Orléans hastened to tell his daughter of a departure that mightily relieved them both; but to his great surprise when he emerged, he found that the curé had stationed himself with his back to the door, declaring that he would guard the entry for fear of being tricked over the Sacraments. What is more, he stayed there four days and four nights, save for brief periods when he sought food and rest at his nearby lodging; and he then always left two priests on duty until his return. Once the danger was passed he raised the siege.

Mme la Duchesse de Berry had by then been safely delivered of a baby girl,[1] and needed only to regain her strength, which she did, amid transports of rage against Cardinal de Noailles and the curé, neither of whom she would ever forgive. On the other hand, she grew more and more devoted to the lovers, who openly sneered at her and stayed with her only for personal gain.

Rions, as I have already described,[2] was a penniless younger son, though he came from a good enough family. He was the grandson of a sister[3] of the Duc de Lauzun, whose adventures with La Grande Mademoiselle are known to all.[4] The likeness in their situations inspired Lauzun to relive the past in the person of his willing nephew, whose absolute dominion over the imperious princess, whom he so cruelly victimized, rendered possible the idea of a marriage. It was Lauzun, indeed, who had recommended the brutal treatment that every day reduced her to tears. He had a theory that Bourbons enjoyed being bullied and ill-treated, and that it was the only way by which they could be ruled. The dangers of Mme la Duchesse de Berry's confinement; the horrible dilemma thrust upon her of having to choose between the Last Sacraments and parting with her lover; fear of the devil that sent her into hysterics at each clap of thunder, emboldened them to act quickly. Both Rions and Mouchy were marvellously well disposed to do the deed, for both saw its advantages. They had been terrified by recent events, and believed that should they reoccur the outcome would be their own banishment. Fear of the devil might bring about a similar result, and while Rions had all to gain and nothing to lose by seizing that incredible chance, Mouchy fixed her hopes on a union which she would have done much to bring about. Neither of them, being sure of their mutual passion, saw any threat to their secret pleasures. I shall break off here, for their preparations were only beginning at the time of Mme la Duchesse de Berry's illness, and this is not the moment to go further.

[1] Nothing seems to be known about this child. Boislisle believes that, like the rest of the Duchesse de Berry's children, she died in infancy.

[2] See p. 59 above.

[3] Diane Charlotte de Caumont-Lauzun, Marquise de Nogent (1632–1720).

[4] See pp. 459 et seqq. below; also *Saint-Simon at Versailles*, p. 11. Mlle de Montpensier, 'La Grande Mademoiselle', was Louis XIV's first cousin, and fell madly in love with Lauzun. After much opposition the King consented to their marriage, but Lauzun backed out in the hope of winning better terms. He went so far in the end that he was imprisoned for ten years in the fortress of Pignerol, but returned to favour by his daring rescue of Queen Mary of Modena and her son the Old Pretender, whom he helped to escape from England to France.

Mme la Duchesse de Berry was deeply distressed at the way in which the entire nation, including the common people, had regarded her illness and the events connected with it. She now endeavoured to win popularity by reopening the Luxembourg gardens to the public. You will remember that for a long time past she had kept them closed.[1] Everyone was pleased and made use of them; but nothing more. She also vowed to wear white mourning for the next six months, which Society thought vastly amusing, considering the circumstances.

On the evening of Saturday, 15 April 1719, the day before Low Sunday, Mme de Maintenon, that notorious siren, passed away at Saint-Cyr.[2] Had this event occurred some years earlier, what an upheaval there would have been in Europe! It passed unnoticed at Versailles, so close at hand; and in Paris was scarcely mentioned. I have said so much already of this too famous and disastrous woman that there remains only to describe her life after the death of the King. Yet her influence was so powerful, so devastating, during thirty-five years without intermission,[3] that everything appertaining to her, even in the last years of her retirement, has some interest.

She withdrew to Saint-Cyr at the very moment of the King's death,[4] and had the good sense to announce that she was dead to the world, never afterwards setting foot beyond the walls of that convent. She saw no one from outside, except for a very few whom I will now mention, asked no favours for herself, made no recommendations, never meddled in anything where her name might appear. Mme de Caylus,[5] Mme de Dangeau, Mme de Levis saw her, but not very often; the two last seldom, and only rarely stayed to dine with her. Cardinal de Rohan visited her each week, also the Duc du Maine, who spent three or four hours with her alone. When he was announced, she was wreathed in smiles, embracing her darling (for so she called him) with the utmost tenderness, though he stank to high heaven. The Duc de Noailles called fairly often, but that pleased her less; his wife not so frequently, although she was Mme de Maintenon's niece, and she always appeared nervous and reluctant. Her welcome seemed to match her expectations. The Maréchal de Villeroy called when he could spare the time, and was always smilingly received. Cardinal de Bissy very rarely visited her; one or two obscure and fanatical bishops sometimes put

[1] See p. 77 above. In the seventeenth and eighteenth centuries, the French royal palaces and their gardens were always open to the public. It was felt as a shocking deprivation when the Duchesse de Berry shut her gates.

[2] When they told Mme de Maintenon that she was dying she is supposed to have said, 'Mourir c'est le moindre moment de ma vie'—and what a life! In our time, she might have said, 'At this stage death could not matter less!'

[3] Saint-Simon greatly exaggerates Mme de Maintenon's influence in the government of France.

[4] See II, pp. 497, 501.

[5] Mme de Maintenon's cousin, converted by her to Roman Catholicism. She wrote the *Souvenirs de Mme de Maintenon* that are so often quoted.

in an appearance, more often the Archbishop of Rouen (Aubigny),[1] Blouin very occasionally, and now and then the Bishop of Chartres (Moustiers de Mérinville), the diocesan and superior of the convent.

Once a week, the Queen of England, when she was at Saint-Germain, dined with her; but from Chaillot, where much of her time was spent, she never came. They had similar armchairs set facing one another, and for dinner, a table laid for two was placed between them with the first course upon it and a hand-bell. It was the schoolgirls who waited on them and poured out the wine; bringing fresh plates and a second course when summoned by the bell. The queen always gave them some little present. When the meal was finished they cleared and removed the table; they brought the coffee, and afterwards took that away also. The queen and Mme de Maintenon would then spend two or three hours alone. They kissed at parting. Mme de Maintenon advanced two or three steps to receive or take leave of her; the schoolgirls, waiting in the ante-room, would escort her to her coach, and loved her dearly because she was very gracious to them. They were especially fond of Cardinal de Rohan also, for he never came empty-handed, but brought enough cakes and sweetmeats to feast them for several days. Such trifles pleased her immensely. Yet even with so few visitors, no one dared to call without first sending to know whether the day and hour would suit. Only her darling was always sure of a welcome; but scarcely a day passed without her receiving some visitor.

When no one came and in the mornings, she filled the hours by writing and reading a great number of letters, almost all to or from the superiors of religious houses and seminaries, abbesses, or even ordinary nuns, for she still retained her passion for directing people's affairs and, since she wrote extraordinarily well and readily, she enjoyed dictating. Mme de Thibouville, born a Rochechouart,[2] gave me these details; having no future, she had been sent to Saint-Cyr as a child. She told me that apart from her personal maids (no manservant of hers entered the convent), Mme de Maintenon had two, sometimes three elderly ladies, and six younger ones to attend her, and that she often changed them, old and young alike. Mme de Rochechouart was one of the young ones. Mme de Maintenon grew fond of her and confided in her a little, so far as the difference in their ages allowed; and because she thought her clever, with a good handwriting, always used her for dictation. She did not leave Saint-Cyr until after Mme de Maintenon's death, and continued to mourn her sincerely, although she was left nothing. Her marriage, forced on her by her total want of means, was not a happy one.[3] Thibouville had squandered his wealth in

---

[1] Claud Maur d'Aubigny (died 1719), Count-Bishop of Noyon 1701, Archbishop of Rouen 1707.

[2] Louise Elisabeth de Rochechouart-Montigny (1702–1772). She married the Marquis de Thibouville in 1751.

[3] Henri-Lambert d'Herbigny, Marquis de Thibouville (born 1710, he died at some time after 1776). He was a writer of romances, a playwright, and a friend of Voltaire.

idleness, sold his regiment as soon as war seemed imminent, and behaved so ill to his wife that she was compelled to seek refuge with her brother the Bishop of Évreux.[1] The country house of that diocese is only a few miles from La Ferté; we constantly visited each other, and they often stayed entire months with us. All this would be of little interest; but when it comes to something which I neither saw nor handled myself, I like to say whence and how I knew it.

Mme de Maintenon, as she had done at the Court, rose and retired extremely early, spending long over her prayers, and in reading devotional books. She often made the schoolgirls read aloud some work of history, and greatly enjoyed hearing them discuss it, and instructing them. Mass she heard from a tribune adjacent to her room, and often attended the services, but she rarely sat in the choir. She took Communion not, as Dangeau says in his memoirs, either every day or at midnight, but twice a week, usually between seven and eight in the morning, returning afterwards to her tribune, where she remained a long time on such days. Her dinner was plain but tasty, elegantly simple, yet plentiful in every way. The Duc de Noailles kept her supplied with game from Saint-Germain and Versailles, and the administration sent her fruit. When there were no visitors she ate alone, served by the girls who attended her, and three or four times a year—no more—she let them sit down to eat with her.

The reverend mothers, their deputies, and all the other officers of the convent were appointed by her, and she daily received a short account of their doings. In all matters of importance the superior took orders from her. Though they called her simply Madame, hers was the ruling hand; and although she was courteous and gentle to the nuns of Saint-Cyr, and kind to the children, everyone trembled before her. No abbess-Daughter of France was ever more absolute, more implicitly obeyed, more feared and respected; yet she was loved by nearly all. The visiting priests were equally submissive to her rule. She never discussed anything concerning the government or the Court with the girls; but often praised the late King to them, never mentioning intrigues, cabals, or scandals.

You will recall that after the Regency was proclaimed, M. le Duc d'Orléans called on Mme de Maintenon, at Saint-Cyr, and actually promised her—her, Mme de Maintenon—that the monthly pension of four thousand francs allowed her by the King would be paid as punctually as before, on the first day of each month. She thus received a royal pension of forty-eight thousand francs a year, and I never heard that she had renounced her previous salary as governess of the King's children by Mme de Montespan, not to mention the emoluments of second lady to Mme la Dauphine Bavière.[2] Certainly the Maréchale de Rochefort, who had been

---

[1] Pierre Jules César de Rochechouart-Montigny (1698–1781), Bishop of Évreux from 1733, of Bagneux from 1755.
[2] Monseigneur's wife, who died in 1690.

the first lady, was still receiving hers. In addition, Mme de Maintenon owned the estate of Maintenon, as well as other properties. Saint-Cyr, at its foundation, had undertaken to support her in retirement with all her servants and carriages, and to feed them, men and horses alike, free, gratis and for nothing, so long as she wished to keep them. All this was faithfully carried out, even down to her firewood, charcoal, tapers and candles; in a word, she did not pay a sou for anything except her clothes and liveries. Her outside staff consisted of a butler and a footman, pantry and kitchen men, and grooms for her eight carriage horses and the one or two kept for riding. Indoors, she had Mlle d'Aumale,[1] her personal maids, and the young ladies mentioned earlier; but they were the schoolgirls being educated at Saint-Cyr. She thus had no expenses save for her charities and the wages of her servants.

The Duc du Maine's disgrace at the *Lit de Justice* held at the Tuileries was the first blow to her health. It would not be too much to say that she must have been aware of that charming creature's plots and manœuvres, and that her hopes had borne her up. When he was arrested, she succumbed. A persistent fever developed, and caused her death, sound in mind and spirit, at the age of eighty-three.

Mourning for her loss was not general, even at Saint-Cyr, and beyond its walls the event was hardly known. The only grief that reached my ears was that of Aubigny, Archbishop of Rouen, her supposed cousin, who was mad enough to die of a broken heart. Her death so deeply distressed him that he fell ill and shortly afterwards followed her.

Law was still achieving miracles with his Mississippi Scheme. A special language had been evolved to express its transactions and the method of dealing in the stock; but I shall not try to explain either that or the rest of its finances. Everyone fought to buy the stock, and immense fortunes were made almost overnight. Law was continually besieged by suppliants and flatterers; his door was forced, people entered by the windows from his garden, and fell down the chimney into his study. The talk was all of millions. Law, as you know, came to me every Tuesday morning between half-past eleven and noon.[2] He often pressed me to accept stock without payment, and a sleeping partnership, so as to give me several millions' worth. Very many people of all sorts and conditions were making vast sums, and Law would no doubt have seen to it that I grew rich more quickly and to an even greater extent; but I never would consent. He then tried Mme de Saint-Simon, but met with an equally firm refusal. Fortune

---

[1] Marie Jeanne, Demoiselle d'Aumale (1683–1756). First a schoolgirl of Saint-Cyr, she was Mme de Maintenon's secretary at Versailles. Her account is rather different, for she says that Mme de Maintenon's fare was very plain indeed, with only one course, although at Versailles she had been accustomed to living in luxury. 'It is true that she was always a very frugal eater.' Mlle d'Aumale says also that her horses and carriages had all been sold and the grooms thanked and dismissed.

[2] See p. 80 above.

for fortune, he would sooner have enriched me than others, on account of my friendship with the Regent, and thereby have forced me to become his friend also. He had indeed spoken to the Regent, hoping to win me by that means, and M. le Duc d'Orléans had approached me more than once; but each time I had evaded him.

One day M. le Duc d'Orléans made an appointment to meet me at Saint-Cloud, so as to take the air after he had been working there, and we both sat on the balustrade before the Orangery, looking down the slope of the wood, towards Les Goulottes.[1] He spoke again of the Mississippi bank, urging me to accept stock from Law. I refused once more, but he continued to press me, producing one argument after another, until at last he grew angry, saying that it was mere vanity to refuse what the King offered (all was done in his name), when so many other persons of my rank and condition urgently desired it. I said that such a refusal would be stupid and impertinent, as well as conceited, and was not my way. Therefore, as he was so pressing, I would explain my true reasons. Not since the reign of King Midas had I heard of anyone who could turn all he touched into gold, and I did not think that even Law had this talent. All his ability was, I believed, no more than clever trickery, a brilliant exhibition of juggling, a robbing of Peter to pay Paul, by which some people became rich at the expense of others. Sooner or later, I declared, it would be seen for what it was; enormous numbers would be made bankrupt, and then how, and to whom, would restitution be made?[2] I added that I abhorred the idea of touching other people's money,[3] and that nothing on earth could persuade me to do so now, not even at second-hand.

M. le Duc d'Orléans was at a loss how to answer; but he none the less continued to argue, still harping on my refusing the King's gift. My impatience suddenly gave me a most happy thought. I said that being so little inclined to consent, I might suggest something which in other circumstances I could never have mentioned. It had come to me suddenly, for the first time, as he spoke. I then referred to what I had told him long ago, in one of our idle talks, namely, how my father had been ruined defending Blaye against the forces of Monsieur le Prince,[4] when he had besieged that fortress for a year and a half. My father had paid and fed the garrison, furnished the supplies, cast the cannon, maintained five hundred gentlemen within the walls, and otherwise expended large sums in saving

---

[1] The ponds at the lower end of Saint-Cloud park. See note, p. 208 above.

[2] The Mississippi Scheme was a national joint-stock company of France, and the country was therefore responsible to the stockholders.

[3] No wonder that everyone, even King Louis XIV, respected the little duke's ferocious honesty. This passage explains why Mme de Coëtanfao left him her all (see II, pp. 410–412). He might have made a better Controller of Finances, had he accepted the post, than he believed.

[4] At the time of the *Fronde*, the revolt of the nobles during the minority of Louis XIV. This passage may explain Saint-Simon's ferocity whenever his governorship of Blaye was attacked. He must have felt that he had a double right to it.

it for the King, without laying waste the surrounding country, or touching any funds, except his own. After those troubles he had been sent an order for five hundred thousand livres, but had never received a sou because M. Fouquet[1] was arrested at the very moment when he was about to arrange for payment. I said to M. le Duc d'Orléans that if he cared to reimburse me for that sum, and the loss incurred by our having been unable to touch it for so long (a loss far greater than the original amount, allowing for interest), I would most gladly accept it as an act of justice and, on payment, would return the bills to be burned in his presence. M. le Duc d'Orléans readily consented, and spoke to Law on the following day. Thus I duly received my money, and burned the bills one by one, before M. le Duc d'Orléans, in his study. That was the money which enabled me to make the improvements at La Ferté.

Pécoil[2] died at this time. He was a most tedious old creature, a maître des requêtes who had never learned to sum up a case, or administer a province, but died immensely wealthy, completely unknown, leaving an only child, a daughter. This story may seem somewhat irrelevant here, but its awful nature forbids its omission. Pécoil's grandfather was an immensely rich Rouen shopkeeper. His father, a merchant of Lyons, worked so prodigiously hard and was so overwhelmingly stingy that although he made millions, he lived cold and hungry, scarcely clothing himself and his family, but all the time watching his pile increase. He dug a cellar under his house at Lyons, on purpose to store his gold, with every imaginable safeguard, including several doors, the keys of which he alone possessed. The last of these doors was made of iron, fitted with a secret lock, known only to himself and the locksmith. It was a highly complicated piece of machinery, and without the key the door was impossible to open. From time to time, he would descend to view his pile and add to it, with the result that his family, who noticed his occasional disappearances holding a candle end, suspected the existence of a miser's hoard; but none dared to follow him. One day he vanished and did not return. His wife and son, and their few servants, looked everywhere for him, and, when he was not to be found in his usual haunts, guessed that he had gone to the cellar. They knew only its outer door, concealed in a dark corner of the ordinary wine-cellar. With immense difficulty they broke this down, to find another similar door behind it, and after that, the iron one. They knocked and called and shouted, not knowing how to unlock or burst it open. When there was no reply, they were frightened and did their best to force it; but it was too thick and too well fixed to yield. With the help of neighbours and workmen, and after long and arduous labour, they

[1] Nicolas Fouquet (1615–1680), Marquis de Belle-Isle, the Surintendant des Finances, and minister of State, who was disgraced for his *luxe insolent et audacieux* and imprisoned by Louis XIV in the Fortress of Pignerol from 1664. He is supposed to have said at the time of his arrest, 'They are making a great mistake; I had made my pile and was about to make theirs.'

[2] Claude Pécoil de Villedieu (1665–1719).

managed to break their way through, to find iron safes protected by stout bars, and the wretched old miser lying dead beside his hoard. His arms were torn; despair was still depicted on his livid countenance; the candle end beside him was burned out, and in his hand was the key of that same door, whose secret, after so many safe entrances and exits, had finally baffled him. A truly horrible death in every kind of way. Indeed, it is so awful, and the miser's punishment so fitting, that I thought it should not be forgotten.

In the year following Pécoil's death, the Duc de Brissac married his daughter[1] who had become a great heiress. For a long time past the Brissacs had not been fastidious in their alliances, although they appeared none the richer. Money flies; filth remains behind.

Mme la Duchesse de Berry, as I have recounted, fell ill on 26 March, and Easter Day was 9 April. Easter week, following after Holy Week, was a dismal time for her to be in Paris, on account of the scandal mentioned above. For one thing, M. le Duc d'Orléans's visits were dreary and infrequent. Her secret marriage to Rions had been the cause of violent quarrels and floods of tears, which she decided to avoid by taking up residence at Meudon on Easter Monday. No use to urge the danger of catching cold, the jolting of the coach, or the change of air so soon after a grave illness. She could not endure Paris another moment, and departed, followed by Rions, most of her ladies, and the greater portion of her personal servants. It was at that point that M. le Duc d'Orléans told me of her determination to announce her marriage. Mme la Duchesse d'Orléans was spending a few days at Montmartre, and we were strolling in the little garden of her apartments. The marriage itself did not so much astonish me; it was her frenzied desire to proclaim it that seemed more strange. M. le Duc d'Orléans spoke of his distress and anger; of Madame, who wished to go to all lengths in opposing her, and of Mme la Duchesse d'Orléans's extreme vexation. It was indeed fortunate at that juncture that officers were leaving every day for service on the Spanish frontier, and that Rions would also have gone, had it not been for Mme la Duchesse de Berry's illness.

M. le Duc d'Orléans considered that the best way of delaying matters was to be rid of him. I cordially agreed, and next day, he was sent such peremptory orders to join his regiment that he dared not disobey. He left immediately; but M. le Duc d'Orléans, though he had not yet been to Meudon, put off his visit another few days. He and his daughter feared one another, and Rions's abrupt departure would not make her less angry. She continually asserted that she was rich, independent, and a widow, rehearsing all she knew of La Grande Mademoiselle's conduct when that lady had wished to marry Rions's great-uncle, M. de Lauzun; loudly

[1] Catherine Marie Pécoil (1707–1770) married Charles Timoléon Louis de Cossé, Duc de Brissac, in 1720.

proclaiming all the estates and honours which she would demand for him, once the marriage was announced, and flying into torrents of abuse when her father tried to dissuade her. There had been disgraceful scenes at the Luxembourg, and worse took place at Meudon, on the few occasions when he visited her. She was firmly determined to announce her marriage forthwith; and all that cunning, tact, gentleness, threats, entreaties, or M. le Duc d'Orléans's strongest arguments could effect was the faint possibility of some further delay. If Madame had had her way, the whole affair would have been ended long before the Meudon journey, by M. le Duc d'Orléans's throwing Rions from an upper window of the Luxembourg.

That ill-advised excursion, those violent tantrums, were not designed to restore the health of one so lately returned from the gates of death. Yet an urgent desire to hide both her real condition and the quarrel with her father, the rarity of whose visits had become noticeable, induced her to give an open-air supper on the terrace, at seven in the evening. She was warned in vain of the dangers of the night air to one in such delicate health, for she was convinced that this feast, coming so soon after a grave illness, would remove all suspicion of a confinement, and persuade people that she and her father were still on the same loving terms as in the past. The supper did not achieve that object. There resulted mishaps caused by her condition, and an intermittent fever, which frustration over the marriage did nothing to dispel. She tired of Meudon, blaming the air and the house, as those who are sick in mind and body so often tend to do. She distressed herself because M. le Duc d'Orléans came so seldom, and Madame and her mother hardly at all, despite her serious illness. Her pride suffered more than her affections, for she had cared very little for those royal ladies, and was now beginning to hate them. Towards her father, her sentiments were not very different, but she still hoped to win him over, remembering how great her influence had once been.

Bad though the draughts and joltings of a journey must be to one in her condition, nothing could stop her moving from Meudon to La Meute, on 14 May, slung between two sheets,[1] in a large coach. She hoped that its nearness to Paris might persuade M. le Duc d'Orléans to visit her more often, and her mother also, if only for the sake of appearances. The journey was painful, attended by further mishaps made worse by the jolting; and neither the air of La Meute, nor many different remedies had any power to relieve her, except during short intervals. Later the attacks became extremely violent. Alternations of fear and hope succeeded one another until the beginning of July, and at that time, when her comfort was short-lived and her pain so long-enduring, the eagerness to announce her marriage somewhat subsided. Thus M. le Duc d'Orléans, and even her mother and Madame, who was spending the summer at Saint-Cloud, went more often to see her.

[1] As though in a hammock.

As July went on, the danger became more acute, with continual mishaps, bouts of pain, and fevers. On the 14th, these symptoms increased, giving rise to serious alarm, and the night was so much disturbed that they wakened M. le Duc d'Orléans, at the Palais Royal. At the same moment Mme de Pons[1] sent Mme de Saint-Simon a note, begging her to come and take up residence, which my wife immediately did, going at once to La Meute and remaining there until the end. She found that the danger was indeed very grave. They had bled Mme la Duchesse de Berry from the arm and foot earlier that day, and her confessor had been summoned. The illness lasted another week, until 21 July, and her death was very horrible. The time has now come to describe it.

The long periods of pain, wearing her down, did not persuade her to protect her life in this world by the necessary treatment, or to reflect on the life so soon to come. At last, parents, priests, and doctors were obliged to use language that princesses of her rank hear only at times of extreme crisis. But Chirac's[2] impiety frustrated their efforts. None the less, since his was the only dissenting voice and the rest continued to plead with her, she consented to submit to their advice for this world and the next. She received the Sacraments with the doors thrown wide open, and talked with the priests and doctors of her soul and health. But to both she spoke royally. When that performance was over and she was once more among her intimates, she boasted of her strength of mind, asking if she had not done well, and given an example of how to die nobly and bravely.

Shortly afterwards she dismissed them all, save only Mme de Mouchy, to whom she gave the key of her jewel-box, asking her to fetch the case of rings, which the latter brought and opened. Mme la Duchesse de Berry then made her a present of it, having already given her many other tokens; for apart from her regular salary, scarcely a day had passed since the princess's illness without her having extracted presents of money or gems, the jewellery being the least valuable. This ring-case, in itself, was worth more than two hundred thousand écus, and Mouchy, greedy though she was, was so overcome that she showed it to her husband. It was evening; M. and Mme la Duchesse d'Orléans had just left; Mouchy's reputation was not good, and they feared to be accused of theft. They therefore decided to mention the gift to the persons least biased against them in a house where they were generally hated and despised. Thus gradually the thing became known and eventually reached the ears of Mme de Saint-Simon, who thought it her duty to inform M. le Duc d'Orléans immediately. Mme la Duchesse de Berry's condition that night was such

[1] Marie Guyonne de Rochefort-Théobon, Marquise de Pons, was the Duchesse de Berry's second lady.

[2] Pierre Chirac (1650–1732), professor of medicine at the University of Montpellier. He was a pupil of Fagon whom he succeeded in 1718 as Director of the Jardin des Plantes. In 1715 he had been appointed the Regent's chief physician, and became Louis XV's doctor in 1730.

that no one at La Meute went to bed; everyone sat waiting in one of the drawing-rooms. Mme de Mouchy, perceiving that the affair was being talked of and having a bad effect, came to Mme de Saint-Simon in a great state of alarm to tell her what had occurred, drawing the ring-case from her pocket as she spoke. Mme de Saint-Simon called to some of the nearer ladies and in their presence (which was why she had called them) advised Mme de Mouchy to take it at once to M. le Duc d'Orléans. Such counsel, given before witnesses, was exceedingly mortifying, but the Mouchy promised to abide by it and, returning to her husband, went up with him at once to their bedroom.

Next day they called at the Palais Royal and asked to speak to the Regent who, having been alerted by my wife, immediately received them, dismissing the small company assembled in his study,[1] for it was still very early. Mme de Mouchy, her husband at her side, paid her respects as best she might, to which M. le Duc d'Orléans's sole reply was to demand the ring-case. This she drew out of her pocket and handed to him. M. le Duc d'Orléans took it, opened it, looked carefully to see that nothing was missing, for he perfectly knew the contents; shut it; took a key from his pocket, and locked it in a drawer of his writing-table. He then dismissed them with a nod, without uttering a syllable. Nor did they speak, but made their bows and retired ashamed, never again to set foot at La Meute. Soon afterwards, M. le Duc d'Orléans went there, and after a short conversation with his daughter talked privately to Mme de Saint-Simon, thanking her for all she had done, and assuring her that the ring-case would be safe in his keeping; yet so furious was he at the Mouchys' presumption that he referred to them in the salon in most unflattering terms; whereupon everyone clapped, including the valets.

Whether or not it was the departure of the Mouchys that had a salutary effect on Mme la Duchesse de Berry, I do not know, for she never mentioned them again; but soon afterwards she appeared to examine her conscience and expressed a wish to receive Our Lord once more. That second time, she took the Sacraments with a piety very different from her behaviour on the first occasion. Her chief almoner, the Abbé de Castries,[2] Archbishop-elect of Albi, officiated and went to the parish church of Passy for the Eucharist, returning with it escorted by M. le Duc d'Orléans and M. le Duc de Chartres. His address was short, well composed, moving, and so eminently suitable that it was the admiration of all who heard it.

In the last extremity, when the doctors could do no more and were ready to try anything, someone mentioned a certain Garus[3] and his elixir,

---

[1] A contemporary source speaks of M. and Mme de Mouchy, in the last days of the princess's life, as having been seen removing several bundles in the night-time. 'When they left they were enormously rich but totally dishonoured.'

[2] Armand Pierre de La Croix (1629–1747): he became Archbishop of Albi in that same year, 1719.

[3] See note 3, p. 235 above.

much in vogue at that time. The King later purchased the recipe. Garus
was accordingly summoned and arrived soon after. He found Mme la
Duchesse de Berry too bad for any certain cure; but he gave her the elixir,
and it succeeded beyond expectation. All that remained was to continue
with it. Above all, he insisted that nothing whatsoever should be given her
save by his own hand, and a firm order to that effect was issued by M. and
Mme la Duchesse d'Orléans. The improvement continued to the point
where Chirac began to fear for his reputation. He seized his chance when
Garus lay asleep on a sofa, and with his usual impetuosity made her swallow
a purge, on his own authority. The two nurses on duty, the only other
persons present, dared not protest. His wickedness was equalled only by
his audacity, for both M. and Mme la Duchesse d'Orléans were in the
adjoining room at that very time. Scarcely any interval elapsed before Mme
la Duchesse de Berry sank into a worse state than before taking the elixir.
Garus was sent for and woken. As soon as he saw her in convulsions, he
cried out that she had been given a purge—no matter what, for in her
condition it was sheer poison. He tried to leave, but was prevented and
taken before M. and Mme la Duchesse d'Orléans. A fearful quarrel then
ensued, with accusations by Garus, and insolence from Chirac who
defended his action with unequalled effrontery—he could hardly deny it,
seeing that the nurses, after being questioned, had told all. Meanwhile
Mme la Duchesse de Berry, unattended, approached her end. She lasted
the remainder of that day, and died on the stroke of midnight. Chirac, when
he saw her death-agony, crossed the room, and bowing rudely to the foot
of the bed, where the curtains were drawn back, wished her a happy
journey, or words to that effect. He then immediately left for Paris.[1] The
miracle was that there were no repercussions, and that he continued in his
post as first doctor to M. le Duc d'Orléans.

Never, since M. le Duc d'Orléans had been so casual (to use no harsher
word) as to tell his daughter my advice on a matter vitally important to
them both,[2] had I seen her, save on ceremonial occasions. Yet Mme de
Saint-Simon sent for me when she saw that the end was near, and that
M. le Duc d'Orléans had no one in whom to confide. In truth, I did
think that my presence comforted him a little, and that it relieved him
to unburden himself to me. I spent nearly the entire evening with him.
He asked me to take upon myself the ordering of everything that must be
done after Mme la Duchesse de Berry's death, the opening of her body,
the concealment of any pregnancy, all the details that would otherwise
need his ruling, so that he might be spared the pain—everything, indeed,
even including the funeral arrangements. He spoke wholly as a friend, gave
me no precise instructions, and told all the princess's household as he
passed that I had full authority, and must be obeyed implicitly. He said

[1] Saint-Simon would have heard all these details from his wife.
[2] See II, pp. 181–182.

further that Mme de Mouchy was no longer to be considered a member of the household, desiring me, and Mme de Saint-Simon also, to see that if she returned she did not enter La Meute, or have a seat in the coaches escorting the body to Saint-Denis, or the heart to Val-de-Grâce. I thought there should be no bodyguard, Holy Water, or other pomps; that the procession, though suitable, should be extremely simple, and that at Saint-Denis, especially, where some ceremony was inevitable, there should be no oration. When I gently explained the reason, which he well understood, M. le Duc d'Orléans agreed to everything.

Of the funeral I said as little as possible, and meanwhile kept him walking up and down the suite of rooms on the garden side, away from the bedroom where his daughter lay dying. Much later, as Mme la Duchesse de Berry grew progressively worse, having been unconscious since Chirac administered that poison, exactly as the Court physicians had poisoned the Maréchal de Boufflers, at Fontainebleau, and with the same result,[1] M. le Duc d'Orléans went into the bedroom and stood by her pillow, where the curtains had been opened. I let him stay only a few moments, and then gently took him into the study, where we were alone. All the windows were wide open; he stood leaning on the iron railings, his tears flowing so fast that I feared lest he choke. When this onset had somewhat abated, he began to speak of life's sorrows and the short duration of our greatest joys. I said such words as God put into my mouth, with all the tenderness, eloquence and affection of which I was capable. Not only did he listen; but he answered me and continued the conversation.

After we had been there an hour, Mme de Saint-Simon came quietly to warn me that the time was come to remove M. le Duc d'Orléans, more especially since the only way lay through the bedroom. My wife had remembered to order his coach, and it was waiting. It was with great difficulty that I contrived to move him, so plunged was he in most bitter grief. At last, however, I managed to persuade him to cross the bedroom without stopping, entreating him to return at once to Paris, which he reluctantly consented to do. He desired me to remain and give the orders, and begged Mme de Saint-Simon with the utmost courtesy to be present when they affixed the seals. I then saw him to his coach, and he drove away. I told Mme de Saint-Simon of his instructions regarding the opening of the body, in order that she might see them carried out, and I dissuaded her from staying longer in the bedroom, where only horror remained.

Mme la Duchesse de Berry died as the clock struck, at midnight, on 21 July, just two days after Chirac's abominable crime. M. le Duc d'Orléans was the only one to feel genuine grief. A few appeared sorry, but those with private means seemed not to regret her. Mme la Duchesse d'Orléans was relieved, but behaved with entire decorum. Madame, on the other hand, made little attempt to hide her lack of feeling; and although M. le Duc

[1] See II, p. 191.

d'Orléans was truly afflicted, he soon consoled himself. His servitude was ended; above all, he no longer had to dread the announcement of the marriage to Rions and its consequences, which would have been worse even than he feared, for the poor princess was found to be with child. Nothing but misery would have attended knowledge of that, and the fact was therefore carefully concealed.

At five next morning, that is to say five hours after her death, La Vrillière came to La Meute and affixed the seals, in the presence of Mme de Saint-Simon. She then stepped beside him into her coach; the people needed for sealing followed in La Vrillière's, and they went to seal, first at Meudon, then at the Luxembourg, after which they reported to M. le Duc d'Orléans at the Palais Royal. Mme de Saint-Simon returned to La Meute, where an even more terrible night awaited her because of her duties at the opening of the body.[1] I myself went to report to M. le Duc d'Orléans that his orders had been carried out. The body lay unguarded in the chapel of La Meute, and a succession of low masses followed one after another during the morning. I took up residence with M. and Mme de Lauzun, at Passy, so as to be near La Meute without actually sleeping there, and nearly every day I went to see M. le Duc d'Orléans. Because of the absence of ceremony, mantles and mantillas were not obligatory at the Palais Royal. People wore black, but dressed otherwise as usual. Mme la Duchesse de Berry died intestate, and gave no presents, save for what Mme de Mouchy managed to filch from her.[2] She had been receiving an allowance of seven hundred thousand livres, apart from the great sums extracted from M. le Duc d'Orléans since the beginning of the Regency. The King's mourning was for six weeks; the Palais Royal's for three months (out of respect for her rank), and Mme de Saint-Simon draped for six.[3] You will remember that from an excess of courtesy she had draped for other deaths, at the times when M. le Duc de Berry had draped.[4]

On the day before the funeral, M. le Duc d'Orléans told me of his own accord that the King would continue Mme de Saint-Simon's full salary—namely twenty-one thousand livres, *per annum*. I thanked him, asking at the same time, as a personal favour to my wife and myself, that he should also continue the salaries of Mme la Duchesse de Berry's other ladies, to which he instantly consented. I then went to La Meute to tell Mme de Saint-Simon what I had done. She immediately sent for the ladies to come to her in her room, saying that I had arrived with news for them. But I was wicked enough to wait until all were assembled before I told them of the Regent's extreme generosity, for he had allowed them to keep their

---

[1] As lady-in-waiting, she had to receive the heart in her hands and place it in an urn. See II, p. 240, for the possible full horror of this service.

[2] The Saint-Simons did receive a certain amount of the princess's furniture and some jewellery. The finest object was a beautiful silver mirror.

[3] The horses and coaches covered with black cloth, and black hangings on the drawing-room walls.   [4] See II, pp. 236–237.

lodgings at the Luxembourg also. Their joy was great and not constrained, and they all kissed me. I advised them to go next day and thank M. le Duc d'Orléans personally. They did so and were most graciously received. Mme de Saint-Simon took that occasion to give up her own apartment at the Luxembourg which, as you know, she had never used. They had hitherto refused to let her give it up, for they did not wish it to appear that she had no room at the Palace.

You may picture the feelings of Rions when he heard the news. It brought his romantic adventures to a most terrible conclusion, at the very moment when his wildest dreams seemed about to materialize. More than once he contemplated suicide, but was held back by the compassion of his friends. He sold his governorship and his regiment after the campaign was over, but his friends did not desert him, for with them he had always been gentle and courteous. He was thus able to continue living among them in comparative comfort; but it must be admitted that he remained in the background and was never heard of again.

Mme de Saint-Simon who, as you know,[1] had been compelled (and I also) to consent to her becoming Mme la Duchesse de Berry's lady-in-waiting, had never at any time seen the smallest hope of ever quitting that odious employment. She had been shown every consideration and granted all the freedom possible; but that did nothing to make the post less distasteful, and she therefore felt all the joy, not to say the intense relief, of her unexpected deliverance from a princess only twenty-four years old. Yet the exhaustion of that final illness and the days following the princess's death brought on a malignant fever that kept my wife for six weeks in acute danger, at the Passy house which Fontanieu lent her on her journeys to and from Forges-les-Eaux. It was two months before she recovered. This mishap drove me nearly out of my mind, and kept me for all that time a prisoner, never leaving the house—indeed, scarcely leaving her bedroom, hearing nothing and seeing no one except close relations and a few most intimate friends. When she began to improve, I asked M. le Duc d'Orléans if he would lend us some rooms in the château, at Meudon. He gave us the entire palace, fully furnished. We spent all of that summer there, and many other summers too, for it is a most delightful spot, and vastly convenient for all manner of excursions.[2] We had intended to entertain only our friends there, but the nearness to Paris brought us crowds of visitors, and the house was often filled to overflowing, not counting our more transitory visitors.

Mme du Maine received permission to remove to a château near Chalon-sur-Saône, to which La Billarderie escorted her. The Duc du Maine was at the same time allowed to hunt near Doullens; but not to spend the night

---

[1] See index, II, under Mme de Saint-Simon.

[2] The gardens were laid out by Le Nôtre. They spent there the summers of 1720, 1721, 1722, and 1723, when their daughter, the poor deformed girl (as crooked as a vine), was married to the Prince de Chimay. What must Saint-Simon have felt, lording it at Monseigneur's home, where the cabal of his bitter enemies had plotted against him in the old days!

away. Meanwhile Cellamare's secretary, having at last obtained leave to return to Spain, was arrested en route and confined in the fortress at Saumur. This was because the Duchesse du Maine had at last spoken, admitting many things, perhaps only so as to keep others secret; for, as I said earlier, I am quite convinced that M. le Duc d'Orléans knew many of her hidden plans, and would have known all had it not been for the Abbé Dubois. Be that as it may, in a signed statement to M. le Duc d'Orléans she confessed that the Spanish plot had been a reality, and named many of her accomplices. She expressed profound contempt for the smaller fry arrested, confirmed the aspirations of the Duc de Richelieu to surrender Bayonne and an entire regiment of the guards; but most of all blamed Laval,[1] as being the ringleader, their confidential agent, and sole go-between with Cellamare. Finally, she admitted that they had fully intended to stir up a revolt in the provinces against the government, and to bring it down, thereafter declaring the King of Spain Regent, and placing him at the head of the French army. They had won strong support in Brittany, in exchange for promises that the Spanish king would restore all the independence that province had enjoyed under Anne of Brittany; and on that account, the rebellious Bretons had agreed to welcome troops sent by Spain, and deliver up to them Port-Louis. Many persons were named, but I never discovered whether they included members of the Paris and Rennes parlements. If she also accused certain members of the Court, who appeared mightily disturbed, no one was arrested; but once again, I received no certain information.

When they questioned Laval, at the Bastille, he flew into a passion against the Duchesse du Maine, calling her every name under the sun, swearing that she was the last person he would have expected to be so weak and dishonourable as to inform on her friends, declaring he had not seen her, except publicly, for the past ten or twelve years, but eventually stating that she had inveigled him into taking part in the plot. He was thereupon induced to give further details, which reached the ears of M. le Duc d'Orléans, and of no one else, so far as I could judge, and even he did not hear all. One thing did emerge, namely that one night after supping at the Arsenal, Mme du Maine had set out secretly for a meeting with Cellamare. She had taken no servants; a few trusted allies rode inside and behind her coach, with Laval on the box instead of her usual coachman. They had no torches, and thus collided with another carriage, becoming so firmly entangled that they had all the trouble in the world to disengage, and were in mortal fear of being recognized.

Such were the avowals that won greater freedom for M. and Mme du Maine, and sent Cellamare's secretary into captivity at Saumur. They also

[1] Guy André de Montmorency, Marquis de Laval (1682–1745), known as 'Chinstrap' (*la Mentonnière*). Saint-Simon says he wore one partly because of a wound, partly so as to be noticed.

marked the beginning of an intrigue that deceived no one, since it was accompanied by assurances that the Duc du Maine had known nothing from start to finish; that the conspirators had been infinitely careful to keep him in ignorance because he was a coward (in trying to defend him they did not mince their words); that had he known and taken fright, all would have been lost and very probably confessed to M. le Duc d'Orléans. That piece of nonsense was Mme du Maine's idea; but M. du Maine abetted her with all his might, swearing to his entire ignorance, blindness, and utter imbecility in never even suspecting the existence of any plot.

M. le Duc d'Orléans told me all this before mentioning it to the Regency Council. To me, he appeared to scoff at the whole affair, ridiculing more especially the play-acting of M. and Mme du Maine. I only smiled, replying rather sarcastically that on the whole I would bank on her success because nothing is more effective than preaching to the converted, and thereupon I changed the subject. We had not discussed them for some considerable time. I knew that I was right, but knew also that the Abbé Dubois's influence was still paramount. You shall see what happened later, and to what point they succeeded in their mummery.

M. le Duc d'Orléans chose this time to give the King a charming present, which he was of the right age to appreciate. He handed over to him La Meute, as a pleasure house, and a place for picnics. The King was enchanted. He felt that he now had something of his very own, and it soon became his greatest treat to go there and consume bread and milk, fruit and salads, and to play his boyish games.[1] When the house changed hands, a new governor was appointed, and the Duc d'Humières mentioned Pezé's name.[2] I immediately had him appointed. He was clever in making it more and more delightful to the King, and at the same moment he received the post of Captain of the Bois de Boulogne; both appointments having previously been held by Rions.

Towards the end of October, M. le Duc d'Orléans (I cannot think who suggested the idea to him, for he was incapable of imagining it himself) desired the King to call him 'Uncle', when addressing him, instead of Monsieur, and this the King did thereafter. The late King had not admitted kinship with anyone except Monsieur and M. le Duc d'Orléans, whom he called respectively *Mon Frère* and *Mon Neveu* when he spoke to or of them. He never referred to his grandchildren or to Monseigneur. Very rarely he would say *Mon Fils*, but never on any occasion *Ma Sœur* in speaking to or of Madame.

Bezons, Archbishop of Rouen,[3] now entered the Regency Council,

[1] It was the fashion for the rich to have small country houses, near Paris, where they could go to drink fresh milk, and eat fruit and vegetables from the garden.

[2] Hubert de Courtavel, Marquis de Pezé (1680–1753). He already knew the little King well, having been a *gentilhomme de la manche* since 1716. His duties then were to walk close enough to the King to catch him by the sleeve if he tumbled.

[3] Armand Bazin de Bezons (1655–1721), Archbishop of Bordeaux 1698, of Rouen 1719.

where important matters were no longer debated or settled. The Abbé Dubois, since becoming secretary of State, had attended for foreign affairs; he was now made a full member. The increasing uselessness of this Council, which M. le Duc d'Orléans openly derided, not caring whom he appointed, made me acutely aware of the danger of his private sessions with Dubois, when all decisions were taken and from which (such was Dubois's influence) no information emerged, save to those needed to execute the orders. I therefore spoke out, saying that the Regency Council was a disgrace and an indignity to the original members; that the conferences in his study were a mistake, giving, as they did, more scope for the tongues of his enemies than when the nation's business was transacted in full Council, as in the early years of his regency. I declared that people could not feel the same confidence, and that suspicions might arise that could later be used to turn the King against him, requiring explanations and imputing evil motives which it would embarrass him to be forced to deny.

M. le Duc d'Orléans was the kind of man to admit very readily the truth of what one said, but the last person in the world to take any action. He said now that I might well be right; but considering the men who formed the Council, it was plain that their judgment could not be trusted. I smiled, and asked whose fault that was. 'True enough,' said he, 'but now that they are appointed, what can I do?' 'What can you do?' I replied, 'Something most necessary and at the same time quite easy; but you must be firm, and not care for their hurt feelings. They would not care for yours, as you well know. You must form a new Council of not more than four members, with yourself to make a fifth. Choose whom you wish, but such that the country may esteem and trust them. Let them be of whatever rank you please, but in order that they may be unbiased, attach them to no other department. Above all, hide nothing from them. Beware of little secret conferences with one person or another, especially with the heads of departments, who might use them for their own purposes. Now is your chance,' I urged, 'for everyone, including the members themselves, is well aware that the size and composition of the present Council renders it useless. They would infinitely prefer to see it formed anew, rather than leave the nation's affairs in the hands of the Abbé Dubois. You will not find it hard to choose your men. Since the King's death you have had ample opportunity to divide the strong from the weak, and to know the characters and ambitions of all possible candidates. Choose therefore, and reflect carefully; but act quickly for you have nothing more to learn, only to consider the various men and decide between them. I believe that you must do this; and to help you, I solemnly declare (and you know I never lie) that I should refuse a seat on a new Council. This will show you that my own ambitions are not involved; that I speak only for the good of the State and your own advantage.'

M. le Duc d'Orléans, with me by his side, took three or four turns up
and down the little gallery outside his winter study, head bent, saying
nothing, as was his custom when reflecting. He then turned to me, saying
that I was right and he would think about it. 'Think by all means,' said I,
'but not too long, for the facts are clear, and you have only to choose and
act.'

I left him thoughtful and disturbed. He knew how much my proposal
would vex the Abbé Dubois, and Dubois was his master. Yet he had
admitted the futility of the Regency Council, and the general discontent
that the Abbé should handle State affairs. As for the danger, if indeed he
was aware of it, the Rubicon had already been crossed; he had let himself
be bound to the English; neutral towards the Imperials, and half-engaged
in a most stupid, most disastrous war with Spain, whose only outcome
would be a personal quarrel with King Philip, and still closer ties with
England and the Emperor. That was exactly the result desired by the
unspeakable Dubois, for the sake of gaining a hat and becoming France's
first minister. This at least my proposal would have scotched, had it been
adopted in time, for a new Council would have known Dubois's intentions
and have stopped him. I saw, alas!, that it was only a dream, and that M.
le Duc d'Orléans would never be persuaded to act. I knew him too well to
hope or despair of anything ever coming from him.

The marketing of stock in the Bank of the Indies, now commonly called
the Mississippi Bank, had for some months past been taking place in the
Rue Quincampoix, from which all carriages and horses had been banned.
The business had so greatly increased that there were crowds all day long.
Guards had been set at either end, and drums and bells were sounded at
seven in the morning and in the evening, to mark the opening and closing
of the bank. On Sundays and feast-days the guard was doubled to keep
people out; such wild excitement was never known before. M. le Duc
d'Orléans proceeded to distribute vast amounts of stock to all the generals
engaged in the war with Spain, and to other ranks also. A month later, the
value of certain coins was three times lowered; this was followed by a
reminting of the entire coinage. Day by day, Law's bank and his joint-
stock company gained in favour. People trusted both completely, rushing
to turn their estates and houses into paper, with the result that everything
but paper cost more than ever before. Everyone's head was turned.
Foreigners envied our good fortune, and moved heaven and earth to share
it. Even the English, so clever and skilled with their banks, companies and
trade, caught the infection, and lived to repent it bitterly.

Meanwhile Law, despite his calm and sagacity, had begun to resent his
inferior status, and to think that his fame deserved the highest place.[1]
Dubois and M. le Duc d'Orléans were of the same opinion. Yet there was
no possibility of advancement for him without the removal of two great

[1] Law's ambition was to be Controller-General of the French finances.

obstacles. First, he was a foreigner, secondly, a heretic; and while the first might be dealt with by naturalization, the second could not. Thus conversion was essential, by a trustworthy converter, pledged not to inquire too deeply, or to fail in the attempt. Dubois had the very man, as it were up his sleeve; none other than the Abbé Tencin,[1] whom the devil has since hoisted to such incredible heights—for in very truth he sometimes abandons his general rule and rewards his own, so that others may be dazzled into obeying him.

This Abbé Tencin was a priest of no account, the great-great-grandson of a goldsmith,[2] son and brother of presidents of the Grenoble parlement. His real name was Guérin, Tencin being that of a small property which had served to ennoble the entire family.[3] He had two sisters, one of whom[4] lived in Paris, moving in high Society, the wife of a certain obscure M. Ferriol. The other,[5] a professed nun, was for many years with the Augustines of Montfleury, in the neighbourhood of Grenoble. Both were pretty, lively, and vastly agreeable. Mme Ferriol was the kinder and more amusing; Mme Tencin scintillated, but was an adventuress and a thoroughgoing wanton. Her charms brought all Grenoble society to her convent, where access was easy, and the conduct of the nuns such that no reproaches by Cardinal Le Camus[6] could reform it. The chief attraction was that of finding, at the end of the prettiest walk imaginable, a pleasant house for which all the best families had provided nuns. The liberties they enjoyed, which Mme Tencin thoroughly exploited, served only to make her impatient of her few remaining chains;[7] she found a nun's habit, the vestige of a rule (though almost totally ignored), a cloister (though freely visited by both sexes) from which she could seldom absent herself, to be intolerable burdens for one who wished to cut a figure in the world and felt ripe for intrigue. She therefore fabricated some form of an excuse and departed, resolved never to return.

[1] The Abbé Pierre Guérin de Tencin (1679–1758). Abbot of Vézelay 1702, Doctor of the Sorbonne 1705, Archbishop of Embrun 1724, Cardinal 1739, minister of State 1742.

[2] Pierre Guérin, the goldsmith who founded the family fortune, and lived in the sixteenth century.

[3] It was the land that was ennobled, a Seigneurie, a Comté, a Duché, according to the number of soldiers its owner was traditionally bound to raise for the King in wartime. Owners took their titles from their estates—hence the particule, *de*. Yet Saint-Simon never allowed the '*de* to grace the Tencins. Others might say 'de Tencin'; to him they were still from the gutter.

[4] Marie Angélique de Tencin (1674–1736) married Augustin de Ferriol, Comte de Pont-de-Veyle (1662–1737). She knew Voltaire, and had been the mistress of Vauban and of Torcy.

[5] Claudine Alexandrine Guérin de Tencin (1682–1749), called Mme de Tencin. Nuns, like the cooks in Edwardian households, were always given the status of married women.

[6] Cardinal Étienne Le Camus (died 1707) was Louis XIV's almoner and Bishop of Grenoble. He gained his hat in 1686. When he tried to apply a severer rule to the convent of Montfleury, the nuns raised such an outcry about cruelty that he was forced to give way.

[7] Saint-Simon means her religious duties. In 1698, when she was sixteen, she had been placed in the convent because money was lacking for a dowry. She was freed from her vows in 1712. Though irreligious, she had principles. 'I regard self-love,' she wrote, 'which is the origin of all movement, as the celestial fluid in which we swim.'

Mme Tencin and her brother the abbé were one in heart and soul, if they may be said to have possessed either. She was his *alter ego*, and he hers. He so well supported her by his tact and cunning that he kept her afloat for many years in good Parisian Society, fully sharing in her diversions and intrigues, despite the fact that her religious status remained, and that she was generally known as 'Tencin the nun'. Her adventures none the less caused a scandal; yet brother and sister lived together throughout that period,[1] and managed so skilfully that no one openly attacked the worldliness and debauchery of a professed nun, who had shed her habit on her own authority. Volumes might be written of this unworthy pair who, despite such great handicaps, contrived by charm and intelligence to make excellent friends. Towards the end of the late King's life, Rome was at last persuaded to release Mme Tencin from her vows, appointing her cannoness of some convent, which I know not, for she never visited it. That happy solution produced no appreciable change in her name, dress, or behaviour, and provoked no scandal. Thus matters stood until after the King's death, soon after which she became the Abbé Dubois's mistress. It was not long before she was also his confidant, then his guide in many of his secret enterprises. They concealed their relationship for some considerable time, during the period when Dubois needed some semblance of respectability; but when he was made archbishop, and later cardinal, she appeared as his official mistress,[2] openly ruling his house, and holding court at her own as the true fountain of all favours and fortunes. It was she who started her beloved brother on the road to power by introducing him to her then secret lover, who received him with open arms, as one who would support him wholeheartedly and be infinitely useful.

The Abbé Tencin himself had a bold and crafty mind that enabled him to pose as a man of prudence and sagacity. He had endless patience, directed always to his self-appointed goal,[3] never swerving, never dismayed by obstruction, ever ready with ideas and expedients that falsely gained for him a reputation for ability. Immensely cunning, hypocritical, tactful, flattering, discreet, sweet or bitter as the times required, he was a master of intrigue, with a sovereign contempt for honour and religion while carefully maintaining an appearance of both. Above all, he hungered for wealth, not

---

[1] Gossip and street ballads accused them of incest, and not even Mme de Tencin denied the rumour. In eighteenth-century France, incest and accusations of incest seem to have been not uncommon among the 'best people'; for example, the Regent and his daughter, Voltaire and his niece. In fact, the Tencins did not live together, but next door to one another, in the Rue Neuve-Saint-Augustin, near the Porte Saint-Honoré.

[2] To be fair to Mme Tencin, it would seem that Saint-Simon exaggerates. She was not publicly Dubois's mistress; it was publicly known that he was her lover, which is a rather different thing.

[3] The Abbé Tencin's goal was not so much his as his sister's for him. He wrote to her, 'Ten years of life are more to me than earning a fortune.' He did not really want to be a cardinal, still less France's first minister; his real desire was to be allowed to live quietly in his diocese, tending his flock; which he managed to do only after his sister's death.

from avarice or any wish to make a show, but purely as a means of delivering himself from his own nonentity.[1]

Such was the apostle whom Dubois sent to proselytize a man of Law's quality. They were already well acquainted; for having, from the beginning, been aware of Mme Tencin's influence, Law had striven to cultivate her good will, and she, ever following her own and her brother's advantage, had allowed him to stuff them both with paper, which she then very prudently had turned into gold.[2] Things had reached this point when the question arose of restoring to the Church's bosom a Protestant or an Anglican, for Law did not rightly know what he should be called. As you may imagine, the task was not a hard one; but they had the good sense to be secret. Thus nothing emerged for certain, and they were spared the customary interval for instruction and for belief to take root. They also avoided some of the scandal and mockery inevitable with such a conversion by such a missionary.

It seems to me that I have long passed the time when I should have described the situation between myself and Fleury, Bishop of Fréjus. We had gone different ways in different company during the late King's lifetime; and though we had friends in common, I had had no dealings with him. But there was no ill feeling on either side, and when we chanced to meet we were very civil, without overstepping the bounds of pleasantry in general conversation, and without desiring closer acquaintance. When he left his diocese to become the King's tutor, we were differently employed. Vincennes was a further separation, and it was not until some months after the King's arrival in Paris that we caught more than a passing glimpse of one another. I have reason to believe that Monsieur de Fréjus was not content with that situation.

As you may remember, it was Mme de Levis who had helped to win him his appointment. She was lively, highly strung, passionately partisan, judging everyone by the light of her affections or, contrariwise, loathing them with as little reason. In truth, she was mad about Monsieur de Fréjus, but mad in all innocence, for despite her raptures, or the reverse, there never was a woman more honourable, virtuous, pious, and well principled. She was the Duc de Chevreuse's daughter and therefore my dear friend, and she had always been on the closest and most affectionate terms with Mme de Saint-Simon. One evening when we were chatting together, she began to talk of Monsieur de Fréjus, reproaching me for not liking him. I showed my surprise, for I had no reason to like or to dislike him. That, however, did not satisfy her, and she several times returned to the subject. I answered amiably enough, having no cause to do otherwise, and at last he addressed me himself, in the King's room, where we had a short con-

[1] 'No matter what you say,' he wrote to his sister, 'you will never convince me that I am worth very much.'
[2] She made a fortune which brought them a handsome income for the rest of their lives.

versation. A few days later he appeared at dinner-time, inviting me to return and dine with him. Thereafter he came fairly often, sometimes staying to dinner, and I frequently spent part of the evening with him. As I said earlier,[1] he conversed well and was most excellent company, having lived all his life in scholarly and well-bred Society. When we came to know one another better, general conversation gave place to discussions on many important matters.

One evening, shortly after he took up his tutorial duties, I was with him when they brought in a package. It was late, and he was sitting beside his fire, in his dressing-gown, with his nightcap on his head. I rose to go, so as to let him open his parcel; but he prevented me, saying that it was only the King's essays, returned corrected by the Jesuits.[2] In truth he needed the assistance of their scholarship, for all he knew was how to behave in good Society and to be charming to ladies, in the *ruelles*.[3] Hearing him mention the King's essays, I inquired somewhat disapprovingly whether he intended to teach him much Latin; but he said no, only so much as to render him familiar with that tongue. After that, we agreed that history was what he should learn thoroughly, and more especially the history of France. I was then struck with an idea, which I immediately mentioned, of a means by which the King might imbibe a vast amount of learning all his life, in a most agreeable manner. I proceeded to explain how Gaignières,[4] a man of great wisdom and scholarship, had spent his entire life research-ing into history, and, with much diligence, huge expense, and many journeys for that sole purpose, had amassed an enormous collection of portraits of men and women of all sorts and conditions who had become famous in France since the time of Louis XI, including a small number of foreigners. I had seen part of this collection at his home; but there were so many that he could not hang them all, not even in the great house where he lived alone, opposite the Hospital for Incurables. When he died, Gaignières had left all this valuable and instructive accumulation to the King.[5]

In the young King's schoolroom, at the Tuileries, there was a small door

[1] In a character-sketch, 1698, not included in this version, Saint-Simon describes him as 'extremely handsome, marvellously well made in his youth, and still retaining that appearance to the end of his life, when his face became, if possible, even more pleasing. Modest and discreet, he had the ability and good fortune to be at first suffered, then welcomed in the very best Society, and to find protectors and influential friends among the most important men and women at the Court, in the administration, and high in the King's favour.'

[2] The Jesuit teachers at the college of Saint-Louis-le-Grand.

[3] The space between the bed and the wall, where visitors sat when they called on ladies lying in their beds. The wittiest conversations and the most lively were supposed to take place in the *ruelles*.

[4] François Roger de Gaignières (1642–1715). He had been an equerry of the last Duc de Guise. A historian, he formed a collection of engravings and drawings, as well as of painted portraits.

[5] Gaignières presented his collection to Louis XIV in 1711, four years before the King's death.

leading into a long and splendid gallery[1] that remained altogether un-furnished. The doorway was filled in, and the gallery itself had been roughly partitioned to form a dormitory for the Maréchal de Villeroy's servants. I asked Monsieur de Fréjus whether lodgings might not be taken for them in the neighbourhood—a thousand francs would have gone far to cover the cost; then, with the door reopened, the entire gallery could be hung with Gaignières's pictures, now probably rotting in some damp warehouse. The tutors of the small boys who paid their court to the King could show them the portraits, and encourage them to find out more by reading history and memoirs; and by that means they would chatter about them as they followed the King. Monsieur de Fréjus, leading His Majesty through the gallery, would further instruct him, and thus teach him history, with many anecdotes useful for a king to know, and which he would hear in no other way. He would be struck by the unfamiliar faces and costumes, and so find it easy to remember the names and dates of the sitters. The other boys' interest would stimulate him to outshine them, for he would take pride in knowing more than they.[2]

Religion and politics would not falsely colour the birth, lives, and actions of persons so long dead, and thus the King might gradually come to learn of good deeds and bad, how fortunes are won and lost, of the intrigues which cunning men may use to gain their ends by deceiving, in-fluencing, or confounding kings—in a word, all the modes of the Court, of which the lives of those men and women would furnish examples. Such pleasant collective instruction might continue up to the reign of Henri IV; when the King should be put on his honour, by making him understand that the knowledge of those persons who lived after must be for him alone, because the immediate descendants of their families and friends might still be alive. I ended by declaring that this form of education might later prove to have been the best of all, for it could continue throughout his life, and the very sight of a portrait would serve to remind him. Monsieur de Fréjus appeared delighted, but nothing was done, and it was borne in on me that there would be no change. I therefore said no more of portraits or the gallery, where the Maréchal de Villeroy's servants remained in possession.

One day towards the end of the year, I was working as usual with M. le Duc d'Orléans when, after a quarter of an hour, he interrupted me to complain most bitterly of the Maréchal de Villeroy. He was wont to let fly at him from time to time; but on this occasion his anger was extreme. He sprang up suddenly, declaring that he had gone too far (those were his words), that he wished and was determined to dismiss him, and, im-mediately afterwards, that he desired me to become the King's governor.

[1] In the wing of the Louvre that runs along the Quai des Tuileries.
[2] This would have been the education which Saint-Simon himself would best have liked. 'I had a natural love for reading and history... I have often thought that... had they encouraged me to make it my serious study, I might indeed have made something of myself.' See I, pp. 3-4.

Though completely dumbfounded, I kept my head, merely smiling, and saying that he must not give that a second thought. 'What?' he exclaimed, 'I have already thought of it, and am quite decided. It should have been done long ago. What have you against it?' and so saying he began to stride up and down, or rather to spin like a top round and round in his little winter study. I asked if he had sufficiently reflected, and he thereupon gave me his reasons for dismissing the Maréchal and putting me in his place—reasons far too flattering for me to record them here. I let him finish and then spoke, refusing to be interrupted.

I agreed with all he said of the Maréchal de Villeroy because there was no gainsaying his complaints or his conclusions; but I did most strongly oppose his dismissal. I reminded M. le Duc d'Orléans of my reasons for opposing the Duc du Maine's removal from his post as superintendent; how sensible he had thought them, and how he had yielded only to the importunities of Monsieur le Duc. I compared that situation with the present one, trying to show him the difference between dismissing even a powerful man when the princes and great mass of the people detested him, and removing another who, though stupid and worthless, was adored by Society and the rabble because he appeared harmless. I expanded on all this for some considerable time, giving many other reasons, and answering all his arguments.

M. le Duc d'Orléans was shaken but still unconvinced. He tried to move me by stressing the great honour, and praising me to the skies. I expressed my gratitude, being truly conscious of the extreme distinction, and his graciousness in offering it. But at the same time, I was in no way dazzled. I once more reminded him of what had happened at the King's death, how King Louis had added a codicil to his will, written with his own hand, by which the education of his successor was taken out of the Regent's hands. Even had he not done so, I added, it was highly desirable that these posts should be beyond the Regent's control, for should the young King die, and he, M. le Duc d'Orléans, succeed because of the Renunciations, all those dreadful suspicions and accusations might be revived. For that reason, I said, he should never, in any circumstances, appoint a friend to any post connected with the King's education or his service, especially not one who was known to be deeply attached to himself. He had seen the wisdom of my arguments on that earlier occasion. Looking back at all that had happened since then, and particularly to the banishment of the Duc du Maine, my reasons appeared still better now, and, as things stood at that moment, I was the last man in all France whom he should choose. Moreover, if I accepted, I should be doing him a cruel disservice.

I have never known a man more ready with his answers than M. le Duc d'Orléans, even when he had nothing worth saying. Now, however, he was so much surprised, so much impressed by my words, or by the firmness of my refusal, that he was reduced to silence as he marched seven or eight steps up, and the same number down, his study which, as I have said, was very small indeed. I remained standing, leaving him to his reflections, for I did not wish to trouble him with useless repetition. There was a long pause, after which he declared that there was much good sense in what I had said, but that the Maréchal de Villeroy had become so intolerable, and I so well suited to the post, that he found it hard to change his mind, but would none the less think again. I thereupon exclaimed that as far as I was concerned that was the end, for most certainly I should never become the King's governor. He spoke again, but not so firmly, and I contrived gradually to convince him, until he at last agreed to put it out of his mind, and leave the Maréchal de Villeroy in office. Yet despite my advice he allowed his displeasure to appear, with the result that the Maréchal treated him with unutterable haughtiness. I was sorry for it, but dared not reproach him, for fear of his changing his mind and dismissing him. In any event, things were going so badly, with the Abbé Dubois clearly master of the country, and the shameful conclusion to the affair of M. and Mme du Maine, that I felt too much disgusted to interfere further. Thenceforward I saw M. le Duc d'Orléans only briefly, when the need arose, taking care to give the inquisitive no reason to suspect me. So ended the year 1719.

CHAPTER VI

1720

The Duchesse du Maine's excuses deceive no one – Adventures of the Abbé d'Entragues – Beginnings of the failure of Law's bank – Dubois, becoming Archbishop of Cambrai, is first ordained, then consecrated at Val-de-Grâce – M. le Duc d'Orléans attends that ceremony – Death of Madame la Duchesse – Catastrophe of the Comte d'Horn – Birth of the Infante Philip – Death and oddness of the Marquise d'Alluyes – Law's bank: the State edict of 22 May – The Regent wishes me to take the seals – I refuse them – The seals removed from Argenson and returned to Chancellor Daguesseau – Retirement of Argenson – Operations of the stock market – Death of Dangeau – His Mémoires – Marriage of the Duc de Lorges to Mlle de Mesmes – Law's departure

THE YEAR BEGAN with a perfectly ridiculous piece of mummery by which no one was deceived—not the public, nor those at whom it was aimed, nor even the actors themselves, except perhaps Madame la Princesse, who was of a nature to be gulled by anything. You will remember that the treacherous Abbé Dubois had given M. and Mme du Maine ample time, and more, in which to destroy their papers and make their plans, after Cellamare's arrest and before their own. Both had behaved in character. Mme du Maine, shielded by her sex and birth, took all the blame upon herself at her interrogation. Having no fear of losing her head, or of any long term of imprisonment, she had told all frankly, perfectly reassured by the example of the Princes de Condé in earlier times, who had escaped lightly after doing far worse.[1]

Her husband, on the other hand, no longer protected by the rank and dignity of a prince of the blood, trembled for his life. He continually asserted his total ignorance; and since he had seen none but his trusted allies, and Cellamare only in the strict seclusion of Mme du Maine's boudoir, he had nothing to fear from documents or depositions. When he was informed of his wife's confession, he flew into a rage, abusing her for treachery and folly, cursing fate for giving him a conspiratorial wife bold enough to act without him, who thus had made him appear guilty when all the time he was perfectly innocent. From then onwards, he would not hear her name mentioned, and after they were released and allowed to write and

---

[1] During the nobles' rebellion (the *Fronde*) against Mazarin, 1648–1653.

visit, would neither receive her letters nor show her any sign of life. Such was the situation when they were brought nearer Paris. The Duc du Maine was taken to Clagny, a house quite close to Versailles, originally built for Mme de Montespan.[1] Mme du Maine returned to Sceaux. They each saw M. le Duc d'Orléans separately, but did not stay in Paris, and since the Abbé Dubois thought it was time to win merit in their eyes and end their disgrace, all went to perfection at their audiences.

During their stay at these country houses, where they received few callers, Mme du Maine falsely gave it out that she had made several attempts to see her husband, but had each time been rebuffed. They kept up this pretence from the month of January, when they first arrived at Clagny and Sceaux, until the end of July. They then decided to risk a further advance; for trusting in the good offices of the Abbé Dubois, they were counting on their eventual restoration, and planning to visit Paris, which they could not do without sharing a lodging.

They carried to such lengths this trumped-up quarrel that their two sons, who arrived at Clagny a few days after the Duc du Maine, were kept from seeing their mother for several weeks. Thereafter permission was given for rare visits, but on no account were they to sleep at Sceaux. When the time came for the farce to end, this is how it was done. Madame la Princesse made an appointment to meet M. du Maine at the house of a certain Landais,[2] paymaster-general of the artillery. She came accompanied by the Duchesse du Maine, but left her sitting in the coach. She then informed M. du Maine that she had a lady with her who desired of all things to meet him. The affair was not hard to manage since all was pre-arranged, and the duchess was immediately sent for. There was a scene of reconciliation, enacted privately between the three of them, who were closeted a long while together. For the finale, they stayed apart, but visited one another more and more frequently, gradually coming closer until, at last, the Duc du Maine returned to live with her at Sceaux.

During those six months the Bastille was slowly emptied of the persons involved in this affair. Some were sent into easy exile for short periods. Laval fared worse or, to speak truly, was less well treated. He had been the moving spirit, externally, of the conspiracy and knew all the secrets of the Duc and Duchesse du Maine; and they so thoroughly blackened his character at their interrogations, at least in those parts which were read aloud at the Regency Council, that there was no possible doubt of his guilt. He emerged from the Bastille in a rage, and never afterwards forgave Mme du Maine, for which she cared nothing, in the manner of all princes and princesses when they no longer need people. They believe they own the world, and owe no duty except to themselves. The events of all periods

[1] His mother.
[2] Étienne Landais de Montroy, paymaster-general of the artillery, of which the Duc du Maine was Colonel-General.

and the conspiracies that occur in each century show how true this is and point the moral.

Another event that occurred at this time deserves mentioning, because of the extraordinary life and oddness of the person concerned. The Abbé d'Entragues[1] had always been accustomed to mix in extremely high Society. His real name was Balzac; I do not know how they came to be called d'Entragues, for the Balzacs originated at Illiers. Be that as it may, this man's family were Crémeaux, gentlefolk in a very small way, hailing from near Lyons. The manner of their getting into Society was through the marriage of his brother to the half-sister of Mme de La Vallière, a mistress of the late King. Mme la Princesse de Conti,[2] who never forgot her mother or her mother's family, protected them, and thus the Abbé d'Entragues was brought into good company, for which he was as to the manner born, with an additional touch of pleasant eccentricity that made him highly entertaining. He was that by nature, but one could not rely on his amiability, for he was a mischief-maker, loving to meddle and set people by the ears, which caused his banishment from several great houses. He acquired abbeys and priories, but never received the Order.

The Abbé d'Entragues was tall, exceedingly handsome, but of an unwonted pallor, which he increased by constant bleedings, and referred to as his delicate complexion. He was in the habit of sleeping with his arms suspended over his head, so as to improve the beauty of his hands, and always, though he wore an abbé's dress, put it on in such an unorthodox manner that people stared at him. More than once he was exiled for debauchery, and on one occasion was sent to Caen at a time when the *Grands-jours*[3] were being held there. Le Peletier de Souzy[4] happened to be one of the judges, and since he had some slight acquaintance with the abbé, he thought it would be polite to visit him. He called on him at midday, and was shown into a scrupulously clean bedroom, with a bed to match, the curtains all opened. Sitting up in bed, doing tapestry work, was a person very elegantly attired, wearing a lady's mob-cap with a lace frill and several knots of ribbon securing it, a set of jewels, cascades of ribbons falling from the throat, a flounced bed-jacket, and patches. Believing that he had strayed into a harlot's chamber, Le Peletier recoiled, apologizing, towards the door, which was not far; but the person called him, begged him to approach, gave his own name, and burst out laughing. It was the Abbé d'Entragues himself, who often slept thus accoutred, and always

---

[1] Bernard Angélique de Crémeaux, Abbé d'Entragues (1650–1733). He was Abbot of Joux-Drieux, a small abbey in Beaujolais, and had been exiled from Paris, for debauchery, 1694–1700.

[2] The Dowager Mme la Princesse de Conti, to whom this refers, was the legitimized daughter of Louis XIV and Mme de La Vallière.

[3] Under the Ancien Régime, judges from the Paris Parlement held periodical sittings to try offences in the provinces, more especially crimes committed by the nobles.

[4] Michel Le Peletier de Souzy (1640–1725). He was director-general of fortifications, 1691–1715, and a member of the Regency Council. See index, II.

with a lady's nightcap and ribbons perched more or less firmly on his head. There are so many stories of him that one might never end the telling of them. Yet he was a man of parts, excellent in conversation, well read, with a good memory, even some learning, and a most pure and elegant turn of phrase. He was, moreover, remarkably abstemious, except regarding fruit and water.

At the time of which I speak, he spent his life in Mme la Princesse de Conti's drawing-room, or with Beringhem, the master of the horse, and in some other great houses where he was still received. Suddenly it was learned beyond all shadow of doubt that he had taken Communion one Sunday with the Dutch ambassador's household.[1] He actually boasted of it, saying that he loved taking Communion with his brothers. What was particularly shocking was that he came of a Catholic family and until that moment had seemed unable to fix his attention on any form of religion. The scandal caused by this piece of folly, and the outcry among the clergy prevented M. le Duc d'Orléans from ignoring the matter, as he would have wished to do. Shortly afterwards he felt obliged to have him arrested and taken to the Bastille. In the interval, however, the abbé had taken ship and left the country. From Anchin, where he disembarked, it was a quick and easy journey to Tournai, but for some unknown reason he continued on to Lille and reported himself to the commandant. Couriers had been sent to alert the frontier forts, and Lille, one of the nearest, was already on the watch. The commandant forthwith arrested him and sent word to M. le Duc d'Orléans, who ordered his imprisonment in that fortress. Such incarceration was not at all palatable to the abbé. He speedily recanted, and was allowed to return to Paris. Nothing more was done to him, nor were his benefices confiscated, and since no one believed that anything serious could emanate from so frivolous a man, he was welcomed back to the drawing-rooms of Madame la Duchesse, Mme la Princesse de Conti, and Mme du Maine, as well as to the other great houses he had been wont to frequent, as though he had done nothing wrong. For some time thereafter he made a point of carrying an enormous breviary whenever he attended mass; then gradually he relapsed into his former ways. Yet despite his depravity and strange habits, and the gambling that often led him into trouble, he continued all his life to give generously to the poor, and, notwithstanding the fruit and ices that he consumed in such vast quantities, lived free of infirmities for more than eighty years. He bore with courage and piety the long illness from which he eventually died, and thus ended in most Christian fashion a life that in other ways was very far from the Christian ideal.

[1] It was a crime against the Church to take Communion with heretics, and was punishable by death. In 1766, the Chevalier de La Barre was tortured and most cruelly executed because he would not remove his hat to a religious procession. He was judged guilty of being a heretic because of this and other such blasphemies.

Law's system was drawing to its close. Had they been content to allow him only his bank, keeping it within safe and prudent limits, they might have doubled the money in the realm and afforded immense assistance to commerce and private enterprises. Had the bank at all times been ready to meet its creditors, the notes it issued would have had all the value of coins, and sometimes have been more convenient, on account of the greater facility of transport. Yet, as I had told M. le Duc d'Orléans in his study, and boldly stated in the Regency Council during the debate on the bank, such an undertaking might be good in itself, but could function effectively only in a republic, or a constitutional monarchy such as England, where the finances are in the control of those who provide them, supplying as much or as little as they think fit, and in the manner that best suits them. In France, with its absolute monarchy, there must inevitably be less stability and therefore less confidence, in the proper sense of the word. An absolute monarch, or those acting in his name, a mistress, for example, a minister, a favourite, or worse a great national disaster such as the late King experienced in the years 1707, 1708, 1709, and 1710, might entirely destroy a bank whose attractions are obvious, yet too insecurely based. If to the solid merits of such a bank are added, as indeed they were, the mirage of a Mississippi Scheme, a joint-stock company, a technical language, a trickster's method of extracting money from Peter in order to pay Paul, the entire establishment, possessing neither gold-mines nor the philosopher's stone, must necessarily end in ruin, leaving a tiny minority enriched by the total ruin of all the rest of the people. That, in fact, is what actually happened.

One factor that greatly hastened the collapse of the bank and of Law's whole system was the irresponsible generosity of M. le Duc d'Orléans, who gave away, almost indiscriminately, vast amounts of stock because he could not resist importunate demands, even from persons whom he knew to be his enemies and utterly despicable. He gave liberally to all who asked; not only that, he let money pass into the hands of those who openly sneered at him, and praised only their own daring. This was scarcely believable, even by those who saw it with their own eyes. Posterity will think it a lie, and we ourselves will come to remember it as though it had been a nightmare. In the end, so much stock was bestowed on those greedy spendthrifts who demanded more and more, yet were always on the verge of penury because of their love of luxury, their lawlessness, and neglect of rank, that paper itself became scarce, the mills being unable to provide sufficient.

In view of this, you will perceive how shamefully abused was that bank which was meant to serve as an ever present resource, constantly needing most delicate adjustments so as to enable it to meet its contractual obligations. That was the question I tried to discuss with Law when he visited me each Tuesday morning. Time and again he put me off, before confessing that he was worried, and complaining nervously of the Regent who, so he said, was playing ducks and drakes with the finances. I knew more than he believed, which prompted me to persist, questioning him ever more closely regarding his balance sheet. After that, perceiving that there could be no further concealment, he stated mildly enough that he had sufficient funds, if only M. le Duc d'Orléans would allow him to manage them. That, however, failed to convince me.

Before long confidence in the bank diminished; its notes became first unpopular, then discredited. It was soon necessary to compel their acceptance, and at the first show of force, the public lost all hope. An edict was then passed forbidding the use of gold or silver coins, on the pretext that from the time of Abraham until the present day, nations had greatly sinned by exchanging coins and the precious metals that composed them. It was argued that paper served the purpose equally well, and that, when we paraded our gold and silver, we did immense harm to less fortunate peoples by making them jealous of our wealth and superiority.

The bank's inspectors were then authorized to search the great houses, even including royal palaces, and to confiscate all the gold and silver écus that they found, leaving only coins worth twenty sous or less, to a total of two hundred francs, for use in giving change, and in buying food and other necessities. Strict orders were issued against hoarding, and dire punishments were threatened. As a result, everyone obediently took their coins to the bank, fearing lest a servant betray them. As you may imagine, no one saw any justice in the bank's assumption of such despotic power, and it was accordingly used even more tyrannically. Private houses were searched, and spies employed to bring offenders to trial. The daily life of the community had never before, in all history, been so much obstructed. It was by a miracle rather than by any action of the government that there was not a revolution, and that from the millions ruined or dying of starvation nothing was heard beyond groans and supplications. The tyranny was too flagrant, too thoroughly iniquitous to continue for long, and soon the authorities felt obliged to resort to further issues of paper-money, and new feats of juggling. The public recognized these for what they were, but submitted rather than risk a ban on keeping even twenty écus in the safety of their homes. The dread of harsher measures to follow made people glad to accept the lesser evil. There were indeed many other prohibitions and restrictions, all aimed at replacing one kind of bank note by another. The intention was always the same, to bring loss to the holders of earlier issues. Yet those holders had been forced to accept the notes, and they formed the great bulk of the nation.

Such affairs occupied the time of the finance department, and the entire life of M. le Duc d'Orléans. It all ended by Law's being driven from the country, a sixfold rise in the price of bread and other foodstuffs, a ruinous increase in wages and salaries, and the destruction of commerce, both public and private. At the expense of the whole nation, a few nobles suddenly acquired vast wealth and dissipated it just as quickly, becoming in the twinkling of an eye even poorer than they had been before, and, in the process, enabling the lawyers' clerks to make their fortunes. In the confusion, millions were amassed by the lowest of the low—assistants of tax-farmers, and bankers' agents, who promptly and skilfully enriched themselves by the Mississippi Scheme and its disastrous consequences. Many years after M. le Duc d'Orléans's death, the government was still occupied with such problems; indeed, despite a considerable increase in the value of land, it is not too much to say that France may never completely recover.

On Sunday, 18 February, the King attended the Regency Council for the first time. He spoke neither on entering, nor during the meeting, nor even when he left, except when M. le Duc d'Orléans, fearing lest he might be bored, suggested his going, and then he only said that he preferred to stay until the end. After that he came, not every time but fairly often, and always stayed the whole time, without fidgeting or interrupting. His presence made no difference, because his armchair always stood alone at the head of the table, for M. le Duc d'Orléans had an ordinary *tabouret* like the rest of us, whether the King came or not. A few days later the Duke of Berwick[1] joined the Council. There were protests because of his being a foreigner; but foreigner or no, he was outlawed by his own country and an exile; a Frenchman by adoption who had lived thirty-two years in France, serving continually in our army; a duke and peer; a Marshal of France; a Grandee of Spain; a general in the armies of both countries, and of proven loyalty. Furthermore, considering the kind of business then done at the Council, its composition mattered very little. We were fifteen already; the Duke of Berwick made us sixteen—that was all. One day when the King attended his little cat followed him, jumping up on to his knee and thence on to the table.[2] The Duc de Noailles made a terrible outcry because he was afraid of cats, and M. le Duc d'Orléans set about removing it; but I smiled, saying, 'Oh! leave it, Sir; it merely makes us seventeen.'[3] At that, M. le Duc d'Orléans laughed aloud and looked at the assembled company who laughed with him. The King joined in the laughter, and reminded me of it next morning at his *petit-lever* as though he understood the joke; but he said only a couple of words. The tale was all round Paris in the twinkling of an eye.

At this time there was a vacancy at Cambrai, caused by the death of Cardinal de La Trémoïlle. Cambrai was the richest see in all France, and

[1] James Fitzjames, Duke of Berwick (1671–1734), natural son of James II and Arabella Churchill, Marlborough's sister.

[2] The King often brought his cat to meetings of the Council. The members called it his colleague.

[3] Saint-Simon was becoming increasingly tired, depressed, disillusioned. The tone of the memoirs alters. He seems to have given up hope for the Regent and the better government of France, and to be hankering for a Court and rank and splendid ceremonial. His eyes turn to Spain, and when the opportunity presents itself in the following year, he is most eager to seize it.

one of the highest posts in the Church. The Abbé Dubois was no more than tonsured;[1] but a stipend of a hundred and fifty thousand livres was a great temptation, and he may have envisaged it as a long step towards that cardinalate which he so longed for. Yet bold though he was, and firm as his hold had become over M. le Duc d'Orléans, he preferred to use a subterfuge rather than ask for the archbishopric outright. He thus told M. le Duc d'Orléans that he had had a happy dream, in which he had seen himself Archbishop of Cambrai. Perceiving his intention, the Regent turned on his heel, without answering. Dubois, increasingly embarrassed, stammered and tried to change the subject; then somewhat recovering, he asked point-blank why he should be refused, since by that one stroke His Highness might make his fortune. M. le Duc d'Orléans, not usually over-scrupulous in the appointment of bishops, was shocked, even somewhat alarmed. He turned to Dubois saying contemptuously, 'You, Archbishop of Cambrai! A man like you!', making him feel not only his commonness, but also his notoriously dissolute way of life. Dubois however had the bit between his teeth, and dashed away quoting precedents. There were unhappily plenty to choose from among the vermin, eccentrics, and perverts appointed by Godet, Bishop of Chartres, who had filled the dioceses with his seminarians, most of them from the gutter, and all utterly worthless. M. le Duc d'Orléans was shaken; less by such hollow arguments than by his inability to stand against a man whom he dared not even contradict. He tried to escape by exclaiming, 'You shark! Where will you ever find another willing to consecrate you?' 'Oh!' said Dubois, 'if that is all, the deed is as good as done; for there is a man in the next room who will be glad to officiate.' 'Who the devil can you mean?' exclaimed the Regent, 'No one would dare.' 'Supposing I produced him,' replied Dubois, 'would that remove the last objection?' 'Well, name him,' said the Regent. 'Why, your own first almoner.[2] He is outside at this very moment, and you will see that he is delighted. I will go quickly to tell him the good news.' So saying, Dubois knelt to kiss M. le Duc d'Orléans's knee, leaving him speechless, vanished into the adjoining room, where he seized hold of the Bishop of Nantes, whispering that he had Cambrai and wished him to officiate (to which Monsieur de Nantes at once consented), and went bounding back to tell M. le Duc d'Orléans that his first almoner had agreed to consecrate him. He then thanked, praised, flattered, clinched the matter by taking the appointment for granted, and thus convinced the Regent that it was beyond his power to object further. That is how the Abbé Dubois was promoted to Cambrai.[3]

[1] He had taken only the first step preparatory to entering the priesthood. For the title Abbé, see note 2, p. 53 above.

[2] Louis de La Vergne, Abbé de Tressan (1670–1733), Bishop of Nantes 1716, Archbishop of Rouen 1723, first almoner of the Duc d'Orléans since 1706.

[3] This story is not confirmed by contemporary sources; but Saint-Simon may have heard everything from the Regent.

There was an appalling scandal, and despite all his effrontery, Dubois felt considerably embarrassed. As for M. le Duc d'Orléans, he was so much ashamed that he would hardly speak to him—which everyone noticed. The next difficulty for Dubois was having to take Holy Orders, though he flattered himself that for him the path would be smoothed, more especially as Cardinal de Noailles[1] so much needed his services in the, to him, agonizing matter of the constitution. Dubois was never more mistaken; material considerations were never of any moment with that prelate. The abbé's vices were well known to him. It horrified him to think of moving a finger to assist him in taking Holy Orders, although he fully understood the effect of a refusal on a man so powerful with the Regent, and sure to feel deeply and personally insulted. M. de Noailles knew that he must bear the weight of Dubois's displeasure for the remainder of his life; yet nothing deflected him. Looking sad and humble, but quite immovable, he refused to sign a dispensation for the minor orders. No words escaped him; he was content to do his duty with all the charity and forbearance which the circumstances allowed. You may well believe that Dubois was affronted and that he never forgave the cardinal, who was none the less universally applauded, with paeans of praise and admiration, which he would gladly have forgone.

So the Abbé Dubois was obliged to look elsewhere, and his eye lit on the Maréchal de Bezons's brother,[2] whose devotion to the Regent had brought him rich rewards. He had recently been transferred from the Archdiocese of Bordeaux to that of Rouen, in which lay Pontoise, only a few leagues distant from Paris. To Dubois, eager to save time, and spare himself the trouble of a long journey, Bezons seemed likely to be more malleable than Cardinal de Noailles; and so he proved, for the dispensation was granted without delay. Dubois then obtained the Pope's consent to his receiving all the minor orders at one and the same time, and himself dispensed with the need for the preparatory retreat. He drove, one morning, four or five leagues out of Paris, to the parish church of Pontoise, near Rouen, where Tressan, Bishop of Nantes, M. le Duc d'Orléans's first almoner, bestowed on him, *extra tempora*, during the celebration of his first mass, the orders of sub-deacon, deacon, and priest; for which service Monsieur de Nantes was rewarded, after Bezons's death, with the reversion of the Rouen Arch-bishopric. There was a great outcry against both prelates, and the reputa-tion of Archbishop Bezons, who had hitherto been justly esteemed and honoured, was left somewhat tarnished.

On the afternoon of the day on which the Abbé Dubois took all three minor orders at once, a meeting of the Regency Council was convened at the old Louvre—measles being rampant everywhere else, including the

[1] Cardinal de Noailles was also Archbishop of Paris, and would have been expected to officiate in his own diocese.
[2] See note 3, p. 255 above.

Palais Royal, it could not be held as usual at the Tuileries. The members were surprised at being summoned in the absence of Dubois, who invariably attended to say what he pleased on foreign affairs. They were still more astonished when he appeared after all, having wasted no time in prayer and solemn thanksgiving. Here was another scandal, reviving and increasing the earlier one. He arrived, as the Duc de Mazarin jestingly remarked, 'hot-foot from his first Communion'. All the Council members, including M. le Duc d'Orléans, stood in little groups in various parts of the Council chamber. I was at the farther end, talking to M. le Prince de Conti, the Maréchal de Villars, and another, I forget whom, when I suddenly noticed the Abbé Dubois, wearing a short coat, and behaving quite as usual. We were not expecting him, and so naturally we exclaimed. This made him turn in our direction, to see M. le Prince de Conti advancing upon him with the sardonic grin he had inherited from his father, but without his father's good-humoured grace, commenting out loud on the Holy Orders taken so rapidly that morning, the sudden return, and the consecration so soon to follow, turning it into a mock-sermon that might have made any other man lose countenance. Not so Dubois. He let the prince say on; then coldly replied that if he were better versed in the scriptures he would feel less surprise, remembering the ordination of Saint Ambrose,[1] which he proceeded to describe at enormous length.

I had ceased to listen. From the moment when he first mentioned Saint Ambrose I had fled to the other end of the room. It appalled me to have to class them together, and I feared lest I be impelled to tell him to hold his tongue. My temper was rising; I knew that soon I should be describing how Ambrose was seized and ordained against his will, in mortal fear; indeed telling the whole story of the violence done to him. That impious comparison became the talk of Paris, with what effect you may imagine. The appointment to Cambrai and the ordination both took place towards the end of February.

The consecration was planned on the grandest scale, and M. le Duc d'Orléans had promised to attend it. The shock and scandal, plus the tremendous preparations, produced a surge of indignation against him. I therefore visited him on the eve of that loathsome ceremony, and at once explained what had brought me, reminding him that I had not reproached him for the Cambrai appointment because, as he well knew, I never spoke once things had been settled. I spoke now, I said, only because I had learned that he meant to attend the consecration next morning. In all friendship, I thought that he should be made aware of the scandal caused by that impious ordination, attended by splendour unparalleled for a man of Dubois's birth, position, and way of life. I added that I would not reproach him for things past, only make sure that he realized what horror he

---

[1] Saint Ambrose was the prefect of Milan, and only a catechumen when he was made bishop by universal acclamation, and forced to accept in spite of all his protests.

had aroused, and persuade him, if possible, not to add the last straw by his presence.

I said further that the general opinion, formed by his habits and conversation, was that he had no religion and made no bones of advertising that fact, and that he proposed to attend the ceremony for the sole purpose of mocking God and insulting His Church. The effect would be disastrous, because people, believing, as they rightly did, that Dubois was using him to serve his own vanity, would come to hate and despise the Regent himself. Verily and indeed, I continued, Dubois had already received so much that he need not degrade his master in the eyes of France and later of all Europe.

I ended by entreating him not to go. I said, as he was well aware, that Dubois and I were on the worst of terms, and that I was the only person not invited; none the less, if only he would promise, and keep his word to be absent, I would myself attend the consecration and stay the entire time, no matter how shocked and unhappy I might be. He would see at once that such an action on my part would be put down to a servile desire for reconciliation with Dubois—I who had taken pride in the fact that never in all my life had I toadied anyone.

This entreaty, so fervently pronounced, was most attentively heard. I was astounded when M. le Duc d'Orléans said that I had opened his eyes; still more so when he clasped me to him, exclaiming that I was a true friend, and indeed he would not go, I had his solemn promise as to that. He was not at all impatient, nor anxious for me to leave. I knew him through and through, and when I went, it was of my own accord, feeling very glad to have turned him from an action so disgraceful and unprecedented. Who would ever have imagined that he would break his word? But you shall hear what transpired.

Although I firmly believed him, yet, knowing his weakness and changeability, and the nature of the Abbé Dubois's hold over him, I thought it prudent to make doubly sure before leaving, and I accordingly sent a footman to the Palais Royal, keeping my coach ready and the horses harnessed. What was my mortification when the man returned saying that the Regent had just stepped into his coach and departed for the consecration, with all the pomp and circumstance of some great State occasion. I had the horses unharnessed, and went to bury myself in my study.

Next day, I learned from a favourite bedfellow[1] of Mme de Parabère, the reigning mistress although unfaithful, that she had lain with M. le Duc d'Orléans between two sheets, at the Palais Royal on the previous night (this never happened in his room, only in hers). He had praised me in a way I shall not repeat, speaking feelingly of my love for him; declaring

---

[1] The word is *coucheur*. Saint-Simon's use of it is said to be his own invention. It occurs in the dictionary of the Académie only as *bon* or *mauvais coucheur*—people easy or hard to get on with.

that because of my urging he would not attend the consecration, and expressing his gratitude. Parabère had added her mite of praise, agreeing that I was right, but had said that he should none the less go. M. le Duc d'Orléans said she must be mad. 'Mad or not,' she replied, 'go you will.' 'But I tell you I shall not.' 'Oh! but you will.' 'This is absurd,' said he, 'You say that M. de Saint-Simon is right, so why should I go?' 'Because I wish you to.' 'Ah! that is different,' he rejoined. 'But why should you care? What is this all about?' 'Oh!' said she, 'Because . . . just because . . .' 'Because! that is no answer! Tell me the real reason, if so be you can.' Then after some further argument, she said, 'Well, if you absolutely must know, it is this. You remember that the Abbé Dubois and I had a tiff three or four days ago, and that we are still on bad terms. He is a fiend for knowing all, and he will certainly discover that we spent this night together. If you miss his consecration tomorrow he will think it my doing, and never forgive me; and he will make so much mischief between you and me that we shall quarrel. I do not want that to happen, which is why you must go, in spite of M. de Saint-Simon.' After that the Regent put up a very weak resistance, then consented; and, to her, he faithfully kept his promise.

Parabère spent the following night with her fancy-man, and told him all, thinking it extremely funny. For similar reasons he repeated the tale to Biron, who told it me next evening. We commiserated with one another on the Regent's enslavement; but I never afterwards mentioned the affair to him, nor he to me, though he seemed mortally ashamed of himself. Whether it was Biron who told Dubois of my endeavours, or whether Parabère sought to win his favour for changing M. le Duc d'Orléans's mind, I never discovered. Be that as it may, Dubois somehow learned the truth and bore me a grudge for the rest of his life. Belle-Isle later informed me that Dubois had told M. Le Blanc that of all the impediments I had put in his way, sometimes endangering his entire career, nothing had so deeply wounded him—truly to the very quick—as my effort to prevent the Regent from attending his consecration; of which it is now high time to speak.

Everything about it was magnificent in the extreme, designed to show the incredible height to which he had risen, and the abject servitude to which he had reduced his master. Val-de-Grâce was the place chosen, as being a royal monastery, the grandest in all Paris, and with the most famous church. Cardinal de Rohan, always glad of an opportunity to snub Cardinal de Noailles, offered of his own accord to officiate. Needless to say that a prelate of such high rank, Bishop of Strasbourg, and eminent in every kind of way, was a consecrator far exceeding the Abbé Dubois's highest hopes. It is only the first honour that is hard to obtain. Regarding the two assistant bishops, Nantes was a necessity, in view of the services he had rendered at the ordination. For the other, Dubois thought it behoved him to find a man beyond reproach of any kind. His eye fell on Massillon the famous Oratorian father,[1] whose virtue, scholarship, and brilliance in the pulpit had won him the see of Clermont; for now and then a good priest had filtered through among the vast number of bad ones who were made bishops. Massillon, cornered, dazed, and helpless, saw all the shame of the proposal, tried to excuse himself, but dared not refuse. What else could he have done? a man of such small account at that period, standing alone against the Regent, his minister, and Cardinal de Rohan. Yet he was blamed, and greatly so, by the world at large, especially by the rich in all sections of Society, who in this monstrous affair were for once united. The more moderate, in great numbers, only pitied him, and gradually people came to understand that he could not have done otherwise than accept.

The church was most splendidly decorated; all France was invited; none dared to be absent, and everyone whose health permitted remained throughout the entire ceremony. Tribunes were especially screened for ambassadors and other Protestant diplomats. One of the most magnificently adorned was reserved for M. le Duc d'Orléans and M. le Duc de Chartres, who accompanied him. Some were kept for ladies and, as M. le Duc d'Orléans's tribune was within the walls of the monastery, it was open to all comers, and arranged, inside and out, with tables piled high with refreshments of all kinds, with officers preparing and distributing them in profusion. The fuss and bustle continued all day because of the great number of tables, laid for persons of lesser degree, and indeed, for anyone who cared to enter and stuff himself. M. le Duc d'Orléans and his staff acted as ushers, seating and welcoming persons of distinction and escorting them to their carriages, while his junior officers took equal care of less important guests. Meanwhile the whole of the watch, and the entire force of police, were kept busy arranging the entry, standing, and departure of countless numbers of coaches, in an orderly fashion and with all possible dispatch.

At the consecration service, during which the conduct of both the consecrated and the spectators left much to be desired, especially on leaving, M. le Duc d'Orléans expressed to every high-ranking person whom he encountered his intense gratification at their presence. He then went off to Asnières to dine with Mme de Parabère, who was in raptures at having persuaded him to witness the ceremony, at which, by all accounts, he had behaved from start to finish in a less than seemly fashion. During the service, his officers had invited all the prelates, important abbés, and distinguished guests to dine with him at the Palais Royal. Two tables, each seating thirteen persons, were prepared in one large room of his State

---

[1] Jean Baptiste Massillon (1663–1742), Bishop of Clermont 1717, member of the French Academy. He belonged to the religious society of the Oratory, famous for its preachers and scholars.

apartments, for the members of high Parisian Society; and several others, equally well furnished, were set up in adjoining rooms for those of lower rank. M. le Duc d'Orléans presented the new archbishop with a diamond of great price to serve for a ring. The entire day was a kind of triumph that won neither men's approval nor the blessing of Almighty God. I saw none of it, and M. le Duc d'Orléans and I never so much as mentioned it afterwards.

Madame la Duchesse,[1] sister of M. le Prince de Conti and of Mlle de La Roche-sur-Yon,[2] died on 21 March, in Paris, at the Hôtel de Condé, at the age of thirty-one, after a very long illness, and a marriage that had lasted seven years. Much has already been said of her and of her total want of self-control. She was pitied, but not mourned. The princes of the blood, having at last been defeated in their efforts to let the bodies of their princesses lie in state, continued their practice of hasty burial. The service at the Hôtel de Condé was meagre in the extreme; after which she was swiftly taken to the Carmelite church in the Rue Saint-Jacques, and there buried. The procession was very grand. Mlle de Clermont[3] accompanied the body, with the Duchesses de Sully and Tallard, as requested by Monsieur le Duc and his mother. Some days later, Monsieur le Duc received visits of condolence, with the usual precaution of a supply of mourning garments in the ante-room, and all the affectation and impropriety of this novel practice, which I mentioned when it was first introduced.

The Comte d'Horn[4] had been in Paris for two months past, leading a shameful life of gaming and debauchery. He was twenty-two and exceedingly well-built, a member of the great and ancient house of Horn, recognized since the eleventh century among the princely families ruling in the Low Countries, and thereafter distinguished by a succession of famous names. Antoine Joseph, Comte d'Horn, with whom we are concerned, was no more than a one-time captain of cavalry, dismissed the service for bad conduct, and a great embarrassment to his mother and brother. They had heard so much to his discredit since his arrival in Paris that they sent a confidential agent with money to pay his debts and persuade him to return. Should he fail, the agent was to appeal to the Regent, their kinsman through Madame, to have him sent home immediately. As ill luck would have it, this gentleman arrived on the day after the crime which I will now describe.

---

[1] Marie Anne de Bourbon-Conti (1689–1720), sister of Louis Armand II de Bourbon, Prince de Conti, and first wife of Louis-Henri de Condé, Duc de Bourbon (1692–1740). She is not to be confused with her mother-in-law the Dowager Madame la Duchesse, daughter of Louis XIV and Mme de Montespan, who did not die until 1743, and appears very frequently in earlier volumes.

[2] Louise Adélaïde de Bourbon-Conti, Mlle de La Roche-sur-Yon (1696–1750).

[3] Marie Anne de Bourbon-Condé, Mlle de Clermont (1697–1722). She was the present Monsieur le Duc's sister, and daughter of the Dowager Madame la Duchesse.

[4] Antoine Joseph, Comte d'Horn (1698–1720).

On the Friday before Good Friday (22 March), the Comte d'Horn went to the market in the Rue Quincampoix, desiring, or so he said, to purchase a hundred thousand écus' worth of stock, and for that purpose requested a jobber to meet him at a hostelry. The jobber came armed with his wallet and certificates to find the Comte d'Horn awaiting him in the company of two men, his so-called friends. They at once attacked the unfortunate man; the Comte d'Horn stabbed him repeatedly with his dagger, and seized his portfolio; one of the friends, seeing that he still lived, quickly finished him off. The people of the inn heard the noise and came running, not fast enough to prevent the murder, but in time to overpower and seize two of the assassins; the other ruffian escaped in the struggle.[1] The police were sent for and the culprits taken to the Conciergerie. This abominable crime, committed in broad daylight, caused an immediate sensation, and several important members of the Horn family went to M. le Duc d'Orléans, begging for mercy. For as long as possible he avoided seeing them, having rightly given orders for justice to be done promptly and impartially; but at last the parents gained an audience, pleading that their son was mad, even claiming that he had a lunatic uncle, and asking for him to be confined in Petites-Maisons,[2] or with the Charity Fathers of Charenton, who also housed lunatics. All the answer they received was to the effect that one could not too quickly be rid of lunatics when they carried madness to the point of murder. Their petition refused, they pleaded the fearful disgrace of a trial and its result on an illustrious family, claiming kinship with all the reigning sovereigns of Europe. M. le Duc d'Orléans replied that the disgrace was in the crime, not in the punishment.[3] They then represented that he himself was their kinsman. 'Well, Sirs! so be it!' he exclaimed, 'Let us share the disgrace.' Law and the Abbé Dubois, who were greatly concerned for the safety of the brokers, encouraged M. le Duc d'Orléans to stand firm, which was his own inclination, if only so as to escape from the continual cries for mercy.

The trial was held with all imaginable speed, and the sentence was the wheel—no less. The parents, having lost hope of saving the criminal, turned all their thoughts to changing the sentence. Some of the family came to see me and begged for my assistance, although I was not of their kin. They told me that the wheel would bring down all their family and connections in the Low Countries and Germany; for it appeared that enormous importance was there attached to the form of execution for persons of quality. Beheading brought no shame on the families concerned, but the wheel inflicted such deep disgrace that uncles and aunts, brothers, sisters, and cousins, down to the third generation, were refused admittance

[1] The ruffian who escaped was known as d'Étampe, or du Terne. His real name was Lestang.

[2] In the Rue de Sèvres, on the site later occupied by the Bon Marché store.

[3] The Regent was quoting Corneille, from Le Comte d'Essex, 'La crime fait la honte, et non pas l'échafaud.'

to all the noble religious communities. Thus apart from the shame, members of such families were deprived of all hope of becoming canonesses or prince-bishops, and were inevitably ruined. This argument deeply impressed me, and I promised to do my best with M. le Duc d'Orléans, but without offering much hope.

It so happened that I was about to spend Holy Week at La Ferté; but I went first to M. le Duc d'Orléans to explain what I had just learned. I said that anyone pleading for the Comte d'Horn's life, in consideration of the eminence of his family, would be acting selfishly, and thinking of them alone. On the other hand, those who insisted on demanding death by the wheel were equally wrong-headed. It appeared to me that there was a middle way, commendable to them who so much loved him, that would satisfy both the demands of justice and the public's more moderate expectations, yet at the same time avoid bringing disgrace and ruin upon an illustrious line. I added that M. le Duc d'Orléans would earn the devotion of all that family and of their connections and friends, instead of the bitter resentment they would certainly feel whenever one of them aspired to enter a noble religious order as, at that very moment, the Comte d'Horn's sister[1] wished to do. It was perfectly simple. All he had to do was to revoke the warrant for death on the wheel, and issue another for beheading. Justice would then be done, and everyone be well satisfied.

M. le Duc d'Orléans gladly consented. He admitted that I was right; saw all the advantage of averting the anger of so many distinguished persons, while at the same time fulfilling the law's requirements, and promised to act on my advice. I told him that I was about to go to La Ferté, and warned him that Law and Dubois would try to change him, since they were both eager for the wheel. He promised to be firm; and knowing him so well, I could see he meant it. I therefore took my leave, and departed next day, as I had arranged.

It all happened as I had foreseen. Dubois and Law made a set at him and twisted him round, with the result that the first news I had on reaching La Ferté was that the Comte d'Horn and his accomplice de Mille had publicly been broken alive upon the wheel, and had died upon it, both on the same scaffold, at four in the afternoon of Holy Tuesday, after first having being put to the question. The outcome was as I had prophesied. The entire Horn family, and all the other great families of the Low Countries, not excluding the German nobility, were angry and indignant, and gave full vent to their feelings. Some of them even nourished thoughts of a terrible revenge. Long after M. le Duc d'Orléans's death, I encountered a number of their kin who could not bring themselves to speak of him without showing the fury they still harboured against his memory.

The Queen of Spain was delivered of a prince whom they named Don

---

[1] Marie Josèphe, Demoiselle d'Horn (1704–1738), who afterwards married the Marquis de Saint-Floris.

Philip.[1] The blue ribbon was at once dispatched to him, following the custom of the late King, who had in this way honoured all the sons of the King of Spain, treating them as though they were Sons of France, although in fact they were no more than sons of a younger Son, and consequently only Grandsons.[2] Maulévrier-Langeron,[3] whose family name is Andrault (nephew of the Abbé de Maulévrier whom I have mentioned elsewhere),[4] was appointed to take the ribbon and be the King's envoy in Spain. It was his uncle who obtained the appointment for him. The family come from Bourbonnais,[5] and are very distantly connected with the House of Condé. This particular member was deeply attached to the Duc du Maine. As you shall see if God allows me to describe my embassy to Spain, M. le Duc d'Orléans might have made a better choice.

The Marquise d'Alluyes[6] died at this time, at the Palais Royal, in Paris. Her name was Meaux du Fouilloux, and she had been maid of honour to Madame, Monsieur's first wife.[7] In 1667, when no longer young, but still beautiful, she had married the Marquis d'Alluyes, who was exiled for his part in the Voisin affair.[8] He died childless, in 1690, after being allowed to return to Paris, though without ever obtaining permission to see the King. The Marquise, a close friend of the Comtesse de Soissons, spent her entire life immersed in love-affairs, and when age forbade them for herself, lived just as passionately those of other people. She was a woman totally devoid of malice. Her only intrigues were of the heart; and these she enjoyed so much that until the moment of her death she was the receptacle for the secrets of all the gallants of Paris, who came each morning to confide in her. She doted on Society, and gambling; had little in the way of fortune, and spent everything she possessed at cards. Every morning she held interviews with the young blades who called to tell her the news of the town, or their own adventures. Then she would send out for a slice of ham or pie, or sometimes for a little salt pork and some patties, and would eat them there and then, before them all. In the evening she supped and played cards wherever she could gain an entry; and so she lived, plump and hearty, free

---

[1] Philippe de Bourbon (1720–1765), Duke of Parma. In 1739, he married Louis XV's eldest daughter (Marie Louise) Elisabeth de France (1727–1759).

[2] Philip V, second son of Monseigneur le Grand Dauphin, ranked as a Son of France because his father, had he not died in 1711, would have succeeded Louis XIV. The title carried no further than Grandchildren of France, which was the rank of Philippe II, Duc d'Orléans. His duchess made great efforts (see II, p. 37) to have their children rated as Great-grandchildren; but it was not allowed.

[3] Jean Baptiste Louis Andrault de Langeron, Marquis de Maulévrier (1677–1754). He became a Maréchal de France in 1745.

[4] Charles Andrault de Langeron, Abbé de Maulévrier. He died this same year. See index, I.

[5] Bourbonnais was the ancient province of France which had Moulins for its capital.

[6] Bénigne de Meaux du Fouilloux, Marquise d'Alluyes (died 1720).

[7] Henrietta of England (1644–1670), daughter of Charles I and Henrietta Maria of France, first wife of Louis XIV's brother Philippe I, Duc d'Orléans, the Regent's father (his court name was Monsieur).

[8] La Voisin, the sorceress, see I, p. 45; the affair led to the suspected poisonings of 1672.

from all infirmities, until she died at over eighty after a very short illness. So ended a long life without care or constraint and entirely given up to pleasure. As for esteem, she sought for none, save only for the reputation of being in the highest degree loyal and secret. Thus everyone liked her, but one never encountered women at her house. It is because her life was so strange that I was induced to recount it.

The King began to ride a horse at a walk, and very soon cantered for a short distance. He also began learning to shoot.

May 22nd of this year, 1720, was famous for the publication of an edict by the council of State, regarding the stock of the India (now called the Mississippi) Company and the notes issued by Law's bank. By its terms, the value of both stock and notes was to be reduced month by month, until at the end of the year they would stand at half their original value. In the language of bankers and bankrupts, this meant showing a light pair of heels; indeed, it so clearly indicated flight that people imagined things to be far worse than they were in reality, because the measure was no remedy, even in a desperate situation. Argenson, who at Law's request had obtained first the finances, then the seals, and who had obstructed him in every possible way, now thought it expedient to resign. He was generally suspected of having issued the decree, partly from malice, partly because he foresaw an inevitable collapse. There was a most violent disturbance. Every rich man thought himself irretrievably ruined, either immediately or in the not so distant future; every poor man saw himself beggared. What little confidence still remained in Law was totally destroyed; not a vestige of it could ever be revived.

On Wednesday, 29 May, La Houssaye[1] and Fagon, counsellors of State and intendants of the finances, went to Law's bank accompanied by Trudaine, the merchants' provost. At the same moment, Le Blanc, a secretary of State, called on Law to inform him that M. le Duc d'Orléans had dismissed him from office as controller-general of the finances, thanking him for his services, and advising him that since many people in France wished him harm, a reliable officer would be detailed to protect him against a possible attack. Besenval,[2] a major of the Swiss Guard, shortly afterwards arrived with sixteen men of that regiment, to stand guard day and night in Law's house. Dismissal and a bodyguard were the last things that Law had expected; but he remained imperturbable on both counts, and in no way abandoned his accustomed phlegm. It was not until the following day that the Duc de La Force escorted him to M. le Duc d'Orléans, entering by the front door; but the Regent would not see him then. Next day, Sassenage[3] let him in by the back; and thereafter Law

[1] Félix Le Pelletier de La Houssaye (died 1723). In 1719 he had become head of the Regency Council, and in 1720 succeeded Law as controller-general of the finances.

[2] Jean Victor, Baron de Besenval (1671–1736). He married a Polish lady and became the French ambassador to Poland and Sweden in 1722.

[3] Ismidon René, Comte de Sassenage (1670–1730). He had been Monsieur's first valet in 1694, and was a member of the Regent's household.

worked quite openly with the Regent, without any kind of concealment, and treated with the usual kindness. On Saturday, 2 June, Besenval and his Swiss were withdrawn. The stock market in the Rue Quincampoix was closed, and reopened in the Place Vendôme, where there was more room and no need to interrupt the traffic. The inhabitants, however, suffered some inconvenience.

In the midst of these happenings, M. le Duc d'Orléans, much displeased with d'Argenson for issuing the edict and thus causing all the commotion, determined to remove the seals from him. He told me about this one afternoon, when I came from Meudon to work with him. He explained his reasons as though his mind were made up, and at once offered to give them to me. I could not help laughing. He said he saw nothing to laugh about, for there was no one else. I expressed surprise at this, to me, most shocking proposal, as though there were not many among the vast body of magistrates who would be capable and worthy of holding the seals, or, failing that, one of the prelates, rather than to a nobleman who knew nothing of the rules, regulations, or forms proper to their administration. He said it was all quite straightforward, merely a routine to be followed, which I might learn in half an hour after taking the office. When I insisted on his finding someone else, he took up the Court Almanach, and patiently read out name after name from the list of the principal magistrates, explaining his reasons for excluding all of them. Thence he passed to the Regency Council, going through a similar process with each member, and thereafter to the prelates, but in lesser detail, for truly, there was none worth his consideration. I did dispute some of those he had rejected from among the magistrates, more especially the Chancellor;[1] but he was adamant. I said I perfectly understood that for a magistrate the seals were worth a fortune, and that because of the power and rank which they bestowed, and for the glory attaching to the family, they were impossible to resist. I, however, was uninterested in such honours. The seals would be no adornment to my family, or in any way change my rank, dress, or conduct. They would, on the other hand, expose me to the mockery of all observers who saw me cudgelling my brains to learn the rudiments of office. Furthermore, I was loath to risk my conscience, honour, or his most precious friendship, by sealing or not sealing, haphazard, the various edicts and proclamations which he might send me. The Regent was not impressed; yet I would not budge, though the discussion lasted three long hours. I several times attempted to return to Meudon, but on each occasion he prevented me. At last, he did consent to let me go, on condition of my being willing to see two unnamed persons, whom he proposed to send to Meudon next day, and against my promise to listen to them, and hear them out, in the hope that they might move me. There was nothing for it but to agree; and only then did he very grudgingly let me go.

[1] Referring to Chancellor Daguesseau, who was living in exile at Fresnes.

No speechmakers appeared next morning; but halfway through dinner, to which I always had many guests, I saw the Duc de La Force enter with Canillac.[1] It surprised me to see Canillac, for I had never had any close acquaintance with him. He had been to my house four or five times in the first fortnight of the Regency, but never since. We had eyed one another from opposite ends of the table at meetings of the Regency Council, after he had become a member; but we did not meet elsewhere. As you will recall, he had delivered himself over to the Abbé Dubois, the Duc de Noailles, and Stair, and was heart and soul with the Parlement. You also know his character. Their arrival did not lengthen the meal, for they ate as though they were in a hurry, and had scarcely drunk their coffee before they asked to be taken to my study. There they proceeded to ride roughshod over me, so I could not doubt M. le Duc d'Orléans's having repeated to them word for word our very long conversation of the previous day. M. de La Force then began what was not so much a discourse as a series of lectures, and by no means short ones. Canillac followed him. He enjoyed public speaking and spoke well, but interminably, and without any kind of constraint. Their whole argument was the need to be rid of Argenson, who had issued the edict of 22 May out of jealousy, for the sole purpose of destroying Law, regardless of the danger in which it placed M. le Duc d'Orléans. It was impossible, or so they said, to appoint anyone from the Parlement because, since the Tuileries *Lit de Justice*, that body had become increasingly hostile to the Regent. The keeper of the seals must be the Regent's firm friend, a man of proven loyalty, able to exert a restraining influence on intriguers, and generally feared and respected. In desiring me, they did me great honour; but when people wish to overcome, they will say anything. None the less, they described me as a man of sense and parts, courageous, with an unsullied reputation for honour and truth, and with a total disregard of personal advantage. They reminded me that I was known to have refused either stock or notes, or any other part in Law's scheme; that my hands were clean regarding the finances, although I understood them; that I was careful of the royal authority, yet would speak out fearlessly in defence of the remonstrances and other rights of the Parlement, while firmly keeping that body under control. Lastly, they urged me to save the Regent from the effects of his weakness and good nature which, as things were at present, would certainly be the ruin of him.

When M. de La Force began yet another speech, I proposed continuing the conversation (which had already lasted nearly three hours) in the open air, on the terrace walk leading to the Capuchin friary. As we proceeded, M. de La Force tried discreetly to tempt me with the pleasures of humiliating the Parlement and the premier président, in revenge for the affair of the bonnets. Canillac had removed himself out of earshot while this was

[1] See note 4, p. 10 above. Perhaps Canillac came because he was the Regent's friend.

going on; but whether accidentally or on purpose I did not discover. He soon returned, however, and towards the end joined in with the light touch of a clever man who, without straying from the path, is ready to use any trifle to gain his ends. The perfect weather and the fine view from the terrace allowed some respite from the grave discussion, until at last we reached the end of the walk and the so-called Bastion. There we sat; but although the view from that spot was still finer, the main theme was immediately resumed.

Were I to repeat all they said, this would never end. Suffice it to remark that these two gentlemen assaulted me as though the fortunes, the health, the very life of M. le Duc d'Orléans depended on my acceptance. Yet I remained firm, not yielding a single inch. At last night fell, and you must remember that the month was May, and the weather the most perfect imaginable. I suggested returning. All the way, they plied me with appeals to my better nature, and reminders of my distress should disasters occur which I might have prevented; but they both looked defeated. When we reached the château, I was extremely careful to avoid my study, taking them at once to join the company, so as to be free at last of those two noblemen who, in seven long hours, had quite exhausted me. Their coach was waiting—it had been ready a long time. They stood for a moment conversing with my guests, then took leave of me and returned to Paris.

I never discovered what had possessed M. le Duc d'Orléans; nor why Canillac was so eager to persuade me. I believe His Royal Highness acted in good faith, wishing to give the seals to a loyal friend who would help him be firm in dealing with the Parlement. M. de La Force would have been glad to take the seals from the bench of magistrates, and see them placed in the hands of a duke who would love to obstruct and mortify them. The Abbé Dubois, with whom I had been on even worse terms since the episode of his consecration, and without whose consent nothing was done, might well have wished to see me fall into some foolish quarrel with the Parlement, and then have interceded with the Regent to my detriment. Such were my reflections after that long conference at Meudon.

My resolute refusal and the hopelessness of trying to change me were reported to M. le Duc d'Orléans at a time of crisis when further delay was impossible. There ensued a hurried conference, to which I was not bidden, between the Regent, the Abbé Dubois, and Law, with the result that the last named was sent to Chancellor Daguesseau, who was known to be bored to death in his exile at Fresnes. The Chevalier de Conflans,[1] Daguesseau's cousin and close friend, a strong man and brilliant in argument, went also, representing M. le Duc d'Orléans, whose first gentleman he was. When they arrived, Law explained the circumstances and sounded the Chancellor, who seemed tractable enough, especially

[1] Philippe Alexandre, Chevalier de Conflans (1676–1744).

after vague hints that his exile might otherwise continue even beyond the Regency. His three years at Fresnes had done much to soften the nature of this man of fifty who, having risen so young to the highest office of all, had hoped to enjoy its sweets for very many years, and meanwhile promote the interests of every member of his family. Exile had dashed these hopes; indeed, he found himself in a far worse position than if he had remained a mere procureur général. Conflans played upon sentiments that were not unknown to him, and had become more intense with the passing years. Thus Law's flattering speeches fell on ears well disposed to hear them; the Chancellor agreed to all. The public, when the news broke, remained unimpressed, simply exclaiming, *Et homo factus est*.

M. le Duc d'Orléans, having been in no doubt regarding the success of their mission, had sent the Abbé Dubois, on Friday, 7 June, to reclaim the seals from Argenson, who returned them on the afternoon of that very day, at the same time handing in his resignation. The Chancellor had returned to Paris during the night, and at midday followed M. le Duc d'Orléans to the Tuileries, where the King gave him back the seals. Law's responsibility for their return, and for bringing him out of exile, made the first blot on a hitherto untarnished reputation that thereafter steadily diminished, until, in the coming years, it was lost altogether.

Meanwhile Argenson had not wasted his time. Born poor, he retired a very rich man; his young children all endowed with offices to step into when they reached maturity; even his brother[1] amply supplied with benefices. Argenson relapsed into an idleness so complete that it cost him his life,[2] as often happens with those who outlive their careers. His retirement was highly improper, for he had long made his home in a rented suite of rooms in the outer wall of a women's convent, which he had furnished as fully and as handsomely as though it had been a town residence. He had been in possession of them for many years, and had slept there whenever possible. He had procured endowments for this convent and privately gave them very large sums of money; all this for the sake of the prioress, a Mme de Veyny, with whom he claimed cousinship and devotedly loved; and indeed, she was a most charming and intelligent woman, of whom no one said a reproachful word.[3] His entire family courted her, despite what was truly shocking, that during all the time when he was lieutenant of police she left her convent if ever he fell ill, and stayed in his house to nurse him. After his retirement he continued to wear the uniform and badge of his post, and retained the rank of keeper of the seals, but only at his home. He seldom went out, except on rare occasions to see M. le Duc d'Orléans (who still kept a regard for him), entering by the back

---

[1] François Élie de Voyer de Paulmy, Abbé d'Argenson (1656–1728), made a counsellor of State for the Church in 1719; Archbishop of Bordeaux from 1720.

[2] Argenson died in 1721.

[3] On the contrary, it would appear that people were deeply shocked by their intimacy.

offices. The Abbé Dubois also showed him some consideration, and several times visited him, whereas he went only once to see the Chancellor. It was this same convent that Mme la Duchesse d'Orléans so gladly continued to support after his death.

On 5 July, the Council issued a decree forbidding people to own or hoard precious stones, or to sell them to anyone but foreigners. You may picture the commotion; for this particular measure, grafted on to others of the same kind, was plainly intended to compel an exchange of all valuables against the discredited banknotes. In vain did M. le Duc d'Orléans, Monsieur le Duc, and Madame try to convince the public that they were setting an example by the disposal of vast quantities of jewels in other countries. They did indeed send some away, but only, as it were, on a visit. No one was duped; each one carefully concealed his own jewellery, which was possible in small amounts, and far more easily managed than with gold and silver plate. This sudden disappearance of jewellery was not of long duration.

Shortly after the publication of this measure, another was prepared establishing the Indies Bank as a trading company, capable of guaranteeing the exchange of six hundred millions in banknotes, at the rate of fifty millions a month, during the first year. This was Law's last resource. It had become necessary to substitute something real for the mirage of the Mississippi, especially since the famous decree of 22 May had proved so disastrous for the paper money. What was now envisaged was the formation of an actual Indies Trading Company (the name given to what had previously been known as the Bank of Mississippi). Yet although the tobacco monopoly and numerous other vast sources of revenue were assigned to the new company, it was still unable to meet the demand for payment of its notes—and this despite all the measures taken to lower their value which, incidentally, had ruined great numbers of people by the reduction of their savings.

New expedients were urgently required. None was found, save only this shift of turning the bank into a commercial undertaking; in other words, under cover of a vague, innocent-looking title, bestowing on it the monopoly of the nation's trade. You may picture how this measure was greeted by a people already tried beyond endurance by the ban, on pain of most severe penalties, against possessing more than five hundred silver écus, and by the visits of inspectors with search warrants, who left them with nothing but paper for their daily needs. The result was twofold; first, popular anger increased to such proportions that it seemed a miracle when it subsided without causing a revolution in Paris. Secondly, the Parlement, basing itself on public resentment, firmly refused to register the new decree.

On 15 July, the Chancellor, at his private house, showed the draft of this decree to deputies from the Parlement, who refused to accept it, though he kept them until nine o'clock at night. Next day, it was laid before the Regency Council. M. le Duc d'Orléans made an excellent speech (he was incapable of making a bad one, no matter how rotten the cause). No one else spoke; they merely bowed their heads, and so it was decided to send the edict to the Parlement for registration on the following day, 17 July.

On the morning of that same 17 July, such vast crowds collected in front of the bank and in the nearby streets to obtain money for their marketing, that ten or twelve people were suffocated. Three of the bodies were borne to the gates of the Palais Royal, where the mob set up a great clamour for admittance. A detachment of the King's guard was hurriedly dispatched from the Tuileries. La Vrillière and Le Blanc each separately harangued the crowds. The lieutenant of police promptly appeared with a section of the watch; the dead were removed, and with soft words the crowd was persuaded to disperse. The King's guard then returned to the Tuileries. By about ten o'clock, when the worst was over, Law took it into his head to go to the Palais Royal, but they hurled abuse at him all along the way; so much so, indeed, that M. le Duc d'Orléans thought it unsafe for him to return and gave him a lodging in the palace. Law's coach returned, however, and stones were thrown shattering the glass; his house also was attacked, amid a great noise of breaking windows. The news reached us so late at the Jacobins' end of the Rue Saint-Dominique that by the time I reached the Palais Royal there was nothing to be seen. I found M. le Duc d'Orléans with a very small company, looking monumentally calm, and plainly showing that to be otherwise would greatly displease him. Thus I did not stay long, having no business, and nothing to confide.

It was on that same morning that the edict was taken to the Parlement and refused registration; but they sent a deputation to M. le Duc d'Orléans, explaining their objections, which made him very angry. Next day, a royal proclamation was posted up, forbidding assemblies, on pain of heavy penalties, and announcing that on account of the previous day's disturbance the bank would remain closed until further notice. This measure succeeded better than it deserved, for how were people expected to live in the meantime? That nothing unruly occurred served only to show the mildness and obedience of the people when subjected to such cruel trials.

Troops were none the less brought into Paris from Charenton, where they had been working on the Montargis canal; a force of cavalry and dragoons was stationed at Saint-Denis, and the King's regiment was encamped on the slopes above Chaillot. Money was sent to the bakers of Gonesse, as an inducement to make them come as usual to Paris; but lest they refuse to accept banknotes, as most of the merchants and craftsmen were doing, the Guards had orders to stay on the alert, and the musketeers to remain in barracks and keep their horses saddled and bridled.

M. le Duc d'Orléans sent for me at five that afternoon. He told me most of what I have recounted here, complained bitterly of the Chancellor for being too lenient with the Parlement, and once again reproached me for refusing the seals. I said, with all due respect, that I begged to differ, for if the Parlement was so stubborn with one of their own kind—a leader whom they loved, and knew to love them—they would be perfectly inflexible with one whom they hated and regarded as having been forced on them. M. le Duc d'Orléans ceased to grumble over the seals. He declared that he was now resolved to punish the Parlement, and saw no better way of doing so than by sending them into exile at Blois. I said that might serve, failing something better. Not that I could suggest anything; but because I foresaw that although exile might indeed be a punishment, it would neither convert nor subdue them. The Regent argued that the magistrates who were accustomed to living in Paris with their families and in the comfort of their homes, would soon grow tired of separation, not to mention the expense and loss of fees. All this was true, and since there was no other suggestion, I agreed. Soon afterwards, however, the idea of Blois was given up, and Pontoise substituted; and thus, because Pontoise is very close to Paris, the whole theory of punishment was nullified. The only result was to display once more the government's weakness, and make a mockery of M. le Duc d'Orléans.

In the meantime, the stock-jobbers were very active in the Place Vendôme. Everyone had been tempted to speculate in the Mississippi Scheme, and there was a race to see who first could fill his pockets with millions, by the help of M. le Duc d'Orléans and Law. The princes and princesses of the blood set a marvellous example. Of all the people in a position to acquire as much stock as they desired, only the Chancellor, the Maréchaux de Villeroy and de Villars, the Ducs de Villeroy, La Rochefoucauld, and myself had consistently refused to accept anything. The two Marshals and La Rochefoucauld were perpetually scheming and working against the government, and the Duc de Villeroy gained much by the salt-tax.[1] They had thus formed themselves into a kind of party, and were rapidly becoming something of a menace. La Rochefoucauld was not of the calibre, either by nature or his office, to do much himself, but as a millionaire, inordinately proud of his grandfather, and with an attachment to the Duc de Villeroy passing that of brotherly love,[2] he followed the Villeroys' lead in everything. His air of aloofness, coupled with his aversion for the Regent, though he invariably grovelled in his presence, aroused great hopes in the Parlement.

One day when the Maréchal de Villars happened to be crossing the

---

[1] He probably administered the farming of that tax, and the monopoly would now go to Law's bank.

[2] François VIII, Duc de La Rochefoucauld (1663–1728), grandson of François, Duc de La Rochefoucauld (1613–1680), author of Les Maximes. He was the Duc de Villeroy's brother-in-law. Their wives were sisters, daughters of Louvois.

Place Vendôme in a superb coach, crammed with pages and lackeys, he had difficulty in forcing a way through the crowd. He thereupon stuck his head out of the window and hurled abuse at the stock-jobbers, haranguing the people in his blustering way about the public disgrace. He was heard in silence until he rashly exclaimed that, thank God, his own hands were clean, when someone shouted out, 'What about your advice?',[1] and the whole crowd took up the cry. Villars, shamed out of his usual truculence, sank back into his coach and succeeded in crossing the Place at walking speed, while shouts and jeers followed him the whole way, and far beyond in the nearby streets, greatly diverting Paris at his expense. There were no complaints.

In the end, the stock market became too much of an encumbrance, and was transferred to the great garden of the Hôtel de Soissons;[2] which was by far the best place for it. M. and Mme de Carignan,[3] to whom that house belonged, raked in money from every side. Profits of as little as a hundred francs (incredible as this might seem, were it not public knowledge) were not too small for them. I do not mean for their servants, but for themselves, and millions from the Mississippi Scheme, not counting other vast sums acquired elsewhere, they did not think above their deserts. In very truth, they carried the art of amassing wealth to the ultimate limit, and by the vilest and most shameful methods. By this last device, they gained huge rents, new facilities, and very great rewards. Law, their intimate friend, after spending several days at the Palais Royal, returned to his own home and received visitors in great numbers. The King several times reviewed the troops that had been brought into Paris, and they were afterwards sent back. The regiments encamped at Charenton returned to Montargis, to work once more on the canal.

Philippe de Courcillon, so-called Marquis de Dangeau, died in Paris on 9 September, aged eighty-four. He was a person of no real account, but because of his remarkable memoirs, curiosity compels me to describe him at some length. His rank was extremely recent, originating in the district of Chartres, and his family were Huguenots. He early became a Catholic, having set his whole mind on the business of making his mark and a very large fortune. Among all the ills brought to France by the rule of Cardinal de Mazarin, gambling for high stakes was a bane to which people of all kinds and conditions soon grew accustomed. Mazarin drew amply from that source of revenue, and found it one of the best means of ruining the nobles whom he loathed and despised, as he did the entire

---

[1] In 1708, before the Battle of Oudenarde, Villars had publicly advised the King that the best policy for monarchs was to let the people hope for much, and give them as little as possible.

[2] Where the Bourse now stands.

[3] Victor Amadeus of Savoy, Prince de Carignan (1690–1741), and his wife Victoire Françoise of Savoy (1690–1766). She had been known as Mlle de Suse, and was a bastard daughter of Victor Amadeus II, Duke of Savoy, father of the Duchesse de Bourgogne and of Philip V's first wife.

French nation. Indeed, Mazarin would have wished to destroy all who were great in their own right, and his policy was steadily continued long after his death, with the result we now see, one that most surely presages the imminent end and dissolution of our monarchy.[1]

Thus gaming was all the rage at the Court, in Paris, and elsewhere, at the time when Dangeau[2] first thought of advancing in Society. He was a big man and exceedingly well built, but became grossly fat in his old age. His face was pleasant enough, though it suggested what indeed he displayed —such mawkishness that it made one vomit. He started with nothing or very little, but applied himself to learning all there was to know of the games then in fashion, *piquet*, *loo*, *ombre*, *commerce*, *hoc*, *reversis*,[3] *brelan*, with the result that he rarely lost, even at *lansquenet* or *bassette*.[4] The knowledge thus gained was worth a fortune to him, for his winnings enabled him to worm his way into some of the great houses, and later to the Court, in very good company. He was affable, obliging, flattering, with all the air, manners, and wit of a man of breeding; settled his debts promptly and in full which, with the help of some enormously lucky coups, was the making of him and the foundation of his great wealth,[5] for no one ever suspected him of cheating; indeed, his reputation remained unspotted throughout his life.

The need to find people able to stake high enough for the King's and Mme de Montespan's tables gained him those entries; and Mme de Montespan once remarked pleasantly that one could no more help liking than making fun of him, which was perfectly true. People liked him because he never said a spiteful word of anyone. Truly, even apart from his honesty at cards, he was a very decent kind of man, strictly honourable, and always willing to oblige. In other ways, he was so appallingly dull, so unbearably sentimental, so gushing over trifles, especially where they even remotely touched the King, or persons in office or favour, so meanly truckling to such people and, after his elevation, so blown up with pride and pomposity, making such a to-do over his so-called nobility, that no one could help ridiculing him.

Once established at the King's table, he used it for his advancement,

[1] He is not foretelling the French Revolution, but the extinction of the nobility which, to him, meant the final disaster.

[2] Dangeau was born in 1638, so that his beginnings were long past. He had been colonel of his regiment of infantry (not so grand as the cavalry) in 1665 and Governor of Touraine in 1667. He was also made a member of the Academy in 1680.

[3] *hoc* was a card game; for *reversis*: see II, p. 215n.

[4] *lansquenet* and *bassette* were both card games. The first was entirely a matter of luck (for earlier references, see index); *bassette* had four players, one of whom dealt the cards: it was an early form of whist.

[5] Mme de Sévigné wrote, in 1676, of Dangeau's play, when he played with the King and Mme de Montespan, 'He thinks only of the matter in hand, and thus wins when the others are losing. He never loses a chance; he is never careless, or absent-minded; in short he defeats luck by good play. The result is two hundred thousand francs in ten days, a hundred thousand écus in a month, and all this is noted down in his receipt-book.'

having early discovered that nothing could be gained without money. I believe, for example, that he paid M. de Vivonne (this happened in 1670) for the governorship of Tours and Touraine, and he soon afterwards purchased one of the two appointments of reader to the King because it gave him the entrées, so useful in the reign of Louis XIV. He thus used money to launch himself as a spectator of the *petit coucher*, a provincial governor, and a member of the King's card-parties with Mme de Montespan. Although not remarkably intelligent, save in his cultivation of High Society, and his choice of company, he liked to dabble in verse-making. In those days, the King sometimes amused himself setting rhymes for his courtiers to match. Dangeau desired of all things to possess a lodging at Versailles, which was hard to come by in those early years. One day, playing cards with Mme de Montespan, he sighed for a room in his sickly sentimental manner, just loud enough to reach the ears of the King and that lady. They did hear, and were much amused. It then entered into their heads to tease him unmercifully by offering him the most salacious rhymes they could devise; and, sure of failure, promised him a lodging if he succeeded before the end of the game. It was the King and Mme de Montespan who were caught, for the Muse was on Dangeau's side. He earned his lodging, and immediately obtained it. He had been a captain of cavalry, and then colonel of the King's regiment; but being less well adapted for war than for courts—though no one thought him a coward— he was employed on missions to some of the German princes, and later in Italy. He was then made a groom-in-waiting of Madame la Dauphine, and received the Order at the grand promotion of 1698.

In 1682, Dangeau had married the immensely rich daughter of one Morin the Jew, thus becoming a brother-in-law of the Maréchal d'Estrées.[1] By her, he had an only daughter whom he married to the Duc de Montfort, elder son of the Duc de Chevreuse, which considerably inflated him. When his wife died, he discovered that he had sufficient wealth to re-ally himself with a Gräfin von Löwenstein,[2] first lady to Mme la Dauphine, and a niece of Cardinal von Fürstenberg. There was an appalling commotion when Madame and Madame la Dauphine saw the arms of the Palatinate coupled with those of Courcillon on Mme de Dangeau's carriage; but they could do nothing about it, and Dangeau thought himself Elector already. Mme de Dangeau had no fortune, but possessed a charming face and figure, and most delightful manners. It was a real pleasure to see Dangeau peacocking it in black mourning for one of his wife's deceased relations, and reciting all their dignities and honours. At last, by constant reinforcement he managed to ennoble himself, affecting all the airs of nobility in a way to make people die of laughing; which is

[1] The Maréchal d'Estrées and Dangeau married sisters, Marie Marguerite and Anne Françoise, daughters of Jacques Morin, known as Morin the Jew. See II, p. 334.
[2] See index, I and II, under Dangeau, Marquise de.

why La Bruyère[1] remarks, in his admirable *Caractère de Théophraste*, that Dangeau was not a genuine lord, only 'school of'.

I was in his bad books for a long time because of an uncontrollable burst of laughter, which I think he never forgave. He did the honours of the Court with extreme lavishness, keeping open house and table every day on a most magnificent scale to all persons of distinction. One day, he invited me to dine. Several ambassadors and other foreigners were present, also the Maréchal de Villeroy, his particular friend. Dangeau carefully turned the conversation at the dinner-table to governorships and governors of provinces; then, amiably embracing the entire company, he announced, 'One must admit that of all of us provincial governors, only M. le Maréchal still retains complete authority in his district.' My eyes met those of Mme de Dangeau. She smiled; I did far worse although I honestly tried to control myself, for he was a decent sort of man, and I had no wish to offend him. It was just too much for me.

He really was the best fellow imaginable; but honours turned his head, and that was what covered him with ridicule. It was far worse after his second marriage; for his natural mawkishness grafted on to a courtier's servility, and overlaid by the snobbishness of a pseudo-lord, formed a whole that reached its summit with the grand-mastership of the Order of Saint Lazarus, which the King gave him in the hope of entertainment.[2] King Louis was kind to him, but loved to mock him, well understanding his sentimentality, conceit and ineptitude. That favour set the entire Court laughing at his expense, in the most unseemly fashion, as he aped the King's bearing at the ceremonies of the Order, all the while believing himself to be universally admired. He was a member of the French Academy and a Conseiller d'État d'Épée. His wife was head of the palace ladies on account of her husband's being a groom-in-waiting and the only titled officer. Mme de Maintenon thoroughly approved of her. Her birth, virtue, and pretty face; a marriage very much to the King's liking and very little to hers, in which she behaved like an angel; the respect due to her uncle the cardinal, and to her husband's office, were all to their advantage, and his election was generally acclaimed. As regards the Saint Lazarus, it is only just to admit that he put the monastic house[3] to a most unselfish purpose, good though it was, for he turned the whole of it into a school for the sons of poor gentry, who learned there, free of all expense, everything becoming to their condition, and were excellently well fed and supported.[4] After this necessary introduction, let us turn to his *Mémoires*, which serve perfectly to describe the man.

From the moment when he first appeared at the Court, that is to say at

[1] Jean de La Bruyère (1645–1696).
[2] This happened in 1693.
[3] His official residence, the monastic house of the order, was at Boigny, near Orléans.
[4] In 1698, Dangeau founded a school, in the Rue de Charonne, for the young knights of the Order of Saint Lazarus, and paid for the education of six of them.

the time of the Queen-mother's death,[1] he wrote down every night the events of the past day, and faithfully continued in that practice until he died. He wrote without comment, as though reporting for the gazette, giving us little more than the bare facts with their exact dates, hardly a word of their causes, still less of intrigues, or of the part played by individuals. The servility of a humble courtier truckling to the great or the favoured; a diffusion of the most insipid and despicable praise, especially for the King's most trivial acts; agonies of fear and sentimental concern over hurting people's feelings (particularly those of ministers and generals), appear on every page—a day rarely fills more than one—and are monstrously sickening. It is hard to conceive how he could have had the patience, the endurance required to compile such a work, writing every day over a period of fifty years in a style so meagre, dry, tight, constrained and careful, describing no more than bare events, and most contemptibly barren.[2]

Yet one must say that Dangeau would have found it impossible to write memoirs of real merit, for which an author needs to know the inner life and working of the Court. Although he seldom quitted Versailles, and then only briefly; though he was a man of some consequence in Society; though people liked and even esteemed him, where his honour and secrecy were concerned, it is none the less true that he knew nothing about anything, and took no part in any affairs. His life was entirely frivolous and superficial, as are his *Mémoires*. He knew what the public knew—no more, and seemed perfectly content to share only in the pleasures and the feasts. Vanity made him very careful to mention this fact on all occasions, but he played no active rôle in them. It is true that his friends, some of them persons of distinction, occasionally confided in him; but he seldom alludes to this. Such friends, and they were few, were too well aware of his essential levity to waste much time on him.

He was a man of less than average intelligence; entirely futile, incompetent in every kind of way, apt to mistake the shadow for the reality, full of windy words that completely satisfied him. His whole mind was set on behaving well, avoiding hurt to other people's feelings, the constant

---

[1] Saint-Simon says 'the Queen-mother' (Anne of Austria, wife of Louis XIII), who died in 1666, and later that Dangeau's memoirs covered fifty years; but he was making a careless slip. He meant Louis XIV's wife, Maria Teresa of Spain, who died in 1683. Boislisle mentions that *Le Journal de Dangeau* was begun in April 1684, and ended in August 1720—just over thirty-six years later.

[2] Saint-Simon's rage at Dangeau's fountains of praise sometimes exploded. 'Maudlin, servile, stinking, lying in his throat!' he scratched in his copy of the *Mémoires*, at the passage describing Mme de Maintenon. Yet when he was first given them to read by the Duc de Luynes, in 1730, he read them through and through in spite of finding them 'suffocating, sickly sentimental'. Perhaps Dangeau's perfect calm may have pricked his conscience; perhaps he was envious of his election to the Academy. One of Dangeau's most insipid entries is as follows, 'I learn that little Corneille has died today. He was famous for his plays.' Other entries: 'Monseigneur took a bath today'; 'The King went shooting', all without comment. None the less, Dangeau's memoirs were valuable to Saint-Simon in his revision, helping him to establish dates and facts. His irritation may also have set light to the splendid pyrotechnics of his own passion.

emission of flattering puffs, in order to win, keep, and enjoy some kind of regard, never perceiving that, from the King downwards, everyone mocked him and set traps for him, into which, more often than not, he fell headlong. Yet his *Mémoires* are full of things that never reached the newssheets. They will greatly improve with time, and be of valuable assistance to those who desire to write more fully, because they will confirm dates and save mistakes. Indeed, they display with most admirable precision the outward events at the Court, the daily routine and all that appertained to it, the various occupations and diversions, the part played by the King, and the life of the courtiers. Nothing could be more desirable than for historians to possess such records of all reigns since the time of Charles V, if that were possible, for they might shed a beam of light through the cloud of nonsense that has been written of the past.[1]

Just two lines more on this prodigious writer. He never concealed the existence of his journal, because no one had any reason to fear it; but no one saw it until after his death. It has not yet been printed; but his grandson the Duc de Luynes, who has it in his keeping, has allowed a few copies to be made. Dangeau who thought nothing beneath his dignity, and liked to figure everywhere, had canvassed for and early obtained a place in the French Academy, of which, when he died, he was the oldest member. He was also a member of the Académie des Sciences though he had no competence whatsoever.[2] It made him immensely proud to belong to those institutions, and he everywhere sought the company of learned men. Yet in his *Mémoires* he shows such gross ignorance of the dukedoms and other ranks at the court of Spain that one is really shocked. He endured the big operation for fistula and nearly died of it, and was cut for an enormous stone. The first operation left him without the least disability, and he lived many years after the second, restored to perfect health, and with no adverse effects. Two years before his death he was cut a second time; but the stone was not a big one, and he was feverish only a few hours. In a month he had recovered, and continued thereafter in robust health. At the end, old age, perhaps boredom for want of the Court and High Society, carried him off after a very short illness.

About half-way through the Parlement's sojourn at Pontoise, I was working alone one afternoon with M. le Duc d'Orléans when he informed me that the premier président had asked his consent to the marriage of his eldest daughter to the Duc de Lorges.[3] My anger and surprise was such

---

[1] Saint-Simon does seem here to be acknowledging something of a debt to Dangeau, and is fairer to him than elsewhere. Perhaps he realizes that in view of the use he made of him, he has done him less than justice.

[2] Dangeau had been made an honorary member of the Académie des Sciences in 1704. This did not mean that he was expected to have any professional qualifications.

[3] The Duc de Lorges (1683–1758), Mme de Saint-Simon's brother. His first marriage had been to Chamillart's daughter whom Saint-Simon loved and used to call *ma grande biche* (my big sweetheart).

that I rose suddenly and hurled my *tabouret* from one end to the other of the little winter study. All my life I had striven to do the essential services for this brother-in-law of mine, not out of love for him—I knew him too well for that—but solely to please Mme de Saint-Simon. I had procured for him the captaincy of the Guards, much to my own discomfiture,[1] had obtained a regiment free of cost for his elder son, and had received precious little gratitude. Let me add that after the death of M. le Maréchal de Lorges, I had given up to him without argument ten thousand écus that should have come to Mme de Saint-Simon, and had lived thereafter very amicably with him. I had thus no reason to expect that he would choose for his second wife the daughter of a man whom I openly regarded as my enemy; whom I refused to bow to, spoke of without restraint, and publicly insulted on every possible occasion, most frequently at the Palais Royal, for I never, or hardly ever, saw him elsewhere. I therefore did not mince my words in speaking to M. le Duc d'Orléans of a marriage so violently repugnant to me; and when he saw my outraged feelings, he did not laugh at the torrents of abuse that burst from my lips; but, contrariwise, admitted that I was right.

I had only recently extricated the Duc de Lorges from a considerable trouble. He owned a house in Livry village, where he imagined he could do as he pleased. Not content with driving Livry[2] to desperation over his hunting—and Livry was the captain and lord of that district, whom I had frequently pacified on his account—he took it into his head to clear, in front of one of his garden gates, a prodigiously wide road running the entire length of Livry forest, using so many labourers that the work was done before anyone had noticed it. You may imagine the cries of the keepers of the woods and forests;[3] the protests of the intendant,[4] and the ruinous costs and annoyance had there been a prosecution. M. le Duc d'Orléans, however, had imposed silence on the officials for love of me, and immediately issued a post-dated order of the Council for the cutting and clearing of the King's timber. Such was my reward. I returned at once to Meudon and told Mme de Saint-Simon of this monstrous alliance. She, too, was horrified. I declared that neither she nor I would ever again see her brother or his intended, bidding her inform M. and Mme de Lauzun that if they signed the contract or attended the wedding, we would not speak to them again for the rest of our lives. In public, I uttered my

---

[1] In 1715. There had been a most appalling row between Saint-Simon and the Roucys who were also after the job. Saint-Simon had obtained it from the Regent; the Roucys said that he had said that the Regent had said that he was not going to degrade the Guards by giving them an untitled captain. In the end the Roucys won. M. de Lorges was neither upset, nor grateful; Saint-Simon said he cared only for pleasure. It was a very long time before anyone spoke to anyone.

[2] Louis Sanguin, Marquis de Livry (1684–1723). He was the Duc de Beauvilliers's son-in-law.

[3] Encouraging poachers and frightening the game!

[4] Fagon was the local intendant of finances.

thoughts without restraint or any choice of words. Mme la Maréchale de Lorges[1] and the Lauzuns did not sign the contract, nor did they attend the wedding, which took place at Pontoise with all the grandiose display usual to the premier président, who invited the members of the Parlement, and obliged them all to sign the contract.

Nothing of all the rumpus I was making escaped the premier président or his family; but their reply took the form of sorrow at my anger, with repeated hopes of appeasing me, and great deference very contrary to their normal arrogance. Let us finish with all this at once. Somewhat later, in the mistaken belief that their meekness had slightly mollified me, they dispatched various friends to address me in such a humble spirit that I should feel obliged to hear them. The only response they got from me was a constant stream of abuse. What at last wore me down, for they could not win me over, was something near and infinitely precious to me: Mme de Saint-Simon's silent and unceasing flow of tears.

She neither ate nor slept. Her delicate health declined visibly. Her sad condition, which only a reconciliation could alleviate, set me in a turmoil, with outbursts and passions that defy all description—a veritable battle between my tender love for one whose grief was sapping her vitality and breaking my heart, and the thought of forgiving two men who, for most excellent reasons, I found wholly odious and contemptible. In the end, I offered myself a living sacrifice for the preservation of Mme de Saint-Simon; and thus, six months later, a reconciliation did take place.

I allowed the contract to be signed, and consented to meet the new Duchesse de Lorges, alone except for the Duchesse de Lauzun, and at the Hôtel de Lauzun. The interview took place standing. My manner was extremely casual. Next day the premier président visited me in full dress uniform, overflowing with compliments and expressions of enormous respect. I was cold, but polite, as I had promised. On the following day, his sister Mme de Fontenilles,[2] the Bailli de Mesmes,[3] and some of their close relations called at our house, and I received them, frigidly, but with sufficient courtesy. The premier président called for the second time, I having positively declined to receive his son-in-law. Yet I knew that I must meet that person before Mme de Saint-Simon would cease from weeping, and at last I agreed even to that. She brought him to me. My greeting was abominable, but the best I could manage in the circumstances. I went afterwards to visit the premier président, who welcomed me with ardour and almost excessive politeness, sparing neither honours nor gratitude, and swallowing his pride in a profusion of compliments.

---

[1] The Maréchale de Lorges was Saint-Simon's mother-in-law. The memoirist was apt to disapprove of her because she was rather common for her husband's lean acres (manure). See I, pp. 61–62.

[2] Louise Marie Thérèse de Mesmes, Marquise de Fontenilles (1668–1755).

[3] Jean Jaques, Bailli de Mesmes (1674–1741). In 1714, he had been the Vatican ambassador to France.

Mme de Lorges and her sister[1] returned my call, accompanied by Mme de Lauzun, soon after my visit to the bride at the Hôtel de Lauzun, then, one after another, I visited the premier président, his sister, his brother, and his mother-in-law.[2] He expressed a great desire to give some kind of a nuptial feast in my presence and that of Mme de Saint-Simon, for he had seen her each time he had called on me, and had seen my children also. I consented even to that. The banquet was excellent and sumptuous, with the premier président and his family directing their words and attentions in the way best calculated to please me. Mme de Saint-Simon was so eager to give a party in return that I could not refuse her. The premier président, who had not dared to expect so much, nearly expired with joy. The same persons were invited, and I strained every nerve to do the thing reasonably well. So ended the fearful quarrel between me and the premier président—a quarrel that had kept us publicly at loggerheads since the affair of the bonnets, and had started afresh with this marriage. In later days he visited me from time to time; then gradually more often, and towards the end of his life I sometimes returned his calls. You may well imagine that these visits were purely matters of courtesy, and that the conversation was of little interest.[3] With Mme de Fontenilles, on the other hand, we struck up a friendship, as we discovered her great merits, her virtues and talents, and the pleasure and safety of her acquaintance. The attachment and affection thus formed has never flagged.

The year ended with the hasty, secret departure of Law, who by then was penniless and had to be sacrificed to public opinion. His flight became known only because Argenson's eldest son, the intendant at Maubeuge, was stupid enough to arrest him. The courier he sent to publish that action was at once returned to him with a severe reprimand for ignoring the passports which M. le Duc d'Orléans had dispatched later. Law's son went with him; they made for Brussels, where the Marquis de Prié, Governor of the Austrian Netherlands, welcomed and entertained them. They did not stay long with him, however, but continued their journey to Liège and thence to Germany. Law offered his services to several of the German princes, who thanked him, but made no use of him. After some further delay, he crossed the Alps and visited certain Italian courts, none of which detained him. He then retired to Venice where, once again, he found no employment.[4] His wife and daughter followed him some months later. I never heard what became of them, nor, for that matter, of his son.[5]

---

[1] Henriette Antoinette de Mesmes, Marquise de Lautrec (1698–1764).

[2] Mme de Fontenilles, the Bailli de Mesmes, and Mme Feydeau de Brou, the premier président's mother-in-law.

[3] On the other hand, he says elsewhere that he gleaned most precious information from him, especially about what the King said when giving his will into the keeping of the Parlement.

[4] Law left Venice in 1721, and returned to England by a circuitous route through Germany and Denmark. He had to leave after a few months, to escape from his creditors. He returned to Venice by way of Germany, and lived there until his death in 1729.

[5] Law's son entered the service of Austria and died in 1734. A younger son was arrested in 1721 and sent to the Bastille for debts to the Bank amounting to three and a half million.

I have said elsewhere and I now repeat that there was nothing greedy or knavish about Law. He was a good, kind, respectful man, whom excessive fame and good fortune had not spoiled, and whose bearing, coaches, table, and way of life were such as to offend no one. He suffered with patience and admirable constancy the frustration of all his plans, until at last, towards the end, finding himself obstructed everywhere, while still valiantly seeking some means of procedure, he grew hard, ill tempered and often rude in argument. He was a schemer and a calculator, always balancing one thing against another, and extraordinarily knowledgeable and learned in such ways, the kind of man who, without ever cheating, continually won at cards by the consummate art (that seemed incredible to me) of his methods of play.[1] His bank, as I have already remarked, would have been excellent in a republic or in a country such as England, where the people control the finances. Regarding the Mississippi, he was deceived, for he truly believed that there were rich possibilities in America. He argued like an Englishman, failing to understand how little suited our fickle nation was to great commercial enterprises. Lack of experience, the greed of those eager to make vast fortunes without delay, the difficulty of working under an authoritarian government without firm principles, in which one minister's work might be totally destroyed by his successor, were all against him. Something which I could never understand was his desire to abolish, first the coinage, then precious stones, and to replace them by paper money; nor do I think that such a thing has ever been attempted since, centuries ago, Abraham paid for Sarah's sepulchre in pieces of silver.

Law's system was indeed so complicated that no one could fathom its workings; he explained it clearly enough, and with a good delivery, but despite that there was a lot of English mingled with his French. He spent several years at Venice, in much straitened circumstances, and, having lived, in decent poverty, a quiet and virtuous life, died there in the Catholic faith, piously receiving the Sacraments of the Church.

So ended the year 1720.

---

[1] Argenson says in his *Mémoires*: 'Law thought himself a great adept; indeed, many trustworthy people who knew him in Venice, have assured me that he knew an infallible way of winning at cards.'

CHAPTER VII

1721

A straight talk with the Regent – I shake his faith in the Abbé Dubois – M. le Duc d'Orléans's fatal weakness – He tells all to Dubois and is angry with me – I violently reproach him – Manœuvres for Dubois's hat – Death of the Duchesse de Sully – Death of Pope Clement XI – Alberoni's downfall and exile – He recovers himself at Rome – Death of Chamillart, Desmaretz, d'Argenson, Mézières, and the Abbé de Lionne – M. le Duc d'Orléans confides to me the secret of the King's coming marriage to the Infanta, and that of Mlle de Montpensier to the Prince of the Asturias – I ask for and obtain the embassy to Spain – The King's illness – The King is told of his marriage – Announcement of the marriage of Mlle de Montpensier – My embassy is announced – My retinue – I leave for Madrid – My journey over the Pyrenees – My first audience of Their Catholic Majesties – Grimaldo – The instruments are signed – My official audience – The signing of the contracts – Maulévrier's treachery – Illuminations – The Court Ball – A private audience – We are allowed to see Their Majesties in bed – The king and queen go to Lerma – My visit to the Escorial – I fall ill with smallpox and recover – Daily life of the King and Queen of Spain – Their characters – Sport – Nuestra Señora de Atocha – The Mall – Life in Madrid – Tactics for obtaining a grandeeship and a Fleece – Letters from the Regent and Dubois to the King of Spain and Grimaldo – A sad reflection

ONCE THE ABBÉ DUBOIS, for so I shall continue to call him despite his consecration as archbishop, had made himself the absolute and acknowledged head of all the country's affairs, M. le Duc d'Orléans no longer told me everything. Yet not even Dubois could entirely destroy our long, intimate, and confidential friendship. One afternoon, when I was working alone with the Regent, he spoke of the approaching treaty between Spain and England, explaining terms by which great advantages accrued to England at Spain's expense, and transferred to that country all the special privileges which France had gained at the accession of King Philip, most of which we had retained, even after the Peace of Utrecht. It is true that we had lost the slave-trade; but the licensed-ship,[1] and many other valuable benefits had remained to us. These the English now claimed, and were

---

[1] This refers to a clause in the treaty allowing the English to send one merchant vessel a year into the ports of Spanish America.

obtaining, for Dubois made no more bones about relinquishing them than he did about Spain's ruining herself in order to gratify England.

At the beginning of the Regency, and many times thereafter, I had said how deeply I resented our subjection to the English. It had become more than I could bear. I could no longer control myself, and I therefore made M. le Duc d'Orléans fully aware of the immense harm he would do to France, and Spain also, if he allowed those terms, and of how one day both the King and the nation would hold him personally responsible for letting the Abbé Dubois sell them out to the English, who would certainly keep a firm hold on anything they thus acquired.

There followed a tirade from me, far longer and more violent than I shall here recount. M. le Duc d'Orléans was most deeply impressed. He argued; then agreed with me on many points, and finally admitted that I was in the right. Much encouraged, I asked him to consider where Dubois's interests lay. As I had often remarked, that priest's whole mind was set on a cardinalate, although M. le Duc d'Orléans with real or simulated indignation had threatened to clap him in irons if ever he caught him harbouring such notions. Be that as it might, I continued, I had no kind of objection to Dubois's hat; he would not be the first cad,[1] nor yet the hundredth, to achieve one; moreover, a Regent of France was great enough so to reward whomever he pleased, particularly his late tutor, now risen to be Archbishop of Cambrai, and first minister. What I could not bear was the thought of his being made a cardinal by the Emperor's authority, and at the request of the King of England. Dubois, I said, solely in order to induce the English to espouse his cause, was resolved to ally the Regent with them and start a war between France and Spain, against all his country's interests. At the same time, he had exposed the Regent to most appalling dangers, as M. le Duc d'Orléans himself had glimpsed during the Cellamare conspiracy, and would have seen most clearly had a war resulted. 'Thereafter,' I added, 'Dubois has placed you at the mercy of the English, and is now ready to give them France, Spain, and the trade of every European country, all for the sake of his hat.'

Never had I seen the Regent more deeply disturbed. Placing his elbows on the table and burying his head in his hands, he remained silent for several moments, with his nose almost resting on the table-top.[2] It was his usual attitude when sitting and profoundly moved. Suddenly he stood up, took a few steps still without uttering a word, then, speaking as though to himself, he exclaimed, 'I must dismiss the rogue.' 'Better late than never,' I replied, 'but you will not do anything.' He continued to pace up and down without addressing me, while I studied him intently, reading in his

---

[1] *Cuistre violet* was the name for bishops—'purple cads'. Odd, because blue was the episcopal colour, with the green and gold hat-tassels that are still worn today.

[2] The Regent's nose was apt to rub the table. He was so near-sighted that his pen was always getting hooked up in his wig.

whole countenance, his absolute conviction, nay, his earnest desire, struggling with the knowledge of his weakness and his subjection to the Abbé Dubois. Two or three times over, he repeated the words 'I must be rid of him', and because I knew him so well, I saw by his tone and manner how terrible was this conflict between his need to take action and his insurmountable fear of having no strength to act. I clearly perceived that nothing more was needed to persuade him of the necessity for Dubois's dismissal; but that no words of mine could fortify him. I therefore thought it best to leave him, and thus relieve him from the distress and shame of having a witness to his anguish. I said I had no more to add; but he scarcely answered, letting me go without argument, which was quite contrary to his usual custom when deeply disturbed. I was glad to have done my duty by speaking so strongly, but had little hope of any good result.

Let us now be done with this sad affair; it is too shocking, too absorbing to bear interruption. Nearly three weeks passed without my noticing any change in M. le Duc d'Orléans's attitude. In our working hours he mentioned neither foreign affairs nor the Abbé Dubois, and I was most careful to avoid references to either. Yet I discovered that on the day following our conversation there had been a quarrel between him and the abbé, so long drawn-out in its successive stages that the neighbouring rooms had been shaken by the noise, despite the empty ante-rooms in between. I also learned that M. le Duc d'Orléans had appeared pre-occupied and extremely cross, very different from his usual self, for he never showed and rarely felt ill humour. Dubois, so they said, was more disagreeable and less tractable than ever before. I guessed that there had been alternations of resolution and weakness, with reproaches and out-bursts leading to no conclusion; for it would have been easy to dismiss the fellow without an audience, or any temptation to be weak. I accordingly imagined that the Regent's infirmity of purpose had proved greater than his most urgent needs, and that Dubois remained his master.[1] I was not mistaken.

Three weeks later, when I went to work with him, I found him striding up and down the farthest of his state apartments, next the corridor to his private suite. He received me so coldly, so unlike his usual self, that I straightway inquired the reason, for I clearly perceived that he held something against me. He hesitated, faltered; I pressed him; suddenly the abscess burst. He said, since I must know it, that he was very angry with me, vomiting forth (truly the only words with which to describe his manner) that I tried to rule him, and would never go counter to my personal wishes. I had refused the finances, the headship of the council for internal affairs, after that, the seals, and three times over I had refused to save him from his worst affliction by becoming the King's governor. 'Is that all?' I inquired.

[1] No doubt the Regent's drunken debauches had undermined his will-power.

'All!' said he, 'is that not enough?' 'Very well, Monsieur,' I replied. 'Let us start with the refusals since they at least are facts; after that we will come to your vague assertion that I try to make you do my bidding.

'Regarding the first two refusals, the one you most minded was that of the finances; and indeed you were monstrously vexed; yet had I accepted you would have been far more so. My objection was my total want of experience, and a deep-seated loathing of all such matters. I should have made mistakes at every turn, and there are no trivial errors in matters of finance. Knowing nothing of that department's ordinary business, how could I have understood Law's operations? And if all M. de Noailles's flattery and subservience to the Parlement did not appease them, how do you suppose they would have treated me, after the affair of the bonnet, and my quarrel with the premier président? That, Monsieur, will dispose of the finances. Moreover, it has never yet been thought a crime to refuse high office on a sincere plea of incapacity. Had any other man been concerned, I might well have said that the refusal merited praise, for not many would be so honest.

'As for the interior, I refused that council because it would have been too hard, too great a labour for me to familiarize myself with the details of all the trials, lawsuits, and regulations concerned, and report on them at the Regency Council. Do you not remember how unambitious I appeared when you first established the councils and how, when you asked me which one I desired to head, I replied then that it was for you to decide, but I thought I might do least harm as an ordinary member of the council for the interior? You laughed at me for that, and graciously offered me a seat on the council of which you yourself were president. This is why I say that you did not mind my refusals, more especially since you have had no reason to complain of d'Antin, whom I proposed as a replacement.

'Now for the seals. First of all, I have never understood why you were so determined that I should take them, when this meant insulting the entire magistrature by giving them a nobleman wholly ignorant of the duties involved. Why choose such a man to represent you at the Parlement, to be answerable for its remonstrances and other decrees, to preside over it, deliver speeches, proclaim the King's will after a *Lit de Justice*, when all these matters would be extremely hard, if not impossible, to combine with the rank and functions of a peer? Why, above all, select the one peer who is a bitter enemy of a premier président with whom he would daily have to confer? Still less could I understand your fickleness in wishing to remove the seals from a Chancellor to whom you had recently returned them. I must submit that my refusal was wise; for as a result the seals remained with Chancellor Daguesseau, and you will agree that no harm has come of it.

'All that now remains is the post of King's governor. Do you not perceive that this high and powerful office must tempt any man of my age with a family to provide for, and no other support than his rank as duke and peer? Do you not think that it would tempt me above all, who was never on such terms with the Maréchal de Villeroy that I need hesitate to supplant him, more especially since I have neither desired nor asked for the post? Can you truly believe that I should refuse this high place, with all the honours, influence, and respect attaching to it, not to mention the very substantial rewards—and refuse it three times[1]—without the strongest possible reasons? The chief of all was that series of terrible rumours, of which I need not remind you. In God's name, Monsieur, only consider, and you will surely do me justice.'

At first, M. le Duc d'Orléans had let me speak freely. Either he had found my defence unanswerable, or he had not minded my refusals until prompted by the Abbé Dubois. On the issue of the governorship, however, the pinpricks inflicted on him by the Maréchal de Villeroy, and fears of the King's future attitude, had considerably alarmed him. He could not forgive me for refusing to assist him and he reproached me again with renewed bitterness, forcing me to repeat myself; but at much greater length than before. At last after a long and angry exchange, I managed to make him admit that my refusal did not deserve so much rancour. Thereafter it was not impossible for me to refute the more general accusations that I did only what suited me, and tried to make him do my pleasure at all times.

I reminded him how despite all my unwillingness I had agreed to join the finance council; how I had begged him, time and again, to release me, pleading my most reasonable aversion because of incapacity, my total ignorance of the Duc de Noailles's methods and my utter abomination of that individual. I said I failed to understand why he should want me, and that I had joined only at his command, continually protesting my uselessness in matters of which I knew nothing. I begged him to remember all the other occasions when he had ordered my obedience, and how unwillingly I had submitted, especially when he had commanded me to see Law once a week to discuss the Mississippi Scheme, though he knew full well that I had opposed it with all my might, both in his study and at the Council.

'Against all my pleading and warnings,' I continued, 'you used your supreme authority to make me visit Mme la Duchesse d'Orléans after the Tuileries *Lit de Justice*, and apprise her of her brother's disgrace. Now, just as I expected, she has quarrelled with me. Indeed, Monsieur, I have never refused you anything that was at all possible, and you cannot mention one refusal which you now consider unjustified. As for inducing

---

[1] The need for brevity obliged the editor to omit two other long passages when the Regent tried to thrust the governorship upon Saint-Simon. Perhaps the temptation to accept had really been very great and the refusal heroic. The post would have given Saint-Simon all the glory he desired, and a second chance to mould a King of France. One feels that this conversation may have been the final blow to his hopes for the Regent, and perhaps to his love. After this he could not escape quickly enough.

you to serve my pleasure, have I ever asked of you anything for myself or my family? Regarding others, have I ever solicited anything improper or likely to harm your reputation in selecting men for offices? And how often have I ignored my own preferences—witness the nominations I have made for heads of councils? Consider affairs of State, and remember that the causes on which I set my heart were invariably defeated, the bastards' rank, for example, the affair of the bonnet, so outrageous, so often and solemnly promised me, all the other disputes with the Parlement, the attacks on yourself, the dangerous and quite unjustifiable encroachments of those so-called nobles. In all these troubles you were duped, and suffered greatly in escaping from them; and worse followed, as I had foretold. You will not deny that you always repented, for, in your study, you told me so yourself. Please remember that though nothing was ever so vitally important to me as those particular issues, once they were settled I remained silent, and when you later tried to reopen the discussion, I always changed the subject. Was that, Monsieur, inducing you to please me? In all that most deeply affected me you did the reverse; yet I think you have never found me less devoted, nor less concerned for your interests. It appears to me that these answers should be more than sufficient. I await your further observations, if any, for I think I have nothing to fear.'

M. le Duc d'Orléans was silent. He had listened, head bent, as was his way when troubled or embarrassed, sometimes pacing up and down, sometimes standing motionless. At last he spoke, turning to me with a smile, and declaring that everything I had said was true, and that I must now forget it. I had been right in imagining that they had shown my refusals in a different light and that he had been vexed; but he had spoken frankly. Now we must put the whole incident behind us and change the subject. 'With all my heart,' I replied, 'but you must allow me some candour in return. You repeated to the Abbé Dubois, did you not, all my remarks concerning the Anglo-Spanish treaty, and his improper conduct in uniting the King of England with the Emperor, and the Emperor with the Pope in pursuit of his hat? Did not that unworldly priest immediately present you with these ancient grudges? Come, confess! was it not thus?' 'Indeed,' he replied, looking monstrously ashamed and embarrassed, 'it was exactly so. The Abbé Dubois's harping on all your refusals stung me into a fury.' 'Well! Monsieur,' said I, 'are you satisfied now?' 'Oh! yes,' he exclaimed, 'there is nothing wrong now. I knew it all the time, but he got me confused.'

Let me add a final touch with something that Torcy told me shortly afterwards. Although Dubois made every effort to conceal his Roman manœuvres, Torcy learned so much by the posts[1] that he thought it his duty to warn M. le Duc d'Orléans. He therefore explained in his quiet way

---

[1] Torcy was master of the posts, and censored the letters. Reading foreigners' letters was a most valuable way of gaining information. Frenchmen were careful, and more often than not used codes.

that if the Abbé Dubois were seeking a hat with His Royal Highness's knowledge, he had no more to say; but being uncertain he felt it only right to report what was afoot. M. le Duc d'Orléans burst out laughing. 'Cardinal!' he cried, 'that little worm! You must be joking, he would never dare.' And when Torcy showed him proof, he lost his temper, exclaiming that if Master Impudence had any such notion, he would clap him into a deep dungeon. He several times repeated that phrase, in fact whenever Torcy produced fresh evidence, from foreign letters, of the continuing intrigue. On the last occasion, when the hat was almost won, Torcy heard the same words repeated with equal fury. Yet when he visited the Regent next day, at the Palais Royal, M. le Duc d'Orléans beckoned him into a corner to say, 'By the way, Monsieur, please write to Rome in my name, requesting a hat for Monsieur de Cambrai. Do not delay, speed is essential.' Torcy was dumbfounded; but once the order had been given, the Regent left him with a serenity only equalled by his previous outbursts. It was, as in the old saying, enough to make one's hair stand on end. Torcy was not so much surprised by the Regent's action, for he had suspected something unreal in the threats; it was the sudden transition, in less than twenty-four hours, from prophecies of dungeons, archbishop though he was, to the calm order to write to Rome for his hat. That was how things were done in those days.

The Duchesse de Sully died, aged fifty-six. She was the Duc de Coislin's daughter; niece of the cardinal, and the sweetest woman imaginable, who would have starved to death had it not been for her brother the Bishop of Metz. Her death was not unfitting to her name,[1] for she developed an abscess in a place which modesty forbade her showing to the surgeons. Her maid dressed it for her in private, and later described the symptoms. It was nothing they could not have cured, had they been able to treat her like other women; but no one could overcome her scruples. The maid explained matters through the half-closed door, and did what they ordered; but this method of surgery by proxy soon brought her to the grave. She died a childless widow.

On 19 March, after an illness lasting barely twenty-four hours, Pope Clement XI[2] died, at the age of sixty-one. He was a cardinal for eleven years, Pope rather more than twenty, and a native of Pesaro, where the Albani family is of no great account. His rule has been described so often in these memoirs that it would be superfluous to enlarge upon it, or on his character. He had long been afflicted with abdominal ruptures, and had lived in the expectation of sudden death. He was immensely stout, ruptured also at the navel, and was held together by a kind of silver stomach. Thus the slightest mishap was enough to strike him dead, as indeed happened.

[1] Her name was Madeleine Armande du Cambout de Coislin (1665–1721). She had been a widow since 1712. The disease, he suggests, was proper for a Magdalen.
[2] Giovanni Francesco Albani (1649–1721), Cardinal 1690, Pope from 1700.

His death came as a reprieve for Alberoni, who was a fugitive in Rome, facing a suit to divest him of his hat. At the time of the Cellanare conspiracy, the Regent and Dubois, who regarded him as their personal enemy, had seized the opportunity to procure his banishment from Spain, though exactly how they operated I never discovered, more is the pity. M. le Duc d'Orléans's death occurred so soon after that of Dubois that I had no chance to question him. All I learned was that the moment came when Alberoni's tyranny was no longer endurable to the Spaniards. It was then easy for Dubois and the Regent to bribe the queen's nurse to represent him as being the sole obstacle to peace with France, serving his own interests, sacrificing those of Their Most Catholic Majesties, and preparing to abandon them to the enmity of all Europe.

The plan succeeded; Alberoni, when he least expected it, received a letter from King Philip commanding him to leave Spain within the next twenty-four hours, and meanwhile an officer of the guard was set to ensure his obedience. How Alberoni took those awful tidings I never learned. All I know is that he obeyed, and left Spain by the Aragon road. So little care was taken regarding his papers and possessions, including vast hoards of jewels and silver, that not until several days had passed was the king informed of the disappearance of the original will of Charles II. It was nowhere to be found, and Alberoni was immediately suspected of having made off with that precious document by which King Charles named the Duc d'Anjou to be Philip V of Spain. It was feared lest he might be intending to present it to the Emperor, in a bid to gain favour. They sent after him, but only with the utmost difficulty and most dreadful menaces was he persuaded to disgorge it, among other important papers found missing at the same time; and all the while he uttered indignant protests. The fear of him was so great in Spain that, until that moment, no one had dared to rejoice openly. This final episode seemed like a guarantee against his return, and there followed an unparalleled exhibition of public joy, coupled with imprecations, and reports to the king and queen of crimes he had committed, of which only they had been ignorant.

Tyrants and thieves have their allotted span. They may not last beyond what the eternal Arbiter permits. We have such abundant proof of Alberoni's having been both that no more need be said of that most abhorrent personage. M. le Duc d'Orléans made little effort to hide his delight; Dubois still less. By their efforts the enemy had been overthrown; by his departure the barrier he had erected between King Philip and the Regent was broken, and with it the only obstacle to peace. That in itself brought joy to Italy, Vienna, and London; the allied powers were jubilant; even the Dutch were thankful to be rid of a minister so powerful, double-faced, and rash.

One last wild gesture of rage and despair he did allow himself. As he journeyed through France on his way to Italy, he stopped at Montpellier to write M. le Duc d'Orléans a letter, offering him the means to wage a most foul war against Spain; and from Marseilles on the eve of embarkation he wrote again, repeating his offer and urging the Regent to accept. Arrived at Rome, he went into hiding, but was none the less summoned to appear before the Sacred College. It so happened, however, that despite the Pope's recommendation, that body considered the privilege of voting in conclave far too precious to be removable on any pretext whatsoever. Thus Alberoni kept his hat, even though every cardinal, except the French and Spanish, had loudly protested against his promotion. It seemed to them that to deprive a cardinal of the purple might become a fatal precedent, reducing them below the level of kings and popes, and challenging their most precious asset, independence. If a prince-cardinal or otherwise noble prelate wished to return his hat, in order to marry and found a line, that would pass; to demote a cardinal as a punishment, or because the hat had been unwisely accorded, was something which they refused to countenance. Thus all the efforts of Spain, and all the Pope's authority, proved powerless to bring on the trial. The preliminaries went forward with infinite slowness, and the case was abandoned altogether after Pope Clement's death, which came, as I have already said, as a reprieve to that scoundrel Alberoni.

After a short absence, he rented a magnificent palazzo in the centre of Rome, and returned to live there in great state, with a large retinue, all amply provided for by his plunder of Spain. He found himself a near neighbour of Cardinal del Giudice, and like him faced the residence of the Princesse des Ursins, thus forming a triangle that gave much food for thought to the citizens of Rome. Alberoni, who saw them both into their graves, succeeded in becoming the legate to Ferrara. He held that office for many years although, in Rome itself, he remained of no great account. He still lives there, sound in mind and body, at the age of eighty-six.

Many persons of note died that year (1721), beginning with Chamillart, aged seventy. You have already learned of his career and disgrace, and very many times of his character.[1] Affable, obliging, and modest, he was fair and kind in all his dealings, never arrogant, never spoiled by power or favour, but without much wit, learning, or understanding. He was easily prejudiced and very obstinate, apt to believe that he knew all, but wholly unself-seeking, attached to the King by bonds of genuine affection, never in the least by hopes of promotion. When he returned to Paris, he moved in the best circles of Court and town; gave supper-parties every day, without display, but with drink and victuals of the very best. He did not often go out,[2] except to dine with me, or with one or other of his small band of intimate friends. For two months of every year he went to his estate, at Courcelles,[3] where he was constantly visited by the entire province. He

---

[1] Michel I Chamillart: see index, I and II.
[2] His private house was in the Rue du Coq Héron.
[3] Near La Flèche, on the River Loire.

lived without ostentation, reflecting earnestly on his salvation. Whenever I was in Paris, I dined with him at least once, and called on him every day, though my visits were not of long duration. I was at La Ferté when he died, and mourned him deeply.

On 4 May, Desmaretz died, aged seventy-three, just eighteen days after Chamillart. You have already learned of the vicissitudes of his career. Great Heavens! Could he but see his son![1] After our reconciliation, which you know of, I had been meeting him every day. He was a man of better sense than parts, and appeared more intelligent than he actually was. There was something slow and heavy about him, though he spoke well, and pleasantly enough; but he was a hard man to deal with, with an unmanageable temper, the very reverse of Chamillart, inasmuch as Chamillart had that rare quality of being an excellent friend and no one's enemy. Desmaretz's friendship went with his interests, and far less generously than would best have served them. You already know his character; let this suffice.

Two days later, on 6 May, d'Argenson also died, at his singular retreat in the outer wall of the Convent of the Filles de la Croix, in the Faubourg Saint-Antoine.[2] Enough has been said of him already. Towards the end of his life, he began to sign his name *de* Voyer, instead of le Voyer, which was the proper form.[3] His family, who have accumulated vast riches and the desire to advance themselves in other directions also, have been most careful to imitate their father's later signature, and to cause their children to be so addressed.

Mézières,[4] a lieutenant-general and governor of Amiens and Corbie, died also about this time. He was small, humped in front, and terrifyingly so behind, with a white face very much resembling that of a frog. He had courage, sufficient wit, brazen effrontery, and enough self-confidence to advance himself. He had adjusted to his appearance and could be seen contemplating his image in the mirrors with great complacency. He was gallant, laid siege to the ladies, and thought himself a very paragon, worthy of all the rewards of war and the Court, not excluding those of chivalry. He was a brother of the mother of the Duc de Levis, and had been heard to say that the connection honoured his nephew; yet I learned on reliable authority that his branch of the Béthisy family was only recently ennobled. Mézières and his wife,[5] a past-mistress in intrigue and a most dangerous

---

[1] The son, M. de Maillebois, was made a Maréchal de France in 1741; but he was beaten at the Battle of Piacenza, 1746. Saint-Simon must have added this when he was revising the memoirs after his retirement.

[2] See p. 166 above.

[3] He was Marc René le (or de) Voyer de Paulmy, Marquis d'Argenson. Saint-Simon persists in referring to him simply as Argenson.

[4] Eugène Marie de Béthisy, Marquis de Mézières (1656–1721). His mother was Marie Françoise de Paule de Béthisy.

[5] Eleanor Mary Sutton Oglethorpe.

woman, lined their pockets from the Mississippi Scheme. He left sons and daughters as scheming and quite as malicious as their mother.

Soon after this came the death of the Abbé de Lionne,[1] son of the famous minister and secretary of State, but resembling him in nothing except the name. He had the Abbeys of Marmoutier, Châlis, and Cercamp, and was prior of Saint-Martin-des-Champs, in Paris, where he spent most of his time, hardly seeing anyone, and dying as obscurely as he had lived. He was a libertine, and had been accused of selling his preferments. For a long time past, he had been in the habit of drinking twenty pints of Seine water every morning.

After our abandonment of Spain and, still more, our inducing that country to sign a treaty so eminently gratifying to the English, or rather, to the Abbé Dubois, I frankly confess my failure to understand how a double marriage between France and Spain could follow with so much speed. The secret was kept so well that no other country, no person even, had wind of it beforehand. For some time past the Abbé Dubois had forbidden M. le Duc d'Orléans to discuss foreign affairs with me, and since our recent contretemps the ban had become even more absolute. That however had not prevented the Regent from continually throwing scraps in my direction, but the bare bones only, never any accompanying details. You may well imagine that I did not comment. In the early days of June I went to work with him, as usual,[2] and found him alone, walking in his state apartments. 'Well met!' said he, seizing my hand, 'I cannot keep the secret from you any longer. My dearest wish is to be fulfilled, my very heart's desire. But you must swear not to tell.' Then, with a laugh, 'If Monsieur de Cambrai knew, he would never forgive me.' He at once informed me that he was reconciled with the King and Queen of Spain; that a match had been arranged between the King and the Infanta,[3] and that another would take place immediately between the Prince of the Asturias and Mlle de Chartres.[4]

My joy was great indeed, but my surprise far greater. M. le Duc d'Orléans embraced me, and after enlarging on the enormous benefits to himself, personally, and the absolute propriety of the King's marriage, I

---

[1] Jules Paul, Abbé de Lionne (1644–1721). He was a doctor of the Sorbonne, and King's Almoner 1671–1681. His trafficking in preferments worried his family so much that they gave him a 'tutor' to restrain him, but the tutor behaved even worse. It was Père Tellier who protected them both.

[2] Since they did not discuss foreign affairs, and as Saint-Simon knew nothing of finance and did not wish to become involved in the education of the King, one wonders what they could possibly have found to work at.

[3] Maria Ana Victoria, Infanta of Spain (1718–1781), daughter of Philip V and Elisabeth Farnese.

[4] Louise Elisabeth d'Orléans (1709–1750), called Mlle de Montpensier, not Mlle de Chartres, a title given to an older sister Louise Adélaïde (1698–1743) who was Abbess of Challes. Louise Elisabeth became Queen of Spain when in 1724 Philip V abdicated in favour of his eldest son Louis; but Louis died eight months later, and Philip returned to the throne. (See also note 3, p. 388 below.)

asked him how he had achieved such wonders, more especially the marriage of his daughter. He said it had all happened in a flash, thanks to the Abbé Dubois's uncanny cleverness; that King Philip had been enchanted by his nephew's desire for the Infanta, and that the alliance with the Regent's daughter had been the *sine qua non* of the whole affair. After further rejoicings and much discussion, I suggested that his daughter's betrothal should be kept secret until her departure, and that of the King until the passing years had made consummation possible. This was to allay the fears of other European countries; for the thought of a union between the two branches of the Bourbon family had always alarmed them, and their entire policy had been directed, only too successfully, to keeping them apart. It would be very wise, I urged, to leave those sovereigns undisturbed for as long as possible. Moreover, since the Infanta was only three years old, there would be ample time to calm any fears aroused by his daughter's marriage. 'You are perfectly right,' replied M. le Duc d'Orléans; 'but it is quite useless. The Spaniards are hell-bent on making the announcement at once, and will send us the Infanta as soon as the formal proposal has been received and the contract signed.' 'What folly!' I cried. 'It will set the alarms ringing in every European country. We must stand firm; it is all important.' 'What you say is very true,' said M. le Duc d'Orléans, 'and I agree with you; but they are obstinate and quite determined; we were forced to give way, and now all is settled. The affair is of such vast importance to me, you would not have had me break off for a trifle.' I merely shrugged my shoulders, to show my disapproval of such imprudent haste.

After some further discussion, I began to think of my own fortunes, and of this being an admirable occasion to establish those of my younger son.[1] I said therefore that matters being so far advanced, he would be considering the dispatch of an ambassador to make the formal request and sign the contract; that a nobleman of high rank would be required, and that I begged him to entrust the mission to me, under his personal protection, with a recommendation to the King of Spain to make the Marquis de Ruffec a Grandee of Spain. I said that he had made a peer of La Feuillade, his worst and most audacious enemy, simply because Canillac had desired it, and had furnished him with large sums of money on the absurd pretext of an embassy to Rome when there had never been any intention of sending him. Moreover, he had just made M. de Nevers a duke, a man whom I believed to be in no way my equal, not to mention the countless favours he

---

[1] Armand Jean de Rouvroy de Saint-Simon, Marquis, later Duc, de Ruffec (1699–1754). In 1715, he had married Marie Jeanne Louise Bauyn d'Angervilliers. He was a serving soldier until 1738 and rose to be a major-general—one of Saint-Simon's tiny sons, commonly known as *les bassets* (the dachshunds) at the Court. His father, with his pretensions to superior rank and birth, must indeed have been concerned about this son's title. Louis XIV gave away so many 'courtesy titles' below the rank of duke, or rather sold them, that to be a *petit marquis* had become something of a joke.

had showered on all and sundry, whereas I had only the two small governorships of my inheritance. I plainly saw that he had nothing left for me, and I was not now asking a dukedom for my younger son, though that would not have provoked a scandal like the advancement of M. de La Feuillade and M. de Nevers, whose service had been less than nothing, and of what quality! (which could not be said of my son). 'But I do now beg you,' I concluded, 'to grant me this small favour, of no concern to anyone, that will give my son the rank and standing of a duke, and seem the natural outcome of my mission to Spain.' M. le Duc d'Orléans scarcely let me finish before granting my request. He promised to do all in his power for the Marquis de Ruffec, with many protests of affection, only asking me to keep the matter a dead secret until he gave the word. Apart from the general need for secrecy, I saw that he wanted time to coax his Dubois into swallowing the pill.

After thanking him, I asked two smaller favours, firstly, not to be given the emoluments of an ambassador, but merely the wherewithal to recoup my expenses so that I was not ruined;[1] secondly, to have no other mission, for I did not want to leave him, and from one affair to another gradually become rooted in Spain. My sole desire in going, I said, was to obtain the grandeeship for my younger son, and then return with all speed. This was because I feared that if Dubois could not prevent my appointment, he would try to keep me in exile, so as to be rid of me. I discovered later that my precautions were not needless. M. le Duc d'Orléans granted both these requests with many gracious words to the effect that he could not spare me for long. I thought I had done great things for my line, and returned home well pleased. How often, O Lord!, do men's best laid plans and victories come to nothing![2]

On the last day of July, the King who until then had enjoyed perfect health, woke with a headache and sore throat. Shivering fits later developed, and that afternoon his head and throat grew worse and he went to bed. Next day I called to inquire. I learned that the night had been bad, and that in the past two hours there had been a relapse. Everyone was aghast. Possessing the *grandes entrées*, I went to his bedroom, which was almost empty. M. le Duc d'Orléans was sitting alone by the fire, looking forsaken and unhappy. I went up to him, and then to the King's bed. At that precise moment, when Boulduc,[3] one of the apothecaries, was giving him

---

[1] People said that Saint-Simon made a good thing of his embassy; but in fact, it got him into debt, and he emerged from it even poorer than before. According to Villars's memoirs, the expenses amounted to 840,000 livres.

[2] Saint-Simon is looking back at the death of his elder son in 1746. He was Vidame de Chartres, Marquis and, in 1722, Duc de Ruffec. When he died, his brother inherited that dukedom, so all the pother was for nothing. Despite what Saint-Simon said to Orléans, he gives the impression that he was longing to escape. In Spain, at least, rank still had proper importance.

[3] Gilles François Boulduc (1675-1742), a professor of chemistry at the Jardin des Plantes, and the King's apothecary.

some draught or other, the Duchesse de La Ferté,[1] who had all the entrées because she was a sister of the Duchesse de Ventadour, happened to be leaning over his shoulder. Hearing my approach, she turned, and immediately declared in a voice that was neither loud nor soft, 'He has been poisoned; he has been poisoned.' 'Pray be silent, Madame!' I exclaimed, 'that is a wicked thing to say.' But she still continued to repeat those words, so clear and so loud that I feared lest the King should hear her. Boulduc and I glanced at one another, and I speedily left the bed and that foolish woman, with whom I had never had the smallest acquaintance. I was deeply anxious and distressed while the illness lasted—no more than five days, but the first three very bad—yet I could not but be thankful that I had refused the governorship. Indeed, I became so much agitated by the thought of my situation had I accepted it that I woke every night in a cold sweat. Yet these wakings were a positive pleasure as soon as I realized that it was not so. The King was not ill long, and recovered completely. Thus all was peace and joy once more, with a spate of *Te Deum*s and other signs of public rejoicing. Helvétius[2] received all the credit, for the other doctors lost their heads. During a consultation which M. le Duc d'Orléans attended, he strongly recommended bleeding from the foot, and had his way. A very marked improvement immediately followed, and the complete cure shortly afterwards.

Thury[3] died unmarried at the age of sixty-two, having given, or rather sold, all he possessed to the Maréchal d'Harcourt. They had the same father but were otherwise totally dissimilar. Thury, dark, evil, moody and cynical, had an excellent brain and was both malicious and insolent. Yet despite his bad reputation in Society and the army, he was received in good houses. It is true none the less that the Duc d'Elbeuf, at table, felled him with a shoulder of mutton, leaving a permanent scar on his most unpleasing countenance, though at the time he did not retaliate.

As I had expected, Dubois was infuriated by the news of my embassy, and set himself to ruin and humiliate me by strewing the most absurd and unlooked-for difficulties in my path, from some of which I found it hard to extricate myself. This is to prepare you for what follows; I shall tell more at the time of my departure to Spain. He soon showed me what I might expect from him, and thus absolved me from any need to consider his feelings; yet much prudence was needed, for until I left everything was in his hands, and afterwards also, such was the hold he had acquired over M. le Duc d'Orléans.

[1] Marie Isabelle Gabrielle de La Motte-Houdancourt, Duchesse de La Ferté (1654–1726).

[2] Jean Claude Adrien Helvétius (1685–1755) was appointed physician to the King in 1713. He was a son of Adrien Helvétius who had been Monsieur's doctor (see I, p. 150), and continued to be the Orléans family doctor. He firmly believed in ipecacuanha as a cure for dysentery.

[3] Henri d'Harcourt, Marquis de Thury (1659–1721). His father lived to be 104, dying in 1719.

The time came for the announcement of the King's betrothal, and M. le Duc d'Orléans was in a permanent state of agitation, wondering how he would take the news, for surprises always alarmed him. The Regent was concerned also for public opinion on account of the Infanta's extreme youth. In the end, he chose a day when the Regency Council was to meet, resolving to tell the King beforehand, and thereafter to make the announcement in full council, as of something already decided and fixed. As I saw it, his greatest problem would be with the King who, as I have said, feared surprises and suddenness. A glance or a gesture from the Maréchal de Villeroy could throw him into such confusion that he became speechless. Yet he must consent with a firm 'yes'; for if he remained silent, what could be done at the Council? And supposing he said 'no', what would happen then? Such anxieties kept M. le Duc d'Orléans, Cardinal Dubois, and myself long in consultation. At last we decided that before the meeting (timed for the afternoon), M. le Duc d'Orléans should send for Monsieur le Duc and Monsieur de Fréjus—Monsieur le Duc because he would not object, and lest he be hurt by being kept longer in the dark, Fréjus to flatter his vanity by choosing him in preference to the Maréchal de Villeroy, and to have him ready to comfort the King, should that prove necessary. Monsieur le Duc was surprised, but not displeased, and played his part well. Fréjus was vexed. He perceived that only necessity had won him the honour; praised the alliance in formal words; thought the Infanta too young (which Monsieur le Duc had not minded); declared that the King would probably not refuse, but be neutral; promised to be present for the announcement, and said little else. The need for secrecy was impressed on them both; but from what transpired I feel sure that Fréjus went forthwith to tell the Maréchal de Villeroy, whom he invariably courted in matters where personal interests were not involved.

On the appointed day, we all forgathered at the Tuileries, M. le Duc d'Orléans appearing last, so as to allow time for late arrivals. He drew me into a corner to tell me of his interviews with Monsieur le Duc and Fréjus. After that he moved restlessly about the council chamber, looking for all the world like a nervous man about to storm ramparts. I kept my eye on him, feeling much alarmed as I observed his condition. At last he entered the King's apartments, and I followed. He asked who was present, and when Fréjus was not mentioned he had him summoned. For a time he remained in the ante-room, then went into the study, where Monsieur le Duc already was, with the Maréchal de Villeroy and some junior members of the staff, assistant tutors and such-like. I stayed in the ante-room, considerably disturbed by Fréjus's absence, which I thought boded no good. He came at last in a monstrous hurry, as though aware of his lateness. Soon afterwards people began to emerge from the study, until only M. le Duc d'Orléans, Cardinal Dubois, Monsieur le Duc, the Maréchal de Villeroy, and Fréjus remained. Then, observing that I was the only person of my rank, and the only council member still in the ante-room, I returned to the chamber.

The Maréchaux de Villars, d'Estrées, and d'Huxelles approached me one after the other, asking whether I knew the reason for the secret conference in the King's study; but I declared I knew no more than they did. They stayed talking to me a good quarter of an hour, or so it seemed, for time was passing and I had begun to fear lest there were difficulties and distresses. At last the Maréchal de Villars exclaimed, 'Let us enter, we shall be as well there as here', and we all went into the ante-room, where only the valets and assistants remained. Very soon the study door opened, how or why I did not see for I was standing with my back to it. The slight noise made me turn my head, and I saw the Maréchal d'Huxelles disappear into the room. Villars said, 'Why not follow?' and we all three entered the study. The King stood with his back to the door; M. le Duc d'Orléans faced him, looking flushed; Monsieur le Duc was close beside them, and both seemed peculiarly despondent. Dubois and the Maréchal de Villeroy stood sideways, and Fréjus next the King. I could see his profile and thought he appeared perplexed. We stood as we had entered, at the King's back. I was directly behind him, and I craned forward a little to see his face, but very quickly drew back because he looked very red, and his eyes, so far as I could see them, were full of tears.[1] No one moved, or addressed us when we appeared. Cardinal Dubois appeared calm, but extremely grave. The Maréchal de Villeroy was, as usual, shaking his wig; at least that is how it struck me at first glance. 'Come, Sire!' he was saying, 'you must show willing.' Fréjus bent down, and spoke to the King in a low voice, as though encouraging him; I could not hear his words. The rest were wrapt in gloom. We, the late comers, were astonished by the scene, more especially I, who knew what was afoot. I discerned at length that the King was refusing to go to the council chamber and that they were pressing him; but I dared not make a sign to M. le Duc d'Orléans or Dubois in order to discover more.

So it continued until, a quarter of an hour later, Monsieur de Fréjus, after a few more whispered words, informed M. le Duc d'Orléans that the King would attend the meeting, but needed time to recover. This brought some measure of relief to those anxious faces. M. le Duc d'Orléans declared that there was no hurry, and that no one would mind waiting. He then stepped between the King and Fréjus; bent to whisper; straightened himself; and announced in a louder voice, 'The King has consented to come. I think it would be best to leave him now.' He departed and we all followed him, only Monsieur le Duc, the Maréchal de Villeroy, and Monsieur de Fréjus remaining with the King. On our way out, the Regent seized my arm, and drew me into one of the doorways to whisper that at the first mention of marriage the King had burst into tears; that they had

[1] See p. 426 below.

had all the difficulty in the world to extract his consent, and that he had, as we saw for ourselves, shown an equal disinclination to attend the council. There was no time to say more.

After an interval the King entered with Monsieur le Duc; but his red and swollen eyes were very noticeable, and he seemed dreadfully unhappy. M. le Duc d'Orléans glanced round the assembly; then turned to the King, to ask if he would be pleased to announce his marriage, to which the reply was a bare 'yes', spoken very low; but the four or five members nearest were able to hear him. The Regent then made the announcement and proclaimed the imminent arrival of the Infanta, with a few well chosen words on the suitability of the alliance, and of drawing closer the bonds between the two branches of the royal family, of late so regrettably at variance. His speech was short and he appeared nervous; but, as usual, he spoke admirably. You may well imagine the speeches when he asked for votes. Lastly, he bowed smiling, turning to the King as though inviting him to smile also; and ended by declaring, 'There, Sire! your marriage is duly approved and accepted, and thus a grand and splendid alliance has been established.'

As you will have noticed, M. le Duc d'Orléans had thought it advisable to treat the two betrothals separately, and there was accordingly an interval. But the announcement could not long be delayed, and was made ten or twelve days later. There was no opposition in the Council, although the Maréchal de Villeroy said something about amazement, looking considerably annoyed. Next day, the King called at the Palais Royal, then at Saint-Cloud, to give formal expression to M. and Mme la Duchesse d'Orléans, Mlle de Montpensier, and Madame, of his pleasure at this brilliant, almost unbelievably exalted match. A vast crowd of foreign ministers, and all the best people of Paris and the Court were present.

I must admit that the marriage of the Prince of the Asturias to one of M. le Duc d'Orléans's daughters was the biggest surprise of my life, considering the ill feeling that had for so long existed between him and King Philip. How the Abbé Dubois, whose very name should have been anathema in Spain on account of the terms of the treaty, had dared even to think of reconciling the Regent with the Spanish king, and not only dared but triumphantly succeeded in placing M. le Duc d'Orléans's daughter on the throne of Spain, was a master-stroke of effrontery and an unparalleled achievement. I never learned how the negotiations proceeded, and therefore cannot describe them. All that M. le Duc d'Orléans told me was that his daughter's marriage had been an absolute condition of the King's, and that King Philip was so much a Frenchman at heart that he had made no difficulty. From this I had concluded that being so passionately French, the King of Spain was willing to swallow anything, so long as his daughter might occupy the throne of his forefathers. *Fortuna è dormire*, say the Italians, and so indeed decrees Providence, that rules all and showers upon us blessings beyond human conception. To say truth, no matter what has happened since M. le Duc d'Orléans's death, he certainly profited immensely by these marriages during the short time that remained to him. Had he lived the normal span, both he and France would have benefited to a far greater extent, for in that event, the Infanta would surely have become our Queen.

While all this was happening, I was, as I have said, in the hands of Cardinal Dubois who, loathing my appointment, was determined by hook or crook to ruin and disgrace me. As soon as the betrothals had been announced, I pressed for my nomination, so as to begin my preparations which, as you will remember, I had been forbidden to do for fear of raising an alarm. I believed that there would be no further delay. I was wrong. Despite all my entreaties the ban remained. This was because the cardinal hoped that haste would double my expenses, and that by making me late he might have an excuse to blame me, and give the envious additional cause for complaint. Seeing, at last, that the continual delay was making preparation impossible, I went to the Regent himself, on Tuesday, 23 September, choosing a time when he was in his room at the Tuileries, and I spoke so strongly that he said we need only go to the King. Thereupon he took me into the study, where we found King Louis with his tutors, assistant tutors, and some courtiers who were not asked to leave, and there and then I was appointed. On our return, M. le Duc d'Orléans made me drive with him in his coach to the Palais Royal, where we had our first serious conversation on the subject of my embassy.

Cardinal Dubois was no doubt exceedingly vexed, but further delay was impossible, and on the following day the preparations were begun, wherein he appeared as urgent and as hurried as he had previously been dilatory. He ordered the tailors to be speedy, desired to see examples of the coats for my servants, both liveried and otherwise, insisted on greater magnificence, and demanded that all my own clothes and those of my children be offered for his approval. In his anxiety to be quickly rid of me once I had been appointed, he hired carts[1] from the posting-houses to take the baggage as far as Bayonne, which was an additional expense for me to bear.

He asked the names of my staff, and wished me to take a very large retinue. I mentioned the Comte de Lorges,[2] the Comte de Céreste,[3] my two sons, the Abbé de Saint-Simon and his brother,[4] a major of his regiment[5] who had served with distinction in Spain, and proved infinitely

---

[1] The word is *haquet*, dray, used for transporting wine and bales of goods.

[2] Guy Michel de Durfort, the eldest son of Mme de Saint-Simon's brother the Duc de Lorges by his first marriage. He was seventeen years old.

[3] Louis Buffile Toussaint Hyacinthe de Brancas, Comte de Céreste (1697–1754).

[4] Claude de Rouvroy (1695–1760), later Bishop of Metz, and Henri de Rouvroy, Marquis de Saint-Simon (1703–1739), grandfather of the Comte de Saint-Simon, the nineteenth-century philosopher and socialist. It has been said that his philosophy could be expressed by the words, 'Love one another', a motto which his eminent cousin might not wholly have approved.

[5] A certain Sieur de Girenton.

useful to me (I afterwards appointed him King's lieutenant, at Blaye), an officer of my younger son's regiment,[1] and the Abbé de Mathan,[2] a friend of the Abbé de Saint-Simon, who has ever since remained with my family. You will remember that the Marquis de Brancas[3] was an old friend of mine; Céreste was his brother but younger by twenty-five years and devoted to my children. He was very eager to come with me, his brother also wished it, and I regarded it as an honour. We became well acquainted on the journey, for I found him delightfully mature, excellent company, and very reliable. Mutual esteem led to a close friendship that has become even firmer with the years.

Dubois approved every name on my list; but I was vastly astonished when he sent to tell me that I must include forty officers from my sons' cavalry regiments, and from the infantry regiment of the Marquis de Saint-Simon, and that if I could not raise so many, he would name some himself. I violently protested, saying both to the Regent and to him that it served no kind of purpose to surround me with this huge and costly retinue; that no ambassador had ever before had a military escort, that my mission was a peaceful one in the cause of union and friendship, and that no protection was required; that apart from the futility and expense of feeding and transporting forty officers of the household troops, such dashing young sparks would have a French love of gallantry and amorous adventures that would give me more trouble than all the rest of my mission.

Eminently sensible though my objections were, they were overruled and very ill received. Dubois intended to ruin me, and subject me to all the anxiety and difficulties which he could contrive. He rightly surmised that nothing would better serve that end than to saddle me with forty officers. When that number was not forthcoming I fixed on twenty-nine, and although the cardinal succeeded in emptying my purse, he failed with the other plan, for the officers behaved perfectly, and the desired effect was not produced. Meanwhile, he had sent to Spain, ordering Sartine[4] to furnish everything that could not be brought from France, my stables, for example, complete with mules, coaches, Spanish servants, and provisions, all of which he managed to perfection.

On 23 October, I at last set off, travelling post with the Comte de Lorges, my sons, the Abbé de Saint-Simon, his brother, and one or two others for company. The rest of the party, including the Abbé de Mathan, joined us at Blaye, and M. de Céreste, at Bayonne. We slept at Orléans, Montrichard,[5] and Poitiers. On the way from Poitiers to Ruffec we met the

[1] The Chevalier de Résie (b. 1689).
[2] Louis Guillaume, Abbé de Mathan, who became Abbot of La Croix-Saint-Lefroy, and died in 1769.
[3] See index, II.
[4] Antoine de Sartine. He was paymaster-general of the Spanish navy, and had an English wife, Catherine Wilts.
[5] Montrichard is in Touraine, not far from Amboise.

Duke of Osuna,[1] at Vivonne, and I stepped down to embrace him. Hearing that he was at mass, I went to stand by the church door, and thus, as soon as he emerged, we were able to exchange compliments, embraces, and expressions of pleasure. We then returned to the posting-house, for he, too, was travelling post. There were continual stoppages in the doorways, when I wished, as was only polite, to do him the honours of France. We afterwards went to an upper room where we conversed alone for an hour and a half. Though he spoke monstrously bad French, we were able to understand one another; but he was not communicative.[2] You may well imagine that I kept my ears wider open than my mouth. Eventually we parted with further compliments, embraces, and assurances of friendship. No matter what I said, I could not prevent his escorting me downstairs. On the other hand, nothing would persuade me to enter my chaise until after his departure.

My chaise collapsed with a broken axle as we arrived at Couhé, an estate belonging to M. de Vérac, and I was delayed three hours while they made a new one. I spent the time writing to M. le Duc d'Orléans and Cardinal Dubois describing the above conversation, and then paid a short visit to the château and the park. We did not reach Ruffec until the clocks were striking midnight; but found that a large number of the local nobility and gentry had been waiting for us some hours. I entertained them all to dinner and supper on both days of my stay. From Ruffec it was a two-day journey to La Cassine, a little house built by my father on the edge of the marshes, four miles from Blaye. It was a great pleasure to visit it. I remained there for the eve of All Saints, and for the day itself, and went to Blaye early next morning, to stay a couple of days. Many persons of quality called on me, including nobility and others from the neighbouring provinces, and great banquets were given for us each afternoon and evening of our short visit.

Although the weather was very bad, this seemed to provide an excellent opportunity for visiting the fortress, which I had a great desire to inspect; and I took my son with me because he had the reversion of my governorship. When we crossed to Bordeaux there was such a fearful storm that everyone urged me to wait; but my time was strictly limited and I did not wish to stay longer. Boucher the Intendant of Bordeaux had brought over his magnificent brig, and enough boats to transport my entire suite and the people who had crossed over to Blaye in order to welcome me. Most of them returned with us. I was enchanted by the view of the port and town, with more than three hundred ships of all nations, bedecked with flags,

[1] Joseph Acuña Pacheco y Tellez-Giron, Duke of Osuna (1684–1733), Lord Chamberlain of the King of Spain, ambassador extraordinary to France 1721. He was Saint-Simon's opposite number, sent to France to sign the marriage contracts and return to Spain with Mlle de Montpensier.

[2] The conversation showed that he knew dangerously much of the recent intrigues at the French Court, but was not prepared to discuss them.

and drawn up in two lines for us to pass between, the cannons booming and salutes being fired from the guns of the Château Trompette.

Everyone knows Bordeaux, and therefore no description is needed. Sufficient to say that, after Constantinople, the port is the most beautiful in all the world. There were congratulatory addresses, and a vast number of coaches collected at the quayside to take us to the house of the Intendant, where the magistrates harangued me, in full dress uniform. As many of them were persons of quality, or in other ways distinguished, and since the magistrates of Bordeaux are different from other civic bodies, I turned to the Intendant after making my speech and requested him to let me invite them to supper. They appeared overcome by this courtesy, which they certainly had not expected, and hurried off to change their coats. Impossible to imagine finer banquets or more delicious food than the Intendant offered us both morning and evening, or more delightful hosts than M. and Mme Boucher, as they did the honours of the town and their residence. The Parlement was not in session, and thus the archbishop and the premier président were absent; but I visited the palace and all the other sights. They tried to prevent me from seeing the town hall which is a hideous building; but I insisted on going there because I wished to be particularly civil to the magistrates. They were all there, and when I said that I came less out of curiosity regarding what was reputed to be an ugly building than to see them once more, I thought they appeared vastly pleased.

After bidding M. and Mme Boucher farewell, we set out once more over the moors, and in due course reached Bayonne, where we lodged with d'Adoncourt the extremely able commandant, who contrived to be much loved and at the same time a good servant of the King. My children and I put up at his house; the rest of the party were lodged in the neighbourhood. Changing carriages and reorganizing the bestowal of our luggage[1] delayed us for four days, during which nothing could have exceeded d'Adoncourt's kindness, his simple, easy politeness, and the abundant, well-prepared, most delicious feasts which he provided for us each day and night. He and his officers met us a league from the town, and I, too, was on horseback when we met. The cannon salutes, the speeches, etc., were similar to those at Bordeaux and had to be borne patiently; what is more, it was so everywhere on my return, except only at Blaye, where I expressly forbade it. Druillet, Bishop of Bayonne,[2] visited me, and then returned to us, to dine with the best Society of the town, but not a great number. Next day I called on him; he was a pious and scholarly prelate and exceedingly good company, much loved in his diocese and the surrounding country. I also visited the citadel and the forts, and everything else worth seeing.

---

[1] They were about to cross the frontier into Spain. There had been an outbreak of plague, and quarantine restrictions meant that French waggons and post-chaises would no longer serve.

[2] André Druillet, Bishop of Bayonne in 1707 (died 1727). Saint-Simon would have felt very warm towards him; for he hated the Bull *Unigenitus*, and loved Cardinal de Noailles.

THE SPANISH ROYAL FAMILY. BY GUILLAUME RANC

LOUIS, PRINCE OF THE ASTURIAS

THE PALACE OF BUEN RETIRO AND THE PLAZA
MAYOR, MADRID. ENGRAVINGS

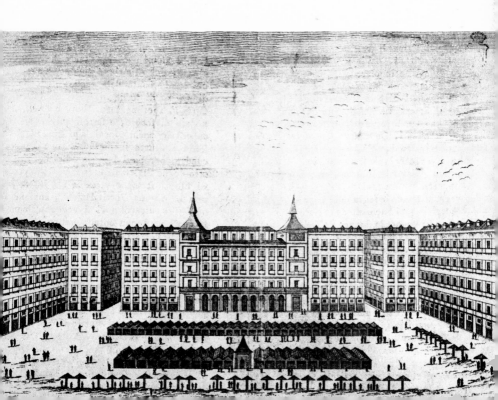

DANGEAU. ENGRAVING AFTER RIGAUD

After quitting Bayonne we crossed the Pyrenees, leaving behind us in France all the rain and wind that had accompanied us until then, and finding clear blue skies and delightful warmth, with views that changed from moment to moment, and were all as fine as possible. We rode on Spanish mules with their long, easy stride. I went a little out of the way to see Loyola,[1] the birthplace of Saint Ignatius, a lonely spot by a broad stream in a narrow defile, with rocky mountains hemming it in on either side. When they are covered with snow, the stream must become a glacier, and in summer a torrent. Four or five Jesuits live there, the very civil and learned custodians of a huge building capable of housing more than a hundred Jesuits and a vast number of pupils, and designed to be the headquarters of their Society.

They showed us the rude home of Saint Ignatius's father, a place with five or six windows, a ground floor for living space, one storey above, and an attic. It might, at the very most, have served for a curé's house, never by any chance have been a château. We saw the room where the saint lay for so long, recovering from his wounds, and where he had the vision of the Society he later founded, also the stable in which his mother had desired to give him birth, in pious imitation of the stable at Bethlehem. Nothing could have been more lowly, cramped, and tumbledown than these two little rooms, yet the gold in them dazzled the eyes and glittered in every corner. In each room there was an altar upon which the Host reposed, and both altars were supremely magnificent.

The present monastery, which they are pulling down, does not amount to much, and holds, at most, a dozen Jesuits. The new church is almost finished, a stately dome of extraordinary height, with matching altars placed at regular intervals around the walls. The gilding, paintings and sculpture cover the whole interior, making it appear extremely rich, yet perfectly discreet. The style is symmetrical and exceedingly fine, and the marble—jasper, porphyry, and lapis-lazuli—is exquisite. The columns, plain, twisted, and fluted, have capitals and ornamentation of gilded bronze. Between the altars are balconies with flights of low marble steps leading up to them and, like the altars themselves, the balustrades are all encrusted with gold. In short, it must be one of the finest buildings in Europe. They gave us some of the best chocolate I have ever tasted,[2] and after spending hours gazing and admiring, we resumed our journey, arriving very late, and with much difficulty, at our night's lodging.

On 15 November, we entered Vitoria, to find a deputation of four provincial officers waiting to receive us with a generous present of excellent wine, named *rancio*. They were gentlemen of rank, heads of the administration, and I therefore asked them to supper, and to dine with us on the

[1] Near San Sebastian.
[2] The Jesuits were evidently great connoisseurs of chocolate. See I, p. 148, for the time when they tried to smuggle gold bars coated with the very best chocolate.

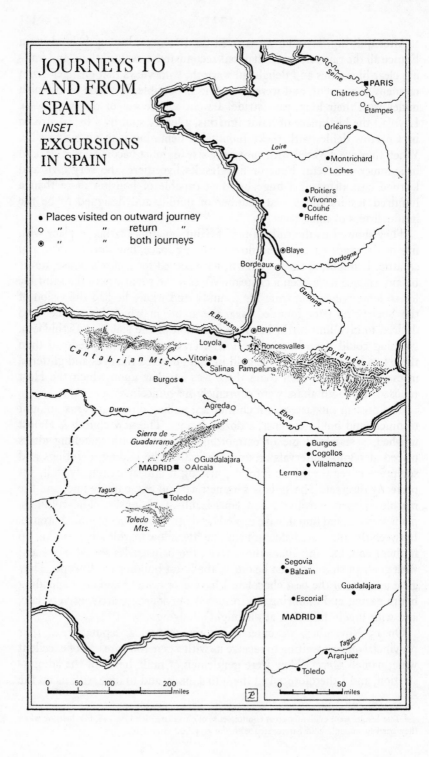

JOURNEYS TO
AND FROM
SPAIN

INSET
EXCURSIONS
IN SPAIN

- Places visited on outward journey
○ " " return "
◉ " " both journeys

following day. They spoke good French; but it surprised me to find Spaniards so gay, and such cheerful company at table. Both in France and in Spain, the cause of my journey made everyone joyful. People thronged the windows and blessed me as I passed. At Salinas, for example, where I did not stay, some ladies, who judging from their houses and appearance at the windows were persons of quality, invited me so charmingly to let them meet, if only for a moment, the man who brought such happiness to Spain, that I thought it only polite to go up to visit them. They seemed enchanted, and I had all the trouble in the world to extricate myself and continue my journey.

At Vitoria, a courier from Sartine arrived, urging me to hurry because Their Catholic Majesties were becoming increasingly impatient. I responded by asking him to have relays reserved for me, no matter what the cost, so that I might press on without further delays.

I arrived at Burgos on the 18th, and longed to remain there at least a day, for my elder son had contracted a high fever, and I was very anxious; but Pecquet,[1] whom I had sent on ahead, now returned, urging me so fervently not to dally that I abandoned my son, leaving most of my retinue with him. The Abbé de Mathan kindly volunteered to stay behind and nurse him, and promised me on no account to leave him. I soon learned the cause of this quite excessive desire for my arrival. It appeared that the queen hated Madrid, and was dying to go to Lerma for the hunting; Pecquet said that M. de Grimaldo[2] and Sartine had done everything possible to persuade her to sacrifice, or at least postpone, that excursion, but that Maulévrier,[3] who was furious at my appointment, had done his utmost to encourage her. He had actually said that if the Duc de Villeroy had been appointed, he would have done more to assist him. The trouble was that he felt strongly antagonistic to any friend of M. le Duc d'Orléans. I resolved not to let him see that I knew anything of all this, but I none the less wrote to Cardinal Dubois to protest.

Thus I left Burgos on the 19th, with my younger son, the Comte de Lorges, M. de Céreste, the Abbé de Saint-Simon, his brother, the major of his regiment, and a handful of servants. We found few post-houses, and such as existed were vastly ill supplied; but we pressed on night and day, without sleep, until we reached Madrid, using whenever possible the carriages of the local officials, and being forced to travel the last twelve

[1] Pierre Antoine Pecquet (died 1762) was a clerk in the foreign ministry, attached to Saint-Simon. He had gone on ahead to Madrid, and it seems that when Philip V heard of his arrival he was furious that the rest of the party were not with him. The exchange of princesses would be delayed, and the weather was getting worse—all because of Saint-Simon's sightseeing and slowness.

[2] Joseph Guttierez, Marquis of Grimaldo (1660–1733). After Alberoni's dismissal, he became first minister of Spain, a counsellor of State, and president of the Council of Foreign Affairs.

[3] Jean Baptiste Louis Andrault, Marquis de Maulévrier, who had been sent with the blue ribbon of the Saint-Esprit for the baby Infante Don Philip (see p. 92 above). He was now the French ambassador.

leagues on post-horses that cost double the money they would have done in France. We arrived on Friday the 21st, at eleven o'clock at night. There were no walls, gates, turnpikes, or any outlying parts of the town; but guards stopped us at our entry to inquire who we were and whence we had come, having been posted on purpose to inform the authorities of our arrival. I was desperately exhausted after travelling all the way from Burgos without resting, and thus, it being very late, I said that we were part of the French ambassador's staff, arriving a day in advance. I learned afterwards that according to the calculations of Sartine, Grimaldo, and Pecquet, we had not been expected until the 22nd.

Early next morning (Saturday, 22 November), Sartine accompanied my secretary to the Marquis of Grimaldo, while I paid the formal calls on ministers that are required of foreign diplomats. Grimaldo, surprised and delighted by my prompt appearance, went at once to the palace to inform Their Catholic Majesties, who were enchanted because of their eagerness to leave Madrid. He then called on me, not waiting for me to call on him, and found me with Maulévrier, the Duke of Liria,[1] and one or two others. Following Grimaldo's example, the chief officers of the court[2] came to my house, as did the Grandees of Spain, the Archbishop of Toledo,[3] and the Grand Inquisitor, Bishop of Barcelona.[4] Nearly all of them bore the empty title Counsellor of State.[5] Castellar the war minister[6] called also that first day, and the Duke of Liria told me that it had been his intention to drive out a league to meet me.

Grimaldo informed me of Their Catholic Majesties' gratification at my arrival, and after many flattering remarks gave me the option of being presented to them that very morning, or later, in the afternoon. I thought it more politic to show eagerness, and we therefore set out at once in Maulévrier's coach, he accompanying us. Thus all the problems regarding first visits—to whom they were due, and the persons who might consider they could justly claim them—were perfectly disposed of, leaving me immensely relieved.

We arrived as the king returned from mass, and were put to wait in a small room between the Grandees' Hall and the Hall of Mirrors into

[1] James Francis Fitzjames (1696–1738), Earl of Tynemouth, Duke of Liria 1716, was Berwick's son. He had married, as her second husband, Catherine Ventura, Duchess of Portugal y Ayala, who became one of the ladies of the new Princess of the Asturias.
[2] The major-domo the Marquis of Villena, the lord high butler the Marquis of Montalegre, the master of the horse the Duke of Arco.
[3] Diego de Astorga y Cespedès had been Archbishop of Toledo since 1720. He had previously been Bishop of Barcelona.
[4] John de Camargo, Bishop of Pampeluna 1716; Bishop of Barcelona and Grand Inquisitor 1720. He died in 1733.
[5] Empty because Alberoni had trained the king never to consult with anyone.
[6] Balthazar Patiño, Marquis of Castellar (1670–1733). Saint-Simon liked him and was delighted when he came as ambassador to Paris in 1730. He was very gay and amusing in conversation as well as being extremely capable. But when he came to Paris he had terribly changed, being afflicted with mild recurrent seizures that made him sad, heavy, and incapable of any continuous thought. He died in Paris, not long afterwards.

which no one enters unsummoned. After a little while the king made his appearance; Grimaldo informed him of my arrival, and he moved towards me preceded and followed by a number of courtiers, but nothing like the crowds at our Court. I bowed very low; he expressed pleasure, inquired about the King and M. le Duc d'Orléans, my journey, and the health of my elder son, whom he knew to be lying ill at Burgos. He then entered alone into the Hall of Mirrors. I was immediately surrounded by the courtiers, all congratulating me and rejoicing at the marriages and the union of our two countries. Grimaldo and the Duke of Liria introduced the gentlemen, nearly all of whom spoke French, and I did my best to reply to their civil speeches.

Five minutes later I received my summons. I entered the Hall of Mirrors alone. It is a vast chamber, but longer than it is wide. The King of Spain, with the queen at his left, stood at the extreme end. I made three low bows, noticing for the first time that the king never wore a hat, except at public audiences, or when he came and went to and from the chapel, as I shall later explain. My audience lasted half an hour (it is always they who dismiss). They spoke warmly of their joy and hopes, saying kind things of M. le Duc d'Orléans, and of their desire for Mlle de Montpensier's happiness. Towards the end, it was the queen who talked most freely, and did me the honour of inviting me to see her children. I followed them alone into the queen's private suite where, in an interior gallery, two ladies and three gentlemen, who appeared to expect us, were waiting. We then entered the rooms of the royal children. I never saw better-looking little boys, nor any more perfectly built than Don Ferdinand and Don Carlos, nor a prettier baby than Don Philip. The king and queen seemed to enjoy showing them off, and made them walk and turn about in front of me, which they did with the utmost willingness. They then presented me to the Infanta, and I tried with all my might to be gallant to her; but indeed, she was charming, with a sensible little face, and no trace of shyness. The queen said that she spoke French quite well already, and the king that she would soon forget Spain. 'Oh! not Spain only,' cried the queen, 'she will forget the king and me, and love only her husband.' At which I made every effort not to be tongue-tied.

Returning to the Hall of Mirrors, the king called me back to present me to the Prince of the Asturias, tall, the ideal for a portrait painter, with beautiful fair hair, a pink and white complexion, a long but pleasant face, and fine eyes set too near the nose. He asked for news of the King, M. le Duc d'Orléans, Mlle de Montpensier, and the probable date of her arrival. So ended my first audience.

Maulévrier escorted me back to my residence, where I found that Don Gaspard Giron,[1] first of the four major-domos, had taken entire charge

---

[1] Gaspard Tellez Giron (1652–1727) had been major-domo to Charles II in 1698, and since then had continuously held high court appointments.

with officers of the royal household to work under him. He had invited a great number of the Spanish nobility and, no matter what I might say, arranged all my entertaining until the following Wednesday, inclusive, with a royal coach drawn by four mules always at my door, attended by a royal coachman and several liveried footmen.[1] I managed to ensure that these favours should not continue longer than three days, but they appeared to be the usual treatment for ambassadors extraordinary. If I enlarge on these honours, it is partly because I thought them so very interesting, but chiefly that you might understand how the immense pleasure given by my mission had made the Spaniards surpass themselves in their welcome and attentions. This warmth and anxiety to please me was evident in every person I met, and so it continued during the entire time of my visit to Spain.

At this point, I think it would be as well to describe the King and Queen of Spain, and to say something also of the Marquis of Grimaldo. My first sight of the king, when I made my first bow, astonished me so much that I was hard put to it to remain calm. Search though I might, I could find nothing in his face to resemble the Duc d'Anjou I had known of old. It had become so long, so changed, so lacking in vitality, compared with what it had been when he left France. He had now a pronounced stoop; his body was shrunken; his chin poked far in advance of his chest; he planted his feet straight, touching one another, and though he moved quickly enough, he crossed them as he walked; his knees were more than a foot apart. When he honoured me by speaking he spoke well; but his speech was so formal, his words so drawled, his expression so vacuous, that I was quite unnerved. A tight-fitting jacket of rough brown tweed (because he was going hunting) did nothing to flatter his figure or his rank. He had a tie-wig swept back off his face, and the blue ribbon of the Order worn over his jacket at all times and seasons, almost concealing the Fleece, which he had on a red ribbon round his neck. I shall say more later of this monarch.[2]

When I first saw the queen (half an hour later, as I have recounted), I was deeply shocked by her face, all pock-marked and scarred by the ravages of smallpox. The court dress of Spain was newfangled, entirely different from the old,[3] and was the invention of the Princesse des Ursins. It favoured young and well-shaped ladies, but was most unfortunate for others because it emphasized all the defects of age and figure. As for the queen, her figure was neither good nor bad, though at that period she was rather thin; but she had beautiful shoulders, and a plump white bosom,

[1] The grandees' mules went at a walk, never at a trot, although Spanish coachmen were famous for their skill. Saint-Simon paying his calls at a fast trot, as in Paris, would have shocked everyone had he not said he was trying to cram in as many visits as possible.

[2] Philip appeared to have become a complete Spaniard; nothing French remained except the ribbon of the Order of the Saint-Esprit worn over all. It was not until later that Saint-Simon realized the terrible homesickness from which he was suffering.

[3] The old style of the Velazquez portraits.

with pretty hands and arms. Her waist was elegant and unconfined, and she was extremely shapely and slender down below.[1] She was rather taller than the average. She spoke excellent French with a slight Italian accent, choosing her words well, and not hesitating at all; the tone of her voice was particularly agreeable. A charming graciousness was in all her words and in her expression, that changed continually according to what she said. She seemed to combine kindness, courtesy even, with great dignity, and the air of majesty that never left her. Perhaps because of that, when one saw her as it were alone (but always with the king, as I shall explain later), one felt at ease. Yet one never forgot her rank, although very soon one became accustomed to her ravaged face. I shall say no more at present, except to stress that by day and night, at work, audiences, or prayer, the king and she were never for one instant apart, save only at official audiences, which they gave separately, at the king's public audiences, at meetings of the council, or in the chapel at the public prayers. All of this I shall describe in due course.

Grimaldo, a Spaniard by birth, looked like a Belgian. He was very fair, short, stout, pot-bellied, with a red complexion, blue eyes, a clever, humorous, even a kind face, and as frank and open as his office would permit. He was exceedingly complimentary, civil, obliging, but at bottom every bit as conceited as our own secretaries of State, with his two little hands pressed over his big stomach, never detaching nor clasping them, but accompanying all he said with their small movements. He was infinitely capable and experienced, a man of honour and loyalty, most devotedly attached to the king and his service, yet a polished courtier. His guiding principle had ever been for a close union with France. There! that will do for the moment regarding this minister, whose confidence and friendship I managed to win, to the great benefit of my mission. We became true friends, and so continued until his death. Let us now return to my embassy.

Tuesday, 25 November, was the day appointed for my official audience. On the previous day, Monday the 24th, I went with Maulévrier to the palace at five in the evening. The Marquis of Bedmar[2] and Grimaldo were waiting to receive us. They escorted us through the Grandees' Hall into a small and most richly decorated room, with carpets of such extraordinary beauty and costliness on the floor that I could scarcely bring myself to tread on them. We found there a table, an inkstand, and four *tabourets*. The two Spaniards did the honours by placing us on the right-hand side. All the documents had been composed, approved, and engrossed long before my arrival, and thus all we had to do was to sign the two instruments and the two copies we had brought with us. We appended our

[1] *par le bas*: is he discreetly referring to her legs, which Queens of Spain were said not to possess? He must have been fascinated to see this woman who six years earlier had quelled and dismissed the redoubtable Princesse des Ursins. See II, p. 398.

[2] Isidore Juan Joseph de La Cueva y Benavides, Marquis of Bedmar (1652–1723). He had been captain-general of the Spanish armies in the Netherlands, and, in 1704, Viceroy of Sicily.

usual signatures to the accompaniment of congratulations, promises, and such rejoicings as may easily be imagined. I was seated opposite the Marquis of Bedmar, and Maulévrier opposite to Grimaldo.

My instructions were to tell Grimaldo that the King of Spain had given pleasure to M. le Duc d'Orléans by appointing Laulès[1] his ambassador to France, and to beg King Philip to grant him some special favour in order to show his approval. I gladly took this opportunity to do Laulès a service, for I had it in my heart to oblige him. I was discovering at every turn how much he had done to make my mission successful, and I could see from the way my words were received that the Spanish court also was well pleased with him. Indeed, Grimaldo wrote at once on the king's behalf, promising him the first suitable promotion, and he very willingly gave me his word not to forget him.

On the following day, Maulévrier, for all that he was our ambassador, put himself to no expense whatsoever. He arrived at my house only a little before the appearance of Don Gaspard Giron with one of the king's most magnificent coaches, drawn by eight admirably dappled grey horses,[2] in which, at the appointed time, we three drove to the palace. Two grooms held every fourth horse by a long rein on the left-hand side. There were no postilions; the king's own coachman drove us with his hat tucked under his arm. Five of my coaches followed, containing all the members of my suite, then twenty more belonging to nobles of the court, sent to do me honour at the request of the Duke of Liria and Sartine, and filled with their gentlemen. The king's coach was escorted by my very numerous footmen in livery, and by the officers of my household, valets, butlers, etc. My gentlemen and secretaries rode in the last of my coaches. Maulévrier's coaches (and there were only two) contained Robin[3] and his secretary, and came last of all. When we reached the square before the palace, I could almost have imagined myself back at the Tuileries, for the regiments of the Spanish guard were dressed, both officers and men, in the uniforms of our French guards; and those of the Walloon guards were like our own Swiss. All were standing to arms, with standards unfurled, drums beating, and the officers saluting with their halberds. The streets were crowded; the booths of the merchants and artisans and all the windows were decorated, and thronged with spectators. People's faces shone with joy, and all the way we heard nothing but benedictions.

[1] Saint-Simon uses the Spanish form. He was in fact Patrick Lawless, an Irishman by birth. He had gone to France in 1720 as the Spanish ambassador, but was not officially appointed until 1721.

[2] Horses in Madrid were the acme of splendour. The grandees were drawn by a four-in-hand of white mules (never more). Grooms drove the leading mule on a rein, walking, and the longer the rein, the higher the rank of the owner. Saint-Simon loved horses: 'Le Barbe à tous crins' (the Barbary with the long mane), 'Le Petit Coureur' that carried him in three of five charges at Neerwinden, 'Capitaine', the grey, on which he rode the last two (see I, p. 28), and the ponies of his boyhood, Norman, Polacre, and Délicieuse, his little bay mare.

[3] Jean Baptiste Robin, one of Dubois's secretaries, who acted as Maulévrier's adviser.

When we stepped down, we found the Duke of Liria, the Prince de Chalais[1] (both grandees), and Valouse,[2] master of the horse, who announced that as Frenchmen born they had come to pay their respects. Caylus[3] might well have made a fourth, but he was not there. The steps were lined with halberdiers and their officers, uniformed like our hundred Swiss, armed with halberds, and performing similar duties. They made a double line across the guardroom and into the room before the presence chamber, the doors of which were closed. All the grandees were assembled there, and a vast number of high-ranking ladies and gentlemen. In fact there was almost as great a crowd as at our Court; but it appeared more formal. In Spain, the head of protocol[4] has fewer duties; the major-domo quite replaces him. In that room, I again received endless compliments and congratulations. Nearly everyone attempted to have speech with me, and so it continued for the next quarter of an hour, at which point the doors of the presence chamber opened for the entrance of the grandees, after which they were once more closed.

I remained with that crowd of distinguished persons while the king came from his apartments and entered the presence chamber by the doors opposite the ones used by the grandees, and by which I was about to enter. Here I must frankly confess that the King of Spain's appearance when I first saw him had impressed me so little that until that very moment I had not begun to compose my speech.

The summons came; the company entered in a crowd before me, and I was left, supported by Don Gaspard Giron on my right hand, and by the head of protocol on the left of Maulévrier, who walked beside me. As we neared the doorway, La Roche[5] came to tell me quietly, on His Catholic Majesty's behalf, that the king hoped I would not be offended if he raised his hat at my first and last bows, but not at my second. He wished, he said, that he might do more for a French ambassador than for others, but it was an old tradition and he dared not break it. I asked La Roche to convey my humble duty, and my thanks for the king's kindly thought, and so saying I stepped through the doorway. The narrow passage forced Maulévrier and the two others to give way, and my mind being altogether occupied with my speech and the splendid scene before me, I did not notice what became of them.

In the middle of the great chamber was a canopy with a backcloth but no

---

[1] Nephew of the Princesse des Ursins. See Chalais in index, I and II.

[2] Hyacinth Boutin, Marquis de Valouse (1671–1736). He had been an equerry of the Dukes of Anjou and Berry, in 1694, and accompanied Philip V to Spain, where he was appointed a master of the horse and first gentleman of the bedchamber.

[3] The Chevalier de Caylus fled to Spain in 1697 because of a duel (see I, p. 255).

[4] The Count of Villafranca (Joseph de Sobremonte y Carnero) (1663–1729) was head of protocol at that time.

[5] Claude Étienne de La Roche (1660–1735), Philip V's head valet and private secretary. He was one of the servants whom the king had taken with him to Spain in 1700.

step, beneath which the king stood; and behind him, some distance away, stood the Duc de Bournonville,[1] Grandee of Spain and captain of the guard. At the extreme end, on my side, was placed the king's major-domo alone, his back against the wall. The grandees lined the remainder of that wall, and the one opposite the king as far as the fireplace, a vast antiquated structure, close by the doors through which I had entered. From the fireplace to those doors, and in front of the remaining wall and windows, as far as the doors used by the king, were ranged row upon row of noble ladies and gentlemen. Some gentlemen of the household, none of them grandees, peered rather furtively through the doorway by which the king had entered, and behind them, a few of the upper servants looked on through the cracks of the doors. The king and the grandees wore hats, no one else was covered.

I paused a moment to survey this incredibly regal scene, wherein no one moved and a profound silence reigned. I then went forward a few slow paces, bowing very low indeed to the king. He uncovered at the same moment, bringing his hat down to the level of his waist. At the centre of the room I made my second bow, turning ever so little as I bent to left and right, to look fleetingly at the grandees, all of whom had again removed their hats, bringing them not so low as at my first bow, when they had copied the king who, at my second, did not move, as he had warned me. I again stepped slowly forward until I was only a few paces away. There I made my third bow, at which he uncovered, as he had done before, with all the grandees following suit. I then began my speech, replacing my hat at the fifth or sixth word, not waiting for the king's command to do so.

[*Saint-Simon's speech, all unprepared as it was, expressed at considerable length the obvious sentiments—mutual happiness, joy at the family and national union, and, of course, all manner of references to the Duc d'Orléans's personal gratification at being reconciled with Their Catholic Majesties, and his pride at the thought of his daughter's becoming Queen of Spain in later years.*]

I ended by mentioning my own delight, and my sense of the great honour of having been appointed to appear before His Catholic Majesty, contributing my small part by placing my name to those happy instruments. I could never forget, I added, from what country His Most Catholic Majesty had sprung, and desired to express my abiding and most profound respect and devotion for his royal person.

If I had been unpleasantly surprised at my first view of the King of Spain, if the conversation afterwards had left me unimpressed, I must say here and now what is the strict and literal truth, namely that the amazement I felt at hearing his reply knocked me almost senseless. To each point of my speech in turn he responded with such dignity and graciousness, such majesty often, such admirably chosen words, and phrases so

---

[1] Michel Joseph, Baron de Capres, later Duc de Bournonville (1682-1752).

apt, judicious, and concise, that I could almost imagine myself listening to our late King, who was a master, well practised in such replies. I shall always regret not having had a notebook so as to have written down those admirable answers. What I here describe is a mere shadow, in no way resembling the extraordinary perfection of the original.[1]

When he had finished, I felt I owed him a word of praise on that subject, and fresh thanks on M. le Duc d'Orléans's behalf. Instead of replying, King Philip honoured me by expressing his pleasure at my appointment to a mission that had brought him so much joy. Then, my hat being off, I presented the officers of the King's regiments who had accompanied me, and he thereafter withdrew, after a few more kind words. I was once again surrounded by the most distinguished people present, showering me with civilities; after which most of the grandees and other persons of quality entered the queen's apartments. A few, however, remained to entertain us while the rest were leaving to take up their positions in the queen's audience chamber. After a short interval, we also were escorted to the adjoining room, and there we waited until she was ready.

The doors then opened and we were admitted. The queen's audience chamber was on the inner side of the little gallery into which I had followed Their Majesties on the day of my first audience. It was as wide but not so long as the outer gallery from which it drew all its light,[2] and was joined to it by a colonnade. We entered at the side adjoining the Infanta's apartments; the queen and her suite entered at the opposite end. It was dark and crowded where we came in, for a barrier had been erected seven or eight paces farther on, where the light was stronger. Between the door and the barrier, which they removed as I approached, a space was left just wide enough for me to pass; and thus I could not see what happened behind me. At the extreme end of the very long chamber, the queen was seated on a kind of throne or, to be exact, in a huge armchair, made bell-shaped by carvings and very highly gilded. Her feet were on a magnificent cushion of unusual height and width, that hid, as I afterwards discovered, some rather low steps. The grandees, ranged along the walls, wore their hats. On the other side, under the colonnade, there were rectangular hassocks, rather long and narrow, only moderately thick, covered in red velvet or satin, or in damask. All were trimmed with gold braid, a hand's width or more, with great golden tassels at each corner. The grandees' wives sat on those of velvet, and the wives of their eldest sons on the satin or damask. They all sat in the same position, propped on their legs and heels. The row of grandees against the wall and the rows of ladies opposite them on the hassocks filled the entire length of the chamber, leaving only a shortish

---

[1] The editor feels that enough is enough, and that readers may prefer to guess at the king's exquisite eloquence.

[2] It was, in fact, what the French called a *double*, like the Saint-Simons' apartment at Versailles: the lining, so to speak, of another room from which all its light was drawn.

space between the barrier and the queen, and another, similar, between the barrier and the door by which I entered.

After pausing a moment to view the richly beautiful scene, I advanced slowly, walking in the middle of the room, until I was level with the second hassock. There I made a very low bow. Continuing forward to the centre of the remaining space I bowed a second time, turning as I did so to allow my eyes to rest on the ladies nearest me; and as I rose, I made the same movement towards the row of grandees, who removed their hats, even as the ladies had slightly inclined their bodies in gracious acknowledgment. I then stepped forward to the foot of the queen's cushion, where I made my third bow, which the queen alone acknowledged with a very low inclination of her body. A moment later, I said, 'Madame', and immediately replaced my hat, to remove it again without taking away my hand, and remaining uncovered during the rest of the audience. The grandees, who had uncovered at my second bow, did not afterwards replace their hats.

My speech was substantially the same as the one I had made to the king, altered only slightly, as befitted the occasion. The queen was simply attired, but sparkled with the most magnificent jewels, displaying all the attributes of queenly grace and majesty, despite the fact that she was suddenly overcome by transports of joy, which she afterwards confessed with some amusement had embarrassed her not a little. When it came to her turn, she none the less spoke very well, mentioning her hopes for the happiness of her daughter, her respectful affection, nay, her passionate devotion to our King, her warm feelings towards M. le Duc d'Orléans, and her desire to see his daughter happy in Spain.

When she had finished, I again bowed low, and retired as swiftly as decorum would allow in order to reach the velvet hassock at the extreme end of the line, and hasten along the row, bending my knee slightly before each lady, and murmuring, '*A los pies de V.E.*', meaning, 'I place myself at Your Excellency's feet', to which each lady responded with a smile and a gentle inclination of her body. It was a race for the swift, which must be completed as they were removing the huge cushion from beneath the queen's feet, and while she rose, descended the steps of her armchair-throne, and walked to the door of her apartments—a distance only half the length of that not very long gallery. One had to be done with the last of the hassocks in time to greet the queen at the door, kneel on one knee, kiss her hand, and utter a sentence or two of gratitude.

I was still not finished with the hassocks when I perceived that the queen had reached the door. She had already shown me such kind cordiality that I thought I might risk a liberty at this happy time. I therefore ran towards her, exclaiming that Her Majesty was leaving too soon, and when she stopped and turned, I declared that I hated to lose a single moment of an honour which I deeply prized. She laughed, and there I was, kneeling on one knee, kissing the ungloved hand which she held out to me, talking most graciously the while. I thanked her, and we had a few moments' conversation in the doorway, during which the ladies left their hassocks and formed a semicircle behind me. With the queen and her attendants gone, I had leisure to pay my compliments to the remaining ladies and gentlemen.

After my return, I was outraged to learn that Maulévrier did not replace his hat during our audiences with the king and queen, which I had not observed since, at both, he had stood some way behind me. I thought this so abominable of him that I resolved to discover the truth from members of my suite, and from the Dukes of Veragua[1] and Liria who were dining with me that day, and had become my friends. All agreed that it had been so; that everyone had been astonished, and that he had not made the smallest gesture towards covering himself. I spoke to him later with all possible civility; but he curtly replied that he had not thought it his duty; that he would find some way to repair the omission, and that he was sorry. When he stepped down from the coach, he had refused to come up to my apartments, where distinguished company awaited us, nor, try as I might, could I persuade him to dine with us.[2] He said he had work to do at home, and would return in time to accompany me to the signing of the contracts. This might have been mere stupidity; but judging by what happened later, it was a thoroughly treacherous action, a snare set for me with malice aforethought.

As you will remember, the articles already signed had been in duplicate, with one copy in Spanish, and one in French. Thus I was under the impression that it would be the same with the actual contracts. My instructions said nothing to the contrary; Cardinal Dubois had not mentioned it, and I had not thought to ask him. I did, however, say something to Maulévrier, who replied that there would certainly be two versions, which reassured me, since Spanish was unknown to me, whereas he and Robin spoke it fluently. I had reminded him that very morning before the audiences, and he had said that the copies were not yet ready, but that I should have the French one before dinner, and since he refused to stay for that meal, I desired him to send it me, which he had promised to do. During the lengthy meal at my house, I twice sent asking for the copy, and on the last occasion he sent word that he was bringing it. When I was ready to leave, and time was pressing, I sent him a messenger on horseback, by whom word came that I should start without him, and

---

[1] Pedro Nuño III of Portugal-Columbus, Duke of Veragua (1676–1733). He had been Viceroy of Sardinia, and minister for the navy 1712, for trade 1715. He was a first gentleman of the chamber.

[2] It was most unfortunate for Saint-Simon that Maulévrier, the French ambassador, should have been such an enemy of the Regent. He really behaved odiously. Saint-Simon said that there was 'nothing under that thick skin except ill humour, vulgarity, and stupidity'. He was hostile all through the mission; the Spaniards noticed it and judged accordingly. Saint-Simon remarked that 'everyone admired my calm contempt and my patience with him'.

that he would meet me at the palace. This proceeding appeared most ill suited to so important an event; not that his two shabby coaches and meagre following would have added much lustre to my procession, but I was surprised, although I took care to conceal my feelings.

The awkward situation in which Cardinal Dubois had so maliciously placed me, by ordering me to take precedence of the nuncio and the major-domo mayor,[1] had made me most punctilious in everywhere giving way to them. I wished to free their minds of any notion that I might, at the crucial moment, try to precede them, for I knew very well that I could not take precedence of either for any length of time. The place of the major-domo mayor at the ceremony was behind the king's armchair and slightly to his right, so as to allow room for the captain of the guard. To station myself there would mean displacing not only him, but also the captain of the guard, and every other person in the line. The nuncio's place was beside the king, his stomach on a level with the right arm of the king's chair. Placing myself there would mean pushing him to one side, against the end of the table, to which he would certainly object, just as the major-domo mayor was bound to resent his own displacement. I resolved therefore to try a middle way by squeezing myself in above the right arm of the king's chair and a little sideways, thus displacing neither but, as it were, slicing a corner off both, making for myself a new place, and covering the entire proceeding with an air of innocent non-comprehension, combined with the eager devotion of a courtier who is determined to converse with the king and hold his attention as long as possible. That was what I did, looking all the while perfectly unconcerned, and the whole manœuvre succeeded marvellously. My only anxiety was for Maulévrier, who should have been standing by my side; but he had not deserved my confidence, and I decided to let him fend for himself.

Thus tormented by questions of places and documents, I left escorted by Don Gaspard Giron, in the king's coach, and with the same retinue as before. I sat alone on the back seat; Don Gaspard alone sat opposite; the cheering multitudes in the streets and windows were as numerous as in the morning. The palace was thronged with the very cream of Madrid Society. All the grandees were present, the nuncio, the Archbishop of Toledo, the Grand Inquisitor, the various secretaries of State, and Père Daubenton the king's confessor. The drawing-room between the Hall of Mirrors and the Grandees' Hall, where the ceremony was to take place, was packed so full that there was scarcely room to move; but intent on my plan, I gradually steered myself through the crowd, saying a word to one person or another,

[1] The nuncio was Alessandro Aldobrandini (1667–1734); the major-domo mayor (grand-master of ceremonies), the Marquis of Villena. To Saint-Simon's dismay, he had been explicitly ordered by Dubois to take precedence of the nuncio at the signing. Diplomatic relations between France and Spain had so nearly been severed that it was considered essential for the French ambassador to be seen to take first place, above the Pope, at this ceremony of recon-ciliation.

until I had come close up against the door of the Mirror Hall, where I remained chatting to those within range. An interval of more than three quarters of an hour ensued, during which I became highly exasperated, trying to conceal my twofold problem amid so many people. The doors then opened and the king and queen appeared, with the Infanta and the princes behind them.

I at once engaged the king in conversation, walking close beside him, and so led him, as it were, to his seat in the Grandees' Hall, taking up the position I had previously selected. The room was arranged as follows: a long table was set crosswise, with one end towards the windows and the other to the doors by which we had entered. It was covered by a carpet on which was an inkstand. Six armchairs had been placed along the side of the table, their backs towards the wall, but leaving a very large space in between, and the arms of the chairs were touching. The king sat on the first armchair on the extreme right, the queen on the second, the Infanta on the third. Next came the Prince of the Asturias, who since the announcement had given her precedence, then Don Ferdinand, and lastly Don Carlos. The governess of the Infanta stood behind her chair because of her extreme youth. No other lady was present, not even the *camerera-mayor*.[1] This straight row was the order of seating even for plays, balls, etc.

The major-domo mayor and the nuncio, who had followed the youngest of the princes, appeared vastly surprised to see me busily conversing with the king by the arm of his chair. I heard the words *signore* and *señor* to right and left, for neither gentleman could speak French. But there I was bowing first to one side, then to the other, smiling gaily the while, as though quite immersed in the joys of the moment, understanding nothing, and returning to the king with such rapturous enthusiasm that they ceased their efforts to distract me. It was only then that I perceived Maulévrier, who was endeavouring to squeeze himself in between the nuncio and myself; but after a little bow, the nuncio had stood firm, and I dared not move (compressed as I was, it would have been extremely difficult), for assisting him to stand above the nuncio would have shown my hand too clearly. Thus Maulévrier remained throughout half-hidden, with only his head visible.

Don Joseph Rodrigo,[2] who stood quite near the table, facing the queen, received the order to read the marriage-contracts. When he was fairly launched, I turned to Maulévrier to ask in a whisper if he had his Spanish copy, and the French one for me. He said they were not yet ready but would soon arrive. 'Not before time!' I exclaimed sharply, turning once more to the king, for I still feared lest my two neighbours should oust me.

[1] The *camerera-mayor* was the Duchess of Linarès. This was the most important post about the queen, and had been held in the time of Philip's first queen by the Princesse des Ursins.
[2] One of the secretaries of State.

The reading was very long; Don Rodrigo declaimed in a loud, clear voice the contract for the marriage of our King with the Infanta, and another document, also in Spanish, giving the names and titles of the ten witnesses, and of all the grandees present. Being somewhat at a loss how to continue my conversation with the king, I conceived the idea of asking for a private audience next day, which he very willingly granted, and I managed to stretch that topic out until the end of the reading.

When all was finished, Don Joseph Rodrigo advanced to the end of the table, intending to offer a pen to the King of Spain; but instead of taking it, the king suggested first reading all the other documents concerned. I therefore said very quietly and with great respect that I thought there should be a French version. Don Rodrigo said that he believed not; whereupon Maulévrier, who until that moment had been silent, said that there was one, and that he would fetch it, and he left the room without another word. Meanwhile King Philip remarked to me that perhaps none was needed, and so saying he called Grimaldo, who approached between me and the major-domo mayor, being allowed by us both as much room as was possible in the circumstances. On the question being put to him, he replied that no French version existed, at which I quietly observed that it would surely uphold the dignity of both crowns to have contracts signed in each language, and at that moment Maulévrier returned. He was in time to hear Grimaldo tell me with the greatest possible courtesy that he thought it would make no difference, more especially since he had seen a letter from Cardinal Dubois to Maulévrier expressly to that effect. I turned full round and gave Maulévrier a look of such blank astonishment as may easily be pictured. He answered, looking guilty, that Cardinal Dubois had indeed said something of the sort in one of his letters. That settled it for me. I declared to the king and queen that I should blindly obey their every command, sweetening those words with all the respect, trust, agreement, and joy in that great day that I could compress into a single sentence, adding that should a French version later be found desirable, Their Catholic Majesties would perhaps not disdain to sign it privately. Meanwhile I had moved as though to draw the contract, lying on the table, nearer to the king's hand; but I took care not actually to touch it, because that was the function of Secretary of State Rodrigo. It seemed from what they said, and their general appearance, that the King and Queen of Spain were much pleased by my demonstration of trust.

Rodrigo at that instant approached the nuncio and, leaning across him ever so little, offered the contract and the pen to the King of Spain. He then went round to the front of the table, and followed along it, moving the document as soon as each royal person had signed. When the king had finished, he pushed the contract before the queen and gave her the pen. She signed, then put it before the Infanta; gave her the pen, and steadied her hand while she wrote, which she did in the prettiest way imaginable.

The queen then took back the pen, stretched in front of the Infanta to give it to the Prince of the Asturias, and moved the document towards him. He signed it, followed by his two brothers, using the same pen, and passing the contract from one to another. The joy accompanying these signatures was really indescribable.

A moment later, when the king and queen had risen, Don Rodrigo came to escort me and Maulévrier to a little table near the window, covered with a carpet, and on it an inkstand. The king and queen arrived there at the same moment, and ordered us to sign in their presence. You do not need me to tell you that there were no chairs, or that we signed standing. Just as I was about to do so where I thought most appropriate, on a level with the youngest of the princes, Don Rodrigo stopped me, indicating the name above. I hesitated, whereupon he explained that it must be so in order to leave room for Maulévrier's name, next to that of the youngest prince. I therefore wrote my name beside the Infante Don Ferdinand, and after saying a few words of respect and joy to the King and Queen of Spain, who were quite close to me, leaning over the table the better to watch me write, I gave the pen to Maulévrier who, after signing, left it on the table. As that order did us greater honour than the one I had been ready to accept, and as it was prompted by the secretary of State, I thought no further resistance was needed, and I briefly thanked Their Catholic Majesties for the honour and pleasure of being permitted to sign in front of them. Praise for the Infanta's goodness, her patience before such a great audience, and her skill in writing, was not forgotten. I then accompanied the king and queen to the door of the Mirror Hall, taking care, on that journey, to show all possible deference to the major-domo mayor and the nuncio, so as to dispel any thought that I had taken and maintained the highest place by design.

To finish once and for all with the matter of the French version, I took Maulévrier with me to Grimaldo's *covachuela*.[1] I had already reproached him, gently and without bitterness, for not telling me of Cardinal Dubois's letter; but he had replied very coldly that he would send for it. When we arrived, Grimaldo repeated with infinite politeness what he had said at the signing, adding that he had conformed exactly to what had taken place at the Paris ceremony, when there had been no Spanish version. He declared, however, that if I persisted in desiring a French copy there would be no difficulty over the king's signature. I thanked him most warmly, for I had no wish to let him, or the King of Spain, see that I had any grievance against Maulévrier. His sullenness, discomfiture, and silence were sufficient proof of guilt.

I returned home after the ceremony which, because of the lengthy readings and the difficulty over the French version, had lasted an inter-

---

[1] A diminutive of *covacha*, meaning a little cave in a rock. It was used for the offices of the *Despacho universal*, in the cellars of the royal palace at Madrid.

minable time. You will perhaps remember that not knowing how to spin out my conversation with the king I had begged for an audience on the following day, and that he had gladly consented. Now such a request, it appeared, was contrary to etiquette at the Spanish court, where ambassadors and others were expected to approach the official concerned, who in due course apprised them of the day and time appointed. Not being aware of this, I was somewhat surprised when an hour and a half after my return, a letter arrived from Grimaldo, asking whether I had something private to impart out of the queen's hearing, and wishing to know what it might be. I at once replied that having found myself in a favourable position I had asked quite spontaneously for an audience, and that if I had not mentioned the queen, it was only because her presence went without saying. I added that I desired only to thank the king; that I had nothing to say that was not for the queen's ears also, and that it would much grieve me were she to absent herself.

While I was thus engaged, Don Gaspard Giron called to take me to see the illuminations at the Plaza Mayor, and I therefore finished my letter in a hurry. We entered his coach, and the principal members of my staff followed us in mine. We went by the back streets so as not to see any reflection from the lights before arriving, and finally reached a splendid house overlooking the square. It was the same house that the king and queen used to watch the festivals.[1] All was dark as we stepped down and climbed the staircase, because they had closed all the shutters; but when we entered the room that faced the square we were positively dazzled, and as we stepped out on to the balcony, my amazement was such that for seven or eight minutes words failed me completely.

The surface area of this square is far greater than anything I have seen, in Paris or elsewhere, and is longer than wide. The five storeys of the surrounding houses are of equal height, each having windows of the same size and the same distance apart, with balconies precisely similar in length and projection, and iron balustrades of the same height and pattern, all of which is exactly repeated on all five storeys. On every balcony two huge torches of white wax were placed leaning against the centre of the returns of the balustrade, not attached to them in any way. The light was extraordinary, the brilliance truly amazing, for one somehow immediately gained an impression of majesty. One could have read the smallest handwriting in the centre of the square and in each corner, even though the ground floors were not illuminated.

As soon as I appeared on the balcony, all the people in the square crowded under the windows and shouted, '*Señor, toro! toro!*' They were asking me for a bull fight, the thing they most passionately enjoyed, and which King Philip had banned from religious motives. Next day, I could do no more than tell him of the shouts, without asking questions, all the

[1] The house was the Panaderia.

while expressing my astonishment at the marvellous illuminations. Don Gaspard Giron and the other Spaniards present were in raptures at my surprise and admiration, and they spread the news all the more gladly because they were not used to being admired by Frenchmen. When I returned, there was scarcely time for supper before leaving once more to go to the palace, where the king was giving a state ball in the Grandees' Hall. It lasted until two in the morning.

This hall, which is vast and most splendidly decorated with bronze and marble, gilding and pictures, was brilliantly illuminated. At the farthest end, opposite the entrance, were placed six armchairs in a row, as at the signing, in which the king, queen, etc., sat in the same order as before. Close beside the right arm of the king's chair and less than six inches farther back, was a folding seat of gilded wood, upholstered in crimson velvet with gold fringes, for the king's major-domo mayor, who sat down at the same moment as the king. At the left side of the youngest Infante's armchair was a hassock, similarly placed, covered in black velvet without any gold, and with black tassels at each corner. This was for the queen's *camerera-mayor* in her widow's weeds, slightly mitigated because the queen could not support the nun's complete apparel that is the required outfit for Spanish widows, unless and until they re-marry. That accounted for the black of the hassock, which would otherwise have been of crimson velvet fringed with gold. This lady might equally well have had a folding chair, but she preferred a hassock, and it denotes similar rank. Behind the armchairs were gilt *tabourets*, covered in red velvet with gold fringes, for the captain of the king's guard, the chief butler, the queen's major-domo mayor, the governess of the Infanta, and the Duke of Popoli, governor of the Prince of the Asturias. Behind the armchairs on the duenna's side, but not immediately opposite her back, were two gilt folding chairs, of red velvet with gold fringes, to which Don Gaspard Giron conducted Maulévrier and me. There was no screen in front of us,[1] which was an extremely high honour, and thus, having nothing to interrupt the view, we were able to observe the whole beauty of the scene, and see the dances as well.

Somewhat lower than the duenna and a short distance from the wall stood a row of *tabourets* like our own, intermixed with hassocks; and there were other *tabourets* and hassocks of damask or red satin, similarly gilded and fringed, for the wives of the grandees and of their eldest sons. Grandees' wives sit always on velvet, the rest may choose between the damask or satin *tabourets* or hassocks. These seats extended almost half the length of the hall on one side; the remainder of the space being occupied by ladies of quality, matrons and maids, seated upon the huge carpet that covered the entire hall. Some ladies stood, if they so wished, and right at the end of the line, in the last places of all, were the queen's

[1] Screens like Venetian blinds through which people could see, yet not be seen.

young 'companions', as they were called, stationed there for the dances. Opposite this long line of ladies, on the other side of the great hall, stood all the male members of the court, grandees and others, with their backs to the windows but some distance from them, the intervening space being filled by spectators of lower rank, as was the space between the ladies and the wall at their backs. At the lower end, on the men's side, were the king's four major-domos in a rectangular formation, to give the directions. Facing the row of armchairs, at the extreme end, the dancers stood waiting, amid grandees and other noblemen, the officers who had accompanied me to Spain, and privileged spectators. Behind them a barrier had been placed across the room, to hold back the crowd of onlookers.

In a room beside the entrance doors, all manner of refreshments were set out, with wines and cakes in great profusion and variety, yet all displayed in perfect order. In the hurly-burly of the country dances, anyone might enter and take away something for the ladies. Jewels sparkled magnificently; I must honestly confess that at a first glance our grandest court balls did not approach this one for splendour. What did appear most strange to me was the sight of three bishops in rochets and capes, standing at the end of the room on the men's side. They were the Duke of Abrantes, Bishop of Cuenca,[1] and two bishops *in partibus*, suffragans of the Archbishop of Toledo. Most peculiar also, at a ball, was the garb of the *camerera-mayor*, for she quite openly held an enormous rosary, and while she laughed and chatted about the ball and the dancers, was all the time mumbling *paternosters*, letting them drop from her lips at regular intervals during the entire time of the ball. Another thing I thought very inconvenient was the complete lack of seats for any gentlemen, except Maulévrier, myself, and the six officials mentioned above. Not even the dancers had seats; indeed, except for those whom I have specified, there was not one seat in all that vast hall, not even behind the spectators.

The queen, by custom, may dance the set-dances only with the princes, but on this occasion, she opened the ball with the king for her partner.[2] He loved dancing and performed in a manner that astonished me, for he seemed a different man, straightening his back and knees, showing admirable neatness and, truth to tell, grace also. As for the queen, when she and the Prince of the Asturias danced together later, they both had such good figures that I never saw a better-looking couple; few, even in France, could approach them in skill, and none that I have known were even half as good. The two younger princes danced extremely well, considering their youth. In Spain, men and women of every age wear bright colours, and anyone who pleases may dance, even if over sixty, without the least risk of mockery or of appearing eccentric. The youngest

---

[1] John Emmanuel de la Croix of Portugal-Alencastro.
[2] It was Mme des Ursins who, in 1701, persuaded King Philip and Queen Marie Louise Gabrielle to dance at court balls. It was an innovation, quite contrary to tradition.

prince led out the Princesse de Robecq[1] who was not far short of fifty, and looked all her years. She was a Croÿ, daughter of the Prince de Solre and widow of the Prince de Robecq, whom the King of Spain made a knight of the Fleece at Mme des Ursins's request. Mme de Robecq was one of the queen's ladies and reputed to be on excellent terms with her. I had known her intimately before she went to Spain, and had paid her one of my first visits. In the old days we had often danced together, which she appeared to have told the queen, for as soon as her dance with the prince was over (as she was French, the Spanish rules for widows did not apply to her) she advanced the entire length of the hall, dropped a beautiful curtsey before Their Catholic Majesties, and came to dislodge me from my retreat[2] with a deep and smiling inclination. I returned her bow, protesting that she was teasing me. A dispute followed, with many pretty speeches on either side, until at last she appealed to the queen, who called to me saying that both the king and she would like to see me dance. I advanced my age, my appointment, the years since I had last performed—every argument, indeed, that I could think of. All was useless; the king joined in, they both besought me, tried to persuade me that I danced very well, finally ordered me in such a way that there was no disobeying. Nothing remained for me but to do the best I could in the circumstances.

After an hour, the little Infanta was taken to bed. Country dances were frequently interposed between the minuets. The Prince of the Asturias invariably partnered the queen; the king danced rarely; but because in country dances everyone dances with everyone, returning at the end to their own partners, the queen also danced with everyone in turn. I missed as many as possible, for as you will easily guess I scarcely knew a soul.

When all was over, the Marquis of Villagarcia,[3] one of the major-domos and the kindest and most sympathetic of men, who has since become Viceroy of Peru,[4] firmly refused to let me leave without first resting in the refreshment room, where he made me drink a glass of most excellent pure wine because he could see that I sweated abominably after dancing so many minuets and country dances in my very heavy coat. The king and queen and the Prince of the Asturias were exceedingly active and appeared greatly to enjoy the ball. That same night and the one following it I had my entire house illuminated, both inside and out, not having had a moment's leisure in which to give any kind of entertainment, so quickly had the state functions come one after another.

It was not without pleasure that I sat down on the morning of Wednesday the 26th, the day after the signing, to write the dispatches I should have to send home after my audience of thanks—due to take place later that

---

[1] Isabelle Alexandrine de Croÿ Solre, Princesse de Robecq (1672–1739).
[2] *reculade*: a retreat in both senses of the word.
[3] Antoine Joseph de Guzman, Marquis of Villagarcia.
[4] Mexico, in 1734, not Peru.

morning. I had succeeded without difficulty in avoiding proxies, and persuading Their Catholic Majesties, against all custom and etiquette, to sign their names, and this not only on the contract itself, but on a copy, which I sent to our King by the same courier. This was much more than had been required of me, for Cardinal Dubois had demanded only a plain copy, signed by a secretary of State. I had avoided the snare, so cleverly baited, in the matter of the French version, and had emerged victorious in so far that Their Catholic Majesties had perceived the treachery, and had offered to sign a second version if I persisted in desiring one. Lastly I could report the joy occasioned by my embassy, the hosts of visitors to my house on the day after my arrival, including many whose right it was to expect a visit from me before making a call; and I did not forget the tact, if such I might call it, that had resulted in my seizing and keeping the highest place at the ceremony, thus saving me from the terrible dilemma by which Cardinal Dubois had calculated to defeat me. His gushing praise in returning the courier, and the trivial imperfections at which he dared only hint, for example, the scene over the French version, the small size of the table at which we had signed, the fact that I had not yet been to the Church of Nuestra Señora de Atocha, showed clearly enough the chagrin beneath all his flowery compliments. Yet you shall see that he took his revenge upon my purse, and that it was no fault of his if I did not return without that prize that had been my sole reason for desiring this embassy.

Right at the end of that same Wednesday morning (the 26th), I was admitted alone (for Maulévrier had excused himself) to the audience which I had requested of the King of Spain. Even as I approached Their Catholic Majesties, I could see how great a service the Marquis of Grimaldo had rendered me by desiring an answer to his letter of the previous evening; for the queen stepped towards me even before I had bowed to the king, exclaiming with a most imperious air, 'Now, Sir! Let us have no nonsense. You wish to speak to the king alone; I shall stand by the window, and you may safely proceed.' I replied in the same way as to Grimaldo, adding that in very truth, had I had the infelicity to find her absent, I should have been obliged to request a private audience of her also, to express similar thanks for all the events of the past day. 'No, no!' she declared petulantly. 'I will leave you with the king, and return when you have done.' And so saying she reached the window in a couple of agile leaps, as it were; for it was some considerable distance away, on account of the vast size of the Mirror Hall in which I was alone with Their Catholic Majesties. I dashed after her, protesting that I would not so much as open my mouth until she had returned to the king who, all that time, had remained immobile. At last she consented to believe me and went back to stand beside him, I following her. He would, in any case, have told her all, and had I spoken to him alone she would never have forgiven me. I then thanked them for all their kindness to me personally, pending the time when I should have the honour of transmitting the thanks of our King. You may well imagine that what I say here in two words I greatly expanded in speaking to Their Catholic Majesties. When I had finished the queen burst into praise of the King of Spain, inviting me to admire everything about him, even including his beauty, while all the while he stood silently smiling. At last he asked if I was sending a courier, to which I answered that I was, indeed, and a special one, for a document signed by their hands was far too precious to be treated in the ordinary way. It appeared to me that this was what they wished, and that my reply had gratified them.

The conversation became more general, as they led me to the windows to admire the beautiful view over the Manzanares, the Casa del Campo nearly opposite, and the country beyond. They then spoke of the court and I expressed my pleasure at having been allowed to see them at all the appointed times. Thereupon, the queen, after glancing at the king, very kindly said that that was not necessary; for me there need be no appointed times or customary hours. I might come whenever I so desired, without an audience or any special reason; that they would be enchanted to treat me as a member of the family, and that I should give them pleasure by taking liberties. I replied as best I might to such a totally unexpected favour, and in rather less than an hour my audience ended.

That same afternoon, the king and queen drove in state to Nuestra Señora de Atocha. This is a national shrine at the extreme end, indeed almost outside the town, adjoining the park of Buen-Retiro.[1] The cathedral is a vast edifice, but only moderately beautiful compared with other Spanish churches. Descriptions of architecture are not in my line, but I think it would be a pity to leave undescribed the procession for the visit of the king and queen, since Spanish sovereigns drive there whenever some calamity has occurred, or there is an occasion for public thanksgiving. This then is their order of march: a royal coach containing the four major-domos; three plainer ones for the gentlemen of the chamber; one more ornate for the master of the horse, the king's butler, and the captain of the guard, and an empty royal coach. There follows a state coach containing the king and queen alone, and after it one of the queen's coaches empty. Then should come another for her master of the horse and her major-domo mayor; but that coach serves no purpose at present because the major-domo mayor refuses to step down for her master of the horse who, in the royal coaches, should have precedence of him and everyone else. Thus the queen's officer is obliged to travel in the royal coach containing the king's master of the horse, and to take precedence immediately after the captain of the guard. This difficulty has made his coach superfluous, and it no longer figures. After the queen's empty coach comes the private coach of the *camerera-mayor*, drawn by four mules, with her own arms and liveries,

[1] The King of Spain's holiday house, very necessary when the 'foul air' needed changing at the palace in the centre of Madrid. See II, p. 319.

escorted by her own footmen, and with her equerry riding beside the right-hand door. She sits alone within. Two of the queen's coaches come next filled with her ladies, and two others, rather plainer, with the maids of honour. Last of all comes a very plain coach indeed, in which sits the *azafata*[1] quite alone; then two similar coaches for the 'companions'.

The coach in which the king and queen sit has eight horses and a postilion, and is surrounded by walking royal footmen. Officers of the horse guards and royal equerries ride beside the doors, and a vast number of guards march both before and behind, with kettledrums beating and trumpets sounding. The regiments of the Spanish and Walloon guards are drawn up in battle array on the palace square, while others line the streets headed by their officers, saluting with standards unfurled and very many drums beating. The pace is extremely slow. The drivers of the royal coaches and that of the *camerera-mayor* drive hat in hand. The other coachmen wear hats.

The longest part of the route is through one of the finest, widest, and straightest streets of Madrid, in which are great numbers of jewellers' shops. All of these were decorated with a brilliant display, in rising tiers, of costly and beautiful objects. Booths along the way were similarly decorated. The balconies, of which there are a great number in Madrid, and all the windows of every floor were hung with large and magnificent carpets; cushions lay on the sills, and the windows themselves were crammed with spectators and ladies in their smartest dresses. On the return, the streets were all as beautifully illuminated as the Plaza Mayor. I must here comment on the admirable order maintained throughout, for although the streets were full of people, they never seemed overcrowded or obstructed. It was the most wonderful sight I ever saw, so full of regal majesty and splendour, and so perfectly orderly.

The grandees all went to Nuestra Señora de Atocha to await the king, and it was my belief that Maulévrier and I should have accompanied them. For once, however, Maulévrier acted wisely in consulting the Marquis of Montalegre, the comptroller of the household, he being the person most expert in the ceremonies and etiquette of the Spanish court. He thought that we might constitute a difficulty, and advised us not to go. We therefore watched the procession and the return from the same house in the Plaza Mayor from which I had seen those wonderful illuminations. I think that there might have been some problem about finding a place for us, because the king sat in a tribune and not among the grandees in the body of the church. This trouble would not have arisen in the chapel, where the place of ambassadors is well established. I find that I have forgotten something which I should have mentioned earlier, namely that the precedence of the queen's major-domo mayor presents no difficulty at public audiences, when he stands with the grandees, if such he be (as he most often is), and makes no claim to any other distinction.

[1] Her Italian maid who had followed her from Parma.

On Thursday, 27 November, the day of the king and queen's excursion to Lerma, and the day after the public thanksgiving at Nuestra Señora de Atocha, Maulévrier woke me very early indeed, with dispatches that had just arrived, and copies of them, made for me. This courier brought the news of Mlle de Montpensier's departure from Paris on the 18th, the list of stages on her journey, her sleeping places, the members of her suite, the expected date of her arrival at the frontier, and the names of those who were charged with the exchange of the two princesses.

The courier could not have come at a more timely moment. The court was leaving that same day, and the glad tidings relieved us mightily, for the king and queen were beginning to be vexed as well as impatient, and complained of the delay every time they saw us, quite unmoved by our attempts at reassurance. Maulévrier and I therefore resolved to lose no time in giving them the news, and we immediately set out for the palace. I had intended to invite Grimaldo to escort us, both on account of the earliness of the hour, and because it was his right; but Maulévrier thought we should do best to go straight to restore the king's tranquillity. He was sure that Grimaldo would understand, and that if Their Catholic Majesties were not yet visible we might wait in the *covachuela*. They could not think ill of us, he said, for our anxiety to bring them good news. Reminding myself that being on such excellent terms with Grimaldo I could explain all, I gave way, and we made straight for the Mirror Hall, which at that hour was deserted. We scratched noisily on the doors so as to attract attention, and a French valet opened to us, declaring that the king and queen were still in bed, which did not surprise us, but we asked him to inform them immediately that we desired the honour of an interview. Now it is unheard of for anyone, except those in most intimate service, and very rarely for them, to see Their Catholic Majesties in bed. Indeed, only Grimaldo comes to work with them in the morning; no one else at all, not even the high officers of the court and government. The valet none the less departed, and returned to say that Their Majesties wished us to know that although it was against every rule and custom, they would be glad for us to see them in their bed.

We accordingly crossed the entire length of the Mirror Hall; turned left into a fine large room, then immediately left again, into a tiny interior, partitioned off from the greater chamber and drawing its only light from the door, and two small windows set high up in the partition wall. There was a bed, at most four and a half feet wide, trimmed with crimson damask and narrow gold fringes. It had four short posts, and the curtains were drawn back at the foot and on the king's side. He lay almost flat, supported on pillows, and wearing a little bed-jacket of white satin. The queen sat upright at the king's left, holding a piece of embroidery. Skeins of wool lay near her hand, and the rest of the bed was strewn with papers, as was also an armchair, very near the head, on the king's side. Both he and the queen wore nightcaps, and she also was wearing a bed-jacket. They lay between sheets, very imperfectly covered by this mass of papers. They cut our compliments short, the king sitting up a little and asking somewhat crossly what had happened. We were quite alone, for the valet had disappeared after showing us the door. 'Good news! Sire,' I cried, 'Mlle de Montpensier left on the 18th; a courier has this moment arrived, and we came at once to tell Your Majesty.' Their faces were suffused with joy as they rained questions on us regarding her route and stopping-places, and the date of her arrival at the frontier, all to the accompaniment of comments and discussion. We told them everything that had occurred in Paris, the honours done to the Duke of Osuna, and to Mlle de Montpensier herself after the signing; the public rejoicing, the ball, in short all that could best portray the great delight, in which the King had shared, and M. le Duc d'Orléans's deep sense of the honour done to his daughter. As you may guess, it was a very large subject, and well covered both by us and by Their Catholic Majesties, who often interrupted one another as they questioned us and discussed various points. As a result, we were with them more than an hour. They seemed highly gratified by our description of the extraordinary honours, and the joy of the entire nation. I say 'our description', but Maulévrier contributed very little, not understanding the true inwardness of customs and differences. After our dismissal, we descended to the *covachuela* to tell all to the Marquis of Grimaldo, and remained with him nearly two hours.

We then dined at my house, returning to the palace in time to see the king and queen leave for Lerma. Once again they showered me with kindnesses. Both of them, more especially the queen, asked me, two or three times over, not to delay in following them, and I promised to be at their coach door when they arrived. After they had gone, I went home to finish my dispatches and send the courier back, giving him at the same time one copy of the marriage contract, signed by the king and queen, in their own hands.

I purposely omit many of the smaller matters regarding which Cardinal Dubois wrote to me,[1] because the illness to which I soon afterwards succumbed made it impossible for me to attend to business until the wedding day of the Prince of the Asturias. I shall also omit the acute embarrassment Dubois caused me, purely out of malice, by increasing my expenses tenfold. You will remember that I had refused any emoluments, on condition of my not being left out of pocket, but having my exact expenses repaid me, and no more. From the very start, Cardinal Dubois had been determined to ruin me, though all the while he uttered reassuring promises. He wished to be revenged for my having obtained the embassy

---

[1] There follow scores of pages describing almost incomprehensible diplomacy, details of trivial intrigues, harking back to Alberoni's time and the relationship between the Regent and Philip V. To addicts of Saint-Simon they have their charm, but are too long for this abridgment.

against his advice, indeed despite his best endeavours. In the end, he did succeed in ruining me; but let it be said for my honour and for that of France, he did not have the pleasure of dishonouring me in Spain, from which I departed when my task was done without owing a sou to anyone, or in any way reducing the state in which I had begun and which I was resolved to maintain. My only retrenchment was to send home nearly all the officers of the King's regiments, wished on me, as you may recall, by that pious prelate.

The Spanish court, travelling at tortoise-speed, was not due to arrive until 11 December at Lerma, a beautiful little market town situated on a small tributary of the river Douro, in a charming valley about six leagues south of Burgos. The palace was originally built in 1625 for Philip III's first minister, the Duke of Lerma, who died a cardinal. It is a magnificent edifice both in size and architecture, with a splendid suite of state apartments and a horseshoe staircase, and is connected to the town by a decorative courtyard with an inner court leading out of it, which unfortunately is on a steep incline. As the palace is sited on a hill, the first floor is at ground level at the back and gives on to a very large tract of land that in any country where gardens were prized might have been made into something exceedingly beautiful, more especially since there is a delightful view across the valley and over the wood that adjoins the palace on its own level. This wood is of great size, close-packed with undergrowth, but light, being full of stunted trees, most of them green oaks.

The palace has rooms sufficient only for the servants and personal attendants, and villages are therefore commandeered in the neighbourhood to lodge grandees and ambassadors. I had the choice of several, and from the description settled on Villamanzo, just half a league north of the town, overlooking it beyond the little valley, which one crossed by a footpath and a stone bridge. The curé's house was prepared for me alone: small, airy, pretty, with new chimneys especially added for my comfort. The rest of the village was taken for my companions and servants. It was all most agreeable for we were the sole inhabitants, apart from the curé and the village folk. Their houses gained greatly by the improvements, and they were so pleased with us that they made friends with all our servants. We did them no kind of harm, and gave them presents on parting; thus they developed an affection for us and regretted our leaving—some even wept. It was, however, an excursion that proved disastrous to my economy and the pockets of my entire household. The excellent reports of the hunting had caused the king and queen's eagerness to go to Lerma and there await the arrival of the future Princess of the Asturias.

On 2 December, I left Madrid to rejoin the court, and on the way stopped at the Escorial, with the Comtes de Lorges and de Céreste, my younger son, the Abbé de Saint-Simon, his brother, and the two senior officers of the King's regiment, whom I kept with me during all my mission to Spain. I was furnished with letters from the King of Spain, the Marquis of Grimaldo, as well as from the nuncio to the prior, who is also governor of the Escorial, requesting him to show me the glories of that great and famous monastery, and allow me to see whatever else I wished. I had been warned that without a recommendation from the nuncio, neither King Philip's order nor that of his minister, nor yet my official position would have had much effect. Indeed, I was once again to suffer from the boorishness and futile reverence for the past of most unmannerly custodians. They are a black and white order, greatly resembling the Celestines,[1] grossly idle, low-born, practising no austerities. In the number of their monasteries, none of which are abbeys, and their wealth, they roughly correspond to the French Benedictines. The Escorial, their most famous house, is a marvellous assemblage of all sorts of buildings, and contains a vast collection of treasures—paintings, sculpture, vases of all description, precious stones, dispersed throughout with no kind of order. I shall not attempt to list them, for that is not my subject. Suffice it to say that the most ardent connoisseur of all these arts might study unremittingly for three whole months and still not have seen all. The shape of a gridiron governs the entire plan of this splendid edifice, in honour of Saint Lawrence and the battle of Saint Quentin, won on his feast-day by King Philip II,[2] who watched the fighting from a neighbouring hill, and vowed to build a monastery there if his troops should prove victorious. There is not a door, lock, utensil, dish, or plate that is not stamped with the gridiron.

The distance from Madrid to the Escorial is almost identical with that from Paris to Fontainebleau. The landscape is flat, and as one nears the monastery, which takes its name from a large village about a league away, it becomes almost completely uninhabited. There are no houses in the immediate vicinity. The apartments of Their Catholic Majesties are in the handle of the grid. Their high officers of state, not excluding the queen's ladies, are housed in the monastery itself, on the arrival side, which is most ill-designed for lodging courtiers.

The church, the grand staircase, and the great cloister filled me with awe. I admired the style of the dispensary and the pleasant garden, although, to say truth, this is not more than a long terrace. The Pantheon frightened me by the impression it gave of horror and solemnity. The great altar and the sacristy dazzled me with their richness. I did not greatly care for the library and still less for its guardians; but the monks received me everywhere with much politeness and gave me a good supper, although cooked in the Spanish way. The prior and another fat monk did the honours. After that first supper, my own servants prepared our meals, but that same fat monk always brought us some dish which it would have been discourteous to refuse, and he always ate with us. Indeed, he never

---

[1] An order founded in 1296 by Pietro di Murrone, who later became Pope Celestine V.
[2] 10 August 1557.

left us, but acted everywhere as our guide. We communicated with him in abominable Latin, to supplement French, which he barely understood, nor were we better in Spanish.

In the sanctuary near the high altar, behind the stalls of the celebrant priests and their assistants, was a row of glass windows, nearly on a level with the floor of the lofty sanctuary. They belonged to a suite of rooms constructed by Philip II for his own use, and in which he died. He heard the services through them. I desired to visit those rooms which one entered from the back, but they refused to show them to me. Although I declared that by order of the king and the nuncio they were bound to show me all, they still refused. They affirmed that the rooms had been shut after the death of Philip II, and that no one since then had entered them. I said I knew that Philip V and his staff had seen them. They admitted as much, but declared that he had forced them, threatening to break down the door; that he had seen them only once, and that they never had, nor ever would, show them to any other. I failed to comprehend such foolish superstitions, but I could do no more and, in any event, I knew from Louville,[1] who had been one of the party, that the entire suite consisted of those five or six dark little rooms and some privies, very roughly put together, and without wall hangings or furniture at the time when he saw them. Thus I did not lose much by failing to inspect them.

On the way down to the Pantheon, I observed a door in the wall on the left-hand side. The fat monk said that it was the rotting-room,[2] and opened it. We climbed five or six steps in the thickness of the wall, and entered a long, narrow chamber, where there was nothing to see apart from the white walls, a large window at the end by which we had entered, and a smallish door facing us. The only piece of furniture was a long wooden table in the centre, on which the corpses are laid and prepared. For each body, a hole is cut in the wall, and the corpse is there enclosed until it has rotted. They cover the hole so that no trace of it remains in the shining whiteness of the marble, although the whole room is brilliantly lit. The monk showed me the whereabouts of M. de Vendôme's body, near the opposite door; and I perceived from his face and expression that that gentleman was unlikely to emerge. The bodies of the kings, and of those queens who bore children, are recovered after a certain time, and placed without ceremony into niches prepared for them in the Pantheon itself. Those of the Infantas and the barren queens are taken to an adjoining room, which I shall now describe, and remain there in perpetuity.

This second chamber is arranged exactly like a library; but instead of the shelves being adapted to fit variously sized books, they are made for coffins piled one above another. The heads are towards the wall, the feet at the

---

[1] An old and great friend of Saint-Simon, and of Philip V when he was the Duc d'Anjou. He had been one of those who accompanied him to Spain, in 1701. See index, I.

[2] *le pourrissoir.*

edge of the shelves, and they are inscribed with the name of the person enclosed. Some coffins are covered in velvet, others in brocade, but they are packed so close that one sees nothing of this, except at the feet. Despite the chamber being windowless, there is no smell, and it is not in the least funereal. We read the inscriptions within view, and the monk read others aloud for our benefit. Thus, commenting and discussing, we made the tour. At the extreme end, the coffin of poor Don Carlos[1] attracted our attention. 'We all know why and how he died,' I said. At those words our fat monk began to bluster, maintaining that he had died a natural death, and inveighing against what he called false rumours. I smiled, and agreed that it would indeed be false to say that they had cut his arteries. At those words, our monk lost his temper, and fell to ranting and raving in a perfect transport of rage. At first I merely listened in silent amusement; but then I described how soon after his first arrival in Spain, the king's curiosity had been aroused to the extent of having the coffin opened, and that I knew from one of the onlookers (Louville again) that Don Carlos's head rested between his legs, Philip II having had him beheaded at the prison, before his very eyes. 'Well! what of that?' exclaimed the monk, by this time completely beside himself. 'It would appear that he richly deserved it, for King Philip had the Pope's permission.' And he began to proclaim the king's justice and piety, and the absolute authority of the Pope, accusing all who thought differently of being heretics. Such is the fanaticism in countries of the Inquisition, where they regard knowledge as a crime, and ignorance and stupidity as the paramount virtues. Although my office protected me, I did not care to argue with the old fatty.[2] I simply laughed, and motioned to my companions to be silent. The monk was thus able to relieve his feelings, and it was a long while before he had calmed himself sufficiently to see that we mocked him, although we said nothing. At last, still fuming, he showed us the rest of the chamber, and we then descended to the Pantheon itself. There they paid us the supreme compliment of lighting the two tiers of candles in the magnificent chandelier that hangs from the centre of the roof. We were dazzled, for not only could the smallest handwriting be read with ease, but everything was clearly visible in the most distant corners.

I spent three days at the Escorial, lodged in a fine large apartment, with my companions equally well housed. Our monk, who had remained in a bad temper since the day of the rotting-room, only recovered his composure at breakfast before our departure. We left him without regret, but far otherwise the Escorial, where we had found so much to interest and delight us. On the road, we encountered the Marquis of Montalegre, and

---

[1] Son of Philip II, and the hero of Verdi's opera *Don Carlos*. The facts are not those of Schiller's story, or of the opera. He was suspected of plotting to murder his father, tried, and found guilty, but sentence of death was not recorded. He died shortly afterwards, 24 June 1508. Rumour had it that he was poisoned or strangled, but no evidence was ever produced.

[2] *ce piffre de moine.*

arrived at the same moment at the place where we were to dine. He sent immediately to invite me and my gentlemen, for he also had a large retinue, and promptly entertained us to such a vast and excellent meal of Spanish food that we later regretted the simple dinner which my own people had prepared for us.

At nine o'clock, we reached our village of Villalmanzo, where I found all imaginable comforts, as did my companions. My elder son, still convalescent, had already arrived from Burgos with the Abbé de Mathan. We had a merry supper, and I made plans for a long walk next day, and for amusing myself reconnoitring the village and its surroundings. That night, however, I developed a fever that worsened during the day, and on the following night became so acute that there was no question of my being able to wait on the king and queen when they arrived at Lerma on the 11th. The illness increased with such rapidity that I was thought to be in grave danger, and then, suddenly, *in extremis.* They bled me, and shortly afterwards smallpox, of which the country was full, declared itself. The weather that winter was such that whereas it froze hard for twelve or fourteen hours every day, there was glorious sunshine from eleven in the morning until close on four o'clock, and at midday it was too hot to go out. Where the sun did not beat directly down on some object such as a wall, there was never any sign of thawing, and the cold was all the fiercer because the air was exceptionally pure and bracing, and the sky perfectly and continuously serene.

The King of Spain, who lived in fear of smallpox, and with good reason believed in no doctor except his first physician,[1] sent this gentleman to me as soon as he learned of my illness, with orders not to leave me for a single moment until I was cured. Thus I had five or six persons nursing me, apart from the servants, and one of the wisest and best doctors of all Europe, who was, moreover, most excellent company. He never left me day or night, and had three skilful surgeons to assist him. I was completely covered with eruptions of a non-malignant kind, and once the spots had appeared there was no serious relapse. The gentlemen who treated me, and their valets, were kept separate at their meals and allowed no intercourse with the rest. Even the cooks who prepared my food were kept apart from the cooks who did nothing for me. Every day, the king's doctor brewed new remedies in case of need; but he used none of them, beyond making me drink, for my only beverage, water into which oranges in their skins had been thrown, cut in half, and gently simmered before my fire. Very occasionally, a spoonful or two of a sweet, pleasant-tasting cordial was given me at the time of the worst suppurations, and later a little Rota wine, and clear broth, mainly of beef or partridge. Nothing lacked in these people's care of me, their only patient; and nothing lacked for my entertainment when I was well enough to seek diversion, for they were the

[1] John Higgens, an Irishman, who died in 1729. He had been Philip V's doctor since 1717.

best company imaginable, and this at a time when convalescents from this particular malady are apt to feel depressed and neglected. Right at the end, they bled and purged me once only, after which I lived an ordinary life, but in a kind of solitude.

During the long interval when my illness kept me from all business, the Abbé de Saint-Simon undertook everything, even the dealings with Cardinal Dubois, Grimaldo, Sartine, and others. I therefore came to the conclusion that the best way to occupy myself in my six weeks of enforced idleness was to make a brief catalogue of everyone at the Spanish court, as it existed during the six months of my visit to Spain, giving details of their characters, fortunes, and official duties. . . .[1]

This leads me naturally to describe the private lives of the King and Queen of Spain, for nothing more deeply affects great and small alike than the daily routine of their rulers.[2] This is well known to all who, because of office or favour, become part of the inner circle, and to those outside also who are well enough trusted to be kept fully informed by the initiates. Let me add in passing, from my own more than twenty years' experience of court life in one form or another, that such knowledge is a guide to all that happens, and is sadly lacking in all Histories and most Memoirs, which would be far more valuable and interesting did they not neglect it as being mere triviality, unworthy of inclusion in a serious work. What is more, I am firmly of the opinion that ministers of State, favourites, and those other few of all ages who by their work or service are brought into daily contact with the monarch, will fully share my conviction.

The queen, when she first arrived in Spain, had but one idea, to fill the void occasioned by her prompt dismissal of the Princesse des Ursins; and the king, whose temperament urgently needed a spouse, and whose conscience prevented his seeking relief elsewhere, gave her, in that direction, all the encouragement she could desire. He had long been accustomed to a continual *tête-à-tête*, or at the most to a third person; but the queen's choice was severely limited. Having no friends among Spaniards, she soon turned to Alberoni, the only man she knew well, who shared her interests by being a native of Parma, and was, like herself, intensely ambitious. He had been her sole adviser since she left her home and, at the beginning at any rate, was the only man in whom she could confide. It was not long before he had stepped into the place which Mme des Ursins had held under the former queen, with the difference of sex removing the absurdity; making him capable of being first minister in name

---

[1] The 'brief catalogue' fills nearly two hundred pages of the Édition de la Pléiade, and far more in the Chéruel and Boislisle editions. The length and dullness of this insertion has led to the omission of the Spanish journey from many books of extracts.

[2] The Duc de Beauvilliers used to say that the absolute regularity of Louis XIV's life was of immeasurable assistance in the conduct of affairs of State. One had only to look at one's watch and consult the almanac to know anywhere in France exactly what the ruler was doing at any moment of the day.

as well as deed, and finally bringing him a cardinalate. To gain those rich rewards, Alberoni had followed the methods which Mme des Ursins found perfectly successful, the same which clever men who aspire to dominate kings invariably practise in a manner highly profitable to themselves, but most detrimental to their masters, and thoroughly pernicious for their kingdoms, subjects, and governments.

Where Alberoni was concerned, he had no more to do than encourage the king's fatal addiction to the prison in which Mme des Ursins had gradually enclosed him, first with the late queen, then, after she died, with herself alone. The new queen and Alberoni followed her example, keeping King Philip entirely to themselves, and making him inaccessible to everyone else. After the dismissal of Alberoni, the queen grew tired of her self-inflicted confinement, and tried several times to loosen her chains, but all in vain. The king's habits had by that time become too firmly established; they were second nature, and she soon despaired of ever freeing herself. This then is how they lived, at all times, in all places, and at every season of the year:

The King and Queen of Spain perpetually shared a bedroom, and one small bed, such as I described when, with Maulévrier, I was permitted to see them therein. In the fevers and maladies that afflicted either of them, even during confinements, they remained together; and at the time when the late queen was devoured by scrofula, the king still continued to sleep with her until a few days before her death. At nine each morning, the *azafata* drew back their curtains, followed by a single French valet[1] carrying a tray with a bowl of *chaudeau*[2] upon it. When I was recovering from smallpox, Higgens explained to me what this is, and had some prepared for me to taste. It is a smooth mixture of broth, milk, and wine, the last predominating, with one or two egg-yolks, sugar, cinnamon, and a clove or two. It is white, sweetish, and very highly flavoured. It would not be my choice, yet it is not unpalatable. People sometimes add crusts of bread or toast, and then it becomes like thick soup; otherwise it can be drunk like a broth, which was the way preferred by the King of Spain. The mixture is somewhat greasy, but extremely hot, and a most excellent restorative after the night before, in preparation for the night to come.

While the king consumed this light repast, the *azafata* handed the queen her tapestry work, helped Their Majesties into their bed-jackets, and placed on the bed the papers from the neighbouring chairs. She then retired with the valet and the breakfast tray. Grimaldo entered upon the hour, having been alerted in his *covachuela*. Sometimes, if their prayers were not yet finished, they would sign to him to wait by the door, for he

[1] The name of the valet was Valois. Saint-Simon includes him in his catalogue of the Spanish court.

[2] This drink, corresponding to an egg-flip, used to be brought to married couples on the morning after their wedding. M. Gonzague Truc, editor of the Édition de la Pléiade, says that La Fontaine in *L'Ivrogne et sa Femme* mentions a *chaudeau* 'strong enough to revive Lucifer'.

entered alone and the bedroom was excessively small. Grimaldo then spread his papers out on the bed; drew from his pocket an inkstand, and started to work with the king—and with the queen also, for her embroidery never deterred her from offering advice. They worked for a longer or shorter time, according to the amount of business or conversation. Grimaldo thereupon collected his papers and withdrew, crossing the empty room from which the bedroom was partitioned, into another where stood a valet. This man, seeing him leave, went back through the empty room to alert the *azafata* who immediately went to give the king his slippers and dressing-gown. His Majesty then crossed the empty room to a closet where he dressed, attended by three French valets (always the same) and either the Duke of Arco or the Marquis of Santa-Cruz, sometimes both. No one else was ever present at that time. When all was ready, one of the valets went to summon Père Daubenton from the Mirror Hall, and he joined the king in that closet, from which all signs of the *lever* had been hastily removed by those same valets, who did not reappear. If after the valets had gone, the king nodded to the two noblemen, they also left; but that rarely happened. Usually they remained standing by the door while the king spoke to Père Daubenton in a window.

As soon as the king had departed, the *azafata*, alone with the queen, put on her stockings and handed her her dressing-gown. This was the only time when they could speak privately; but it was never more, and sometimes even less, than a quarter of an hour. Had they spent longer together the king would have known, and have wished to hear the reason. The queen then crossed the empty room into a fine large chamber where her ladies waited for her *toilette*: the *camerera-mayor*, two palace ladies, two maids of honour (changed weekly), and her dressers. Very occasionally a third lady, or a maid of honour off-duty, also attended. When the king had finished dressing, and had spoken with Père Daubenton, which did not usually take long, he joined the queen at her *toilette*, followed by the two lords-in-waiting. The infante also appeared with their governors and, after the marriage of the Prince of the Asturias, his bride came too, with her duenna the Duchess of Montellano,[1] and perhaps one or other of her ladies.

Hunting, excursions, the fine coats of the king and the infante provided the main topics of conversation, interspersed with gentle rebukes from the queen to her ladies for some lack of attention in her service, or for ill conduct or impiety, for she held them on a very short rein. They were discouraged from going much into Society; their friends were watched. In order to gain the queen's favour they had often to be confined, but not too long in labour, or too frequently indisposed. Most important of all, they must go to prayers once a week. Cardinal Borgia had the entrée to the queen's *toilette*, and was often present, bringing life to the proceedings by

[1] Luisa de Gand y Sarmients, Duchess of Montellano (1654–1734).

his jokes. The entire ceremony lasted three-quarters of an hour, the king and everyone else standing. When they left, the king went to the door that connected the Mirror Hall with the ante-room of the Grandees' Hall where the court was assembled, and gave his orders through the half-open doors to the very few whom they concerned.

This was the time for private audiences to foreign ministers and the noblemen who desired them. These persons were introduced one by one into the Mirror Hall, where the king received them quite alone. Once a week, on Mondays, there were public audiences, a practice that cannot be too much admired, provided it is not abused. Instead of the doors being half-open, they are left wide apart for everyone to enter. The king, followed by his courtiers, then walks through the whole suite of rooms to the great chamber where the ambassadors present their credentials and grandees are invested. He then sits in an armchair, with a table at his right hand, on which is ink and paper. When someone he knows desires private speech with him, their request is granted. The words, 'This audience is secret', are proclaimed, the grandees remove their hats and file bowing past the king into the adjoining room. The captain of the guard stands in the doorway, advancing his head a little round the half-shut door, so as to watch the king and the person with him. When that person rises from his knees, he perceives it, and re-enters with all the rest, who take up the same positions as before. I never attended a public audience without there being at least one secret interview, and sometimes two or three. In the short time before the wedding, the grandees invited me to assume precedence as though I were a Spanish duke, and I accepted. Afterwards, I had the double right, as a duke and peer of France and as a Grandee of Spain. My second son attended with me after his investiture.

After the audience, or after diverting himself with the queen when there was none, the king and queen went together to the chapel. They went alone, and were alone in their tribune where an altar had been erected. There they heard mass together, and took Communion, both together, never separately, usually once a week, after which they heard a second mass. When they returned, or very shortly after, their dinner was served. They ate always in the queen's room, and had supper there also, in whatever residence they happened to be, but they had different dishes. The king ate very little, the queen abundantly because she liked eating and enjoyed a variety. He had always the same, some plain soup; capons, chickens, pigeons, roast or boiled, and invariably a roast fillet of veal; no fruit, cheese, or salad, rarely any cakes or pastries. The meal was never without meat; it occasionally included eggs, raw, or cooked in various ways, and both he and the queen drank nothing but Champagne wine. Dinner over, they prayed together.

An hour later, they left their rooms by a short public passage, and down a little stairway to their coach, returning by the same way. I often saw them in that corridor as they went or came, and the queen always had some pleasant word for those who stood there. On their return, if they had not picnicked in their coach, they ate some morsel in the palace. For the king it was a piece of bread, or a large biscuit with some wine and water. The queen ate pastries and fruits in season, or perhaps a little cheese. The Prince and Princess of the Asturias and the children followed them into the queen's room with their attendants, as at her *toilette*. They withdrew in less than a quarter of an hour, and Grimaldo entered. This was the time for serious work. It was also the moment for the queen to confess, if she so desired; but apart from matters relating to her confession, there was no time for talk. The room she used was next the one in which the king worked, and if he thought her too long, he would open the door and call to her. When Grimaldo left, they prayed together or read a devotional book until their supper, which was served like their dinner. At both meals, more dishes were cooked in the French style than in the Spanish, or even the Italian. After supper, conversation or prayer carried them on until bedtime. Their *coucher* was like their *lever*. As a final touch, Their Catholic Majesties shared a privy in all their residences, with their *chaises-percées* placed side by side.

Thus their lives were a continual *tête-à-tête*. When they travelled it was at a snail's pace, and by such very short stages that the time ordinarily spent hunting was enough to take them their day's journey. Night after night they rested on the road, in houses specially arranged to match their palaces in every detail. In their coaches they were also alone, *tête-à-tête* in a vast conveyance belonging to the queen, with seven glass windows, and a red velvet cover, like those used by royalty in France, tacked over all.

If this description should seem long drawn-out, it is because such a life might well be unbelievable to those that had not witnessed it—this monotonous routine, so strictly ordered, so perfectly regular by day and night, wherever they happened to be. This endless togetherness, day in, day out, rarely interrupted even for a moment, might appear completely unbearable. Its influence on State affairs and the lives of individuals was enormous, for it will be obvious that no one, whoever he might be, could speak to the king apart from the queen, or to the queen out of his hearing, so inordinately jealous were they both. That is what gave the *azafata* such great importance, because when putting on her stockings, or during the public audiences, she could give the queen a letter. That, moreover, was the only moment when the queen could see someone from outside, whom the *azafata* smuggled in, after taking due precautions. Yet it was a practice she discouraged, for she feared discovery and its consequences. But in those short periods she could at least receive and read letters, and write notes herself, you may imagine with what haste, and what care to keep no scrap of paper.

As for the character of Philip V, he was not born with any superiority of intellect, nor did he possess the least trace of what is called imagination. He was cold, silent, sad, and sober, knowing no pleasures except hunting, fearing Society, fearing even himself, seldom coming forward, seldom attracted to others, solitary and retiring by preference and habit. Yet he was none the less sensible and upright, and imbued with a fair understanding. Although apt to be stubborn, and on such occasions impossible to influence, he was, in general, very easy to advise and guide.

He had little sense of danger. During his campaigns, he allowed them to place him where they wished, displaying no sign of fear, even under fire; and it amused him to notice if others were alarmed. He was equally unfeeling when under cover and far from danger, for it never struck him that his own valour might be questioned. On the whole he enjoyed campaigning, but cared little whether he went or stayed at home, and, present or absent, he left his generals to decide everything, offering them no advice. He was inordinately vain, and could bear no opposition. What made me so sure that he loved flattery was that the queen never ceased from praising him, even for his appearance. She asked me one day at the end of an audience that had turned to conversation whether I did not think him very handsome, the best-looking man I had ever seen. His piety was a habit, engrained by conscience, fear, obedience to the rules; but he had no real understanding of religion. The Pope, when he was not resisting him, was to him a divinity. He had the gentle manners of the Jesuits, whom he devotedly loved. His health was excellent, but he examined it continually, and lived in a permanent state of alarm. A doctor such as the one whose fortune was made by Louis XI[1] would have become rich and powerful in his service; fortunately his own physician was already wealthy, and a most honourable man.

King Philip was a good man, and not a hard master. He was kind to those who attended on him, and even to some of the noblemen who did not. His love for France was most apparent. He felt gratitude and veneration towards the late King, love for the late Monseigneur, and affection for his brother the late Dauphin whose loss he continued to mourn. I never heard him mention other members of the royal family, or ask for news of any of the courtiers, save only the Duchesse de Beauvilliers,[2] of whom he spoke with affection.

His scruples concerning his throne were hard to understand, or to reconcile with his thought of returning, should any tragedy occur, to the throne of his fathers which he had more than once most solemnly renounced. The facts were that he could not get out of his head the Queen's[3] renunciations when she married Louis XIV, and all the oaths sworn to

[1] Saint-Simon is referring to Jacques Coitier (died 1505), whom Louis XI made president of the Chambre des Comptes.
[2] Widow of the Duc de Beauvilliers, who had been his governor.
[3] His grandmother Maria Teresa (1638–1683), daughter of Philip IV of Spain. See I, p. 136, note 2.

affirm them; neither could he comprehend how Charles II could legally have bequeathed a monarchy that was not his absolute property, in the sense that a private person may own land and freely dispose of it in his will. Thus he firmly believed that he was a usurper, and Père Daubenton was obliged to wage daily battles with him on that account. So thinking, he nourished the hope of returning one day, partly because he would have preferred to rule and live in France, partly also to quieten his conscience by abandoning Spain.[1] No doubt such thoughts were confused in his mind, but those are the facts, and only the impossibility of taking action prevented his leaving Spain altogether. They played a large role in his decision to abdicate, which he was already contemplating when I went to Spain.[2] As you may imagine, he never mentioned that difficult subject to me, but others kept me fully informed, although between Grimaldo and myself not a word was uttered.

As for the queen, she was quite as eager as the king to leave Spain, which she detested, and longed to reign in France, should a calamity occur. She thought she might live there a less enclosed and a happier life. She had been brought up most harshly by her mother in an attic of the palace at Parma, and never allowed into Society. Even after the announcement of her great alliance, the Duchess let her appear only on rare occasions, and then kept her always within sight. She was endowed with naturally quick wits, and a charm which she had learned to control. Everyone who knew her was astonished at the way in which good sense and intelligence compensated in her for ignorance of Society, affairs, and personalities. The attic in Parma and the perpetual tête-à-tête in Spain, had prevented her from gaining any real experience. No one can therefore deny her perspicacity in detecting from what little she observed the underlying truth about people and affairs. This rare gift might have been hers in perfection had ill temper not marred it; but ill-tempered she was, and one must admit that anyone living her life would have been the same. She knew her strength and capabilities, but did not allow pride, or a foolish love of display, to weaken them. Normally she was simple, calm, even merry, with a natural gaiety that sparkled up despite the eternal constraints of her life; and if she showed bad and sometimes bitter temper as a result of repression, she was far otherwise in general, and, indeed, quite exceptionally charming.

Coming to Spain, as she did, with the fixed idea of dismissing Mme des Ursins and replacing her in the government, she acted so quickly to gain

---

[1] King Philip's conscience tortured him. Alberoni is said to have reported that he often threw himself weeping upon his knees before the figures in the tapestries, begging them to forgive him his sins.

[2] See Renunciations in index. Philip, who must surely have counted his son also as a usurper, continued to reign until 1746. He died on 9 July of that year, having for a long time been sunk in a mental stupor reminiscent, perhaps, of the gloomy apathy of his father Monseigneur le Grand Dauphin.

control, not only of that but of the king also, that she very soon was
mistress of both. Regarding State affairs, nothing could be hidden from
her, for the king worked only in her presence; she read and discussed
with him every paper, and was present at all private audiences; thus
there was little she did not know. As regarded the king, she knew all, for
their continual togetherness had given her the opportunity to learn him
thoroughly, as it were by heart. She could thus foresee setbacks and
prepare against them by gentle words, judge the strength of opposition, if
any, the cause and the best means of removing it, the times to give way so
as to return later, the times to stand firm and carry all by force. All such
means were needed, powerful though she was, and, dare I say it, the
king's own nature was her strongest weapon, and one which she sometimes used against him. Then there were nocturnal refusals arousing
tempests;[1] the king shrieked and threatened, sometimes did worse. She
held firm, wept, and on occasions defended herself. On the morning after,
everything was in turmoil. The very small entourage, approaching first
one and then the other, often never learned the cause. Peace returned on
the following night, and it was seldom that the queen was not the gainer.

Her life thus alternated between severe restraint, and outbursts so
violent as to defy imagination. Though her influence was very great, she
needed constant vigilance, wiles, stratagems, and patience to maintain it. It
is not too much to affirm that, successful though she was, the price she paid
was too great; but so active was she, so fixed, so determined to gain her
ends, and those ends appeared to her so vital, that every sacrifice seemed
to her worth while.[2] Her prime ambition was by all means to save herself
from the miseries of life as a Spanish queen-dowager, or an unknown fate
at the hands of a successor who was not her own son.

There soon developed secondary aims that made her first objective seem
easier to accomplish. Several princes were born to her, and thereafter all
her thoughts turned to making them independent sovereigns in the lifetime of King Philip, with the intention of providing herself with kingdoms
which she might retire to, and rule after his death. Day and night she
meditated on this grand design, for the foreign policy of Spain must hinge
upon it, supporters be acquired, and given posts with powers and duties
to make them capable of assisting her. Nothing could have been more
damaging to Spain than this frantic chase after foreign thrones for the
queen's children, when combined with the impossibility of ever seeing the
king without her. She was so fearful of any thwarting of her desires, and
had such a superficial acquaintance with State affairs, that every proposal
seemed suspect to her if it did not immediately coincide with her plans.

[1] Madame wrote that on such occasions she took refuge in a little bed on castors that had
belonged to the late queen.
[2] She was known as 'the termagant'. Her great desire was to expel the Habsburgs from Italy,
and turn over their kingdoms to her sons. In the event, all she gained was the Two Sicilies for
Don Carlos.

She would stiffen at once, and although she could sometimes be moved, it was only after devious approaches, great tact, and tedious delays that wasted much precious time, and sometimes ruined the whole undertaking. Had it been permitted to see her alone and spend time with her, she had sufficient intelligence and sense to understand and argue with good judgment. She might then have been persuaded, but the king being always present, this was impossible, for she deeply feared lest he be impressed by contrary arguments and use them against her. Thus she would have no explanations, refusing everything, even proposals that might have assisted her, because she could not foresee the outcome. In view of her attitude, Spanish ministers immediately gave way, fearing disgrace or the loss of their offices, while foreign ambassadors likewise stopped short, knowing full well the uselessness of persistence; all of which did immense damage to the affairs of Spain.

In matters of purely domestic importance, especially in the granting of posts and favours, she did not always have her way; but in preventing their bestowal she invariably succeeded. Her skill and tact in dealing with the king were incomparable, as she gradually brought him round to share her likings and aversions. She seldom moved directly, but prepared the ground far ahead, edging her way by twists and turns, advancing or retiring in accordance with the king's looks, replies, and moods, which she knew so well that she never erred. Her praise, flattery, and sweetness were unfailing —never a sign of boredom, never a glimpse of her heavy burden. In everything that did not affect her aims, the king was always right, no matter what he might say or do, and she anticipated his wishes so constantly, so gladly, looking so happy, that no one could have imagined that they were not always to her liking. Yet he held her on so short a rein that she was never able to quit his left side. Often have I seen her at mall,[1] carried away by some story or conversation, walk a few paces slower than the king, until she had fallen five or six steps behind. Then he would turn and, that instant, she would be beside him in two little bounds, continuing the discussion with the few gentlemen who had followed them and who, like myself, moved quickly up to regain the lost ground. I shall have more to say in due course regarding the game of mall.

You will have observed from this description of the life of the King and Queen of Spain that no vestige remained of the ancient etiquette of that court. It had fallen altogether into disuse, for if the gentlemen could show themselves only for brief moments, there was no time at all for the ladies, no councils, or working hours with any but the one minister. Nearly all the posts about the court had been abolished, the chief steward (one of the three highest offices) and the gentlemen of the chamber no longer had functions or powers; their titles were empty, their keys of office like

[1] The game of pall-mall, played in a long avenue (hence the name of the London street), in which a ball was driven through iron hoops with a mallet.

those of broken watches. Thus, fewer and fewer came to the palace; even the Marquis of Montalegre, the chief steward and captain of the halber-diers, was very seldom to be seen there. Alone of the three high officers, the master of the horse had lost very little, since his functions regarded the exterior, which applied also to the first equerry. It had been the work of the Princesse des Ursins to discontinue gradually the councils which the king normally attended, and make valueless the court etiquette and the functions of its various officers. It was part of her plan to keep the king enclosed and remove all possibility of gentlemen speaking to him pri-vately; and it was the same with the queen and her ladies. For similar reasons, she had taken the utmost care in selecting palace ladies, maids of honour, and women-of-the-bedchamber, filling the lower posts, so far as was possible, with Irishwomen and other foreigners. After Mme des Ursins's departure there was no revival of former etiquette or functions. The *camerera-mayor* who succeeded her had no private hour with the queen, and was reduced, like her major-domo mayor, to attending her at her *toilette* and her meals.

Here I must repair an omission in what I said of the master of the horse and the first equerry. Whenever the king was away from the palace, and picnicking or dining in a village (not on journeys, but out shooting or driving), should he wish to drink a sup, or wash his hands; should he desire to put on a coat or waistcoat, or change his shirt, so needing to undress and dress again, it was the master of the horse and the first equerry who served him. They thus appropriated to themselves the duties of the chief butler, even if he were present, and those also of the gentlemen-in-waiting, which was one reason why those officers were disinclined to follow the king on such excursions.

It is now time to speak of shooting and pall-mall.

Shooting was the everyday diversion of the king, and therefore had also to be the queen's chief delight. The procedure never varied. Their Catholic Majesties did me the extraordinary honour of bidding me join them on one occasion, and I went in my coach. Thus I saw everything perfectly, and to have seen one occasion was to have seen all. Wild boar and deer are not found on the plains; they need to be sought after near the mountains, where the country is too rough for hunting in the sense that we know it in France. The plains themselves are so dry and hard, so full of deep, hidden clefts, that the best stag- or greyhounds would be exhausted as quickly as the hare they pursued, and have their feet scratched, or even maimed into the bargain. Moreover, the whole country is so covered with strong-smelling herbs that the hounds would derive little assistance from their noses. The king had quite ceased to care for taking flying shots or stalking game, and since he no longer rode a horse, all his hunting was confined to shooting driven game.

The Duke of Arco, as master of the horse, was comptroller of every day's sport. It was he who chose the terrain, on which two vast leafy hides[1] were constructed back to back, almost entirely roofed over, and provided with large windows at nearly breast height. The king, the queen, the captain of the guard, the master of the horse, and four loaders all packed into the first hide, with a score of shot-guns and the means to load them. In the other, on the day that I was present, was the Prince of the Asturias, who had arrived in his coach with only the Duke of Popoli and the Marquis of Surco.[2] Also in that hide was the Marquis of Santa-Cruz and the Duke of Giovenazzo (the queen's major-domo mayor and her master of the horse), Valouse, two or three officers of the bodyguard, and myself, with a great number of guns and men to load them. A solitary palace lady, in waiting on the queen, sat quite alone in still another coach, from which she did not stir, having brought with her, as her sole consolation, a book, and a piece of embroidery, for none of the party ever approached her.

Their Majesties and this attendant retinue made the journey at full speed because it was at least three or four leagues, quite twice as far as from Paris to Versailles. They stepped down at the hides, and the coaches with the unfortunate palace lady, and all the horses, were taken far away, completely out of sight, for fear of alarming the game. Two, three, even four hundred peasants had been enlisted on the previous night to surround the area, and begin hallooing at early dawn from far away, so as to rouse and frighten the animals, and drive them gently towards the hides. No one was allowed to move or even whisper, every coat had to be concealed, everyone stood in complete silence. This continued, while we waited, for more than an hour and a half, which I did not find particularly amusing. At length we heard distant halloos; soon after groups of animals began to pass within long or short range of our guns, and the king and queen immediately blazed away in all directions. This sport, or to be more exact this butchery, lasted more than half an hour, as we watched them kill or cripple stags, hinds, roe-deer, wild boar, hares, wolves, badgers, foxes, and martens in vast numbers. The king and queen shot first; then, more often than not, they allowed the master of the horse and the captain of the guard to have their turn; but since we could not tell who had fired each shot, we had to wait until there was silence from the king's hide before letting the prince shoot, and then it often happened that he had little to aim at, and we nothing at all. None the less, I managed to shoot a fox, perhaps somewhat sooner than was polite, wherefore, feeling rather ashamed, I apologized to the Prince of the Asturias, who burst out laughing, joined by all the others, but in a most civil manner.

As the peasants approached, drawing closer together, the shooting

---

[1] *deux grandes feuillées*: the alternative meaning, 'camp latrines', is well known to French soldiers of today.

[2] Ferdinand of Roncamonte y Figueroa, Marquis of Surco, a gentleman-in-waiting (died 1735).

continued, and ended only when they were almost level with the hides, still hallooing because there was nothing behind them. At that point, the carriages returned, the occupants of the two hides emerged and mingled; the bag was dragged up for the king's inspection, and then loaded on to the backs of the coaches. During this time, the talk was all of the day's sport. On this particular occasion, they bore away a dozen or more animals, also several hares, foxes, and martens. Darkness overtook us soon after leaving the hides. Such was the amusement of Their Catholic Majesties on every working day. The peasants received payment, and the king gave them a little something extra as he stepped into his coach.

Nuestra Señora de Atocha, or simply Atocha, as it is most often called, is a miraculous image of the Blessed Virgin, in the glittering chapel of a rather ordinary church, in the magnificent Dominican monastery outside Madrid but only a gunshot from the farthest houses, and adjoining the park of Buen-Retiro Palace. This image is held in such veneration by the inhabitants of Madrid and Castile that all services of public prayer and thanksgiving are held before it. From time immemorial, the king has never embarked on a long journey without first praying there (known as bidding farewell to Nuestra Señora de Atocha), and the same on his return. The value of the gold, precious stones, lace, and costly silks adorning the statue is fabulous. One of the greatest ladies in the land is selected as its lady-in-waiting, a much prized honour, and a very costly one, for it requires forty or fifty thousand livres annually to furnish lace and rich materials, out of which the monastery later derives a handsome profit. I shall not now comment on this cult. The Duchess of Alba, wife of the Spanish ambassador to Paris, was lady-in-waiting at the time of my mission. She died a few days after my arrival, and I never learned who succeeded her.

Evening services are often held before the Lady of Atocha, and the king and queen frequently attend them, driving there without ceremony through the outskirts of Madrid, and not entering the body of the church or the monastery. An unpretentious side door to the main building leads up by fifteen steps into three rooms (the central one being the largest) that open into a long gallery overlooking the chapel. The royal family and their necessary attendants use one of the two smaller rooms; the other is for their following—a very few. I was there, awaiting Their Majesties on almost every occasion, and I never saw more than a dozen courtiers (always the same), apart from those whose duties compelled their attendance. Palace ladies and maids of honour, but by no means all of them, followed the queen; but if she afterwards went to the Mall, only one lady accompanied her; the rest, including the *camerera-mayor*, returned. Three or four monks, heads of the order, received Their Majesties and watched them leave.

I never in my life saw such gross, obese, vulgar, and offensive creatures as those monks. Pride shone in their eyes and suffused their countenances.

The presence of Their Majesties abashed them not at all, not even when addressing them. I speak as to their expressions, tone, and general appearance, for they spoke only Spanish, which I did not comprehend. What surprised me so much that I could scarcely believe my eyes when first I saw it, was the insolent, almost brutal way in which they pushed their elbows in the faces of the ladies; and then how, as though at a signal, the ladies would curtsey very low, humbly kissing the monks' sleeves, and curtseying again, to all of which the monks made no return, at the very most throwing some arrogant word in their direction, without the smallest suspicion of a bow. I even saw a few gentlemen kiss their sleeves in a furtive kind of way; but I never saw a monk offer his sleeve to any one of them. Although this extraordinary performance was repeated each time the king visited Atocha, it always surprised me, and I never became accustomed to seeing it.

After prayers, the king more often than not drove to the Retiro Park, followed by his gentlemen. They left the coaches at the end of the Mall, a beautiful, wide, and extremely long alley, where the king played at pall-mall with the master of the horse and the first equerry, the Marquis of Santa-Cruz, or some other nobleman. He always took three complete turns, both up and down. The queen walked beside him the entire time, changing sides, when necessary, so as to be always on his left. The game was very pleasant because the atmosphere was so delightful. No one entered the Mall itself except the noblemen, and the lady attending the queen. All the rest lined the sides. We followed Their Majesties, and all the way the queen addressed remarks with charming informality to one or other of the gentlemen, even joking with them from time to time, and amusing the king with her pleasantries. She sometimes embarrassed Valouse by making him her butt, and thus increased the gaiety. She would then pretend to attack the Duke of Arco, setting Santa-Cruz against him, and encouraging them to quite fierce repartee. Then the master of the horse would make some retort, speaking to her freely, and in jest. If one of the players tripped, or mishit, everyone laughed and teased him unmercifully, with the result that the time spent in the Mall often seemed too short by far. The king, ordinarily so grave, would smile, and on rare occasions make some short remark. He played well and gracefully, and the queen never ceased admiring him. At the conclusion of the final turn, the coaches were brought to the end of the Mall, and everyone went home. From mid-February to mid-April, when there was the close season for shooting, pall-mall, with sometimes a walk to follow, helped almost every day to fill the void.

Life in Madrid was of two kinds for persons without occupation. I mean for Spaniards and the foreigners established there. The Spaniards did not dine out, idled away their time at home, and saw very little of one another. They rarely visited each other's houses; still more rarely those of foreigners. Occasionally they would give a *conversazione* for a group of five or six invited guests, leaving the front doors open in case others should appear. When I paid my official calls, I sometimes found these in progress. They would sit together talking for three or four hours, but seldom played cards. Chocolate would be brought and placed at their elbows, with sweet biscuits, creams, and water-ices. Spanish ladies held receptions of a similar kind. In good weather many people took an airing along the fine road that leads to Buen-Retiro,[1] or strolled beneath the trees and among the fountains beside the Manzanares.[2] They very rarely invited foreigners and, in fact, scarcely mixed with them at all. The foreigners, men and women alike, dined and visited freely, as we do in France, and very frequently entertained one another in their respective houses. The courtiers at first showed their disapproval, but since there were no other diversions they soon ceased to object. Compared with Paris, very few monks or priests were to be seen in the streets, despite the fact that Madrid is full of monasteries and convents.

It is the custom for ladies to send from time to time to inquire after the health of highly placed noblemen. This is known as a *recado*, and according to the same custom, the recipient of the *recado* must call on the following day, or very shortly after, to thank the lady concerned. This often happened to me, and when I visited, I sometimes found the lady alone. One lady on whom I frequently called, without the excuse of a *recado*, was the Dowager-duchess of Osuna,[3] a daughter of the last Constable of Castile. She lived in great state, in a magnificent house, superbly furnished. She was devoted to M. le Duc d'Orléans, and had seen much of him when he was at Madrid; thus he had charged me to visit her and convey his respects. She had a private theatre, complete in every detail; not so deep, and slightly smaller than our one in Paris, but far more beautiful, and most particularly convenient because the boxes communicated with one another in the stalls and the circle. This noble dame would not have been unwelcome in Paris Society, for she spoke excellent French, and combined to perfection the arts of conversation, with the manners of a very great lady, which indeed she was. I also regularly visited several other ladies.

The first on whom I called was the Marchioness of Grimaldo. No one had warned me of the way in which Spanish ladies received. I entered to find her sitting at the extreme end of her drawing-room, facing the door, with a group of ladies and gentlemen on either side. She rose when she saw me, but remained anchored to the spot, making a little bob as I approached her, after the fashion of nuns. When I left, she bobbed again, without moving an inch forward. It was the custom of the country. The men come forward a certain distance to meet one, and again when one leaves, according to one's

---

[1] The street called the Paseo de Atocha.
[2] The Prado.
[3] Maria Remigilda de Velasco y Benavides, Duchess of Osuna (1683–1734).

rank, for in Spain everything is fixed by rule. Yet one is wearied by all the compliments that, to a far greater extent than in France, speed or delay the process of departure. Each side knows exactly the distance to be covered, for nothing that is said may alter that. Thus the compliments serve no purpose whatsoever, yet one party would incur blame and the other feel justly offended, if all were not done according to the rules. This does not prevent continual stoppages, with the result that very often the compliments take up as much time as the visit itself. It really becomes insufferable. I speak of course of formal calls! When acquaintance has been established, people's behaviour to each other is much as in France. Ladies never visit gentlemen; but they may go to their houses when invited for concerts, balls, fireworks, or such-like, and should there be supper as well as refreshments, they sit down to table and eat with the company.

I must, however, state that Spaniards are unequalled for their courtesy, distinguished manners, and readiness to oblige; always provided that a person's rank and conduct merit such attentions. Conversely, there are no people more sensitive, or better able to express their displeasure and contempt, if they have reason to believe that they are meeting with rudeness. I say when they have reason, for they have too much dignity to take offence at trifles, and they readily forgive foreigners, so long as they do not seem conceited or overbearing. Maulévrier and I constantly experienced this both with the highest nobility and with people of no importance; but the manners in either case were totally dissimilar.

It is now time to take up once again the thread of my story, interrupted by descriptions of so much that is fascinating and unknown to France. You will recall that my sole reason for desiring the Spanish embassy was to gain for my younger son a grandeeship, and thus fortify the cadet branch of my family. Nothing else would have taken me to Spain; but a secondary objective was a Golden Fleece for my elder son, to give him the pleasure of returning with a decoration, at his age a great prize. I left Paris with full permission to avail myself of every opportunity, and with M. le Duc d'Orléans's promise to write, recommending me to the King of Spain, and using King Louis's name, in support. Strong recommendations were also to be forthcoming from Cardinal Dubois to the Marquis of Grimaldo and Père Daubenton. I had spoken to both those gentlemen in the whirlwind of affairs, ceremonies, and rejoicings, and had received great encouragement. On every subject except the Bull *Unigenitus* the Jesuits wished to support me, and had informed Père Daubenton to that effect, since they believed they would need me for some time to come. A French grandeeship mattered little to them; but they were anxious that I should know they were assisting me. Grimaldo was honesty itself; he had come truly to care for me, and had given me many proofs of friendship, as you will doubtless remember. His great hope was that the union of our two countries through the royal marriages would influence the conduct of their governments. In Spain his only ally was the king, and he therefore looked to France for support, or at least neutrality, since he well knew the faithlessness and caprice of Cardinal Dubois. Grimaldo may have thought that by thus sealing our friendship he could rely on my services with M. le Duc d'Orléans. I believed it no harm to allow him to be so persuaded, in order that I might extract a favour very natural in the circumstances, of no great significance, and, where he was concerned, totally inoffensive.

I considered that the actual wedding-day would be the perfect moment. Once that were passed the enthusiasm for me might cool, relationships might even become strained, and highly disagreeable. Since my arrival at Madrid, I had done everything possible to please and (dare I say it?) had abundantly succeeded, more especially because I had striven to keep some sort of measure in my courtesies, paying particular attention to rank and office, and not allowing myself to be blinded by riches. None the less, I needed the help of M. le Duc d'Orléans's recommendation to the king, and the letters of Cardinal Dubois. I had never doubted the Regent's good will, but much misdoubted that of his minister, as I had good reason to do. Their letters should have reached Madrid at the same time as myself; but days passed and they did not arrive. What made me especially impatient was that after I had read them, I should need time to reflect on how to use them to the best advantage. I was prepared for Cardinal Dubois to be treacherous, and to show a lack of interest that is often worse then outright obstruction. I feared also that being unable to prevent M. le Duc d'Orleans from writing to the king, he might offer to compose the letter, making it so feeble and ineffective that although the Regent might wish to alter it, in my absence he would not dare. Being of that mind, I resolved to strengthen my defences with the entire Spanish court, as well as with the minister and confessor, and the king and queen themselves. I hoped to make myself so agreeable to Their Catholic Majesties as to put them into a mood to bestow favours.

A few days before going to Lerma, letters came from Cardinal Dubois regarding my affair. Nothing could have been more eager, more encouraging, offering advice, urging me to seek every possible means of furthering my desires, assuring me meanwhile that letters of recommendation from M. le Duc d'Orléans and himself would be forthcoming in plenty of time. Amid the sweet scent of flowers, one got a whiff of his innate falseness; but I had reckoned on that, and had done all that honour and prudence would permit in order to offset it. I accordingly took kindly the compliments he showered upon me, and left for Lerma determined to press on with my cause, not relying on the promised letters, but ready to extract from them every possible advantage.

Soon after my arrival I fell ill, as you already know, and remained for six weeks in exile. During that long interval the Abbé de Saint-Simon undertook all my correspondence, even with Dubois. It was not until the end of my quarantine that the long-awaited letters came, and when they did so, fulfilled my very worst expectations. Cardinal Dubois had written to Grimaldo with so many twists and turns, here a sentence expressing urgency, there another protesting the paramount importance of the king's inclinations, all couched in such flowery language that the original request was completely smothered. M. le Duc d'Orléans's letter was for the king's private ear, and, though you will scarcely credit it, was even feebler than Dubois's effusion. Like a pencil draft that has been left out in the wet, it was so obscure and unintelligible that it produced no effect whatsoever. Respects, caution, moderation, unwillingness to influence in any way, assurances of a great desire only to please, gave the impression of a debt being paid as a matter of form, with a total indifference as to the outcome. You may well imagine that these letters hugely distressed me, for although I had foreseen Cardinal Dubois's ill will, it now appeared far greater than I had previously thought possible.

Yet there the letters were, and use had to be made of them. The Abbé de Saint-Simon accordingly wrote to Grimaldo enclosing them (for I dared not write myself on account of the danger of infection), and Grimaldo, after mature reflection, took a strong line, to my enormous surprise, not to say alarm. His reply was to the effect that such letters of recommendation would do more harm than good, and must be suppressed. Meanwhile, King Philip should be encouraged to believe that by honouring me he would please M. le Duc d'Orléans, all the more so because he had not requested it, and because I, myself, who had ample excuse, seemed not to have asked him to do so. Grimaldo assured me that there would be no difficulty in obtaining for me the grandeeship and the Fleece, without mentioning any letters from the Regent or Dubois. After discussing the matter with Higgens who knew the terrain and really wished to help me, I decided to rely entirely on Grimaldo's kind offices and, as you shall see, he amply succeeded.

In recounting the extraordinary way in which I got my wish, I am very far from desiring to appear ungrateful to M. le Duc d'Orléans. Had he not, despite Dubois's absolute prohibition, told me the secret of the royal marriages, I should never have been in a position to ask for my embassy. I did at once ask for it, telling him my true reasons for desiring it, and he granted my request there and then, for that particular purpose, promising to recommend me to King Philip, but swearing me to secrecy because he needed time to persuade Dubois to swallow the pill. Had I not agreed, the embassy would never have been mine, and all chance of the grandeeship and the Fleece would have been lost for ever. Thus the prince's affection and trust in me proved more powerful than the spell cast over him by his miserable tutor; and if later he yielded to the knavish tricks by which Dubois attempted to ruin me, that must be put down to his essential weakness and the cardinal's rascality. I was thereby caused great distress, and much personal loss, but the harm was far greater to France and to the prince himself. On this sad and only too veracious reflection I end this year, 1721.

CHAPTER VIII

1722

Exchange of the princesses – Pitiful gifts – I have audience of Their Catholic Majesties and the Prince of the Asturias – The king, the queen, and the prince go incognito to meet the princess at Cogollos – The wedding – I become a Grandee of Spain of the first class, with permission to choose one or other of my sons to share the honour with me – My elder son obtains the Golden Fleece – I propose, on my own volition, a public bedding for the Prince and Princess of the Asturias – I gain my wish – Illness of the Princess of the Asturias – Investiture of my younger son – Anxieties – Strange behaviour of the princess – Fêtes and illuminations – Chocolate in Lent – I visit Toledo – The Mozarabic mass – Aranjuez – The excellence of buffaloes' milk – Confirmation of Don Philip – The king and queen's extremely private excursion to Balzaïn – Cardinal Dubois's plot – I force an entry into Balzaïn – Segovia – I follow Their Majesties to La Granja – My farewell audiences – Most singular conduct of the princess – I leave Madrid – At Châtres, Dubois asks my consent to disgracing the Duc de Noailles – I refuse it – I resign my peerage in favour of my elder son – Long conversation with the Regent and Dubois – Marriage of my daughter – The Court returns permanently to Versailles – Disgrace of the Maréchal de Villeroy – Disappearance of the Bishop of Fréjus and the King's distress – Cardinal Dubois determines to be made First Minister – Agonizing conversations with the Regent – Dubois is appointed – The coronation – No duke will attend – Disgraceful novelties – The two crowns – Death of Madame

THE YEAR BEGAN with the exchange of princesses on the Isle of Pheasants, in the little River Bidassoa that separates the two kingdoms. A simple wooden pavilion had been built there, on a scale very different from the one put up at the same spot in 1659, for the signing of the Peace of the Pyrenees. The exchange took place on 9 January, with a presentation of gifts from King Louis to the Spanish escort, after which the princesses and their new households continued their journeys in opposite directions. I spent an hour in conversation, at Lerma, with the Marquis of Santa-Cruz and the Duke of Liria, who described it all in great detail and in the most lighthearted manner imaginable, especially Santa-Cruz. He was guarded with reference to the presents, but smiled despite himself as he showed me his, at which I could not help shrugging my shoulders. We neither of us made any comment, but, in truth, the few small stones were of very poor quality. Seeing that Santa-Cruz had been in charge of the entire proceedings, you may well imagine what the other gifts were like. The Spaniards openly laughed at them, until I thought I should have died of shame. This was not the time for economies; fifty thousand écus ought to have produced something more worthy of the monarch who gave them, but no matter how high blind fortune raises them, upstarts[1] must always have their pickings.

When all was ready for the exchange, the Infanta left Oyarzun,[2] and Mlle de Montpensier Saint-Jean-de-Luz, and with their retinues arrived on the same day on opposite banks of the river. They crossed at the same moment to the Island of Pheasants, remaining there only long enough to embrace and sign the necessary documents. Then, also at the same moment, they departed towards their new homes. The Infanta was now attended by the Prince de Rohan; Mlle de Montpensier by the Marquis of Santa-Cruz. The Spanish party then spent the night at Oyarzun, and the French at Saint-Jean-de-Luz, as before. They left again on the following day. The poor Queen-dowager of Spain nearly ruined herself with most magnificent presents and, urged thereto by her extreme poverty, had stooped in almost servile fashion to Mlle de Montpensier, treating her as though she were married, and already Princess of the Asturias, visiting her at her lodgings and offering her an armchair. I made the most of the unhappy queen's endeavours, in order to persuade the King and Queen of Spain to send the considerable sums due to her, which were much in arrears, and I did at last extract a fairly large payment, but that was once and for all; I could afterwards do no more for her.

Immediately after leaving Bayonne, the Prince de Rohan, whose celebrations had not extended even so far as a dinner-party, took a post-chaise and swiftly returned to Paris, where he described the event and as much of the Infanta as he had seen, or had wished to see. The Marquis of Santa-Cruz, on the other hand, sent a courier to Lerma and travelled in company with Mlle de Montpensier, who was alone with her Spanish household, all her French ladies, and even her maids, having without exception left her at Bidassoa—a very wise arrangement. The Infanta, on the other hand, because of her extreme youth, had been allowed to keep her governess, Doña Maria de Nieves, for a few years. She was a lady in whom the Queen of Spain placed the greatest confidence. The governesses of Spanish Infantas are not high-ranking like those of royal children in

---

[1] This is a dig at the Prince de Rohan, in charge of the French princess until she was handed over to the Spaniards, and a member of the Lorraine family which Saint-Simon so abominated. He had been responsible for the presents, and had further infuriated the memoirist by trying to have himself styled 'Highness' on the contracts of exchange. Saint-Simon, who foresaw that attempt to claim precedence, asked Santa-Cruz to see that he added neither 'Highness, nor Excellency, nor even Excellentisime Seigneur to his name'. This passage is very funny, but sadly too long for inclusion.

[2] Near Irun.

France; but are chosen from among maids of honour, women-of-the-bed-chamber, and such-like.

While Mlle de Montpensier was terminating her journey, my exile also was drawing to a close. It ended precisely two days before her arrival at Lerma. Their Catholic Majesties' kindness to me daily increased, as did the attentions of their court, who had assembled in such great numbers that the royal couple were prevented from enjoying the solitude to which they were accustomed at Madrid, and in their holiday palaces. They had therefore removed to Ventosilla, a small castle, in a village a few leagues from Lerma, with the bare minimum of attendant courtiers, and returned only on 15 January, in readiness to welcome the princess. They had the goodness to inform me that they wished to see me the very day that my quarantine ended; but knowing the king's fear of smallpox, I waited for an express command, which I should have to obey, although at that time I was still very red,[1] partly owing to the intense cold, and despite all the drugs which they had used to cause the spots to fade. Thus it was not until 19 January that I went to Lerma for the first time, to make my bow, and thank Their Majesties most sincerely for all the care they had taken of me.

The formality of the audience soon turned to a conversation. They did me the honour to tell me of Cardinal Borgia, who had arrived a few days earlier from Rome and was full of gossip. As we were talking, the king stopped suddenly, laughed, looked at the queen, and said that the cardinal had told them the drollest thing imaginable. I smiled inquiringly, but dared not question him. He turned once more to the queen, saying, 'Shall we tell him? Perhaps it's rather too naughty?' 'Why not?' replied the queen. 'Very well!' said the king, 'but you must promise not to tell a soul.' I did promise, and I kept my word absolutely. I tell the story here for the first time, after the death of King Philip, and of all the other people concerned, and thus I shall let it be known only to readers, if after my death these memoirs should happen to see the light. By that time no one will remain who could personally be offended. What the king graciously revealed to me was that, according to Cardinal Borgia, Cardinal de Rohan, for all his splendour and celebrated charm, was not greatly respected at Rome because he went to such absurd lengths, for a man of his advanced age, in caring for his complexion. It was said that he washed in asses' milk to make his skin softer and whiter. This he tried to keep secret, but it became known none the less; the pious were shocked, and the rest laughed at him. Thereupon the king and queen supplied their own comments, and all three of us laughed heartily, for King Philip told the story well, and his remarks were exceedingly funny. I assured them that I was not shocked, having known for many years the truth regarding that so-called Father of the Church. I said no more then; for it was not

[1] Red because the spots had not entirely faded.

the moment to speak of the Bull *Unigenitus*, from which Cardinal de Rohan had extracted immense profit for himself and for his family.

My audience ended with all imaginable graciousness on the part of Their Catholic Majesties. I was also vastly gratified by the eager desire of their entire court to congratulate me on my recovery. I then went to pay my respects to the Prince of the Asturias, who received me just as kindly. They all appeared to be enchanted by the news of the princess's arrival, and said that they could not wait to see her. Indeed, I learned when I returned to dine at my house that the king and queen, and the prince also, had put on ordinary clothes and had gone unescorted in one of the Duke of Arco's coaches, to Cogollos, a dirty little village four leagues from Lerma, in order to see her incognito. The duke whispered to Santa-Cruz to tell her ladies not to curtsey, and then greeted the princess, extending his addresses so as to give his royal escort sufficient time to look at her. He later asked her permission to present a lady and two gentlemen who of all things desired to pay their respects; but one lady alone with two gentlemen, in the retinue of a third, gave away the secret. The princess guessed rightly; tried to kiss their hands, and was immediately enfolded in tender embraces. The remainder of the visit was occupied with most affectionate greetings on the one hand, and expressions of respect and gratitude on the other. After a quarter of an hour so spent, Their Catholic Majesties returned very late to Lerma, in the same coach.

I had arranged with Maulévrier, who dined with me that day, that he was to call for me from his lodgings, a league distant, between six and seven next morning, and that we should go in procession with all my coaches and our respective retinues, to salute the princess at Cogollos. There and back it was an eight-league journey. We should need to hurry so as to return in time to snatch a bite before going to Lerma for the princess's arrival. We thus set out at seven o'clock punctually, with the mules going at a spanking pace. She was not yet dressed when we arrived; but I was presented, and afterwards introduced the Comte de Céreste, my sons, the Comte de Lorges, and the MM. de Saint-Simon. The Duchess of Montellano, her other ladies, and Santa-Cruz all tried in vain to persuade her to address a word to us; but they made up for her silence by all possible courtesies. We had no time to lose, and thus made a quarter of an hour suffice for the official visit, returning very quickly to my house to eat a hurried meal that was served to us on the instant. We then went to Lerma, where fortune had favoured us, as we had no more than half an hour to wait.

As soon as we arrived, I went upstairs to visit the Marquis of Grimaldo, notwithstanding that I had seen him only the night before. His room was at the farther end of a vast hall, part of which had been arranged as a chapel. There would be a fresh encounter with the nuncio, and I feared lest he might remember what had happened at the signing. I did not wish to give Dubois any cause to reproach me.

The king's prie-dieu was immediately opposite the altar, a short distance
from the steps, in exactly the same position as the King's prie-dieu at
Versailles, only nearer the altar, and with a couple of hassocks placed side
by side. The chapel was empty. I took up my position by the right-hand
side of the king's chair, at the extreme edge of the carpet but not upon it,
and while standing there, I received better entertainment than I had any
right to expect. Cardinal Borgia, pontifically attired, stood facing me, at
the epistle-side of the altar, learning his lesson between two surpliced
chaplains who held a vast tome open before him. He strove to read aloud,
but failed all along the line; the chaplains corrected; he lost his temper;
rated them; started afresh; was again corrected, and at last grew so angry
that he turned upon them and shook them by their surplices. I laughed
until my sides were splitting, for being so busy and in such difficulties he
was in no state to notice me. Spanish weddings take place in the afternoon,
and, as with their christenings, the ceremony begins at the door of the
church. The king and queen arrived with the prince and princess and the
entire court, whereat His Majesty's presence was loudly proclaimed. 'They
must wait,' cried the cardinal furiously, 'I'm not ready for them.' And to
wait they were obliged, while the cardinal continued his lesson, still raging,
and as red as a turkey-cock. At length he consented to go to the door, and a
rather long pause ensued. I was greatly tempted to follow him, but felt it
necessary to keep my place. I lost some of the fun, however, for the king and
queen were laughing and talking as they took their places, and the courtiers
were laughing also.

When the nuncio approached, he made a gesture of immense surprise,
saying, 'Signore! Signore!' but being determined not to understand, I
pointed laughing to the cardinal, reproaching him for not having instructed
him better, for the honour of the Sacred College. The nuncio knew French
well enough, but murdered it in speaking. The laughter, and my air of
sublime innocence caused such a happy diversion that he had no time to do
more, especially since Cardinal Borgia gave us even greater occasion for
mirth as the ceremony proceeded. He lost all track of his place in the book,
and forgot what he was doing; thus the chaplains were continually correct-
ing and putting him straight, while his snorts of rage made the king and
queen, and the other witnesses, quite unable to contain themselves. All
that I could see was the backs of the prince and princess as they knelt on
their hassocks, between the prie-dieu and the altar, and the face of the
cardinal making the most fearsome grimaces. Luckily for me, I had only
the nuncio to deal with, the major-domo mayor having taken up his
position on the other side of the prie-dieu. There was a great crowd of
grandees behind us, and the remainder of the chapel was so full of
distinguished persons that there was barely room to move.

Amid all the diversion caused by that unhappy cardinal, I noted how
well content the king and queen appeared at witnessing the solemnization

of this marriage. When the service, not a long one, was over, Their Catholic Majesties, who had been the only persons to kneel (with the exception of the bride and bridegroom, who knelt when necessary), rose and retired to the left-hand corner of their carpet, where they spoke together in an undertone for perhaps the length of a *credo*. The queen thereafter remained where she was, but the king came to me, still standing where I had been throughout the service. His Majesty then did me the immense honour to say, 'Monsieur, I am much pleased with you and the manner in which you have conducted your mission to me. I wish to give you some token of my pleasure, esteem, and friendship, and I hereby make you a Grandee of Spain, of the first class, and not you only, but one or other of your two sons to be a grandee also, bearing the title at the same time as yourself; and I make your elder son a Knight of the Golden Fleece.' I instantly knelt to kiss his knees, trying to express my gratitude, and show by my devotion, most humble duty, and profound respect my great desire to be worthy of the favours he so graciously bestowed on me. I then kissed his hand, and turned to summon my children, using the few moments before they reached my side to reiterate my thanks. I addressed my younger son, telling him to kiss the king's knees, in gratitude for the favours showered upon us both. He also kissed the king's hand and, as he rose from his knees, King Philip said that it had pleased him greatly so to honour us. I afterwards presented my elder son to thank him for the Fleece; but he did no more than bow extremely low, and kiss hands. That done, the king returned to the queen and I followed him with my sons. I bowed very low before her, expressing my particular thanks; then I presented first the younger, and only secondly the elder. The queen greeted us most graciously and with many kind words, after which the royal couple, with the prince and princess, returned to their apartments. I longed to follow them, but we were immediately surrounded by a crowd of courtiers eagerly congratulating us. I was most careful to respond to all in the most polite and becoming manner, and although I had been far from expecting to receive the honours at that particular time, Grimaldo having been exceedingly vague, it did seem as though every member of that large court was glad, and wished me well.

For more than an hour, my sons and I were completely encircled, and long afterwards persons of lower degree, who had been unable to approach us earlier, came up to offer their congratulations, and I tried, according to their various ranks, to receive and answer them as graciously as I had done the others. I did not attempt to conceal my joy, and my sense of the great honour done to my second son; yet neither did I forget to express my pride at the promotion of the elder to be of the noble company of the Golden Fleece. At the same time, it distressed me not to see Grimaldo among the crowd, and as soon as it became possible I went up to his room and thanked him from the bottom of my heart. Truly, I was overjoyed to have gained my sole desire in undertaking this embassy, and I owed all to Grimaldo.[1]

Let us now retrace our steps for a matter which I left unmentioned for fear of interrupting the narrative. The Spaniards' modesty and soberness prevent their witnessing the bedding of a bridal pair. After the wedding breakfast there is general conversation for a short time, and then everyone goes away, even including the closest kin of both sexes and all ages. The bride and bridegroom undress in different rooms, and go to bed unwitnessed, save by the few necessary attendants, for all the world as though they had been married a long time. I knew of this custom, and had received no orders concerning it. None the less, considering our own ways in such matters, I could not regard as firmly based any marriage not followed by consummation, at least presumptive.

It had been agreed, because of the prince's age[2] and delicate constitution, that he should not cohabit with the princess until Their Catholic Majesties so advised, which would not be for at least another year. I mentioned this concern of mine to Grimaldo, at Lerma, but all in vain. Spaniard-like, he tried merely to quieten my scruples about something he thought unalterable. Apart from the fact that I had only a few moments' talk with him, I thought it best to say no more; indeed I allowed him to believe he had convinced me, for should he suspect me of wishing to persuade the king, he might put in his word beforehand. None the less I was determined to pursue the matter; at the worst I could only fail; no one else would know of my endeavours. Thus in my audience, at Lerma, when we had finished the business on hand, I began to speak of the wedding and, one thing leading to another, of its consummation, strongly approving the decision to postpone this. Thence I turned to M. le Duc d'Orléans's joy at hearing the news, and I proceeded once again to rehearse his sense of the extraordinary honour, more especially the precious token it gave of a return to Their Catholic Majesties' favour. I paused there to see the effect of my little speech, and since it appeared good, I was emboldened to add that notwithstanding the modest ways of Spain, Their Majesties might wish, on this august occasion, to adopt the French practice and witness the bedding of the young couple. I reminded the king how, in earlier days, he had attended the bedding of Mgr and Mme la Duchesse de Bourgogne, who only long afterwards became one flesh.

They heard me out, and did not interrupt, which I thought a good omen. They exchanged looks. The king said to the queen, 'Well! what do you think?' 'But, Monsieur, what do you?' she replied. At that I spoke again, saying that I would not for the world give them a false impression; I

---

[1] 'The King of Spain has given the Golden Fleece to the Duc de Saint-Simon's elder son, and has made the younger a Grandee of Spain. These are splendid wedding gifts, and will enormously raise the prestige of the family—something they much need.' *Mémoires* of Mathieu Marais.

[2] The prince was fourteen, and the princess twelve years old.

had received no written orders on that subject, nor had it been discussed. What I had taken the liberty of suggesting was entirely my own idea, the fruit of solitary reflection, moved, or so I firmly believed, by my loyalty to both crowns, as a good Frenchman and a good Spaniard also, for the purpose of cementing the union of the two monarchies so firmly that not even Austria would dream of trying to part them.

My reasoning appeared to carry weight. Their Catholic Majesties turned to one another, saying a few words in a whisper, after which the king asked, 'Supposing we consent, how will you proceed?' I replied that nothing was simpler; His Majesty had only to remember the wedding of Mgr le Duc de Bourgogne. At the same time, it would be wiser not to let the decision be known until the day appointed, lest there be objections from people who hated changes and might, at first, fail to understand the important reasons. If Their Majesties decided to go forward, it would be quite sufficient to let the news seep out very quietly at the state ball immediately before the *coucher*. During a public function there were not likely to be objections, and those who wished to pay their court by witnessing so interesting and novel a scene would be alerted in time. Their Majesties alone, with the small attendance necessary, would watch the undressing and see the couple put to bed. On either side of the bed, at a level with the pillows, would sit the Duke of Popoli, on the prince's side, and the Duchess of Montellano, on the princess's. The curtains on all three sides should be drawn back as far as possible, and both wings of the door flung wide open. The entire court should then be allowed to enter with all the rest, and to draw near the bed, until the room was crammed to full capacity. A good quarter of an hour would be time enough for all to have leisure to see, after which the curtains should be closed in the presence of all the people, and they would then depart. Meanwhile the Duke of Popoli and the Duchess of Montellano must be extremely careful to insert their heads behind the closed curtains, so as not, even for a single moment, to lose sight of the prince and princess. When the very last person had gone beyond the ante-chambers, the prince should be made to rise and go escorted to his own rooms.

The king and queen greatly approved of my plan, and after a little more discussion, they promised me to act as I had suggested; whereupon I most humbly thanked them. I had every reason to believe that they were convinced by my arguments, and not displeased by what, in Spain, was a novel and outlandish affair, for soon afterwards they were laughing with me over the absurd habits of Cardinal de Rohan, as I have described.

On the day after the wedding, when I was relatively free from callers and congratulations, I took my sons to Grimaldo's room. Half-way up the stairs I was overtaken by one of the three French valets, sent to tell me that the king had ordered four *tabourets* to be placed in one of the window recesses, during the ball, to accommodate me, Maulévrier, the nuncio, and my elder son, who was recovering from a second bout of illness, contracted at our lodging while I was having smallpox. That most kind attention deeply touched me; but I concluded that so to distinguish my son, who was neither a duke nor a grandee, might easily distress the other grandees and perhaps upset all the Spaniards. I therefore begged the king, with all the respect and thanks imaginable, to allow my elder son to return home before the ball, on the excuse that he was still very poorly and needed his rest. I thus evaded an honour that might have caused great annoyance.

We continued up the staircase to Grimaldo's room. After we had all thanked him, I sent away my sons, and then said that not having seen him after my audience, I wished to tell him what had happened; though he no doubt had already heard the news. I explained everything to him, rehearsed all my arguments, spoke of M. le Duc d'Orléans's pride and joy, and my own deep sense of Their Majesties' gracious kindness. Grimaldo, like a sensible man, and perhaps having some personal liking for me, took it all remarkably well, saying that to follow so well established a precedent could do no possible harm, but that the court might well be horrified. He promised, however, to spread the news during the ball, and even to support me by explaining the reasons. He kept his word absolutely, and with so much success that no one dared be scandalized by this great and surprising innovation. Neither then, nor later, was it censured by anyone of any condition whatsoever.[1]

Feeling vastly pleased with myself, I went to sup with the Duke of Arco, who had invited all the distinguished Frenchmen, and many of the best people at the court. The cooking was in the Spanish style, but it included a most excellent *olla podrida*,[2] which made up for some of the other dishes to which we were less accustomed, and there was a most delicious wine from the district of La Mancha. The wines and oil made by the noblemen on their estates for their own consumption are very good indeed, and cast a sad reflection on the laziness of the common people, whose produce is evil-smelling beyond words. There were also little green hams, such as one rarely meets with in Spain, and then only in the houses of the Duke of Arco and two other noblemen. They come from pigs reared in small enclosures covered with thick undergrowth, in which the vipers proliferate that are their only nourishment. These hams give off a most delicious odour, and taste surprisingly spicy and invigorating.[3] A more exquisite dish you cannot imagine. The supper was long and abun-

---

[1] Saint-Simon wrote rather differently to the Regent. 'This innovation', he said, 'greatly surprised the Spaniards, and some people were even scandalized.'

[2] *Olla podrida*, literally 'rotten broth', a stew of hashed meat and vegetables. So much stew and soup was eaten in France at that period that Saint-Simon probably felt at home with it.

[3] Vipers may appear doubtful food to modern ears, but in the eighteenth century they were considered to be strengthening and revivifying and were much in demand for rich old invalids. The Duke of Marlborough, after his stroke, was given viper broth every day by the Duchess. The best vipers came from France.

dant; the company very joyful and polite; the service lavish, and admirably efficient. After taking our leave, we all went into the king's apartments, where everything was in readiness for the state ball.

Half the court were already assembled, the rest appeared soon after. We did not have long to wait before Their Majesties and Their Highnesses entered, and the queen opened the ball with the Prince of the Asturias. The arrangements were as I described them on the occasion of the Madrid ball. The nuncio, Maulévrier and I, seated on our *tabourets*, watched the dancing from the window recess; but I had little time for rest, as I was constantly in demand for the minuets and country dances. My coat was monstrously heavy and I was very tired after the displacements of that day and the previous one, but it was the day of the wedding, and I had just obtained honours far greater than I had had any right to expect. It was thus a festival for me also, and it would have been churlish ever to refuse. The ball, though as gay as possible, lost nothing of its stateliness and dignity. It lasted until two in the morning. The only persons seated were the nuncio, Maulévrier and myself, for no other ambassador went to Lerma. The Duke of Abrantes, Bishop of Cuenca, stood all the time, with a neighbour bishop, two bishops *in partibus*,[1] suffragans of Toledo,[2] and the Grand Inquisitor (who had attended the wedding without officiating). They remained for its entire duration, wearing rochets and capes, and holding their mitres in their hands. The news of the public *coucher* broke during the ball; I observed considerable surprise, but no disapproval. Everyone stayed to witness the novel event.

When the ball was over we all followed the king and queen to the princess's apartments and waited in the ante-chambers. Only the necessary attendants entered her bedroom. The *toilette* did not take long; Their Majesties and the prince were extremely merry.[3] It all went just as I have described, and I returned to Villalmanzo and my bed, of which I felt in urgent need.

I could not rest there long, however, for next morning, 21 January, I had to return early to Lerma for the Velation service.[4] In Spain, weddings take place after dinner or in the evening, and the nuptial mass, when the bride and bridegroom stand under the marriage canopy, is held the following day. I went first to visit the Marquis of Grimaldo, and then took up my former position shortly before the court arrived. The king's prie-dieu, and the hassocks for the prince and princess were arranged as on the previous day, and Cardinal Borgia, splendidly attired, was again repeating

[1] *In partibus infidelium*: in heathen lands. Titular bishops for countries where there was no Roman Catholic hierarchy.
[2] One was Bishop of Toledo, the other of Madrid.
[3] Saint-Simon does not say that the princess enjoyed herself. If she felt miserable and embarrassed as well as ill, and thought him to blame, it might partly explain her later conduct.
[4] When the bride and bridegroom stood beneath the marriage-canopy. Hence the name, Velation.

his lesson with the two chaplains; but this time, he had only to put on his chasuble when the king and queen entered, followed by the prince and princess, hand in hand. The nuncio, arriving at the same instant, greeted me very civilly as he took his place beside me. He seemed to have accepted the situation. Maulévrier who, at the wedding, had stood a pace or two behind me, was absent. It afterwards appeared, though he said nothing about it, that he had returned to Madrid. The cardinal said low mass; but was just as much confused as on the day before, and made a terrible botch of the remaining ceremonies. After all was over, I accompanied Their Majesties on the return, laughing and joking with them over the cardinal's discomfiture, and I asked permission to take my leave of them after their dinner, because they were returning to Madrid. I forgot to mention that the bridal canopy was held up by two of the king's almoners, called pages of the *cortina*. I believe the name comes from the fact that until the reign of Philip V, the entire recess in which the king's prie-dieu was placed when he attended mass was enclosed by curtains, called in Spanish *cortinas*, and it was the duty of the king's almoners to lift a corner whenever necessary, so as to allow him to smell the incense, kiss the Gospel, etc.

I dined with the cream of our French society at the house of the Duke of Arco, amid a great company of high-ranking persons. The banquet was as magnificent as on the previous day, and I remembered to do full justice to the *olla podrida*, and those delicious viper-hams. The Spaniards were enchanted to see a Frenchman enjoying saffron, more especially because at my own dinner-parties it was always present in many of the dishes, and they could see that it pleased me. Most unfortunately, I could not be persuaded to share their taste for dipping their bread into the salt-cellars. It was a favourite habit; but I thought it neither nice nor pleasant tasting. It was a long and merry dinner.

After a short time spent in conversation I went to take my leave of the king and queen, to thank them once again for the public *coucher*, with most sincere gratitude for the honours bestowed on me and on my sons. I then bade them farewell until I waited on them after their return to Madrid. So much business had accumulated that I decided to devote all the following day to my letters, and to leave on the 23rd, the day after the departure of the court. It was indeed a hard task to explain to M. le Duc d'Orléans and Cardinal Dubois how I had managed to do without their letters, and alone and unassisted had obtained from Their Catholic Majesties in the most charming manner possible all the honours after which I so greatly hankered. I had no fears where M. le Duc d'Orléans was concerned. His carelessness in small matters (and often in greater ones) set my mind at rest regarding him. With Cardinal Dubois it was different, for he had composed both letters with the sole intention of destroying my hopes, and he would, I was sure, do his best to set M. le Duc d'Orléans against me. I therefore wrote a short and cheerful letter to the prince, of the kind he enjoyed reading, but full of gratitude to them both, addressing towards Cardinal Dubois especially such a torrent of thanks as to assure him that the letters, not presented, but read by Grimaldo to Their Majesties, were solely responsible for my receiving such favours. The thing was done. No matter now to whom the credit went. Being unable to do worse, he took it with good grace, congratulated me, and gave it out that he had been delighted to do me this service.

The Princess of the Asturias towards the end of her journey had been seriously indisposed. Red spots had appeared on her face, and later turned to erysipelas; soon afterwards a fever developed. When I went to the palace after the court's return, I found Their Majesties in a state of alarm. I did my best to calm them, saying that the princess had already had measles and smallpox, and that it would not be surprising if she felt the effects of her long journey and the great change that had come into her life. They were not convinced, and next day I found them still more anxious. The mishap was a considerable annoyance to them, for all the festivities had to be postponed, and the great hall of the grandees that had been emptied of furniture for a state ball, remained in that condition a very long time. The queen asked me if I had seen the princess. I replied that I had inquired at the door of her room. That however was not enough, for she ordered me to see her, and the king supported her. Now nothing goes more contrary to the customs of Spain than for a man, even a close relation, to visit a lady in bed. Reasons of State had provided sufficient excuse for the marriage *coucher*, but there was none that I could find for violating the proprieties now, and I believed that the Spaniards would attribute such a visit to my vanity, and be immensely shocked. I therefore did everything possible to avoid going, but in vain. On each of the three following days they asked if I had seen her. Prevaricate as I might, they knew I had not done so, and that all the efforts of the Duchess of Montellano to persuade me to enter had been useless. They then both of them scolded me, saying that they desired me to see her myself, and report on the remedies and treatment being given her. The king called on her twice a day, the queen much more often, and they unbent so far as to feed her themselves with the soups and other nourishment which she was required to take. I declared that if their desire was that M. le Duc d'Orléans should know of their goodness and kindness to his daughter, there was no need for me to see her, I was already sufficiently well posted and full of confidence, and I could tell him truly that she was better nursed than she would have been in his house. On the third day, however, they became really angry at my stubbornness, and gave me their absolute command to go every day to see her. There was nothing for it but to obey them.

Next day I visited the princess, and was introduced by the Duchess of Montellano. The erysipelas did appear very extensive and very red. Her ladies said that her throat and bosom were covered by it, and that although the fever was not high it still persisted. Despite my protests they made me inspect the rash with a candle, and retailed the diet and remedies prescribed by the doctors. I went straight back to report to the king and queen, for they had insisted on my seeing them alone each day since our return from Lerma. They immediately asked what I thought of the princess. Then after more conversation regarding the disease and its treatment, the king exclaimed, 'But you do not know all. I must tell you that she has two greatly swollen glands at her throat; that is what worries us; because we cannot tell what to make of them.' I took his meaning at once, and instantly replied that I could understand his deep anxiety, but that truly there was no cause; for although I could not deny M. le Duc d'Orléans's debauchery, I could honestly affirm that it had had no bad consequences, his health having been so uniformly excellent, beyond any suspicion, that never for a single day had he failed to appear in his customary manner. I had lived all my life on such intimate terms with him that the smallest misfortune resulting from his pleasures could not have escaped me. I added that Mme la Duchesse d'Orléans enjoyed equally good health, and that none of her children had ever given occasion for alarms of such a nature.[1]

Towards the end of my speech, I observed that the king and queen, who had been listening with rapt attention, appeared much comforted. They both said they felt truly relieved, knowing, as they did, that I would not wilfully deceive them. The king then added that there was a further cause of anxiety in that the mortal illness of the late queen had begun with just such a swelling of the neck glands, which was later diagnosed as incurable scrofula. I replied to this that according to medical opinion in France, the late queen's glands were the effects of a goitre contracted in her own country,[2] where the proximity of the Alps seemed to make such a condition general; even her sister Mme la Duchesse de Bourgogne had not escaped it. The cause of the princess's illness was, I thought, completely different since none of her ancestors had been similarly afflicted. It seemed to me far more probable that her swollen glands were the result of the erysipelas and would shrink as she recovered. This long conversation ended with my once again receiving orders to visit the princess every day, and to write in detail to M. le Duc d'Orléans, describing their love and care for her, not on any account allowing him to perceive the nature of their terrible suspicions. That, they said, must be kept a profound secret between us.

Two days later, when I had the honour of calling on them after my visit to the princess, I could see that they were still very anxious, although they tried to conceal it. After mentioning once more the swollen glands, they

---

[1] In these veiled words Saint-Simon lets the reader see clearly enough that the king and queen feared lest she was syphilitic through the sins of her father.

[2] Savoy. Philip V's first wife and the Duchesse de Bourgogne were sisters, daughters of Victor Amadeus II, Duke of Savoy. See genealogical table, II, p. xvii.

told me they had bidden Higgens write to Chirac,[1] M. le Duc d'Orléans's
family doctor, to ask his opinion as being better acquainted with her
constitution. They said they hoped Chirac would dispense with compliments and the restraints of medical etiquette, and give his advice
honestly and frankly. At that point, I felt obliged to write in similar terms
to M. le Duc d'Orléans and to Cardinal Dubois, informing them of the
situation, but not mentioning the reason for Their Majesties' dreadful
anxiety. Of that I wrote only to M. le Duc d'Orléans, a private letter, in my
own hand. It was for Chirac to deal with in writing to Higgens, if so be that
he considered it advisable.

[*Saint-Simon had taken very seriously the fears of King Philip and the queen. 'I
think, Monseigneur,' he wrote to the Regent, 'that you should know the truth of the
king's and queen's anxiety concerning the princess. They did me the honour to confide
it to me in secret, for they dread its becoming generally known. The fact is that she
has two swollen glands on her neck close to her ears, and that the fatal illness of the
late queen gives cause for alarm. What worries them also is that although she has
been regular for the past eleven months (but not to any great extent), this has not
served to drain them, and from what she says, she has had frequent attacks of the
erysipelas from which she is now suffering. Though I am not a doctor, I have tried to
calm them by mentioning the princess's age, at which swollen glands are far less
serious than with older persons. Indeed, children very often suffer from them. I said,
moreover, that when she is older and her system better regulated, nature will be more
able to dissipate them at those periods. None the less, you must realize that their
disquiet is greater than they admitted, though they did not dissemble, for when she was
bled, her blood was putrid, and it will be necessary to work steadily and unremittingly
in order to restore her health. I had best tell all to Your Royal Highness. Her blood is
in such a state that it appeared to me possibly to be the cause of the fears which they
were perhaps too much embarrassed to state clearly. What I told them regarding your
good health, and that of Mme la Duchesse d'Orléans (which in such a case would
depend on yours) immediately restored their confidence, even to the point of saying
many courteous things of Your Royal Highness, which you will perhaps pardon me
for saying that you have not always deserved in these matters. However that may be,
their minds are now at ease regarding the suspicions which I perceived in them, and
which they now assure me never entered their minds.'*]

While the illness continued, I could not avoid seeing the princess each
day, and afterwards reporting to Their Majesties. Yet in all that time she
never addressed a single word to me, although her ladies and the Prince
of the Asturias, who was often present, did everything to persuade her.[2]
Once she had begun to recover, and her glands were less swollen, I simply

---

[1] See p. 32 above.
[2] She would not speak to him at their first meeting either (see p. 373 above). Perhaps, because
of the Maines, she had learned to dislike him; perhaps it was because of the Saint-Simons'
troubles with her sister the Duchesse de Berry; perhaps the Duchesse d'Orléans, who was
cross with Saint-Simon, had upset her. In any event, poor child, she, like her sister, was not
entirely sane.

appeared before Their Majesties as they returned from hunting, and said a word as they passed.

The investiture of my younger son took place on 1 February, which happened to be the eighty-seventh anniversary, to the very day, of my father's reception by the Parlement as a duke and peer of France. It caused a slight altercation between the Duke of Arco who, as his sponsor, took the date from the king and so informed the grandees, and the Marquis of Villena who claimed this to be the prerogative of the major-domo-mayor. I have already described this beautiful ceremony, and shall therefore say only that the Duke of Arco, who as master of the horse invariably travelled in the king's coach, of course alone, had the extraordinary goodness to come to fetch the Marquis de Ruffec and myself in his own carriage, with his personal liveries, and the coach of the Duke of Alba,[1] his assistant at the ceremony, following after. Nothing that I could say would induce these gentlemen to step before us into the coach, or sit on the back seats. They performed their official services with the greatest attention and courtesy, and very graciously took upon themselves the task of inviting the guests to the dinner at my residence, doing the honours there far better than I ever could have done. I was highly flattered to see so large a company of grandees and other noblemen at the investiture; indeed, they assured me that no one had ever seen a larger attendance, and on returning home we were forty-five at table, either grandees, or persons most highly distinguished in other ways, with many tables set for those of somewhat lower rank. Coming and going from the palace, I had the same escort of liveried servants and coaches that had been attached to me for my first formal audience, when I had claimed the hand of the Infanta, and I felt sure that this equal pomp and ceremony much impressed the Spaniards.

In the chapel afterwards, from my own seat on the ambassadors' bench, I had the pleasure of seeing my second son on the bench of grandees. Since we were to share the honour during my lifetime, I had thought it only right to let one investiture suffice for both. As for Maulévrier, disagreeable though he had been in this matter of the grandeeship, I decided that his office was of more importance than my contempt, and I therefore invited him to dinner, although ambassadors do not normally attend investitures. He refused with extreme rudeness, but I would not be put off. There were an incredible number of courtesy visits to be paid and received (one calls twice on each grandee, first to invite him to the ceremony, secondly with invitations to the dinner, for him and his eldest son); but I none the less took my son to call on Maulévrier, and after that he did consent to come. He looked, however, more than ordinarily glum and unamiable, in contrast with the Spaniards who, to reflect my own joy, adopted a most un-Spanish air of gaiety and freedom, as well as hugely enjoying my food, for they ate and drank much more than was

[1] Francisco Alvarez of Toledo y Beaumont, Duke of Alba (1663–1739).

usual at Spanish banquets. Next day, my son and I had to return the visits of all the grandees and other distinguished persons who had dined with us.

Meanwhile, the temper of the Princess of the Asturias grew steadily worse as her health improved, and I learned from her household that despite all the queen's kindness, she could not be induced to visit her. All day long she sat amusing herself by looking out of her bedroom window, so that everyone might see she was recovered. She had been given the Infanta's apartments, and thus was on the same floor as the queen, separated from her only by that inner gallery which I have had occasion to describe; yet she would not listen to her ladies' advice regarding her conduct, and gave even the queen short answers in response to the gentlest remonstrance. All this the queen told me, bidding me go to her, to see if I might help to make her more tractable. I replied that I was sadly aware of the situation, and could not hope to succeed where Her Majesty had failed; but after hearing more—she telling me all, and I adding further details which she did not deny—I took the liberty of saying that there had been too much of spoiling. The princess must now be taught her duty, and that if consideration for M. le Duc d'Orléans were restraining them, not only would I take full responsibility, but most emphatically declare that he would approve of all it might please Her Majesty to say or do to the princess, and be obliged to her. As they well knew, he was infinitely grateful for Their Catholic Majesties' renewed favour and, in his daughter's own interests, would wish her to learn speedily how best to please them.

This speech was well received; and since I had already visited the princess in bed, there was no reason for not returning. Moreover, her stubborn refusal to leave her room was becoming tiresome because it meant postponing the festivities to which everyone was eagerly looking forward. I accordingly called on her two or three times, but was unable to extract more than a brief yes or no, and not always so much when I inquired about her health. I therefore adopted the ruse of telling her ladies, in her presence, all that I should otherwise have addressed to herself. The conversations were thus as good as lessons, although she took no part in them. Yet she was persuaded to visit the queen once or twice, although in *déshabille* and with a very bad grace.

The Grandees' Hall, meanwhile, was still cleared for the ball in honour of a princess who refused to attend. The king and queen, as I have already said, loved dancing; the ball was a pleasure to which they, the Prince of the Asturias, and all the courtiers looked forward impatiently; the princess's behaviour was becoming known and was having the worst possible effect. I could see that the king and queen were losing patience, and I therefore went to her once more to speak through her ladies. I said that her health appeared sufficiently robust to allow her to enjoy the pleasures awaiting her; I described the ball, saying how splendid it would be, how beautiful, how perfectly suited to someone of her age, how much the king and queen loved to dance, how impatiently they waited to hear that she was well enough to go. Suddenly the princess spoke, though I had not addressed her, crying out like a spoilt child, 'Me go? Indeed, I shall not!' 'Very good, Madame,' said I, 'so you refuse! You will regret it, for you will miss a ball at which the entire court looks forward to greeting you, and you both wish and need to please the king and queen too much to forgo such an opportunity.'

She was not looking at me from where she sat; but directly I had finished she turned her head, and in a voice of such determination that I never heard it equalled, she stated flatly, 'No, Monsieur, I say again, I will not go. The king and queen may do as they wish. They love dancing; I hate it; they like getting up late and going late to bed; I go to bed early. Let them go their own way, and leave me to go mine.' I laughed, saying that I knew she was only teasing, but that I was too old to be caught that way, because at her age people did not lightly give up balls, and because she was too intelligent to deprive the court and public of this magnificent spectacle, or refuse the king and queen, for that would be monstrous discourtesy at her age, and so soon after her arrival. Her ladies supported me, and the conversation continued, although the princess no longer appeared to be listening.

When I left, the Duchess of Montellano and the Duchess of Liria followed me. They wished to tell me of their alarm at seeing such resolute stubbornness in a child of twelve, refusing duty and pleasure in a strange land, quite alone among foreigners. I myself was even more appalled, for I imagined most terrible consequences. Even so, I did my best to reassure the ladies, saying that the effects of her illness and her natural petulance might be the cause; but that with returning health all might still be well, though this I was far from believing. When I next saw the king and queen, however, I was careful not to offer such an excuse, and when he displayed annoyance, I took the liberty of saying that I did not imagine he would let himself be inconvenienced by a child's whim, due surely to her illness, or deprive himself, his court, and the public, of a spectacle as delightful and splendid as this ball would be. For my own part, I continued, I should be deeply disappointed, since the first ball which I had attended had been a very great pleasure. 'Oh! we cannot have it without the princess,' he replied. 'But, Sire, why not?' said I, 'Your Majesty gives the ball for his own pleasure, and as part of the general rejoicings. It is not for the princess, though she may provide the occasion, to govern Your Majesty's diversions. If she thinks herself well enough, she will come; if not, let the ball be held without her.'

While I thus spoke the queen was nodding and winking at me, and I therefore went on to say that everything must be, first and last, as Their Majesties pleased, since they were the sole reason for such festive occasions.

Great though the prince and princess undoubtedly were, they could be no more than chief courtiers, enhancing the splendour of a ball, never its object. The trust Their Majesties deigned to place in me encouraged me to beg them not to let the princess imagine that the ball was for her, and could not take place without her. If it were magnificent enough to do honour to Their Majesties, she might discover her relative unimportance, and that, in my opinion, was vital both for her education and her future happiness. The queen at first eagerly supported me; but when the king said nothing, she quietly changed the subject. At the end of the audience, as the king turned from me after my bow, she again winked and nodded to show that I had done well; then pointing with her finger as though prodding him, she gave me to understand that I must continue. That being so, I hurried over my dinner so as to return before they went out hunting, and I quite loudly asked the queen when the ball would be, because I was longing for it. She replied, suiting action to the word, that we should ask the king, and inquired if he had heard me. 'Very well! I shall see,'[1] he answered. These few remarks brought them to the top of the nearby staircase, by which they always came and went, and I remained at the top because there was scarcely room for two to descend it side by side.

On the following day I was there once more. The queen told me that the ball was cancelled and orders were given to put everything to rights; but she motioned to me to speak to the king, which I did, begging him to grant me the ball as a personal favour. We were by then at the top of the narrow stairs; but she signed to me to follow, and I accordingly squeezed myself in beside the page who held her train, talking aloud of the ball, for the king to overhear. A moment later, however, she turned towards me, looking, if I may venture to say so, somewhat shamefaced, and signed to me to say no more. It appeared that the king had made an observation; but the passage was dark and I had perceived nothing. On the landing, where it was wider, the queen joined the king. I remained where I was. They conversed in an undertone, and then the queen called me to her, saying, 'Now all is settled; there is not to be a ball; but to relieve his feelings' [those were her very words] 'the king will give one tonight, after supper, in the state apartments and only for the household; but the king wishes you to come.' I thanked her with a very low bow, at which she said again, 'You will be sure to come, won't you?' I replied to this favour as best I might. The king said, 'At least there will be only ourselves'; the queen added, 'We shall be able to dance as we please, without any formality.' They then continued the descent, and I saw them enter their coach.

The ball was in the inner gallery. Only the lords-in-waiting were present, the master of the horse, the various major-domos, the palace ladies, maids of honour, and companions. The king and queen and the Prince of the

[1] King Philip was copying his grandfather Louis XIV, who invariably said, 'I shall see', to the requests of courtiers.

Asturias enjoyed themselves enormously; a great many minuets were danced and an even greater number of country dances, and they kept it up until three in the morning, at which point Their Majesties retired. It was then that I first saw and handled at leisure the famous pearl, *La Peregrina*,[1] which the king that evening wore in his hat, suspended from a magnificent diamond clasp. This pearl, of the finest quality imaginable, is exactly the same size and shape as those tiny musk-pears, called 'seven in the mouth'[2] that ripen towards the end of the strawberry season. The name shows their size, although no ordinary mouth could possibly hold more than four without choking. This pearl is as thick and as long as the smallest of such pears. It is also unique. They say that one similar to it, the other earring, was the one which Mark Antony, in an access of love, dissolved in vinegar for Cleopatra to swallow.

Despite the fact that the princess's apartments were next to the inner gallery, she made no appearance, not even for a moment. My prediction to Their Majesties had been only too correct, for she continued to behave outrageously in every way, except in affairs of the heart, and when she returned to France as a childless widow, there was time to know her for what she really was.[3] I have described the ball here, so as to finish with the princess; let us turn now to the other festivities in honour of the double marriage.

The first occasion was on 15 February, when there were illuminations and fireworks in the palace square. I have mentioned the extraordinary beauty of the previous illuminations, and these fireworks were no less splendid. They lasted an hour or more, in full force, varying continually between landscapes, hunting-scenes, magnificent arches, fortresses, and palaces. Brilliant rockets in great numbers continually shot up rivers of fire and dropped cascades of fiery rain. In a word, every effect calculated to reinforce and enhance the spectacle or add to its wonders, was continually displayed at full strength, never failing or pausing even for a moment. One had not eyes enough to see the whole of it. Our finest displays are as nothing by comparison.

Next day, Their Catholic Majesties drove in state to Nuestra Señora de Atocha, as I have already described; but this time it was in a coach of glass and gilded bronze, with the Prince and Princess of the Asturias seated in front, and a following of thirty coaches full of grandees and courtiers. I did not go, and neither did Maulévrier, bearing in mind the advice given by the

[1] The story of this famous pearl is that it was originally found off the Isthmus of Panama by a negro diver, who was given his freedom as a reward. It then went to the King of Spain, and is said to have been worn by Mary Tudor (Mary I of England) at her wedding to Philip II in 1554.

[2] Boislisle speaks of 'little muscat or *sept-en-gueule* pears, the smallest variety of all. The flesh is reddish-brown, like butter-pears, musk-scented, ripe towards the end of June.'

[3] See note 4, p. 310 above. A few months after Louis's death she returned to France and lived at the Luxembourg Palace, where she scandalized everyone by her violent speeches and conduct. Soon afterwards she retired to a convent.

Marquis of Montalegre on the earlier occasion. On their return, the king
and queen drove through the illuminated Plaza Mayor, and stayed there for
some time; I was in one of the windows. When they reached the palace, the
square was most brilliantly lit. I had the honour of being invited to stand
on the balcony with Their Majesties, and was near them at the firework
display mentioned above. After a little while, however, I went to another
window that had been reserved for my sons and my suite, and I returned to
the king's balcony only in time to accompany Their Majesties to their
apartments.

There was another pageant held in the great square, beneath the
illuminations, which the king watched from the balcony, as before, and I
watched also from a balcony on the opposite side, in company with the
nuncio, Maulévrier, and my entire suite. I have elsewhere described how
all five storeys of the surrounding houses, the roofs, and the centre of the
square itself were crammed to bursting point with spectators, all without
the least impropriety or disorder. On this occasion the scene was a naval
battle, between a Turkish vessel and a Maltese galley that won the victory
after a long fight, and then set fire to the Turk after boarding her. The
sea was so perfectly imitated, the motion of the ships so life-like, the
manœuvres so deftly carried out, so correct and varied as the final assault
was mounted and the victory won, that the end appeared always in doubt,
and one could almost imagine that one saw the real thing. The battle lasted
more than two hours and never ceased to be fascinating. The boarding of
the vessel was marvellously done, with the attackers beaten off time and
again before the end. The final display of fireworks before the palace was
different, but quite as beautiful as on the first occasion, and Their Catholic
Majesties did me the honour to keep me with them a very long time.

Lent brought the festivities to an end, after which Their Majesties left
the palace to stay for a while at Buen-Retiro. It happened also to be the
anniversary of the death of the late queen (referred to as the Savoyana),
which was celebrated at the Church of the Incarnation, a large and beautiful
edifice, although it forms part of a convent. The grandees were of course
invited, including my second son and myself, but none of the ambassadors.
On the previous evening I had attended vespers, in company with the Duke
of Liria. There was no one in the body of the church, and we therefore
proceeded to the sacristy, where we found some of the grandees. Soon
afterwards others arrived, and when we numbered fifteen or more, someone suggested taking our seats and sending for the priest to begin the
service. When the moment came to move, however, no one would pass
before me, and had I gone first I should have placed myself at the head of
the bench of grandees. After various civilities, I spoke out, saying that I
knew how great an honour it was to be a grandee, and their equal. At the
same time, I was also a French ambassador, and were I to accept their
courtesy, a precedent would be made for other ceremonies and other

ambassadors. Proud though I was of my high office, it was only transitory; I cared far more for the permanent and hereditary rank of a Spanish grandee, and therefore asked, nay, entreated them to let five or six go in before me and sit higher on the bench. Then, I said, they would not be setting an example which they might later think unfortunate. They thanked me sincerely and consented. The Duke of Medina-Celi entered first, four or five others followed him, then I and the rest, and we sat in that order. The king's music played as a prelude to vespers; the bishop, enrobed, took his seat, and twenty more grandees entered one after another.

Next day many more of us attended the mass sung by the king's choir, conducted by the same prelate. My politeness had made a deep impression. All the grandees were gratified, and many of them spoke to that effect. But I was not there in my rôle of ambassador, and I think it was only right to have acted as I did.

I shall not describe Retiro, since every book concerning Spain deals with it at length. Let me say only that to my way of thinking it is as grand as the palace in Madrid, of greater size, and far more comfortable. There are a number of courtyards, one of which is kept private, like the one reserved, in France, for the 'honours of the Louvre', as a place where the coaches of cardinals, ambassadors, and grandees may stand. There is also the makings of a fine park, if the trees were better shaped, and the water for the ponds and fountains more abundant. It reminded me very much of the Luxembourg in Paris, the same shape, the same terraces, layout, basins, and fountains. The Mall is very fine and prodigiously long. As I have already said, the king played there every day at that season when he did not go hunting. One day when I accompanied them it greatly surprised me to see the queen taking frequent pinches of snuff. I remarked that it was strange to find a King of Spain who indulged in neither snuff nor chocolate. The king said that, in truth, he never took snuff; whereat the queen made excuses for herself, saying that she had tried hard to give it up for the king's sake, but was ashamed to say that she had failed. The king said he drank chocolate in the morning with the queen, but only on fast days. 'On fast days, Sire!' I exclaimed. 'Chocolate for fasting?' 'Certainly,' said the king. 'Chocolate is permissible.' 'But Sire!' I protested, 'that means eating something nice, sustaining, even nourishing.' 'I tell you,' said the king crossly, turning rather red, 'that it is allowed; the Jesuits say so, and they have it for every fast. Of course they do not steep their bread in it as on other days.' I held my tongue, for it was not my place to give him instruction; but I silently marvelled at the morals of those worthy fathers, the rules they laid down, the blind obedience which they exacted from high and low alike, the pettiness of their teaching when compared with the sublime maxims of the Gospels, their knowledge of the principles of religion, and the comfortable blindness in which they kept the kings whose guides they were supposed to be.

At this time I took a week's holiday for a journey on which I had set my heart when I first thought of going to Spain. I wished to see Toledo because it interested me very much;[1] and I particularly wished to see the famous cathedral, with all its treasures, and the great belfry that brings in a revenue of five millions. I wished also to see the spot where the Councils of Toledo were held, for many of their decrees were accepted by the Church as a whole, because of the vast learning and holiness of the great majority of their members. Above all, I wished to see and hear the so-called Mozarabic mass, which is retained only in Toledo, where Cardinal Ximenes[2] established it permanently in one of the cathedral chapels, and in seven parishes that practise no other rite. This is the mass that must have been said before the eighth century, since it is earlier than the conquest of part of Spain by the Arabs (or the Moors, as they call them locally), which occurred in the early years of that century. The Moorish invasion was led by Count Julian, in revenge for the violation of his daughter by Roderic, King of Spain.[3] Before I left, I made my arrangements with the Archbishop of Toledo, with whom, as you know, I was on very friendly terms.[4]

Although Toledo is nearly twenty leagues from Madrid, our relays were so well spaced that it took us no more than a day's journey, and we arrived very early. The road is picturesque, open, and level, but the city of Toledo is in the foothills of the mountains. When we reached the outskirts, beneath the great rock on which stand the ruins of the ancient castle, they made me turn my back on the town to visit the Franciscan monastery where the famous Councils were held. I had scarcely set foot to ground before I was surrounded by the heads of that establishment, who eagerly pointed out a barred window in the castle, from which, so they said, King Roderic had first seen Count Julian's daughter who had lived on the site of the monastery. There and then he had conceived for her the passionate love that had turned out so tragically for him and for all Spain. This tale did not impress me very deeply, especially as the window and its surroundings seemed to me to be far less than a thousand years old. The monks then conducted me to their church that looked somewhat uninteresting, with a new and rather commonplace façade. Hardly had I entered before they

[1] There may have been another reason for the excursion, apart from sightseeing, for he had written on 22 February, to the Duc d'Orléans, 'I want to see whether prayers said for you in the Mozarabic tongue may be more efficacious than prayers in Latin or French.' The Mozarabs were lawful Christians under the rule of the Moors.

[2] Ximenes (or Jimenez) de Cisneros (1436–1517). Born in Castile, he became Queen Isabella's confessor in 1492, Archbishop of Toledo 1495, cardinal 1507. He was Grand Inquisitor of Castile, 1506–1516. Ferdinand's minister, and was appointed Regent after the king's death. He was no doubt a great statesman, but Saint-Simon's admiration seems somewhat out of character because one of Ximenes's actions was to quell a revolt of the grandees, and destroy their feudal power. The Larousse encyclopedia says he was pitiless in his repression of heretics.

[3] Roderic, the last of the Visigoth Kings of Spain, was defeated by the Moors at the Battle of Guadalete, 711; but that battle may never have occurred, and the whole legend is most uncertain.

[4] See p. 324 above.

stopped me to ask whether I had observed nothing miraculous. All I could see was a life-size crucifix over the altar, the figure, as is usual in Spain, wearing breeches and a wig; but that did not surprise me for I had seen many like it. I stood gazing at it in silence, trying with all my might to discover what they meant. 'Well! the arms!' they cried; and then I did notice that while one arm was stretched out in the usual manner, the other was hanging down. I inquired what this could signify. 'A great and continuing miracle,' they solemnly declared, and immediately, but giving neither date nor any description of the church at the relevant time, they told me how a rich man had gotten a young girl with child, on a verbal promise of marrying her. He had later denied this promise and laughed at her; whereupon she and her parents, having no written proof, challenged him to repeat his denial publicly, before the crucifix. No sooner had the young couple knelt before it than the left arm detached itself from the cross and lowered itself gently to the position it now occupied. After which the onlookers had cried, 'A miracle! a miracle!' and the young man had married her. Although my ambassadorial status gave me protection from the Inquisition, I thought it more prudent to avoid making a scandal in a foreign country so dominated by superstition, and I accordingly swallowed this legend to the best of my ability. They then led me to the high altar to say a short prayer, and next proceeded to compel me to examine all the chapels, one after another. There was a miracle attaching to each of them, and I had to marvel at them all. After each chapel, I begged to be taken to see the Council chamber, the sole reason for my visit; but they said, 'A moment! a moment! You must first see this chapel; it is truly miraculous.' As I went and listened to one tale after another, my enthusiasm rapidly diminished, and at last, when they had shown all and told everything, they confessed that nothing remained of the Council chamber and that only six months earlier they had demolished the last traces in order to build a kitchen.

I flew into such a rage that it was all I could do to abstain from striking them hard. I turned my back on them, reproaching them bitterly for what had almost been sacrilege, and I entered my coach without any polite speeches, firmly refusing to set foot within their monastery. Such is the fate of precious antiquities through avarice or ignorance, or for the sake of expediency, and no one, not the police nor any private person, ever troubles to have them preserved. The loss of this one did most deeply distress me.

The Archbishop of Toledo had arranged for me to sleep at his palace, and I immediately went there. Céreste, the Comte de Lorges, my sons, the Abbé de Saint-Simon and his brother, the Abbé de Mathan and the two senior officers of our regiments had come with me, and they also were lodged in the palace and the adjoining houses. Two nephews of the archbishop received me, and servants, sent especially by him, waited upon us. Both nephews were canons, and the younger was particularly civil and intelligent. We conversed in Latin; but the elder, despite the fact that he was an inquisitor, thought I was speaking some strange tongue which he could not understand, and begged me to speak Latin. That was because we Frenchmen pronounce words quite differently from the Spaniards, Italians, and Germans; later on, however, we did manage to communicate with one another. They showed us all possible courtesy, and never, even for a moment, became wearisome. The archbishop's palace was not commodious; all the rooms were dark and depressing, and it was very sparsely furnished. They offered us a great variety of dishes, but without meat of any kind.[1] There was a full meal every morning and evening, but the evening meal was lighter.

Lent, in Castile, is a most irksome period. Because of laziness and the distance of the sea, salt-water fish are impossible to obtain. There are a few fish in the larger rivers but none at all in the smaller ones, which dry up in summer. There are also no vegetables except garlic, onions, cardoons,[2] and some herbs, nor is there any milk or butter. They do have salt-fish, and it might not be so bad if only the oil were better, but during Lent, one can smell it in every street of Madrid, for everyone eats it, young and old, men and women, nobles, commoners, and the rabble. One is thus reduced to eggs served in all imaginable ways, and chocolate, which is the one luxury. Besugo is the only sea-fish eaten in Madrid. It comes from Bilbao at Christmas time, and everyone is delighted when it first appears. It is the same size and flavour as a mackerel or herring, has the same firm and delicate flesh, and tastes very good. The Spaniards eat it for feasts and fasts alike and never grow tired of it; but towards the start of Lent it turns sour, and soon after becomes uneatable. The food we had at Toledo was therefore not very palatable, and was cooked in the Spanish way; but there was plenty of it, and they could have done no better.

Next day, I went out early to visit the church, or rather the two churches, for the two separate chapels, symmetrically placed, are fully as large as churches. One is called the Chapel of the Old Kings, the other, of the New Kings. They contain magnificent tombs, and both have beautiful big choirs on a level with the high altars, with numerous richly carved stalls, where masses are said at the same time as in the cathedral, and yet no sound disturbs or interrupts the three separate services. The sacristy is so vast, so full of enormously valuable treasures, that it might well pass for a fourth church. They showed me the imperial cope of the Emperor Charles V, made of cloth of gold of great width, with a foot-long train, all studded with black two-headed eagles; the cloth of the hood appeared to have been particularly sumptuous and most richly embroidered, with great loops of the same material, and huge golden hooks. They opened for me one of many cupboards containing the most precious vestments of all. To the

[1] Because it was Lent.
[2] Rather like artichokes; they grow by the Mediterranean.

thickly padded border of one particular cope was attached the beautiful diamond badge of the Saint-Esprit, which the late King sent to Cardinal Portocarrero.[1] Surrounding it was a chain of most magnificent diamonds, on which hung the Golden Fleece worn always by Charles II, and which, shortly before his death, he presented to this cathedral—in the circumstances, two thoroughly useless gifts. I shall not stay to describe the architecture or the treasures that provide some of the most interesting pages in books about Spain, for indeed whole volumes are devoted to them. Let me only remind you that the burial place of Cardinal Portocarrero is marked by a simple inscription on the floor of the choir, at a place where it is constantly trodden underfoot. In obedience to his express wishes, there is no coat of arms; it bears only the words, *Hic jacet cinis, pulvis, et nihil.*[2] On the wall above, however, there is a splendid and worthy epitaph.

Despite its being Lent, the archbishop had sent orders for the Mozarabic mass to be sung and celebrated for my benefit, with as much pomp as though it were already Easter. The chapel in which this rite was first established has its own choir, situated near the lower end of the nave. They had placed a prie-dieu for me there with a carpet and four cushions, two for my knees below, and two above for my elbows, and another similar prie-dieu for my younger son. This is the usual procedure for cardinals, ambassadors, and grandees in all the Spanish churches. We were conducted to them in procession. They had been set on the Gospel side, quite near the altar. So although I was kneeling I could see everything. The Comtes de Lorges and Céreste, my elder son, the Abbé de Saint-Simon and his brother had only bare hassocks.

I watched and heard this mass with the greatest interest; but shall not describe it because I have seen it fully explained in Cardinal Bona's book,[3] and other liturgical publications. They escorted me afterwards to the choir because I wished to attend that service. One thing that appeared very odd to me was to see a kind of white flag flying from the highest pinnacle of the great belfry, a prodigiously tall and wonderfully decorated structure. I thought at first that we might be at the anniversary of the cathedral's dedication; but they undeceived me very quickly by informing me that the flag was in honour of Cardinal Borgia. It seems that as soon as a canon of Toledo, or the archbishop, is made a cardinal, a flag is flown from the belfry, and if it should chance that several canons have become cardinals, they fly a flag for each of them, and they are not taken down until death.

After our return from church, and before dinner, it was announced that two canons had called to pay their respects in the name of the chapter. At

---

[1] See I, p. 212.
[2] 'Here lie ashes, dust, and nothingness.' See I, p. 489.
[3] Giovanni Bona (1609–1647), a native of Piedmont, was made a cardinal in 1669. He wrote several books, including a liturgical treatise.

the same time, they warned me that one of them was named Pimentel,
Archdeacon of the Cathedral of Toledo, a member of one of the most
illustrious families of Spain. They also told me that he had a stipend of
eighty thousand livres from his prebend, and that he had refused the
archbishoprics of Seville and Saragossa. What is more, he was head of the
diocesan Inquisition. He was accompanied, they said, by another canon of
very good family, whose prebend brought him an annual sixty thousand
livres. You will observe how well endowed the Spanish canons are, in
comparison with our own. The room where I was became crowded with
my own people, many gentlefolk from the town, for the corporation had
called on me, the archbishop's nephews, and his higher officials. We
were all standing. I stepped forward a few paces to greet the canons;
I had given them chairs, set side by side; I took one opposite them. In
sign language I invited them to replace their hats, and we all three covered.
Everyone else continued to stand, for want of chairs. The canons wore
long coats, and hats. As soon as I had replaced my hat, I took it off again
and opened my mouth to thank them for coming. Instantly, Pimentel
was on his feet, bowing, hat in hand. He said '*Domine*', giving me no time
to utter a word, sat down, covered, and proceeded to deliver a most
admirable address in extremely good Latin, that lasted for more than a
quarter of an hour. I can scarcely describe my surprise and confusion.
How could I answer in French a man who did not know the language? On
the other hand, how answer him in Latin? I did manage, none the less. I
had been straining my ears while he was speaking, and mentally framing
my reply. He ended with a bow similar to the one he had made at the start
and, as he bent low, I could see my young men watching me and inwardly
chuckling at the plight they thought I was in—and they were not mistaken.

Once Pimentel was seated, I removed my hat; I rose; I said '*Domine*.'
Sitting down and replacing my hat, I shot a glance at the young ones, who
seemed flabbergasted[1] at my daring, for they had not been expecting it. I
then made out as best I might in Latin, most probably murdering it with
terrible mistakes, but continuing bravely to answer him point by point,
ending with expressions of gratitude and compliments to the chapter, the
deputies, and finally to the representative of the whole Pimentel family,
touching ever so delicately on his birth, modesty, and scorn of high office,
as evidenced by his refusal of two rich and famous archbishoprics. Such
an ending made them forgive my bad Latin and pleased them vastly, at
least so I heard later, and I did not speak any less long than Pimentel. As I
made my final bow, I took another look at my young men, who looked
stunned. They had not thought very much of my Latin; it was my courage
and persistence which they admired, and they told me so afterwards in no
measured terms. There was a short silence, after which the canons rose to

---

[1] *eplapourdi*: a word Saint-Simon uses elsewhere. It was Normandy slang, which he probably
learned in the nursery from his Norman nurse.

go, and I escorted them almost to the farthest end of the adjoining room. The nephews and the rest of the company all congratulated me on my eloquence in Latin. I do not imagine that they really thought me fluent, no more did I; but at least I had managed to extricate myself.

We soon afterwards dined. The stewards, the waiters, and the footmen who poured out the wine and changed our plates all looked to me so much like Jesuits that I dared not ask for anything. I had noticed earlier that every one of the Archbishop of Toledo's servants, even including his grooms and coachmen, wore clerical attire exactly like priests, and that it was the garb worn by Jesuits since the time of Saint Ignatius, their founder. After dinner, I returned the visit of the two canons but, perhaps from politeness, word was sent that they were out.

From Toledo, I went to Aranjuez, a journey as long as from Paris to Meaux. Although the governor was away, they lodged me at his house, a fine large building quite near the castle. It is the only place in all Castile where fine trees grow, in great numbers. By whichever way one enters the town, one drives along an avenue about a league long, and many have a double row of trees. In all, there are twelve or thirteen such avenues, leading from all directions into a great square, and down many of them one sees far beyond to the distant horizon. These avenues are crossed by others, and where they intersect there are squares that resemble shady cloisters or small grassy fields, on either side of which the roads run out into the country to a distance of a league or more.

The castle is a vast building with spacious state apartments, above which are lodgings for the more important courtiers. The extensive garden is encircled by the river Tagus, and bordered by a narrow terrace that runs beside the stream, which at that point is not wide enough for boats. There are fine large lawns and some splendid avenues, the rest of it being broken up with groves of trees, shady arbours, and fountains in the form of birds and animals, including some that drown any admirer who stays to contemplate them. The water comes from underground springs, and falls in an abundant stream from the false birds perched among the trees, and the mouths of the animals and other statues. One is made wet through in an instant, and it is impossible to escape. Indeed, the entire garden is laid out in the old-fashioned Flemish manner, and was designed by Flemish gardeners, specially imported for that purpose by Charles V. Accustomed as we are to the excellent taste of Le Nôtre in the French gardens, we cannot help finding the gardens at Aranjuez somewhat vulgar; yet in Castile they are very charming because of the trees and the water. One thing that did greatly shock me was to see a mill on the Tagus, less than a hundred paces from the castle. It lies astride the river, and its noise is heard everywhere.

Behind the governor's house is a park intersected by wide avenues and stocked with deer, buck, and wild boar in great numbers. The undergrowth, which is very thick, is purposely kept low for the benefit of the animals. We walked along a path for a short distance to a kind of gap in the fence, protected by a strong wooden grille, that overlooked a grassy arena, surrounded by trees. A servant climbed high up beside this gate, and blew a whistle. Immediately, the whole arena was filled with wild boar and their young, of all ages and sizes, including some truly enormous specimens. The servant then threw down a great quantity of corn, on which the animals fell with every sign of voracious hunger, coming quite close up to the grille, many of them snarling, with the larger ones pushing the smaller out of their way, while the young retreated to the protection of the trees until the big boars had had their fill. This little diversion kept us amused nearly an hour. Thence we drove in an open carriage down the same wide avenues to the place they call 'The Mountain and the Sea'. There is a tiny little hill, standing alone, from the top of which one may discern the entire countryside, with all the immense number of avenues and the enclosures formed where they intersect. It is a most agreeable view. Almost the whole of the flat top of this hill is occupied by a large ornamental sheet of water—a marvel, in Spain, though in other countries one would not think much of it. It is edged with stone, and there are little boats, like galleys and gondolas, in which Their Catholic Majesties sometimes go on the water and amuse themselves with fishing, for the pond is well-stocked. At one side is a large park, or menagerie, in which is kept a flock of camels, and another of buffaloes. Next morning, some of the royal keepers brought a most beautiful camel for me to see. It was saddled and fully laden, and they made it kneel down in front of me to be unloaded of a great quantity of vegetables, and green stuff for salads, also eggs and carp, some of them three feet long, and all very large and fat; but I thought later that they tasted no better than our own, in other words, they were flabby, tasteless, and full of small bones. I was lodged at the king's expense and spent there the whole of one day.

It seemed a charming spot in springtime, and should be delightful in summer, but it appeared that no one stayed there then, not even the villagers, who shut their houses and go elsewhere when the great heat begins. They told me that the valley is liable to cause very dangerous fevers, and that those who recover are left in a decline as bad as after any serious illness, and apt to last for seven or eight months. The court, for that reason, spends no more than six weeks or perhaps two months there, in springtime; and seldom, if ever, returns in the autumn. From Aranjuez back to Madrid, the road was fairly good. It is about the same distance as from Madrid to the Escorial, but you need to cross Madrid in order to go from one palace to the other.

On my return the king and queen asked my opinion of Aranjuez. I praised it highly, as indeed it merited; but in my description of all I had seen, I mentioned the mill, and my surprise at its being allowed to stand so close to the castle, blocking the view, and, worse still, making an intolerable racket. I said that no ordinary person would put up with it for a moment. The king, however, was not pleased. He quickly replied that it had always been there and did no one any harm. I at once changed the subject, and we continued to speak for some considerable time of all the pleasures of Aranjuez. I had tasted buffalo milk there for the first time, and had found it excellent, better by far than any other. It is light and sweet, a little thicker than the best cream, without the slightest flavour of the animal, cheese, or butter. I often wondered why they did not keep a herd at the Casa del Campo, so as to accustom Madrid to its deliciousness.

On 7 March, the Infante Don Philip received the sacrament of confirmation at the hands of Cardinal Borgia, having been baptized the day before, with the Prince of the Asturias standing godfather. It was a week before his second birthday, which made me think the whole affair rather premature. On the following day, he was made a Knight of Saint James, and Commander of the rich district around Aledo.[1] This was how they did it. The Marquis of Bedmar, President of the Council of the Orders of Chivalry, Knight of Saint James and of the Saint-Esprit, sat on a velvet chair with gold fringes, facing but not near the altar, with a table covered by a rich carpet on which stood a crucifix and the Bible, etc., at his right hand. Twenty or more Knights of Saint James, grandees and others, sat in two rows on either side, on carpet-covered benches, according to their rank in the Order, with the most senior at the ends nearest to the Marquis of Bedmar. They wore ordinary dress, and over it the great cloak of Saint James, made of a white woollen material and extending down to the heels, with the sword of Saint James embroidered in red on the left side. The cloak is left open in front like a monk's cope, and is tied at the neck by thick cords of white silk, arranged so as to hang in loops over the left side, descending rather lower than the embroidered badge, and ending with two large pompons of white silk, in shape much resembling the green pompons that one sees in the heraldic arms of bishops, on the hats. All the knights wore hats,[2] and the spectators stood behind them. The king and queen, with the Prince and Princess of the Asturias and their retinues, were in a tribune, and I had been placed in another, above them, with my own people.

The Marquis of Santa-Cruz came from the sacristy bareheaded, on the epistle side, carrying the baby prince. He passed along the back of the row of knights on that side, with a small following, none of them knights, and stood for a few moments in the space between the head of that bench and the table; whereupon the Marquis of Bedmar, without removing his hat,

---

[1] A village in Murcia.

[2] Saint-Simon appears astonishingly interested in the hat-drill. It plainly had as much significance in Spain as it had in France, where Louis XIV had twenty different degrees of saluting with his hat, and the affair of the bonnets was of such shattering importance.

appeared to turn and speak to him. Santa-Cruz made some reply; he then stepped forward, still bareheaded, and kneeled before Bedmar, who remained covered, as did the knights on the two benches. After a very short time, Santa-Cruz, still carrying the little prince, went to stand in front of the table, and appeared to swear an oath, which did not take long. He then returned to stand before the Marquis of Bedmar. Bedmar had his back turned to me, and I was thus unable to hear whether or not he spoke; but I think that he did. Santa-Cruz, who faced me, did not speak.

Soon afterwards, Santa-Cruz turned the little prince in his arms so that his back was towards Bedmar. Two members of the prince's following produced a tiny cloak similar in every way to those of the other knights. Bedmar grasped it with both hands, placed it on the little prince's back, and then took him upon his knee, while the Marquis of Santa-Cruz stepped back a few paces. Simultaneously, the Marquis of Montalegre, steward of the order, and the Duke of Arco, master of the horse, rose from the benches and solemnly advanced side by side, followed by the Marquis of Grimaldo (also a knight) bearing the gold spurs. All three were hatless. When they stood before the Marquis of Bedmar, they bowed low, which the Marquis of Santa-Cruz had not hitherto done, on account of holding the prince. The Marquis of Montalegre and the Duke of Arco then took the spurs; buckled or attached them somehow to the prince's heels and immediately removed them.

After that, the Marquis of Santa-Cruz took the prince again into his arms and returned whence he had come. When Bedmar had seen him re-enter the sacristy he rose, removed his hat, and bowed to the knights, who removed theirs also, rising together at exactly the same moment. They then withdrew in no particular order. What did amaze me was the absolute quiet and stillness of the little child, who was as yet in the care of women. Despite being surrounded by men with strange faces and unfamiliar garb, he allowed himself to be carried into church; put on someone's knees; dressed by a stranger in a cloak; his heels, or that part of him, touched by spurs, and carried out again, without weeping or expostulating, but looking around at all those unknown persons without fear or impatience.

Next day, the 9th, the king and queen went quite alone for four days' holiday to Balzaïn. Their only courtiers were the Duke of Arco, the Marquis of Santa-Cruz, the Count of San-Esteban-de-Gormaz, captain of the bodyguard, Valouse, the Princesse de Robecq, a palace lady, the queen's nurse, and one of the 'companions'. I saw them off early in the morning, and soon after dinner began my round of farewell calls, intending to take formal leave of Their Catholic Majesties when they returned from Balzaïn. During my very first visit, however, I was informed that a long-awaited courier had arrived, bringing answers to letters and instructions regarding many matters which Cardinal Dubois had not until then found time to consider. I went home at once. The first letter I opened was from

Dubois, giving me an account of the happenings in Paris on the arrival of the Infanta, and of all the celebrations, so that I might describe them fully to the King and Queen of Spain. There was a packet of letters from the whole Orléans family, answers to mine telling of the wedding of the Princess of the Asturias—and very slow they had been in coming. I found also what I had urgently been expecting, a letter from M. le Duc d'Orléans to King Philip, thanking him for the honours done to me, and others from Cardinal Dubois to Père Daubenton and the Marquis of Grimaldo, on the same subject. Nothing in this packet, or in the other which I am about to describe, explained the cause of the long silence for which the cardinal, as usual, made profuse apologies.

It was the second packet that had demanded such great speed. From it, it appeared that Cardinal Dubois had been feeding Cardinal de Rohan with expectations of becoming the first minister, and that Cardinal de Rohan had been silly enough, before leaving Rome, so to inform the Pope and several cardinals. It had thus become general gossip, although no one in Rome was fool enough to believe him.

Dubois, since his promotion, had modestly abstained from attending the Regency Council, nothwithstanding that he was now secretary of State for foreign affairs, as well as being master of all the rest. Although in earlier days he had invariably been present, he did not yet feel strong enough to fight unsupported the battle for personal precedence. Like a new-born chick, he was trailing his shell behind him. It was for that reason that he had given Cardinal de Rohan to understand that before becoming the first of all ministers, he must have held some lesser ministry, and that he should immediately ask M. le Duc d'Orléans to appoint him to the Council; coming, as he did, hot-foot from Rome, after giving, so Dubois affirmed, most notable service, he would surely not be refused—Dubois himself would see to that. Rohan was thus to be made the stepping-stone by which Dubois might join the Council—his subsequent ejection would not be hard to contrive. Standing firmly on Rohan, Dubois would be secure against the taunts, odious comparisons, and jibes of those members who would feel insulted by his company. The objections would be to both, as prelates, and Cardinal de Rohan, as the senior, would bear the brunt of them. The personal element would thus entirely disappear, since Rohan's rank made him wholly acceptable. Dubois had only to shelter modestly behind Rohan's skirts, and enjoy the victory he had gained for the whole cardinalate.[1] That, indeed, is what happened.

Having been, thank the Lord, three hundred leagues from the scene of action, I cannot explain the details. The dukes, as usual, were cheated; but such of them as were members of the Regency Council ceased to attend the meetings, and so also did the Chancellor. The cream of the joke was

[1] In Boislisle there is a note to the effect that by putting Rohan on the Council, Dubois hoped to stop his grumbling which had never ceased since first he went to Rome.

that the Marshals of France resigned also, though none of them, until then, had ever disputed anything with the cardinals. Dubois was enchanted. He seized the occasion to persuade the Regent (quite without foundation) that the dukes' objection to the cardinals was no more nor less than a cabal directed against him and his administration. The courier was sent post-haste to tell me of the event, and Cardinal Dubois's personal letter must not be omitted from these memoirs. Indeed, it warrants being given in full, so as to disclose the extraordinary cunning of that pestilential serpent.

Paris, 2 March 1722

Monsieur

You will no doubt already have learned of the disturbance at the Regency Council, on the occasion of M. le Duc d'Orléans's inviting Cardinal de Rohan to become a member [Dubois was appointed at the same moment, but modesty kept him silent regarding that]. Had the quarrel arisen merely over the precedence of cardinals against that of dukes and peers, I might not so much have regretted your absence. It was, however, a pretext concocted by a cabal, the leader of which is a man [the Duc de Noailles] who proved unable to retain your esteem, and now appears to harbour malice against His Royal Highness, with the intention of bringing down his government and destroying his works. [His works! Oh, Dubois!] I have never more sincerely wished for your presence, nor more urgently desired the support of your wrathful indignation. I beg you, Monsieur, not to doubt the truth of my words until you have seen the situation for yourself, for then you will feel disposed to show your zeal on the side which you deem best fitted to serve the country's interests, the recent alliance of the two crowns, and the upholding of M. le Duc d'Orléans himself. [He is referring to what he said above, about *destroying his works*; but he knew them all the time to be his own doing.] Let me add for your own security that, should the plot succeed, I am sure of your being, if not their first victim, then certainly their second. This disturbance leads me naturally to think of your return. I am, however, persuaded that your presence is still needed—at Madrid; and it seems to me that the only way to give you the liberty which you must earnestly desire, is to suggest your gaining a favourable reception for M. de Chavigny.[1] From what I hear this may not be easy, since they say that people have given bad reports of him. He does not, in fact, merit them, and until M. le Duc d'Orléans sends

---

[1] Anne Théodore Chavignard de Chavigny (1687–1771). He was the son of a Beaune attorney; had been on a diplomatic mission to Genoa, and was now to replace Saint-Simon as ambassador extraordinary at Madrid. Saint-Simon was not pleased. Chavigny was common. His real name was Chavignard; by dropping a couple of letters and changing another he tried to pass for one of the aristocratic Chavignys. It was the Jesuits who had duped everyone and had him presented to the King who cared nothing for good families or good old names. Dubois was plainly not hopeful of securing Saint-Simon's best endeavours on his behalf.

a new ambassador to Spain, he is the only man capable of obeying the instructions you will issue when you leave. I trust, Monsieur, that you will consent to gain favour for him, and a hearing, and secure for him permission to approach Their Catholic Majesties. After making these arrangements, you may return at your leisure. I find myself in two minds, torn between the great services you are rendering in Spain, and the support you will give, in France, to His Royal Highness. Also, if I may venture on a personal touch, between my desire to cultivate your recently most kind acquaintance, and to show you, if that were possible, fresh proof of my own esteem and attachment.

The falseness in every line of this letter leaps to the eye. Dubois, though sheltering behind Cardinal de Rohan, dreaded the antagonism of so large a group of peers. He knew his master's weakness, his contempt for precedence and reason; he knew that M. le Duc d'Orléans would be guided by circumstances and bow to superior numbers; that twelve or fifteen of the highest in the land would far outweigh, in his eyes, two cardinals, one of whom was powerless, the other his own creation. The Chancellor's authority was an even greater embarrassment. Dubois's plan was therefore to submerge the Regent's fears in the far more serious dread of a plot to overthrow him. He had learned in England the art of bringing to light a dangerous plot, in order to extract from the Parliament more troops and money than it would otherwise be disposed to grant. In like manner, he produced this supposed cabal, aimed, so he said, at nothing less than the destruction of the Regent and his government. Yet the real question was far otherwise, so simple, so totally unconcerned with politics or the administration, that Dubois might have strangled it at birth had he not introduced this dangerous and useless novelty, the appointment of cardinals to the Regency Council. But such an exclusion would have excluded him also, and although the Council was no longer of any consequence, he needed to be first there, and to dominate it. He had not the patience to wait the few remaining months before the King's majority, when the Regency Council would automatically cease to be.

As a final inspiration, he attached to this supposed conspiracy a plot to break the new alliance between France and Spain by returning the Infanta; and it was for the purpose of convincing the Regent that he sent me that urgent courier, bringing me an explanation, and orders to go at once to the king and queen, with the assurance that all was well. In a second letter, Dubois urged me not to delay, but to seek out Their Catholic Majesties immediately, in whatever palace they might be.

I read these letters and re-read them. I reflected on them in solitude and came to a firm decision, resolving not to be the cardinal's dupe, or hazard the good opinion I flattered myself I had earned, in Spain, by pretending an imaginary cabal to be a reality. Time would soon show its non-existence. It was invented to force the Regent's hand, and the orders sent me were designed to persuade him of imminent danger.[1] On the other hand, I was reluctant to lay myself open to reproaches for disobedience, and I therefore resolved to gratify Dubois by forcing my way into Balzaïn, where no witness would hear my words.

I went first to Grimaldo, who was at work in his *covachuela*, and quickly explained the situation. I did not mention the word cabal, but said that the Regent feared lest the resignation of so many important members of his Council might wrongly impress Their Catholic Majesties. I added that a courier had been sent to obviate that possible mischance, and had brought me instructions to see Their Majesties without delay, no matter where they might be. Grimaldo smiled at the undue urgency. He remarked that the king and queen would not be interested; they had no intention, so he said, of becoming embroiled in the quarrels at the French Court, or of interfering in any way. His advice to me was to wait for Their Majesties' return, in four days' time. They had left for Balzaïn only that morning with the bare minimum of attendance; there was an absolute ban on joining them; the king would certainly be both displeased and embarrassed to see me there. I agreed with all he said; but stressed that, knowing Dubois as he did, he must see that I should be reproached for tardiness, and accused of being out of favour, since I had not been invited to Balzaïn. I then handed him the second letter, the one that contained no more than a curt order to report instantly to Their Catholic Majesties, no matter where they might be. Grimaldo read and pondered over this, admitting, when he returned it, that he saw the difficulty, but scarcely knew how to advise me. We spent a little more time discussing Cardinal Dubois's character, after which I entreated him to write the king a letter, explaining the situation, and begging him to be so indulgent as to see me. Come what might, I was determined to go to Balzaïn next morning, for I preferred to risk King Philip's passing annoyance, rather than be disgraced at my own Court, where Cardinal Dubois ceaselessly tried to ruin me. Grimaldo shrugged his shoulders, saying that, in the circumstances, mine might be the better way, and that fortunately a courier for Balzaïn was about to leave at that very moment, to whom he would give a letter. I thanked him much for his help, and returned to arrange my journey, sending relays ahead of me, and saddle mules to wait farther along the road.

I was gone, next day, before six in the morning, and was much astonished to find the gates of Madrid still closed; the keys on the outer side, and the keeper a hundred yards beyond. Luckily the walls were not high at that point, for we had to make a groom scale them, and even then he had great trouble in finding the porter to let us out of the town. The Comte de Lorges, my younger son, the Abbé de Saint-Simon, his brother, and a major of his regiment accompanied me. Céreste thought it too thankless a task.

[1] Boislisle says that the cabal was a pure invention of Dubois's.

Towards midday we arrived at the foot of the pass over the Guadarrama, having been climbing steadily for about as long as from Paris to Senlis. We left the carriages there, and mounted our mules. I never saw a lovelier road, nor one that would be more alarming in a coach. In front was a solid wall of rock of immense height, up which a smooth but narrow road made a zigzag, but not too sharp ascent, in such a way that it was quite easy to converse with those immediately above and below. Both mountain and road were thickly covered with snow, and the trees that grew profusely between the rocks had their branches so laden with icicles that they sparkled like clusters of the most beautiful and brilliant jewels imaginable. There was something strange and magical in that awe-inspiring scene. At last, after innumerable twists and turns we reached the summit. It had not much of a plateau, and the descent was far shorter and easier. Balzaïn was situated about half-way down, in a narrow valley, a fair distance from the foot of the pass.

Balzaïn was built by the Moors, and was burned deliberately in the reign of Charles II, who went there too often for his people's liking. It has never been restored; what remains are the tiny remnants of a large and beautiful castle, with an unimpressive garden, and nothing remarkable in the surroundings. We dismounted near a tumbledown building that had once been connected with the castle, to which there is now no covered approach. We were shown into the Duke of Arco's office, where his stewards were working; but they very civilly left the room, after placing wicker chairs for us close to the fire, which we badly needed, and offering us refreshments, for which we thanked them. It was only four in the afternoon, and we had to wait an hour and a half before the return of Their Catholic Majesties from La Granja, now called San Ildefonzo. The Duke of Arco's kitchen was in the adjoining room; above were four cell-like bedrooms for the three noblemen and Valouse, and on the ground floor, next the kitchen, was a narrow slit which the duke used as a dining-room. As soon as we were warned of Their Majesties' approach, we went to see them step down from their coach. Grimaldo had written of our coming, and we were expected. The king's manner was cold, not to say sour, and he did not utter. The queen looked embarrassed, but was slightly less unkind. She spoke a few words to me. The retinue, on the other hand, were as welcoming as could be. The king and queen then climbed up a wooden stairway with hand-rails. It was an outside staircase, like that in any peasant's cottage, so narrow that they had to go in single file. At the top was a square balcony, large enough to hold five or six people huddled together, leading directly into the royal bedroom, with nothing beyond it except a privy, and one other room. That was the full extent of their lodging, with a few tiny rooms above and below, and on the ground floor their kitchens, and the King's study.

When they had reached the little balcony, Their Majesties stopped to wait for me, and I asked leave to speak with them. The suite stayed outside and in the adjoining room, and I thus found myself quite alone with them. They moved towards the window because the light was fading fast. 'Well! Sir, what is this urgent matter?' said the king crossly. I began with apologies for arriving without permission, and briefly explained my firm orders and the happenings at the Regency Council; but I mentioned no cabal. I said merely that the cause of the resignations was the appointment of the cardinals; that the administration was not weakened thereby; but that M. le Duc d'Orléans wished to keep Their Catholic Majesties informed of every event because of the great regard he felt for them. The king, still vexed, remarked that it did not warrant the journey, and could perfectly well have been kept until his return to Madrid. I looked at the queen, saying that it was very hard having to deal with Cardinal Dubois, for he would have come down on me for the least delay, being convinced, probably with good reason, that had I been in France, I also should have resigned. The queen laughed, remarking that she could well understand the dilemma. She then turned to the king, saying that there was no great harm, save in having given me so much trouble, and at once questioned me regarding the affair, but very briefly and simply. King Philip appeared somewhat mollified. He declared that such matters did not interest him, for he had no desire to become involved with the French Court; especially not with its problems and quarrels. I ended by telling them of the arrival of the Infanta and of all the celebrations, which pleased them immensely and put him in a better temper. The arrangements for her welcome delighted them particularly, and more especially the King's having driven out so far from Paris to meet her.

After a very short conversation, by the end of which they had become perfectly cheerful, the queen suggested summoning the suite in order to tell them the news, and she bade me call them to come in. She then told them all, just as I have described, adding that I must read out to them the full account. Then she suddenly broke off to ask very kindly where I should find lodgings for myself and my party. The Duke of Arco promptly offered me supper and a bed; but appeared to hesitate over accommodation for the others. All this was accompanied by a profusion of compliments paid with the utmost courtesy by the Duke of Arco and the Marquis of Santa-Cruz; the king also said a few words, and the queen was most animated. I wished no one to be inconvenienced and, in any case, there was no room for my party. I therefore asked leave, and was permitted, to go on to Segovia and seek lodgings there, and that was how it was settled. The Duke of Arco would have kept us all to supper, but I managed to excuse myself, and he lent us a coach with room for four persons to take us the rest of the journey. While all this had been happening, the queen was speaking to the king in an undertone; she now turned to say that they would let us go only on condition of our returning next day to dine with the Duke of Arco, and afterwards following them to La Granja, where the king wished to show me his new gardens and buildings. King Philip joined in the invitation, looking pleased and serene, and the queen was kindness itself. We then took our leave and departed for Segovia, a distance approximately equal to that from Paris to the old Porte de la Conférence, at Sèvres, across a very flat plain, after climbing a gentle slope. They had given us a mounted escort, with torches.

Those of my company who went on horseback arrived first. We met them in the road, they having found it impossible to persuade any door to open. People had shouted at them from the upper windows as though they had been thieves and murderers. Notwithstanding our coach and escort, we had a similar reception wherever we knocked, and thus began to fear that we should spend the night supperless upon the streets. At last we created such a disturbance at the door of one very large house that after many threats and entreaties from the upper windows, the inhabitants took courage from our numbers and the royal liveries of our escort, and opened to us. You may picture our relief. They led us upstairs and showed us rooms and beds. That was a great thing; but when we spoke of supper, they had no bread, no meat, none of the etceteras. Our dinner on the way had been meagre in the extreme, and we had not thought it necessary to bring food for the evening. It took much time and trouble to appease our unwilling hosts, who already thought badly of us for disturbing their sleep, and to collect the wherewithal for supper at so late an hour, in a country where there are neither inns nor hostelries. In the end, however, after much patience, we ate and slept not too badly.

Curiosity caused me to waken early. My windows gave me a near view of the great Roman aqueduct that seems carved from a single block of stone, and has never ceased to carry water from the neighbouring mountains to every quarter of the large and well-built town, where there are fine squares and churches and wider, lighter, straighter streets than in any other of the Spanish towns I visited, except Madrid and Valladolid. As one approaches the aqueduct one is conscious of its immense height, higher than the tallest ones around Versailles and Marly. There are no archways, only a few doors to give access where necessary; and the vast size of the stones from which it is constructed is truly amazing. The joins are almost imperceptible; hardly a trace of them can be seen. I was fascinated to see this marvellous structure that has stood safely for so many centuries.

The town is at the end of a beautiful and fertile plain extending for four or five leagues, and is sheltered by the mountain which, at that place, is extremely lofty and very rocky. At the opposite end, overlooking the plain, stands the castle of Segovia which, like Vincennes, fills the double function of being a royal palace of vast size, richness and beauty, and also a prison for crimes against the State. Unlike most of the Spanish palaces, it has a fine large courtyard; the royal apartments are admirably extensive, with well-considered decorations of great magnificence and beautiful workmanship. The gold in them is thick and dark, and as shining as on the day when it was first applied. There are charming painted ceilings, and the exquisite painting on the immense number of walls, doors, windows, and ceilings reminded me forcibly of those at Fontainebleau with, on balance, a distinct preference for Segovia. The state apartments overlook a narrow river that winds its way close by the castle, and thence across all that beautiful plain to the line of mountains of varying shape and height.

On the top floor of the prison, which is seven storeys high, adjoining the castle and sharing the same courtyard, is confined that famous itinerant monk whom M. de Chalais[1] brought to Paris closely guarded, and veiled in the deepest mystery, as I have earlier described.

[*This event (not included) happened in 1708. Saint-Simon says that in revenge for Orléans's outrageous jest when he toasted them, at supper, as the 'con capitaine and con lieutenant', Mme de Maintenon and the Princesse des Ursins had an itinerant Spanish monk arrested and taken very secretly to Paris, and before Louis XIV. He there confessed to having been the Duc d'Orléans's accomplice in a successful plot to poison the royal princes. Nothing of course was proved, since the royal family was not poisoned, but died of measles. The story did, however, increase suspicions harboured against the Duc d'Orléans at that time, and greatly add to his unpopularity. The monk was sent back to Spain and imprisoned, as described, at Segovia, where Saint-Simon, who was of course deeply interested, said that 'he subsequently lived as debauched a life as was possible between the four walls of a criminals' gaol'.*]

He was later sent to Segovia under strong guard, and has never since left that prison. I learned from the man in charge of the prisoners that this monk was insatiable of romances, and scarcely less so of meat and wine; that he swore and blasphemed unceasingly, and spent his time howling with rage, or else singing to keep up his spirits. He complained bitterly of the injustice of the Spanish courts, but would never tell the reason for his incarceration, from which he had many times tried to escape—this being the cause of his confinement on the top storey. It seemed that he had never accustomed himself to prison life, and behaved like a madman. The warder appeared to me to be quite out of patience with him because of his impiety and disgusting love of debauchery; he said that he gave him more trouble than all the rest of the prisoners. I did everything possible to gain a sight of him at his window, but without success. At least he could enjoy a lovely view. He was given all the books he desired, and as much food and wine as he cared to have; but was allowed to see no one, nor have anything that might enable him to write. Our

[1] Louis Jean Charles de Talleyrand, Prince de Chalais (1680–1757). He was the son of the brother of Mme des Ursins's first husband, and had attached himself to her in Spain. See index, I and II.

morning having been spent in this interesting manner, we left for Balzaïn in the same coach by which we had come.

It was one in the afternoon by the time we reached the Duke of Arco's room, and shortly afterwards we were given an abundant and most excellent meal, although nearly all was cooked in the Spanish way. The Marquis of Santa-Cruz, the Count of San-Esteban-de-Gormaz, and Valouse dined with us, and the Duke of Arco most nobly did the honours with all imaginable politeness. We sat long at table with super-excellent wines, very good coffee, good appetites, and good talk. Those Spanish noblemen were enchanted to see me fall upon their national dishes with so much gusto. Soon after dinner, they conducted us to the foot of the wooden staircase, by which the king and queen descended to enter their coach. They greeted me very warmly indeed. The king appeared quite reconciled to my being at Balzaïn, and both he and the queen obviously enjoyed the thought of showing me their building works at La Granja, which is Spanish for The Grange. That, indeed, is what it is, no more, set on a lonely site once belonging to the monks of the Escorial, and about a league from Balzaïn.

The king had used the little house for hunting, and liked its solitude. The convenience of having unlimited water, and an abundance of game had persuaded him to buy it from the monks and to build there a palace for his retirement; for as soon as the Prince of the Asturias was old enough, King Philip intended to abdicate in his favour, as he later did. This intention, however, was known only to the queen and Père Daubenton, who both of them dreaded it of all things and, by gentle pressure, did all they could to change his mind.

The Duke of Arco and the Marquis of Santa-Cruz left the rest of the company in order to escort us. The road wound through the valley, often crossing pretty streams and deep gullies as it neared the foot of the high range of mountains over which we had ridden on our way from Madrid. As we neared La Granja the valley narrowed, though it remained open country. We approached the building at one side; the frame was already constructed, the roof in place, and there were divisions for the rooms. By that time, they were working on the interior, but masons were still needed, and the gardens were only roughly laid out. The chapel, as big as a cathedral, was just beginning to rise from the ground, and there were to be lodgings for a chapter and clergy, though these had not yet been started. There were also foundations for a collegiate church, dedicated to Saint Ildefonso,[1] whose name is given to the great new palace. At this point it would be desirable to give you some notion of the place which became so famous when Philip V retired there during his short abdication.

It would be hard to find a less agreeable spot, or to have better succeeded

[1] Saint Ildefonso (600–667), a disciple of Saint Isidore of Seville (c. 560–636), was Arch-bishop of Toledo 657.

in rendering it dismal, not to say hideous, by the siting of the castle. It is a long and very large edifice with windows back and front, placed almost at the foot of an extremely smooth and gentle slope that rises gradually to the edge of the Segovia plain, which this almost imperceptible gradient entirely conceals. Had the castle been placed twenty or thirty yards higher, it would have enjoyed a wonderful view of the town and aqueduct, besides allowing for a terrace to overlook the gardens in the most delightful way imaginable. As it has been erected, it is on the same level as the valley floor and only that is visible, while the back windows at every stage are so close to the rise that anyone who leant out would feel he could almost touch it. It appeared to me that the ground floor was intended for guardrooms, with halls for dining-tables, and other rooms to serve as lodgings. The entire first floor was for the occupation of Their Catholic Majesties, and divided into fine rooms of varying sizes, but all spacious. The back, obscured as I have described, is for offices and privies, with lodgings for the *camaristas* and the necessary domestic staff. At the end, there will be galleries cut into the chapel walls; but these are not yet begun. We did not see the upper floor. The staircase is vast and will be beautiful, set in the centre of the building. To its right and left are charming concealed stairways, which we used.

Opposite the chapel, and only a few yards from the castle, was a rather large edifice enclosing courtyards and other smaller buildings. It was intended for stables and outhouses, and to serve as lodgings for the gentlemen of the household and the court officials. Its nearness to the castle astonished me, and I said as much to the queen; but she merely replied that they liked to hear the bustle of the comings and goings. The real reason, which I did not then perceive, was that seeing and hearing the life of those surrounding them somewhat alleviated their boredom. The gardens extended to the mountains, no great distance, but on either side they were already very large, and have since been made still wider, until now they fill the entire breadth of the valley. They had planted whole avenues of fully grown trees, as the late King did at Marly. There were low terraces edged with stone slabs surrounding lawns, and shrubberies still scarcely higher than the ground, with ornamental lakes, canals, and innumerable ponds of every size and shape. Waterfalls and fountains produced all manner of watery effects from the clearest, purest water imaginable, in incredible abundance. The fountains sprayed out jets of every shape and size, some of the single ones being as thick as a man's thigh, and at least twice the height of the beautiful one at Saint-Cloud that made King Louis so jealous, and which everyone else most rightly admired.

It sometimes happens that the worst features have their uses, and thus the long range of mountains that so restricts the view from these gardens has a kind of terrible beauty that provides a setting for the castle. A mule can bring down from them a load of snow and ice in a matter of two hours, coming and going; for the entire chain abounds in gushing springs at every level, even above the snow-line. Vast numbers of orange trees have been planted in the gardens, set into urns of bronze, or the most rare varieties of marble, and all are embellished with carvings in low relief, with bronze and marble statues as fine as any you will see at Versailles or Marly. There are workshops where the best sculptors procurable from France and Italy were busily at work; but with all their charm and elegance of design, these gardens have one serious disadvantage, namely that the ground is hardest rock, with only a thin crust of soil covering it. This means that pick-axes, and sometimes gunpowder, are needed to excavate the lakes and ponds, the holes for planting trees, and the ditches for sunken fences. The rocks then have to be removed long distances on mule-back, and good soil brought back to fill the holes excavated for the trees; and this must be done for any new plantations or ponds that may be added in the future, if they extend the gardens. It is not only the expense, though this must be enormous; the worst of it is that no matter how deep they make the holes, the roots of the trees will continue to spread, and some will descend perpendicularly. Then, as soon as they touch the rock they will wither; the new soil will dry up and cease to provide moisture to feed them, and the result will be that in a very few years' time they will all be dead.

I saw no signs of any courtyard or entrance. They said that the two ends of the garden and the foot of the little hill rising to the plain of Segovia would provide the boundaries, and that there would be a lodge with a gate at either end. The main entrance would be at the side where we arrived, and only a narrow paved road would separate the castle from the gardens, nothing more. The nearest habitation was a gamekeeper's wretched little cottage, about half a league distant; there was no other house for a very long way, which evidently delighted the King of Spain, and brought favourable comments from the queen also. With my companions, I had the honour to follow Their Catholic Majesties wherever they went, first through the house, and then the gardens, all day long without any repose. They enjoyed showing me everything, and I enjoyed paying my court to them by admiring the various beauties, and the marvellous waterworks that are truly unique. Conversation never flagged all day, with Valouse most talkative, the queen always charming, and the king putting in an occasional word. They were so gracious as to speak also to my retinue, and were very happy giving their orders personally, and making themselves known to those who had charge of the buildings and gardens, under the direction of the Duke of Arco, who was controller of the whole project.

When we returned to Balzaïn, the king ordered me to follow him to his room, where, alone with him and the queen, I took my leave, afterwards thanking the gentlemen, more especially the Duke of Arco, who, with the best will in the world, had done so much for our comfort. He lent us the same coach and mounted escort for our return to Segovia, and next day it took us to the foot of the pass where our mules awaited us. We found our carriages where we had left them on the other side, and that same evening we arrived at Madrid. On the following morning I visited Grimaldo to recount our adventures; but I did not fail to mention that although the beauties of La Granja had charmed me, I was most unpleasantly impressed by the environment and situation of the castle. He said he had been sure that everything would turn out for the best, and was delighted that, after his first show of annoyance, the king had wished to show me his new buildings, and that the excursion should have quite restored me to favour. Grimaldo did not disguise his real opinion of the buildings and their situation, which we continued to discuss for some considerable time.

On 13 March, Their Catholic Majesties returned to Buen-Retiro. The arrival of my courier, my sudden journey to Balzaïn, despite the absolute prohibition, the whole day I had spent there, and all the kindnesses and favours shown me since my arrival in Spain had given rise to an absurd rumour, so widely spread that it took me entirely by surprise. It was said that I should shortly quit the post of French ambassador in order to become first minister of Spain. The common people who had enjoyed our lavish spending—for none of my party had given cause for complaint on that score—took to cheering me in the streets, congratulating me openly, even pursuing me into shops. They formed a crowd around my house, until I dispersed them as quickly and politely as possible, by assuring them that there was no truth in the rumour, and that I was about to return to France. I must however confess that such marks of esteem and popularity did not displease me, but what most moved me was a scene with the Marquis of Montalegre, steward of the household. When I met him at the entrance to the state apartments at Buen-Retiro, he rushed to embrace me, exclaiming that he was quite overjoyed to learn that I was remaining to be first minister. I thanked him for this strong proof of his esteem, but explained that I was leaving in a few days; whereupon he cast me a look of intense anger and indignation, turning sharp upon his heels and vanishing without so much as a bow or a single word in reply. Several other noblemen also congratulated me, and I answered them in the same way.

I must now repair a slight omission, although at this point it is somewhat out of place. I forgot to mention that for the journey over the pass, coming from and going to Balzaïn, the king and queen always used the queen's huge state coach, the one with seven glass windows. This meant that on the road over the mountains there was, almost the entire way, no more than two inches of solid ground between the wheels and the precipice. In many places, indeed, the outer wheels overhung the void for one or two hundred paces, sometimes even more. Vast numbers of peasants were pressed into service to hold the coach upright by means of long ropes, working in relays, and clambering over the rocks with all the discomfort and peril imaginable, both for the coach and its occupants. Nothing was ever done to improve the road, and the king and queen were never in the least alarmed. The ladies following them, however, nearly died of fright, notwithstanding that their coaches were made extremely narrow for that especial journey. As for the gentlemen, they rod on mule-back. I shall not comment of this most surprising custom.

On 21 March, I had my official, farewell audience of the king and queen separately. Once again the dignity and excellence of the king's speech took me by surprise. They were both infinitely gracious to me, and expressed their regret at my departure, as did the Prince of the Asturias. But there followed an event of a very different order which, ridiculous though it was, I cannot help recounting. When I and my retinue arrived for our final audience with the Princess of the Asturias, we found her standing upon a dais, with her ladies on one side, and on the other a group of grandees. I made my three bows and my complimentary address. I then waited for her to reply; but all in vain, for she never uttered a word. After a short silence, I tried to give her the means to reply by asking what messages she had for the King, the Infanta, Madame, and M. and Mme la Duchesse d'Orléans. She looked at me, and then let such a loud belch escape her that the entire room echoed with it.[1] I was so much surprised that it quite staggered me. Then came another as loud as the first. I did not know which way to look, having the greatest difficulty in preventing myself from laughing; but when I glanced to right and left, I saw them all with their hands to their mouths and their shoulders shaking. A third explosion, even more violent, created complete havoc, and sent me and my party flying in fits of laughter that were all the greater for having been so fiercely suppressed. Spanish gravity was altogether lost; chaos reigned, no bows were made, for every one of us, bursting with laughter, was doing his best to escape, while the princess remained perfectly serious, making no attempt to communicate with me in any other manner. We stopped in the adjoining room to give vent to our mirth and speak freely. It was not long before the king and queen learned the story of my audience, and they spoke of it in the Mall, after dinner. They were the first to laugh, which gave the rest their freedom, of which they took full advantage I received and paid a vast number of courtesy visits, and, since one is easily gratified, I came to the conclusion that I should be truly missed.

The greater part of these last days, I spent with those, especially Grimaldo, who in this short space of six months had allowed me to believe they were my friends. Great though my joy was at the thought of seeing Mme de Saint-Simon and my friends in France, I could not leave Spain without sorrow in parting from so many who had given me strong proofs of their affection, and from a nation which I had learned to esteem, even to

---

[1] Madame had written of her just before she went to Spain: 'she has the nastiest manners of any child I know. . . . I promise you that I shed no tears in bidding her farewell.'

respect, with particular gratitude to many gentlemen and ladies of high rank. With several of them I corresponded for a considerable time, and with Grimaldo, for the remainder of his life. My respectful, grateful devotion to the King and Queen of Spain persuaded me to take the honour of writing to them on all suitable occasions, more especially when I felt obliged to express my acute distress at the return of the Infanta.[1] I consulted the Bishop of Fréjus regarding this, resolved that if he should forbid me, I would ask Laulès to give my letter into their hands. They several times honoured me with most gracious replies, and whenever Spaniards of high rank came to visit France with their permission, they invariably directed them to assure me of their continued favour.

I left Madrid on 24 March, taking the Pampeluna road, and sleeping one night at Guadalajara, where the Princesse des Ursins met with disaster,[2] and where I visited the pantheon of the Duke of Infantado, as I have earlier described. The Governor of Pampeluna called at my lodging and tried to persuade me and all my company to sleep and sup at his house. After innumerable compliments, he allowed us to remain where we were, but only on condition of our all going to supper with him. The meal appeared on the instant; very lavish, cooked in the Spanish way, most evil-tasting. Our host's manners were polite, well-bred, and easy, and we were treated to a reputedly marvellous dish, which turned out to be a vast bowl filled with cods' roes, fried in oil. It was not worth eating and the oil was bad; but I ate all I could manage, out of politeness. We thanked the governor, who escorted us back to our lodging, returning next morning to bid us farewell.

A little farther on, we hired mules for the crossing of the Pyrenees. This way the road is shorter and easier than by Vitoria; but even so it was very rough because the Spaniards (although they levelled it for the passage of artillery after they gained a French king) had deliberately broken it up when the Abbé Dubois, in order to please the English and so gain his hat, forced M. le Duc d'Orléans to make war on Spain.

We slept next at Roncesvalles, a horrible place, quite fallen into ruins, the loneliest and most dismal spot that I encountered during the entire journey. The church is profoundly uninteresting, and so are the remains of the ancient monastery, where we lodged. The Abbé called on me wearing a long green cloak, which I thought extremely odd. We did not stay long. They showed us Roland's sword and other fictitious relics. Early on the

---

[1] In 1725 Louis XV was 15 and more than ripe for matrimony; Maria Ana Victoria was only five, and the marriage was not to be celebrated and consummated for another ten years. It was decided that the Infanta must be sent back to her parents, whatever offence this caused them, and a marriageable wife chosen for him. The bride chosen was twenty-two-year-old Marie Leczinska, daughter of Stanislas I, the deposed King of Poland. The rejected Infanta married in 1729 Joseph of Braganza (1714–1777), King of Portugal from 1750.

[2] Actually, disaster overtook the Princesse des Ursins seven miles farther on, at Jadraqué: see II, pp. 397–398.

following day we left that unpleasant place, reaching Bayonne on Maundy Thursday, in rain that had never for a moment ceased to pour since we left the mountains. Apparently rain dare not pass the Pyrenees; I had seen scarcely any in Spain, where the sky is usually cloudless and there is seldom any wind. D'Adoncourt,[1] despite our protests, insisted on lodging us, and gave us the most sumptuous and delicious meals. I attended the cathedral services on all the Holy Days, and received all the honours due to a provincial governor. I had the honour to pay my court more than once to the Queen-dowager of Spain, who commanded me to dine on Easter Day at her town house. The Sieur de Bruges[2] did the honours with the utmost courtesy, and because they knew I was starved of fish, they offered it to me in great variety and such admirable condition that I chose it in preference to meat. I went later to thank the queen and take my leave of her, and she thereupon presented me with a very beautiful gold sword, but without diamonds, for which she apologized. The bishop absolutely insisted on our dining with him next day. There was good company, good food, and an abundance of fish, for which I still found ample space.

On 13 April we reached Loches, about five in the afternoon, and I decided to sleep there because I had a host of things to tell the Duchesse de Beauvilliers, who was at one of her estates only six leagues away.[3] After writing my letter to her, I sent it by special courier, so as to run no risk of its being opened. I arrived fairly early at Étampes, on the 14th, and slept there; and on the 15th, by ten o'clock in the morning, I was at Châtres,[4] where Mme de Saint-Simon was due to dine and sleep, so that we might have all the pleasure of meeting again and being together, telling each other all, at leisure and alone, as we could not hope to be, in Paris, during the first days after my return. She arrived an hour later, escorted by the Duc d'Humières and Louville, at the little château lent us by the Duc d'Arpajon. The day spent there seemed very short to us, and so did the morning of the next one, 16 April.

While we were talking, at ten in the morning, Belle-Isle[5] appeared. After many congratulations and expressions of good will, with praise for my conduct in Spain, and my letters, he gave me a short description of the situation at the Court, saying nothing of precedence and little of the cabal, but offering the Duc de Noailles as the most dangerous opponent of M. le Duc d'Orléans and his government. He took great care to remind me of my deep aversion, and impress me with my need to seize this opportunity to ruin him for ever. He continued by mentioning Dubois's excellent opinion of my merits, and how he had been sent with all dispatch by the cardinal

---

[1] Dominique Stuart d'Adoncourt. He was in command of the Roussillon army and an old friend of Saint-Simon's.

[2] André Druillet, comptroller of the queen-dowager's household. See also p. 371 above.

[3] She had an estate at Saint-Aignan-sur-Cher.

[4] Now Arpajon.

[5] See note 4, p. 233 above.

to acquaint me with what had happened, in the belief that my love for France, and my personal attachment to M. le Duc d'Orléans, would lead me to support Cardinal Dubois in his further plans, for which he had eagerly been awaiting my return; in other words, the dismissal of the Duc de Noailles and the cancelling of his appointment as first captain of the bodyguard.

This discussion, on that one subject, lasted more than an hour, and ended with my begging for time in which to reflect further. Belle-Isle dined with us almost immediately after, for we wished to arrive very early in Paris, and he left before us.

I stayed no longer than was required to change coaches before going to the Palais Royal and straight to Cardinal Dubois. He hurried out to meet me, giving me the warmest welcome possible, and taking me at once, without pausing or returning, to M. le Duc d'Orléans, whose greetings were quite as warm, and infinitely more sincere. He was in his smaller study at the end of the gallery. We sat down at his writing-table, I facing him, the cardinal at one end. I told them many things and answered a host of questions. I then spoke to M. le Duc d'Orléans of the Princess of the Asturias and her conduct towards Their Catholic Majesties, and of their kindness and patience. After these grave matters, I amused him with the story of my farewell audience, and he laughed heartily. He then told me of the resignations from the Council of Regency, whereat the cardinal mentioned the cabal, without going into details, but saying that His Royal Highness could not have done otherwise than dismiss the Chancellor. I let him finish, and then replied that I found it all most disturbing, but that having only just arrived, I needed to learn more. Turning at once to face M. le Duc d'Orléans, and speaking to him alone, I said that since the Chancellor was banished to Fresnes for an action which I myself would probably have taken, I hoped His Royal Highness would not object to my visiting him without delay. These words silenced the Regent and made him look down, while the cardinal, flushed with anger, looked wildly in every other direction. I do not for a moment believe that they hoped to persuade me back to the Council, but they were surprised at my firm support of the men who had resigned; and my frank declaration of loyalty to the Chancellor had stung the Regent personally, and embarrassed the cardinal in his rôle of courtier. I was not displeased with the state to which I had reduced them, nor with the longish silence that resulted. Before departing, I asked permission of the Regent to resign my peerage in favour of my elder son. It seemed wrong to me that, destined by birth to succeed me as a duke and peer, he should not enjoy similar rank to that which I had gained for his younger brother with the Spanish grandee-ship.

I went from the Palais Royal to the Tuileries to make my bow to the King, at his supper, after which I made him the same request. Thence I returned home to inform my son, who took the title Duc de Ruffec,[1] and I there and then made him a present of the jewels surrounding the King of Spain's portrait, which Grimaldo had brought me after my first audience. The stones were valued at eighty thousand livres by the best Parisian jewellers. It was the most expensive present ever given to an ambassador by the King of Spain, and I had great pleasure in ordering a most magnificent 'Fleece' to be made for him.

I had scarcely arrived home before it became necessary to conclude a marriage for my daughter[2] that had been proposed before my departure for Spain. Some women are so constructed that life is happier for them if they live it unwed, on the revenues from the dowry they would otherwise have received. Mme de Saint-Simon and I had good reason to think that our child was such a one, and we had decided to treat her in that way. My mother,[3] however, thought differently, and she was accustomed to rule. It seemed that the Prince de Chimay[4] believed that in my present situation I might do marvels for him, if he married my daughter. I had frankly revealed my mind to him, and had shown him how little reliance should be placed on such expectations; and I refused to take any action until after my return, so as to give him ample time, in my absence, for further reflection. He had, however, continued to press Mme de Saint-Simon, and she had not discouraged him. Shortly after my arrival, he became so importunate that I could no longer withhold my consent, and the wedding took place at Meudon, with as little ceremony and as few guests as was possible in the circumstances. His family name was Hénin-Liétard; his forebears the Comtes de Bossu were famous for their splendid alliances, their rich estates in the Low Countries, and the high offices which they held under Charles V, and more recently. Their ambition was to trace their ancestry back to the ancient princedom of Alsace, though their own line was old and famous enough to require no such questionable embellishments. The present Prince de Chimay did notable service in Flanders, during the war that followed the death of Charles II. He then went to Spain, where he paid his court to the Princesse des Ursins, and she made him a Spanish grandee. Later, he returned to France and married the Duc de Nevers's daughter, who died a few years after, leaving him childless. He was extremely handsome, with a most agreeable countenance, while

[1] Until then his title had been Vidame de Chartres, Marquis de Ruffec.

[2] Charlotte de Saint-Simon. See I, p. 83; II, p. 342. She was horribly deformed and a hypochondriac.

[3] His mother, Charlotte de l'Aubespine, was eighty at that time; but Saint-Simon hinted once before, at the time when his wife was objecting to being made the Duchesse de Berry's lady-in-waiting, that she was a veritable dragon. See I, p. 83n; II, p. 74n.

[4] Charles Louis Antoine de Hénin d'Alsace, Prince de Chimay (died 1740). His first wife had been Diane Gabrielle Victoire Mazzarini-Mancini, daughter of the Duc de Nevers. He was Governor of Luxembourg, and first peer of Hainault, a lieutenant-general of Philip V's armies, captain-general of artillery in the Spanish army of the Low Countries, and a Grandee of Spain 1708.

VERSAILLES IN 1722. BY JEAN BAPTISTE MARTIN

THE CORONATION OF LOUIS XV AT RHEIMS, 25 OCTOBER 1722.
BY JEAN BAPTISTE MARTIN

THE GRAND TRIANON FROM THE AVENUE, 1722. BY PIERRE DENIS MARTIN

THE REGENT, PHILIPPE D'ORLÉANS, WITH A PORTRAIT
OF MME DE PARABÈRE. BY NICOLAS DE LARGILLIÈRE

THE 'LIT DE JUSTICE' HELD ON 22 FEBRUARY
1723 WHEN LOUIS XV REACHED HIS MAJORITY.
BY NICOLAS LANCRET

Photo : Lauros- Giraudor

his manners and bearing were those of a very great nobleman, which indeed he was by the size and number of his estates (though most of them were in the hands of his creditors, and his finances generally were in a state of great disorder). Yet he was a man without principles who, for all his valour and fine talk, conducted himself and his affairs most improperly, being a prey to all manner of whims and ambitions. The Duchess of Sforza, in whose drawing-room he spent every evening during his earlier marriage, truly predicted all that I later discovered of him.

[*In this second marriage, he certainly appears to have been both brave and calculating. This is what the Duc de Luynes says about it in his* Mémoires : '*It is altogether too strange a marriage to pass without remark. Mlle de Saint-Simon is so dwarfish, so deformed, so frightful to look at that M. and Mme de Saint-Simon had had no thoughts of marriage for her, and sought only to hide her from view. M. de Saint-Simon was a great favourite of the late M. le Duc d'Orléans; which appears to be the reason why M. de Chimay asked for his daughter's hand. M. de Saint-Simon, in his usual emphatic style, answered with a minute, almost exaggerated (if that were possible) description of his daughter's imperfections, adding that if M. de Chimay was relying on his reputed influence over M. le Duc d'Orléans, he had best understand once and for all that his future father-in-law would have nothing to do with any affair that might concern him. M. de Chimay none the less persisted. He lived for some years in Paris, seeing his wife from time to time, for she continued to live, as before, in her father's house.*']

Only a few days afterwards there was another wedding at our Meudon home: that of the Abbé de Saint-Simon's sister with the Comte de Laval,[1] at that time no more than a maréchal de camp, but now a Maréchal de France. His name and that well-deserved reward for long and distinguished service make any comment from me unnecessary. Mme de Saint-Simon had always kept a kindly eye on this young girl, and had invited her to stay during my absence in Spain. She was extraordinarily pretty, with a gentle, modest air that was most charming. Her nature was better even than her looks, for she was bright and agreeable, with a piety and virtue that have never been challenged. In the highest Society she was perfectly at home, and her conduct has been the greatest assistance to her husband in his career. He was seeking an alliance and a family capable of advancing him. A small governorship went to him on his marriage,[2] and his bride received a pension.

The decision was at last made for the King to leave Paris and thenceforward hold his Court at Versailles. He drove there in state, on 15 June, and the Infanta followed him next day. They occupied the apartments of Louis XIV and the late Queen, and the Maréchal de Villeroy had his

---

[1] The marriage was between Guy Claude Montmorency, Comte, later Maréchal, de Laval, and Marie Elisabeth de Rouvroy de Saint-Simon, the daughter of Eustache Titus, Marquis de Saint-Simon: see II, pp. 265–266.

[2] The governorship of Philippeville.

lodging in the offices behind the King's studies. Cardinal Dubois was in sole charge of the château, as M. Colbert, and after him M. de Louvois, had been in their day. He was making great strides towards that goal of all his ambitions, the post of first minister, and for that reason aimed, so far as it was possible, at ousting M. le Duc d'Orléans. In Paris, many of those without hope of a lodging at Versailles, or of going there, except seldom and briefly if at all, had free access to the prince. The change would interfere with his supper-parties among his *roués* and the women who were little better. Dubois well knew that the prince would return to them whenever possible, and he therefore planned to hinder him by continually presenting matters requiring a decision. Such frustrations were sure to bore and annoy M. le Duc d'Orléans, and be most effective in inclining him to hand over responsibility to Dubois, as first minister, thus purchasing his own liberty. Nothing then would prevent the Regent's return to Paris, his box at the Opéra, and his odious suppers, and the cardinal would be left to reign in his stead.

Although my return from Spain, and my conduct towards those who had left the Council, had greatly displeased Cardinal Dubois, and although my opposition to the arrest of the Duc de Noailles was something for which he never forgave me, he thought it premature to display any ill will. Thus nothing hindered my familiar intercourse with M. le Duc d'Orléans (Dubois actually spoke of it with a show of approval mixed with deference); but where State business was concerned, or any matter greater than trifles or Court affairs, I was kept in utter darkness, save for scraps dropped by M. le Duc d'Orléans in our private talks, without any encouragement from me. On several occasions the cardinal offered to keep me fully informed; he wished all the concealment I was encountering to appear to be the Regent's doing. None the less, apart from the fact that the prince told me so much that it was plainly not he who desired secrecy, I knew Dubois too well to be duped by his offers and his praise. He was really at a loss how to separate me from M. le Duc d'Orléans; he feared my opposition to his appointment; he wanted to keep me out of State affairs, but at the same time thought he needed to flatter me. Thus it was that he overwhelmed me with amiability, and surpassed himself whenever we happened to be together with the Regent. In so doing his plain intention was to show His Royal Highness that he did his utmost to mollify me, making it harder for me to oppose his plans, and reducing the effect of any arguments of mine in matters where we disagreed.

One such very soon presented itself, the proposed exile of the Duc de Noailles. Dubois thought it best to say nothing to me, but M. le Duc d'Orléans mentioned it as something he was being urged to do. I asked why, but he offered no reason beyond that of the supposed cabal; whereupon I declared that I had been shown no proof of any conspiracy, and even had there been one, why banish the Duc de Noailles rather than the others? Until then, I continued, he had remained content with exiling the Chancellor; that in itself was sufficient of a bombshell and might well have been dispensed with; to descend upon someone else without producing further cause would be tantamount to threatening the Maréchaux de Villars, d'Estrées, Tallard, Huxelles, even the Maréchal de Villeroy in person, for they were the reputed leaders of the so-called plot. To make enemies of so many important personages, held in such high esteem, appeared suicidal to me. As for M. de Noailles himself, in my opinion, he was of the wrong kind to be gelded, but should either be left entire, or totally obliterated. I could see no reason or justice in destroying him then—a man who, along with his whole family, was so firmly and nobly established, who had for so long enjoyed the Regent's trust, and controlled his country's finances—without clear proof of some dreadful crime for which he faced the law. A man like Noailles would not rot in exile. The King's majority was near; when he returned, his post of captain of the guard would bring him constantly before the King, and his clever brain would devise some means of making himself agreeable, so as to win favour for M. le Duc d'Orléans's enemies. His Royal Highness would then regret having alienated him without due cause, especially since he would be capable of revenge. I said finally that in view of my known detestation of the Duc de Noailles, my opinion should be worth that of a dozen neutral persons.

This question of exile hung for a week in the balance, during which time the cardinal did everything possible to work on my hatred and self-interest. I had no desire, however, to further his ambitions; nor would I indulge my loathing at the expense of M. le Duc d'Orléans. The delay was not for long. Five weeks later, or thereabouts, when I believed that all was for- gotten, I went to the Palais Royal, for from Meudon where we lived, I saw M. le Duc d'Orléans either at Versailles or in Paris, on the days appointed for my visits. I was much surprised to find La Vrillière waiting alone in the little gallery outside the study, for it was not his time, and I asked him what had brought him. He said he had a message for M. le Duc d'Orléans. I at once entered the study, where I found the prince looking somewhat disturbed, and I asked him also why La Vrillière was in the gallery. 'It is to do the deed,' he answered. 'What?' I said, 'What deed?' 'The exile of the Duc de Noailles,' said he. 'No!' I exclaimed, 'not after all I said and all my arguments! Truly, Monsieur, you have not reflected'; and I began to rehearse once more the most important reasons. We had been standing; but immediately he began to walk, head down, round and round in that tiny study, as he always did when something bothered him. This exercise and my speech, interspersed with some feeble replies, lasted a good quarter of an hour. Then there was silence, as he stood, his nose pressed up against the window pane; after which he turned to face me, saying dismally, 'It is too late now.' I could see that there had been a struggle and that he knew I was right; but also that he had feared the cardinal too much to withstand him. I shrugged my shoulders and lowered my head, remarking that it was for him to decide and that I hoped he had done wisely. Thereupon he opened the study door, called La Vrillière, and spoke to him for a few moments, almost through the crack of the door. Thus the deed was done, and that same evening the Duc de Noailles received his marching orders. Next morning he went to his estates near Turenne, and there played the martyr, carrying the bishop's cope in religious processions, and singing in the parish choir. Everybody there made mock of him, as did the Parisians when it became known, for in order to pay his court to the Regent, he had kept an actress there since the beginning of the Regency, after having most assiduously read his breviary, kept his Lents, and attended the services in the chapel from the time of his return from Spain until the late King's death, all in order to be reconciled with King Louis and his aunt de Maintenon, in which last he failed.

With the Duc de Noailles exiled, Cardinal Dubois still had to rid himself of the Maréchal de Villeroy, his most formidable opponent. Each day that passed without the announcement of his new post seemed an age to him; but try as he might, he could not persuade M. le Duc d'Orléans to issue the dismissal, and to act with Villeroy still in office was too dangerous. The Maréchal was certain to create a most fearful uproar at the news of the first ministership, which would be the signal for many others to protest, who without him might have stayed mute. Such anxious thoughts and the seeming hopelessness of ever finding a solution occupied Dubois's entire mind and made him even worse tempered, while the affairs of State remained wholly neglected. At last he determined to make a final effort to win over the Maréchal; but not daring to proceed alone, he pressed Cardinal Bissy into his service, encouraged by that prelate's conduct in the matters of the constitution and the King's confessional, so recently given over to the Jesuits. Dubois accordingly confided to him his difficulties, the uncalled-for malevolence of the Maréchal de Villeroy,[1] his own vain efforts at appeasement for the honour of the State, and the sake of appearances. He then urged the good which only Bissy might effect by curbing the Maréchal's constant rudeness, and disposing him to regard Dubois as in no way meriting such rancour.

A mutual attachment to Mme de Maintenon, the intrigues around the constitution, and a hatred of Cardinal de Noailles had united Villeroy and Bissy in a close alliance. That smug, self-seeking prelate now eagerly seized the chance to assist a colleague. High though he had climbed, his present rank was to him no more than a step on the ladder to even greater heights, for now that two cardinals were members of the Regency Council, he saw no reason why he should not make a third. He thus turned all his mind to appeasing the Maréchal de Villeroy, and with such perfect success that he soon extracted a message of peace. Picture the two cardinals in bliss,

---

[1] Ever since the cardinals were admitted to the Council.

with Dubois instructing Bissy to say the most agreeable things to Villeroy, coupled with assurances that the desire of his heart was to pay him a visit. Bissy relayed that most pleasing statement; but Villeroy, not to be out-done in a show of willingness, offered instead to accompany him when calling on Cardinal Dubois.

It so happened that they selected a Tuesday morning, when some unusual business, I forget exactly what, had caused me, at that precise moment, to go to M. le Duc d'Orléans at Versailles.[1] It was the day of the cardinal's weekly audiences to the foreign ambassadors, who were waiting their turns in the great drawing-room before his study, for since time immemorial it has been the custom to see them in the order of their coming, so as to avoid quarrels over precedence. Bissy and Villeroy arrived to find Dubois closeted with the Russian minister. The servants desired to inform him of an event so altogether extraordinary as the presence of the Maréchal de Villeroy, but that the Maréchal would not allow, and he sat down with Bissy to wait, on one of the sofas. Shortly afterwards Dubois appeared with the departing ambassador, and immedi-ately espied the sofa with its noble burden. All else became invisible to him. He rushed forward, eager to do public homage, full of regret for having been forestalled, when he had only waited for a day to be named, entreating them both to enter his study, explaining to the waiting am-bassadors that the Maréchal de Villeroy's duties and his zeal forbade his leaving the King for more than a moment.

The conversation began with an exchange of compliments, to a suitable accompaniment by Bissy. There followed protests of good will from Cardinal Dubois, and soft replies from the Maréchal. As time went on, however, the sweet sound of his own voice led Villeroy to speak frankly, then to speak home truths, and gradually, warming to his work, to utter harsh and bitter verities that had all the ring of insults. Dubois, in his amazement, pretended at first to misunderstand; and Bissy, with the Maréchal's venom increasing, rightly thought it time to intervene by reminding Villeroy of the original purpose of the visit. But the rising tide of his eloquence had borne him away, and there burst from his lips a perfect stream of abuse, coupled with most violent accusations. In vain Bissy tried to quieten him; nothing he could say had the effect of soothing, indeed, it seemed to excite Villeroy to still more extravagant flights. By this time, Dubois was too much distressed to speak, and Bissy, though justifiably angry, was helpless, because in losing his temper the Maréchal had blocked the only exit. Shouting more and more loudly, he proceeded to threats, swearing that now things were in the open there could be no going back; sooner or later, he said, he would do Dubois an injury, of that he gave him fair warning. 'You have the power!' he exclaimed. 'Everyone crawls to you;

---

[1] Saint-Simon's knack of being present 'at the precise moment' of great events seems almost uncanny.

no one dares oppose you. Noblemen count for nothing with you! Believe me, if you want safety, you had better use your power to arrest me—that is, if you dare!' And he then proceeded to pile Pelion on Ossa by defying and insulting his victim, who honestly believed he had as much chance of invading heaven as of arresting the great Maréchal de Villeroy. You may well imagine that Bissy had not remained silent; he now seized Villeroy by the shoulders; pushed him towards the door; opened it; thrust him through it, and removed himself also. Dubois followed him, more dead than alive. He had to assume a good face for the benefit of the ambassadors; but though all three did their best to compose themselves, not one of the waiting ministers doubted that an appalling quarrel had taken place. Versailles was soon ringing with the news, and the Maréchal enlightened everyone still further by boastful accounts, amid derisive laughter, of his defiance and challenge.

I had been working and chatting a long time with M. le Duc d'Orléans. He had gone to the privy, and I was standing behind his desk tidying his papers, when Cardinal Dubois burst into the room, his eyes starting out of his head. Seeing me alone, he shouted rather than inquired where the Regent had gone. I said he was in the privy, and asked what had happened to send him so distracted. 'I'm ruined, I'm ruined!' he cried, scurrying to the privy door; and he spoke so loud and so explosively that M. le Duc d'Orléans heard him and emerged almost running to ask what was the matter and join me at the table. Dubois's explanation (his habitual stammer greatly increased by anger and fright) was far more detailed and took much longer even than this account of mine. He ended by declaring that after so many insults, such a vile and unmerited attack, he could neither conduct the business of the State, nor even appear at the Court while the Maréchal de Villeroy still remained. M. le Duc d'Orléans must choose between them.

I can scarcely describe M. le Duc d'Orléans's consternation, or mine for that matter. We could not believe our ears; we thought we must be dreaming. He turned, looking horribly dismayed, to ask my opinion, and I imagined he did so because I had formerly opposed the Maréchal de Ville-roy's removal. I said nothing. He continued to press me. At last I stated that I had always thought it dangerous to dismiss him, and was still so minded, although the King's being near his majority somewhat eased the situation. Now, however, after this appalling scene, I was convinced of its being far more of a risk to leave him with the King, for no one could be sure that he might not draw his sword against the Regent himself. His challenge seemed like the words of a man who knew he deserved arrest but believed no one would dare to make the attempt, and, being so persuaded, had become ungovernable. Since the first day of the Regency, he had conspired against the Regent; all His Royal Highness's endeavours had failed to appease him, and now he had come into the open with a challenge that was no less than rebellion. Such was my opinion, for which His Royal Highness had asked. As for action: it needed reflection to see how to proceed with a suddenness that would leave him no time for self-defence.

Next day when I visited M. le Duc d'Orléans, I found him in conference with Cardinal Dubois and Monsieur le Duc, who had already learned of the quarrel. Dubois departed soon after, and M. le Duc d'Orléans sat down at his writing-table, with Monsieur le Duc and myself on the opposite side, for the time had come to establish our plans. After a brief introduction, the Regent called upon me to speak, and I repeated my views as shortly as possible. Monsieur le Duc said he agreed with me, for if Villeroy were left in office the only hope for us would be a moonlight flit—those were his very words.[1] We then began to discuss ways and means.

I said we had two problems, a pretext for the arrest, and the manner of it. A pretext was entirely necessary, one strong enough to convince the doubters, and silence even his best friends. Most important of all, we must not let it appear that his dismissal was in any way due to his attack on Dubois, monstrous though that was. The public, who loathed Dubois, would recall his gutter-origins and instantly take sides with his illustrious attacker; the punishment would appear out of all proportion, and provoke a public outcry. Fortunately, I declared, M. le Duc d'Orléans already had the perfect weapon in his grasp. He would remember, I said, how often he had complained of the impossibility of ever speaking to the King alone, or even of having a few private words with him, in his crowded study. If ever he made such an attempt, Villeroy would step forward and, in the sight of all beholders, insert his head between them. Later, if an explanation were demanded, he would say that as the King's governor he could permit no person, not even the Regent of France, to be alone with him, even for a moment. That, I declared, was sheer impudence, when the person concerned was the Regent, a Grandson of France, and the King's closest kin. It was also completely outrageous at a time when, for the good of the State, M. le Duc d'Orléans needed to instruct the King on matters that might be discussed only in private, to the exclusion even of the Maréchal de Villeroy. To make governorship an excuse for interfering between the King and the Regent was to arouse the most wicked and unnatural suspicions, which was something no one could forgive, and seemed to provide a perfect reason for action.

M. le Duc d'Orléans, I added, must lay a trap, and when Villeroy was caught, demand an explanation. Then, with all respect to the King, he should take a high tone, but not too much, only sufficient to make Villeroy feel his authority, acting in the King's name. In his present state of arrogance, neither the Maréchal nor anyone else would expect an arrest to follow, so accustomed were they to the prince's patience. I had scarcely

---

[1] *N'y avait qu'à mettre la clef sous la porte*: to go without leaving an address. It is possible that Saint-Simon invented this expression.

finished speaking before the Regent exclaimed, 'You have taken the words out of my mouth. Had you not spoken, I was about to suggest it. Do you not agree, Monsieur?' said he then, turning to Monsieur le Duc. That prince nodded assent, and so the matter was settled.

I returned that same evening to Meudon, where many of Mme de Saint-Simon's friends and mine often slept, and where it had become the fashion to dine or sup on the journey to Paris or Versailles. We thus always had much company. All the talk was of the quarrel, and people blamed the Maréchal de Villeroy; but no one mentioned consequences because M. le Duc d'Orléans's forbearance made them appear so unlikely.

On the evening of Sunday, 12 August, M. le Duc d'Orléans went to work with the King, as he was accustomed to do several times a week, and because it was summer, the hour chosen was after his ride, from which he returned early. The work on this occasion was to explain the disposal of vacant posts and benefices, the appointment of magistrates and intendants, and the reasons for various nominations. When they had finished, M. le Duc d'Orléans desired to take the King alone into one of the back studies for a private talk. Villeroy objected. M. le Duc d'Orléans, having set the trap, watched with enormous pleasure to see it close. He then politely explained that the approaching majority made it entirely necessary for him, in whom the supreme authority had reposed, to instruct the monarch on many matters in private talks, to which no third party, no matter what his office, might be admitted. Only consideration for the Maréchal de Villeroy's feelings had postponed these sessions, and now the Regent had cause to think that the delay had been too long.

Villeroy, furiously shaking his wig, replied that he very well knew what was due to the Regent, the King and, for that matter, to his own office. He was responsible for the King's person and must therefore know all, which was why there could be no private talks with His Royal Highness; as for sessions tête-à-tête in another room and out of sight, that was something which he absolutely refused to allow. At those words, giving him a cold stare, M. le Duc d'Orléans said, as though speaking to a servant, that he forgot himself, and had best mind his words when addressing the Regent of France. Then, adding that the royal presence had spared him a well-merited reprimand, M. le Duc d'Orléans bowed low and left the room. M. de Villeroy accompanied him a few yards, muttering and gesticulating angrily; but the Regent went on his way, seeming neither to see nor hear, leaving the King vastly astonished, and Fleury trying to hide a smile. The general opinion was that despite his arrogance, Villeroy was at heart no more than an abject courtier, and that he had now learned the difference between insulting Cardinal Dubois, and challenging M. le Duc d'Orléans in the royal presence. That indeed was true, for less than two hours later he was heard to say how distressed he would be if M. le Duc d'Orléans thought him in any way discourteous. He had only done his duty, Villeroy added, and would call next day to explain matters. He believed that His Royal Highness would understand.

For reasons of security all the necessary plans had been made the day before. Nothing remained but to give the orders when the hour of the Maréchal's visit became known. Beyond M. le Duc d'Orléans's bedroom was a large room with four tall windows leading out into the garden, on the same level and only two paces distant. One pair was on the side opposite the fireplace, the other in the wall that faced the entrance. All four opened like doors and extended from floor to ceiling. It was a corner room, used as a waiting-room for courtiers, and stood at right angles to the little study where M. le Duc d'Orléans habitually worked, and where he used to see the more distinguished persons who desired an interview. When the time came, Artagnan,[1] captain of the grey musketeers, knowing what he had to do, stationed himself in this large room, with several officers of his own regiment and some veterans at hand, in case of need. All knew that something was brewing, but not a word of the real truth. Officers of the light horse were lined up outside the windows. They, too, were in total ignorance, and so also were the many members of M. le Duc d'Orléans's staff, on duty in his bedroom as well as in the waiting-room.

Everything was in readiness when noon came and the arrival of the Maréchal de Villeroy amid the usual commotion. He was, however, alone, for his chair-men and following had been made to wait some distance off, beyond the guardroom. Picture him making an entrance, stopping, looking around, advancing a few steps with a great show of politeness for the benefit of spectators. He demands to know the whereabouts of M. le Duc d'Orléans, and is told that he is working in his study. He thereupon begins to shout, declaring that the Regent will see him immediately, or he will force an entry and ask the reason why. At that precise moment La Fare, captain of M. le Duc d'Orléans's guard, steps in front to prevent him, and asks for his sword. The Maréchal is convulsed with rage, and all the bystanders are agog. Le Blanc appears with his carrying-chair, hitherto concealed, and plants it before him. Villeroy shouts for help; his legs fail him; he is toppled into the chair; the doors are closed and, in the twinkling of an eye, he is carried into the garden by one of the side windows, with Artagnan and La Fare on either side, and light horse and musketeers before and behind. The pace quickens. They dash down the steps of the Orangery, on the shrubbery side, to find the gates open and a coach-and-six standing without. The chair is set down. The Maréchal, still fuming, is forced into the coach. Artagnan climbs in beside him. A musketeer officer gets up in front with a King's gentleman in ordinary; twenty mounted musketeers with their officers surround them. 'Whip up, coachman!' and they are gone.

[1] Joseph de Montesquiou, Comte d'Artagnan (1650–1729), already mentioned, II, p. 263. Not Alexandre Dumas's hero, but a captain of Saint-Simon's old regiment.

When all was peace again, M. le Duc d'Orléans experienced some embarrassment in breaking the news to the King. He entered the study, and dismissed the courtiers, leaving only those whose posts gave them a right to be present, but they were not many. At his first words, the King flushed scarlet and his eyes filled with tears; he thrust his face into the back of a chair and did not say a word, refusing all attempts to persuade him to go out or play a game. At supper he would scarcely touch his food; but wept bitterly, and afterwards, he had a sleepless night. Next day and on the one after (the 14th) things were very little better.

That same day, as I left the table after dinner, one of my footmen informed me that a courier had come with a letter from Cardinal Dubois, but that he had thought it best not to give it me at the table. I opened it. The cardinal besought me to go to him immediately at the offices of the Steward of Versailles, and to bring a trusty servant who could ride faster than the post to La Trappe, after our conference. He said I was not to rack my brains, for he would tell all when we met. I at once sent for my coach, but it was like an age before it arrived because the stables, at Meudon, are a long way from the new château, where we lodged. The demand for a courier to ride to La Trappe completely bewildered me, for I could think of nothing capable of distressing Dubois, so soon after Villeroy's arrest. Could this concern the constitution, or some traitor hiding in the monastery? All manner of strange ideas filled my mind on the journey to Versailles.

When I arrived, I saw Cardinal Dubois waving and gesticulating at an upper window, and by the time I had alighted he had hurried down to meet me at the foot of the steps. His first words were to ask if I had brought the courier, and I indicated a servant of mine who knew his way everywhere, from having been so long in my service. Dubois was well acquainted with him, this man having kept him company in my waiting-room when, as 'little Abbé Dubois', he came to my house so often in days gone by. As we mounted the staircase, he told me of the King's distress, apparently much augmented by the sudden disappearance of the Bishop of Fréjus. He had not been at Versailles on the previous night, and no one knew anything, save that he was neither at Villeroy nor on his way thither. The King was utterly prostrated by his departure, and everyone else was troubled because, unless he had taken refuge at La Trappe,[1] his whereabouts could not be imagined. Dubois took me straight to M. le Duc d'Orléans, who was alone and deeply concerned, pacing up and down in his study. As soon as he saw me, he cried out that he did not know what would become of him, or how to pacify the King, who kept calling for Monsieur de Fréjus, and would listen to no explanations, but cried out continually that he was deserted.

---

[1] Fleury, having been Villeroy's assistant, might well have wondered where the next blow would fall.

After a spate of jeremiads amid a most marked absence of ideas, Dubois begged me to go and write to La Trappe. In M. le Duc d'Orléans's study all was confusion, everyone was speaking at once; it would have been impossible amid all that noise to sit down and write at his table, as I so often did when we were alone. My lodging was in the new wing and probably shut, for no one expected me that day, and I accordingly decided to go to Pezé's[1] room close by, and write there; but I had scarcely finished before Pezé himself appeared, calling out, 'No need for a letter; he's found, he's found! Come back at once to M. le Duc d'Orléans.' He then proceeded to explain that one of the prince's staff who knew that Fréjus was a friend of the Lamoignons, had met Courson[2] in the great courtyard as he came from a meeting, and had asked if he had any news. Courson replied that he could not imagine the reason for such a to-do. Fréjus had merely gone to Bâville to sleep; whereupon M. le Duc d'Orléans's gentleman had taken Courson to His Royal Highness's study.

When Pezé and I returned all was quiet. Cardinal Dubois was advising M. le Duc d'Orléans to give the King the good news, and tell him that he was sending to Bâville to fetch back his tutor. The Regent thereupon departed, and I waited with Dubois. When he reappeared, it was to say that the King was comforted and that Fréjus would return next morning. On the following day, M. le Duc d'Orléans gave him the warmest of welcomes, made light of everything, coaxed away his fears, explained that it was only in order to spare him that he had not been warned of the arrest. All of which was made easier by Fréjus's hatred for the Maréchal with his rudeness, jealousy, and sudden whims. In his heart, Fréjus was glad of Villeroy's exile and of the chance to rule the King unhindered. He was asked to explain to the King the need for Villeroy's dismissal, and to promise to work loyally with the Duc de Charost, the newly appointed governor. It subsequently appeared that Villeroy had convinced King Louis that without his vigilance he would have been poisoned, and that had been the reason for the tears. When Fréjus also vanished, the King became almost frantic, believing that his removal was designed to facilitate the murder. With Fréjus's prompt return, half his terrors were allayed, and continued good health dispelled the remainder.

The Maréchal de Villeroy was allowed a week at Villeroy to rest and recover. Then, since parted from the King he presented no kind of danger, he was sent to Lyons where, in the few years remaining to him, he fulfilled his functions as governor of the town and province. It was none the less thought prudent to keep a close watch on him, and Liboy[3] was

---

[1] Hubert de Courtavel, Marquis de Pezé (1680–1753), who had been one of the King's gentlemen since 1716.

[2] Guillaume Urbain de Lamoignon, Comte de Courson (1674–1732). He was the eldest son of Monsieur de Bâville, and grandson of that hated Bâville who was the cruel Intendant of Languedoc. See I, pp. 212f.

[3] See note 2, p. 121 above.

accordingly sent to limit his authority by a show of vigilance and restraint
that effectively served to destroy his prestige. When he arrived at Lyons he
refused the honours, for much of his old arrogance had gone. The long
distance from Paris and the Court, the total absence of protest, gave him no
cause for hope, and induced him to be prudent for fear of harsher treatment. With Villeroy banished, the last obstacle in Dubois's path was
removed. Nothing now remained but to proclaim him first minister. He
had gathered all the power into his own hands and brought his master to
the point of not daring to move, still less take a decision without his
knowledge and consent. Cardinal Dubois's desires, in other words his
advantage or convenience, now became the sole object of the government
of France. M. le Duc d'Orléans saw the situation and understood it; he
was thenceforward no more than a puppet dancing to the cardinal's tune,
and against him he had no defence.

The situation caused general dismay, but so great was the fear of this
all-powerful man, whose ambition knew no bounds, that no protests were
heard. All were terrified of him. I suffered most because of my love for
France, my attachment to M. le Duc d'Orléans, and my realization of what
the outcome would be; for I plainly saw that there was no remedy, knowing
him as I did, and being so often in his company. Yet although the usurper's
power was supreme, he still feared and respected me. He had been unable
to destroy entirely the confidence which M. le Duc d'Orléans reposed in
me, his old familiar friendship, his liking for me, dare I say the comfort he
felt in seeing and talking to me, even when most constrained—and he
sometimes overstepped those limits. For my part, my free-speaking, my
sincerity, let me say once more, the lack of ambition which allowed me to
consider only the welfare of France, and my affection for the Regent,
obliged the cardinal to treat me with a politeness he showed to no one else,
thus compelling me to preserve the decencies with him.

On the next occasion when the day came for me to work with M. le Duc
d'Orléans, I went to Versailles at four o'clock, my usual time, and an hour
when he was alone. I spoke to no one, but went straight to him in his study.
After a few minutes in general conversation, I put my papers on his table;
he sat down, and I took a chair opposite him, as was my custom. I thought
he looked worried and abstracted, and indeed he asked me several times to
repeat myself—he, whose mind was ordinarily far ahead of mine, who
loved to joke on the gravest matters, especially with me, saying outrageous
things to try my patience, and then bursting into laughter because I always
got angry. This unaccustomed solemnity gave me the opportunity to ask
him, after a time, what the matter was. He stammered something out,
paused, but did not explain further. I smiled at him, and inquired whether
it concerned the rumour that he was about to make Cardinal Dubois first
minister, for I thought the direct question might save him embarrassment.
He cheered up immediately, saying that Cardinal Dubois was certainly

longing to be appointed. As for himself, he added, he was sick of work, and sick and tired of the formality at Versailles, where he had no diversions in the evening. In Paris, he was at least free by supper-time, and might have company after his work was done, or when he quitted his little box at the Opéra. It was more than he could bear to wear himself out with work all day long, and then die of boredom when evening came. He was, he said, much disposed to cast the burden on a first minister who would give him rest during the day, and allow him to spend his evenings in Paris. I laughed, protesting that he had explained enough, and that his arguments were amply conclusive. He saw that I was teasing, and declared that I could not know how tired he felt at the day's end, and that the awful dullness of the evenings were almost as fatiguing. In Mme la Duchesse d'Orléans's drawing-room, it was indescribably tedious, and he had nowhere else to go.

I said that because of the terms I had lately been on with Mme la Duchesse d'Orléans, I could not comment; but I did think it lamentable that he, the Regent, so witty, so cultivated, such good company when he wished to please, could find no better entertainment. I reminded him of the late Prince de Conti,[1] and of how the King had hated him, and shown it so publicly and continually that everyone had known. Thus he was of no importance and, worse still, every courtier was aware that to seek his company was to provoke the King's anger. Yet so greatly was he esteemed and respected that his room, at Versailles, was crowded every morning, and no sooner did he appear in the drawing-rooms at Marly than he was surrounded by the best people at the Court, eager to converse with him agreeably for the next two or three hours. In the daytime the prince was never at a loss for diversion, though he neither hunted nor gambled, nor was ever found in low company; his debauchery[2] was always with persons of quality, and of such sterling worth that they adorned every table. In short, like Orpheus with his lute, he made the rocks and trees come to him.

I asked M. le Duc d'Orléans what stopped him from imitating that prince, than whom he had far superior wit and attainments. He talked better of past history, the wars and the Court, was equally, indeed more, courageous, had commanded armies, and knew the true story of events in Spain. M. le Duc d'Orléans had fully as much charm; could tell a tale equally well, and over and above these advantages, he was greater by far than M. le Prince de Conti had ever been, for he held the reins of government and was the fount of honours. That alone was enough to bring the world to his feet and allow him to choose the company that best pleased him. He had only one thing to do, I continued, prefer good to bad in every kind, study how to distinguish and attract the best, and sup with them merrily but with restraint. Let him reflect that his present ways became

[1] For the character of François Louis de Bourbon, who died in 1709, see I, pp. 420–421.
[2] *débauches*, according to the *Dictionnaire de l'Académie*, 1718, meant 'polite merriment during meals'—'*une honnête réjouissance dans un repas*'.

disgraceful after the age of eighteen or twenty. The racket, the language devoid of all decency, were utterly degrading, while drunkenness effectively banished any last shred of dignity or good breeding that might still cling to him. Everyone was repelled by the lewdness and vulgarity of his disgusting friends, so much so, indeed, that it had come to be considered a merit not to be one of them. My conclusion was that if he was bored at Versailles it was from choice, for the best people and the wittiest company would flock to him, once they could be sure of avoiding filth, blasphemy, and drunkenness. I ended by entreating him to remember that for years past I had said nothing of his personal conduct. I should not mention it now had he not forced me by showing me the awful abyss into which he would fall, if boredom alone drove him to appointing a first minister.

M. le Duc d'Orléans listened to me patiently, elbows on the table, head sunk between his hands—his invariable posture when worried or unhappy. He listened, as I say, to my earnest reproaches for a far longer time than it has taken me to record them. When I had quite done, he admitted that all I said was true, but that there was even worse to follow, for he had lost all desire for women, and wine had become nothing less than odious to him. 'Fie! Monsieur, for shame!' I exclaimed, 'You have indeed gone to the Devil, if you are prepared to lose your soul in this world and the next for the sake of vices that tempt others, not yourself. Disgusted with wine; dead to Venus's charms,[1] what pleasure can you find in such debauchery, unless you love to hear belching and obscenities that would make all decent people stop their ears?' For a few moments I was silent, before entreating him, for the last time, to compare his present life of debauchery with the polite diversions suitable to his age and rank and office, the kind of pleasures that would draw all honourable men to his side, in joy at seeing him at last leading a life more becoming to the master of the nation's affairs, and of all private fortunes. Then they would cease to be haunted by the dread of seeing the young King follow his bad example, and indulging in vices that could be tolerated in most very young men, but were wholly inadmissible in kings, who needed to comport themselves better in every way than their subjects. I asked him to reflect on what the Court, Paris, France, and foreign nations would think to see a Regent of his age[2] and proven abilities abdicating, so to speak, in order to have leisure for debauchery. I warned him that he would be delivering himself over to his enemies who might persuade a young and inexperienced monarch to dismiss the minister of his appointment, and replace him by one more to their liking. If alarms and suspicions should then arise, where would be his defence? I spoke of his great-uncle Gaston d'Orléans, spending his last years imprisoned at Blois, dying unhappy and alone, and if one might dare to say so of a Son of France, despised by all.

[1] One cannot help suspecting that in revision Saint-Simon's style bolted with him.
[2] The Regent was forty-nine.

[Saint-Simon would not have described this interview in such minute detail—minute even for him—had he not thought it of immense importance. It was, in a sense, a turning point in their relationship, for he was giving the Regent a last chance; his refusal to take it killed the last vestiges of Saint-Simon's respect. We are shown the hopeless weakness of Orléans's nature, worn out perhaps by his 'orgies', and his tragic, incompetent administration. He has been called the fossoyeur *(gravedigger) of the monarchy. Yet despite Saint-Simon's judgment and reproach, uttered with all the force and sincerity of which he was so notoriously capable, his affection for his friend did not diminish. The memoirist's character has been distorted in the published extracts by endless examples of his hatreds and his malice; it is a good thing to see another side.*

The unrelenting loathing that Saint-Simon and Madame felt for Dubois sprang from their belief that when he was Orléans's tutor he deliberately corrupted him, in order to destroy his will, and gain influence for himself.]

At that point I concluded that I had said enough, perhaps too much, and I waited anxiously for the outcome. After a pause, M. le Duc d'Orléans sat upright. 'Well!' said he, 'I shall have to grow cabbages at Villers-Cotterets,'[1] and rising, he began to pace up and down, with me beside him. I asked how he could be sure of being left to plant them in peace—or in safety. Judging from past history, he might well be accused of conspiracy, should the King begin to fear him. After a few more turns round the little room, he admitted that reflection was required, and then continued his circling for a dozen turns or more without uttering a word.

When he came near the wall by the corner of his writing-table, where two *tabourets* stood (I can see the spot even now), he took my arm and pulled me down on to one of them, himself taking the other. Then, turning to face me, he asked most earnestly if I remembered Dubois when he was merely the servant of Saint-Laurent, and thought himself supremely fortunate to be so much. He then rehearsed all the various steps and stages of his rise to power, until the day on which we spoke. 'And he is not yet satisfied,' he cried, 'He persecutes me to make him first minister, and I am sure that will not content him; though what the devil can he hope for next?' Then, as though answering his own question, 'Make himself God Almighty, I suppose, if that could be.' 'Oh! no doubt of that,' I replied, 'that is for certain. But now, Monsieur, you who know the man, are you willing to be the step by which he rises over you?' 'No, most certainly I shall stop him,' he cried, and once again the silent pacing of his study began. I, too, said nothing, so full was I of that 'I shall stop him', coming immediately after such strong words, and the sudden recital, so abruptly terminated, of the life of Cardinal Dubois *ab incunabulis.*[2]

At length he sat down in his usual place at the table, I facing him, also seated, and he resumed his customary posture, with his head deep sunk between his two hands. For more than a quarter of an hour he thus remained, not stirring or opening his mouth, and I also remained silent,

---

[1] The Regent's country house.   [2] *ab incunabulis:* from the cradle onwards.

though I did not cease to observe him. Suddenly he lifted his head, and without otherwise moving thrust it towards me, saying in a low and sheepish voice, with a look to match, 'Well! Why wait any longer? Why not make the announcement?' Such was the result of our conversation. 'Monsieur!' I exclaimed, 'What a thing to say! Who is pressing you? Will there not always be time? At least reflect on what we have been saying, and then let me show you what becomes of first ministers and of the rulers who appoint them.' He silently hid his face and gave no further utterance. I was stunned by that sudden firmness coming so soon after his dispraise of Dubois's ambition; but I decided that arguments were of no avail. If any hope remained, it would come only with postponement. It was not a long pause, for soon afterwards he said, 'Ah! well, come back tomorrow, punctually at three. We will talk again; there is time enough.' I took up my papers and moved to go; but he came hurrying after me and opened the door as if to call me back, saying, 'Come without fail, at three. Promise me you will come.' He then once more closed the door.

Next day, 22 August, I arrived punctually at three, to find M. le Duc d'Orléans alone and pacing, but looking far more cheerful. 'Well!' said he, 'What more have we to discuss? It seems to me that we covered everything, and that nothing remains except to make the appointment.' I fell back a couple of steps, remarking that he had decided very rapidly on a matter of such prime importance. He replied that he had given thought to all my words, but in the end, had resolved it was killing him to work all day, be bored all night, and badgered by Cardinal Dubois at all hours. I retorted that the last was the true reason and that I was not surprised to find the cardinal so pressing. What did surprise me was his success with a man as suspicious as M. le Duc d'Orléans, and I besought him to reflect once more, on one or two matters, in particular.

First, he might do much less work and visit the Opéra whenever he pleased without promoting Dubois. The cardinal was already so powerful that no one dared approach the Regent without his consent; thus His Royal Highness's frequent absences would not be much noticed. Secondly, despite his almost supreme power, Dubois was in a perilous position, for he was perched like a bird on a branch, liable to be swept away in a trice if he displeased the Regent. To grant him a title, with letters patent enregistered by the Parlement, would protect him from summary dismissal until the proper forms had been gone through, and he had been given the chance to appeal. I entreated M. le Duc d'Orléans to consider the difference between a man who wields power by leave of his master, and one whose title is established by public proclamation, and registered with due ceremony at the Parlement. I paused, but he merely looked worried and said nothing.

To anyone other than M. le Duc d'Orléans, I might have stressed the peril of making as his first minister a man who, by money, flattery, or toadying, would control every avenue of approach to the King, so as to be the paramount influence when he came of age. M. le Duc d'Orléans would by then have lost his authority over his one-time servant, and find himself exposed to dismissal or exile, in exactly the way that Gaston had been treated by Mazarin. That, however, was something which the Regent in his spellbound condition was plainly incapable of understanding. In any case, I had already risked enough in fruitless opposition to Cardinal Dubois—more especially since M. le Duc d'Orléans would never be able to hold his tongue. I therefore fell silent and waited to see what would transpire. The pacing continued for seven or eight turns; the prince was evidently disquieted, his head was down, and he said nothing. He returned to sit at his writing-table in the same attitude as before, I facing him, only the table between us; but the silence was not broken, for I was resolved not to be the first to speak.

At last he raised his head to look at me, reminding me (as though there were any need!) that I had more to say regarding the office of first minister. I replied that he knew the history of his own country and of the neighbour-ing States too well to need reminders of the calamities caused by their first ministers in Hungary, Vienna, England, and Spain, with the sole and shining exception of Cardinal Ximenes, although even he was not wholly proof against the poison of Flanders. It would, I said, be a waste of time to trace the careers of other first ministers, with the long list of revolts and destruction wrought by their ambitions and self-seeking, or to describe the scorn and hatred accruing to their masters because of their greed. Even Henry VIII of England was great only after the disgrace of Cardinal Wolsey. Think how, in France, the cleverest, most suspicious, most artful, most cautious of all our Kings was betrayed by Cardinal Balue[1] to the Duke of Burgundy . . . and how, when Louis XI at last returned to his senses, he shut Balue, cardinal though he was, into an iron cage, and kept him so confined for many years, taking good care never to appoint a successor.

Louis XII, twice brought to the verge of ruin. . . . The death of the Duc de Guise. . . . The Emperor Charles V, his peace and security destroyed by the Cardinal of Lorraine. . . . Louis XIII—even Richelieu was not exempt from the desire for aggrandizement. . . .[2]

A longish silence followed this strong speech of mine. M. le Duc d'Orléans's head still remained buried in his hands, sinking lower and lower until it almost touched the table.[3] He raised it at last, looking dis-mally across at me; then once more looked down, seemingly much ashamed, and remained for some time longer in that posture. He then rose and

---

[1] Cardinal Jean de La Balue (1421–1491). He was secretary of State to Louis XI, who imprisoned him for conspiring against him with Charles the Bold.

[2] This sally into past history occupies twelve pages of the Pléiade edition and is extremely repetitive. It is typical of Saint-Simon's digressions. No doubt he did not speak it all in the same breath. It was probably greatly enlarged in revision.

[3] Can it be that he was sleeping?

wandered about the room, still without a word. But what was my consternation when he broke the silence! Stopping suddenly, he turned towards me without raising his eyes, and in a low, unhappy voice exclaimed, 'We cannot go on like this; he must be appointed at once.' 'Monsieur,' I said, 'you are very kind and very wise; what is more, you are the master. Have you orders for me at Meudon?' I immediately made my bow and withdrew whilst he was still exclaiming, 'But I shall see you soon, shall I not?' To that I made no reply, simply closed the door.

Next day, Cardinal Dubois was duly appointed first minister by M. le Duc d'Orléans, who presented him to the King as such during their working hours.

The day of the coronation was fast approaching.[1] From all that had gone before since the beginning of the Regency I foresaw only too well that this moment, when the rank and place of the peers should be most apparent, would be made a source of further humiliation to them. The first blow had been struck by the edict of 1711 that conferred upon the princes of the blood, and failing them on the royal bastards, the right to represent senior peers at the King's coronation, in place of other dukes. The ignorance, baseness, and malice of the Grand-master of ceremonies;[2] Cardinal Dubois's desire to bring confusion and abasement everywhere, in order to elevate the cardinals by contrast; a similar love of disorder on the part of M. le Duc d'Orléans, on the principle of divide and rule, would complete the task. None the less I made soundings, asked questions, argued and pleaded, meeting nothing but vagueness, stammering, and minds made up. Cardinal Dubois, who appeared to have learned of my discontent from M. le Duc d'Orléans, made suggestions, and required me to believe in miracles. He dreaded what might happen. His desire was to content me and let the other dukes be submerged. He asked to know what part they should play. I refused to answer until I had spoken to them—though I had sworn never again to interfere. When he pressed me, I spoke my mind. He stammered out first yes, then no, and fell back on general praise for the rank, the rules of precedence, the propriety, nay, the need of their presence at the crowning with all due dignity, but he did not enter into details. I said words alone guaranteed nothing; that to attend the coronation at the risk of meeting humiliation, or worse, would never be by my advice, and that if M. le Duc d'Orléans wished the dukes to be present, he must have everything written down, and must sign two copies, giving one to the Grand-master of ceremonies, with instructions to see that all was done to

[1] The coronation was of huge importance to Saint-Simon. There was in it a moment symbolic of the rôle set apart for peers in the old order, in their function as the monarch's advisers, supporters and defenders. When the King left the altar to go to his throne, Charlemagne's crown was held over his head by the hands of the dukes and peers, so that at one moment he seemed, to the witnesses, to 'disappear, encircled by a hedge of dukes'.

[2] Thomas III, Marquis de Dreux-Brézé (1677–1749).

the letter. The other copy should be given to whichever of the dukes he cared to select.

Dubois, who had no intention of giving any such undertaking, since his hope was to entice the dukes into a trap, protested against documents and advised the spoken word. I said shortly that the affair of the bonnet, and other affairs also, had taught the dukes to place no reliance on words or spoken promises, no matter how often repeated. He must therefore choose between a document, and dispensing with an order which he regarded as useless, except to swell the Court. The cardinal cooed at me in honeyed even respectful tones (which cost him nothing), and did his utmost to win me over. He sent Belle-Isle and Le Blanc to me next day, to urge that my absence would be too conspicuous; that he earnestly wished for my presence; that he would procure me all manner of honours. M. le Duc d'Orléans asked if I would not change, and though he dared not press me, or preferred not to do so, did what else he might to secure me. When at last they saw that they would fail, Dubois himself spoke to me, imploring me not to dissuade the other dukes, and to believe that their absence might appear disloyalty. I said that those who prevented their attendance by not issuing proper orders had best think again; that—as had been proved too often—I had no influence over the dukes; I only knew what they should do, and I would stand by that.

I had less trouble than I expected in ascertaining that none of them was going, save those whose official duties made the journey essential, and none, even of those, would be in the cathedral at Rheims, at any of the services in other churches, at the State banquet, or in the processions, unless their duties required it of them. They were ready to sacrifice curiosity to a sense of fitness, which they did most loyally and with scrupulous exactitude. When I was sure of what would happen, I took my leave of M. le Duc d'Orléans four or five days before the King's departure, and bade farewell also, looking very grave, to Cardinal Dubois, for I had decided to go to La Ferté, and I left next day. Both protested vigorously against my going; but when they saw I would not be moved, they tried instead to make me come to Villers-Cotterets where M. le Duc d'Orléans was holding high festival. I replied humbly that since I could not attend the solemn ceremonies at Rheims, I should think myself very much out of place at Villers-Cotterets, and I stood firm against all their persuasion. I had previously confirmed with the dukes that, except for those whose duties made it necessary, none of them would go either to Paris or Rheims, and so it was. Thus I left for La Ferté five or six days before the King's departure, and returned about ten days after he did.

The chaos at the ceremony defies description,[1] and was most offensively at

---

[1] It will be seen that Saint-Simon's concern was wholly and solely for precedence. Nothing else seems to have mattered to him. Perhaps, for him, the exclusion of the dukes at such a moment symbolized the end of France. It must have shown him the absolute defeat of all his own efforts and hopes for the new reign.

variance with the traditions of precedence. This showed most clearly in the condition of the persons commanded to attend, and that of those who received no order; for the intention to exclude anyone with a claim to rank or nobility was most perfectly apparent. No less evident was the plan to replace them by administrators and even by their clerks, these two sections being summoned by name and especially invited, as were none of the nobility, except those few who held offices reserved for men of high rank. In Rheims cathedral there was similar disorder at the services, and with the same intention. I shall not attempt to describe it in detail, for if I did so I should never end, even though I mentioned only the coronation, the banquet, and the ceremony of the Order.

I never learned what claims had been made by the bastards; but neither the Duc du Maine, nor his two sons, nor yet the Comte de Toulouse made the journey to Rheims, and the Comte de Toulouse when pressed to attend flatly refused, and remained at Rambouillet. Of the six cardinals then in Paris, only Cardinal de Noailles was not summoned. That tribute Dubois thought he owed to Cardinal de Rohan and the constitution, both having done him such excellent service, at Rome, in the cause of his hat; for by excluding Cardinal de Noailles, Rohan would find himself heading the row of five bishop peers.

Ecclesiastical peers had a double right to the highest places on their side of the cathedral—no dispute about that with the lay peers—since theirs was the chief function in the ceremony. The Archbishop of Rheims being the officiating prelate, the other five bishop peers joined him in the same row, and acted as chief officiants. This constituted two unanswerable claims to precedence. The tradition of earlier coronations provided a third. Cardinal Dubois was anxious for his cardinalate to appear, and to be first with the consent of his colleagues the other cardinals. He did not therefore wish to seat them behind the Ecclesiastical peers, yet dared not place them in front, for fear of disrupting the entire ceremony. He accordingly had the cardinals' bench placed somewhat behind that of the bishops, but pushed up so high towards the altar that the last of the cardinals (who happened to be Polignac) was not hidden by the Archbishop of Rheims, or by the supporting priests who stood near him. Thus the archbishops and bishops and their attendant clergy had benches behind that of the prelate peers, and were placed farther back than the bench of cardinals.

On a line with the benches for archbishops, bishops and other clergy of lower degree, were three benches on which sat ten counsellors of State, ten maîtres des requêtes, and, so that nothing should be wanting to dignify the occasion, ten of the King's secretaries.

Opposite the prelate peers sat the lay peers; no one at all faced the cardinals. Behind the lay peers were three Marshals of France, appointed to carry the regalia.[1] You will recollect that the Maréchal d'Estrées,

---

[1] The three Marshals of France were d'Estrées, Huxelles, and Tessé; the regalia (les trois honneurs) were the crown, the sceptre, and the hand of justice.

appointed to bear the crown, became a duke and peer only on 16 July 1723, when he succeeded the childless Duc d'Estrées, M. de Nevers's son-in-law.

Below the 'honours-bench' and slightly farther back was a bench reserved entirely for secretaries of State, with nothing before them except the end of the peers' bench. It is indeed true that for one short moment a *tabouret* for the Duc de Charost was placed in the space between; but only for the very brief period when he was acting in his capacity as the King's governor—an office that does not normally figure at coronations.

Behind the bench for the three Marshals sat the Maréchaux de Matignon and de Bezons. The remainder of their bench (which was behind that of the secretaries of State) and other benches still farther back were filled with gentlemen of the Court, who came out of curiosity, for none was bidden. Thus, on the one side were counsellors of State, maîtres des requêtes, and King's secretaries, and on the other, secretaries of State, all especially invited and excellently placed, while persons of rank, uninvited, were treated as mere spectators and seated higgledy-piggledy, as chance or the whim of the Grand-master of ceremonies decreed. They served only to fill empty spaces whereas, even down to royal clerks, every quill-driver had superiority over the highest nobility of France.

The first four choir-stalls nearest the altar, on either side, were occupied by the four Knights of the Order appointed to carry the four parts of the offertory,[1] and by the four barons, guardians of the Ampulla. One filthy trick was the deliberate lie inserted by the Grand-master of ceremonies, in a book printed and published a few months earlier, to the effect that my father had been one of these bearers at the coronation of Louis XIV. Despite all that I said, stated, and affirmed, swearing that this was a blatant error, and that the person referred to was my uncle,[2] not my father who, at that time, was loyally fighting for the King against the rebels of Bordeaux, the lie went uncorrected in a book stuffed with lies for an express purpose. A decision had been made. It had been determined, on this most solemn occasion, not in any way to differentiate between those who were both dukes and peers, and those other nobles who were not of the peerage of France, and a man had been chosen ready to comply with leaders whose sole intent was their imagined personal advantage. The Maréchal de Tallard, a duke but not a peer, was put to head the Comte de Matignon, M. de Médavy (later Maréchal de France), and Goësbrand, all four being Knights of the Order. Thus was created the monstrous precedent of combining a Maréchal de France with three others who were not so, in a function that, until then, had never been fulfilled by a Marshal, still less by one who was also a duke.

---

[1] The four parts of the offertory were a jar of wine, a gold wafer, a silver wafer, and a red velvet purse containing thirteen gold coins.

[2] Charles de Rouvroy, Marquis de Saint-Simon (1601–1690).

As for seating opposite to them the four barons guarding the holy Ampulla, here was a totally novel abuse, perpetrated so as to gratify their curiosity to witness the crowning. To have placed their four squires with pennons unfurled, on four low chairs immediately below them, was the ultimate disgrace, seeing that neither the princes of the blood nor any other office-holder was allowed either squires or pennons.

One other most glaring error, committed at no previous coronations, was a matter of such enormous significance that I cannot but think it was deliberate. Two crowns are always used at coronations, the great crown of Charlemagne, and another made especially to fit the King's head, and studded with precious stones. The larger one was purposely made too big for a man to wear, so that it might be supported by eleven peers, each holding it by one hand over the head of the King at the moment when he is crowned by the Archbishop of Rheims. Then, still supporting the great crown, the peers lead the King to his chair by the rood-screen, where his enthronement takes place. Considering the vast size of the great crown, it could have been intended for no other use; but in the published account of the coronation there is no mention of the peers' holding it over the King's head—an omission that is evidently deliberate.[1]

The second crown is kept by the rood-screen. As soon as the King is seated, Charlemagne's crown is handed to the bearer, and the King himself takes the smaller one and sets it upon his own head, removing and replacing it at various times during the service. When he goes to the altar for communion and returns, he leaves the small crown on his prie-dieu by the rood-screen, and, once again, the peers support Charlemagne's crown above his head. I am not aware if the published account is wrong there also, but it would be extraordinary indeed were it not.[2]

At the royal banquet there was an error in the procedure, or else a mistake in the published account, for if that is correct, there were two novelties never before seen at a coronation banquet. The error (or the mistake in reporting) is that when the King first returned from the

[1] The two crowns are now kept in the Louvre. This is what the official account of the coronation of Louis XIII has to say: 'Cardinal de Joyeuse took the great crown from the altar, and alone raised it two hands' breadth above the King's head without touching him, and immediately all the peers placed their hands under it to support it, and then the same Lord Cardinal holding it with his left hand, blessed it. After the benediction, the Lord Cardinal alone set the crown lower, upon the head of the King, and all the peers joined hands upon it. . . .'

Despite the proved incapacity of the peers to govern France in the Regency councils, Saint-Simon remained confirmed in his opinion that the welfare of France depended on having, not an absolute monarch, subject to human weaknesses and temptations, nor one assisted by professional administrators, whose ruling temptations would be personal ambition and personal gain; but a king advised and supported by the peers of the realm who, because they owned the land, would gain most by the prosperity of the country as a whole.

To lose, at the coronation of a new king, the symbolic reminder that this was the tradition, was to lose all he believed in and had struggled for.

[2] If Saint-Simon's ghost was looking down to see the coronation of Elizabeth II, so perfectly conducted by the premier duke and peer of England, it must have made him still more conscious of les funestes charmes de l'Angleterre.

cathedral to his rooms, his gloves were removed and burned because they had touched the Holy Oils, and his shirt also, for the same reason. He is then stated to have changed his clothes, put on again his kingly mantle, and continued to wear his crown. The removal and burning of the gloves is correct, and has always been the practice when the King returns for the first time to his apartments. The shirt is also burned, but only when the King returns after the banquet, and finally divests himself of all his coronation robes. Although some kings may possibly have changed their shirts, they have invariably replaced all the other garments worn by them in church, before proceeding to the royal banquet. To do otherwise would be an error and a novelty. If there were no error, it was a very grave mistake to have described it thus, and a most careless omission not to have said exactly what the King, when going to the banquet, wore beneath his kingly mantle.

I shall not mention all the other mistakes and omissions, for they were legion. Nor shall I attempt to describe the splendid entertainments given for the King by M. le Duc d'Orléans and Monsieur le Duc, at Villers-Cotterets and Chantilly.

Madame, always so strong and most magnificently healthy, had not been feeling well for some time past, even to the point of believing that she was about to contract a fatal illness. The intense love for all things German, which she most sincerely felt, made her care far more deeply for her daughter and her daughter's children than for M. le Duc d'Orléans and his. She was dying to see Mme la Duchesse de Lorraine and the grandchildren she had never met, and eagerly looked forward to being with them, at Rheims, at the time of the coronation. Since, however, she felt more and more sickly as the time approached, she hesitated over the journey, and finally decided to go several days in advance of the King, so as to have more leisure, and she made the Lorraine family aware of her intentions.

You will recollect that after Monsieur's death she had taken back into her service the Maréchale de Clérambault and the late Comtesse de Beuvron,[1] having always been deeply fond of them, despite Monsieur's hatred of both, and his insistence on their dismissal. Now the Maréchale de Clérambault firmly believed that she could see into the future by the method of pin-pricks which, thank God!, I neither understand, nor shall attempt to describe. It was, at any rate, an art in which Madame placed great faith. That being so, she consulted the Maréchale regarding her journey to Rheims, and received the following reply, very firmly given: 'Go, Madame; you may safely go, I feel quite well.' This was because the pin-pricks had assured her that Madame would outlive her. Thus comforted, Madame journeyed to Rheims, and was lodged with Mme la Duchesse de Lorraine and her children, in the beautiful Abbaye de Saint-Pierre, where the King twice visited them. She witnessed the coronation and

[1] Louise Françoise Bouthillier de Chavigny (1640–1724), and Lydie de Rochefort de Théobon. See I, p. 185.

the ceremonies of the Order on the following day from a tribune with her daughter and grandchildren; but on her return to Paris lost the Maréchale who died on 27 November, in her eighty-sixth year, having, until then, enjoyed the health, strength, and radiance of a woman of forty.

She was one of the most brilliant women of her day, and the most cultivated, although she rarely allowed that to appear. She knew the true inwardness of the most interesting events at the Court, in former days; but kept most stubbornly silent concerning them. This was a habit she had contracted from having, in her youth, kept silence for a whole year, thus curing herself of a most dangerous disease of the chest. She drank nothing but water, and precious little even of that. When at leisure, she could be so charming that one longed to be with her always. I often saw her so in the company, at most, of three or four people, in the drawing-room of her dear friend the Chancelière de Pontchartrain. She had a way with her, a wit, a special turn of phrase, an aptness that made her enchanting, yet withal, she was most perfectly unaffected. Until her last illness, she almost invariably wore full dress going to and from the Court; moreover, she was rich in the extreme, although most monstrously parsimonious. In the corridors and galleries of Versailles she wore a black velvet mask, for though without pretensions to beauty or daintiness, she said it kept her complexion fresh, and that the air brought her out in spots. She was the only lady to wear such a mask; but when one met and bowed to her, she never failed politely to remove it. Gambling she adored, but played only *commerce* for the lowest stakes; yet she would have been perfectly happy to continue playing all day and all night. Perhaps I have said too much of this lady; her singularity set the ink flowing.

Madame was all the more affected by the death of this old, familiar friend because the pin-pricks, as she well knew, had invariably prophesied that though she would survive, it would not be for long. As it turned out, her death followed very soon after. Dropsy, becoming evident very late, made such swift progress in the next few days that she prepared for death, showing great courage and piety. She liked the Maréchale de Clérambault's brother, the late Bishop of Troyes,[1] to be with her nearly all the time, in that brief period, and remarked to him, 'Monsieur de Troyes, we were a tough couple, the Maréchale and I.' The King visited her, and she received the Sacraments. She died at Saint-Cloud, at four in the morning of 8 December, in her seventy-first year, leaving in her will firm instructions not to open her body,[2] or to have any funeral pomp. Thus, on the 10th of that same month, she was taken to Saint-Denis in an undraped coach, proceeded, surrounded, and followed by mounted pages from the royal stables, the bodyguard and Swiss of M. le Duc d'Orléans, and her own footmen bearing torches.

---

[1] (Denis) François Bouthillier de Chavigny (c. 1665–1730), Bishop of Troyes from 1697.
[2] Madame wrote that opening the body after death never did anyone any good.

Madame, on the whole, was more of the nature of a man than of a woman. She was stout, courageous, a thorough German, frank, straight-forward, good, and kind. Her manner was of the noblest; she was a great lady in all her ways, and yet small-minded to a degree in matters concerning the respect due to her.[1] Hating Society, she kept herself shut away from the Court, perpetually writing letters, except for the brief moments when she held court in her drawing-room. For the remainder of the time, she was alone with her ladies. Hard, brutal, apt to take aversions, she had sudden outbursts that were truly alarming, and no one was safe from them. Although possessed of sufficient intelligence and wit, she had no tact, no charm, no gentleness. As I have already said, she was intensely jealous of all her rights, and capable of the meanest actions in protecting them. Her figure resembled that of a Swiss guard, and yet she could be a most loyal and tender friend. M. le Duc d'Orléans loved her and respected her deeply. He never left her during her last illness; but although, throughout his life, he had visited her regularly, she was quite without influence. He was, none the less, most sincerely grieved by her death; for I was alone with him several hours on the following day, and I saw him weeping bitterly.

So ended the year 1722.

[1] On her deathbed, it is reported that she said to one of her ladies who kissed her hand, 'You may kiss me properly now. I am going to a land where all are equal.'

CHAPTER IX

1723

Emptiness of the coming year – Death of Madame la Princesse – The King proclaims his majority – Secret marriage of the Comte de Toulouse – Reinstatement of the Bastards – Death of Cardinal Dubois – His character – His bouts of rage – Death of Premier Président de Mesmes – Sad deterioration in the health of M. le Duc d'Orléans – I speak to Fréjus – Death of the Duc de Lauzun – His character and adventures – Death of M. le Duc d'Orléans – Monsieur le Duc becomes First Minister – Obsequies of M. le Duc d'Orléans – The Comte de Toulouse makes his marriage public – Novion becomes Premier Président of the Paris Parlement. Conclusion

THIS YEAR, whose end marks the limit which I have set for these Memoirs, will be neither as long nor as detailed as those preceding it. I was embittered by the changes in the coronation service; I foresaw the complete restoration of the bastards; I felt heartsick to see the Regent in hopeless bondage to his scoundrelly minister, and the State fallen victim, without hope of deliverance, to the ambition, avarice, and caprices of that wicked man. Familiar though I had always been with the abnormal weakness of will of M. le Duc d'Orléans, the thought of it had taken ever firmer hold on my mind since the moment when, after all that I, and he himself, had said, he had appointed Dubois first minister. Truly, the manner of the appointment was such that it would be incredible had one not witnessed it, as I did, and faithfully recorded it. I could not approach the unhappy prince without repugnance, for I knew that in him great and useful talents lay buried, and I therefore felt what the bad Israelites had said of manna, in the desert, '*Nauseat anima mea super cibum istum levissimum.*'[1] I could hardly bring myself to speak to him; he perceived it; I saw that it distressed him; he tried to win me back, yet dared not mention State affairs, except lightly and fleetingly, for he could not bear altogether to avoid them. I scarcely troubled to answer, but changed the subject without delay; and I reduced the length and frequency of our sessions, bearing his reproaches with a stony front. In very truth, what had I to say or discuss with a Regent who no longer ruled himself, let alone a kingdom where only confusion reigned?

Cardinal Dubois, when we met, went out of his way to be ingratiating.

---

[1] Numbers xxi, 5: 'Our soul loatheth this light bread.' (Authorized Version.)

He did not know how to be rid of me. The long-established, never interrupted attachment between M. le Duc d'Orléans and myself had become so strong that, having more than once tested it, he despaired of causing a rupture. His plan was now to weary me by imposing on his master a secrecy most foreign to our old habits; but which cost the Regent more than it did me, because it went against his nature, and because, I venture to say, he had gained much in the past from confiding in me. As for myself, I was glad to be spared his confidences, knowing that no good would come of them either for the State, or the honour and advantage of M. le Duc d'Orléans, who was by then totally immersed in his Paris pleasures, and bound hand and foot to his first minister. Conviction of my complete uselessness drove me further and further into retirement; although I did not for one moment believe that different conduct would be dangerous, or that Dubois could coerce the Regent into exiling me, as he had done the Duc de Noailles, nor yet that he would mistreat me in such a way as to make me go voluntarily. Thus my life went on as before; that is to say, I continued to see M. le Duc d'Orléans, always in private, but at ever longer intervals. Our discussions were brief and impersonal; we never spoke of State affairs, and on the rare occasions when he mentioned them, I at once changed the subject, answering in such a way as to cut him short. Behaving in that fashion, and harbouring such deep resentment, you may easily imagine that I was of no influence, and that my account of the coming year will lack the personal touch of a good and truthful memoir, and be as arid as the information in the gazettes.

The death of Madame la Princesse[1] followed closely upon that of Madame, for she died in Paris, on 23 February, at the age of seventy-five. They were cousins and close friends. Their grandfather, a son-in-law of James I of England, was that Elector Palatine who lost his electoral estates and title, and died an exile in Holland, for having attempted to become King of Bohemia.

Madame la Princesse was immensely rich in lands and money. She was ugly, humpbacked, somewhat twisted, very dull, but also exceedingly pious, gentle, and of a patience which she had had constantly and painfully to exercise during the forty-five years of her married life. When she became a widow, she altered, redecorated, and entirely refurnished the Petit Luxembourg, which until then had been a monstrosity; but when one visited her, the only entrance was by a kind of chicken-ladder that led into a poky little dining-room, in the corner of which was a door opening into a most magnificent drawing-room, at the end of the long suite of rooms that comprised the rest of the apartment, which they never showed. All the ceremonies proper to her rank were performed at the Petit Luxembourg, where she died; but there was never any question of her ladies forming a guard of honour. That

---

[1] Anne of Bavaria, widow of Henri Jules de Bourbon, Prince de Condé, and mother of Monsieur le Duc. She was Madame's first cousin, her father having been the Prince Palatine Edward of Bavaria, brother of Madame's father the Elector Palatine Charles Louis.

presumption when previously essayed had failed completely, and the princes of the blood seemed at last to have surrendered their false claim.

On 19 February, at Versailles, the King received M. le Duc d'Orléans's congratulations on his majority, and announced the creation of three new peerage dukedoms.[1] On the following afternoon, he drove in state to the Tuileries and, on the 22nd, held a *Lit de Justice* at the Parlement, to hear his majority proclaimed. The session ended with the registration of a new edict against duelling, then becoming prevalent. At the Tuileries, on the 23rd, the King heard addresses by various important bodies, and by others also who were entitled to harangue him. On the 24th, he went to visit Madame la Duchesse and the two daughters of Madame la Princesse who had died on the previous evening. People were surprised when he called also on her sister the Duchess of Brunswick; but his visits extended no further, and did not include the princes and princesses of the blood, or the grandchildren of Madame la Princesse. He returned to Versailles on the 25th, in the same state as on the outward journey.

It had long been known that the Comte de Toulouse was attracted by the Marquise de Gondrin[2] when he had met her taking the waters at Bourbon. She was the sister of the Duc de Noailles, whom he neither liked nor respected, and the widow, with two sons, of the elder son[3] of d'Antin, with whom he had always been connected in matters of business and friendship, since both were children of Mme de Montespan. Mme de Gondrin had been made a palace lady shortly before the death of Madame la Dauphine. She was young, lively, very much a Noailles, with a beautiful neck and shoulders, an agreeable face, and untouched by any breath of scandal. To preserve secrecy,[4] the Comte de Toulouse seized on the moment of the *Lit de Justice* at the Parlement, which neither he nor Cardinal de Noailles now attended. The Maréchale de Noailles drove alone with her daughter to the archbishop's palace; the Comte de Toulouse arrived with d'O at the same time; the cardinal said mass and performed the ceremony in his private chapel, and they all returned as they had come. The news did not spread, nor was anything even suspected, more especially as the Comte de Toulouse had always shown a strong disinclination for matrimony.

The Regency Council was disbanded, and a new State Council formed consisting only of M. le Duc d'Orléans, M. le Duc de Chartres, Monsieur le Duc, Cardinal Dubois, and de Morville, a hitherto unemployed secretary of State,[5] to whom Dubois had handed over his previous post at the department of foreign affairs.

---

[1] Biron, Levis, and La Vallière.

[2] Marie Victoire Sophie de Noailles (1688–1766). It turned out to be a happy marriage.

[3] Louis de Pardaillon, Marquis de Gondrin, died in 1712. Their two sons were the Duc d'Épernon and the Marquis de Gondrin.   [4] One wonders why all the secrecy.

[5] Charles Jean Fleuriau, Comte de Morville (1686–1732). He had been procureur général at the Grand Conseil of 1711, ambassador at The Hague and a counsellor of State in 1721. He was also a member of the French Academy.

M. le Duc d'Orléans, who esteemed nothing and ground honours and favours beneath his heel, had given the *grandes entrées* indiscriminately to all who asked; wherefore the numbers had become so great that it was no longer a privilege, and the crush had begun to incommode the King. Cardinal Dubois, quite as eager to dominate the King as he had ever been to rule M. le Duc d'Orléans, sought to prevent as many as possible from having free access to His Majesty, and thus took the first opportunity to make the desired changes, on the pretext of restoring order, and relieving the King from embarrassment in his private hours. I have already explained, before the death of the late King, what the entrées allowed, and how rare and precious a favour they were in his day, because they gave opportunities for speaking privately with the late King who was so chary of granting audiences. Whenever, in his leisure hours, a man possessing the entrées approached to speak to him, the other courtiers moved aside.

Cardinal Dubois's first move was to desire all those who possessed the *grandes* or *premières entrées*[1] to return their warrants. Only the Maréchal Duc de Berwick and Belle-Isle were excepted; Berwick because, having accepted the Spanish embassy, his influence might be discounted, and Belle-Isle because Dubois wished to delude him before finally ruining him. In the event he failed with both, for Berwick did not go to Spain, and Belle-Isle after long confinement to the Bastille, and exile at Nevers, returned to the Court and made an enormous fortune. Both kept their entrées. I was one of those deprived, and M. le Duc d'Orléans permitted it.[2] I returned my warrant as soon as asked, for I would not stoop to beg; and I never uttered a word either to Dubois, or to M. le Duc d'Orléans, who would have been mightily embarrassed.

Thus, with the two exceptions above mentioned, the entrées were reduced to office-holders and those few who had had them in the late King's reign. Cardinal Dubois much enlarged the family circle which, in Louis XIV's day, had been restricted to Monseigneur, his sons, Monsieur, M. le Duc d'Orléans, the Duc du Maine, and the Comte de Toulouse. Dubois claimed this entrée for himself, as of right, and in order to disarm censure, extended the circle to include the princes of the blood, the Duc du Maine, his two sons, and the Comte de Toulouse. The princes now had the right to enter the private apartments at any time when the King was not working, and they were highly delighted; for, in the past, they had never had more than the bedroom entrée. These family entrées have remained ever since with the princes and the bastards, and it would be hard now to dislodge

---

[1] In the old days the *grandes entrées* had been granted to very few as a most signal favour. The possessors entered the King's private suite with footmen throwing back both sides of the big double doors. The *premières entrées* holders had to enter by the *derrières* (the back offices). When they wished to attend the King's *lever* or his *coucher*, they entered with all the other courtiers; but they could at any time slip alone into the King's study, using the backstairs, unless there was a Council meeting, or the King was working with a minister.

[2] Saint-Simon had had his entrées since 1717.

them, even if the King, as he easily might, became bored or irritated by their presence.

This was the first step towards the re-establishment of the bastards and the Duc du Maine's sons in all the rank, honours and privileges which they had enjoyed at the time of the late King's death. Everything was returned to them by a royal proclamation, enregistered at the Parlement. All that was refused them was the right to the succession, the title of princes of the blood, and the high seats at the Parlement. In every other way they were made to appear equal to the princes, and were given the same entrées. One would surely have imagined that after their recent and well-deserved disgrace this would have satisfied them; but not so, and Mme la Duchesse d'Orléans was the least content of all. They clamoured for nothing less than the restoration of the three honours withheld from them, and made yet another demand, namely that all these privileges should descend by inheritance to their children. Dubois, however, hesitated to do violence to the princes' feelings in such delicate matters. His aim was to remain on good terms with both sides, but to keep them at loggerheads in order to rule them, favouring first the one and then the other, as best suited his interests. The peers voiced their protest—always the last hope of the oppressed. It was this event that completed my estrangement from the cardinal and M. le Duc d'Orléans, to whom, since it was plainly useless, I made not the smallest reproach. None of us visited the bastards to congratulate them on their disgraceful restoration which, considering the past, was a most monstrous error on the part of M. le Duc d'Orléans.

On 11 June of this year, the King went into residence at Meudon; the pretext was the need to clean the Château de Versailles,[1] but the real reason was the convenience of Cardinal Dubois. Meudon was more than half-way on the road from Versailles to Paris, where he wished to flaunt himself by presiding over the Church Assembly, and he thus was spared some of the bumping over cobbles. His debauches were causing him constant and most acute discomfort, which was greatly aggravated by the shaking of a coach, though he took immense trouble to conceal his pain. During this excursion to Meudon, the King held a review of his *Maison*,[2] an occasion which the first minister's pride would not allow him to miss. It cost him his life. He rode a horse, the better to savour his triumph. He suffered acutely, and made his disease so much worse that help became necessary. In the deepest secrecy, the most famous doctors and surgeons were consulted; their predictions were most sinister, and despite all his precautions, their constant visits and occasional indiscretions soon revealed the truth. He managed once or twice, but not more often, to

---

[1] On account of the '*mauvais airs*', caused by over-population and inefficient plumbing, three months was the longest stay advisable in any of the royal residences.

[2] *La Maison du Roi*: the famous regiments of the King's household troops. See index, I.

make the journey to Paris, in the effort to seem as usual; but he was all the time in agonies of pain. On 10 August he died, at Versailles.

He had striven with all his might to keep the world in ignorance, regularly attending the Council, making engagements to see ambassadors in Paris, and then defaulting, refusing to see people at his residence, and turning like a fury upon anyone who tried to accost him as he was borne in his chair from the old château to the new, where he was lodged.[1] On Saturday, 7 August, his condition was so bad that the surgeons and doctors advised an immediate operation, without which, they said, he could not live more than a few days. It appeared that the abscess had burst into his bladder on the day when he had ridden on horseback, and that the discharge of pus would cause gangrene, if it had not already done so. They declared that he must go at once to Versailles; but the shock of the fearful news so overcame him that during the whole of that Sunday he was too ill to be moved, even in a litter. On Monday the 9th, he was borne thither at five in the morning.[2]

After allowing him a short rest, the doctors, wishing to begin the operation, suggested that he should receive the Sacraments. The advice was not taken in good part, for ever since the day of the review he had been in a continual storm of rage; and after the Saturday when the operation was first mentioned, his fury had increased. None the less, he did send for a certain friar at Versailles, and was closeted alone with him about a quarter of an hour. A man as rich as he, and as well prepared, needed no more; and, in any case, the confessions of first ministers have a degree of licence.[3] When they returned to his room, the doctors again suggested Communion, at which he exclaimed that this was easily said, but that for cardinals there was a special service; he did not know what it was, and they must send to Paris, to ask Cardinal Bissy. They looked at one another, understanding that he wished to delay; but since the need was so pressing, they still proposed starting at once, whereupon he sent them packing.

Seeing that there was mortal danger in the slightest postponement, the faculty sent to Meudon for M. le Duc d'Orléans, who came immediately, in the first coach he could find. He exhorted Dubois to submit, then inquired whether there was any risk. The reply was that no promise could be made, but that if nothing were done he would be dead in two hours—perhaps even less. M. le Duc d'Orléans returned to the bedside and begged to such good effect that a consent was extracted. The operation was accordingly begun at five o'clock, and lasted five minutes. It was performed by La Peyronie,[4] who became the King's first surgeon after the

[1] At Meudon.
[2] The King was staying at Meudon, which was why Dubois had to be moved. No one was allowed to die where the King was in residence.
[3] Saint-Simon may have been thinking of Cardinal Mazarin's last confession.
[4] François Gigot de La Peyronie (1678–1747), son of a doctor of Montpellier. In 1733 he was appointed first surgeon to the King.

retirement of Maréchal, who was present the entire time, as was Chirac, and other eminent doctors and surgeons. Dubois screamed and roared in a most horrible manner. M. le Duc d'Orléans entered as soon as all was over, and was informed by the doctors that from the nature of the wound and that which had issued from it, the patient had little time left. In fact, he died precisely twenty-four hours later, on Tuesday, 10 August, at five in the afternoon, storming against the faculty, whom he never ceased to abuse.

They had offered him Extreme Unction, and also Communion, but he would have neither, nor would he endure the presence of a priest, ending his life in black despair, and transports of rage at the necessity for leaving it. Fortune thus played him a low trick, by letting him purchase success so dearly, at the cost of endless labour, intrigue, and agonies of mind; showering upon him quite disproportionate grandeur, power, and riches, only to snatch them away after four short years, when his star was in the zenith—I am reckoning his success as beginning from his appointment as a secretary of State, but if one dates it from his cardinalate, two years was all he had. He died the absolute ruler of his master, less like a minister than the wielder of supreme power. He was superintendent of the post office, cardinal, Archbishop of Cambrai, and Abbot of seven different abbeys, for towards the end he became perfectly insatiable, and was making preparations to seize Citeaux, Prémontré, and several other monasteries. It was later discovered that he was also receiving an English pension of forty thousand pounds sterling.

Out of pure curiosity I reckoned up his income, and I thought it might be of interest to give you my findings. In order to avoid any possible exaggeration, I have minimised the revenues coming from his benefices, appointments, and pension:

Cambrai	120,000 livres
Nogent-sous-Coucy	10,000 „
Saint-Just	10,000 „
Airvault	12,000 „
Bourgueil	12,000 „
Bergues-Saint-Vinocq	60,000 „
Saint-Bertan	80,000 „
Cercamp	20,000 „
	324,000 „
Premier Ministre	150,000 „
Les Postes	100,000 „
	250,000 „
English Pension @ 24 livres to the £	960,000 „
Total	1,534,000 livres

I believe that on top of all this he received twenty thousand livres annually from the Church, for his cardinalate, but the exact amount I never discovered. He made vast sums with Law, most of which were used in Rome, to procure his hat; but there still remained a prodigious amount of money. He had, moreover, enormous quantities of the finest silver and gold plate, most of it beautifully and elaborately ornamented, exceedingly fine furniture, superb jewels, the most magnificent harness from several foreign countries, and wonderfully beautiful coaches. The food at his table was in every way delicious, rich, and abundant, and although he himself ate little, by inclination and for a regimen, he did the honours vastly well. What incredible riches! Raised up from the gutter! What a fall! Truly to him may be applied the psalmist's words: 'I have seen the wicked in great power, and spreading himself like a green bay tree. Yet he passed away, and lo! he was not: yea, I sought him, but he could not be found.'[1]

On the evening of the Wednesday, the day after his death, he was removed from Versailles to Paris, and taken to the chapter-house of the Church of Saint-Honoré, where they buried him a few days later. The various colleges of which he was a member held services for him, as did the Church Assembly whose president he had been. There was also a service at Notre-Dame, in recognition of his rank as first minister. Cardinal de Noailles officiated, in the presence of judges of the higher courts. No funeral orations were made anywhere, for no one ventured to speak in his praise. His brother, an unassuming person, now found himself the inheritor of vast wealth, of which he spent very little, although he did employ a part of it to build a kind of mausoleum, a handsome but simple memorial with a very Christian inscription placed at the end of the church where the cardinal was buried. The rest of the money he gave to the poor, fearing lest it should bring a curse upon him.

There are many examples of great fortunes being made, some of them by men of little account, but never by one so entirely devoid of the requisite talents as was Cardinal Dubois, if one discounts his gift for low and secret intrigues. His mind was mediocre in the extreme, his learning unremarkable, his capabilities non-existent. In appearance he was much like a ferret, but also looked ill-bred. His preaching was highly disagreeable, enumerating point after point, always with hesitancy, and with insincerity written large upon his countenance. His morals were too bad for concealment; his transports not to be excused as madness; his head was incapable of holding more than one subject at a time, and he of conceiving or following any line of action save for his personal advantage. Nothing to him was sacred; he had no respectable attachments, but was outspoken in his contempt for loyalty, promises, honour, truth, and integrity, openly priding himself on his scorn for moral principles. As lustful as he was ambitious, he desired to accumulate all the good things of life for himself

[1] Psalm xxxvii, 35, 36.

alone; thought only of himself, cared nothing for what did not benefit him personally, pronouncing it folly to act or think otherwise. Yet at the same time, he was sweet-spoken, a toady, a trimmer, admiring, fawning, changing his tactics with consummate ease, ready to assume different, sometimes contradictory personalities in order to succeed, but still never managing to charm. In marshalling his arguments he was headlong, gusty, sometimes unintentionally obscure, with little of reality or truth in his reasoning. Disagreements invariably followed; nothing went easily for him. None the less, when he so desired, he could jest gaily enough, and tell a pleasant tale; but he spoiled all by his manner of speaking, and even that might have passed had it not been for the stammer which his falseness had made habitual; for he could never be certain how he would reply.

It is scarely believable that with so many serious defects, the one man he should have been able to charm was M. le Duc d'Orléans, who had so much wit, such clear judgment, such a gift for seeing into a character. Dubois gained his affection when he was his tutor, and later won him over by encouraging his eagerness for freedom, the so-called fashionable world, and the temptations of debauchery, commending his scorn for rank and power, destroying his soul with the fine-sounding maxims of atheistical writers, ruling his mind and will to such a degree that the unhappy prince could never break free from him, any more than he could free himself from the opinions contrary to all reason, truth, and conscience, which he tried so hard to conceal. Once having gained the mastery, it was Dubois's most cherished task, by hook or by crook, to keep his place with the one on whose favour all his hopes and ambitions depended. Not that these rose very high at the beginning, when he was no more than valet to the Curé of Saint-Eustache and Saint-Laurent's assistant; yet they were none the less considerable for an underling of his condition.

To watch the prince continually, to work upon his abnormally weak nature, became his prime object, and also his best hope. It was awareness of M. le Duc d'Orléans's easygoing character that buoyed Dubois up during his various exclusions, the most serious of which occurred at the beginning of the Regency, and you will recall how skilfully he restored himself to favour. Beguiling his master with the secret intrigues in which he was so adept, he induced him to believe in the marvels of uniting with England, an alliance that caused, and still causes, the State great harm. Then, playing upon M. le Duc d'Orléans's personal ambitions, he first bullied him, then wedded him to the notion that should the King die young, the two usurpers[1] would need to hold together; and M. le Duc d'Orléans allowed himself to be influenced by the chatter of Canillac, the

[1] George I a usurper because of the Old Pretender; the Regent would become one if he seized the throne after Louis XV's death, for Philip V, despite the 'renunciations', would have been preferred by very many Frenchmen. Considering the sudden deaths of so many members of the royal family in 1711–1712, it would not have been natural to build with any certainty on the life of the little King.

cunning of the Duc de Noailles, and the commanding airs of the Earl of Stair, which he seemed to find so impressive. Yet for all that, he never desired the crown. That is the extraordinary truth, which I cannot too often repeat because it was continually and most clearly made evident to me; and I call it extraordinary because even had the crown descended to him free of all controversy, he would have felt the burden of it, the restriction, the embarrassment, to a far greater degree than any gratification. Thus had come about the need for a close attachment between himself and Dubois, and the reason why it had to be kept secret.

Step by step, displaying no trace of ability, no care save for his own interests, Dubois rose to be secretary of State. The road to supreme power was thereafter both short and easy. Thenceforward, his mind was fixed on preventing his master (whose slippery nature he well knew) from eluding him. He exhausted himself with spying, watching at every moment to mark what the prince was doing, the length of every audience, his mood, his countenance, his remarks after interviews and parties of pleasure, the persons he had met and their remarks also, afterwards combining and digesting all the information thus received. With deliberate intent he set himself to spread alarm and fear so as to discourage people from going directly to the prince himself, and to upset the plans of any who had dared to make them without his prior consent. Diligent application to this self-appointed task, and an outward show of continual involvement with State affairs, robbed him of his leisure, with the result that he became un-approachable, except at public audiences, or at those rarely granted to foreign ambassadors. As a matter of fact, very few of these managed to see him, for most were reduced to waiting in corridors, on stairways, or in the rooms through which he made his secret exits, and therefore expected to find no one.

On one occasion he threw on the fire a great packet of letters, come from all parts of the world, and all sealed. As he did so, he exclaimed with pleasure at being able to 'catch up with the work'. After his death, several thousand unopened letters were discovered. Indeed, all his work had fallen into arrears; but no one, not even the foreign ambassadors, had dared to complain to M. le Duc d'Orléans, nor did that prince, completely given over to his pleasures and never off the road between Paris and Versailles, cast a thought to State affairs. He was enjoying his freedom too much for that, more especially since Dubois was careful to keep his portfolio stocked with sufficient trifles to fill the King's working hours with the signing of orders for agreed expenditure, or warrants for appointments to vacant benefices.[1] Dubois had taken no firm decisions; everything was

---

[1] Saint-Simon says that when Louis XIV was alive his Tuesday morning's work with the Finance Council consisted entirely of 'signing warrants (instead of leaving this to the Surin-tendant des Finances) in settlement of disputes between individuals on matters of appoint-ments, or prize-money'.

in chaos. You do not need ability to govern like that. Two words to the heads of departments, a few moments spent in providing the King's councils with unimportant dispatches, the rest gone over with M. le Duc d'Orléans, and then allowed to remain in abeyance, such was the entire work of that first minister, apart from his investigations into M. le Duc d'Orléans's private life. All the rest of his time was spent in parades, speech-making, and quarrelling; for the transports of rage, with filthy and abusive language, from which neither men nor women, whatever their rank, were safe, protected him from a vast number of audiences. Most people preferred to deal with lower officials or to abstain entirely, rather than expose themselves to his furious insults. You would scarcely credit the treatment received by ambassadors, prelates, ladies, and otherwise distinguished persons at such interviews.

The appalling scenes created by Cardinal Dubois, more especially after his rise to power, at which time he altogether ceased to restrain himself, would fill a volume. I shall recount no more than a few, just so as to give some examples. When the fit seized him, he would go round and round the room, climbing over tables and chairs, never letting his feet touch the floor, and M. le Duc d'Orléans told me several times that he had often watched him when so engaged. When Mme de Cheverny[1] was widowed and retired to the Incurables, her post as governess to M. le Duc d'Orléans's children was given to Mme de Conflans.[2] Shortly after the coronation, Mme la Duchesse d'Orléans inquired whether she had called on Cardinal Dubois to inform him of her appointment. Mme de Conflans said no, she had seen no reason for a visit since the post was so remote from State affairs. Mme la Duchesse d'Orléans none the less insisted, on the grounds of M. le Duc d'Orléans's close attachment to the cardinal. Whereupon Mme de Conflans protested, finally remarking that she did not wish to be exposed to the affronts of a madman who insulted everyone. She was a woman of spirit, with the courage to defend herself, and though always polite, she could be as proud as any peacock. Mme la Duchesse d'Orléans, however, laughed at her fears, saying that she only had to announce her appointment, and that such a courtesy was bound to please him. Picture her then leaving Versailles immediately after dinner, and arriving in Dubois's huge audience-chamber, in which eight or ten people were waiting to speak to him where he stood by the hearth rating an unfortunate lady in the most filthy and abusive language. Mme de Conflans was panic-stricken. She was not big at any time; she now shrank still further; yet she pulled herself together and stepped up to the cardinal, as the other lady retired. As soon as he perceived her, he asked her sharply what she wanted. 'Monseigneur,' said she, 'Ho! so it's Monseigneur now, is it?' he inter-

[1] Marie de Johanne de Saumery, Comtesse de Cheverny (1652–1727). She became the younger children's governess in 1716.
[2] Louise Françoise de Jussac, Marquise de Conflans.

rupted, 'That will not serve, Madame.' 'But, Monseigneur,' she tried again. 'What the hell do you mean; do I have to say it twice?' he burst out again, 'When I tell you that something will not serve, that is so, and no more about it.' 'Monseigneur,' Mme de Conflans made this third attempt so as to explain that she wanted nothing; but at the first word, the cardinal took her by the shoulders, turned her about, and gave her a great push in the back. 'Go to hell!' he shouted; 'leave me in peace.' Mme de Conflans, thinking she would fall in a dead faint, fled weeping furious tears, and arrived in that condition before Mme la Duchesse d'Orléans to tell her, through sobs, of her encounter. Everyone was well accustomed to Dubois's tirades, but this one appeared so extremely funny from her account that a burst of laughter completed her indignation and left her vowing that she would never again go near that impossible man.

On the first Easter Day after he was made a cardinal, he woke at eight and rang his bell as though he would break it. Picture him cursing his servants in the most horrible manner, spitting out all imaginable filth and abuse, shouting at the top of his voice because they had not wakened him. He had desired to say mass, he declared, and with all he had to do, could scarcely now find the time. The best thing he could have done after such preliminaries was to omit it altogether, and so far as I am aware, he never did say mass after his promotion.

He took as his private secretary a man named Venier, whom he had caused to be unfrocked, extracting him from the Abbaye de Saint-Germain, where he had been a lay-brother for twenty years administering the finances with prudence and ability. Venier soon learned not to stand on ceremony with him; but spoke his mind whenever the occasion demanded. One morning the cardinal asked for a paper that did not come readily to hand, and immediately began swearing, blaspheming, shouting at his clerks and, as though he had not already enough of them, threatening to enlist twenty, thirty, fifty, a hundred more, all the while creating an appalling rumpus. Venier remained silent, as Dubois called him to witness how ill he was served for the wages he paid, and then, losing his temper a second time, demanded an answer. 'Monseigneur,' said Venier, 'have just one clerk more, and let his sole task be to curse and rage for you. You will see that all will then be well; for you will have plenty of time in which to discover that you are very well served.' At this the cardinal laughed, and all was peace again.

Every night he ate a chicken. That was all his supper, and he ate it alone. I do not know how it happened, but on one occasion his servants forgot it. As he went to bed, Dubois remembered, and rang his bell, ranting and roaring at his people, who listened unmoved. Picture him yelling for his chicken at the top of his voice, and damning his servants for being so late. Picture also his astonishment at being told he had already eaten it; but that if he so desired, another might be spitted. 'What is that?' he cried. 'You say I have eaten it?' A firm assent persuaded him that the facts were not otherwise—but they mocked him. I say no more; this will suffice to show his monstrous character, and the relief which persons of all kinds and conditions experienced at his death. I may truly say that all Europe felt relief, not excluding his own brother, whom he treated like a negro slave, on one occasion threatening to dismiss an equerry for lending a coach to take him across Paris.

Most relieved of all was M. le Duc d'Orléans. For some time past he had been groaning under the burden of that heavy yoke and the slavery it entailed. Not only could he no longer issue orders or make decisions; it had become useless to express wishes on great or small matters. In everything he was forced to abide by the cardinal's rulings, and at the least opposition Dubois would become transported with fury, scolding and rebuking him as though he were a mere commoner. Poor M. le Duc d'Orléans had begun to discover that he was alone, and his isolation showed him the extent of the cardinal's power, and the eclipse of his own. He feared Dubois; he could no longer endure him; he longed to be rid of him. One observed this every day in a thousand different ways; yet he neither dared to act, nor knew how best to do so. Deserted and spied upon, he had no one in whom he could confide, and the cardinal, to whom all was reported, redoubled his tantrums so as to hold down by fear what he had gained by cunning. It was hopeless for him to try to retain his power by other means.

Immediately after his death, M. le Duc d'Orléans returned to Meudon and reported to the King, who straightway desired him to take charge of the nation's affairs, and appointed him first minister. He took the oath next day, and the warrant was at once sent for registration to the Parlement. This sudden decision for which M. le Duc d'Orléans was totally unprepared, came about because of the Bishop of Fréjus's fear lest someone else receive the post. As I have already related, the King loved M. le Duc d'Orléans because he treated him with enormous respect, and allowed him, in their work together, to feel himself to be the fount of honour in making selections for the appointments. What is more, he never bored him, nor let their working hours encroach upon his pleasures. Despite all his tricks and his wiles, Dubois had never won the King's affection or become intimate with him, and it was plain to all, even to the near-sighted, that the King felt the strongest aversion for him. This distressed the cardinal, and made him redouble his endeavours to please; but apart from his affected airs, and the unpleasantness of his manners when trying to be most amiable, he had two enemies attached to the King, both of them eager to frustrate him. One of these was the Maréchal de Villeroy, until his dismissal; the other, a far more dangerous antagonist, was Fréjus, whose ambition made him loathe the cardinal, and who had been firmly resolved to destroy him, should M. le Duc d'Orléans fail.

A man still more corrupt, were that possible, than Cardinal Dubois followed him a fortnight later. Premier Président de Mesmes, aged sixty-one, who had already been afflicted by apoplectic seizures, now suffered one that finished him for good in less than twenty-four hours, during which brief period no one could extract from him the least sign of life.[1] I say more corrupt than Dubois because of his foul and most notorious duplicity and because, being of rich and noble birth, he had no need to make a fortune —unlike Dubois who was of the very dregs. Not that this excused him, but he had that much more temptation than Président de Mesmes, who had only to enjoy the honourable fruits of his birthright. I have so often had occasion to acquaint you with his hateful and most despicable character that I may now safely refrain from any further soiling of the paper. You already know how they forced me to be reconciled with him after the Duc de Lorges's disgraceful marriage with his daughter[2]—a match which he had every cause to repent later, as he several times confessed to me.

All this time I had been living quietly at La Ferté with most excellent company, and had seen no reason to leave there when couriers arrived bringing me news of Cardinal Dubois's death, and urging me to return. Another then arrived, dispatched by the vanity and greed of the premier président's daughters, begging me to return immediately to ask M. le Duc d'Orléans for a pension on their behalf. Once again I yielded to the kindness and piety of Mme la Duchesse de Saint-Simon, who desired of all things that I should not refuse them that service, and I accordingly left for Paris a few days later. The Court had gone back to Versailles on 13 August, and it was there that I found M. le Duc d'Orléans.

As soon as I entered his study, he came forward to greet me, asking anxiously if I had meant to desert him. I replied that whilst his cardinal lived I had found myself to be supremely useless, and had taken advantage of that situation to enjoy my freedom and a rest. Now that the obstacle had so gratifyingly been removed, I was once again his most obedient servant. He made me promise to take up my old life with him, as it had been before, and without ever mentioning the cardinal he began to talk of current affairs both at home and abroad, explaining the problems, and describing the concern of England and Holland regarding a new company of merchant-bankers being formed, at Ostend, by the Emperor. They were anxious to have it suppressed, in the interests of their trade. M. le Duc d'Orléans discussed with me the advantages to France in this matter, and gave me his views on the best way of promoting them. I thought him well content, cheerful, glad to return to work. When we had exhausted the subject, and spoken of the King, with whom he was greatly pleased, I introduced

[1] The doctors would have done everything to put life back into him by rude shocks, such as shakings, walking up and down, and emetics, partly so that he might be shriven, partly on the principle that makes one shake a watch to set the mechanism going. See the death of Monsieur, I, pp. 158–159.

[2] See II, p. 355.

the question of a pension for the daughters of the premier président. He burst out laughing, recalling the vast sums which he had lavished upon their father, or been robbed of by him, and proceeded to laugh at me for pleading their cause in so unlikely a suit, especially in view of my relationship with their late father. He then, in one short and admirable phrase, delivered his funeral oration. Let me frankly admit that I did not persist in something which I also considered to be wholly absurd, and which was no business of mine. From then onwards, I was on the same terms with M. le Duc d'Orléans as we had been before Dubois's appointment as first minister, and he continued to place all his confidence in me. I must, however, confess that I did not make any great effort to influence him.

The new part of Meudon had been returned to me, fully furnished when the Court again took up residence at Versailles, and on the same terms as before the King's visit. The Duc and Duchesse d'Humières were our guests there, in very good company. The Duc d'Humières asked if I would take him one morning to Versailles, as he wished to thank M. le Duc d'Orléans.[1] The Regent was not dressed when we arrived, but still in the cupboard under the stairs, which he had made his privy. I found him there, sitting on his *chaise-percée*, surrounded by two or three of his gentlemen and valets. His appearance terrified me. His head was hanging; his face purple-red; he was so dazed that he did not even see me enter. When his servants announced me, he slowly turned his head, scarcely raising it at all, and asked in a thick voice what brought me so early. I told him. I had gone in to beg him to come quickly to the room where he dressed, so as not to keep the Duc d'Humières waiting; but I was so horrified that I could not explain. I drew Simiane,[2] his first gentleman, into the window recess, and expressed my surprise and alarm at M. le Duc d'Orléans's condition. Simiane replied, however, that for a long time past he had been so in the early morning; that today was no different, and that my distress was because I did not ordinarily see him at such times. He would be better, said Simiane, when dressing had shaken him awake. None the less, when he did emerge, he seemed to me very little recovered. He received the Duc d'Humières's thanks looking heavy and bewildered; and he (always so gracious, so polite, so adept at turning the pleasant and appropriate phrase) scarcely uttered a word. We withdrew a moment later.

M. le Duc d'Orléans's condition gave me much food for thought. For months past secretaries of State had been telling me that he would have signed no matter what in the early morning, had they presented it. This was the effect of his supper-parties. More than once in the past year when we were working alone together, he had suddenly disappeared, explaining

---

[1] Louis François d'Aumont (1670–1751) became Duc d'Humières by his marriage to the hereditary duchess. He was the younger son of the Duc d'Aumont, and wished to thank for the governorships of Boulogne and Boulonnais which he had inherited after the death of his father.

[2] François Antoine, Marquis de Simiane-Esparron (1674–1734).

that Chirac continually purged him because his stomach was always so full that when he sat down to his evening meal he had no appetite, notwithstanding that he ate nothing early in the morning, and no more than a cup of chocolate between one and two in the afternoon, in public, at the time when everyone saw him.[1] I had spoken my mind to him on that account, but nothing that I said would have made the smallest difference. I knew, what was more, that Chirac had spoken plainly to him regarding the continuance of his supper-parties, saying that they must very soon lead to a fit of apoplexy or to dropsy of the chest, for his breathing at such times was impeded. Thereupon he had exclaimed in horror at the last named disease because it was slow, suffocating, disabling, showing the approach of death. He said that he would far prefer apoplexy which came as a surprise, and killed instantly without giving one time to think. What other man, in those circumstances, would have preferred sudden death to one that would give him time to collect his thoughts? He might even have resolved to live instead of die, and have done what was necessary to that end by leading a sober, healthy, decent life that might, considering his robust constitution, have continued for very many years of highly enjoyable existence. But alas! the unhappy prince was doubly blind.

I was at this time in close touch with the Bishop of Fréjus, and since it appeared only too likely that a replacement in charge of State affairs might be needed, I much preferred that he should be the man. I therefore sought him out, explaining the state of M. le Duc d'Orléans's health as I had observed it that same morning, predicting that his death was fast approaching and would be very sudden. I then advised him to lose no time, but at once to make plans with the King so as to be appointed first minister, should the post fall vacant. I said there would be no difficulty, since he had ample proof of the King's affection for him (indeed, there was no one else King Louis cared for half as much); and their long daily sessions would give him ample opportunity to make arrangements to step immediately into office. I thought he appeared extremely grateful for this piece of advice and my ambitions for him; but he behaved modestly, as though conscious that the rank and post were far above his station.

This was not the first time I had mentioned the possibility, but never before had it been an immediate issue. Fleury now said that he had given it much thought; but had concluded that the appointment of anyone other than a prince of the blood would create a public outcry, and that Monsieur le Duc was the only possible candidate. I exclaimed violently at the danger of appointing a prince of the blood, whom no one would dare oppose, and whose friends would line their purses. I reminded him that the late King would never have one in his councils for fear of giving him too much power. And how compare a mere seat on a council of a governing King, fiercely jealous of his supreme authority, and the place of first

[1] See p. 158, above.

minister with an inexperienced boy-King, governing in name only? If such a first minister were also a prince of the blood he would, in very truth, be an absolute ruler. I recalled how greedily the princes had plundered the finances, how stubborn they had been in support of Law, and of everything that promoted their interests, how bold in the accumulation of wealth.[1] That should show him the kind of stewardship to be expected from a prince of the blood, more especially from Monsieur le Duc, who combined avarice with stupidity, obstinacy, and insatiable ambition, and whose friends were even more self-seeking, as well as cleverer, than himself. Under such administrators France, and Fleury also, would fall victim to the personal ambitions of that entire circle. He did not contradict me; saying only that there was still much good in Monsieur le Duc, who was honourable and upright, and had shown him friendship. The true reason was, however, that the descent from M. le Duc d'Orléans to a commoner would be altogether too great, too much for his successor to bear, when he had to face the envy and jealousy of the whole world. A prince of the blood, on the other hand, stood so far above the rest (especially Monsieur le Duc who was the only one of suitable age) that he would not be troubled; and a further consideration was that he was neither acquainted nor familiar with the King although, having replaced M. du Maine as superintendent of his education, he should have been both. He would thus need the good offices of all those in the intimate circle. Fleury, after reflecting long on all these matters, had finally concluded that Monsieur le Duc was the only possible choice.

His last words silenced me. I replied that he was better placed to see the entire picture, and that I must be content with having warned him, although I much regretted his refusal to take the office. I shall leave you to imagine the expressions of gratitude, friendship and confidence with which his reply was seasoned.

I returned to Meudon with the Duc d'Humières, well persuaded that Fréjus was restrained only by fear. I thought him as eager as any man to wield supreme power, but that as a protection against envy great enough to overthrow him, he had devised the strategy of sheltering behind a prince of the blood, being fully satisfied that Monsieur le Duc, the only one of an age to take office, would soon prove in every way incapable. Under his protection Fréjus would be first minister in all but name, the King's tutor and sole possessor of his affection. In those circumstances, Monsieur le Duc would not dare to attempt anything without his support. Thus without jealousy or scandal, and conserving a suitably modest demeanour, he would swiftly gather the power into his own hands. Any endeavour on my part to foil this well-laid plot would be like running my head against a wall. I did not therefore tell him that Mme de Prye and the rest of

[1] Madame la Duchesse and the Prince de Conti had each extracted millions in paper money from Law, 'for all the world as though they drew water from a tap'.

Monsieur le Duc's intimates were certain to destroy him, for in their lust after power and profit they would fill Monsieur le Duc with a longing for independence that would very quickly result in Fréjus's dismissal. I did, however, relate all the above to Mme de Saint-Simon, from whom I kept nothing secret, relying, as always, on the great commonsense that has so ably supported me all through my life. She agreed with me on every point.

On 19 November, the Duc de Lauzun died, at the age of ninety and six months. The very close attachment between the two sisters whom we had married, and constant residence at the Court, where we four had a pavilion permanently allotted us on all the Marly excursions, meant that we lived in one another's pockets. After the King's death we met almost every day, and invariably dined together, either at my house or at his.[1] He was such an extraordinary person, so eccentric in every way, that La Bruyère is right to say in *Les Caractères* that the vicissitudes of his life defy imagination. To those who knew him well, even in old age, the remark seems to fit exactly; which is why I have decided to describe him at length.[2]

M. de Lauzun was small and fair, extremely well built, with a noble air, a countenance that sparkled with intelligence and inspired respect, but was without charm—at least, so I was told by his contemporaries. Overflowing with ambition, whims, and fancies, he was covetous of everything, always wanting more, never content with what he possessed. He had no education, no culture, no intellectual graces or refinement. By nature he was melancholy, unsociable, violent; lordly in all his ways, essentially spiteful and malicious, and made more so by jealousy and ambition; yet when he made a friend, which was rare, he himself was a good one, and a good kinsman also. Quick in making enemies, even with persons of no importance, he was cruel to their defects and in discovering and mocking their absurdities. He was courageous in the extreme and most dangerously rash. As a courtier, he was insolent, mocking, and servile to the point of cringing, ready to use any mean trick, plotting and labouring with infinite care in order to gain his ends, therefore dangerous to ministers, feared by everyone at the Court, uttering biting remarks with a wit that spared no one.

When he first appeared at Court, he was poor and without prospects, a younger son, a mere boy from Gascony, who arrived fresh from the provinces with the title of Marquis de Puyguilhem. The Maréchal de Gramont, his father's first cousin, gave him a home. Gramont was a man of the highest importance among the courtiers of his day, a friend of the Queen-mother and of Cardinal Mazarin, and colonel of the guards. His eldest son, the Comte de Guiche, was the very flower of valour and

---

[1] At that time Lauzun was living at the Quai Malaquais, and Saint-Simon, who had moved from the Rue des Saints-Pères in 1714, in the Rue Saint-Dominique.

[2] Since cuts were necessary, the editor made it a rule to exclude events that happened before Saint-Simon's time at the Court as he had them only by hearsay, while he is always telling us that the only important matters are what passed beneath his eyes, or through his hands. Lauzun's exploits are, however, so famous that it seemed wrong to omit them.

chivalry, a great favourite with the King, and with the cardinal's niece the Comtesse de Soissons,[1] in whose drawing-room the King was permanently rooted. M. de Guiche presented the Marquis de Puyguilhem, who in a remarkably short time became a favourite also, being given the King's dragoon regiment, quickly promoted to be brigadier-general, with the new rank of colonel-general of dragoons especially created for him.

The Duc de Mazarin, who had retired from the Court in 1669, wished to sell his commission as grandmaster of artillery. Puyguilhem was the first to hear of it, and begged it from the King, who gave his promise; but only on condition of absolute secrecy for the next few days. At the end of that time, Puyguilhem, who had the entrées, waited for the King to leave the finance council, in the empty room, between the council chamber and the one where all the courtiers were gathered. He there saw Nyert, the head valet on duty,[2] who asked what he wanted. Puyguilhem, sure of success, seized the opportunity to gain a friend by confiding to this servant the news of his appointment. Nyert congratulated him, pulled out his watch, saw that there was still time to act, as he said, in a rather urgent matter for which the King had given orders. He tore four steps at a time up the narrow stairs at the top of which was the tiny room where Louvois worked—at Saint-Germain, there were so few and such small rooms that the ministers and most of the courtiers lodged at their private houses in the town. Nyert burst into this office of Louvois's to inform him that Puyguilhem was to be made grandmaster of artillery immediately after the council, and he repeated what he had been told.

Now Louvois detested Puyguilhem, the friend of his rival Colbert. It alarmed him to imagine a haughty favourite in a post so closely touching the war ministry, his own department. He therefore embraced Nyert, sent him flying back, took up a few papers to offer an excuse, went down to find Nyert and Puyguilhem in the above mentioned room. Nyert, apparently much astonished, remarked that the council was still sitting. 'No matter,' said Louvois, 'I must go in, I have urgent business for the King', and so saying, he entered. King Louis was surprised; he asked what brought him, then rose and approached him. Louvois drew him aside into a window recess, and there informed him that the news had spread of Puyguilhem's new appointment, and that that gentleman was waiting in the adjoining room for the King to confirm it. Louvois continued that although His Majesty was the absolute master of his favours and selections, he felt it his duty to say that Puyguilhem, so arrogant and capricious, would be sure to reorganize the entire artillery; that this post was inextricably connected with the work of the war department; that nothing would run smoothly

[1] Olympe Mancini, Comtesse de Soissons (1639–1708). She was a niece of Cardinal Mazarin.
[2] Pierre de Nyert (1597–1682). He was a musician, and in 1638 had been head valet in charge of the wardrobe of Louis XIII. Saint-Simon is speaking of a time very many years before he came to the Court, in fact thirty-seven years before he was born.

between a grandmaster of artillery and a secretary of State who cordially disliked each other, and that one of the disadvantages would be their having constantly to refer their quarrels and arguments to the King for settlement.

The King was greatly vexed to learn that his secret had become known to the very man from whom he had most wished to hide it. He turned to Louvois saying with extreme gravity that nothing as yet was settled, dismissed him, and returned to his seat at the council. The meeting soon afterwards ended and the King went to mass; he noted Puyguilhem, but passed by without a word. That gentleman, completely mystified, waited all the rest of that day; but when the time came for the King's *petit coucher* and there was still no announcement, he brought the matter up. King Louis replied that it was not yet time, but that he would see.[1] That ambiguous answer and the curt manner of its utterance put fear into Puyguilhem's soul. He was a great stealer of hearts and had a way with the ladies; he therefore went to Mme de Montespan and, confiding his trouble, implored her to act. She promised miracles, and with that hope kept him happy for some days longer.

At last, tired of waiting and wholly unaware of the reason for his disappointment, he took a course so rash that it would be unbelievable had it not been vouched for by the entire Court of that day. It so happened that Puyguilhem was sleeping with one of Mme de Montespan's favourite maids—for he baulked at nothing that would serve him for warnings and protection. He now resolved upon the most hazardous enterprise ever conceived. In all his various love-affairs, the King never failed to spend the night with the Queen. He was sometimes late in joining her, but he never missed, and thus, for convenience, he went to bed with his mistresses in the afternoon. Puyguilhem persuaded the above mentioned waiting-maid to hide him beneath the bed on which the King would lie with Mme de Montespan. She did so, and by their talk he learned of how Louvois had prevented his appointment; of the King's extreme anger at the telling of his secret; of his decision to refuse Puyguilhem on that account, and more especially in order to avoid having to mediate between him and Louvois in their quarrels. Puyguilhem heard all that was said by the King and his mistress, and perceived that she who had promised him marvels was doing him every imaginable disservice. One cough, the smallest movement, the faintest noise would have revealed the presence of that daredevil; and then what would have become of him? It is the kind of thing that makes one laugh and shudder all at the same moment.

He was luckier than he deserved, for they did not notice him. At length the King and his mistress rose; the King put on his clothes and returned to his apartments; Mme de Montespan attired herself for the rehearsal of a ballet, at which the King, the Queen, and the entire Court were to be

[1] See note, p. 387 above.

present. The maid extracted Puyguilhem, who apparently felt no need to adjust his dress, for instead of returning to his room, he posted himself outside Mme de Montespan's door. When she emerged he offered her his wrist, asking in soft, respectful tones whether he might dare to hope that she had remembered him. She assured him that indeed she had spoken and, in the most gratifying manner possible, enumerated the various services she had rendered him. Now and again he stopped her, plying her with eager questions designed to lead her to still higher flights. After which, putting his mouth to her ear, he told her she was a liar, a trollop, a whore, a piece of dog-filth, repeating to her, word for word, the whole of her conversation with the King. Mme de Montespan was so flabbergasted she had no strength left for utterance, and only just managed to continue walking without displaying the fact that her legs and entire body were all a-tremble. When they arrived at the rehearsal room where the Court was assembled she fainted quite away. The King flew to her side in high alarm, and they had great difficulty in reviving her. She told him what had happened that same evening, vowing that only the devil himself could have informed Puyguilhem. King Louis was furious because of the injuries she had suffered, but remained completely at a loss to discover how Puyguilhem could have known.

As for Puyguilhem himself, so much incensed was he at losing the artillery that relations between him and the King became uncomfortably strained. It was a situation that could not have endured. At the end of a few days he used his entrées to seek the chance of a private word, and seized it when it came. He spoke of the artillery, and boldly reminded the King of his promise. The answer came that this no longer applied. The promise had been given on condition of secrecy, and Puyguilhem had blabbed. At those words Puyguilhem drew his sword and broke it across his foot, furiously exclaiming that he would not serve a prince who so basely failed to keep his word. Thereupon the King, transported with rage, took what may well have been the finest action of his life. He turned away, opened the window, and flung out his cane, saying that it would grieve him to be obliged to strike a gentleman. Then immediately he left the room.

Next morning, Puyguilhem, who had not dared to show himself in the meanwhile, was arrested in his bedroom and taken thence to the Bastille. It so happened, however, that he was a close friend of Guitry,[1] a great favourite for whom the post of grandmaster of the wardrobe had been especially created, and that Guitry was brave enough to intercede for him. He managed to persuade the King that Puyguilhem's disappointment was so great it had quite distracted him, with the result that King Louis's heart was softened. He presented the artillery to the Comte de Lude, a Knight of the Order whom he greatly relished because they shared the same tastes

[1] Guy de Chaumont, Marquis de Guitry. He was made a counsellor of State in 1657, and grandmaster of the wardrobe in 1669.

in gallantry and hunting. Du Lude sold his post of first gentleman of the chamber to the Duc de Gesvres in order to pay for the artillery, and the King obliged Gesvres to offer his former post of captain of the bodyguard to Puyguilhem, as a consolation. At this incredibly swift return to favour, Puyguilhem had the hardihood to refuse Gesvres's offer, hoping for something better; but even this did not finally affront the King. Guitry saw his friend at the Bastille next day, and with enormous difficulty persuaded him to accept the King's bounty. In a moment he was freed and allowed to return to Saint-Germain, where he saluted the King, took the oath on his new appointment, and sold the colonelcy of dragoons.

He had been governor of Berry since 1665. I shall not here recount his adventures with La Grande Mademoiselle, who gives so artless a description of them in her memoirs; or his supreme folly in not immediately marrying her after gaining the King's consent—especially since his only reason for postponement was to secure the royal liveries and celebration of the wedding during the King's mass. In the event the delay proved fatal because it gave time for Monsieur and Monsieur le Prince to persuade the King to retract. Mademoiselle fumed and raged, but Puyguilhem, who by his father's death had become Comte de Lauzun, offered his marriage as a willing sacrifice to the King thereby showing more prudence than appeared altogether necessary in the circumstances.[1] He had by then received the captaincy of the hundred *gentilshommes à bec de corbin*[2] in succession to his father, and had been promoted to lieutenant-general.

He was in love at that time with Mme de Monaco,[3] a crony of the first Madame[4] who selected her when, as a Daughter of England, she received the King's permission to appoint, like the Queen, a superintendent of her household. The appointment made Lauzun wildly jealous[5] and furiously angry with her. One afternoon, that summer, he went to Saint-Cloud and found Madame and all her court sitting on the floor for coolness in the heat, and Mme de Monaco, half sitting, half lying, with one hand outstretched, palm upwards. Lauzun, flirting with the ladies, turned suddenly with a movement so skilful that he planted his heel on Mme de Monaco's open palm. Then, suddenly executing upon it a neat pirouette, he departed. That lady, however, had sufficient self-command not to cry out or complain.

Shortly afterwards he did far worse, when he discovered that the King

---

[1] It is generally supposed that a secret marriage had already taken place, but there is no proof of this.

[2] They carried gilded battle axes shaped like ravens' beaks and formed part of the famous household troops, the *Maison du Roi* (see index, I), so justly feared in the wars of Louis XIV.

[3] Catherine Charlotte de Gramont, Princesse de Monaco (1639–1678).

[4] Henrietta of England (1644–1670), first wife of Philippe I, Duc d'Orléans.

[5] The second Madame wrote later: 'I would not put my hand in the fire and swear that Mme de Monaco never slept with the King. . . . Lauzun had a love-affair with her, but a secret one. He had forbidden her to glance amorously at the King, but once he happened to be in the same room when they were flirting, and he was so overcome with jealousy that . . .' and she tells this same story.

was enjoying some kind of affair with her, and the fact that at a certain hour Bontemps brought her, wrapped in a cloak, up the concealed staircase and on to the landing outside the back door of the King's offices, where also was a privy standing immediately opposite. Lauzun arrived early and went into hiding in the privy, securing himself with the hook behind the door, and able to watch through the keyhole for the critical moment when the King unlocked his door, put the key on the outside, and then re-entered closing the door after him. Lauzun waited a while listening at the King's door, then, giving the key a double turn, he swiftly withdrew it from the lock and threw it into the privy, once more enclosing himself therein. Soon afterwards Bontemps, arriving with the lady, was vastly surprised to find no key. He knocked gently but without effect, then struck harder until the King arrived. Bontemps said the lady was there, but no key, and asked him to open. The King said he had put the key outside. Bontemps searched on the floor, while the King, trying to force the door, found that it was locked and double-locked. Picture all three of them highly astonished and completely bewildered. A conversation ensued through the keyhole, trying to determine what had happened. The King became exhausted wrestling with the lock. In the end they had to bid one another farewell with the door between. And there was Lauzun listening to every word they said, and watching them through the keyhole of his privy, as safely protected by the hook as though he had been about his normal business. And all the while he was in fits of silent laughter, vastly enjoying the absurd predicament.

In 1670, the King decided to take the ladies on a triumphal journey to inspect his Flanders fortresses. He was guarded by an entire army corps and all the troops of his *Maison*, such a vast body that the alarm was raised in the Low Countries, and he had all the trouble in the world to calm their fears. He gave command of the whole to the Comte de Lauzun, with the rank of general. It was an occasion on which Lauzun shone particularly, showing himself extremely capable, gallant with the ladies, and most lavish in his spending; but such glory and the accompanying proof of high favour gave Louvois food for reflection. That minister now joined with Mme de Montespan, who did not forgive Lauzun for his eavesdropping or his atrocious insults, and together they succeeded in reminding the King of the broken sword, and the insolent refusal of the captaincy. They made Lauzun appear as forgetting his place, enticing Mademoiselle to the point of being about to marry her, so that he might become possessor of her great wealth, a man whose headstrong nature would be a perpetual danger, and who was even then attracting the devotion of the army by his open-handed bounty. They further accused him of disloyalty, in that he had continued to be friendly with the Comtesse de Soissons,[1] even after her dismissal

---

[1] She was involved in the trial of the poisoner Voisin. Saint-Simon has got something wrong since the marriage was not abandoned until the end of 1670, and the execution of Mme Voisin did not take place until 1680.

from the Court, under suspicion of most horrible crimes. Considering the savage treatment which they brought down upon him, they must have imputed some of those crimes to Lauzun himself.

They continued their pursuit throughout the whole of 1671 without Lauzun noticing any change in the manner of the King or Mme de Montespan, who continued to behave to him with their wonted friendliness and consideration. He was something of an expert on precious stones and the various methods of setting them, and Mme de Montespan often consulted him. One afternoon in mid-November 1671, he returned from Paris, where he had been to examine some jewels for her. He stepped down from his coach and went straight to his room. The Maréchal de Rochefort, captain of the guard, entered upon his heels, and placed him under arrest. Lauzun, astounded, asked to know the reason, demanded to see the King or Mme de Montespan, or at least to write to them. All was forbidden. They removed him to the Bastille, and shortly after to Pignerol, where he was confined in a dungeon. His post of captain of the bodyguard was given to M. de Luxembourg, and his governorship of Berry to the Duc de La Rochefoucauld who, after Guitry's death, also became master of the robes.

You may imagine Lauzun's state of mind, hurtled in the twinkling of an eye from the loftiest heights to the deepest dungeon in the fortress of Pignerol, without having been given the least notion of his offence or allowed to see anyone. He managed to keep his health for a considerable time, but at last became so ill that he felt the need for a confessor. I have often heard him tell how much he dreaded to be sent a bogus priest, and how to protect himself he had stubbornly insisted on a Capuchin.[1] He used to say that when a friar arrived, he took a firm grip on his beard at both sides, and tugged with all his might, so as to be sure there was no trickery. He was kept at Pignerol for five years.[2]

Necessity teaches prisoners new skills. There were many others in the cells above and on each side of Lauzun, and they had devised a means of communication. This had led to the boring of well-concealed holes, so as to hear better, then to increasing them in size until they were large enough for a man to pass. Fouquet, the one-time minister of finance, had been confined there since December 1664, and when he learned of Lauzun's presence in the dungeon below, he most ardently desired to see him; for when they last had met, Lauzun had been no more than a youth, striving to become a courtier. Those prisoners who had become acquainted with Lauzun now proposed to hoist him up through one of the tunnels, which Lauzun gladly accepted, for he was no less eager to see Fouquet. Picture them together, and imagine Fouquet's stupefaction as he heard the story of this younger son who, when he last had seen him, thought himself incredibly lucky to be sheltered by the Marquis de Gramont, and who had

[1] Because they all wore long beards.
[2] Nearly ten years, from December 1671 to April 1681.

since become colonel of dragoons, captain of the bodyguard, and an army general.[1] Fouquet, more and more astounded, began to doubt Lauzun's sanity, and when he heard the rest, the grandmastership of artillery, so narrowly missed; the events that followed, culminating with the King's consent to his marriage with Mademoiselle; how that had miscarried, and the vast riches that would have been Lauzun's had it taken place, he became convinced of his madness. Thereupon all hopes of an attachment vanished, at least on Fouquet's side, for he regarded Lauzun's adventures as mere fiction, and all the news he brought of the Court and Society as worthless.

The lot of the unfortunate Fouquet was shortly afterwards much improved, for his wife and some of the officers of the garrison received permission to visit him. One of his first remarks was to pity poor, unhappy Lauzun, once so full of promise, who had evidently been imprisoned to conceal his madness. You may imagine his feelings when they told him that Lauzun's stories were no more than the truth. After a time, Lauzun also was moved from his dungeon to a bedroom, and was given the same privileges as Fouquet, which meant that they could visit one another at their pleasure. I never learned what occurred, but when Lauzun left Pignerol he was Fouquet's enemy, and thereafter did him all the harm possible, even to persecuting his family after Fouquet's death,[2] which everyone considered most reprehensible.

No one had expected Lauzun to be confined for long, but he was not released until 1681, and even then was not allowed to emerge from Anjou and Touraine. Some considerable time later, he received permission to return to Paris, on condition of never coming within two leagues of wherever the King was in residence. Once established there, boredom led him to gambling for vast sums in which he proved amazingly lucky, and a most daring and skilful player. Monsieur, who occasionally paid short visits to Paris, invited him sometimes to play at the Palais Royal, then in the summer months to Saint-Cloud. Lauzun lived for several years after that fashion, winning a fortune, and lending with great generosity. Yet, though he dwelt so near the Court and mingled with the best people, he was strictly forbidden to approach more closely. At last, unable to endure this restriction, he begged the King's leave to go to England where huge fortunes were made playing for the highest imaginable stakes. The King consented, and Lauzun departed, furnished with so much money that he became extremely popular, and was no more miserable than he had been in Paris.

[1] In the French service there were naval as well as army generals (for example, the Comte de Toulouse was a naval general).

[2] The rumour was that Lauzun, who could not leave any woman unseduced, had exerted undue pressure on the Fouquets' youngest daughter when she visited the prison with her mother.

King James, ruling in England at that time, gave him a most honourable welcome. The revolution was already impending, and erupted eight or ten months after Lauzun's arrival. It would almost seem that it had been arranged on purpose to serve him, for everyone knows how much it profited him. James II, uncertain of his fate, betrayed by his friends and his ministers, forsaken by his people, with the Prince of Orange the idol of the army and the fleet, entrusted his family to the care of Lauzun who brought the queen and the Prince of Wales in safety to Paris. The queen in her letter of thanks to King Louis included a passage to the effect that her joy at being safe under the King's protection was somewhat tempered by being forbidden to present the man who had rescued her. The King's answer was that he, too, was grateful to the Comte de Lauzun, and would testify as much by receiving him forthwith and restoring him to favour. And so it was indeed, for when she presented him at Saint-Germain, he was treated with the utmost graciousness, given back his entrées, and promised a lodging at the Château de Versailles, which he immediately received. You may imagine his feelings at that triumphant return from outer darkness. He also received a lodging in the Château de Saint-Germain, when that became the residence in France of King James.

Lauzun, skilful courtier that he was, drew the maximum of profit from both courts, using his connection with the English one as a pretext for speaking often to our King, and for bearing his messages. In the end, he succeeded so well that he was permitted to receive the Order of the Garter from the hands of the King of England, at a ceremony at Notre-Dame. King Louis also gave him leave to serve King James with the rank of general, and entrusted the French contingent to his command when that monarch made his second expedition to Ireland. In that campaign the Battle of the Boyne was lost; but in spite of that defeat, the Comte de Lauzun received on his return the letters patent of a dukedom, which were registered at the Parlement in May 1696. What a marvel! But not even that would have compared with a royal marriage to La Grande Mademoiselle, the ownership of most enormous wealth, and the rank and privileges of a Duke and Peer of Montpensier! What a pedestal to have scaled and, had there been children, to what heights might he not have risen!

He was in every way a most extraordinary man, and he delighted in emphasizing his strangeness, even among his family or with his valets. He would often pretend to be blind and deaf, so as to see or hear more than people imagined, and diverted himself by teasing fools (even those of high rank) by jabbering nonsense at them. His manner was deceptively quiet, restrained, gentle, even humble-seeming; but in that honeyed voice of his he made remarks of devastating aptness, either angrily or mocking, never more than a word or two, with a look sometimes of such innocence that he appeared not to be aware of what he had said. Everyone feared him, and though he had a vast acquaintance, he had few or no friends. Yet he

deserved to have friends because of his eagerness to oblige when he could
be of service, and his readiness to open his purse. He loved to entertain
distinguished foreigners and to do the honours of the Court; but ambition
was the canker that ruined his entire career. He was, all the same, a very
good and dependable kinsman.

I have spoken of his moods, his unforgettable jibes, his unlikeness to
other men. Let me now give you an example of his uncertain temper. In
the year before the King died, we had arranged a marriage between a
great-niece of the Maréchale de Lorges and the Comte de Poitiers, last
survivor of that illustrious house, immensely rich, and with vast estates.
Both were orphans. The wedding was from Lauzun's house, and he
entertained us all. A year later, almost at the moment of the King's death,
the bridegroom died, which was a thousand pities for he was full of
promise. In the following summer, M. le Duc d'Orléans reviewed the
Maison du Roi on the plain that bounds the Bois de Boulogne, on the side
opposite to Passy, where M. de Lauzun owned a very pretty house.[1] He
made an excursion there with a number of distinguished guests, and I
joined them on the night before the review. Mme de Poitiers, being very
young and having seen nothing, was dying to watch the parade; but she
dared not appear in public during this the first year of her mourning. The
company eagerly discussed ways and means, and concluded at last that
Mme de Lauzun might safely take her concealed at the back of her coach,
and that was how the matter was decided. Amid the ensuing laughter, M.
de Lauzun returned from Paris, where he had spent the day, and everyone
turned to tell him the joke. No sooner had they spoken than he flew into
such a violent temper that he lost all control, forbidding the whole plan,
his mouth almost frothing, uttering most scathing things to his wife, not
only in harsh terms, but furiously, most hurtingly, almost raving. She began
quietly to mop her eyes. Mme de Poitiers sobbed, and the entire company
was in extreme discomfort. The evening seemed to take a year to pass and,
compared with the supper, the most solemn refectory meal was an occasion
of merriment. Lauzun sat grim and furious in the midst of profound silence.
No one uttered, save for a word at long intervals to an immediate neighbour. At dessert he left the table and retired to his bedroom. Thereafter
people endeavoured to find excuses for him, or to say something calculated
to relieve the tension; but Mme de Lauzun very wisely and politely
discouraged them, and promptly arranged for card-tables so as to prevent
further discussion.

Next morning I went to M. de Lauzun's room, expressly to give my
opinion of the scene on the previous evening. He allowed me no time to
do so. No sooner did he see me than he stretched out both arms, exclaiming that he was mad and did not deserve a visit, but should rather be sent
to the Petites Maisons.[2] He went on to praise his wife to the skies (as she

[1] Called Les Sablons.   [2] The lunatic asylum of Paris.

truly deserved), declaring that he was unworthy of her, not fit to kiss the ground beneath her feet, proceeding to call himself by every name under the sun, and then, with tears in his eyes, assuring me that he merited pity rather than anger. He was more than eighty years old, he said, with neither kith nor kin; he had been captain of the guard, but were he to become so once more he could not fulfil the duties; yet to his shame and sorrow he must confess that he kept reminding himself of the old days, and in all the years since he had lost that appointment, he had never managed to forget it, console himself, or pluck the dagger from his heart.[1] Whenever the memory returned it put him in a temper, and to hear that his wife proposed taking Mme de Poitiers to see a review of the bodyguard, in which he no longer had any place, had quite turned his head and reduced him to the frenzy which I had witnessed. He dared not appear after such an exhibition; he begged me on his knees to ask his wife to forgive a foolish old man who was dying with misery and shame. This sincere and most painful confession touched my heart. My only thought was how to comfort and set him up again. Reconciliation was not hard; but it was not without difficulty that we persuaded him to leave his room, and for days afterwards he appeared shamefaced—or so they told me, for I left that same evening, my occupation in those days allowing me very little leisure.

I have often reminded myself of that occasion, reflecting on how disastrous it is to become intoxicated with social success, and the wretched plight of this man, whom neither wealth nor domestic bliss, nor the attainment of high rank, nor old age, nor yet bodily weakness could separate from the cares of this world, and who, far from tranquilly enjoying his gains and contemplating his great good fortune, exhausted himself with vain regrets and profitless resentment. Lauzun could never persuade himself that, with death so near, the regaining of that post which he so passionately longed for would be a mere delusion, binding him still more firmly to the life he was about to leave. People die as they have lived; it rarely happens otherwise. How vitally important it therefore is to try to live so as to be done with worldly ambition before it and life both forsake us, and to exist trying and hoping always to make a good end.[2] Lauzun's foolish longing to be once more captain of the bodyguard so ruled his existence that he frequently wore a blue uniform trimmed with silver lace that, without being an exact copy of the full dress of a guards' officer, approached it as closely as he dared. Yet, though no one had the temerity to say so, it was far more like the livery of the royal hunt-servants, and might have made him look very silly had not his eccentricities become familiar to Society, where he was greatly feared.

---

[1] Yet when he was 90, Lauzun was still breaking in horses.

[2] M. Truc, editor of the Pléiade edition, says that Saint-Simon revised this part of his memoirs when he was seventy-five years old. These do, indeed, read like the thoughts of an old man.

Despite all his scheming and servility, he was ready to turn on anyone with a blistering remark uttered in the gentlest of voices. Ministers, generals, rich and successful persons and their families were most often maltreated. He, as it were, assumed the right to say and do what he pleased, and no one dared to attack him. Only the Gramonts were safe, for he never forgot the hospitality and protection they had given him in earlier days, and he loved them, cared for them and treated them with respect. The old Comte de Gramont took advantage of this immunity, and did vengeance for the entire Court by railing at him on every possible occasion; Lauzun never replied in kind nor took offence, but he did quietly avoid his company. He was of great assistance to his sisters' children, for example that most worthy priest the Bishop of Marseilles,[1] who gave such notable service in the time of the plague, sparing neither his strength nor his fortune. Lauzun asked M. le Duc d'Orléans to give him an abbey, but when benefices were shortly afterwards distributed, Monsieur de Marseilles was forgotten. Lauzun, feigning ignorance, asked the Regent if he had been so good as to remember him. The Regent appeared discomfited. M. de Lauzun, as though helping him out of a difficulty, murmured in soft, respectful tones, 'Never mind, Sire, next time he will do better,' a piece of sarcasm that left M. le Duc d'Orléans speechless, as Lauzun smilingly retired.

On one occasion he prevented a whole series of promotions to the rank of Marshal of France, merely by ridiculing the nominees. He said to the Regent in those same quiet tones that if, as was rumoured, only decrepit generals were to be advanced, might he mention that he himself was the oldest and most decrepit of all and, moreover, had commanded armies as a full general. They could not proceed after that. He was actuated by envy and spite; but because his remarks were so apt and so bitter, people often repeated them.

We were very closely associated in our lives; he even rendered me, of his own volition, some real and very friendly services, and I treated him always with every care and consideration, as he did me. Yet I did not altogether escape his malicious tongue, and one jest of his bid fair to ruin me. I still cannot imagine how I escaped. The King's health was failing; he knew it; he was beginning to think of times to come. Society did not smile on M. le Duc d'Orléans; but the time of his greatness was visibly approaching. All eyes were upon him, and watching him suspiciously. They were watching me also, who for so long had been the only courtier publicly attached to him, and plainly enjoying his entire confidence. M. de Lauzun came to dine with me, but found me already at table with guests who apparently were not to his liking. He went on to Torcy, with whom at that time I had no acquaintance. He also was at table, with many guests

---

[1] Denis François Xavier de Belsunce-Castelmoron, Bishop of Marseilles (1671-1755). His mother was Anne de Caumont-Lauzun, Marquise de Castelmoron (1682-1731). The plague at Marseilles, which began in 1709, did not end until the time of the Regency.

unfriendly to M. le Duc d'Orléans, including Tallard and Tessé. 'Monsieur,' said Lauzun to Torcy, with the gentle deprecating air he so often assumed, 'have pity on me, pray; I tried to dine with M. de Saint-Simon, but found him at table with a large gathering, whom I took good care not to join. I had no wish to be at the centre of a Cabal,[1] and thus I come to you in the hope of dinner.' Everyone burst out laughing, and in the twinkling of an eye the tale had reached Versailles, so that Mme de Maintenon and M. du Maine heard it within the hour; yet nothing was ever said. It was of no use to be angry; I took the whole matter as though a cat had scratched me, and never let Lauzun see that I knew anything.

Three or four years before he died, he had a malady that put him *in extremis*. We all visited him assiduously; but he would see no one except Mme de Saint-Simon, and her only once. One day when he was very bad, Biron and his wife[2] had the temerity to enter his room on tiptoe, and conceal themselves behind the curtains of his bed; but although they felt sure of being unobserved, Lauzun had seen them in the mirror over the fireplace. Now he did not mind Biron, but the wife he detested, notwithstanding that she was his niece and his heiress. He thought her self-seeking and inquisitive, and her manners in other ways deplorable, in which matter Society agreed with him. Their surreptitious entry shocked him deeply, for he realized that in her anxiety to inherit, she could not wait to learn how ill he really was. He therefore resolved to give her cause for repentance, and himself some amusement. Picture him then talking aloud, as though he were alone, uttering fervent prayers to God, entreating forgiveness of his past life, seemingly quite convinced of death's approach, vowing that since pain and fatigue barred him from doing penance, he would at least ensure that all his worldly goods should go to the hospitals, to atone for his sins. He ended with a thanksgiving to God for showing him this, the only means by which he might gain salvation after a long life without religion. All this was uttered in a voice so penitent, so sincere, so resolute, that Biron and his wife were fully convinced of his intention to cut them out of their inheritance and fulfil his pious purpose. They had no desire to hear more; but went quite panic-stricken to tell the Duchesse de Lauzun of their cruel disappointment, and beg her to gain them some concessions. The patient, however, had already summoned the lawyers, and Mme de Biron was at the end of her tether. You may well imagine that such was Lauzun's intention. He kept the lawyers waiting, then bade them enter and dictated a new will that was a death blow to Mme de Biron. Yet he would not sign it at that time, nor did he ever do so. He enormously enjoyed the drama, and laughed over it with his cronies when he was better, for despite his age and the gravity of his illness, he recovered completely.

[1] A reference to the Meudon Cabal. See index, I, under cabal.
[2] Mme de Biron was the daughter of Lauzun's sister, Mme de Nogent.

He had the strength of iron with the deceiving appearance of delicate health. He dined and supped heartily every day, eating excellent viands and many dainty dishes, always in cheerful company both morning and evening. He partook of everything, both fish and meat, guided only by his appetite, and with no curb put on that. In the morning he drank chocolate, and in his room there were always on some table or other dishes of the fruits in season, sweet cakes (in earlier days), along with beer, cider, lemonade, and frozen drinks of various kinds. During the afternoon, he ate and drank continually and encouraged others to do likewise. He went to bed each night immediately after getting up from table. I remember one occasion of many when he dined with us after the above-mentioned illness. He then ate so heartily of fish, so many vegetables, so very much of everything else provided, despite all our protests, that when evening came we sent to discover tactfully whether he had not a bad attack of indigestion. He was at table; again eating heartily!

His last illness came on suddenly, almost instantaneously, with cancer of the mouth, that most dreadful of all maladies. He bore it until the end with almost incredible patience and fortitude, without complaint, ill-humour, or outbursts against anyone—he who normally had been irritated even by himself. When he saw that the disease was growing worse, he retired to rooms he had rented for that purpose in the monastery of the Augustine friars, which could be entered from his house. There he was able to die in peace, safe from Mme de Biron and all other ladies except his wife who, with one of her maids, had permission to go to him at any time. His only thought in this last place of retirement was to turn to good account his terrible plight, devoting his remaining days to pious talk with his confessor and some of the friars, reading books of devotion, doing all that is best calculated to prepare for death. When we saw him, there was no unpleasantness, no misery, no suffering; only courtesy, peace, and quiet conversation. He appeared indifferent to events in the outside world, though he sometimes talked of them, but only, it seemed, for something to discuss, as he spoke little and with difficulty. He moralized very rarely, still more seldom mentioned his illness; but over and above all, during those two long months, his quiet courage never faltered.[1] In the last ten or twelve days, however, he would no longer receive his brothers-in-law or his nephews, and very quickly sent his wife away. He received the Last Sacraments in a highly edifying manner, retaining his consciousness until the very end.

On the morning before his death, he sent for Biron and informed him that he had done for him all that Mme de Lauzun had desired, bequeathing to him all his possessions apart from a modest legacy to Castelmoron, his other sister's son,[2] and rewards for his servants. He emphasized the fact

---

[1] His long imprisonment must have taught him patience.
[2] Charles Gabriel de Belsunce, Marquis de Castelmoron (1682-1739). His mother was Anne de Caumont-Lauzun. She had been a year older than Lauzun.

that whatever he had done for Biron since his marriage, and all that was in his will, was due entirely to Mme de Lauzun, to whom Biron should be eternally grateful. As his uncle and as testator, Lauzun charged him never to cause her the smallest pain or anxiety; never to obstruct her wishes, nor ever to sue her in the courts for any cause whatsoever. Biron himself told me all this on the following morning, in the same words which I use here. He said that Lauzun, as soon as he was finished, had bidden him farewell in a firm voice, and had dismissed him. Very rightly he had refused all pomp for his funeral, and was buried quietly at the church of the Petits-Augustins. He had held none of the King's appointments, excepting his ancient captaincy of the *becs-de-corbin*, a post that was abolished two days after his death. A month earlier, he had sent for Dillon,[1] King James's chargé d'affaires, a general with a distinguished record, and had given back to him the collar of the Order of the Garter, and an onyx Saint George surrounded by large and perfect diamonds, asking for them to be returned to King James.

I perceive, at this point, that I have let my pen run on in describing this personage. The violent extremes of his life, and the close acquaintance brought about by our kinship appeared to warrant my making him better known, more especially since he figured too little in public affairs to be mentioned in the later histories. There is another reason, however. I draw near to a moment which I dread recording because my desires cannot harmonize with the truth. They are indeed most ardent, and therefore afflict me most deeply, for the facts are terrible, allowing no possibility of finding any extenuating circumstance. Horror of reaching this dreadful moment has checked me, compelled me to seize any pretext for delay, frozen my pen. You will readily understand that we approach the death of M. le Duc d'Orléans, and the manner of it. What an appalling event to have to describe! coming, as it did, after our long and intimate attachment that lasted throughout his life, and will remain with me for the rest of mine, piercing my heart with fear and grief for him.[2]

It makes one tremble to the very marrow of one's bones to harbour the fearful suspicion that God in his anger may have taken him at his word. You will remember that, only a short time before, he had said that he feared a slow death whose arrival would long be foreseen (yet that is a precious boon, if knowledge of how to use the interval is granted also), and that he would infinitely prefer to die suddenly. Alas! he obtained his wish, in a death still more sudden than that of Monsieur,[3] whose constitution resisted longer.

---

[1] Arthur, Lord Dillon (1670–1733), an Irishman in the service of the Old Pretender.

[2] The terrible thought that he had died unshriven, with all his sins upon him, facing the prospect of eternal damnation. Saint-Simon seems to be giving us a rare glimpse of true religious feeling.

[3] His father, Philippe I d'Orléans. See I, p. 159.

On 2 December, I went after dinner from Meudon to Versailles, in order to work with M. le Duc d'Orléans. I spent three-quarters of an hour with him in his study, walking up and down, discussing the matters he was to bring later that day to the attention of the King. I saw no change in him. For some time past, his body had become stouter and heavier, but his mind and his reasoning powers were as clear as ever. I then returned to Meudon, and sat for some time conversing with Mme de Saint-Simon. At that season we had not many guests, and accordingly, when I left her in her drawing-room, I retired to my study. When an hour had passed, I heard shouts and a sudden disturbance, and saw Mme de Saint-Simon, greatly alarmed, bringing me one of the Marquis de Ruffec's grooms, sent from Versailles to inform me that M. le Duc d'Orléans was in an apoplectic fit. I was deeply concerned, but scarcely surprised, for, as you know, I had been expecting this for some time past. I began to agitate for my carriage, which kept me waiting some time, because the new château is far from the stables. As soon as it appeared, I flung myself in, and drove off at full speed.

At the park gates a second courier sent by the Marquis de Ruffec stopped the carriage to tell me that all was over, and I remained there half an hour, absorbed in my grief and my reflections. At the end of that time I decided to go to Versailles and, there arrived, I went straight to my apartment and locked myself in. Nangis,[1] who was eager to become master of the horse, had succeeded me with M. le Duc d'Orléans, and being quickly dismissed, was succeeded by Mme de Falari,[2] a lovely adventuress married to another of the same kind, a brother of the Duchesse de Béthune. She was one of the unhappy prince's mistresses. His portfolio was ready to be taken to the King, and he had been talking to her more than an hour, waiting for the appointed time. It had almost arrived; they were sitting close together, side by side in two armchairs,[3] when he suddenly toppled sideways upon her, and never afterwards showed the smallest sign of consciousness, not even so much as a gleam. Falari, as you may well imagine, was terror-stricken; she called for help at the top of her voice, and continued to call in vain. When no one came, she did her best to support the wretched prince on the adjacent arms of the two chairs, ran first into the big study, then into the bedroom and ante-rooms and, still finding no one, out into the courtyard, and thence into the lower gallery. It was the hour when M. le Duc d'Orléans worked with the King; his servants therefore believed that as there would be no callers he would not need them, for he always went upstairs alone, by the small staircase that led from his 'cave' (in other words from his privy) into the last of the

---

[1] Louis Armand de Brichanteau, Marquis de Nangis (1682–1742). See index I and II.

[2] Marie Thérèse Blondel d'Haraucourt (1697–1782). She was the Duc de Falari's second wife.

[3] It is possible that Saint-Simon may have drawn a decorous veil over the scene. Other sources suggest that the situation was far more shocking.

King's ante-rooms, where a secretary awaited him with his portfolio, having entered by the grand staircase and through the guardroom. Falari managed at last to collect some servants, but no medical assistance, and she sent those who came first to hand to fetch doctors. By an evil chance, or rather, as Providence had ordained, the tragic event had taken place when everyone was busy each with his own affairs, or else paying visits; thus a good half-hour elapsed before any doctor or surgeon arrived, or any of M. le Duc d'Orléans's personal valets. As soon as the faculty observed him, they pronounced it hopeless; but they none the less stretched him at full length upon the floor and bled him there and then. Despite all their endeavours, he remained to all appearances unconscious. No sooner did the news break than people of every kind and condition came running until both the big and small studies were crowded. In less than two hours all was over, and almost at once the rooms became as empty as they had previously been full. When help arrived, Falari returned to Paris with all possible speed.

La Vrillière was one of the first to be informed of the apoplexy. He hastened to tell the King and the Bishop of Fréjus, and then immediately went to Monsieur le Duc, therein acting like a skilled courtier, ready to turn every crisis to personal advantage, for he had a shrewd suspicion that that prince would be the next first minister.[1] After urging Monsieur le Duc to take the necessary steps, he hurried home to draw up letters patent (just in case they should be required) in the same form as those which had been used for M. le Duc d'Orléans. News of the death was brought to him the moment it occurred. He sent word of it to Monsieur le Duc, and himself went at once to the King's apartments, where the imminence of the danger had brought together all the most important people. Fréjus, at the first news of the seizure, had settled Monsieur le Duc's appointment with the King, whom he had no doubt begun to prepare when the deterioration in the Regent's health first became apparent. Thus when Monsieur le Duc arrived and entered the King's study, the greatest of the courtiers were allowed to enter also. It was noticed that the King seemed very sad, and that his eyes were red and full of tears. When the last person had entered, the doors were immediately closed. Fréjus said loudly to the King that at this moment of the tragic loss of M. le Duc d'Orléans (whose praise occupied no more than two sentences) His Majesty could do no better than ask Monsieur le Duc to take upon himself the burden of State affairs, and assume the office of first minister in M. le Duc d'Orléans's stead. The King said nothing, merely gave consent to Fréjus by a nod; whereupon M. le Duc expressed his thanks. La Vrillière, delighted with himself for acting so promptly, had ready in his pocket a copy of the oath

[1] Revising so long afterwards, Saint-Simon may have forgotten what happened. According to contemporary accounts, it was Monsieur le Duc himself who brought the King the news and arranged his own appointment.

which M. le Duc d'Orléans had taken on his appointment. He produced it at this moment, proposing out loud to Fréjus that this might be a suitable time. The King assented, and Monsieur le Duc was accordingly sworn. He soon afterwards departed, followed by the company assembled in the King's study, for all in a moment he had become the man of the hour.

M. le Duc de Chartres, a degenerate and a libertine, was in Paris with one of his kept women from the Opéra.[1] He received the courier sent to bring news of the apoplexy, and on the road encountered another, who informed him of his father's death. No crowds hastened to greet him at the door of his coach, only the Ducs de Noailles and Guiches made manifest their desire to serve him wherever they could best assist. He treated them like nuisances, rid himself of them with all possible speed, and hurried upstairs to find his mother. To her he said that two fellows had set a trap for him; but since they had forgotten to bait it, he had escaped without difficulty. That magnificent display of intelligence, shrewdness and tact gave promise of all the qualities that this prince has later developed. His friends did their best to persuade him that he had made a bad mistake; but to no purpose, he continued in the same way.

As for me, after a wretched night, I attended the King's *lever*, not so much to be seen as to speak a word to Monsieur le Duc in a quiet and becoming manner. I had been closely concerned with him since the Tuileries *Lit de Justice*, though he had greatly displeased me by his weakness in consenting to the rehabilitation of the bastards. At *levers*, he always stood by the centre window, opposite which the King dressed, and since he was immensely tall, one distinguished him easily behind the mass of people who surrounded the King. On this particular day the crowd was very great. I made a sign that I wished to speak, and he at once broke through the throng to come to me. I drew him into the window recess nearest the door, and there explained that I would not try to pretend I was not heart-broken; but at the same time hoped he would believe me when I said that had the choice of a first minister been mine, he should have had my nomination; whereat he thanked me with many expressions of cordial regard.[2] I then said that in M. le Duc d'Orléans's portfolio were several documents which I ought to explain to him now that he had assumed office; I therefore begged him to send for me at whatever time he pleased and, since I was in no condition to face the world, to have me admitted by the small door from the great gallery, by which means I might avoid the crowd in his apartment. He most readily consented, but later that same day excused himself with the utmost graciousness, on the

---

[1] It is said that he was actually at the Opéra at the time of the Duc d'Orléans's death, following in his father's footsteps and in a similar situation.

[2] In fact this was not the case, for in another passage Saint-Simon tells how he first went to Fleury and tried to make him seize the appointment. The thought of a prince of the blood in a position of such power was not welcome to the duke, who feared further attempts to suppress his fellow peers.

grounds of its being his first day in office, for not there and then fixing an hour to suit my convenience. I well knew that particular little door and the study in question, because that same apartment had been Mme la Duchesse de Berry's on her marriage. It was on the top floor of the new wing, and very near my own, which was on the same level, facing the staircase.

Immediately afterwards I went to the Duchess of Sforza, who had remained one of my dearest and most intimate friends although I had long since ceased to visit Mme la Duchesse d'Orléans, for reasons which I recounted at the appropriate time. I told her that in this tragedy that had come upon us, I considered it my duty, because of the respect and affection I bore the late M. le Duc d'Orléans, to join my tears with those of the people most closely attached to him, his senior staff, even his bastards, though I knew none of them, and that it would seem vastly improper to except his widow. Mme de Sforza, I said, knew my situation regarding that lady, also the fact that I had no desire to change it; none the less, on this sad occasion, it appeared to me only right to visit her at her home. Provided I might have the satisfaction of doing the right thing, it was totally indifferent to me whether she received me or not. I then asked Mme de Sforza to discover whether Mme la Duchesse d'Orléans would see me, and if yes, whether she would do so fittingly, for I had no concern either way. She assured me that Mme la Duchesse d'Orléans would be glad to see and to welcome me, and went immediately to deliver my message. When she returned with a cordial reply I went at once to pay my visit. Mme la Duchesse d'Orléans was in bed, surrounded by her ladies and some of her chief officers. M. le Duc de Chartres was there also, with a suitably decorous air that compensated for lack of grief. She spoke of the general lamentations, not mentioning our private quarrel; but that was by my desire. M. le Duc de Chartres retired to his own rooms; our languid talk dragged on until I could decently end it, and I then followed him to the apartment that had been his father's until he became the Regent. They said he was busy. I returned three times during the course of the morning. On the last occasion his head valet appeared ashamed and, despite all my protests, went to announce me. M. le Duc de Chartres then came to the door of his study, where he had been closeted with persons of no importance—I forget whom, but they were of the kind he preferred. I beheld a man highly embarrassed, resentful, not distressed, but so confused that he scarcely knew what he did. I paid my condolences in the plainest, strongest language possible, and in a loud voice. He apparently regarded me as a vulture, loosed upon him by the Dukes of Guiches and Noailles, for he did not condescend to reply. I waited a few moments; then seeing that nothing could be expected from that semblance of a man, I made my bow and withdrew, without his making the smallest effort to accompany me, as he should have done, the whole length of his apartment; whereupon he turned and bolted back into covert.[1] I must add that as I left, I cast my eye around the assembled company, and that they all appeared vastly astonished. I then returned to my room, not at all comforted by my tour of the château.

I was about to leave the table when one of Monsieur le Duc's footmen came to tell me that he was ready to receive me. He led me straight through the little door and into the study. Monsieur le Duc came to meet me on the threshold, closed the door, drew forward an armchair, and took another for himself. I spoke of the matters I had mentioned, and after some more general conversation, we came to the events of the day. He told me that he had visited M. le Duc de Chartres after the King's *lever*, and having paid the necessary compliments had offered his condolences; he had gone on to expressions of friendship and of his sincere devotion to the memory of M. le Duc d'Orléans, promising to do everything in his power to support and assist his son. When M. le Duc de Chartres remained silent, he had repeated his assurances and offers of assistance, but all he had been able to extract was a single dry word of thanks, and a look of such discourtesy that he had quickly left. I told him of my experience that same morning, and we lamented together. He then spoke to me with great kindness and civility, urging, nay bidding me to visit him often. I replied that knowing how his time would be taken up with business and callers, I should feel some scruples about disturbing him. I would, however, come when I had something to impart, and I begged him, since I was not accustomed to wait in ante-rooms, to order his servants to tell him of my arrival, and to announce me at the first possible moment. I gave him my word to be neither long nor importunate. There followed protestations of friendship, compliments, assurances, etc., etc. This all lasted about three-quarters of an hour, after which I fled quickly back to Meudon.

On the following day Mme de Saint-Simon visited Versailles in order to pay her court to the King after the sad event, and to call on Mme la Duchesse d'Orléans and her son. Monsieur de Fréjus came to her as soon as he learned that she was at the château, for she did not stay there long. Through all the charming things he said to her, she felt she discerned a wish to see me in Paris rather than at Versailles. No more was needed to confirm in me a resolution, already decided on when I first perceived the deterioration in M. le Duc d'Orléans's health. Thereafter I made Paris my home,[2] fully determined not to appear before the new administrators, save on those rare occasions when necessity or politeness required, and then for a brief moment only, with the dignity appropriate to a man of my condition,

---

[1] The Duc de Chartres was twenty years old.

[2] Saint-Simon was born at the Hôtel de Selvois, in the Rue des Saints-Pères, on 16 January 1675. The house no longer exists, but it was at the corner of the Rue Saint-Dominique. He lived there after the death of his father until 1714. He then took another house close by, also in the Rue Saint-Dominique, where he wrote the greater part of the Memoirs. In 1746, three years after his wife's death, he moved to the Rue du Cherche-Midi. When that house was sold in 1750, he settled in the Rue de Grenelle, and died there on 2 March 1755.

and of all that I once had been. Happily for me, I did not at any time lose sight of the complete change in my situation and, to say truth, the loss of Mgr le Duc de Bourgogne and all that I had seen of government had destroyed in me any ambitions of that nature. That beloved prince had been snatched from me at the age of my father when he lost Louis XIII; that is to say, my father was thirty-six and his King forty-one; I, at thirty-seven, lost a prince not yet thirty who was about to ascend the throne and restore justice, order and truth to his people. Thereafter came a head of State healthy enough to have lived a century, as we both were, he and I, and he was no more than six months my senior. I was thus already prepared to outlive my own day, and had tried to make the most of it.

Monseigneur had died aged forty-nine and a half, and M. le Duc d'Orléans lived two months longer. I compare these almost equal life-spans because of the relative situations of the two princes until Monseigneur's death. Such is life and the vanity thereof.

The death of M. le Duc d'Orléans made a great stir both at home and abroad; but in foreign countries he was far more highly esteemed and far more deeply mourned than by Frenchmen. Although foreigners, in particular the English, had suffered by his weakness, they had learned by experience to recognize the breadth and soundness of his understanding, the nobility of his mind, his remarkable sagacity, his skill and wisdom in statecraft, the dexterity of his manœuvres in constantly changing circumstances, his superiority to his ministers and to the ambassadors of foreign powers, the delicate perception he brought to the unravelling of State affairs, and the consummate skill with which, when he so pleased, he could swiftly answer questions of all kinds. These are rare talents in government, and caused him to be feared and treated with respect by foreign envoys, and his gracious ways that could lend charm even to refusals made him still more agreeable to them. What is more, they prized his native courage.

The brief interlude during which he had fallen under the spell of that wretched Dubois and had nearly been destroyed, served only to raise him in the regard of foreigners, for they compared the conduct of affairs when he controlled them with their state when directed by his first minister. When Dubois died and the prince once again took the helm, he displayed all the skill they had been wont to admire, and the weakness which had been his chief defect was not so evident to distant eyes.

The King loved him for his unfailing respect, the efforts he made to divert him, the way he spoke and worked with him. He wept for him and was most truly grieved by his loss; indeed, he never afterwards spoke of him (and he mentioned him repeatedly) without expressing his esteem, affection, and regret, for the truth had emerged despite all the lies and slanders with which they had attempted to smother it. Monsieur le Duc, who gained so much by his death, maintained throughout a most decent and dignified bearing; Madame la Duchesse was admirably controlled, the bastards, who were not bettered by the change, had no cause to show rejoicing. Fréjus, on the other hand, could scarcely contain his delight. He could be observed sweating under the need for concealment; his happy, unspoken desires were visible at all times; despite his best endeavours, his entire countenance was radiant with joy. Since emotions are destructive to reason, the Court was not greatly divided. There were some who saw clearly after the manner of the foreigners, bearing constant witness to his charm, his approachability, his unfailing patience, the quiet way in which he would listen, the kindness that came so naturally to him. Others, a greater number, were equally sorry, but less for his loss than because they understood the character of his successor and knew also his friends. The vast majority mourned him not at all. Some had belonged to opposing factions, others had been shocked by his debauches, and the habit he had deliberately formed of not keeping promises; many were malcontents, mostly with grudges that had no real foundation, and these included a host of incompetents such as exist in every sphere, and, at Courts, are prevalent. Such people always believe that their fortunes and ideas deserve better success, but are no more than foolish devotees of mere innovation.

In the churches, canting hypocrites, and even some who were truly devout, rejoiced to be delivered from the public scandal of his life and the encouragement it gave to libertines. Both Jansenists and supporters of the constitution, moved by folly or ambition, united in expressing their relief. The former, though at first they had been hopeful, had since suffered worse than under the late King. The latter were furious at not being allowed free rein to destroy once and for all the maxims and liberties of the Gallican Church, or establish the supremacy of bishops, thus reverting to the days when episcopal authority made prelates feared by all, even by the King himself. Together they exulted at the removal of a superior intelligence, ready to sacrifice individuals, but firmly resisting all their attempts to push on towards their final goal. Under a successor, they hoped that they might dare to act more boldly.

The Paris Parlement, the provincial assemblies, and the entire body of magistrates did not forgive M. le Duc d'Orléans for those displays of authority which were forced on him by their abominable encroachments. Although by impudence and cunning they had contrived to avoid the worst effects, they were not in a position to make further advances. Their dearest wish still remained unfulfilled; thus their joy was unconstrained at the passing of a government from which they had extorted so much. They could not endure the thought of not having extorted all, or changed their status from that of a simple court of justice to that of a Parliament on the English lines, but with the upper house in complete subservience.

The army, forcibly crammed with commissioned officers of all ranks, and showered with Saint-Louis crosses, all too often, like the promotions, bought from administrators or their mistresses, had been reduced to a state of near destitution by cheese-paring and a discipline so pedantically harsh that service had become a veritable slavery. An increase in pay had made no difference to infantrymen and troopers because of the inflated price of the most common necessities. Indeed, this most important, widely distributed, and very large section of the nation was in a worse state than ever before, under the tyranny of departments and of weak or contemptible officials. How would they not rejoice at any change that could lighten their burden, tend towards the good of the service, and properly evaluate merit and devotion!

Lastly, the people of Paris and the provinces had been driven to desperation by the cruel action of fiscal decrees, and the continual juggling with taxes designed to remove all their money. No private fortune was safe, confusion reigned in every family already distressed by the prodigious increase in all prices, whether for luxuries or sheer necessities. For years past they had groaned under this oppression, after early hope of deliverance and relief in which extreme need and urgent longing had driven them to trust. No one who valued security of any kind but was desolated by the deceits practised, seeing himself, despite all his care, falling again and again into traps and snares, watching his patrimony and savings melt away before his eyes, without protection of his rights by the law, and at his wits' end how to feed and bring up his family.

This abnormal, but general disorder was the direct result of all the different shifts and expedients in the finances—vain attempts to repair the ruinous situation at the death of Louis XIV. Yet it was not calculated to make the public regret the man whom they thought had been responsible. Acting like children, they furiously kicked the block of wood that had struck their feet, disregarding the careless passer-by who, by dropping it, had been the sole cause of their pain. I had seen only too clearly that such would be the result of the new organization, or rather disorganization of the finances, and I had tried to shift the responsibility from M. le Duc d'Orléans's shoulders by proposing a meeting of the States General, to which he agreed until the Duc de Noailles, for personal advantage, dissuaded him, as I recounted at the appropriate time.[1] Years later, the scales fell from many people's eyes, M. le Duc d'Orléans was mourned with most profound regret, and at long last received the credit which he so truly deserved.

On the day after M. le Duc d'Orléans's death, his body was taken from Versailles to Saint-Cloud, and next day the ceremonies were there begun. M. le Comte de Charolais,[2] with the Duc de Gesvres and the Marquis de Beauvau[3] his train-bearer, drove to Saint-Cloud in a royal coach, with an

---

[1] See p. 6 above.

[2] Charles de Bourbon-Condé, Comte de Charolais (1700-1760). He was the second son of Monsieur le Duc (1668-1710).   [3] Pierre Madeleine, Marquis de Beauvau (1663-1734).

escort of the guard. M. le Comte de Charolais, as the King's representative, sprinkled Holy Water, and was received at the coach door by M. le Duc de Chartres with, at his personal request, the two sons of the Duc du Maine. The heart was conveyed from Saint-Cloud to Val-de-Grâce by the Archbishop of Rouen, chief almoner of the defunct prince, with M. le Comte de Clermont,[1] prince of the blood, sitting at his left, the Duc de Montmorency,[2] son of the Duc de Luxembourg, on the front seat, and the customary following of retainers. M. le Prince de Conti went with the Duc de Retz,[3] son of the Duc de Villeroy, in the State procession from Saint-Cloud to Saint-Denis. The Chevalier de Biron,[4] M. le Duc d'Orléans's master of the horse, rode on horseback with the captain of the bodyguard. All the remaining officers of the household travelled in coaches. The obsequies were postponed until 12 February.

M. le Duc de Chartres, now become Duc d'Orléans, and M. le Prince de Conti wore deepest mourning for that ceremony, the Archbishop of Rouen officiated, and Poncet, Bishop of Angers,[5] spoke a funeral oration that did scant justice to the greatness of his subject.[6]

The King visited Mme la Duchesse d'Orléans and Madame la Duchesse at Versailles, and similarly honoured M. le Duc de Chartres, who was the only prince of the blood to receive a visit. Also visited were Mme la Princesse de Conti, Mlle de Chartres, and Mme du Maine.

On the day after M. le Duc d'Orléans's death, the Comte de Toulouse announced his marriage to the Duc de Noailles's sister, a widow with two sons by the Marquis de Gondrin, d'Antin's elder son. She had been one of the late Dauphine's ladies. The jealous and the fools, in whom this world abounds, grumbled and protested when they saw her assume her new rank. As you well know, I had no cause to love the Duc de Noailles, and have never guarded my tongue in speaking of him. Yet truth requires me to say that considering the Noailles's birth there is no reason to exclaim when one of them marries a prince of the blood. No one, at least, can deny the vast difference between a Noailles and a Séguier, the one, for example, whom we saw queening it as Duchesse de Verneuil, on the occasion of the marriage of Mgr le Duc de Bourgogne;[7] dining at the King's table by

---

[1] Louis de Bourbon-Condé, Comte de Clermont (1709-1771), younger brother of the Comte de Charolais.

[2] Charles François Frédéric II, Duc de Montmorency, later Duc de Luxembourg (1702-1764), a grandson of the great Duc de Luxembourg.

[3] Louis François Anne de Neufville, Marquis, later Duc, de Villeroy (1695-1766).

[4] Louis Anne de Gontaut, Comte de Biron (1701-1780). In 1746 he became Duc et Pair, and, in 1757, was made a Marshal of France.

[5] Michel Poncet de La Rivière (1672-1730), a member of the French Academy.

[6] This oration was not printed, at the request, it is said, of the Regent's son. Perhaps it resembled the following: 'He died eight or nine years too late for the welfare of the State and the people, on account of all the harm he did, and the irreparable and general poverty he brought to the entire nation. Thus the people have good reason to rejoice greatly at his death. He was an evil prince.'

[7] See I, p. 98.

special invitation for the wedding breakfast, and in full possession of all the privileges since enjoyed by the Comtesse de Toulouse.

A booby replaced a rogue in the office of Premier Président of the Paris Parlement. He was the personal choice of Monsieur le Duc, who much relished the Gesvres family, and hoped to win favour with the Parlement by promoting Novion,[1] the most senior of the présidents-à-mortier, but the worst possible candidate for the post. He was not rude or unjust after the manner of Premier Président de Novion his grandfather, but all he knew of the law was the basic procedure. It must be admitted that his speeches were super-excellent, but apart from proficiency in that dull art, nothing more was forthcoming from him. He was an obscure, solitary, uncouth kind of fellow, who cared for no one, and grew desperate when he had to grant an audience. A curse to his family and to all who had to deal with him, he was, in very truth, unendurable to others and, by his own admission, a great trial even to himself. That was how he appeared in an office where his work brought him in contact with the Court, his fellow magistrates, and the public, against whom he kept his door so firmly barred that he was virtually unapproachable. Yet while litigants grumbled about his brusque manner when they did manage to reach him, he himself would go abroad 'taking the air', as he phrased it, in the house he had occupied before becoming premier président. There he would chat with his neighbour a wheelwright, in the doorway of his shop, because, so he said, he was the most sensible man alive.

One poor suitor, a man of no account, despaired of ever being able to see him in order to request an audience. In the end he took to wandering about the Palais de Justice, not knowing who to ask or where to go for help. He found himself in the stable yard,[2] and saw a man in shirt-sleeves who was watching them grooming the horses, and roughly demanded to know why he was there and what he wanted. The wretched suitor explained very humbly that he had a most worrying case, and badly needed to settle it, but no matter how hard he tried he could not get near Monsieur le Premier Président who was, by all accounts, a veritable curmudgeon. The man in shirt-sleeves asked if he had his claim, and if so to give it him, promising to do his best to see that it reached the premier président. The suitor drew it from his pocket, thanked him for his kindness, remarking at the same time that he doubted whether anyone could extract an audience from one so strange and so moody as M. de Novion. He then departed. Four days later he was informed by his attorney that his suit would be heard in two days' time, which came as an agreeable surprise. He accordingly presented himself, with his lawyer, at the Great Chamber, ready to plead his cause. What, however, was his astonishment when he saw his shirt-sleeved friend

---

[1] André III Potier de Novion, Marquis de Grignon (1659-1731). He was a cousin of the Duc de Gesvres, whose family name was also Potier.

[2] The *basse cour* or stable yard contained the outhouses and privies.

sitting on the bench, in the premier président's robes! He nearly fell over backwards, terrified at the thought of what he had said, at a time when he believed he was addressing a nobody. The end of the story is that he won his case there and then. Such was Novion.

And now, at last, I reach the limits I had set for these Memoirs. None such can be valuable unless they be true, none true unless written by a man who saw and handled the matters of which he writes, or knew of them from a person worthy of implicit trust who himself had seen and handled them. What is more, the writer must love truth to the point of being ready to sacrifice all for its sake. Here, I may venture to commend myself, and I am fully persuaded that no one of all those who knew me would deny it. This love of truth was, indeed, the thing most prejudicial to my career. I often realized it, but I have preferred truth to all else, and could never bring myself to stoop to any deception; moreover, I have cherished truth even against myself. You will clearly have perceived the errors (sometimes most glaring) into which I was led by my affections or for the good of the State, which I have ever set before all other considerations, and always above personal advantage. To take one example among many of which I did not write because they concerned only myself, you will recollect that I continued to press for the finances to be given to the Duc de Noailles because, most mistakenly, I believed him to be the ablest, richest,[1] and most competent of the available nobility; and this was at a time when his black treachery to me had become known. You will also remember all that I did to save the Duc du Maine, against my keenest desires and interests, because I thought it dangerous to attack both him and the Parlement at the same time, and the Parlement was an urgent issue that could not be deferred. Let those suffice. I will not stay to mention many other such incidents which may be found in the Memoirs at the moments when they occurred, always provided that they added something to the description of current affairs or the life of the Court and Society.

There remains the question of impartiality, that vital quality, which is held to be so difficult, I venture to say impossible, for an author writing of what he has seen and handled. One is attracted by honourable and truthful persons; provoked by the rogues who swarm at Courts, and made still more angry by those who do one harm. A stoic is a fine and noble conceit. I therefore do not pride myself on being impartial; it would be useless. It will be all too evident in these Memoirs that praise and blame flow freely over those who stir my emotions, and are used more temperately concerning those to whom I am indifferent; yet I have always been a staunch supporter of the virtuous and fiercely against dishonest people, according to their degrees of vice or virtue. Nevertheless, I will give myself this much credit, which I believe the content of these Memoirs will not gainsay, that I have been

[1] Being so rich, he would not have been tempted to feather his own nest first, as Fouquet was suspected of doing.

infinitely watchful of my likes and dislikes, more especially of the latter, so as to keep the balance when writing of people, not only to avoid exaggeration, but to forget personal prejudice, regarding myself as my own enemy, rendering exact justice, and letting the truth everywhere prevail. Only thus could I be assured of remaining strictly impartial. I believe that there is no other way.

As for the accuracy and truth of what I have reported, the Memoirs themselves bear witness to the fact that almost every matter contained in them was handled by me personally, and that the rest I have learned from those who dealt with them. In each case I have given names; these names and my intimate relationship to the bearers of them are above suspicion. When I have received information through less reliable channels, I have mentioned it, and have not been ashamed to confess it when I knew nothing. Thus the Memoirs are authoritative, and at first hand. No one can ever doubt their truth and authenticity; and I think I may say that none heretofore has contained so wide a range of subjects, treated more thoroughly, in greater detail, or combined to form so instructive and curious a whole.

Since I shall not be there to see, it does not greatly affect me; but should these Memoirs ever be published, I have no doubt they will arouse most violent animosity. Everyone cares for his family, his interests, his claims, his dreams, and in these matters will brook no contradiction. We love the truth only when it flatters us, and in these things it flatters very few. Those whom one praises are not grateful—truth demanded it. Those, in far greater numbers, of whom one speaks otherwise become still more furious when censure is supported by facts. Moreover, at the time of which I have written, especially towards the end, everything was fast sinking into decadence, confusion, and a state of chaos that has ever since increased.[1] These Memoirs, on the other hand, are redolent of law, order, truth, and firm principles, and clearly expose all that is the reverse, which now more and more prevails with most ignoble, yet supreme power. In such circumstances there is bound to be a general revolt against a mirror that reflects the truth. These Memoirs were not written for those serpents who corrupt a country, and destroy it with their unsteady minds, their private interests, and in all the various ways by which its ruin can be speeded; they are written for those who seek enlightenment so as to be forearmed. Such men, unhappily, are being deliberately swept aside by those in power and office, who fear nothing so much as exposure by persons who have no other motives than justice, truth, reason, order, and wise government, and whose efforts are all directed to the public good.

One thing remains to be said concerning my conversations with many different persons, in particular with Mgr le Duc de Bourgogne, M. le Duc d'Orléans, M. de Beauvilliers, the various ministers, the Duc du Maine on

[1] Saint-Simon wrote this when he was revising his Memoirs, 1739-1749.

one occasion, three or four times with the late King, latterly with Monsieur le Duc and other eminent men, wherein I have quoted the opinions which I expressed, and the advice I received, gave, or disputed. There are so many recorded that I could well understand it if a reader unacquainted with me were tempted to range them with the invented speeches that historians sometimes put into the mouths of generals, ambassadors, senators, or conspirators, in order to give verisimilitude. I do however assure you, with all the truth that has hitherto guided my pen, that all these conversations are recounted with most scrupulous exactitude, precisely as they occurred, and that had I anything with which to reproach myself, it would be for having toned down my account rather than fortified it. Memory may perhaps have failed regarding the exact wording—animated by the subject and occasion, one speaks more vehemently than one writes. Let me only add, with all the confidence I expressed above, that no one of all those who have known and lived with me will doubt the truth of these reports, no matter how highly coloured they may appear, and none will fail to recognize my living image.

One thing that provokes me about Memoirs is that when the reader ends them he loses sight of the principal characters, and knows nothing of their after-lives. One would like to know what happened to them, without being put to the trouble of seeking elsewhere, which laziness might forbid, no matter how great the urge to learn more. That information I have a mind to give, if God allows me sufficient time. There will not be as much detail as when I was at the centre of affairs. Although Cardinal Fleury told me all I wished to know of foreign matters, and usually was the first to speak of them; although he revealed also some of the affairs of the Court, I followed them with the supreme indifference that I have felt towards ministers and other well informed persons. I have thus every reason to fear that such a supplement to the Memoirs will make very dull reading, unenlightened, vastly different from what has gone before; but you may at least discover what became of the various persons mentioned in the Memoirs, until the death of Cardinal Fleury, for that is all my aim.

Shall I say a word of my style, the negligences, the repetitions of the same word at too close intervals, the profusion of synonyms, above all, the obscurity caused by overlong sentences, perhaps also by repetition?[1] I have known these defects; I could not avoid them. Carried away by my subject, I have cared little for the manner of the rendering, so long as it was well explained. I never became a scholar; I never cured myself of writing fast.[2]

---

[1] In this respect, the translator has deliberately avoided repetitions and grammatical errors, and put in some stops. The general reader needs also to be considered, if the purpose of the translation is to be achieved.

[2] 'He wrote so fast that the torrent of his ideas could not keep pace with his pen, so swift was he in hatred, so quickly bowled over by laughter, so suddenly moved by enthusiasm or affection. Reading him you feel that you are living a month in the space of an hour.' Henri Taine, *Journal des Débats*, 1856.

Improving my style by revision would have meant recasting the entire work, and I had not the strength for such a labour; it might even have proved a waste of time. To correct well one must write well; you will have seen that I cannot pride myself on that. My only thought has been for accuracy and truth. I venture to state that both are most strictly adhered to in my Memoirs; they are their very soul and guiding light, and for their sake my style merits your kind indulgence. There is all the greater need, since I cannot promise to do better in the supplement.[1]

[1] The supplement was never completed, or has been lost.

Inscription engraved on copper, from Saint-Simon's coffin, which was destroyed during the Revolution.

Cy Gît
Louis Duc de Saint-Simon, Pair
de France, Comte de Rasse,
Grand d'Espagne de La
Première Classe, Marquis
de Ruffec, Comte de La
Ferté-Arnaud, Vidame de
Chartres, Gouverneur des
Ville, Citadelle et Comté
de Blaye, Bailly et Gouverneur
de Senlis, Chevalier des
Ordres du Roy, cy devant
Du Conseil de Régence dès
Son Etablissement, depuis
Ambassadeur Extraordinaire
En Espagne, Décédé le 2 Mars
1755, Agé de 80 ans ou environ

Requiescat in pace

POSTSCRIPT

LOUIS DE ROUVROY DE SAINT-SIMON was born at Versailles, in the middle of the night of 16 January 1675. His father, aged sixty-nine, was Claude de Saint-Simon, Captain of Versailles, Master of the King's Wolfhounds, First Gentleman-in-Waiting, and had been made a duke and peer by Louis XIII. His ancestry, so he claimed, traced back to Charlemagne. His second wife, Saint-Simon's mother, was thirty-four, a dragon who ruled her son and his family all her life. 'My mother was accustomed to decide for us.'

Although Louis XIV was the monarch at whose Court Saint-Simon lived as a Duke and Peer of France, Louis XIII was the King he venerated. His portraits were displayed in the family residences, and a ring with the King's likeness set in diamonds was handed down from father to son; what is more, every time Saint-Simon spoke his name, he added the pious invocation, *de triomphante mémoire*.

Louis de Saint-Simon's education began at home, under a tutor René de Gogué, who reported that he was apt to fly into rages, bad at Latin, and inattentive. He liked reading, however, especially history books and the memoirs of great men. His father, who instilled into him the niceties of etiquette, the proper privileges due to a duke and peer, the rules for claiming an armchair, a straight chair, or a *tabouret* at the Court, and the *precise* angle of the back when bowing to the King (not too high, carefully not too low, just exactly so), did not have him taught arithmetic; 'I never learned even the first principles.' He was a lonely little boy, enjoying solitude and the society of the elderly, not mixing easily with boys of his own age, or attracted by the lives they led. Easily his closest friend was the King's nephew Philippe, Duc de Chartres, later to succeed his father, Philippe I, as Duc d'Orléans, and later still, Regent of France during Louis XV's minority. It was a devoted, lifelong friendship on terms of such equality as there might be between men so different in rank. In after years, Orléans's debauchery and drunkenness, which ruined his career and spoiled his mind, disgusted and saddened Saint-Simon, but nothing weakened his steadfast affection, or the complete confidence and rather casual fondness which Orléans felt for him. The two boys played together in the nursery and shared some of their lessons. Saint-Simon's greatest pleasures in those early days were asking questions of ancient dukes and duchesses about the

Court in their day, and the annual excursion with his father to Saint-Denis, to attend the memorial service for Louis XIII, though it sometimes turned out that they were the only persons present.

In 1690, when he was fifteen, he wrote his first essay, a description of the Dauphine's funeral, giving the order of the ceremony and precedence. In the following year he went to study philosophy and equitation at the famous academy of the Sieurs de Rochefort, where the cavalry training was very much on the lines of the present Spanish Riding School at Vienna. It was all-important in war to persuade your horse to do some of the fighting—kicking out with all four iron hoofs, trampling down your enemy, or extricating you with a giant leap from a circle of infantry. He conceived the idea of writing his Memoirs. He was presented to Louis XIV who thought him undersized, but consented to his joining one of the three companies of musketeers, the officer-training regiments. In 1692, his father died, leaving him unprotected, virtually alone in the world, with no one to turn to, except his mother.

During the next two years, Louis de Saint-Simon, now himself a duke and peer, fought in the wars. He bought a cavalry regiment and charged bravely five times at the Battle of Neerwinden, on Capitaine, Petit Coureur, and the excellent bay horse with clipped ears and tail. When the armies went into winter-quarters, he was chosen to be the spokesman for seventeen of his fellow-peers in a lawsuit against his own commander-in-chief, the great Maréchal de Luxembourg, the eighteenth duke in seniority, who dared to claim precedence to which he was not entitled. During the intervals, Saint-Simon was beginning to collect notes and material for his great work, and arranging his family papers. His mother now thought it time for him to marry—he was nineteen years old, and had inherited his father's governorships and an income of 100,000 livres. He looked about for a suitable father-in-law, noble, rich, and well placed at the Court; his choice fell first on the Duc de Beauvilliers—'It is you and the duchess whom I wish to marry, not your daughters, whom I scarcely know.' When it appeared that all nine of them were determined to be nuns, he fell back upon another duke, the Maréchal de Lorges, and successfully courted his elder girl Marie Gabrielle de Lorges ('cette perle unique'), with whom he lived happily ever after. When not at war, he spent his entire time at the Court under the King's eye, hoping for employment, walking, dancing, shooting hares, attending levers, soupers, and couchers.

In 1699, he took the first of his notebooks for the opinion of the Abbot of La Trappe, his spiritual director. The verdict was for him to continue with his Memoirs, but in strictest secrecy. He and Mme de Saint-Simon had by this time three children, two boys and a girl, their entire family. The poor girl was deformed and hideous to behold; the boys, so short as to be almost dwarfish, were known at the Court as les bassets.

At the age of twenty-seven, passed over in a general promotion, he sent in his resignation. He had a small house in Versailles town, but no lodging at the château, a great handicap when it was necessary to change into full dress or seek a privy. His father-in-law came to the rescue by lending him a tiny room partitioned off from his own apartment. Meanwhile Saint-Simon was making useful friends: Chamillart the War Minister, the Duc de Beauvilliers the Finance Minister, Pontchartrain the Chancellor. He returned sometimes, after taking due precautions not to be missed at the Court, to his country house at La Ferté Vidame. He also made lifelong enemies, and learned to hate with bitter loathing the King's elder bastard son, the Duc du Maine. He provoked and irritated Louis XIV, but the King could not help respecting him.

1709 was the terrible year of defeats and national disasters, the fearful frost, and the famine that followed. The Meudon Cabal, meeting at the house of Louis Le Grand Dauphin, upheld the bastards and the unspeakable Duc de Vendôme, plotted to dishonour the Duc de Bourgogne and destroy Saint-Simon's friend the Duc d'Orléans. Saint-Simon took up arms on the other side. He was disgraced and contemplated voluntary exile but, in 1710, an audience with the King saved him. Louis XIV was seventy-one.

Mme de Saint-Simon was made lady-in-waiting to the Duchesse de Berry, and they were granted an apartment at the château, arranged for them by the King himself, with a kitchen built out in the yard for their entertaining—an especial favour. For the next two years Saint-Simon prospered. With the Grand Dauphin's death, the Duc de Bourgogne became the heir apparent, and took Saint-Simon as a kind of assistant, adviser, and secretary. They worked together in the new Dauphin's study, drawing up plans for the new reign, with the memoirist busy compiling evidence for the realization of his heart's desire, the restoration of the dukes and peers to their old place in the government of France. 'A glorious and not too distant future opened before me.'

In 1712, came the tragedy of the sudden deaths of the Duc and Duchesse de Bourgogne and their elder surviving son. Saint-Simon was in despair: 'I have had a taste of honey, now I have to die.' He nevertheless turned to what was to come. The future Louis XV was only two years old, and the Duc d'Orléans would be Regent of France, with Saint-Simon his only respectable friend. When Louis XIV died in 1715, they stood virtually alone against the bastards, the Parlement, and the courtiers. Saint-Simon, at the age of forty, prepared to begin a political career. The start was triumphant, with the historic session of the Parlement at which the King's will was declared null, the bastard Duc du Maine was set aside, and the Regent's supreme powers were confirmed. Saint-Simon became an original member of the Regency Council, having refused greater employment.

1718 brought the second great victory of the *Lit de Justice*, when the

Parlement was humbled and the bastards were removed from the succession. This was Saint-Simon's heyday. He was acting as an *éminence grise*, attacking the Parlement, advising on foreign affairs, upholding Law the merchant banker. He refused to become controller of finances. He hated to say no, but confessed to his ignorance of 'even the first principles of arithmetic'. He was far from rich; he saw Law weekly at the Regent's request; but although he believed him to be honest, if mistaken, he refused altogether to accept a present of shares in the Mississippi Scheme, and only with great difficulty was persuaded to take repayment for a loan which the State had owed to his father and never settled. He did not understand money, and distrusted it; it was the Duchesse de Saint-Simon who did their private accounts.

The great adventure of his life was in 1721, when he went to Spain, as plenipotentiary, to be a witness of the marriage-contract of Louis XV to the baby Infanta, and attend the wedding of the Regent's daughter to the Prince of the Asturias. He was made a grandee, conjointly with his second son, and the elder son was given the Golden Fleece. He had refused to take the usual sum given to ambassadors for their 'emoluments', saying that he preferred to be repaid for his expenses, but that he never fully was. When he returned to France, he found that Cardinal Dubois had assumed control of the fast-degenerating Regent, to his explicit exclusion. The coronation of Louis XV approached, and Saint-Simon once more went into battle for the rights and dignities of the Dukes and Peers of France, their place in the government and their symbolic rôle in the crowning ceremony. He was defeated, but in his rage so managed things that not a single duke attended the coronation, except those who had official duties. A new post in the government was created, and Cardinal Dubois became first minister of France.

1723 was the 'sterile year'. The Regent's government collapsed and the Regency Council was abolished. Dubois died. Then came most horrible tragedy, with the Duc d'Orléans, Saint-Simon's beloved friend, dying suddenly, unshriven, in most scandalous circumstances. Saint-Simon was heart-broken, and consumed with terror on his behalf. Monsieur le Duc became the new first minister but had no need of Saint-Simon's assistance. Cardinal Fleury, the King's adviser, hinted to Mme de Saint-Simon that her husband was not wanted at Versailles. He decided to leave the Court for ever.

Between 1723 and 1743, he lived completely retired either at his Château de La Ferté Vidame, or in his Paris house. He wrote and wrote, notes and 'digressions' for his Memoirs, notes on the history of the Duchy-peerages of France. He received the Order of the Saint-Esprit in the promotions of 1728. In 1739, the Duc de Luynes showed him Dangeau's journal, which he covered with furious notes, scratched in the margins and between the lines: 'Infuriating, enough to make one vomit!' and on the description of Mme de Maintenon, 'boring, filthy, stinking, lying in his throat!' The pen nearly tears the paper apart. One may be thankful; had Dangeau not been boring, we might have had no Saint-Simon, no spur to the revision of his own Memoirs. In 1739 he began to revise and edit his work, deciding to bring it to a close in 1723, at the end of the Regency, and announcing a supplement containing the later history of the surviving chief personages. For the next ten years he was immersed in this tremendous labour.

In 1739 came the death of the Marquis de Saint-Simon, his second cousin, whom he had assisted and taken with him to Spain. This was the grandfather of Claude Henri de Rouvroy, Comte de Saint-Simon, the founder of French Socialism, who was born in 1760 and died in 1825.

1743 brought the greatest of all sorrows, the death of his dear wife Marie Gabrielle. On page 1153 of the manuscript there is a line stretching right across the paper, of pear-shaped ink marks, perhaps representing tears. He wrote no more for the next six months. These words are from his will: 'I desire that no matter where I may die, my body shall be brought to the crypt of the parish church of La Ferté and buried there beside that of my beloved wife. And I wish there to be iron rings, hooks, and bands, so that our two coffins may be joined together so close and so firm that they can never afterwards be parted without destroying them both.' At the Revolution, however, the coffins were broken apart, and the bodies thrown into a pauper's grave. That was still a long way ahead. Precisely six months after his wife's death, he began to write again, on the next line, exactly where he had broken off.

He had twelve more years to live. He draped his rooms with black, and his bed with grey. He had enormous debts; even his servants were owed their wages. His embassy had completely ruined him, and the Duchess was no longer there to do the accounts and keep him straight. Day and night, he wrote in his grey-walled study, among his tapestries, his family portraits, and the four portraits of Louis XIII, with that of Cardinal Dubois in the privy, facing his *chaise-percée*. He had twelve thousand history books in his library, from which he steadily made notes, believing that he was excavating the truth for posterity. The friends who occasionally visited him reported that his conversation was fascinating. From time to time he was appealed to by the Court to settle some argument about precedence, and people were staggered by his *savoir maniaque*—his frenzied knowledge. No one, it seems, had any suspicion of his *magnum opus*. His two sons died, in 1746 and 1754. His daughter, a hypochondriac, lived on, married, at her grandmother's insistence, to the Prince de Chimay, despite Saint-Simon's sad conviction that she 'was not made for marriage'.

On 2 March 1755, Louis de Rouvroy, Duc de Saint-Simon, died at the age of eighty. Seals were immediately set upon his house in the Rue de Grenelle, and at La Ferté Vidame, for he was hopelessly bankrupt. There were lawsuits of all kinds; he owed his candlemaker (as might be expected) astronomical sums. Five crates of letters and manuscripts were given to his lawyer for safe-keeping. There were more than three thousand notebooks. In the inventory, pictures also are mentioned, by Veronese, Titian, Correggio, among other artists.

In 1760, the five crates were seized by royal command and secretly stowed away among the archives, in the department of the Affaires Étrangers. Saint-Simon's cousin, Claude de Saint-Simon, Bishop of Metz, his residuary legatee and brother of the late Marquis, applied for permission to examine and catalogue the whole mass of papers. Permission was refused. There were further lawsuits and appeals to the Parlement, and an Academician, the Abbé de Voisenon, a scholar who went by the unhappy nickname *petite poignée de puces*, was appointed by the minister to report on, and give extracts from, the various notebooks.

At this point (1763), the manuscripts were moved from the Louvre to Versailles, where a numbered inventory was made, the work continuing over a period of seven years, during which copies were shown to Mme de Pompadour, who made 'historical extracts' for the benefit of Louis XV's little grandsons, and to Mme du Deffand, whose friends were vastly diverted by the malice, but did not find him witty. In 1781, extracts were published anonymously, in Brussels, under the title, *Pièces intéressantes et peu connues pour servir à l'histoire*. Between the years 1788 and 1818, various unbound extracts, some false, others distorted, of the *Mémoires du Duc de Saint-Simon* appeared, published in France. The Academician Lemontey, who used Saint-Simon's memoirs and quoted copiously from them in his *Histoire de la Régence*, was forbidden to publish, and did not finally receive permission until twelve years later.

In 1819, the then Marquis de Saint-Simon, as head of the family, obtained an audience of Louis XVIII, and begged for the freedom of an ancestor who had been *embastillé* for nearly a century. The request was readily granted, but the archivists still made difficulties. Only a portion of the Memoirs was released, then all eleven portfolios, but not the index, written in the author's own hand. At last, in 1829–30, a still defective edition of the *Mémoires complets et authentiques du Duc de Saint-Simon* appeared. In the next twenty years numerous other editions were published; that edited by Chéruel is accepted as being the original text.

In 1854, Dangeau's journal was published in full, with Saint-Simon's hitherto unpublished notes and additions. Scholars claimed that they had seen a supplement to the Mémoires; but nothing more was ever heard of it, nor of other documents. All the private correspondence, more especially the 518 letters of the Duchesse de Saint-Simon to her husband, the numbered correspondence with the Duc d'Orléans covering a period of nearly forty years, the more than a thousand letters to the nuncio Cardinal Gualterio (a letter every week for twenty years) have disappeared. Can they still be among the Archives? Is Saint-Simon still 'top secret'? According to the records, more than 150 portfolios are missing.

In 1874, the Boislisle edition, which ran into forty-three volumes, began to appear. Thereafter came the Édition de la Pléiade, in seven volumes (1947–61). There have been two other abridged translations into English, one by B. St. John, with a Preface by J. B. Perkins, in 1902, the other by R. P. Wormeley in 1909.

INDEX

NOTE: As in Volumes I and II, it has been found necessary, for reasons of space, to omit names of persons and places occurring only once and of no particular interest in the context: apologies to readers for any resulting inconvenience. 'f' after a number indicates that the name occurs on two, 'ff' on three, 'fff' on four consecutive pages; mentions on more than four consecutive pages are indicated, e.g., 36–45 passim. Subjects discussed over not more than three consecutive pages are indicated by consecutive numbers; if discussed over a longer series of pages, by the first page number followed by 'et seqq'.